RESEARCH METHODS AND INTEGRATION IN THE SOCIAL SCIENCES

Fourth Edition

With contributions by David Desjardins, Edwin B. Holland, and Bill Russell
John Abbott College

Taken from:

Understanding Research
by W. Lawrence Neuman

Basics of Social Research: Qualitative and Quantitative Approaches, Canadian Edition
by W. Lawrence Neuman and Karen Robson

The Essential Guide to Writing Research Papers, Canadian Edition
by James D. Lester, James D. Lester, Jr., and Patricia I. Mochnacz

Qualitative Research Methods for the Social Sciences, Seventh Edition
by Bruce L. Berg

Custom Publishing

New York Boston San Francisco
London Toronto Sydney Tokyo Singapore Madrid
Mexico City Munich Paris Cape Town Hong Kong Montreal

Cover Art: Courtesy of PhotoDisc, EyeWire/Getty Images

Excerpts taken from:

Understanding Research
by W. Lawrence Neuman
Copyright © 2009 by Pearson Education, Inc.
Published by Allyn & Bacon
Boston, Massachusetts 02116

Basics of Social Research: Qualitative and Quantitative Approaches, Canadian Edition
by W. Lawrence Neuman and Karen Robson
Copyright © 2009 by Pearson Education Canada, Inc.
Published by Allyn & Bacon
Toronto, Ontario

The Essential Guide to Writing Research Papers, Canadian Edition
by James D. Lester, James D. Lester, Jr., and Patricia I. Mochnacz
Copyright © 2003 by Pearson Education Canada, Inc.
Published by Addison Wesley Longman, Inc.
Toronto, Ontario

Qualitative Research Methods for the Social Sciences, Seventh Edition
by Bruce L. Berg
Copyright © 2009, 2007, 2004, 2001, 1998, 1995, 1989 by Pearson Education, Inc.
Published by Allyn & Bacon
Boston, Massachusetts 02116

19 17

2009420371

MHB

Pearson Custom Publishing
is a division of

www.pearsonhighered.com

ISBN 10: 0-558-37321-6
ISBN 13: 978-0-558-37321-4

Brief Contents

Contents

Part 1 Introduction to the Research Process

Part 2 Research Methods

PART I

Introduction to the Research Process

CHAPTER 1

Doing Social Research

Taken from: *Basics of Social Research: Qualitative and Quantitative Approaches,* Canadian Edition, by W. Lawrence Neuman and Karen Robson

1

INTRODUCTION

Social research is all around us. Educators, government officials, business managers, human service providers, and health care professionals regularly use social research methods and findings. People use social research to raise children, reduce crime, improve public health, sell products, or just understand their lives. Reports of research appear on news programs, in popular magazines, in newspapers, and on the internet.

This book is about social research. In simple terms, research is a way of going about finding answers to questions. Professors, professional researchers, practitioners, and students in many fields conduct research to seek answers to questions about the social world. You probably already have some notion of what social research entails. First, let us end some possible misconceptions. When we asked students in our classes what they think social research entails, they gave the following answers:

- It is based on facts alone; there is no theory or personal judgment.
- Only experts with a Ph.D. degree or college professors read it or do it.
- It means going to the library and finding a lot of magazine articles or books on a topic.
- It is when someone hangs around a group and observes.
- It means conducting a controlled experiment.
- Social research is drawing a sample of people and giving them questionnaires to complete.
- It is looking up lots of statistical tables and information from official government reports.
- To do it, one must use computers to create statistics, charts, and graphs.

The first two answers are wrong, and the others describe only part of what constitutes social research. It is unwise to confuse one part with the whole.

People conduct social research to learn something new about the social world; to carefully document guesses, hunches, or beliefs about it; or to refine their understanding of how the social world works. A researcher combines theories or ideas with facts in a careful, systematic way. He or she learns to organize and plan carefully and creatively and to select the appropriate technique to address a specific kind of question. A researcher must treat the people in a study in ethical and moral ways. In addition, a researcher must fully and clearly communicate the results of a study to others.

Social research is a process in which people combine a set of principles, outlooks, and ideas (i.e., methodology) with a collection of specific practices, techniques, and strategies (i.e., a method of inquiry) to produce knowledge. It is an exciting process of discovery, but it requires persistence, personal integrity, tolerance for ambiguity, interaction with others, and pride in doing quality work.

Reading this book cannot transform you into an expert researcher, but it can teach you to be a better consumer of research results, help you to understand how the research enterprise works, and prepare you to conduct small research projects. After studying this book, you will be aware of what research can and cannot do, and why properly conducted research is important.

ALTERNATIVES TO SOCIAL RESEARCH

Unless you are unusual, most of what you know about the social world is not based on doing social research. You probably learned most of your knowledge about the social world by using an alternative to social research, based on what your parents and other people (e.g., friends, teachers) have told you. You also have knowledge based on your personal experiences, the books and magazines you have read, and the movies and television you have watched. You may also use plain old "common sense."

More than a collection of techniques, social research is a process for producing knowledge. It is a more structured, organized, and systematic process than the alternatives that most of us use in daily life. Knowledge from the alternatives is often correct, but knowledge based on research is more likely to be true and have fewer errors. Although research does not always produce perfect knowledge, compared to the alternatives it is much less likely to be flawed. Let us review the alternatives before examining social research.

Authority

You have acquired knowledge from parents, teachers, and experts as well as from books, television, and other media. When you accept something as being true because someone in a position of authority says it is true or because it is in an authoritative publication, you are relying on authority as a basis for knowledge. Relying on the wisdom of authorities is a quick, simple, and cheap way to learn something. Authorities often spend time and effort to gain knowledge, and you can benefit from their experience and work.

There are also limitations to relying on authority. First, it is easy to overestimate the expertise of other people. You may assume that they are right when they are not. History is full of past experts whom we now see as being misinformed. For example, some "experts" of the past measured intelligence by counting bumps on the skull; other "experts" used bloodletting to try to cure diseases. Their errors seem obvious now, but can you be certain that today's experts will not become tomorrow's fools? Second, authorities may not agree, and all authorities may not be equally dependable. Whom should we believe if authorities disagree? Third, authorities may speak on fields they know little about, or they may be plain wrong. An expert who is very informed about one area may use his or her authority in an unrelated area. Also, using the halo effect (discussed later), expertise in one area may spill over illegitimately to be authority in a totally different area. Have you ever seen television commercials where an athlete uses his or her fame as authority to convince you to buy a car? We need to ask: Who is or is not an authority?

An additional issue is the misuse of authority. Sometimes organizations or individuals give an appearance of authority so they can convince others to agree to something that they might not otherwise. For example, the Fraser Institute, a "free market" conservative advocacy group funded by major corporations, published a book in 1999 entitled *Passive Smoke: The EPA's Betrayal of Science and Policy.* The book, authored by John Luik and Gio Batta Gori of the Fraser Institute, claimed that the breadth of previous evidence on the dangers of second-hand smoke was based on "junk" research. Nowhere, however, were the authors' long-standing affiliations with the tobacco industry mentioned as obvious conflicts of interest. As well, while both authors have doctorate degrees, only Gori's is in biological sciences; Luik holds degrees in philosophy.

A related situation occurs when a person with little training and expertise is named as a "senior fellow" or "adjunct scholar" in a private "think tank" with an impressive name, such as the Centre for the Study of X or the Institute on Y Research. Some think tanks are legitimate research centres, but many are mere fronts created by wealthy special-interest groups to engage in advocacy politics. Think tanks can make someone a "scholar" to facilitate the mass media's accepting the person as an authority on an issue. In reality, the person may not have any expertise.[1]

Too much reliance on authorities can be dangerous to a democratic society. Experts may promote ideas that strengthen their own power and position. When we accept the authority of experts but do not know how the experts arrived at their knowledge, we lose the ability to evaluate what the experts say.

Tradition

People sometimes rely on tradition for knowledge. Tradition is a special case of authority—the authority of the past. Tradition means you accept something as being true because "it's the way things have always been." Many people believe that children who are raised at home by their mothers grow up to be better adjusted and have fewer personal problems than those raised in other settings. People "know" this, but how did they learn it? Most accept it because they believe (rightly or wrongly) that it was true in the past or is the way things have always been done. Some traditional social knowledge begins as simple prejudice. You might rely on tradition without being fully aware of it with a belief such as "People from that side of the tracks will never amount to anything" or "You never can trust that type of person" or "That's the way men (or women) are." Even if traditional knowledge was once true, it can become distorted as it is passed on, and soon it is no longer true.

Common Sense

You know a lot about the social world from your everyday reasoning or common sense. You rely on what everyone knows and what "just makes sense." For example, it "just makes sense" that murder rates are higher in nations that do not have a death penalty because people are less likely to kill if they face execution for doing so. This and other widely held commonsense beliefs, such as that poor youth are more likely to commit deviant acts than those from the middle class or that most Catholics do not use birth control, are false.

Common sense is valuable in daily living, but it allows logical fallacies to slip into thinking. For example, the so-called gambler's fallacy says, "If I have a long string of losses playing a lottery, the next time I play, my chances of winning will be better." In terms of probability and the facts, this is false. Also, common sense contains contradictory ideas that often go unnoticed because people use the ideas at different times, such as "opposites attract" and "birds of a feather flock together." Common sense can originate in tradition. It is useful and sometimes correct, but it also contains errors, misinformation, contradiction, and prejudice.

Media Myths

Television shows, movies, and newspaper and magazine articles are important sources of information. For example, most people have no contact with criminals but learn about crime by watching television shows and movies and by reading newspapers. However, the television portrayals of crime, and of many other things, do not accurately reflect social reality. The writers who create or "adapt" images from life for television shows and movie scripts distort reality, either out of ignorance or because they rely on authority, tradition, and common sense. Their primary goal is to entertain, not to represent reality accurately. Although many journalists try to present a realistic picture of the world, they must write stories in short time periods with limited information and within editorial guidelines.

Unfortunately, the media tend to perpetuate the myths of a culture. For example, the media show that most Canadians who receive welfare are single mothers (actually, single and childless men are the largest group of recipients), that most people who are mentally ill are violent and dangerous (only a small percentage actually are), and that most people who are elderly are senile and in nursing homes (a tiny minority are). Also, mass media "hype" can create a feeling that a major problem exists when it may not (see Box 1). People are misled by visual images more easily

Box 1 Is the Methamphetamine Panic a Media Myth?

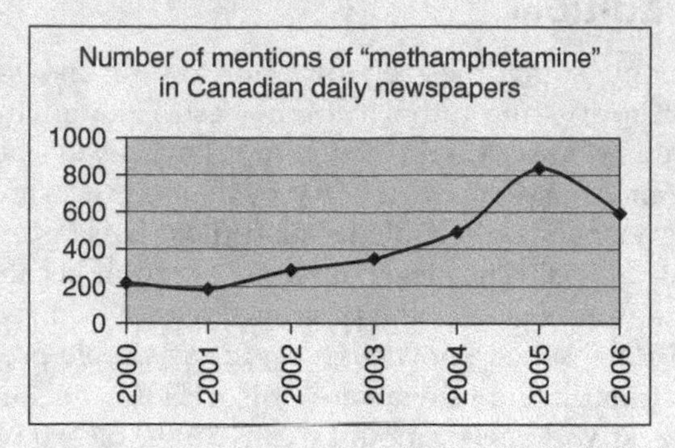

Canadians hear a lot about the dangers of drug use. *Maclean's* magazine and newspapers in all major cities have carried headlines about it. The CBC program *the fifth estate* broadcast a special on this epidemic, entitled "Dark Crystal". Law enforcement agencies in several provinces have begun aggressively cracking down on possession and dealing of methamphetamine and have increased maximum penalties for these offences.

While occasional mention of the street drug occurred in the early 1990s the number of times the word *methamphetamine* has appeared in major Canadian dailies has increased greatly over the last few years. In 2000, for example, there were 218 mentions of the word in major Canadian daily newspapers, and this almost quadrupled in 2005 to 850 mentions. Despite media attention about the risks of "ice" and the numbers of youth at risk of becoming addicts, there is no scientific evidence for this panic. A recent Statistics Canada study on teen drug use found that only 2 percent had tried methamphetamines, compared to 34 percent who had tried marijuana, 4 percent who had tried ecstasy, 1 percent who had tried heroin, and 3 percent who had tried crack cocaine.

Perhaps media reports fueled fear of an explosion of crystal meth addiction among young Canadian people. The drug is cheap, highly addictive, and has become popular among North American rural poor. However, deaths from this drug are relatively low compared to other legal drugs. For example, in 2003, 15 people in British Columbia died due to an overdose of methamphetamine, while there were 337 overdoses attributable to other drugs, including prescription drugs and alcohol.[3] No publicly available figures are available to give evidence to this drug crisis, however.

than other forms of "lying"; this means that stories or stereotypes that appear on film and television can have a powerful effect.

Competing interests use the media to win public support.[2] Public relations campaigns try to alter what the public thinks about scientific findings, making it difficult for the public to judge research findings. For example, a large majority of scientific research supports the global warming thesis (i.e., pollutants from industrialization and massive deforestation are raising the earth's temperature and will cause dramatic climate change and bring about environmental disasters). The media give equal attention to a few dissenters who question global warming, creating the impression in the public mind that "no one really knows" or that scientists are undecided about the issue of global warming. The media sources fail to mention that the dissenters represent less than 2 percent of all scientists or that most dissenting studies are paid for by heavily polluting industries. The industries also spend millions of dollars to publicize the findings because their goal is to deflect growing criticism and delay environmental regulations, not to advance knowledge.

Newspapers offer horoscopes and television programs or movies report on supernatural powers, ESP (extrasensory perception), UFOs (unidentified flying objects), and angels or ghosts. Although no scientific evidence exists for such, between 20 and

50 percent of the Canadian public accepts them as true, and the percentage with such beliefs has been growing over time as the entertainment media give the phenomenon more prominence.[4]

Personal Experience

If something happens to you, if you personally see it or experience it, you accept it as true. Personal experience, or "seeing is believing," has a strong impact and is a powerful source of knowledge. Unfortunately, personal experience can lead you astray. What appears true may actually be due to a slight error or distortion in judgment. The power of immediacy and direct personal contact is very strong. Even knowing that, many people believe what they see or personally experience rather than what very carefully designed research has discovered.

The four errors of personal experience reinforce each other and can occur in other areas, as well. They are a basis for misleading people through propaganda, cons or fraud, magic, stereotyping, and some advertising. The most frequent problem is **overgeneralization**. It occurs when some evidence supports your belief, but you falsely assume that it also applies to many other situations. Limited generalization may be appropriate; under certain conditions, a small amount of evidence can explain a larger situation. The problem is that many people generalize far beyond limited evidence. For example, over the years the authors have known a number of blind people. All of them were very friendly. Can we conclude that all blind people are friendly? Do the six or so people with whom we happened to have personal experience represent all blind people?

The second error, **selective observation**, occurs when you take special notice of some people or events and tend to seek out evidence that confirms what you already believe and ignore contradictory information. People often focus on or observe particular cases or situations, especially when they fit preconceived ideas. We are sensitive to features that confirm what we think but ignore features that contradict it. Psychologists found that people tend to "seek out" and distort their memories to make them more consistent with what they already think.[5]

A third error is **premature closure**, which often operates with and reinforces the first two errors. Premature closure occurs when you feel you have the answer and do not need to listen, seek information, or raise questions any longer. Unfortunately, most of us are a little lazy or get a little sloppy. We take a few pieces of evidence or look at events for a short while and then think we have it figured out. We look for evidence to confirm or reject an idea and stop when a small amount of evidence is present. In a word, we jump to conclusions. For example, we want to learn whether people in a particular town support Mary Smith or Jon Van Horn for mayor. We ask 20 people; 16 say they favour Mary, 2 are undecided, and only 2 favour Jon, so we stop there and believe Mary will win on the basis of a small sampling of town residents.

Another common error is the **halo effect**, when we overgeneralize from what we accept as being highly positive or prestigious and let its strong reputation or prestige "rub off" onto other areas. For example, you pick up a report by a person from a prestigious university, say McGill or Queen's University. You assume that the author is smart and talented and that the report will be excellent. You do not make this assumption about a report by someone from an unknown university or college. You form an opinion and prejudge the report and may not approach it by considering its own merits alone.

HOW SCIENCE WORKS

Although it builds on some aspects of the alternative ways of developing knowledge, science is what separates social research from those ways. Social research involves thinking scientifically about questions about the social world and following scientific processes. This suggests that we examine the meaning of science and how it works.

Science

The term *science* conjures an image of test tubes, computers and people in white lab coats. These outward trappings are a part of science, especially natural science (i.e., astronomy, biology, chemistry, geology, and physics) that deals with the physical and material world (e.g., plants, chemicals, rocks, stars, and electricity). The social sciences, such as anthropology, psychology, political science, and sociology, involve the study of people—their beliefs, behaviour, interaction, institutions, and so forth. Fewer people associate these disciplines with the word *science*. Science is a social institution and a way to produce knowledge. Not everyone is well informed about science.

Scientists gather data using specialized techniques and use the data to support or reject theories. **Data** are the empirical evidence or information that one gathers carefully according to rules or procedures. The data can be **quantitative** (i.e., expressed as numbers) or **qualitative** (i.e., expressed as words, visual images, sounds, or objects). **Empirical evidence** refers to observations that people experience through the senses—touch, sight, hearing, smell, and taste. This confuses people because researchers cannot use their senses to directly observe many aspects of the social world about which they seek answers (e.g., intelligence, attitudes, opinions, feelings, emotions, power, authority, etc.).

The various ways that acquiring knowledge might address the topic of laundry are shown in Table 1.1. Anderson and Robson (2006) found, using scientific inquiry (statistical analysis of data), that while women are primarily responsible for doing laundry, if boys are socialized at a young age to be responsible for their own laundry tasks, they are *more likely* to be responsible for laundry when they are in adult relationships.

The Scientific Community

Science comes to life through the operation of the scientific community, which sustains the assumptions, attitudes, and techniques of science. The **scientific community** is a collection of people who practise science and a set of norms, behaviours,

Table 1.1 Sources of Knowledge

Example Issue:	In the division of household tasks by gender, why do women tend to do the laundry?
Authority	Experts say that as children, females are taught to make, select, mend, and clean clothing as part of a female focus on physical appearance and on caring for children or others in a family. Women do the laundry based on their childhood preparation.
Tradition	Women have done the laundry for centuries, so it is a continuation of what has happened for a long time.
Common Sense	Men just are not as concerned about clothing as women are, so it only makes sense that women do the laundry more often.
Media Myth	Television commercials show women often doing laundry and enjoying it, so they do laundry because they think it's fun.
Personal Experience	My mother and the mothers of all my friends did the laundry. My female friends did it for their boyfriends, but never the other way around. It just feels natural for the woman to do it.
Scientific	Women are more likely to be responsible for laundry, but if boys are socialized at a young age to be responsible for domestic tasks, they are more likely to do them in adulthood.

and attitudes that bind them together. It is a professional community—a group of interacting people who share ethical principles, beliefs and values, techniques and training, and career paths. For the most part, the scientific community includes both the natural and social sciences.[6]

Many people outside the core scientific community use scientific research techniques. A range of practitioners and technicians apply research techniques that scientists developed and refined. Many use the research techniques (e.g., a survey) without possessing a deep knowledge of scientific research. Yet anyone who uses the techniques or results of science can do so better if they also understand the principles and processes of the scientific community.

At the core of the scientific community are researchers who conduct studies on a full-time or part-time basis, usually with the help of assistants. Many research assistants are graduate students, and some are undergraduates. Working as a research assistant is the way that most scientists gain a real grasp on the details of doing research. Universities employ most members of the scientific community's core. Some scientists work for the government, such as Statistics Canada, or private industry in organizations, such as Ipsos Canada, Gallup Canada, Pollara, and Environics. Most, however, work at the approximately 200 research universities and institutes located in a dozen advanced industrialized countries. Thus, the scientific community is scattered geographically, but its members tend to work together in small clusters.

How big is the scientific community? A discipline such as sociology may have about 8000 active researchers worldwide. Most researchers complete only two or three studies in their careers, whereas a small number of highly active researchers conduct many dozens of studies. In a specialty or topic area (e.g., study of the death penalty, social movements, divorce), only about 100 researchers are very active and conduct most research studies. Although research results represent what humanity knows and it has a major impact on the lives of many millions of people, only a small number of people are actually producing most new scientific knowledge.

The Scientific Method and Attitude

You have probably heard of the scientific method, and you may be wondering how it fits into all this. The **scientific method** is not one single thing: it refers to the ideas, rules, techniques, and approaches that the scientific community uses. The method arises from a loose agreement within the community of scientists. It includes a way of looking at the world that places a high value on professionalism, craftsmanship, ethical integrity, creativity, rigorous standards, and diligence. It also includes strong professional norms, such as honesty and uprightness in doing research, openness about how a study is conducted, and a focus on the merits of the research itself and not on any characteristics of individuals who conducted the study.

Journal Articles in Science

Consider what happens once a researcher finishes a study. First, he or she writes a detailed description of the study and the results as a research report or a paper using a special format. Often, he or she also gives an oral presentation of the paper before other researchers at a conference or a meeting of a professional association and seeks comments and suggestions. Next, the researcher sends several copies to the editor of a scholarly journal. Each editor, a respected researcher chosen by other scientists to oversee the journal, removes the title page, which is the only place the author's name appears, and sends the article to several reviewers. The reviewers are respected scientists who have conducted studies in the same specialty area or topic. The reviewers do not know who did the study, and the author of the paper does not know who the reviewers are, which is called "blind" review. This reinforces the scientific principle of judging a study on its merits alone. Reviewers evaluate the research based on its clarity, originality, standards of good research methods, and advancing knowledge. They return their evaluations to the editor, who either decides to reject the paper, or asks the author to revise and resubmit it, or accepts it for publication. It is a very careful, cautious method to ensure quality control.

The scholarly journals that are highly respected and regularly read by most researchers in a field receive many more papers than they can publish. They accept only 10 to 15 percent of submitted manuscripts. Thus, several experienced researchers screen a journal article based on its merits alone, and publication represents the study's tentative acceptance by the scientific community as a valid contribution to knowledge. Unlike the authors of articles for the popular magazines found at newsstands, scientists are not paid for publishing in scholarly journals. In fact, they may have to pay a small fee to help defray costs just to have their papers considered. Researchers are happy to make their research available to their peers (i.e., other scientists and researchers) through scholarly journals. The article communicates the results of a study to which a researcher might have devoted years of his or her life, and it is the way researchers gain respect and visibility among their professional peers. Publishing in academic journals is also an important part of the careers of many scientists, as their careers and contributions to their discipline are often assessed by the scholarly articles they have published. Likewise, the reviewers are not paid for reviewing papers but consider it an honour to be asked to conduct the peer reviews and to carry out one of the responsibilities of being in the scientific community.

You may never publish an article in a scholarly journal, but you will probably read many such articles. It is important to see how they are a vital component in the system of scientific research. Researchers regularly read what appears in the journals to learn about new research findings and the methods used to conduct a study. Eventually, the new knowledge is used in textbooks, new reports, or public talks.

STEPS IN THE RESEARCH PROCESS

Social research proceeds in a sequence of steps. Although various approaches to research suggest slightly different steps, most studies follow the seven steps discussed here. To begin the process, you select a *topic*—a general area of study or issue, such as domestic abuse, homelessness, or powerful corporate elites. A topic is too broad for conducting a study. This makes the next step crucial. You must then narrow down the topic, or *focus* the topic into a specific research question for a study (e.g., "Are people who marry younger more likely to engage in physical abuse of a spouse under conditions of high stress than those who marry older?"). As you learn about a topic and narrow the focus, you should review past research, or the *literature,* on a topic or question. You also want to develop a possible answer, or hypothesis, and theory can be important at this stage.

After specifying a research question, you have to develop a highly detailed plan on how you will carry out the study. This third step requires that you decide on the many practical details of doing the research (e.g., whether to use a survey or qualitative observing in the field, how many subjects to use). It is only after completing the design stage that you are ready to *gather the data* or evidence (e.g., ask people the questions, record answers). Once you have very carefully collected the data, your next step is to *analyze the data*. This will help you see any patterns in it and help you to give meaning to or *interpret* the data (e.g., "People who marry young and grew up in families with abuse have higher rates of physical domestic abuse than those with different family histories."). Finally, you must *inform others* by writing a report that describes the study's background, how you conducted it, and what you discovered.

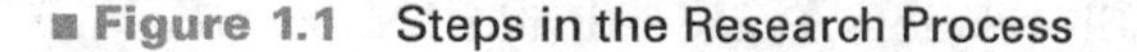

Figure 1.1 Steps in the Research Process

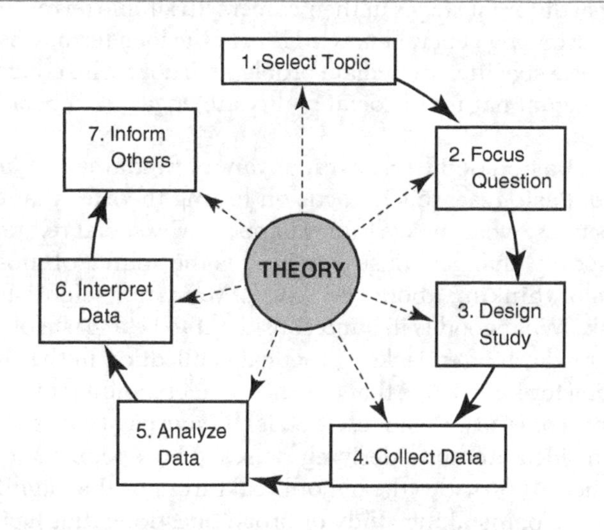

The seven-step process shown in Figure 1.1 is oversimplified. In practice, you will rarely complete one step totally, then leave it behind to move to the next step. Rather, the process is an interactive one in which the steps blend into each other. What you do in a later step may stimulate you to reconsider and slightly adjust your thinking in a previous one. The seven steps are for one research project; it is one cycle of going through the steps in a single study on a specific topic.

DIMENSIONS OF RESEARCH

Three years after they graduated from university, Tim and Sharon met for lunch. Tim asked Sharon, "So, how is your new job as a researcher for Social Data, Inc.? What are you doing?" Sharon answered, "Right now I'm working on an applied research project on day-care quality in which we're doing a cross-sectional survey to get descriptive data for an evaluation study." Sharon touched on four dimensions of social research as she described her research on day care.

Social research comes in several shapes and sizes. Before you begin a study, you will need to make several decisions about the specific type of research you are going to conduct. Researchers need to understand the advantages and disadvantages of each type, although most end up specializing. We can think of the types as fitting into one of the categories in each of four dimensions of research.

The first dimension is a distinction of how research is used, or between applied and basic research. The next is the purpose of doing research, or its goal, to explore, describe, or explain. The next two dimensions are more specific: how time is incorporated into the study design, and the specific data-collection technique used.

The dimensions overlap, in that certain dimensions are often found together (e.g., the goal of a study and a data-collection technique). Once you learn the dimensions, you will begin to see how the particular research questions you might want to investigate tend to be more compatible with certain ways of designing a study and collecting data. In addition, being aware of the dimensions of research will make it easier to understand the research reports by others.

Use of Research

For over a century, science has had two wings. Some researchers adopt a detached, purely scientific, and academic orientation; others are more activist, pragmatic, and interventionist oriented. This is not a rigid separation. Researchers in the two wings cooperate and maintain friendly relations. Some individuals move from one wing to another at different stages in their careers. In simple terms, some researchers concentrate on advancing general knowledge over the long term, whereas others conduct studies to solve specific, immediate problems. Those who concentrate on examining the fundamental nature of social reality are engaged in basic research.

Basic Research. **Basic social research** advances fundamental knowledge about the social world. Basic researchers focus on testing theories that explain how the social world operates, what makes things happen, why social relations are a certain way, and why society changes. Basic research is the source of most new scientific ideas and ways of thinking about the world. Many nonscientists criticize basic research and ask, "What good is it?" and consider it to be a waste of time and money. Although basic research often lacks a practical application in the short term, it provides a foundation for knowledge that advances understanding in many policy areas, problems, or areas of study. Basic research is the source of most of the tools, methods, theories, and ideas about underlying causes of how people act or think used by applied researchers. It provides the major breakthroughs that significantly advance knowledge; it is the painstaking study of broad questions that has the potential of shifting how we think about a wide range of issues. It may have an impact for the next 50 or 100 years: often, the applications of basic research appear many years or decades later. Practical applications may be apparent only after many accumulated advances in basic knowledge that build over a long time period. For example, in 1984, Alec Jeffreys, a geneticist at the University of Leicester in England, was engaged in basic research studying the evolution of genes. As an indirect accidental side effect of a new technique he developed, he discovered a way to produce what is now called human DNA "fingerprints" or unique markings of the DNA of individuals. This was not his intent. He even said he would have never thought of the technique if DNA fingerprints had been his goal. Within ten years applied uses of the technique were developed. Today, DNA analysis is a widely used technique in criminal investigations.

Applied Research. **Applied social research** is designed to address a specific concern or to offer solutions to a problem identified by an employer, club, agency, social movement, or organization. Applied social researchers are rarely concerned with building, testing, or connecting to a larger theory, developing a long-term general understanding, or carrying out a large-scale investigation that might span years. Instead, they usually conduct a quick, small-scale study that provides practical results for use in the short term (i.e., next month or next year). For example, the student government of University X wants to know if the number of University X students who are arrested for driving while intoxicated or involved in auto accidents will decline if it sponsors alcohol-free parties next year. Applied research would be most applicable for this situation.

People employed in businesses, government offices, health care facilities, social service agencies, political organizations, and educational institutions often conduct applied research and use the results in decision making. Applied research affects decisions such as the following: Should an agency start a new program to reduce the wait time before a client receives benefits? Should a police force adopt a new type of response to reduce spousal abuse? Should a political candidate emphasize his or her stand on the environment instead of the economy? Should a company market a skin care product to mature adults instead of teenagers?

The scientific community is the primary consumer of basic research. The consumers of applied research findings are practitioners, such as teachers, counsellors, and social workers, or decision makers, such as managers, agency administrators, and public officials. Often, someone other than the researcher who conducted the study uses the results.

Applied research results are less likely to enter the public domain in publications and may be available only to a few decision makers or practitioners. This means that applied research findings often are not widely disseminated and that well-qualified researchers rarely get to judge the quality of applied studies.

The decision makers who use the results of an applied study may or may not use them wisely. Sometimes despite serious problems with a study's methodology and cautions from the researchers, politicians use results to justify cutting programs they dislike or to advance programs they favour. Also, because applied research often has immediate implications or involves controversial issues, it often generates conflict. In 2002, the *Toronto Star,* working with a York University psychology professor, published an analysis of a database containing police-related incidents. The results supported the idea that the Toronto police engaged in racial profiling—that is, that they stopped Black people more often for no other reason than because they were Black. The research was met with extreme hostility, and the newspaper was sued by the police union. The Toronto Police Service then commissioned an independent review of the *Toronto Star*'s analysis, which was undertaken by a criminal lawyer and a University of Toronto sociology professor, who came up with different results that found no evidence of racial profiling. Who is correct? The debate over the extent of racial profiling in Canadian policing continues to be a very controversial topic in the news and among Canadian academics.[7]

1

Applied and basic researchers adopt different orientations toward research methodology (see Table 1.2). Basic researchers emphasize high methodological standards and try to conduct near-perfect research. Applied researchers must make more trade-offs. They may compromise scientific rigour to get quick, usable results, but compromise is never an excuse for sloppy research. Applied researchers try to squeeze research into the constraints of an applied setting and balance rigour against practical needs. Such balancing requires an in-depth knowledge of research and an awareness of the consequences of compromising standards.

Types of Applied Research. There are many specific types of applied research. Here you will learn about three major types: evaluation, action, and social impact assessment.

Evaluation Research Study. **Evaluation research study** is applied research designed to find out whether a program, a new way of doing something, a marketing campaign, a policy, and so forth, is effective—in other words, "Does it work?"

Table 1.2 Basic and Applied Social Research Compared

Basic	Applied
1. Research is intrinsically satisfying and judgments are by other social scientists.	1. Research is part of a job and is judged by sponsors who are outside the disciplines of social science.
2. Research problems and subjects are selected with a great deal of freedom.	2. Research problems are "narrowly constrained" to the demands of employers or sponsors.
3. Research is judged by absolute norms of scientific rigour, and the highest standards of scholarship are sought.	3. The rigour and standards of scholarship depend on the uses of results. Research can be "quick and dirty" or may match high scientific standards.
4. The primary concern is with the internal logic and rigour of research design.	4. The primary concern is with the ability to generalize findings to areas of interest to sponsors.
5. The driving goal is to contribute to basic theoretical knowledge.	5. The driving goal is to have practical payoffs or uses for results.
6. Success comes when results appear in a scholarly journal and have an impact on others in the scientific community.	6. Success comes when results are used by sponsors in decision making.

Source: Adapted from Freeman and Rossi (1984:572–573).

The most common type of applied research is evaluation research. This type of research is widely used in large bureaucratic organizations (e.g., businesses, schools, hospitals, government, large nonprofit agencies) to demonstrate the effectiveness of what they are doing. An evaluation researcher does not use techniques different from those of other social researchers. The difference lies in the fact that decision makers, who may not be researchers themselves, narrowly define the scope and purpose of the research, with the objective of using results in a practical situation.[8]

Evaluation research questions might include the following: Does a Socratic (one-on-one) teaching technique improve learning over lecturing? Does a law-enforcement program of mandatory arrest reduce spouse abuse? Does a flex-time program increase employee productivity? Evaluation researchers measure the effectiveness of a program, policy, or way of doing something and often use several research techniques (e.g., survey and field research). If it can be used, the experimental technique is usually preferred. Practitioners involved with a policy or program may conduct evaluation research for their own information or at the request of outside decision makers. The decision makers may place limits on the research by fixing boundaries on what can be studied and by determining the outcome of interest. This often creates ethical dilemmas for a researcher.

Ethical and political conflicts often arise in evaluation research because people can have opposing interests in the findings. The findings of research can affect who gets or keeps a job; it can build political popularity; or it may help promote an alternative program. People who are personally displeased with the findings may attack the researcher or his or her methods.

Evaluation research has several limitations: The reports of research rarely go through a peer review process, raw data are rarely publicly available, and the focus is narrowed to select inputs and outputs more than the full process by which a program affects people's lives. In addition, decision makers may selectively use or ignore evaluation findings.

Action Research Study. **Action research** is applied research that treats knowledge as a form of power and abolishes the division between creating knowledge and using knowledge to engage in political action. There are several types of action research, but most share five characteristics: (1) the people being studied actively participate in the research process; (2) the research incorporates ordinary or popular knowledge; (3) the research focuses issues of power; (4) the research seeks to raise consciousness or increase awareness of issues; and (5) the research is tied directly to a plan or program of political action. Action research tends to be associated with a social movement, political cause, or advocacy for an issue. It can be conducted to advance a range of political positions. Some action research has an insurgent orientation with goals of empowering the powerless, fighting oppression and injustice, and reducing inequality. Wealthy and powerful groups or organizations also sponsor and conduct action research to defend their status, position, and privileges in society.

Action researchers are explicitly political, not value neutral. Because the primary goal is to affect socio-political conditions, publishing results in formal reports, articles, or books is secondary. Most action researchers also believe that knowledge develops from direct experience, particularly the experience of engaging in socio-political action.

Social Impact Assessment Research Study. A researcher who conducts **social impact assessment** (SIA) estimates the likely consequences of a planned intervention or intentional change to occur in the future. It may be part of a larger environmental impact statement required by government agencies and used for planning and making choices among alternative policies. He or she forecasts how aspects of the social environment may change and suggests ways to mitigate changes likely to be adverse from the point of view of an affected population. Impacts are the difference between a forecast of the future with the project or policy and without the project or policy. For example, the SIA might estimate the ability of a local hospital to respond to an earthquake, determine how housing availability for the elderly will change if a major new highway is built, or assess the impact on university admissions if students receive interest-free loans. Researchers who conduct SIAs often examine a range of social outcomes and work in an interdisciplinary research team to estimate them. The outcomes include measuring "quality of life" issues, such as access to health care, illegal drug and alcohol use, employment opportunities, schooling quality, teen pregnancy rates, commuting time and traffic congestion, availability of parks and recreation facilities, shopping choices, viable cultural institutions, crime rates, interracial tensions, or social isolation.

For example, many forms of legal gambling have expanded rapidly in Alberta since the early 1990s. Video lottery terminals (VLTs) were introduced into drinking establishments and electronic slot machines were allowed in casinos and racetracks. Gaming revenue rose from $225 million per year in 1992 to $1 545 million in 2003.[9] Provincial politicians sought new sources of revenue without raising taxes and wanted to promote economic development. The gambling industry promised the government new jobs, economic revitalization, and a "cut" in the huge flow of money from gambling. This looked ideal to the politicians: they could help create jobs, strengthen the local economy, and get revenue without raising taxes. While the success of Alberta's economy is unrivalled in Canada at the time of writing, the provincial economic benefits derived from gambling revenue did not come without a cost. The problem of compulsive gambling has increased, particularly among youth and Aboriginal populations (Smith and Wynne, 2002). Compulsive gamblers have low work productivity, devastate their families, and often turn to crime. Were such social results predictable? Yes, if the officials had first had high-quality social impact assessment research conducted. This is rare, however. Officials often accept extravagant claims made by special-interest industry advocates who promise the illusion of getting something for next to nothing. Also, some officials are ignorant or distrustful of social research. The few social impact studies conducted on gambling made accurate predictions, and the outcome was no surprise.

Purpose of a Study

If you ask someone why he or she is conducting a study, you might get a range of responses: "My boss told me to"; "It was a class assignment"; "I was curious"; "My roommate thought it would be a good idea." There are almost as many reasons to do research as there are researchers. Yet the purposes of social research may be organized into three groups based on what the researcher is trying to accomplish—explore a new topic, describe a social phenomenon, or explain why something occurs. Studies may have multiple purposes (e.g., both to explore and to describe), but one of three major purposes is usually dominant (see Box 2).

Exploration. Perhaps you have explored a new topic or issue in order to learn about it. If the issue was new or no researchers had written about it, you began at the beginning. In **exploratory research**, a researcher examines a new area to formulate precise questions that he or she can address in future research. Exploratory research may be the first stage in a sequence of studies. A researcher may need to conduct an exploratory study in order to know enough to design and execute a second, more systematic and extensive study. It addresses the "what?" question: "What is this social activity really about?"

Lavoie, Robitaille, and Hébert (2000) wanted to learn what teens thought about violence in interpersonal relations. They gathered qualitative data from discussion groups with 24 Canadian teenagers, ages 14 to 19, in Quebec. The researchers found that the teens experienced many forms of violence in their social relations. The

Box 2 **Purpose of Research**

Exploratory

- Become familiar with the basic facts, setting, and concerns
- Create a general mental picture of conditions
- Formulate and focus questions for future research
- Generate new ideas, conjectures, or hypotheses
- Determine the feasibility of conducting research
- Develop techniques for measuring and locating future data

Descriptive

- Provide a detailed, highly accurate picture
- Locate new data that contradict past data
- Create a set of categories or classify types
- Clarify a sequence of steps or stages
- Document a causal process or mechanism
- Report on the background or context of a situation

Explanatory

- Test a theory's predictions or principle
- Elaborate and enrich a theory's explanation
- Extend a theory to new issues or topics
- Support or refute an explanation or prediction
- Link issues or topics with a general principle
- Determine which of several explanations is best

teenagers explained the violence and nonconsensual sexual relations by emphasizing individual, couple, and social factors (e.g., the influence of peers or pornography). The teens often blamed the victim and placed the responsibility for violent acts on the victims of violence. The authors suggest that studies of abuse and methods of violence prevention need to be tailored to how teens understand and explain violence.

Exploratory researchers tend to use qualitative data and not be committed to a specific theory or research question. Exploratory research rarely yields definitive answers. If you conduct an exploratory study, you may get frustrated and feel it is difficult because there are few guidelines to follow. Everything is potentially important, the steps are not well defined, and the direction of inquiry changes frequently. You need to be creative, open-minded, and flexible; adopt an investigative stance; and explore all sources of information.

Description. You may have a more highly developed idea about a social phenomenon and want to describe it. **Descriptive research** presents a picture of the specific details of a situation, social setting, or relationship. Descriptive research focuses on "how?" and "who?" questions: "How did it happen?" "Who is involved?" A great deal of social research is descriptive. Descriptive researchers use most data-gathering techniques—surveys, field research, content analysis, and historical-comparative research. Only experimental research is less often used. Much of the social research found in scholarly journals or used for making policy decisions is descriptive.

Descriptive and exploratory research often blur together in practice. In descriptive research, a researcher begins with a well-defined subject and conducts a study to describe it accurately; the outcome is a detailed picture of the subject. The results may indicate the percentage of people who hold a particular view or engage in specific behaviours—for example, that 8 percent of parents physically or sexually abuse their children. A descriptive study presents a picture of types of people or of social activities.

Albas and Albas (1993) conducted a descriptive study of cheating avoidance among Canadian university students. They were interested in how students avoided being labelled as cheaters, focusing mainly on the innocent noncheaters. The researchers thought people used various avoidance strategies in order to avoid being perceived as cheaters and maintain their self-image. The researchers observed and interviewed students, and reviewed written personal accounts of over 300 students gathered over 17 years at a Canadian university. To avoid being seen as cheaters during exams, students exhibited various behaviours, including controlling their eye movement, positioning their books and notes in special ways, sitting in non-suspicious locations during examinations (i.e., not at the back of the examination room), and repressing "creature releases," such as going to the bathroom or even yawning.

Explanation. When you encounter an issue that is well recognized and have a description of it, you might begin to wonder *why* things are the way they are. **Explanatory research** identifies the sources of social behaviours, beliefs, conditions, and events; it documents causes, tests theories, and provides reasons. It builds on exploratory and descriptive research. For example, an exploratory study discovers a trend in lower rates of marriage; a descriptive researcher documents that 10 percent of couples living together are not married and describes the kinds of men and women for which it is most frequent; the explanatory researcher focuses on *why* certain couples are choosing cohabitation over marriage. Wu (1999) conducted an explanatory study to test a theory that says the timing of a first marriage is delayed when preceded by cohabitation. In other words, living together without being married has the effect of postponing the timing of a first marital union. The author noted that certain liberal attitudes may predispose individuals to be open to premarital cohabitation and less likely to marry overall. In his analyses of large-scale survey data from Canada, Wu discovered that timing of first marriage was significantly delayed for women if cohabitation occurred first, and that cohabitation not only delayed first marriage, but affected the attitudes of individuals such that they had less likelihood of marriage overall.

1

Time Dimension in Research

An awareness of how a study uses the time dimension will help you read or conduct research. This is because different research questions or issues incorporate time differently. Some studies give a snapshot of a single, fixed time point and allow you to analyze it in detail (cross-sectional). Other studies provide a moving picture that lets you follow events, people, or social relations over several time points (longitudinal). Quantitative studies generally look at many cases, people, or units, and measure limited features about them in the form of numbers. By contrast, a qualitative study usually involves qualitative data and examines many diverse features of a small number of cases across either a short or long time period (see Figure 1.2).

Cross-Sectional Research. Most social research studies are **cross-sectional:** they examine a single point in time or take a one-time snapshot approach. Cross-sectional research is usually the simplest and least costly alternative. Its disadvantage is that it cannot capture social processes or change. Cross-sectional research can be exploratory, descriptive, or explanatory, but it is most consistent with a descriptive approach to research. The exploratory study by Lavoie, Robitaille, and Hébert (2000) on violence in interpersonal relationships was cross-sectional, based on qualitative data from discussion groups with 24 Canadian teenagers.

■ **Figure 1.2** The Time Dimension in Social Research

Longitudinal Research. Researchers using **longitudinal research** examine features of people or other units at more than one time. It is usually more complex and costly than cross-sectional research, but it is also more powerful and informative. Descriptive and explanatory researchers use longitudinal approaches. Let us now look at the three main types of longitudinal research: time series, panel, and cohort.

Time-Series Study. A **time-series study** is longitudinal research in which a researcher gathers the same type of information across two or more time periods. Researchers can observe stability or change in the features of the units or can track conditions over time. The specific individuals may change but the overall pattern is clear. For example, every year since 1985 Statistics Canada has been gathering data on social trends in the Canadian population using the General Social Survey (GSS). Each year for the GSS, Statistics Canada collects information from several thousand people aged 15 years and older living in private households. The focus of the questions changes annually with each "cycle," with these topic cycles being repeated every few years. For example, the focus of the survey in 1986 was "Time Use," and this topic was again repeated in 1992, 1998, and 2005. Collecting data across several points in time can show us how trends in social life change. In this particular example, it was possible to see the changes in how the average person spends his or her time. Researchers found that, in 1992, the average time it took for people to get from their residence to their place of work was 54 minutes. By 2005, this had risen to 63 minutes. If you multiply this by the number of days that people work during the year, this amounts to 12 full days of commuting per year.[10]

Panel Study. The **panel study** is a powerful type of longitudinal research in which the researcher observes the same people, group, or organization across multiple time points. It is more difficult to conduct than time-series research and very costly; tracking people over time is often difficult because some people die or cannot be located. Nevertheless, the results of a well-designed panel study are very valuable. Even short-term panel studies can clearly show the impact of an event. For example, in 1994, Statistics Canada surveyed over 11 000 people who were contacted four times over one year in order to see if a recent tobacco tax cut would have any effect on the smoking habits of Canadians. Findings revealed that rates of quitting were lower in provinces where the taxes had been cut and that the numbers of new smokers over this period was also higher in these provinces (Hamilton, Levinton, St-Pierre, and Grimmard, 1997).

Cohort Study. A **cohort study** is similar to a panel study, but rather than observing the same people, the study focuses on a category of people who share a similar life experience in a specified time period. Researchers examine the category as a whole for important features and focus on the cohort, or category, not on specific individuals. Commonly used cohorts include all people born in the same year (called *birth cohorts*), all people hired at the same time, and all people who graduate in a given year. Unlike panel studies, researchers do not have to find the same people for cohort studies and only need to identify those who experienced a common life event.

For example, Warman and Worswick (2004) conducted a cohort study to examine patterns of earnings among immigrants to Canada over a 20-year period. They used census data and examined immigrants who arrived in Canada by grouping them into cohorts based on their arrival year. The authors found that there was a steady decline in the earnings of immigrants who lived in metropolitan areas when their earnings were compared to their Canadian-born counterparts over time. They also found, however, that the most recent arrival cohort (1996–2000) fared slightly better than those who arrived in earlier cohorts.

Case Studies. In cross-sectional and longitudinal research, a researcher examines features of many people or units, either at one time period or across time periods, and measures several common features of them, often using numbers. In **case-study research**, a researcher examines, in depth, many features of a few cases over a duration of time with very detailed, varied, and extensive data, often in a qualitative form. The researcher carefully selects a few key cases to illustrate an issue and study it (or them) in detail and considers the specific context of each case. This contrasts with other longitudinal studies in which the researcher gathers data on many units or cases, then looks for general patterns in the mass of numbers.

For example, Bridgman (2002) conducted a case study on providing housing and employment-orientated training to homeless youth in Toronto, Ontario. The study described the details about the lives and conditions of homeless youth, identified several types of homeless youth, and discussed the various challenges that the organizers and participants in the project faced. This case study used various types of detailed qualitative data, with exploratory, descriptive, and explanatory phases to reveal a great amount of unexpected and new information.

Fischer, Wortley, Webster and Kirst (2002), in contrast, used many types of qualitative and quantitative data in their three-year-long case study of a "John school" in Toronto. Their research began by examining the social and political context in which these John schools came into being in Canada, with specific emphasis placed on the laws surrounding prostitution control. John schools were created in the 1990s as programs aimed at those who were charged, for the first time, with attempting to solicit a prostitute. The program typically occurred on a Saturday with various speakers, including a crown prosecutor, former prostitutes, and public health representatives, giving presentations on various topics. Charges were then withdrawn for those individuals who attended John school. The researchers used quantitative techniques, such as surveying the "johns" before and after attending such a program, examining official rates of reoffending, and conducting a large survey of the general population of Ontario about their knowledge of and attitudes toward the program. They also used qualitative techniques by interviewing numerous key stakeholders in the John School program, and conducting an in-depth field study of the John school itself. Through using the case study method and utilizing these various techniques of data collection, the researchers were able to unravel the complex legal, social, cultural, political, and institutional aspects of Canadian attitudes toward prostitution.

Data-Collection Techniques

Social researchers collect data using one or more specific techniques. This section gives a brief overview of the major techniques. In later chapters, you will read about these techniques in detail and learn how to use them. Some techniques are more effective when addressing specific kinds of questions or topics. It takes skill, practice, and creativity to match a research question to an appropriate data-collection technique. The techniques fall into two categories based on whether the data being gathered are quantitative or qualitative.

Quantitative Data-Collection Techniques. Techniques for quantitative data collection include experiments, surveys, content analyses, and existing statistics.

Experiments. **Experimental research** closely follows the logic and principles found in natural science research: researchers create situations and examine their effects on participants. A researcher conducts experiments in laboratories or in real life with a relatively small number of people and a well-focused research question. Experiments are most effective for explanatory research. In the typical experiment, the researcher divides the people being studied into two or more groups. He or she then treats both groups identically, except that one group but not the other is given a condition he or she is interested in: the "treatment." The researcher measures the reactions of both groups precisely. By controlling the setting for both groups and giving only one group the treatment, the researcher can conclude that any differences in the reactions of the groups are due to the treatment alone.

Surveys. A **survey** is done by asking people questions in a written questionnaire (mailed or handed to people) or during an interview and then recording answers. The researcher manipulates no situation or condition; he or she simply asks many people numerous questions in a short time period. Typically, he or she then summarizes answers to questions in percentages, tables, or graphs. Researchers use survey techniques in descriptive or explanatory research. Surveys give the researcher a picture of what many people think or report doing. Survey researchers often use a sample or a smaller group of selected people (e.g., 150 students), but generalize results to a larger group (e.g., 5000 students) from which the smaller group was selected. Survey research is very widely used in many fields.

Content Analysis. A **content analysis** is a technique for examining information, or content, in written or symbolic material (e.g., pictures, movies, song lyrics). In content analysis, a researcher first identifies a body of material to analyze (e.g., books, newspapers, films) and then creates a system for recording specific aspects of it. The system might include counting how often certain words or themes occur. Finally, the researcher records what was found in the material. He or she often measures information in the content as numbers and presents it as tables or graphs. This technique lets a researcher discover features in the content of large amounts of material that might otherwise go unnoticed. Researchers can use content analysis for exploratory and explanatory research, but primarily it is used for descriptive research.

Existing Statistics. In **existing statistics research**, a researcher locates previously collected information, often in the form of government reports or previously conducted surveys, then reorganizes or combines the information in new ways to address a research question. Locating sources can be time consuming, so the researcher needs to consider carefully the meaning of what he or she finds. Frequently, a researcher does not know whether the information of interest is available when he or she begins a study. Sometimes, the existing quantitative information consists of stored surveys or other data that a researcher reexamines using various statistical procedures. Existing statistics research can be used for exploratory, descriptive, or explanatory purposes, but it is most frequently used for descriptive research.

Qualitative Data-Collection Techniques. Techniques for qualitative data collection include qualitative interviews, focus groups, field research and historical-comparative research.

Qualitative Interviews. Researchers conduct **qualitative interviews** with a selection of people in order to gain an in-depth understanding of the meaning of a social phenomenon to a group of people. A researcher conducting qualitative interviews will choose a research topic and then select a fairly small group of individuals with whom to explore this topic (usually less than 30 individuals). Researchers using this technique will get data that is highly detailed and expresses the unique and comprehensive perspectives of the individuals who were interviewed. Qualitative interviewing is often used for exploratory and descriptive studies.

Focus Groups. **Focus groups** are like qualitative interviews, but they are conducted in a group. A group of usually around five to seven individuals is given a topic to discuss and data about the research question are derived from this group discussion. Like qualitative interviewing, focus group research is used mostly for exploratory and descriptive studies.

Field Research. Most field researchers conduct case studies looking at a small group of people over a length of time (e.g., weeks, months, years). A person involved in **field research** begins with a loosely formulated idea or topic, selects a social group or natural setting for study, gains access and adopts a social role in the setting, and observes in detail. After leaving the field site, the researcher carefully rereads the notes and prepares written reports. Field research is used most often for exploratory and descriptive studies; it is rarely used for explanatory research.

Historical-Comparative Research. **Historical-comparative research** examines aspects of social life in a past historical era or across different cultures. Researchers who use this technique may focus on one historical period or several, compare one or more cultures, or mix historical periods and cultures. Like field research, a researcher combines theory building/testing with data collection and begins with a loosely formulated question that is refined during the research process. Researchers often gather a wide array of evidence, including existing statistics and documents (e.g., novels, official reports, books, newspapers, diaries, photographs, and maps) for study. In addition, they may make direct observations and conduct interviews. Historical-comparative research can be exploratory, descriptive, or explanatory and can blend types.

1

CONCLUSION

This chapter gave you an overview of social research. You saw how social research differs from the ordinary ways of learning-knowing about the social world, how doing research is based on science and the scientific community, and about several types of social research based on its dimensions (e.g., its purpose, or the technique used to gather data). The dimensions of social research loosely overlap with each other and provide a kind of "road map" to help you make your way through the terrain of social research. In the next chapter, we turn to social theory. You read about it a little in this chapter. In the next chapter, you will learn how theory and research methods work together and about several types of theory.

KEY TERMS

action research *14*
applied social research *12*
basic social research *12*
case-study research *19*
cohort study *19*
content analysis *21*
cross-sectional research *17*
data *8*
descriptive research *16*
empirical evidence *8*
evaluation research study *13*
existing statistics research *21*
experimental research *20*
explanatory research *17*
exploratory research *15*
field research *21*
focus groups *21*
halo effect *7*
historical-comparative research *22*
longitudinal research *18*
overgeneralization *7*
panel study *19*
premature closure *7*
qualitative data *8*
qualitative interviews *21*
quantitative data *8*
scientific community *8*
scientific method *9*
selective observation *7*
social impact assessment study *14*
social research *3*
survey research *20*
time-series study *18*

ENDNOTES

1. See Rampton and Stauber (2001:247–277 and 305–306).
2. An Ipsos-Reid (Canada) poll of Canadians conducted in 2006 revealed a wide range of beliefs that Canadians had in the paranormal. The study results can be accessed on the Ipsos Reid website: www.ipsos.ca.
3. These figures are from the British Columbia Coroner's Service, which can be accessed at www.pssg.gov.bc.ca/coroners/index.htm. Schacter (2001) provides a summary of memory issues.
4. See Best (2001:15) on advocates and media.
5. Schacter (2001) provides a summary of memory issues.
6. Discussions of the scientific community can be found in Cole and Gordon (1995), Crane (1972), Hagstrom (1965), Merton (1973), Mulkay (1991), and Ziman (1999).
7. See Harvey and Lui (2003) for a detailed discussion of how the data were reanalyzed.
8. Beck (1995) provides a useful overview.
9. See Statistics Canada (2007) *Perspectives on Labour and Income: Gambling*.
10. See Statistics Canada, *The Daily,* July 12, 2006.

CHAPTER 2

Becoming an Ethical Researcher

Taken from: *Understanding Research,* by W. Lawrence Neuman

Corbis Sygma

2

In 1932, the U.S. Public Health Service began a study on how the disease syphilis progressed. The goal was to improve treatment programs for infected African Americans. Six hundred low-income black men in Macon County, Alabama participated in the "Tuskegee Study of Untreated Syphilis in the Negro Male." Of participants, 399 had syphilis and 201 did not have the disease. Researchers never told the participants that the study was on syphilis or that they had syphilis. Instead, they told the participants that they were being treated for "bad blood," a local term for many ailments, including syphilis, anemia, and fatigue. In exchange for participating in the study, the men received free medical exams, free meals, and burial insurance. Researchers instructed local physicians not to treat participants for syphilis. Although the study was supposed to be six months long, it continued for 40 years. Researchers never treated the participants for syphilis, even after a highly effective treatment, penicillin, became available in 1947. They followed the men until death. Untreated syphilis goes through several stages. Second stage syphilis develops three months to three years after onset. It causes fever, swollen lymph glands, sore throat, patchy hair loss, headaches, weight loss, muscle aches, and fatigue. If untreated, it becomes late stage syphilis. This stage damages the victim's heart, eyes, brain, nervous system, bones, and joints. It can produce mental illness, blindness, deafness, memory loss, serious neurological problems, heart disease, and death.

The "Tuskegee Study of Untreated Syphilis in the Negro Male" ended in 1972 because of an exposé by a news reporter. By the time it ended, 28 participants had died of untreated syphilis. One hundred others died due to syphilis-related complications. Participants had infected 40 wives, and 19 children had contracted the disease at birth. The reporter who wrote the story that ended the study had talked to a research interviewer working for the study. The interviewer had been trying to raise ethical concerns with the U.S. Public Health Service for five years, but he could not get top research officials to end the study and provide proper medical care for the participants.

With the media exposé, a national scandal erupted over the study in 1973. After the U.S. Congress held public hearings, the federal rules on ethics in research with humans were overhauled. Eventually, the surviving research participants sued the U.S. government and were awarded $10 million in an out-of-court settlement. Even after the 1974 settlement, it took another 23 years before the President of the United States officially apologized to the surviving research participants.

The Tuskegee syphilis study is one of the most outrageous instances of a disregard of basic ethical principles in research with humans in the United States. Two books, a play, and a dramatic movie, *Miss Evers' Boys* (1997), document this incident. This unethical research and the publicity surrounding it illustrate that research with humans has limits. When you study people, you must follow ethical principles. In this chapter, you will learn about ethical issues that arise when doing social research.

When you conduct research with humans, you do more than simply gather data according to certain procedures; you must do so in an ethical manner. We conduct a study to create knowledge, answer questions, solve problems, or help humanity, but we must always do this in a morally responsible manner. Research ethics includes the concerns, dilemmas, and conflicts over the proper way to conduct a study. Ethics defines what is or is not morally legitimate. This is not as simple as it may appear at first. There are few clear ethical absolutes, but many general ethical principles or guidelines require that you apply judgment. Some principles may conflict with others in practice or ask you to balance competing priorities (see Figure 2.1).

You must balance potential benefits from research—such as advancing understanding and improving decision making—against its potential costs—such as loss of dignity, self-esteem, privacy, or democratic freedoms.

THE ETHICAL IMPERATIVE

You should think of ethics early in the research process, as you plan a study or prepare a research proposal. While conducting a study, you may confront ethical issues and must quickly decide how to act. It is difficult to appreciate ethical issues fully until you actually begin to conduct a study, but waiting until you are in the middle of doing research is too late. You need to prepare ahead of time and consider ethical concerns. By being familiar with ethical concerns, you can build sound ethical practices into a study's design and be alert to potential ethical concerns that may arise. An ethical awareness also will help you to understand the research process.

Researchers have a strong moral and professional obligation to act ethically *at all times and in all situations*. This holds even if research participants are unaware of or are unconcerned about ethics. It holds even if an employer or the sponsor of a study cares little for ethics or asks you to engage in unethical research acts. "The research participants did not care" or "my boss told me to do it" are never acceptable reasons for engaging in unethical behavior.

Most professions (e.g., journalists, law enforcement, medicine, accounting, etc.) have ethical standards. The ethical standards for doing research with humans may be more rigorous than standards in other areas. Being ethical is not always easy. For

Figure 2.1 Balancing Two Priorities When Doing Research

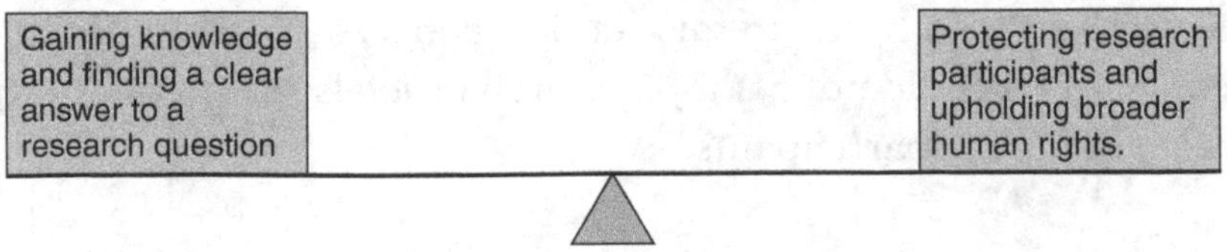

centuries, moral, legal, and political philosophers debated the issues that a researcher may face. Ultimately, ethical behavior begins and ends with you, the individual researcher. The best defense against unethical behavior is a strong personal code of moral behavior. Before, during, and after conducting a study, you will have opportunities to, and *should,* reflect on the ethics of research actions and consult your conscience. Ultimately, doing ethical research rests on your personal integrity.

Given that most people who do research are genuinely concerned about other people, you might ask, Why would anyone act in an ethically irresponsible manner? The most common cause of unethical behavior is a lack of awareness and pressures to take ethical shortcuts. People feel pressures to build a career, publish new findings, advance knowledge, gain prestige, impress family and friends, satisfy job requirements, and so forth. Doing ethical research usually takes longer, is more costly, and is more complex to complete. In addition, there are many opportunities to act unethically, and the odds of being caught are small. Written ethical standards are in the form of vague principles that may not be simple to apply.

If you act ethically all the time, few people will rush to praise you. This is because ethical behavior is expected. However, if you act unethically and are caught doing so, expect public humiliation, a ruined career, and possible legal action against you. To prepare yourself to act ethically, internalize a sensitivity to ethical concerns, adopt a serious professional role, and maintain contact with others who are doing research studies.

Scientific Misconduct

Professional researchers, research centers, and government agencies that fund research all have rules against **scientific misconduct** (see Example Study Box 1: Scientific Misconduct and the Miracle Study). Two major types of scientific misconduct are research fraud and plagiarism. Both are serious ethical violations for which there is never an excuse.

Research fraud is serious deception or lying about data or a study. It happens when a researcher invents data that he or she did not really collect and fails to disclose honestly and fully how he or she conducted a study. Fraud in research is rare but includes significant, unjustified departures from the generally accepted practices for doing and reporting on research. If anyone conducts a study that sharply differs from generally accepted research practice, other people will suspect either incompetence or possible fraud.

Plagiarism is "stealing" someone else's ideas or writings and then using them without citing the source. It is misrepresenting what someone else wrote or thought as your own. If you copy two sentences from someone's research report or use another researcher's questionnaire but fail to report the source, you committed plagiarism. You must put very serious effort into keeping track of sources and properly citing them. Good documentation always allows others to track a source back to its origin.

scientific misconduct violating basic and generally accepted standards of honest scientific research, for example, research fraud and plagiarism.

research fraud to invent, falsify or distort study data or to lie about how a study was conducted.

plagiarism using another person's words or ideas without giving them proper credit and instead passing them off as your own.

Example Study Box 1 Scientific Misconduct and the Miracle Study

In October 2001, a peer-reviewed publication, the *Journal of Reproductive Medicine,* published a study by three Columbia University medical school researchers. Lobo, Cha, and Wirth claimed to have demonstrated that infertile women who had people pray for them became pregnant twice as often as women for whom no one said prayers. The researchers reported that 199 women undergoing in vitro fertilization in Korea, and who had Christian groups in Australia, Canada, and the United States pray for them, conceived at twice the rate as women who did not receive prayer. Researchers never told patients they were part of a study or that anyone was praying for them. Articles touting the findings appeared in newspapers worldwide, and television news programs announced the miracle study.

Serious readers of the study quickly became suspicions due to a lack of details and the use of an unusual and extremely complex study design. Suspicions increased when the researchers refused to share data or to answer questions. Dr. Rogerio Lobo, the lead author, first failed respond to inquiries; next said he did not know about the study until 12 months after it was finished. He then removed his name from the study and stepped down as chairman of the Obstetrics and Gynecology Department. Dr. Lobo had connections with the journal and might have influenced the peer review process. The second author, Dr. Cha, refused to answer questions and left Columbia University shortly after the study appeared. A few years later, another scholarly journal found him guilty of plagiarism. Shortly after the study appeared, Daniel Wirth (a lawyer without a medical degree who had used a series of false identities over the years) pleaded guilty to conspiracy to commit fraud in shady business dealings. Soon it was learned that researchers had failed to get informed consent from participants. Informed consent means a research participant "consents," or voluntarily agrees to be part of a study, and is "informed," i.e., he or she knows something about the study to which he or she is agreeing to participate. This triggered an official investigation by the United States Department of Health and Human Services. Over time, suspicions grew that researchers faked study data and that the study was a case of scientific fraud. The reputations of all the authors, of the sponsoring university, and of the scholarly journal in which it appeared have been irreparably tarnished.

Another study on the healing power of prayer was conducted by Mitchell Krucoff of Duke University and others. It appeared in 2005 in the scholarly journal *Lancet*. In this study, 700 heart patients received prayers by Buddhist, Muslim, Jewish, and Christian congregations around the world. The authors fully disclosed all study details, answered all questions, and obeyed all ethical guidelines. The study design was straightforward, and there was no evidence of fraud. However, this study found that prayer had no effect on healing. The study authors stated that until more research is conducted, we do not know whether prayer has any effect on medical recovery.

Unethical but Legal

Do not confuse being ethical with acting legally. A research action can be fully legal (i.e., not breaking any law) but clearly unethical (i.e., violate accepted standards of ethical research). This happens in other areas of life. You might be a dishonest, deceptive, and untrustworthy person who fails to keep your word and often lies. This makes you an immoral person, but you are not violating a law (unless you engage in deceptive business practices or lie while under a sworn oath). You may not have friends and few people will trust you, but you will not be sent to jail. (See Figure 2.2 for relations between legal and moral actions.)

As shown in Figure 2.2, most research actions are both moral and legal. People can quickly recognize actions that are both illegal and immoral. A few rare instances occur when a research action is illegal but ethical (see Example Study Box 5: Not

■ **Figure 2.2** Typology of Legal and Ethical Actions in Research

	Ethical	
Legal	**Yes**	**No**
Yes	Moral and Legal	Legal but Immoral
No	Illegal but Moral	Immoral and Illegal

Breaking the Confidence Guarantee later in this chapter). More common are legal research actions that violate ethical standards, because ethics are broader than the law. Acting within the law does not guarantee that you are acting ethically in research. You may want to seek guidance about ethics in research. Luckily, there are several resources: colleagues, ethical advisory committees, institutional review boards (discussed later in this chapter), professional codes of ethics (discussed later in this chapter), and published discussions of research ethics.

ETHICAL ISSUES INVOLVING RESEARCH PARTICIPANTS

Have you ever been a participant in a research study? If so, how were you treated? More than any other ethical issue, most attention in research ethics focuses on possible negative effects on the research participants. This is because of past situations of abuse and because total protection for research participants with absolute rights of noninterference would make research impossible. It is important to protect participants in research while still involving them in research studies.

Learning from History **Nazi Doctors**

The Hippocratic Oath that physicians take pertains to the ethical practice of medicine. It says, "Never to do deliberate harm to anyone." During the 1940s, respected scientific and medical experts in Germany violated this Oath. They conducted horrible acts on innocent men, women, and children for the purpose of studying them. The researchers used high research standards and carefully gathered data. They even published results in scholarly journals. Nonetheless, they acted unethically and failed to protect the research participants.

Using the large populations in concentration camps, German researchers gassed, poisoned, and froze research participants to death. They injected participants with typhus and malaria to study the diseases. Researchers purposely exposed people to mustard gas and incendiary bombs to study how they caused injury, and they starved people to death to study the starvation process. At the same time that German research was occurring, the Japanese conducted similar horrific studies on humans at research Unit 731 to improve bacteriological warfare. As many as ten thousand people were research participants, both civilians and prisoners of war. Physicians performed vivisections (opening the body and cutting flesh) and infected prisoners with various diseases and then removed organs to study disease. These procedures were conducted while the patients were alive. Vivisected prisoners included men, women, children, and infants. Prisoners had limbs amputated in order to study blood loss. Researchers froze the limbs (hands, arms, legs) and amputated them for study, or froze intact limbs and then thawed them to study the effects of untreated gangrene and rotting. Researchers also used humans as targets to test grenades, flamethrowers, germ-releasing bombs, chemical weapons, and explosive bombs. Other researchers looked at how long it took a person hung upside down to choke to death.

When World War II ended, the Allies (mostly British, French, and American) brought Nazi doctors before a war crimes tribunal in Nuremburg, Germany. They found many of the researchers to be guilty of "crimes against humanity." The trials resulted in the creation of an international set of ethical standards for conducting research with humans. Postwar trials charged few Japanese researchers with war crimes, and the events of Unit 731 received less publicity. This was because the Pacific War ended later, European involvement was less, and most of the victims were Asians subject to racist views that treated them as less important.

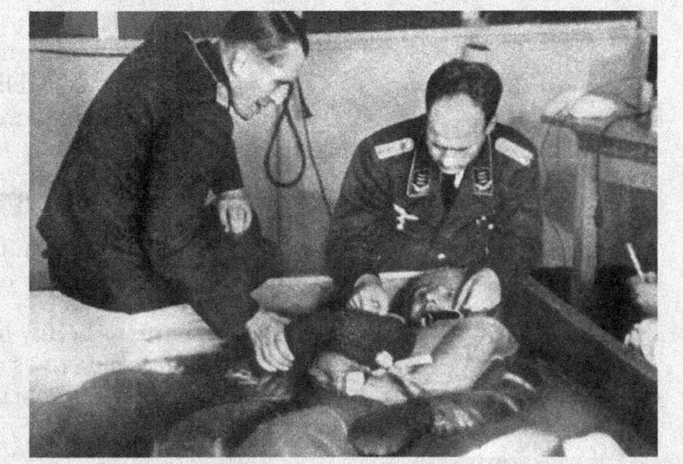

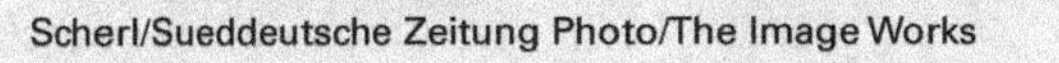
Scherl/Sueddeutsche Zeitung Photo/The Image Works

There are many gray areas in ethics in which you must balance competing values; however, the community of researchers, codes of ethics, and sometimes the law recognize a few clear prohibitions:

- Never cause unnecessary or irreversible harm to research participants.
- Always get voluntary consent from research participants before a study begins.
- Never unnecessarily humiliate or degrade research participants.
- Never release harmful information about specific individuals collected for research purposes.

If you wish to act ethically, follow a simple rule: Always show respect for the research participant. As the person conducting a study, you have a clear ethical responsibility to provide research participants with basic protections.

The Origin of Ethical Principles for Research with Humans

We can trace concerns over the treatment of research participants to medical studies in the early 1900s. This concern expanded after the public learned of gross violations of basic human rights in the name of research. The most notorious violations were "medical experiments" in Nazi Germany and Japan in the 1940s (see Learning from History: Nazi Doctors). Despite the mistreatment of people in the name of research, such as the Tuskegee syphilis study, each exposure of these incidents helped to extend and advance the discussion of ethical principles.

In the syphilis study and in horrific medical experiments during World War II, vulnerable, powerless people suffered in the name of scientific research and advancing knowledge. No one voluntarily agreed to participate in the study, and no one was told what would happen to them. This situation gave rise to the principle of voluntary participation (see discussion later in this chapter). It would be wonderful to report that all such abuse ended in the 1940s. However, incidents of unethical research have reappeared.

Until the 1970s, U.S. medical researchers did not always provide full ethical protection. For example, in 1940 U.S. researchers injected 400 prisoners with malaria to study the disease. They did not tell inmates about the nature of the experiment. Similar studies on malaria continued through 1946. As the U.S. military developed atomic weapons, researchers conducted studies on the effects of radioactive substances on people from the 1940s and the 1960s. In addition to prison inmates, researchers often used U.S. soldiers, hospital patients, or children with mental disabilities as research participants. In one case, researchers put radioactive material in the breakfast cereal of children. In other studies, the U.S. military gave unsuspecting people hallucinogenic drugs, such as LSD, to study their effects. During the 1960s, medical researchers injected patients at the Jewish Chronic Disease Hospital with live cancer cells and injected the hepatitis virus into children with developmental disabilities institutionalized at the New York Willowbrook School. Through the 1970s, researchers tested over 90 percent of new pharmaceuticals on prison inmates, despite increased questions about ethical protections.

Protect Research Participants from Harm

Most discussions about not harming people in research focuses on medical research, but social research can also cause harm in several ways:

- Physical harm or bodily injury
- Great emotional distress or psychological harm
- Legal harm and damage to a person's career, reputation, or income

Certain types of harm are more likely in certain types of research (e.g., in experiments versus field research). As a researcher, you have a responsibility to be aware of potential harm and to take precautions that will minimize the risk of harm to participants. The guiding ethical principle is that no person should experience harm as the direct result of his or her participating in a research study.

Physical Harm. Physical harm is rare in social research studies. The ethical rule is simple: Never—under any circumstance—purposely cause physical harm to a research participant. To be ethical, you must anticipate risks, including basic safety concerns (e.g., safe buildings, furniture, and equipment). This means screening out high-risk participants (those with heart conditions, mental breakdown, seizures, etc.) if you will subject them to great stress. A researcher accepts moral and legal responsibility for injury due to participation in research. You should terminate a project immediately if you can no longer guarantee the physical safety of those involved (see Example Study Box 3: Zimbardo Prison Experiment). Of course, if you do research in a dangerous situation, you also want to protect yourself from harm.

Psychological Abuse, Stress, or Loss of Self-Esteem. Some social research studies place participants in stressful, embarrassing, anxiety-producing, or unpleasant situations. By placing participants in realistic situations with psychological distress, we can learn about people's responses in real-life, high-anxiety situations. However, is it unethical to cause discomfort? Researchers still debate the ethics of the famous Milgram obedience study (see Example Study Box 2: The Milgram Obedience Study). Some say that the precautions Milgram undertook and the great knowledge gained outweighed the potential psychological harm to participants. Others believe that the extreme stress and the risk of permanent harm were too great. Today, no one would conduct such an experiment due to a heightened sensitivity to the ethical issues involved.

Social psychologists who study helping behavior often place participants in stressful, emergency situations to see whether they will lend assistance. For example, Piliavin and associates (1969) studied helping behavior in subways by faking a person's collapse onto the floor. In the field experiment, the riders in the subway car were unaware of the experiment and did not volunteer to participate in it. The study's findings were valuable, but the lack of informed consent (see later in this chapter) and anxiety created were ethically controversial.

Only experienced researchers should consider conducting a study in which they purposely induce great stress or anxiety. They must take all necessary precautions before inducing anxiety or discomfort. This includes consulting with others who have conducted similar studies as well as with mental health professionals. They should screen out high-risk populations, arrange for emergency interventions, and be prepared to end the study immediately if a dangerous situation arises. They must always obtain written informed consent (discussed later in this chapter) and always debrief participants (explained later). Even with these safeguards, they can never create unnecessary stress. *Unnecessary* means beyond the minimal amount required for the desired effect. Any discomfort they create must have a very clear, legitimate research purpose. Knowing what *minimal amount* means comes with experience. It is best to begin with too little stress, risking a finding of no effect, than to create too much. Also, it is best to work in collaboration with other researchers, because involving several sensitive researchers reduces the chance of making an ethical misjudgment.

Legal Harm. A researcher is responsible for protecting research participants from an increased risk of arrest simply because they are in a study. If a risk of arrest is associated with research participation, the willingness of people to participate in research will decline. Potential legal harm is one criticism of the study by Humphreys (1973) (see Example Study Box 4: Humphreys Tearoom Study). A related ethical issue occurs if you learn of illegal activity when collecting data. You must weigh the value of protecting the researcher-participant relationship against potential harm to innocent people if you do not report what you discover. In the end, you, as the researcher, alone are morally and legally responsible.

In field research on police, Van Maanen (1982:114–115) reported seeing police beat people and witnessing illegal acts and irregular procedures but said, "On and following these troublesome incidents I followed police custom: I kept my mouth shut."

Field researchers who study the "seamy side" of society can face difficult ethical decisions. For example, when studying a mental institution, Taylor (1987) discovered the mistreatment and abuse of inmates by the staff. He had two choices: Abandon the study and call for an immediate investigation, or keep quiet and continue with the study for several months, publicize the findings afterward, and then become an advocate to end the abuse. After weighing the situation, he followed the latter course and is now an activist for the rights of mental institution inmates. In some studies, observing illegal behavior may be central to the research project. A researcher who closely works with law-enforcement officials must face the question, Are you an independent professional who ethically protects participants to advance knowledge in the long term, or are you freelance undercover informant who is working for the police and is trying to catch criminals now?

Example Study Box 2 The Milgram Obedience Study

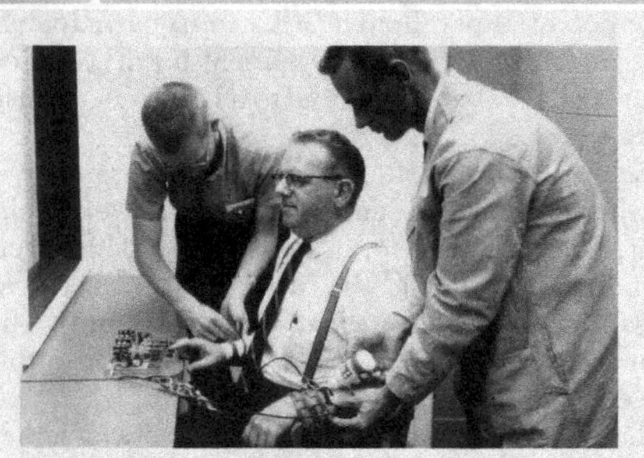

Courtesy of Alexandra Milgram. Copyright 1968 by Stanley Milgram. Copyright renewed 1993 by Alexandra Milgram. From the film OBEDIENCE, distributed by Penn State Media Sales

Stanley Milgram's studies on obedience (Milgram, 1963, 1965, 1974) are widely discussed. He wanted to learn how ordinary people could have carried out the horrors of the Holocaust under the Nazis. The study examined the impact of social pressure on people obeying authority figures. After signing informed consent forms, he assigned a volunteer-participant, in rigged random selection, to be a "teacher" while a confederate working for him was the "pupil." The pupil was located in a nearby room, where the research participant could hear but not see the pupil. The pupil was connected to electrical wires. Milgram told the participant to test the pupil's memory of word lists and to increase the electric shock level if the pupil made mistakes. The shock apparatus was clearly labeled with increasing voltage that indicated its danger. As the pupil increasingly made mistakes and the teacher-participant turned switches, the pupil would make noises as if in severe pain. The researcher was always present and made quiet comments such as, "You must go on" to the participant. As the voltage levels got higher, Milgram reported, "Subjects were observed to sweat, tremble, stutter, bite their lips, groan and dig their fingernails into their flesh. These were characteristic rather than exceptional responses to the experiment" (Milgram, 1963:375). At the end, he told participants what really took place. The "pupil" was actually a confederate who was acting, and no one was shocked. The percentage of "teacher" participants who applied electrical shocks to very dangerous levels was dramatically higher than Milgram expected; 65 percent gave shocks at 450 volts. This study raised ethical concerns over using deception and about the extreme emotional stress participants experienced. Despite the precautions, many people believe that the degree of distress and risk of long-term emotional problems among the participants was too great.

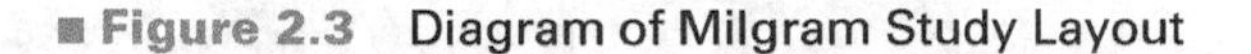

■ **Figure 2.3** Diagram of Milgram Study Layout

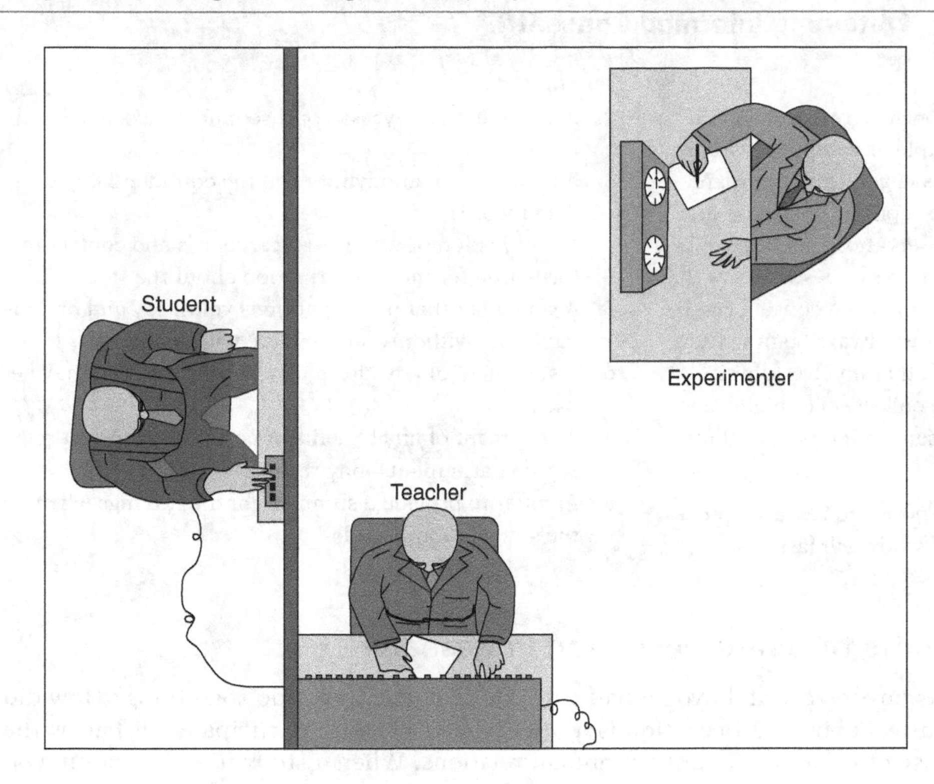

Participation Must Be Voluntary and Informed

A fundamental ethical principle is, Never coerce anyone into participating; participation *must* be voluntary at all times. This is the ethical **principle of voluntary consent**. Permission is not enough. To make an informed decision, people need to know what they are being asked to participate in. Researchers need to make participants aware of their rights. To do this they provide participants with a statement about the study and ask participants to sign it. This is **informed consent**. Government agencies require informed consent in most studies involving people, with a few exceptions. You should get informed consent unless there are good reasons for not obtaining it (e.g., covert field research, use of secondary data, etc.).

An informed consent statement gives a research participant specific information (see Making It Practical: Obtaining Informed Consent) about research procedures and the uses of the data. For survey research, we know that participants who receive a full informed consent statement respond the same as those who do not. If anything, people who refuse to sign the statement are likely to guess or say "no response" to survey questions.

A formal, signed informed consent statement is optional for most survey, field, existing statistics, and secondary data research, but it is mandatory for most experimental research. The general rule is, the greater the risk of causing possible harm to a research participant, the greater the need to obtain a written informed consent statement. There are many sound reasons to get informed consent and very few reasons not to get it.

Informed consent that discloses research details along with the researcher's identification helps to protect research participants against fraudulent research and to protect legitimate research. It lessens the chances that a con artist can use a bogus identity to defraud or abuse research participants, market products, or obtain personal information for unethical purposes.

principle of voluntary consent never force anyone to participate in a research study, participants should explicitly and voluntarily agree to participate.

informed consent an agreement in which participants state they are willing to be in a study and know what the research procedure will involve.

Making It Practical Obtaining Informed Consent

You must get informed consent for most research on humans. Consent upholds the principle of voluntary participation and is mandated in various laws, regulations, and codes of ethics. There are a few exceptions to the use of consent, such as field research observation in a large public setting. In situations such as a survey questionnaire that do not ask for highly personal information, consent can be a short oral statement. Consent must always be in written form with a signature for research that involves physical discomfort, induced stress, or the collection of highly personal information. Informed consent statements contain the following eight elements:

1. A brief description of the purpose and research procedure, including how long the study will last
2. A statement of any risks or discomfort associated with participation
3. A guarantee of anonymity and the confidentiality of data records
4. Identification of who the researcher is and contact information for more information about the study
5. A statement that participation is voluntary and participants can withdraw at any time without penalty.
6. A statement of any alternative procedures that may be used
7. A statement of any benefits or compensation that research participants may receive
8. An offer to provide a summary of the findings when the study is completed

Limits to Using Deception in Research

Has anyone ever told you a half-truth or lie to get you to do something? How did you feel about it? Deception is a mild type of harm to participants; it harms the sense of trust and honesty in human relations. When a study uses deception, voluntary participation and a person's right not to participate can be a critical issue.

Example Study Box 3 Zimbardo Prison Experiment

PG Zimbardo, Inc.

Philip Zimbardo (Zimbardo 1972) designed an experiment on prison conditions. Before the experiment, he gave male volunteer students personality tests and only included those in the "normal" range. He randomly divided the volunteers into two role-playing groups: guards and prisoners. The study took place in a simulated prison in the basement of a Stanford University building. Zimbardo informed participants assigned to play prisoner that they would be under surveillance and would have some civil rights suspended, but that no physical abuse was allowed. He deindividualized (dressed in standard uniforms and called only by their numbers) the prisoners, and militarized (given uniforms, nightsticks, and reflective sunglasses) the guards to make the simulation feel real. He told guards to maintain a reasonable degree of order. Guards served 8-hour shifts while he had prisoners locked up 24 hours per day. The study was to last two weeks. Unexpectedly, participants got very caught up in their roles. The prisoners became passive, depressed, and disorganized. The guards became aggressive, arbitrary, and dehumanizing. By the sixth day, Zimbardo called off the experiment for ethical reasons. The risk of permanent psychological harm, and even physical harm, was too great.

Researchers debate whether using deception is ethically acceptable. Some say it is never acceptable. Others say it is ethical, but only for specific purposes and with strict conditions.

Sometimes an experimental researcher deceives participants or uses misrepresentation for legitimate methodological reasons. The most common use of deception is when you expect that participants would modify their behavior or statements if they knew the study's true purpose. For example, you want to study body posture. If you tell participants you are studying their body posture, they might adjust how they stand or sit because they know this is something you were observing. This could make it impossible for you to learn about their real body posture. Another use of deception is in covert field research. For example, you could not gain access to a research site if you told the truth, so you lie or hide your identity as a researcher. Say you want to conduct a field study on teens who use illegal drugs and commit minor crimes. If you told the teens when you first approached them you were going to carefully observe and study them, they might not cooperate or reveal all their actions.

In any type of study, deception is *never preferable* if you can accomplish the same thing without using it. It is a last resort. Deception is acceptable only within strict limits, if you do the following:

- Show that it has a clear, specific methodological purpose.
- Use it only to the minimal degree necessary and for the shortest time.
- Obtain informed consent and do not misrepresent any risks.
- Always debrief (i.e., explain the actual conditions to participants afterward).

It is possible to obtain prior informed consent and use deception if you describe the basic procedures involved but conceal limited information about specific details. You could inform participants that they will sit alone in a room for 10 minutes, chat with one other participant for 5 minutes, and then complete a 15-item questionnaire, but not tell them your hypotheses or that the other participant in the room is secretly working for you. Experimental researchers often invent stories about the purpose of a study to distract participants from the true purpose of a study. For example, a researcher studying male-female eye contact might tell participants the study is about college student opinions on current affairs.

Some field researchers use covert observation to gain entry to a field research setting. In studies of cults, small extremist political sects, and illegal or deviant behavior, it may be impossible to conduct research if you disclose your purpose. *If a covert stance is not essential, the ethical rule is very clear: Do not use it.* If you are unsure of whether covert access is necessary, then use a strategy of gradual disclosure. Begin with limited disclosure, then reveal more as you learn more about a setting and participants. When in doubt, it is best to err in the direction of disclosing your true identity and purpose.

Covert field research is controversial among researchers. Many feel that all covert research is unethical. Even researchers who accept covert research in certain situations place limits on its use. It is only acceptable when overt observation is impossible. If you use covert research, you must inform participants of the covert observation immediately afterward and give them an opportunity to express concerns.

A downside to deception and covert research are that they increase mistrust and cynicism and lower public respect for doing research. Secretly spying on people without their permission and lying to get information carry real dangers. They are analogous to being an undercover government informer in a nondemocratic society.

Avoid Coercion. Coercion is another issue that creates difficulty in obtaining informed consent. Coercion can be physical, social, legal, professional, financial, or other pressure put on people to agree to participate in a study. The general rule is clear: Never coerce people to participate. This includes offering people a special benefit that they cannot attain other than through participation in a study. For example, it is unethical for a commanding officer to order a soldier to participate in a study, for a professor to require a student to be a research participant to pass a course, or for an employer to expect an employee to complete a survey as a condition of continued employment.

The rule against coercing people to participate in a study can become tricky in specific situations. For example, a convicted criminal faces the alternative of two years' imprisonment or participation in an experimental rehabilitation program. The convicted criminal does not believe in the benefits of the program, but the researcher believes that it will help the criminal. The criminal is being coerced to participate; the alternative is two years in prison. In such a case, the researcher and others must honestly decide whether the benefits to the criminal and to society clearly and far outweigh the ethical prohibition on coercion. Plus, the coercion must be limited. Even so, such decisions are risky. History shows many cases in which researchers forced powerless participants to be in a study allegedly to help them, but later it turned out that the research participants received few benefits but experienced great harm (see the discussion of the Tuskegee syphilis study at the beginning of this chapter).

Perhaps you have been in a social science class in which a teacher required you to participate in a research project. This is a special case of coercion. Usually, it is ethical. The legitimate justification for it is that students learn more about research when they experience it directly in a realistic situation. Such minor, limited coercion is acceptable as long as the teacher meets three conditions:

- The participation in research is attached to a clear educational objective of the specific course.
- Students have a choice of the research experience or an alternative activity of equal difficulty.
- The teacher follows all other ethical principles of conducting research.

Example Study Box 4 **Humphreys Tearoom Study**

Kelly Redinger/Design Pics/Corbis Royalty Free

Laud Humphreys studied male homosexual behavior (Humphreys 1973). He focused on "tearooms"—places where anonymous sexual encounters occur. He observed about 100 men engaging in sexual acts in a public restroom in a park. To do this, Humphreys pretended to be a "watchqueen" (a voyeur and lookout). He also followed research participants to their cars and secretly recorded their license numbers. He next obtained the names and addresses of participants from law enforcement registers by posing as a market researcher. One year later, in disguise, Humphreys used a deceptive story about conducting a health survey to interview the men in their homes. Humphreys kept names in safety deposit boxes and took precautions. He significantly advanced knowledge about the men who frequent "tearooms" and overturned previous false beliefs about them. He learned that most of the men were married and had stable jobs. They were not isolated loners without stable relationships or jobs, as was previously thought. The study generated an ethical controversy. It was covert research based on deception. None of the participants voluntarily agreed to be in the study. Despite precautions, Humphreys put participants at risk of great legal and personal harm. Had he lost control of the names, someone might have used them to blackmail participants, destroy their marriages and careers, or initiate criminal prosecution against them.

Privacy, Anonymity, and Confidentiality

How would you feel if someone learned private details about your personal life and shared them with the public without your permission or knowledge? Because researchers sometimes learn intimate details about participants, they must take precautions to protect research participants' privacy.

Privacy. When you study people, you may learn private details about them. As survey research probes into beliefs, backgrounds, and behaviors, it often reveals intimate, private details. Experimental researchers sometimes use two-way mirrors or hidden microphones to "spy" on a person's behavior. Even if research participants are aware they are in a study, they may not know what a researcher is looking for. Field researchers observe private aspects of behavior or eavesdrop on personal conversations. They have studied people in public places (e.g., in waiting rooms, walking down the street, in classrooms, etc.), but some "public" places are more private than others (consider, for example, the use of periscopes to observe people who thought they were alone in a public toilet stall). Eavesdropping on conversations and observing people in quasi-private areas raises ethical concerns.

When you conduct research, you need to protect the privacy of participants. To be ethical, you can only violate a participant's privacy to the minimum degree necessary and collect private information only for a legitimate research purpose. In addition, you must take several steps to protect the information you have learned about participants from public disclosure. This takes two forms that many people confuse: anonymity and confidentiality.

2

Anonymity. **Anonymity** means to remain anonymous or nameless. No one can trace information back to a specific individual. You can protect anonymity differently in different research techniques. In survey and experimental research, you do not collect names or addresses of participants and refer to them by a code number. If you use a mail survey and include a code on the questionnaire to determine which respondents failed to respond, you are not keeping respondents anonymous during that phase of the study. If you collect completed questionnaires from individuals on which they do not provide their names but you are able to narrow down which person submitted a particular questionnaire based on details about them and a list of name, your questionnaire is not anonymous. You might breach a promise of anonymity unknowingly in small samples. For example, you survey students at a small college of 250 students and ask questions including age, sex, religion, hobbies, and hometown. You notice answers from a 22-year-old Jewish male born in Stratford, Ontario whose hobby is to be on the football team. Such information among a small group allows you to learn who the specific individual is, even if you did not ask his name. This violates a promise of anonymity.

Protecting anonymity in field research is difficult. You learn details about research participants and their names. You can disguise some details and give false names, but even this does not always work. In one community study, researchers invented a false town name, "Springdale," and altered facts to protect the anonymity of the people studied, but they did not do enough. As a result, readers could identify the town and particular individuals when the study appeared as a book, *Small Town in Mass Society* (Vidich and Bensman 1968). Town residents became very upset about how the researchers portrayed them. They even staged a parade mocking the researchers. An additional issue is that when you use fictitious information, the gap between what you studied and what you report may raise questions about what you found and what you made up.

anonymity not connecting a participant's name or identifying details to information collected about him or her.

Confidentiality. Even if you cannot protect anonymity, you should always protect participant confidentiality. Anonymity means that no one can learn the identity of specific individuals. **Confidentiality** allows you to attach the information to particular

confidentiality holding information in confidence or not making it known to the public.

Figure 2.4 Anonymity and Confidentiality

Confidentiality	Anonymity YES	Anonymity NO
YES	Gather data so it is impossible for anyone to link it to any name and release findings in aggregate form.	Privately link details about a specific participant to a name, but only publicly release findings in aggregate form.
NO	Release details about a specific participant to the public, but withhold the name and details that might allow someone to trace back to the person.	**Unethical** Reveal publicly details about a person with his/her name.

2

individuals, but you keep it secret from public disclosure. You only release data in a way that does not permit anyone else to link specific individuals to information. To do this, you present data publicly only in an aggregate form (e.g., as percentages, statistical means, etc.). It is possible for you to provide anonymity without confidentiality, or vice versa, although they usually go together (see Figure 2.4).

Here is an example of each situation listed in Figure 2.4:

- **Anonymity with confidentiality** You conduct a survey of 100 people but do not know names of any of the participants and only release data as percentages of the total.
- **Anonymity without confidentiality** You conduct a field research study and learn a lot about person X but never learn the person's name. You report all the details about the person publicly but alter only a few details to make it impossible for anyone to track down the person to discover the name.
- **Confidentiality without anonymity** You conduct a survey of 100 people and have each person's name listed on his or her questionnaire but only publicly release the data as percentages of the total.
- **Neither anonymity nor confidentiality (this is unethical)** You conduct a survey of 100 people and have each person's name on his or her questionnaire. You publicly release a person's answers with the name, or with enough details to allow easy discovery of the person's name.

Anonymity and confidentiality become more complicated if you study "special populations" (see the discussion later in this chapter). In many large bureaucracies, people in positions of authority may restrict research access unless you violate confidentiality and give them information about participants. For example, you want to study drug use and sexual activity among high school students. School authorities only agree if you give them the names of all drug users and sexually active students. They might say they want to assist the students with counseling and to inform the students' parents. An ethical researcher must refuse to continue. If the school officials really wanted to assist the students and not use researchers as spies, they could develop their own outreach program. Another example is a survey of a company. A company manager asks to see all employee complaints and names of who complained. The supposed reason is to address the complaining individual's concerns. The ethical researcher protects participant privacy and only releases findings without names to protect the employees from potential retaliation.

Privacy rules operate with those to protect participants from legal or physical harm. Draus and associates (2005) protected the participants in a study of illegal drug users in rural Ohio. They conducted interviews in large multiuse buildings, avoided any reference to illegal drugs in their written documents, did not include the names of drug dealers and locations, and did not affiliate with drug rehabilitation services. This is because the rehabilitation services had ties to law enforcement. They (2005:169) noted, "We intentionally avoided contact with local police,

Example Study Box 5 Not Breaking the Confidence Guarantee

Social researchers can pay a high personal cost for being ethical. Washington State University Professor Rik Scarce went to jail. Professor Scarce had studied extremist social-political movements using accepted field research techniques. He introduced himself, slowly gained access and won trust, explained his research interests, and guaranteed confidentiality. He attended a local group's meetings, talked with activists and leaders, and spent time observing. In a second study of extremist groups, Dr. Scarce was studying a radical animal liberation group when police suspected the group leader of breaking into at nearby animal facility, releasing the research animals, and causing $150,000 in vandalism damage. Although some past court rulings appeared to offer social researchers protection, other rulings have not upheld confidentiality protections for social research data. When police asked for all of Dr. Scarce research notes, he followed professional ethical rules and principles. He refused to break the research confidentiality guarantee and hand over his notes or testify to a grand jury about his observations. As a result, he spent 159 days in a Spokane, Washington jail for contempt of court.

Petre Buzoianu/Corbis

2

prosecutors, or parole officers" and "surveillance of the project by local law enforcement was a source of concern."

In a few, rare situations, other principles overrule the principle of protecting research participant privacy. One exception is a clear, immediate danger to a person's safety, such as learning that a participant is considering suicide or plans to injure or kill another person. For example, you study parents, and during an interview with a father, you learn that he is abusing his child physically or sexually. In this case, you weigh protecting participant privacy against harm that the child would experience. The ethical course of action is to protect the child from imminent harm and notify the authorities.

Extra Protection for Special Populations

Some research participants may not be able to give true voluntary informed consent. **Special populations** such as students, prison inmates, employees, military personnel, the homeless, welfare recipients, children, or the developmentally disabled may not be fully capable of giving consent freely. Some may agree because it is a way to a desired good—such as higher grades, early parole, promotions, or additional

special populations people lacking the cognitive competency or full freedom to give true informed consent.

services; others may not understand what research means. If you wish to have "incompetent" people (e.g., children, mentally disabled, etc.) participate in a research study, you must meet two minimal conditions:

- The person's legal guardian/parent grants written informed consent permission.
- You closely follow all standard ethical rules to protect participants from any form of harm.

For example, you want to survey high school students to learn about their sexual behavior and drug or alcohol use. If you wish to conduct the survey on school property, you must obtain permission from school officials and get informed consent from the parent/legal guardian of any student who is a legal minor (usually under 18 years old) as well. You should also obtain informed consent from the research participant. High schools students are a special population that requires extra protections.

Formal Protections for Research Participants

In the United States, the U.S. Department of Health and Human Services Office for the Protection from Research Risks issues regulations to protect research participants. Federal regulations follow a biomedical model and protect participants from physical harm. It is one federal government agency, and technically its rules apply to when federal money is involved, but all other government agencies and most researchers follow its guidance. Most local governments, hospitals, universities, and private companies model their internal policies on the federal rules. Other U.S. government rules require the creation of institutional review boards at all research institutes, medical facilities, colleges, and universities where research with humans occurs. An **institutional review board (IRB)** applies ethical guidelines by reviewing research procedures at a proposal or preliminary stage. Some forms of research are exempt from a formal, full review by the IRB. These include educational tests, normal educational practice, most nonsensitive survey questionnaires, observation of public behavior, and studies of existing public data in which individuals cannot be identified. Submitting a proposal to an IRB for review requires a little extra time and planning. Most IRB members are concerned with upholding ethical protections of research participants. They are an "extra set of eyes" looking at a research design to ensure that participants will be fully protected.

Most professionals (such as physicians, attorneys, family counselors, social workers, and others) have organizations that developed a written code of ethics, peer review boards, or licensing regulations. A **code of ethics** is a written statement of ethical rules that identify proper and improper behavior. Most professional social science associations have codes of ethics that represent a consensus of professionals on ethics. Although not all researchers may agree on every ethical issue, they uphold ethical standards as members of a profession.

We can trace formal codes of research ethics to the Nuremberg Code adopted during the Nuremberg Military Tribunal on Nazi war crimes immediately after World War II. It was a direct response to the cruelty of concentration camp experiments, and it outlines ethical principles and rights of human research participants. These include the following:

- Ensure that participants have voluntarily consented to be in the study.
- Avoid unnecessary physical and mental suffering.
- Avoid any research where death or disabling injury to participants is likely.
- End a research study immediately if its continuation is likely to cause injury, disability, or death.
- Highly qualified people using the highest levels of skill and care should conduct research studies.
- Study results should be for the good of society and unattainable by any other method.

institutional review board (IRB) a committee of researchers and community members that oversees, monitors, and reviews the impact of research procedures on human participants.

code of ethics a written, formal set of professional standards that provides guidance when ethical questions arise in practice.

2

Making It Practical Codes of Ethics

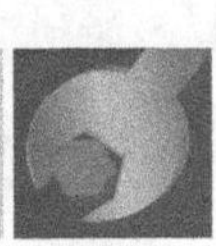

Professional associations promote codes of ethics and hear about possible violations, but there is no formal policing of the codes. The penalty for a minor ethical violation rarely goes past public embarrassment and a letter of complaint. Those who commit a serious ethical violation, even if they violated no law, will face loss of reputation, loss of employment, a ban on the research findings being published, or restrictions from future jobs. Besides making explicit the beliefs of the research community and providing individual researchers with guidance, codes of ethics help universities and other institutions defend legitimate, ethical research against outside political or other pressures. If researchers receive unjustified demands to stop legitimate research or to reveal protected details about research participants, they look to written codes of ethics on websites. If you review the codes of ethics of several professional organizations, such as nursing, social work, public opinion research, psychology, or sociology, you will discover that they are not identical but they do overlap a great deal.

Figure 2.5 Code of Professional Ethics and Practices

We, the members of the American Association for Public Opinion Research, subscribe to the principles expressed in the following code. Our goals are to support sound and ethical practice in the conduct of public opinion research and in the use of such research for policy- and decision-making in the public and private sectors, as well as to improve public understanding of public opinion and survey research methods and the proper use of public opinion and survey research results.

We pledge ourselves to maintain high standards of scientific competence and integrity in conducting, analyzing, and reporting our work; in our relations with survey respondents; with our clients; with those who eventually use the research for decision-making purposes; and with the general public. We further pledge ourselves to reject all tasks or assignments that would require activities inconsistent with the principles of this code.

THE CODE

I. Principles of Professional Practice in the Conduct of Our Work
   A. We shall exercise due care in developing research designs and survey instruments, and in collecting, processing, and analyzing data, taking all reasonable steps to assure the reliability and validity of results.
      1. We shall recommend and employ only those tools and methods of analysis that, in our professional judgment, are well suited to the research problem at hand.
      2. We shall not knowingly select research tools and methods of analysis that yield misleading conclusions.
      3. We shall not knowingly make interpretations of research results that are inconsistent with the data available, nor shall we tacitly permit such interpretations.
      4. We shall not knowingly imply that interpretations should be accorded greater confidence than the data actually warrant.
   B. We shall describe our methods and findings accurately and in appropriate detail in all research reports, adhering to the standards for minimal disclosure specified in Section III.
   C. If any of our work becomes the subject of a formal investigation of an alleged violation of this Code, undertaken with the approval of the AAPOR Executive Council, we shall provide additional information on the survey in such detail that a fellow survey practitioner would be able to conduct a professional evaluation of the survey.

II. Principles of Professional Responsibility in Our Dealings with People
   A. The Public:
      1. When preparing a report for public release we shall ensure that the findings are a balanced and accurate portrayal of the survey results.
      2. If we become aware of the appearance in public of serious inaccuracies or distortions regarding our research, we shall publicly disclose what is required to correct these inaccuracies or distortions, including, as appropriate, a statement to the public media, legislative body, regulatory agency, or other appropriate group, to which the inaccuracies or distortions were presented.
      3. We shall inform those for whom we conduct publicly released surveys that AAPOR standards require members to release minimal information about such surveys, and we shall make all reasonable efforts to encourage clients to subscribe to our standards for minimal disclosure in their releases.

(continued)

Figure 2.5 *Continued*

B. Clients or Sponsors:
   1. When undertaking work for a private client, we shall hold confidential all proprietary information obtained about the client and about the conduct and findings of the research undertaken for the client, except when the dissemination of the information is expressly authorized by the client, or when disclosure becomes necessary under the terms of Section I-C or II-A of this Code.
   2. We shall be mindful of the limitations of our techniques and capabilities and shall accept only those research assignments that we can reasonably expect to accomplish within these limitations.

C. The Profession:
   1. We recognize our responsibility to the science of survey research to disseminate as freely as possible the ideas and findings that emerge from our research.
   2. We shall not cite our membership in the Association as evidence of professional competence, since the Association does not so certify any persons or organizations.

D. The Respondent:
   1. We shall avoid practices or methods that may harm, humiliate, or seriously mislead survey respondents.
   2. We shall respect respondents' concerns about their privacy.
   3. Aside from the decennial census and a few other surveys, participation in surveys is voluntary. We shall provide all persons selected for inclusion with a description of the survey sufficient to permit them to make an informed and free decision about their participation.
   4. We shall not misrepresent our research or conduct other activities (such as sales, fund raising, or political campaigning) under the guise of conducting research.
   5. Unless the respondent waives confidentiality for specified uses, we shall hold as privileged and confidential all information that might identify a respondent with his or her responses. We also shall not disclose or use the names of respondents for non-research purposes unless the respondents grant us permission to do so.
   6. We understand that the use of our survey results in a legal proceeding does not relieve us of our ethical obligation to keep confidential all respondent identifiable information or lessen the importance of respondent anonymity.

III. Standards for Minimal Disclosure

Good professional practice imposes the obligation upon all public opinion researchers to include, in any report of research results, or to make available when that report is released, certain essential information about how the research was conducted. At a minimum, the following items should be disclosed.

   1. Who sponsored the survey, and who conducted it.
   2. The exact wording of questions asked, including the text of any preceding instruction or explanation to the interviewer or respondents that might reasonably be expected to affect the response.
   3. A definition of the population under study, and a description of the sampling frame used to identify this population.
   4. A description of the sample design, giving a clear indication of the method by which the respondents were selected by the researcher, or whether the respondents were entirely self-selected.
   5. Sample sizes and, where appropriate, eligibility criteria, screening procedures, and response rates computed according to AAPOR Standard Definitions. At a minimum, a summary of disposition of sample cases should be provided so that response rates could be computed.
   6. A discussion of the precision of the findings, including estimates of sampling error, and a description of any weighting or estimating procedures used.
   7. Which results are based on parts of the sample, rather than on the total sample, and the size of such parts.
   8. Method, location, and dates of data collection.

From time to time, AAPOR Council may issue guidelines and recommendations on best practices with regard to the release, design and conduct of surveys.

Copy of American Association of Public Opinion Research of Code of Professional Ethics (a pdf file) as revised in 2005.

Summary Review Basic Principles of Ethical Research

- Accept responsibility for all ethical decisions and the protection of research participants.
- Use the research techniques that are most appropriate for a topic or situation.
- Follow accepted methodological standards and strive for high accuracy.
- Detect and remove any threats of harm to research participants.
- Never exploit research participants for personal gain.
- Get informed consent from the research participants before beginning.
- Treat the research participants with dignity and respect at all times.
- Only use deception if absolutely needed, and always debrief participants afterward.
- Honor all guarantees of privacy, confidentiality, and anonymity you make to participants.
- Be candid and honest when interpreting and reporting study results.
- Identify the sponsors of funded research to participants and to the public.
- Release all details of the study procedures with the results.
- Act with integrity and adhere to the behaviors outlined in professional codes of ethics.

The principles of the Nuremberg Code focused on medical experimentation, but they became the basis for the ethical codes for all research with humans.

ETHICS AND THE SPONSORS OF RESEARCH

You might find a job in which you are assigned to conduct research for a sponsor—an employer, a government agency, or a private firm. Special ethical issues can arise when a sponsor pays for research, especially applied research. Some sponsors ask researchers to compromise ethical or professional research standards as a condition for continued employment. If a sponsor makes an illegitimate demand, you have three basic choices: be loyal to an organization and cave in to the sponsor, exit from the situation by quitting, or voice opposition and become a whistle-blower (see the discussion later in this chapter). You need to set ethical boundaries beyond which you refuse a sponsor's demands and choose your own course of action. Whatever the case, it is best to consider ethical issues early in a relationship with a sponsor and to express your concerns up front.

Arriving at Particular Findings

A sponsor might tell you, directly or indirectly, what results you should come up with before you conduct a study. The ethical choice is to refuse to continue if told you must reach specific findings as a precondition for doing research. Legitimate research does not have restrictions on the possible findings. In an ethical, legitimate study, you will not know the findings for certain until after you have gathered the data and completed the study.

Limits on How to Conduct Studies. Sponsors can legitimately set some conditions on research techniques used (e.g., survey versus experiment) and limit costs for research. However, as a researcher, you must follow generally accepted research standards. Often there is a trade-off between research quality and cost. You should give a realistic appraisal of what you can accomplish for a given level of funding. If you cannot uphold generally accepted standards of research, refuse to do the research.

Unfortunately, some sponsors care little for the actual results or truth. They have little respect for research or its ethical principles. To them research is only "a cover" that legitimates a predetermined decision or only a way to deflect criticism. They are abusing the reputation of research and its integrity to advance their own narrow goals. If a sponsor asks you to use illegitimate research techniques (such as a biased sample or leading survey questions), the ethical choice is a refusal to cooperate. In the long run, ethical violations harm the sponsor, researchers, the scientific community, and society in general. You need to decide whether to prostitute your skills and give sponsors whatever they want, even if it is unethical, or be a professional who is obligated to teach, guide, or even oppose sponsors based on higher principles.

Suppressing Findings. Perhaps you conduct a study, and the findings make the sponsor look bad. The sponsor decides to suppress the study's results. This kind of situation happens fairly often in applied research. In one case, a state government created a lottery commission to examine starting a government-sponsored lottery. Some politicians and members of the public asked for a study on the likely effects of a state lottery, so the commission hired a sociologist with expertise in that area. After she completed the study, but before releasing the report to the public, the commission asked her to remove sections of the report that discussed the negative social effects of gambling. They tried to eliminate sections of the report that predicted that the lottery would cause a large increase in compulsive gamblers and the recommendation that the state create social services to help them. The commission ordered and paid for the study, but the researcher felt a professional ethical obligation to show the public the full, uncensored report. Unless she went beyond the commission and released the complete report, the public would see a distorted, biased picture of study findings.

Unfortunately, even the U.S. federal government has a record of suppressing research findings that contradict the political goals of high officials. In 2004, many leading scientists, including Nobel laureates, medical experts, former federal agency directors, and university presidents, voiced their concern over the dramatic increase in the government's misuse of research. A major complaint was that government officials had suppressed important research findings that disagreed with their political goals. In addition, they suppressed findings on the poor safety or pollution records of industries that just happened to be major political campaign contributions. Researchers working for government agencies said that their politically appointed managers had suppressed findings or omitted important technical information to advance nonscientific, political goals that the findings had contradicted.

In sponsored research, you want to negotiate conditions for releasing findings *prior to beginning* the study or signing a contract. It is best to begin with an explicit guarantee that you will only conduct ethical research. It is legitimate to delay the release of findings to protect the identity of informants, to maintain access to a research site, or to protect your personal safety. It is not legitimate to censor findings because a sponsor does not want to look bad or wants to protect its reputation. The researcher directly involved and knowledgeable about a study shoulders a responsibility for both conducting the research and to making its findings public.

Whistle-blowing occurs when a researcher informs an external audience of a serious ethical problem that is being ignored. It is never a first step; rather it occurs after the researcher has repeatedly attempted to inform superiors and fix the problem internally. The whistle-blowing researcher must believe that the situation is a serious breach of ethics and the organization will not end it without public pressure. Whistle-blowing is risky in several ways:

- Outsiders may not be interested in the ethical abuse and simply ignore it.
- Outsiders might not care about ending unethical behavior instead use the exposure of unethical behavior to advance their own goals.

whistle-blowing when a researcher sees unethical behavior and, after unsuccessful attempts to get superiors to end it, goes public to expose the wrongdoing.

Tips for the Wise Consumer Who Paid for a Study?

It is unethical to hide the identity of research sponsor. You should tell study participants who the sponsor is and inform the readers of research reports. Participants in a study have a right to know the sponsor. Telling participants is rarely controversial, but it becomes tricky in a few instances. For example, a pro-choice organization sponsors a study to look at the attitudes of members of religious groups opposed to abortion. The organization asks that you not reveal the sponsor to participants. You must balance the ethical rule to reveal a sponsor's identity against the sponsor's desire for confidentiality and possible bias or reduced cooperation by study participants. In general, unless you have a very clear, strong methodological reason for not doing so (such as reduced cooperation and strong bias), tell participants of the sponsor of a study. If telling participants of the sponsor will create a bias or noncooperation, then wait until after you have gathered the data.

When reporting study results, the ethical mandate is unambiguous: You must always reveal sponsors who fund a study. One study can have multiple sponsors, especially if it is a large one; you should list all the sponsors. Government agencies, foundations, or nonprofit organizations fund most research studies. Here is the sponsor information from the footnote of an article (Kane 2005: 463): "This research was conducted in part under National Institute of Justice grant #1996IJCX0053. Neither the NIJ nor any agencies mentioned in the manuscript bear responsibility for the analyses and interpretations of the data contained herein."

If you see no funding source listed, the study was probably part of the researcher's professional duties or supported by an employer. As you read more research reports, you may notice that certain organizations regularly sponsor studies on a topic.

- Managers will try to protect the organization and discredit the whistle-blower.
- The whistle-blower often experiences emotional distress and strained relations, and even lawsuits.
- Future employers may not trust the whistle-blower and may avoid hiring him or her.

A whistle-blower needs to be prepared to make sacrifices—loss of a job or no promotions, lowered pay, an undesirable transfer, abandonment by friends at work, or legal costs. There is no guarantee that doing the ethical-moral thing will end the unethical behavior or protect an honest researcher from retaliation.

POLITICAL INFLUENCES ON RESEARCH

The ideals of a free, open, and democratic society include advancing and sharing knowledge. People have a right to study and inquire into any question and to share their findings publicly. Ethical issues largely address moral concerns and standards of professional conduct. Most of the time, these are under the researcher's control. Political concerns can also influence and interfere with the research process. Organized advocacy groups, powerful interests, government officials, or politicians may try to restrict or control the direction of research.

In the past, powerful political interests and groups have tried to stop research or the spread of legitimate research findings. They did this to advance their own narrow political goals. They have used their political power to threaten researchers or their employers, to cut off research funds, to harass individual researchers and ruin their careers, and to censor publication of findings that they disliked.

Politically powerful groups have directed research funds away from studying questions that researchers see as important and toward studies of policy positions that favored their own political views. Members of the U.S. Congress targeted and removed funds for individual research projects that panels of independent scientists evaluated as being well designed and critical to advanced knowledge. Why? The politicians personally disliked the study topics (such as sexual behavior of teens, illegal drug users, voting behavior). Politicians are not the only ones interfering with

Example Study Box 6 Political Influence on Crime Research

Savelsberg, King, and Cleveland (2002) conducted a content analysis study on shifts in U.S. criminal justice policy during the last the thirty years of the twentieth century. They looked at articles in leading scholarly journals between 1951 and 1993 to see whether politicians changed how the federal government awards research funds to increase the politicization of criminal justice research. More specifically, they asked whether the government money went to studies that supported specific crime policy ideas advocated by powerful politicians rather than to purely science-based ideas. For example, they asked whether funds directed research away from looking at certain ways to fight crime (altering social conditions, using informal community controls, and emphasizing rehabilitation) and toward others (imposing more formal, coercive police actions and emphasizing punishment). They found that politics had influenced crime research. If the head of a government agency with research funds was politically appointed or funds only were for a crime-fighting policy that was closely tied to political ideology, they called it "political funding." They found that the proportion of research articles listing sponsors classified as "political funding" grew from 3 percent to 31 percent over the nearly 40-year time period they examined. They documented a large-scale shift in research, away from examining the sociological conditions of crime and the effects of rehabilitation and toward a focus on control and punishment (Savelsberg, King, and Cleveland 2002 and Savelsberg, Cleveland and Ryan 2004). This study illustrated how politicians and political movements gained control of government research funding and then politicized it and used the money to redirect the type of research that was conducted.

the free flow of knowledge. Large corporations have threatened individual researchers with lawsuits for delivering expert testimony in public about research findings that revealed to the public the corporation's bad conduct (for many examples, see Mooney 2005).

The powerful in society try to control or censor research out of fear that free, unbiased research might uncover something damaging to their interests. They put a higher value on protecting and advancing their political or economic interests than on the open pursuit of truth. This shows the tight connection between unimpeded, open scientific inquiry and the ideals of open public debate, democracy, and freedom of expression. Censoring and controlling research has always been the practice in dictatorships and totalitarian regimes.

VALUE-FREE AND OBJECTIVE RESEARCH

You have undoubtedly heard about "value-free" research and the importance of being "objective" in research. This is not as simple at it might first appear for the following three reasons:

- The terms *value free* and *objective* have multiple meanings.
- Researchers have alternative ultimate goals for doing research.
- Doing value-free, objective research does not mean that individual researchers are devoid of all values.

Multiple Meanings. *Value free* has two meanings: (1) research without any prior assumptions or theory; and (2) research free of influence from an individual researcher's personal prejudices/beliefs. The first meaning is rarely possible. It means "just facts" without theory or assumptions. Assumptions and theory are in virtually every research study. The best thing is to acknowledge them and make them explicit. Having theoretical assumptions does not prevent study findings from reversing or overturning them. The second meaning is standard practice. It means that an individual person doing the research temporarily "locks up" his or her personal beliefs, values, and prejudices during the research process (i.e., design, data collection, data interpretation). Your personal beliefs should not distort using standard research procedures but can still influence the choice of a study topic or research question or how to publicize or use findings.

Objective has two meanings as well: (1) focus only on what is external or visible; and (2) follow clear and publicly accepted research procedures and not haphazard, invented personal ones. The first meaning is not accurate. We conduct empirical research based on direct or indirect evidence. Although some evidence is not directly visible, such as a person's personality or opinion, you can create measures to make it visible. The second meaning is standard practice. You should always conduct research in an open, public manner that fits with widely accepted procedures.

Alternative Goals. Some professional researchers say they reject value-free research. They mean that they maintain personal values in certain parts of the research process, not that they embrace sloppy and haphazard research or research procedures that follow personal whims. They believe that a researcher should be explicit about his or her values, not that a study has foregone conclusions and automatically supports a specific value position. You should reflect carefully on reasons for doing a study and the procedures used. In this way, other researchers see the values and judge for themselves whether the values unfairly influenced a study's findings.

Devoid of Values. Even researchers who strongly advocate value-free and objective studies admit a place for personal, moral values. Personal, moral views can enter select parts of the process: when choosing a topic to study and how to publicize the findings. Although you must follow standard procedures and contain personal views and values in some parts of the research process, you can still study the questions you believe to be important and make extra efforts to publicize the findings among specific interest groups.

WHAT HAVE YOU LEARNED?

We conduct research to gain knowledge about the social world. The perspectives and techniques of social research can be powerful tools for understanding the world. Nevertheless, with that power to discover comes the responsibility to be ethical. It is a responsibility to yourself, a responsibility to your sponsors, a responsibility to the community of researchers, and a responsibility to the larger society.

The responsibilities of research can conflict with each other. As Rik Scarce (1999:984–985) observed, "Ethics are morality—fundamental rights and wrongs—in practice. They are not . . . legally acceptable statements. . . . They are standards higher than any law." Ultimately, you personally must decide to conduct research in an ethical manner. Research is not automatically moral. Individual researchers must uphold ethical-moral research and demand ethical conduct by others. The truthfulness and use/misuse of the knowledge we gain from research depends on individual researchers like you.

KEY TERMS

anonymity *37*
code of ethics *40*
confidentiality *37*
informed consent *33*
institutional review board (IRB) *40*
plagiarism *27*
principle of voluntary consent *33*
research fraud *27*
scientific misconduct *27*
special populations *39*
whistle-blowing *44*

APPLY WHAT YOU'VE LEARNED

Activity 1

To better understand possible sponsors of research, locate 30 scholarly journal articles on two topics of your choice. For each article, look to see whether there is a sponsor other than the author's employer. You can find this in a footnote at the beginning or the end of an article saying that there was a grant that provided funding. How many of the 30 articles you located had an outside sponsor? For some topics, you may find no article with sponsors. For other topics, a large majority might have sponsors.

Activity 2

Social science fields and related practitioners have professional organizations with a code of ethics. Figure 2.5 provided an example of the ethical code of the American Association for Public Opinion Research. Below is a list of 14 other U.S.-based professional organizations that have such codes.

Select five associations from the list below and look up what their code of ethics says about conducting research. In what areas do they all agree or say the same thing? In what areas do you see differences among them?

Professional Organization	Web Site for Code of Ethics
1. Academy of Criminal Justice Sciences	http://www.acjs.org/pubs/167_671_2922.cfm
2. American Anthropological Association	http://www.aaanet.org/committees/ethics/ethics.htm
3. American Counseling Association	http://www.counseling.org/Resources/CodeOfEthics/TP/Home/CT2.aspx
4. American Educational Research Association	http://www.aera.net/aboutaera/?id=717
5. American Nurses Association	http://www.med.howard.edu/ethics/handouts/american_nurses_association_code.htm
6. American Planning Association	http://www.planning.org/ethics/
7. American Political Science Association	http://www.apsanet.org/513.cfm
8. American Psychological Association	http://www.apa.org/ethics/code2002.html
9. American Society for Public Administration	http://ethics.iit.edu/codes/coe/amer.soc.public.admin.d.html
10. American Sociological Association	http://www.asanet.org/page.ww?section=Ethics&name=Ethics
11. Association for Institutional Research	http://www.airweb.org/?page=140
12. Association of American Geographers	http://www.aag.org/Publications/EthicsStatement.html
13. Marketing Research Association	http://www.mra-net.org/
14. National Association of Social Workers	http://www.socialworkers.org/pubs/code/code.asp

Activity 3

Find out about your college's or university's IRB. If it does not have one, ask your teacher to explain why it does not. If it does, find out who the members are and ask to attend a meeting as an observer when a "nonexempt" social research project is being discussed. Obtain a copy of the informed consent form used and write a short description of the meeting and issues discussed at it.

Activity 4

A whistle-blower can be in any professional field (such as accounting, banking, education, engineering, or medicine), not just doing research. What is common among whistle-blowers is that a professional identifies repeated improper-unethical conduct and, after unsuccessful attempts to remedy the issues, goes public with a revelation about it. What protections, legal, career, or otherwise, does a researcher have if he or she becomes a whistle-blower? Also, what consequences have past whistle-blowers experienced? To address these questions, you may wish to examine laws protecting whistle-blowers or the U.S. government's Office of Research Integrity statement on the issue: http://ori.hhs.gov/misconduct/nprm_reg.shtml. You may also wish to look at a book on the topic, such as Alford, C. Fred (2001). *Whistleblowers: Broken Lives and Organizational Power.* Ithaca, NY: Cornell University Press.

2

REFERENCES

Draus, Paul J., Harvey Siegal, Rober Carlson, Russel Falck, and Jichuan Wang, Jichuan. 2005. "Cracking the Cornfields." *Sociological Quarterly* 46:165–189.

Humphreys, Laud. 1973. *Tearoom Trade.* Chicago: Aldine.

Kane, Robert J. 2005. "Compromised Police Legitimacy as a Predictor of Violent Crime in Structurally Disadvantaged Communities." *Criminology* 43:469–498.

Milgram, Stanley. 1963. "Behavioral Study of Obedience." *Journal of Abnormal and Social Psychology* 6:371–378.

Milgram, Stanley 1965. "Some Conditions of Obedience and Disobedience to Authority." *Human Relations* 18:57–76.

Milgram, Stanley. 1974. *Obedience to Authority*. New York: Harper and Row.

Mooney, Chris. 2005. *The Republican War on Science*. New York: Perseus Books.

Piliavin, Irving, J. Rodin, and Jane Piliavin. 1969. "Good Samaritanism: An Underground Phenomenon?" *Journal of Personality and Social Psychology* 13:289–299.

Savelsberg, Joachim, Lara Cleveland, and Ryan King. 2004. "Institutional Environments and Scholarly Work: American Criminology, 1951–1993." *Social Forces* 82:1275–1302.

Savelsberg, Joachim, Ryan King, and Lara Cleveland. 2002. "Politicized Scholarship? Science on Crime and the State." *Social Problems* 49:327–349.

Scarce, Rik. 1994. "(No) Trial (But) Tribulations: When Courts and Ethnography Conflict." *Journal of Contemporary Ethnography* 23:123–149.

Scarce, Rik. 1999. "Good Faith, Bad Ethics: When Scholars Go the Distance and Scholarly Associations Do Not"*Law & Social Inquiry* 24:977–986.

Taylor, Steven. 1987. "Observing abuse." *Qualitative Sociology* 10:288–302.

Van Maanen, John. 1982. "Fieldwork on the Beat." *Varieties of Qualitative Research.* Edited by J. Van Mannen, J. Dabbs, Jr., and R. Raulkner (pp. 102–151). Beverly Hills, CA: Sage.

Vidich, Arthur, and Joseph Bensman. 1968. *Small Town in Mass Society*, rev. ed. Princeton, NJ: Princeton University Press.

Zimbardo, Philip. 1972. "The Pathology of Imprisonment." *Society* 9:4–6.

PART II

Research Methods

CHAPTER 3

Qualitative and Quantitative Sampling

Taken from: *Basics of Social Research: Qualitative and Quantitative Approaches,* Canadian Edition, by W. Lawrence Neuman and Karen Robson

3

INTRODUCTION

Qualitative and quantitative researchers approach sampling differently. Most discussions of sampling come from researchers who use the quantitative style. Their primary goal is to get a representative **sample**, or a small collection of units or cases from a much larger collection or population, such that the researcher can study the smaller group and produce accurate generalizations about the larger group. They tend to use sampling based on theories of probability from mathematics (called probability sampling).

Researchers have two motivations for using probability or random sampling. The first motivation is saving time and cost. If properly conducted, results from a sample may yield results at 1/1000 the cost and time. For example, instead of gathering data from 20 million people, a researcher may draw a sample of 2000; the data from those 2000 are equal for most purposes to the data from all 20 million. The second purpose of probability sampling is accuracy. The results of a well-designed, carefully executed probability sample will produce results that are equally as accurate as trying to reach every single person in the whole population. A census is an attempt to count everyone in the target population. National censuses take place in Canada every five years with the most recent one occurring in May of 2006.

Qualitative researchers focus less on a sample's representativeness or on detailed techniques for drawing a probability sample. Instead, they focus on how the sample or small collection of cases, units, or activities illuminates key features of social life. The purpose of sampling is to collect cases, events, or actions that clarify and deepen understanding. Qualitative researchers' concern is to find cases that will enhance what the researchers learn about the processes of social life in a specific context. For this reason, qualitative researchers tend to collect a second type of sampling: nonprobability sampling.

NONPROBABILITY SAMPLING

Qualitative researchers rarely draw a representative sample from a huge number of cases to intensely study the sampled cases—the goal in quantitative research. Instead, they use nonprobability or **nonrandom samples**. This means they rarely determine the sample size in advance and have limited knowledge about the larger group or population from which the sample is taken. Unlike the quantitative researcher, who uses a preplanned approach based on mathematical theory, the qualitative researcher selects cases gradually, with the specific content of a case determining whether it is chosen. Table 3.1 shows a variety of nonprobability sampling techniques.

Table 3.1 Types of Nonprobability Samples

Type of Sample	Principle
Haphazard	Get any cases in any manner that is convenient.
Quota	Get a preset number of cases in each of several predetermined categories that will reflect the diversity of the population, using haphazard methods.
Purposive	Get all possible cases that fit particular criteria, using various methods.
Snowball	Get cases using referrals from one or a few cases, and then referrals from those cases, and so forth.
Deviant Case	Get cases that substantially differ from the dominant pattern (a special type of purposive sample).
Sequential	Get cases until there is no additional information or new characteristics (often used with other sampling methods).
Theoretical	Like sequential sampling, but tied to the grounded theory approach.

Haphazard, Accidental, or Convenience Sampling

Haphazard sampling can produce ineffective, highly unrepresentative samples and is not recommended. When a researcher haphazardly selects cases that are convenient, he or she can easily get a sample that seriously misrepresents the population. Such samples are cheap and quick; however, the systematic errors that easily occur make them worse than no sample at all. The person-on-the-street interview conducted by television programs is an example of a haphazard sample. Television interviewers go out on the street with camera and microphone to talk to a few people who are convenient to interview. The people walking past a television studio in the middle of the day do not represent everyone (e.g., homemakers, people in rural areas). Likewise, television interviewers often select people who look "normal" to them and avoid people who are unattractive, poor, very old, or inarticulate.

Another example of a haphazard sample is that of television shows or websites that ask people to phone in or "log in" to vote on topics. Not everyone watches the show or looks at these websites, has an interest in the topic, or will take the time phone or log in. Some people will, and the number who do so may seem large (e.g., 5000), but the sample cannot be used to generalize accurately to the population. Such haphazard samples may have entertainment value, but they can give a distorted view and seriously misrepresent the population.

Quota Sampling

Quota sampling is an improvement over haphazard sampling. In quota sampling, a researcher first identifies relevant categories of people (e.g., male and female; or under age 30, ages 30 to 60, over age 60), then decides how many to get in each category. Thus, the number of people in various categories of the sample is fixed. For example, a researcher decides to select five males and five females under age 30, ten males and ten females aged 30 to 60, and five males and five females over age 60 for a 40-person sample. It is difficult to represent all population characteristics accurately (see Figure 3.1).

Quota sampling is an improvement because the researcher can ensure that some differences are in the sample. In haphazard sampling, all those interviewed might be of the same age, sex, or race. But once the quota sampler fixes the categories and number of cases in each category, he or she uses haphazard sampling. For example, the researcher interviews the first five males under age 30 he or she encounters, even if all five just walked out of the campaign headquarters of a political candidate. Not only is misrepresentation possible because haphazard sampling is used within the categories, but nothing prevents the researcher from selecting people who "act friendly" or who want to be interviewed.

A case from the history of sampling illustrates the limitations of quota sampling. George Gallup's American Institute of Public Opinion, using quota sampling, successfully predicted the outcomes of the 1936, 1940, and 1944 U.S. presidential elections. But in 1948, Gallup predicted the wrong candidate. The incorrect prediction had several causes (e.g., many voters were undecided, interviewing stopped early), but a major reason was that the quota categories did not accurately represent all geographical areas and all people who actually cast a vote.

Purposive or Judgmental Sampling

Purposive sampling is used in situations in which an expert uses judgment in selecting cases with a specific purpose in mind. It is inappropriate if it is used to pick the "average housewife" or the "typical school." With purposive sampling, the researcher never knows whether the cases selected represent the population. It is often used in exploratory research or in field research.

■ **Figure 3.1** Quota Sampling

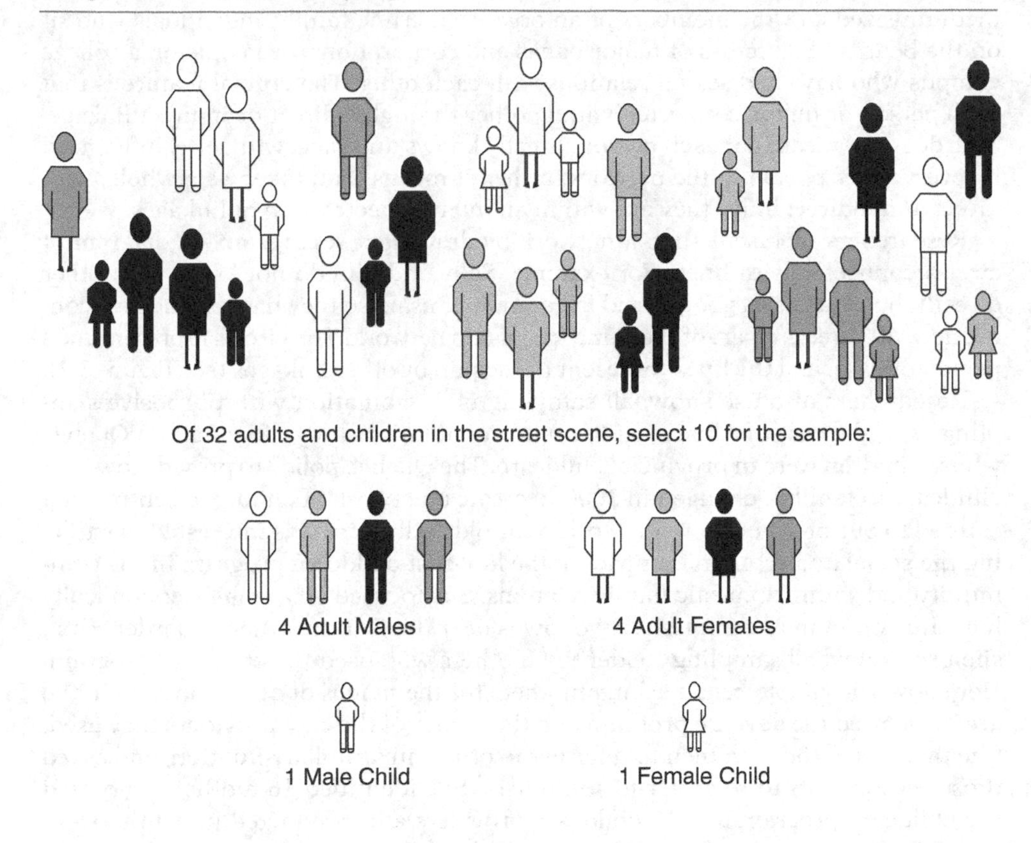

Purposive sampling is appropriate in three situations. First, a researcher uses it to select unique cases that are especially informative. For example, a researcher wants to use content analysis to study magazines to find cultural themes. He or she selects a specific popular women's magazine to study because it is trend setting.

Second, a researcher may use purposive sampling to select members of a difficult-to-reach, specialized population (see Hidden Populations later in this chapter). For example, the researcher wants to study prostitutes. It is impossible to list all prostitutes and sample randomly from the list. Instead, he or she uses subjective information (e.g., locations where prostitutes solicit, social groups with whom prostitutes associate) and experts (e.g., police who work on vice units, other prostitutes) to identify a "sample" of prostitutes for inclusion in the research project. The researcher uses many different methods to identify the cases, because his or her goal is to locate as many cases as possible.

Another situation for purposive sampling occurs when a researcher wants to identify particular types of cases for in-depth investigation. The purpose is less to generalize to a larger population than it is to gain a deeper understanding of types.

Snowball Sampling

Snowball sampling (also called *network, chain referral,* or *reputational sampling*) is a method for identifying and sampling (or selecting) the cases in a network. It is based on an analogy to a snowball, which begins small but becomes larger as it is rolled on wet snow and picks up additional snow. Snowball sampling is a multistage technique. It begins with one or a few people or cases and spreads out on the basis of links to the initial cases.

One use of snowball sampling is to sample a network. Social researchers are often interested in an interconnected network of people or organizations. The network could be scientists around the world investigating the same problem, the elites of a medium-sized city, the members of an organized crime family, individuals who sit on the boards of directors of major banks and corporations, or people on a college campus who have had sexual relations with each other. The crucial feature is that each person or unit is connected with another through a direct or indirect linkage. This does not mean that each person directly knows, interacts with, or is influenced by every other person in the network; rather, it means that, taken as a whole, with direct and indirect links, they are within an interconnected web of linkages.

Researchers represent such a network by drawing a **sociogram**—a diagram of circles connected with lines. For example, Sally and Tim do not know each other directly, but each has a good friend in common, Susan, so they have an indirect connection. All three are part of the same friendship network. The circles represent each person or case, and the lines represent friendship or other linkages (see Figure 3.2).

Researchers also use snowball sampling in combination with purposive sampling as in the case of Albanese (2006) in a qualitative study of women in Quebec whose children were in provincial childcare. The Quebec policy to provide low-cost childcare to families changed in 2000 to create a network of childcare centres that catered to out-of-school care to 0 to 12 year olds. Albanese was interested in studying the social and economic impact of the low-cost childcare program in the community and within domestic family relations. She focused on a small, economically hard-hit community comprising two towns near the Ontario-Quebec border. First, she used snowball sampling to identify mothers who used the childcare program. Her snowball sample began asking mothers for the names of other mothers in the area who used the daycare program and the names of the care providers they used. She then asked those women to refer her to others in a similar situation, and asked those respondents to refer her to still others. She identified 16 mothers who used the childcare program and 17 childcare providers and conducted in-depth, open-ended interviews about their experiences and opinions on the program.

Deviant Case Sampling

A researcher uses **deviant case sampling** (also called *extreme case sampling*) when he or she seeks cases that differ from the dominant pattern or that differ from the

■ **Figure 3.2** Sociogram of Friendship Relations

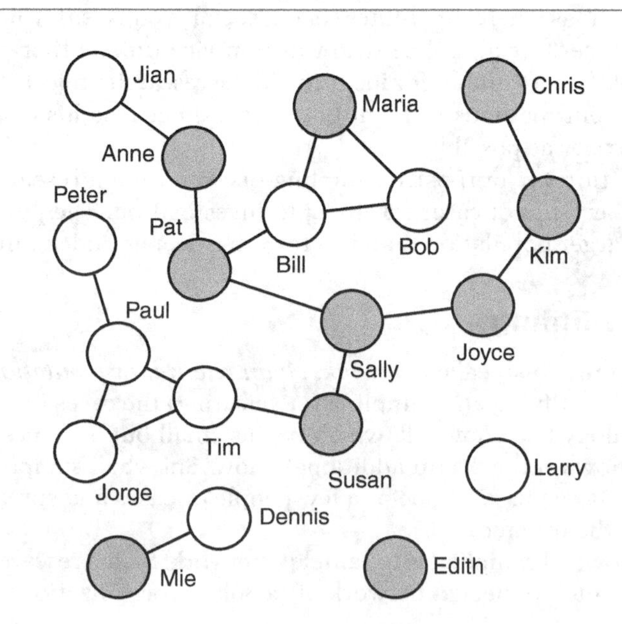

predominant characteristics of other cases. Similar to purposive sampling, a researcher uses a variety of techniques to locate cases with specific characteristics. Deviant case sampling differs from purposive sampling in that the goal is to locate a collection of unusual, different, or peculiar cases that are not representative of the whole. The deviant cases are selected because they are unusual, and a researcher hopes to learn more about the social life by considering cases that fall outside the general pattern or including what is beyond the main flow of events.

For example, a researcher is interested in studying high school dropouts. Let us say that previous research suggested that the majority of dropouts come from families that have low income, are single parent or unstable, have been geographically mobile, and are racial minorities. The family environment is one in which parents and/or siblings have low education or are themselves dropouts. In addition, dropouts are often engaged in illegal behaviour and have a criminal record prior to dropping out. A researcher using deviant case sampling would seek majority-group dropouts who have no record of illegal activities and who are from stable two-parent, upper-middle-income families who are geographically stable and well educated.

Sequential Sampling

Sequential sampling is similar to purposive sampling with one difference. In purposive sampling, the researcher tries to find as many relevant cases as possible, until time, financial resources, or his or her energy is exhausted. The goal is to get every possible case. In sequential sampling, a researcher continues to gather cases until the amount of new information or diversity of cases is filled. In economic terms, information is gathered until the marginal utility, or incremental benefit for additional cases, levels off or drops significantly. It requires that a researcher continuously evaluate all the collected cases. For example, a researcher locates and plans in-depth interviews with 60 widows over 70 years old who have been living without a spouse for ten or more years. Depending on the researcher's purposes, getting an additional 20 widows whose life experiences, social backgrounds, and worldviews differ little from the first 60 may be unnecessary.

Theoretical Sampling

Related to sequential sampling is the concept of **theoretical sampling** is a sampling concept that is tied to grounded theory. With grounded theory, the theory emerges from the data and we don't know how many cases we will need in our study beforehand. Researchers who use grounded theory techniques often employ theoretical sampling, which means that they continue to collect data until no new information emerges. Researchers refer this point where no new themes or information emerges as **theoretical saturation**.

Beck (2002) used theoretical sampling in her study of how mothers of twins coped in the first year after birth. She recruited mothers through a "parents of multiples" group who met monthly at a local medical centre. Because sampling, data collection, and theory development all occur simultaneously in the grounded theory process, Beck continued interviewing until aspects of her emerging theory became "saturated." When she first began interviewing, Beck found that "mothers referred repeatedly to the fact that they could not compare how being a mother of twins was different from being a mother of a singleton because their twins were their only children."[1] In order to saturate the theme of how being a mother of twins was different, Beck sought out additional interviewees who were women with children other than their twins. Once she was able to develop this theme within her data to "saturation point" (i.e. no new information emerged), her sampling was complete.

Using the grounded theory approach requires the researcher to go back and forth between analyzing data, collecting data, and sampling. As the study progresses, the researcher needs to be sensitive to what direction the data are taking him or her and where to go next. This process of going back and forth between data collection, analysis, and decisions about how to proceed is called the **iterative process**. It is unique from other sampling techniques as there is a constant interplay between collecting data, analyzing it, and making decisions about where to go next. The data collection typically continues until theoretical saturation has been met. Imagine it as a cyclical event where there are no predetermined stages of events and where the researcher works with data collection, analysis, and theory development in an interactive and non-linear manner.

PROBABILITY SAMPLING

A specialized vocabulary or jargon has developed around terms used in probability sampling. Before examining probability sampling, it is important to review its language.

Populations, Elements, and Sampling Frames

A researcher draws a sample from a larger pool of cases, or *elements*. A **sampling element** is the unit of analysis or case in a population. It can be a person, a group, an organization, a written document or symbolic message, or even a social action (e.g., an arrest, a divorce, or a kiss) that is being measured. The large pool is the **population**, which has an important role in sampling. Sometimes, the term *universe* is used interchangeably with *population*. To define the population, a researcher specifies the unit being sampled, the geographical location, and the temporal boundaries of populations. Consider the examples of populations in Box 1. All the examples include the elements to be sampled (e.g., people, businesses, hospital admissions, commercials) and geographical and time boundaries.

3

A researcher begins with an idea of the population (e.g., all people in a city) but defines it more precisely. The term **target population** refers to the specific pool of cases that he or she wants to study. The ratio of the size of the sample to the size of the target population is the **sampling ratio**. For example, the population has 50 000 people, and a researcher draws a sample of 150 from it. Thus, the sampling ratio is 150/50 000 = 0.003, or 0.3 percent. If the population is 500 and the researcher samples 100, then the sampling ratio is 100/500 = 0.20, or 20 percent.

Box 1 Examples of Populations

1. All persons aged 16 or older living in Singapore on December 2, 1999, who were not incarcerated in prison, asylums, and similar institutions
2. All business establishments employing more than 100 persons in Ontario, Canada, that operated in the month of July 2005
3. All admissions to public or private hospitals in the province of Ontario between August 1, 2005, and August 1, 2007
4. All television commercials aired between 7:00 a.m. and 11:00 p.m. Eastern Standard Time on three major Canadian networks between November 1 and November 25, 2006
5. All currently practising physicians in Australia who received medical degrees between January 1, 1960, and the present
6. All male heroin addicts in the Vancouver, British Columbia, or Seattle, Washington, metropolitan areas during 2003

A population is an abstract concept. How can population be an abstract concept when there are a given number of people at a certain time? Except for specific small populations, one can never truly freeze a population to measure it. For example, in a city at any given moment, some people are dying, some are boarding or getting off airplanes, and some are in cars driving across city boundaries. The researcher must decide exactly who to count. Should he or she count a city resident who happens to be on vacation when the time is fixed? What about the tourist staying at a hotel in the city when the time is fixed? Should he or she count adults, children, people in jails, those in hospitals? A population, even the population of all people over the age of 18 in the city limits of St. John's, Newfoundland, at 12:01 a.m. on March 1, 2006, is an abstract concept. It exists in the mind but is impossible to pinpoint concretely.

Because a population is an abstract concept, except for small specialized populations (e.g., all the students in a classroom), a researcher needs to estimate the population. As an abstract concept, the population needs an operational definition. This process is similar to developing operational definitions for constructs that are measured.

A researcher operationalizes a population by developing a specific list that closely approximates all the elements in the population. This list is a **sampling frame**. He or she can choose from many types of sampling frames: telephone directories, tax records, driver's license records, and so on. Listing the elements in a population sounds simple. It is often difficult because there may be no good list of elements in a population.

A good sampling frame is crucial to good sampling. A mismatch between the sampling frame and the conceptually defined population can be a major source of error. Just as a mismatch between the theoretical and operational definitions of a variable creates invalid measurement, so a mismatch between the sampling frame and the population causes invalid sampling. Researchers try to minimize mismatches. For example, you would like to sample all people in a region of Canada, so you decide to get a list of everyone with a driver's license. But some people do not have driver's licenses, and the lists of those with licenses, even if updated regularly, quickly go out of date. Next, you try income tax records. But not everyone pays taxes; some people cheat and do not pay, others have no income and do not have to file, some have died or have not begun to pay taxes, and still others have entered or left the area since the last time taxes were due. You try telephone directories, but they are not much better; some people are not listed in a telephone directory, some people have unlisted numbers, and others have recently moved. With a few exceptions (e.g., a list of all students enrolled at a university), sampling frames are almost always inaccurate. A sampling frame can include some of those outside the target population (e.g., a telephone directory that lists people who have moved away) or might omit some of those inside it (e.g., those without telephones).

Any characteristic of a population (e.g., the percentage of city residents who smoke cigarettes, the average height of all women over the age of 21, the percent of people who believe in UFOs) is a population **parameter**. It is the true characteristic of the population. Parameters are determined when all elements in a population are measured. The parameter is never known with absolute accuracy for large populations (e.g., an entire nation), so researchers must estimate it on the basis of samples. They use information from the sample, called a **statistic**, to estimate population parameters (see Figure 3.3).

A famous case in the history of sampling illustrates the limitations of the technique. The *Literary Digest*, a major American magazine, sent postcards to people before the 1920, 1924, 1928, and 1932 U.S. presidential elections. The magazine took the names for the sample from automobile registrations and telephone directories—the sampling frame. People returned the postcards indicating whom they would vote for. The magazine correctly predicted all four election outcomes. The

■ **Figure 3.3** A Model of the Logic of Sampling

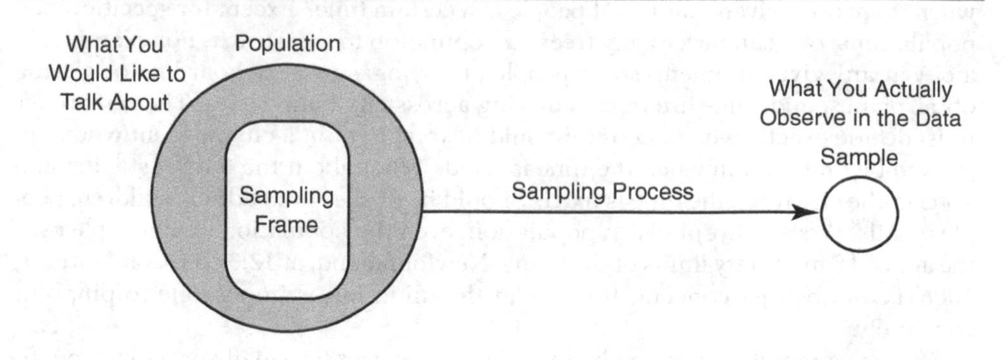

magazine's success with predictions was well known, and in 1936, it increased the sample to 10 million. The magazine predicted a huge victory for Alf Landon over Franklin D. Roosevelt. But the *Literary Digest* was wrong: Franklin D. Roosevelt won by a landslide.

The prediction was wrong for several reasons, but the most important was mistakes in sampling. Although the magazine sampled a large number of people, its sampling frame did not accurately represent the target population (i.e., all voters). It excluded people without telephones or automobiles, a sizable percentage of the population in 1936, during the worst of the Great Depression of the 1930s. The frame excluded as much as 65 percent of the population and a segment of the voting population (lower income) that tended to favour Roosevelt. The magazine had been accurate in earlier elections because people with higher and lower incomes did not differ in how they voted. Also, during earlier elections, before the Depression, more lower-income people could afford to have telephones and automobiles.

You can learn two important lessons from the *Literary Digest* mistake. First, the sampling frame is crucial. Second, the size of a sample is less important than whether or not it accurately represents the population. A representative sample of 2500 can give more accurate predications about a population than a nonrepresentative sample of 1 million or 10 million.

Why Random?

The area of applied mathematics called probability theory relies on random processes. The word *random* has a special meaning in mathematics. It refers to a process that generates a mathematically random result: that is, the selection process operates in a truly random method (i.e., no pattern), and a researcher can calculate the probability of outcomes. In a true random process, each element has an equal probability of being selected.

Probability samples that rely on random processes require more work than nonrandom ones. A researcher must identify specific sampling elements (e.g., persons) to include in the sample. For example, if conducting a telephone survey, the researcher needs to try to reach the specific sampled person by calling back four or five times to get an accurate random sample.

Random samples are most likely to yield a sample that truly represents the population. In addition, random sampling lets a researcher statistically calculate the relationship between the sample and the population—that is, the size of the **sampling error**. A nonstatistical definition of the sampling error is the deviation between sample results and a population parameter due to random processes.

Random sampling is based on a great deal of sophisticated mathematics. This chapter focuses on the fundamentals of how sampling works, the difference between good and bad samples, how to draw a sample, and basic principles of sampling in social research. This does not mean that random sampling is unimportant. It is essential to first master the fundamentals. If you plan to pursue a career using quantitative research, you should get more statistical background than space permits here.

Types of Probability Samples

Simple Random. The simple random sample is both the easiest random sample to understand and the one on which other types are modelled. In **simple random sampling**, a researcher develops an accurate sampling frame, selects elements from the sampling frame according to a mathematically random procedure, then locates the exact element that was selected for inclusion in the sample.

After numbering all elements in a sampling frame, a researcher uses a list of random numbers to decide which elements to select. He or she needs as many random numbers as there are elements to be sampled: for example, for a sample of 100, 100 random numbers are needed. The researcher can get random numbers from a **random-number table**, a table of numbers chosen in a mathematically random way. Random-number tables are available in most statistics and research methods books. The numbers are generated by a pure random process so that any number has an equal probability of appearing in any position. Computer programs can also produce lists of random numbers.

You may ask, "Once I select an element from the sampling frame, do I then return it to the sampling frame or do I keep it separate?" The common answer is that it is not returned. Unrestricted random sampling is random sampling with replacement—that is, replacing an element after sampling it so it can be selected again. In simple random sampling without replacement, the researcher ignores elements already selected into the sample.

The logic of simple random sampling can be illustrated with an elementary example—sampling marbles from a jar. You have a large jar full of 5000 marbles, some red and some white. The 5000 marbles are my population, and the parameter you want to estimate is the percentage of red marbles in it. You randomly select 100 marbles (close your eyes, shake the jar, pick one marble, and repeat the procedure 99 times). Now you have a random sample of marbles. Count the number of red marbles in your sample to estimate the percentage of red versus white marbles in the population. This is a lot easier than counting all 5000 marbles. Let's say your sample has 52 white and 48 red marbles.

Does this mean that the population parameter is 48 percent red marbles? Maybe not. Because of random chance, your specific sample might be off. You can check your results by dumping the 100 marbles back in the jar, mixing the marbles, and drawing a second random sample of 100 marbles. On the second try, your sample has 49 white marbles and 51 red ones. Now you have a problem. Which is correct? How good is this random sampling business if different samples from the same population can yield different results? Let's say you repeat the procedure over and over until you have drawn 130 different samples of 100 marbles each (see Box 2 for results). Most people might empty the jar and count all 5000, but you want to see what is going on. The results of your 130 different samples reveal a clear pattern. The most common mix of red and white marbles is 50/50. Samples that are close to that split are more frequent than those with more uneven splits. The population parameter appears to be 50 percent white and 50 percent red marbles.

Mathematical proofs and empirical tests demonstrate that the pattern found in Box 2 always appears. The set of many random samples is your **sampling distribution**. It is a distribution of different samples that shows the frequency of different sample outcomes from many separate random samples. The pattern will appear if the sample size is 1000 instead of 100; if there are 10 colours of marbles instead of 2; if the population has 100 marbles or 10 million marbles instead of 5000; and if the population is people, automobiles, or colleges instead of marbles. In fact, the

Box 2 Example of Sampling Distribution

Red	White	Number of Samples
42	58	1
43	57	1
45	55	2
46	54	4
47	53	8
48	52	12
49	51	21
50	50	31
51	49	20
52	48	13
53	47	9
54	46	5
55	45	2
57	43	1
	Total	130

Number of red and white marbles that were randomly drawn from a jar of 5000 marbles with 100 drawn each time, repeated 130 times for 130 independent random samples.

Number of Samples	42	43	44	45	46	47	48	49	50	51	52	53	54	55	56	57
31									*							
30									*							
29									*							
28									*							
27									*							
26									*							
25									*							
24									*							
23									*							
22									*							
21								*	*							
20								*	*	*						
19								*	*	*						
18								*	*	*						
17								*	*	*						
16								*	*	*						
15								*	*	*						
14								*	*	*						
13								*	*	*	*					
12							*	*	*	*	*					
11							*	*	*	*	*					
10							*	*	*	*	*					
9							*	*	*	*	*	*				
8						*	*	*	*	*	*	*				
7						*	*	*	*	*	*	*				
6						*	*	*	*	*	*	*				
5						*	*	*	*	*	*	*	*			
4					*	*	*	*	*	*	*	*	*			
3					*	*	*	*	*	*	*	*	*			
2				*	*	*	*	*	*	*	*	*	*	*		
1	*		*	*	*	*	*	*	*	*	*	*	*	*		*

Number of Red Marbles in a Sample

pattern will become clearer as more and more independent random samples are drawn from the population.

The pattern in the sampling distribution suggests that over many separate samples, the true population parameter (i.e., the 50/50 split in the preceding example) is more common than any other result. Some samples deviate from the population parameter, but they are less common. When many different random samples are plotted as in the graph in Box 2, then the sampling distribution looks like a normal or bell-shaped curve. Such a curve is theoretically important and is used throughout statistics.

The **central limit theorem** from mathematics tells us that as the number of different random samples in a sampling distribution increases toward infinity, the pattern of samples and the population parameter become more predictable. With a huge number of random samples, the sampling distribution forms a normal curve, and the midpoint of the curve approaches the population parameter as the number of samples increases.

Perhaps you want only one sample because you do not have the time or energy to draw many different samples. You are not alone. A researcher rarely draws many samples. He or she usually draws only one random sample, but the central limit theorem lets him or her generalize from one sample to the population. The theorem is about many samples but lets the researcher calculate the probability of a particular sample being off from the population parameter.

Random sampling does not guarantee that every random sample perfectly represents the population. Instead, it means that most random samples will be close to the population most of the time, and that one can calculate the probability of a particular sample being inaccurate. A researcher estimates the chance that a particular sample is off or unrepresentative (i.e., the size of the sampling error) by using information from the sample to estimate the sampling distribution. He or she combines this information with knowledge of the central limit theorem to construct confidence intervals.

The **confidence interval** is a relatively simple but powerful idea. When television or newspaper polls are reported, you may hear about something called the margin of error being plus or minus two percentage points. This is a version of confidence intervals. A confidence interval is a range around a specific point used to estimate a population parameter. A range is used because the statistics of random processes do not let a researcher predict an exact point, but they let the researcher say with a high level of confidence (e.g., 95 percent) that the true population parameter lies within a certain range.

The calculations for sampling errors or confidence intervals are beyond the level of this discussion, but they are based on the idea of the sampling distribution that lets a researcher calculate the sampling error and confidence interval. For example, you cannot say, "There are precisely 2,500 red marbles in the jar based on a random sample." However, you can say, "I am 95 percent certain that the population parameter lies between 2450 and 2550." You can combine characteristics of the sample (e.g., its size, the variation in it) with the central limit theorem to predict specific ranges around the parameter with a great deal of confidence.

Systematic Sampling. **Systematic sampling** is simple random sampling with a shortcut for random selection. Again, the first step is to number each element in the sampling frame. Instead of using a list of random numbers, a researcher calculates a sampling interval, and the interval becomes his or her quasi-random selection method. The **sampling interval** (i.e., 1 in k, where k is some number) tells the researcher how to select elements from a sampling frame by skipping elements in the frame before selecting one for the sample.

For instance, let's say you want to sample 300 names from 900. After a random starting point, you select every third name of the 900 to get a sample of 300. My sampling interval is 3. Sampling intervals are easy to compute. You need the sample size and the population size (or sampling frame size as a best estimate). You can think of the sampling interval as the inverse of the sampling ratio. The sampling ratio for 300 names out of 900 is 300/900 =.333 = 33.3 percent. The sampling interval is 900/300 = 3.

In most cases, a simple random sample and a systematic sample yield virtually equivalent results. One important situation in which systematic sampling cannot be substituted for simple random sampling occurs when the elements in a sample are organized in some kind of cycle or pattern. For example, a researcher's sampling frame is organized by married couples with the male first and the female second (see Table 3.2). Such a pattern gives the researcher an unrepresentative sample if systematic sampling is used. His or her systematic sample can be nonrepresentative and include only wives because of how the cases are organized. When his or her sample frame is organized as couples, even-numbered sampling intervals result in samples with all husbands or all wives.

Table 3.3 illustrates simple random sampling and systematic sampling. Notice that different names were drawn in each sample. For example, H. Adams appears in both samples, but C. Droullard is only in the simple random sample. This is because it is rare for any two random samples to be identical.

The sampling frame contains 20 males and 20 females (gender is in parentheses after each name). The simple random sample yielded 3 males and 7 females, and the systematic sample yielded 5 males and 5 females. Does this mean that systematic sampling is more accurate? No. To check this, draw a new sample using different random numbers: try taking the first two digits and beginning at the end (e.g., 11 from 11921, then 43 from 43232). Also draw a new systematic sample with a different random start. The last time the random start was 18. Try a random start of 11. What did you find? How many of each sex?

3

Stratified Sampling. In **stratified sampling**, a researcher first divides the population into subpopulations (strata) on the basis of supplementary information. After dividing the population into strata, the researcher draws a random sample from each subpopulation. He or she can sample randomly within strata using simple random or systematic sampling. In stratified sampling, the researcher controls the relative size of each stratum, rather than letting random processes control it. This

Table 3.2 Problems with Systematic Sampling of Cyclical Data

Case	
1	Husband
2[a]	Wife
3	Husband
4	Wife
5	Husband
6[a]	Wife
7	Husband
8	Wife
9	Husband
10[a]	Wife
11	Husband
12	Wife

Random start = 2; Sampling interval = 4. [a]Selected into sample.

Table 3.3 How to Draw Simple Random and Systematic Samples

1. Number each case in the sampling frame in sequence. The list of 40 names is in alphabetical order, numbered from 1 to 40.
2. Decide on a sample size. We will draw two 25 percent (ten-name) samples.
3. For a *simple random sample,* locate a random-number table (see excerpt). Before using the random-number table, count the largest number of digits needed for the sample (e.g., with 40 names, two digits are needed; for 100 to 999, three digits; for 1000 to 9999, four digits). Begin anywhere on the random number table (we will begin in the upper left) and take a set of digits (we will take the last two). Mark the number on the sampling frame that corresponds to the chosen random number to indicate that the case is in the sample. If the number is too large (over 40), ignore it. If the number appears more than once (10 and 21 occurred twice in the example), ignore the second occurrence. Continue until the number of cases in the sample (10 in our example) is reached.
4. For a *systematic sample,* begin with a random start. The easiest way to do this is to point blindly at the random number table, then take the closest number that appears on the sampling frame. In the example, 18 was chosen. Start with the random number, then count the sampling interval, or 4 in our example, to come to the first number. Mark it, and then count the sampling interval for the next number. Continue to the end of the list. Continue counting the sampling interval as if the beginning of the list was attached to the end of the list (like a circle). Keep counting until ending close to the start, or on the start if the sampling interval divide evenly into the total of the sampling frame.

No.	Name (Gender)	Simple Random	Systematic
01	Abrams, J. (M)		
02	Adams, H. (F)	Yes	Yes (6)
03	Anderson, H. (M)		
04	Arminond, L. (M)		
05	Boorstein, A. (M)		
06	Breitsprecher, P. (M)	Yes	Yes (7)
07	Brown, D. (F)		
08	Cattelino, J. (F)		
09	Cidoni, S. (M)		
10	Davis, L. (F)	Yes*	Yes (8)
11	Droullard, C. (M)	Yes	
12	Durette, R. (F)		
13	Elsnau, K. (F)	Yes	
14	Falconer, T. (M)		Yes (9)
15	Fuerstenberg, J. (M)		
16	Fulton, P. (F)		
17	Gnewuch, S. (F)		
18	Green, C. (M)		START, Yes (10)
19	Goodwanda, T. (F)	Yes	
20	Harris, B. (M)		
21	Hjelmhaug, N. (M)	Yes*	
22	Huang, J. (F)	Yes	Yes (1)
23	Ivono, V. (F)		
24	Jaquees, J. (M)		
25	Johnson, A. (F)		
26	Kennedy, M. (F)		Yes (2)
27	Koschoreck, L. (F)		
28	Koykkar, J. (M)		
29	Kozlowski, C. (F)	Yes	
30	Laurent, J. (M)		Yes (3)
31	Lee, R. (F)		
32	Ling, C. (M)		
33	McKinnon, K. (F)		
34	Min, H. (F)	Yes	Yes (4)
35	Moini, A. (F)		
36	Navarre, H. (M)		
37	O'Sullivan, C. (M)		
38	Oh, J. (M)		Yes (5)
39	Olson, J. (M)		
40	Ortiz y Garcia, L. (F)		

* Numbers that appeared twice in random numbers selected.

Table 3.3 (Continued)

Excerpt from a Random-Number Table (for Simple Random Sample)

15010	18590	00102	42210	94174	22099
90122	38221	21529	00013	04734	60457
67256	13887	94119	11077	01061	27779
13761	23390	12947	21280	44506	36457
81994	66611	16597	44457	07621	51949
79180	25992	46178	23992	62108	43232
07984	47169	88094	82752	15318	11921

guarantees representativeness or fixes the proportion of different strata within a sample. Of course, the necessary supplemental information about strata is not always available.

In general, stratified sampling produces samples that are more representative of the population than simple random sampling if the stratum information is accurate. A simple example illustrates why this is so. Imagine a population that is 51 percent female and 49 percent male; the population parameter is a sex ratio of 51 to 49. With stratified sampling, a researcher draws random samples among females and among males so that the sample contains a 51 to 49 percent sex ratio. If the researcher had used simple random sampling, it would be possible for a random sample to be off from the true sex ratio in the population. Thus, he or she makes fewer errors representing the population and has a smaller sampling error with stratified sampling.

Researchers use stratified sampling when a stratum of interest is a small percentage of a population and random processes could miss the stratum by chance. For example, a researcher draws a sample of 200 from 20 000 university students. He or she gets information from the university registrar indicating that 2 percent of the 20 000 students, or 400, are divorced women with children under the age of 5. This group is important to include in the sample. There would be four such students (2 percent of 200) in a representative sample, but the researcher could miss them by chance in one simple random sample. With stratified sampling, he or she obtains a list of the 400 such students from the registrar and randomly selects four from it. This guarantees that the sample represents the population with regard to the important strata (see Box 3).

In special situations, a researcher may want the proportion of a stratum in a sample to differ from its true proportion in the population. For example, the population contains 0.5 percent Aleuts, but the researcher wants to examine Aleuts in particular. He or she oversamples so that Aleuts make up 10 percent of the sample. With this type of disproportionate stratified sample, the researcher cannot generalize directly from the sample to the population without special adjustments.

In some situations, a researcher wants the proportion of a stratum or subgroup to differ from its true proportion in the population. For example, the 1996 General Social Survey oversampled senior citizens, particularly in the province of Quebec. This oversampling was undertaken so that in-depth analyses of the opinions of and experiences of seniors could be studied. A random sample of the Canadian population would yield relatively few seniors. Statistics Canada and the Quebec Bureau of Statistics conducted a separate sample of seniors to increase the total number to 1250 seniors sampled nationally and 700 sampled from the province of Quebec. The researcher who wants to use the entire sample (not just seniors but all people in the study) must adjust it to reduce the number of sampled seniors before generalizing to the Canadian population. Disproportionate sampling helps the researcher who wants to focus on issues most relevant to a subpopulation.

Cluster Sampling. **Cluster sampling** addresses two problems: Researchers lack a good sampling frame for a dispersed population and the cost to reach a sampled ele-

Box 3 Illustration of Stratified Sampling

Sample of 100 Staff of General Hospital, Stratified by Position

Position	Population		Simple Random Sample	Stratified Sample	Errors Compared to the Population
	N	*Percent*	*n*	*n*	
Administrators	15	2.88	1	3	22
Staff physicians	25	4.81	2	5	23
Intern physicians	25	4.81	6	5	+1
Registered nurses	100	19.23	22	19	+3
Nurse assistants	100	19.23	21	19	+2
Medical technicians	75	14.42	9	14	+5
Orderlies	50	9.62	8	10	22
Clerks	75	14.42	5	14	+1
Maintenance staff	30	5.77	3	6	23
Cleaning staff	25	4.81	3	5	22
Total	520	100.00	100	100	

Randomly select 3 of 15 administrators, 5 of 25 staff physicians, and so on.
Note: Traditionally, *N* symbolizes the number in the population and n represents the number in the sample.

The simple random sample overrepresents nurses, nursing assistants, and medical technicians, but underrepresents administrators, staff physicians, maintenance staff, and cleaning staff. The stratified sample gives an accurate representation of each type of position.

3

ment is very high. For example, there is no single list of all automobile mechanics in North America. Even if a researcher got an accurate sampling frame, it would cost too much to reach the sampled mechanics who are geographically spread out. Instead of using a single sampling frame, researchers use a sampling design that involves multiple stages and clusters.

A *cluster* is a unit that contains final sampling elements but can be treated temporarily as a sampling element itself. A researcher first samples clusters, each of which contains elements, then draws a second sample from within the clusters selected in the first stage of sampling. In other words, the researcher randomly samples clusters, then randomly samples elements from within the selected clusters. This has a big practical advantage. He or she can create a good sampling frame of clusters, even if it is impossible to create one for sampling elements. Once the researcher gets a sample of clusters, creating a sampling frame for elements within each cluster becomes more manageable. A second advantage for geographically dispersed populations is that elements within each cluster are physically closer to one another. This may produce a savings in locating or reaching each element.

A researcher draws several samples in stages in cluster sampling. In a three-stage sample, stage 1 is random sampling of big clusters; stage 2 is random sampling of small clusters within each selected big cluster; and stage 3 is sampling of elements from within the sampled small clusters. For example, a researcher wants a sample of individuals from Mapleville. First, he or she randomly samples city blocks, then households within blocks, and then individuals within households (see Box 4). Although there is no accurate list of all residents of Mapleville, there is an accurate list of blocks in the city. After selecting a random sample of blocks, the researcher counts all households on the selected blocks to create a sample frame for each block. He or she then uses the list of households to draw a random sample at the stage of

Box 4 Illustration of Cluster Sampling

Goal: Draw a random sample of 240 people in Mapleville.

Step 1: Mapleville has 55 districts. Randomly select 6 districts.

1 2 3* 4 5 6 7 8 9 10 11 12 13 14 15* 16 17 18 19 20 21 22 23 24 25 26
27* 28 29 30 31* 32 33 34 35 36 37 38 39 40* 41 42 43 44 45 46 47 48
49 50 51 52 53 54* 55
* = Randomly selected.

Step 2: Divide the selected districts into blocks. Each district contains 20 blocks. Randomly select 4 blocks from the district.

Example of District 3 (selected in step 1):
1 2 3 4* 5 6 7 8 9 10* 11 12 13* 14 15 16 17* 18 19 20
* = Randomly selected.

Step 3: Divide blocks into households. Randomly select households.

Example of Block 4 of District 3 (selected in step 2):

Block 4 contains a mix of single-family homes, duplexes, and four-unit apartment buildings. It is bounded by Oak Street, River Road, South Avenue, and Greenview Drive. There are 45 households on the block. Randomly select 10 households from the 45.

1	#1 Oak Street	16	"	31*	"
2	#3 Oak Street	17*	#154 River Road	32*	"
3*	#5 Oak Street	18	#156 River Road	33	"
4	"	19*	#158 River Road	34	#156 Greenview Drive
5	"	20*	"	35*	"
6	"	21	#13 South Avenue	36	"
7	#7 Oak Street	22	"	37	"
8	"	23	#11 South Avenue	38	"
9*	#150 River Road	24	#9 South Avenue	39	#158 Greenview Drive
10*	"	25	#7 South Avenue	40	"
11	"	26	#5 South Avenue	41	"
12	"	27	#3 South Avenue	42	"
13	#152 River Road	28	#1 South Avenue	43	#160 Greenview Drive
14	"	29*	"	44	"
15	"	30	#152 Greenview Drive	45	"

* = Randomly selected.

Step 4: Select a respondent within each household.
Summary of cluster sampling:

1 person randomly selected per household
10 households randomly selected per block
4 blocks randomly selected per district
6 districts randomly selected in the city
$1 \times 10 \times 4 \times 6 = 240$ people in sample

sampling households. Finally, the researcher chooses a specific individual within each sampled household.

Cluster sampling is usually less expensive than simple random sampling, but it is less accurate. Each stage in cluster sampling introduces sampling errors. This means a multistage cluster sample has more sampling errors than a one-stage random sample.

A researcher who uses cluster sampling must decide the number of clusters and the number of elements within each cluster. For example, in a two-stage cluster sample of 240 people from Mapleville, the researcher could randomly select 120 clusters and select two elements from each, or randomly select two clusters and select 120 elements in each. Which is best? The general answer is that a design with more clusters is better. This is because elements within clusters (e.g., people living on the same block) tend to be similar to each other (e.g., people on the same block tend to be more alike than those on different blocks). If few clusters are chosen, many similar elements could be selected, which would be less representative of the total population. For example, the researcher could select two blocks with relatively wealthy people and draw 120 people from each. This would be less representative than a sample with 120 different city blocks and two individuals chosen from each.

When a researcher samples from a large geographical area and must travel to each element, cluster sampling significantly reduces travel costs. As usual, there is a tradeoff between accuracy and cost.

For example, Alan, Ricardo, and Barbara each plan to visit and personally interview a sample of 1500 students who represent the population of all college and university students in North America. Alan obtains an accurate sampling frame of all students and uses simple random sampling. He travels to 1000 different locations to interview one or two students at each. Ricardo draws a random sample of three universities from a list of all 3000 universities and colleges, then visits the three and selects 500 students from each. Barbara draws a random sample of 300 universities and colleges. She visits the 300 and selects 5 students at each. If travel costs average $250 per location, Alan's travel bill is $250 000, Ricardo's is $750, and Barbara's is $75 000. Alan's sample is highly accurate, but Barbara's is only slightly less accurate for one-third the cost. Ricardo's sample is the cheapest, but it is not representative at all.

3

Probability Proportionate to Size (PPS). There are two methods of cluster sampling. The method just described is proportionate or unweighted cluster sampling. It is proportionate because the size of each cluster (or number of elements at each stage) is the same. The more common situation is for the cluster groups to be of different sizes. When this is the case, the researcher must adjust the probability or sampling ratio at various stages in sampling.

The foregoing cluster sampling example with Alan, Barbara, and Ricardo illustrates the problem with unweighted cluster sampling. Barbara drew a simple random sample of 300 colleges and universities from a list of all 3000, but she made a mistake—unless every institution has an identical number of students. Her method gave each institution an equal chance of being selected—a 300/3000 or 10 percent chance. But colleges and universities have different numbers of students, so each student does not have an equal chance to end up in her sample.

Barbara listed every college and university and sampled from the list. A large university with 40 000 students and a small college with 400 students had an equal chance of being selected. But if she chose the large university, the chance of a given student at that college being selected was 5 in 40 000 (5/40 000 = 0.0125 percent), whereas a student at the small college had a 5 in 400 (5/400 = 1.25 percent) chance of being selected. The small-college student was 100 times more likely to be in her sample. The total probability of being selected for a student from the large university was 0.125 percent (10 × 0.0125), while it was 12.5 percent (10 × 1.25) for the small-college student. Barbara violated a principle of random sampling—that each element has an equal chance to be selected into the sample.

If Barbara uses **probability proportionate to size (PPS)** and samples correctly, then each final sampling element or student will have an equal probability of being selected. She does this by adjusting the chances of selecting a college in the first stage of sampling. She must give large colleges with more students a greater chance of being selected and small colleges a smaller chance. She adjusts the probability of selecting a college on the basis of the proportion of all students in the population who attend it. Thus, a college with 40 000 students will be 100 times more likely to be selected than one with 400 students. (See Box 5 for another example.)

Box 5 Complex Sampling Example

The Canada Campus Survey has been administered on two occasions—in 1998 and 2004—in order to collect information on undergraduate students across Canada. It is funded by the Canadian Institutes of Health Research. In particular, the Canada Campus Survey is a cross-sectional study that collects information on student characteristics, undergraduate drinking and substance use, gambling behaviour, and mental health (Adlaf, Demer, and Gliksman, 2005). Each of the times the survey has been undertaken, the sampling procedure has been different, although the sample sizes have been comparable.

In both years, the target population of the study was the same: undergraduates who were studying full-time at accredited Canadian universities during the academic year in question. The researchers determined that in order for universities and colleges to be eligible for consideration in the study, they needed to meet five criteria: 1) they had to have a Registrar, 2) they needed to have in excess of 1000 degree-seeking undergraduate students, 3) the students needed to physically meet on campus for classes, 4) the college or university was non-military, and 5) the institution was publicly, not privately, funded. There were 64 institutions that met these criteria.

The first time the survey was administered, the researchers used **multistage cluster sampling**. The term "multistage cluster sampling" may seem very complicated, but it is more easily dealt with if you think about what it means. The first thing that you should be able to identify is the *stages,* then the *clusters* within these stages. For the first stage, the researchers first divided Canada into five regional strata (clusters): the Atlantic Provinces, Quebec, Ontario, the Prairie Provinces, and British Columbia. For the second stage, they randomly selected four universities (clusters) from within these strata using probability proportionate to size (PPS) so that bigger universities had a greater chance of being selected than smaller universities and colleges. This left a sample of 20 universities, but not all selected universities agreed to participate—in fact, just 16 did. In the final stage, 1000 students were randomly selected within each of the chosen universities. In the end, 7800 students from 16 campuses were surveyed through a postal questionnaire.

In 2004, a different sampling technique was employed. Unlike in 1998, multistage cluster sampling was not used. Instead a single-stage sample of 350 students randomly selected from each eligible institution was undertaken. In total, 40 of the 64 eligible institutions agreed to take part in the study. Overall, 6282 students from 40 universities participated in the study. Also different from the 1998 study was that participants could participate by mail or by filling out the survey online.

Many comparisons could be made between students in the two years of the study. Findings revealed, for example, that smoking decreased by three percent and the use of hallucinogenic drugs was down by four percent. In both years, however, just under a third of students reported feeling psychological stress and around the same numbers reported patterns of harmful drinking.

Which sample is better? The authors (Adlaf, Demer, and Gliksman 2005) contend that despite the different methods used in both years, the basic characteristics of the

Box 5 (Continued)

sample with regard to age, sex, numbers of students living on campus, and year of study remain very similar.

It should also be noted that the response rates for the different years of the survey were quite different. If you recall, response rates just refer the number of people who responded divided by the total number of people who were contacted to participate. A higher response rate is associated with a more representative sample—i.e., one that is more likely to be characteristic of the target population. In 1998, the response rate was 51 percent. This dropped to 41 percent in 2004. Nonresponse is discussed more in Chapter 9.

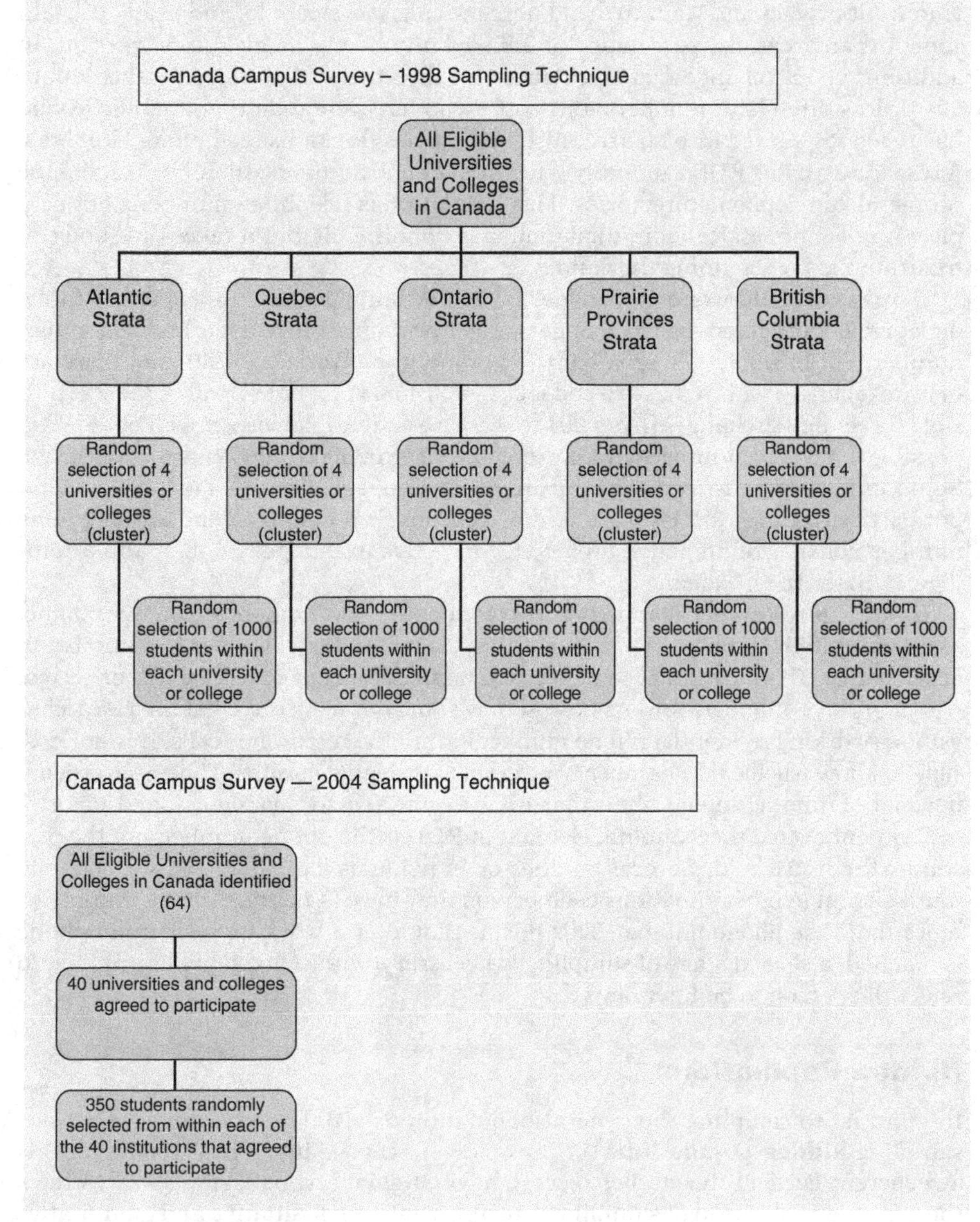

Random-Digit Dialing. Random-digit dialing (RDD) is a special sampling technique used in research projects in which the general public is interviewed by telephone. It differs from the traditional method of sampling for telephone interviews because a published telephone directory is not the sampling frame.

Three kinds of people are missed when the sampling frame is a telephone directory: people without landline telephones, people who have recently moved, and people with unlisted numbers. Those without phones (e.g., the poor, the uneducated, and transients, but also the growing number of those who only use mobile cellular telephones) are missed in any telephone interview study, but the proportion of the general public with a telephone is nearly 95 percent in advanced industrialized nations. As the percentage of the public with telephones has increased, the percentage with unlisted numbers has also grown. Several kinds of people have unlisted numbers: people who want to avoid collection agencies; the very wealthy; and those who want privacy and want to avoid obscene calls, salespeople, and prank calls. In some urban areas, the percentage of unlisted numbers is as high as 50 percent. In addition, people change their residences, so directories that are published annually or less often have numbers for people who have left and do not list those who have recently moved into an area. Also, directories do not list cell phone numbers. A researcher using RDD randomly selects telephone numbers, thereby avoiding the problems of telephone directories. The population is telephone numbers, not people with telephones. Random-digit dialing is not difficult, but it takes time and can frustrate the person doing the calling.

Here is how RDD works in Canada. Telephone numbers have three parts: a three-digit area code, a three-digit exchange number or central office code, and a four-digit number. For example, the area code for Edmonton, Alberta, is 780, and there are many exchanges within the area code (e.g., 433, 468, 467); but not all of the 999 possible three-digit exchanges (from 001 to 999) are active. Likewise, not all of the 9999 possible four-digit numbers in an exchange (from 0000 to 9999) are being used. Some numbers are reserved for future expansion, are disconnected, or are temporarily withdrawn after someone moves. Thus, a possible Canadian telephone number consists of an active area code, an active exchange number, and a four-digit number in an exchange.

In RDD, a researcher identifies active area codes and exchanges, then randomly selects four-digit numbers. A problem is that the researcher can select any number in an exchange. This means that some selected numbers are out of service, disconnected, pay phones, or numbers for businesses; only some numbers are what the researcher wants—working residential phone numbers. Until the researcher calls, it is not possible to know whether the number is a working residential number. This means spending a lot of time getting numbers that are disconnected, for businesses, and so forth.

Remember that the sampling element in RDD is the phone number, not the person or the household. Several families or individuals can share the same phone number, and in other situations each person may have a separate phone number or more than one phone number. This means that after a working residential phone is reached, a second stage of sampling is necessary, within household sampling, to select the person to be interviewed.

Hidden Populations

In contrast to sampling the general population or visible and accessible people, sampling **hidden populations** (i.e., people who engage in concealed activities) is a recurrent issue in the studies of deviant or stigmatized behaviour. It illustrates the creative application of sampling principles, mixing qualitative and quantitative styles of research and often using nonprobability techniques. Examples of hidden populations include illegal drug users, prostitutes, homosexuals, people with HIV/AIDS, and homeless people.

Tyldum and Brunovskis (2005) described ways to measure the hidden population of women and children who were victims of sex trafficking in Norway. They suggested using multiple sampling approaches and thinking in terms of several overlapping populations in which victims are a subset. One population is all working prostitutes. By telephoning all identifiable escort and massage services, then calculating response rates and the number of women per phone, the authors estimated that 600 female prostitutes worked in the Oslo metropolitan area in October 2003. Based on number of months most women work in prostitution and their turnover rate each year, they estimated that 1100 different women work as prostitutes in Oslo in a year. Of these, about 80 percent are of non-Norwegian origin. Victims of sex trafficking are a subset among the roughly 800 non-Norwegians who work as prostitutes who are being exploited by others and working involuntary. A second population is the women identified as victims by law-enforcement officials or non-government service agencies. Law-enforcement estimates depend on the specific level of enforcement efforts and are most likely to identify a small percentage of the most visible and serious cases. Similar difficulties exist with nongovernment service agencies that provide aid to victims. Thus, during the first ten months of 2004, Norwegian police detected 42 sex trafficking victims. This is a subset of all possible trafficking victims. For this population Tyldum and Brunovskis suggested using a capture-recapture method borrowed from biology. In capture-recapture, a percentage of the same cases will reappear across multiple attempts to "capture" cases (with a release after past capture). This percentage recaptured allows researchers to estimate the size of the total population. A third population is that of migrants who have returned to their country of origin. By surveying returnees and estimating the proportion of them who are former trafficking victims, researchers have another way to estimate the size of the hidden population.

In contrast, a less complex technique of studying the hidden population is described by Manzoni and associates (2006). These researchers were interested in studying property crime among opiate drug users outside of treatment in five Canadian cities. Since there is no official sampling frame of illegal opiate drug users, this population was studied using snowball sampling techniques. The participants were recruited through outreach centres, through advertisements, and by posting notices in local social and health agencies. The researcher was able to recruit 677 participants, with each interviewed drug-using participant being paid $20 for an interview.

You are now familiar with several major types of probability samples (see Table 3.4) and the supplementary techniques used with them (e.g., PPS, within-household, RDD, and RDS) that may be appropriate. In addition, you have seen how researchers combine nonprobability and probability sampling for special situations, such as hidden populations. Next, we turn to determining a sample size for probability samples.

Table 3.4 Types of Probability Samples

Type of Sample	Technique
Simple Random	Create a sampling frame for all cases, then select cases using a purely random process (e.g., random-number table or computer program).
Stratified	Create a sampling frame for each of several categories of cases, draw a random sample from each category, then combine the several samples.
Systematic	Create a sampling frame, calculate the sampling interval 1/k, choose a random starting place, then take every 1/k case.
Cluster	Create a sampling frame for larger cluster units, draw a random sample of the cluster units, create a sampling frame for cases within each selected cluster unit, then draw a random sample of cases, and so forth.

3

How Large Should a Sample Be?

Students and new researchers often ask, "How large does my sample have to be?" The best answer is, "It depends." It depends on the kind of data analysis the researcher plans, on how accurate the sample has to be for the researcher's purposes, and on population characteristics. As you have seen, a large sample size alone does not guarantee a representative sample. A large sample without random sampling or with a poor sampling frame is less representative than a smaller one with random sampling and an excellent sampling frame. Good samples for qualitative purposes can be very small.

The question of sample size can be addressed in two ways. One is to make assumptions about the population and use statistical equations about random sampling processes. The calculation of sample size by this method requires a statistical discussion that is beyond the level of this text. The researcher must make assumptions about the degree of confidence (or number of errors) that is acceptable and the degree of variation in the population.

A second and more frequently used method is a rule of thumb—a conventional or commonly accepted amount. Researchers use it because they rarely have the information required by the statistical method and because it gives sample sizes close to those of the statistical method. Rules of thumb are not arbitrary but are based on past experience with samples that have met the requirements of the statistical method.

One principle of sample sizes is this: the smaller the population, the bigger the sampling ratio has to be for an accurate sample (i.e., one with a high probability of yielding the same results as the entire population). Larger populations permit smaller sampling ratios for equally good samples. This is because as the population size grows, the returns in accuracy for sample size shrink.

For small populations (under 1000), a researcher needs a large sampling ratio (about 30 percent); a sample size of about 300 is required for a high degree of accuracy. For moderately large populations (10 000), a smaller sampling ratio (about 10 percent) is needed to be equally accurate, or a sample size of around 1000. For large populations (over 150 000), smaller sampling ratios (1 percent) are possible, and samples of about 1500 can be very accurate. To sample from very large populations (over 10 million), one can achieve accuracy using tiny sampling ratios (0.025 percent) or samples of about 2500. The size of the population ceases to be relevant once the sampling ratio is very small, and samples of about 2500 are as accurate for populations of 200 million as for 10 million. These are approximate sizes, and practical limitations (e.g., cost) also play a role in a researcher's decision.

A related principle is that for small samples, small increases in sample size produce big gains in accuracy. Equal increases in sample size produce more of an increase in accuracy for small than for large samples.

A researcher's decision about the best sample size depends on three things: (1) the degree of accuracy required, (2) the degree of variability or diversity in the population, and (3) the number of different variables examined simultaneously in data analysis. Everything else being equal, larger samples are needed if one wants high accuracy, if the population has a great deal of variability or heterogeneity, or if one wants to examine many variables in the data analysis simultaneously. Smaller samples are sufficient when less accuracy is acceptable, when the population is homogeneous, or when only a few variables are examined at a time.

The analysis of data on subgroups also affects a researcher's decision about sample size. If the researcher wants to analyze subgroups in the population, he or she needs a larger sample. For example, I want to analyze four variables for males between the ages of 30 and 40 years old. If this sample is of the general public, then only a small proportion (e.g., 10 percent) of sample cases will be males in that age group. A rule of thumb is to have about 50 cases for each subgroup to be analyzed. Thus, if I want to analyze a group that is only 10 percent of the population, then I should have 10 × 50 or 500 cases in the sample to be sure I get enough for the subgroup analysis.

Drawing Inferences

A researcher samples so he or she can draw inferences from the sample to the population. In fact, a subfield of statistical data analysis that concerns drawing accurate inferences is called **inferential statistics**. The researcher directly observes variables using units in the sample. The sample stands for or represents the population. Researchers are not interested in samples in themselves; they want to infer to the population. Thus, a gap exists between what the researcher concretely has (a sample) and what is of real interest (a population) (see Figure 3.4).

■ **Figure 3.4** Model of the Logic of Sampling and of Measurement

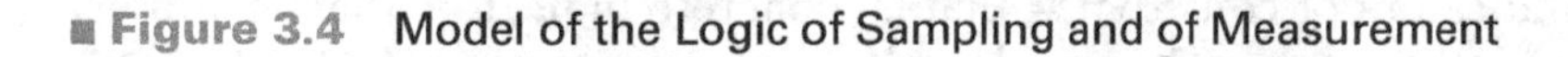

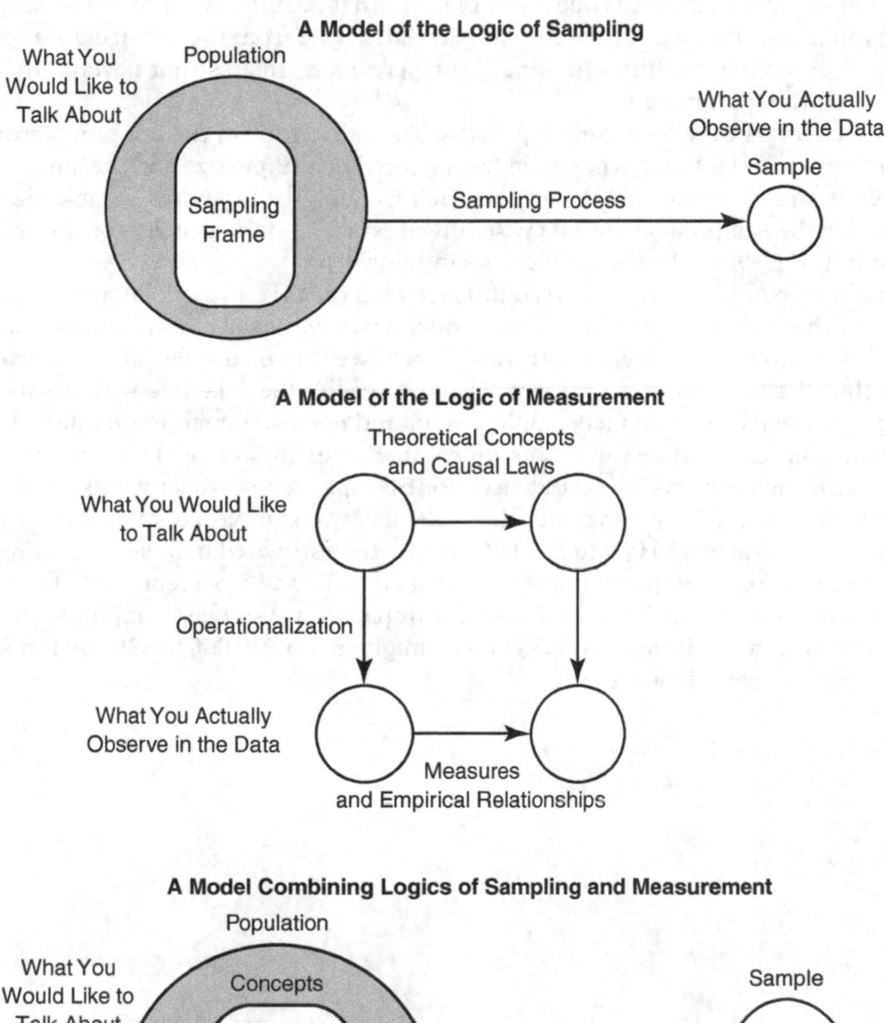

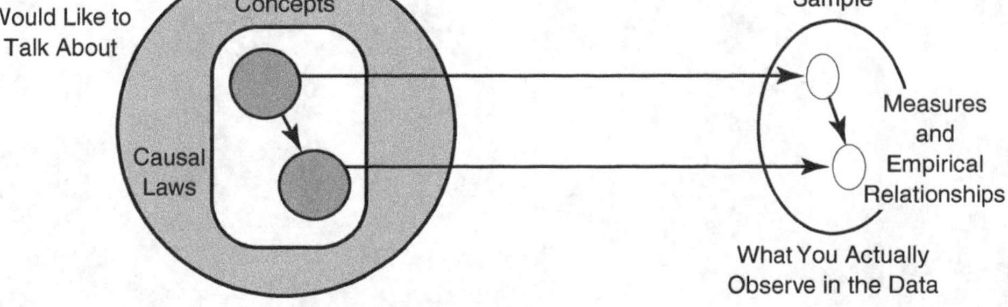

In the last chapter, you saw how the logic of measurement could be stated in terms of a gap between abstract constructs and concrete indicators. Measures of concrete, observable data are approximations for abstract constructs. Researchers use the approximations to estimate what is of real interest (i.e., constructs and causal laws). Conceptualization and operationalization bridge the gap in measurement just as the use of sampling frames, the sampling process, and inference bridge the gap in sampling.

Researchers put the logic of sampling and the logic of measurement together by directly observing measures of constructs and empirical relationships in samples (see Figure 3.4). They infer or generalize from what they can observe empirically in samples to the abstract causal laws and constructs in the population.

Validity and sampling error have similar functions, as can be illustrated by the analogy between the logic of sampling and the logic of measurement—that is, between what is observed and what is discussed. In measurement, a researcher wants valid indicators of constructs—that is, concrete indicators that accurately represent abstract constructs. In sampling, he or she wants samples that have little sampling error—concrete collections of cases that accurately represent unseen and abstract populations. A valid measure deviates little from the construct it represents. A sample with little sampling error permits estimates that deviate little from population parameters.

Researchers try to reduce sampling errors. The calculation of the sampling error is not presented here, but it is based on two factors: the sample size and the amount of diversity in the sample. Everything else being equal, the larger the sample size, the smaller the sampling error. Likewise, the greater the homogeneity (or the less the diversity) in a sample, the smaller its sampling error.

Sampling error is also related to confidence intervals. If two samples are identical except that one is larger, the one with more cases will have a smaller sampling error and narrower confidence intervals. Likewise, if two samples are identical except that the cases in one are more similar to each other, the one with greater homogeneity will have a smaller sampling error and narrower confidence intervals. A narrow confidence interval means more precise estimates of the population parameter for a given level of confidence. For example, a researcher wants to estimate average annual family income. He or she has two samples. Sample 1 gives a confidence interval of $30 000 to $36 000 around the estimated population parameter of $33 000 for an 80 percent level of confidence. For a 95 percent level of confidence, the range is $23 000 to $43 000. A sample with a smaller sampling error (because it is larger or is more homogeneous) might give a $30 000 to $36 000 range for a 95 percent confidence level.

CONCLUSION

In this chapter, you learned about sampling. Sampling is widely used in social research. You learned about types of sampling that are not based on random processes. Only some are acceptable, and their use depends on special circumstances. In general, probability sampling is preferred by quantitative researchers because it produces a sample that represents the population and enables the researcher to use powerful statistical techniques. In addition to simple random sampling, you learned about systematic, stratified, and cluster sampling. Although this book does not cover the statistical theory used in random sampling, from the discussion of sampling error, the central limit theorem, and sample size, it should be clear that random sampling produces more accurate and precise sampling.

Before moving on to the next chapter, it may be useful to restate a fundamental principle of social research: Do not compartmentalize the steps of the research process; rather, learn to see the interconnections between the steps. Research design, measurement, sampling, and specific research techniques are interdependent. Unfortunately, the constraints of presenting information in a textbook necessitate presenting the parts separately, in sequence. In practice, researchers think about data collection when they design research and develop measures for variables. Likewise, sampling issues influence research design, measurement of variables, and data collection strategies. As you will see in future chapters, good social research depends on simultaneously controlling quality at several different steps—research design, conceptualization, measurement, sampling, and data collection and handling. The researcher who makes major errors at any one stage may make an entire research project worthless.

KEY TERMS

central limit theorem *63*
cluster sampling *66*
confidence intervals *63*
deviant case sampling *56*
haphazard sampling *54*
hidden populations *72*
inferential statistics *75*
iterative process *58*
multistage cluster sample *70*
nonrandom sample *53*
parameter *59*
population *58*
probability proportionate to size (PPS) *69*
purposive sampling *54*
quota sampling *54*
random-digit dialing (RDD) *72*
random-number table *61*
random sampling *60*
sample *53*
sampling distribution *61*
sampling element *58*
sampling error *60*
sampling frame *59*
sampling interval *63*
sampling ratio *58*
sequential sampling *57*
simple random sampling *61*
snowball sampling *55*
sociogram *56*
statistic *59*
stratified sampling *64*
systematic sampling *63*
target population *58*
theoretical sampling *57*
theoretical saturation *57*

ENDNOTE

1. See Beck (2002:596)

CHAPTER 4

Research with Nonreactive Measures

Taken from: *Understanding Research,* by W. Lawrence Neuman

BWAC Images/Alamy

What do you throw away? Have you ever gone through your trash to find something accidentally thrown away? Thieves, private detectives, and police investigators comb through trash to gather information. Researchers also study trash to learn about social behavior. Just as archaeologists study bits of broken pottery to learn about ancient cultures and reconstruct social life from long ago, you can learn about people and their behavior by studying what they discard. I sometimes look through trashcans in my classroom and notice many soft drink and beverage containers. Over the years, I have seen changes in the popularity of beverages among my students. Urban anthropologists have studied the contents of garbage dumps to learn about lifestyles based on what people throw away (e.g., liquor bottles indicate alcohol consumption). They found, based on garbage, that people underreport their liquor consumption by 40 to 60 percent (Rathje and Murphy 1992:71). Examine my family's trash and that of our neighbor, and you will discover differences in our respective eating habits, lifestyles, and recreation habits. My neighbor's family eats a lot of carryout fast food and delivered pizza. Their primary form of recreation is to watch television, especially professional sports. They drink a lot of soft drinks and beer. They subscribe to a weekly television guide and a sports magazine. My family eats a lot fresh fruits and vegetables and drinks bottled water and wine. We cook from scratch and almost never eat fast food or drink sodas. Our recreation is to go to the theater and to read books and newspapers. We subscribe to two newspapers, and to one news and one arts magazine. Trash is physical evidence that can become data to inform us about human behavior. It is a form of nonreactive data, the topic of this chapter.

Most quantitative social research, such as experiments and survey research, are reactive. The people who are studied know that they are part of a research study. Reactive research can be problematic. People sometimes modify their words or actions because they are aware that they are in a study. The example of studying trash is a type of **nonreactive research**. The people being studied are not aware of being studied in nonreactive research, but the nature of the data rather than covert or secret data collection and spying makes such research nonreactive. In this chapter, you will learn about four *nonreactive* quantitative research techniques:

Physical evidence analysis
Content analysis
Existing statistics analysis
Secondary data analysis

Quantitative nonreactive research techniques have two advantages: first, people do not act differently because you study them, or because they are aware that data about them is part of a research study. Second, it is often faster and easier to collect data. Quantitative nonreactive research has some disadvantages. With several nonreactive techniques you have limited control over how the data are collected. Also, you often must infer the meaning of data indirectly. You follow the quantitative measurement process to create a nonreactive measure: (1) Conceptualize a construct and create a theoretical definition, (2) develop an operational definition of a variable, and (3) collect empirical evidence.

ANALYZING PHYSICAL EVIDENCE FOR CLUES ABOUT SOCIAL LIFE

As shown in the study on trash that opened this chapter, you can learn about social life by looking creatively at various types of physical evidence. It begins when you notice evidence that indicates a variable of interest. Discarded beverage containers indicate beverage availability and people's taste preferences. The critical thing about nonreactive or **unobtrusive measures** (i.e., measures that are not obtrusive or intrusive) is that people who generate it are not aware of its use in a research study.

Over the years, social researchers used many kinds of physical evidence to create nonreactive measures of variables. They have

- looked at family portraits in different historical eras to see how seating patterns reflected gender relations within the family;
- measured public interest in exhibits by noting worn floor tiles in different parts of a museum;
- compared graffiti in male versus female high school restrooms to examine gendered themes; and
- examined high school yearbooks to compare the high school activities of people who later had psychological problems with those who did not.

Nonreactive data can confirm or reveal different things from direct, reactive data. This happened with the alcohol consumption measure based on the study of trash. We know that people's answers to a survey question do not always match their behavior. Perhaps my favorite music is heavy metal rock. In a survey question, I say my favorite music is classical because I want to appear refined and sophisticated. In an experiment, if given a choice to listen to heavy metal or classical, I pick classical music to present myself as sophisticated and educated. However, you might follow how some researchers studied the listening habits of drivers. They checked the radio stations that drivers had tuned to when cars were taken in for service. If you checked my car radio, you might find that it is never tuned to classical, only to heavy metal rock. Going through my trash for lists of purchases, you see no classical music, only heavy metal rock. At times, nonreactive data can give a more accurate measure of music preference than direct reactive measures.

nonreactive research a collection of research techniques in which the people in the study are unaware that someone is gathering information or using it for research purposes.

unobtrusive measures most nonreactive research measures do not intrude or disturb a person, so the person is unaware of them.

To conduct a study with physical evidence, you need to do the following:

- Identify a physical evidence measure of a behavior or viewpoint of interest.
- Systematically count and record the physical evidence.
- Identify and measure other variables of your hypothesis.
- Consider alternative explanations for the physical data and rule them out.
- Compare the two variables of your hypothesis using quantitative data analysis.

Limitations of Physical Evidence

Physical evidence measures are indirect. This means you must infer or make a cautious "educated guess" from the evidence to people's behavior or attitudes. For example, you infer that leaving a radio station in my car to a station that plays heavy metal indicates my music preference. You do not know whether I set the radio to that station because it has the best weather forecasts or a favorite announcer. You do not know whether someone else who also drives the car likes heavy metal and I never listen to the radio when driving. Perhaps a different person takes the car in for service and changes the radio settings. For these reasons, you need to confirm inferences from nonreactive data with reactive evidence. When you must infer indirectly from data, looking for patterns in a very large sample makes it less likely to be misled by a few unusual situations.

You want to confirm the meaning of a physical evidence measure to rule out alternative explanations. For example, you can measure walking traffic by customers in a store by the amount of dirt and wear on floor tiles. To use this measure, you first must clarify what the customer traffic really means (e.g., Is the floor a path to another department? Does it indicate a good location for a visual display?). Next, you systematically measure dirt or wear on the tiles and record results on a regular basis (e.g., every month). Next, you compare the wear and dirt in one area to wear in other locations. Finally, you rule out alternative reasons for the data (e.g., the floor tile is of lower quality and wears faster, or the location is near an outside entrance).

4

Example Study Box 1 **Data in the Graveyard**

Bob Daemmrich/PhotoEdit Inc.

Have you ever walked through an old cemetery and read what was on the tombstones? You can learn a lot. Writing on tombstones provides data about conditions in the past. In addition to official written records, which may be incomplete or destroyed over time, we can look at the physical evidence on tombstones. Foster and colleagues (1998) examined the tombstones in 10 cemeteries in an area of Illinois for the period from 1830 to 1989. From the tombstones, they retrieved data on birth and death dates and gender. In total, they gathered information from over 2000 of the 2028 burials in the 10 cemeteries. They learned how the area differed from national trends. For example, they found that conceptions had two peaks (spring and winter), and females aged 10 to 64 had a higher death rate than males. Younger people tended to die in late summer but older people in late winter. Cemeteries can also reveal information about family size and relations (e.g., a married adult woman is buried with her parents and not her husband).

Another limitation of nonreactive data is possible privacy violation. You could be violating a person's privacy by noting the stations on a car radio or detailing what is put in his or her trash. The potential for privacy violation means that you must take extra care in collecting data to protect anonymity and confidentiality. For example, you record the make and year of a car and the radio stations, not the owner's name. You observe whether two types of garbage occur together (pizza boxes and beer cans) but not other information in the same trash (a name and address on discarded junk mail).

Creativity is an important aspect of nonreactive research using physical measures. A researcher needs to think creatively about what observations might indicate. Perhaps you notice that people driving bright red or yellow cars seem to speed more than people who drive black or gray ones. You might hypothesize that people who are attracted to bright colors and want to be noticed feel less constrained by rules or laws. If you obtained a radar gun to measure car speed and record car color, you could see whether color and speed are related. You need to be aware of alternative explanations and be cautious in drawing conclusions. Perhaps younger people like brightly colored cars and are also more likely to speed. Age and not the desire to have a bright car could be the real causal factor.

REVEALING THE CONTENT BURIED WITHIN COMMUNICATION MESSAGES

Content analysis is a nonreactive technique that lets you explore both hidden and visible content in communication messages. The *content* can be words, meanings, pictures, symbols, ideas, themes, or any message that the **text** communicates, directly or indirectly. Text appears in all communication media, including books, newspaper or magazine articles, advertisements, speeches, official documents, films or DVDs, musical lyrics, photographs, articles of clothing, and works of art. Professionals in many fields use content analysis, including marketing, communication, education, politics, and public health. Researchers have used content analysis to study the following:

- themes in popular songs and religious symbols in hymns
- trends in the topics that newspapers cover
- the ideological tone of newspaper editorials
- sex-role stereotypes in textbooks or feature films
- how often people of different races appear in television commercials and programs
- answers to open-ended survey questions
- enemy propaganda during wartime.
- the covers of popular magazines
- personality characteristics evident from suicide notes
- social class and identity themes in advertising messages
- gender differences in conversations

You use objective, systematic counting and recording procedures to carry out an analysis of the content in text. This produces quantitative data on the symbolic content that is present in the text. There are also qualitative versions of content analysis that emphasize interpreting symbolic meaning. Here, we focus on quantitative data about a text's content.

Content analysis is nonreactive because words, images, or symbols of text are produced without the creator or author of a communication message being aware that someone someday might study it. Content analysis allows you to uncover aspects of the content (i.e., messages, meanings, bias, etc.) in the text of a communication medium (i.e., a book, article, movie, song, etc.) differently from what you learn in ordinary reading, listening, or watching. With content analysis, you can compare content across many texts and analyze it with quantitative techniques (e.g., charts and

content analysis a nonreactive technique for studying communication messages.

text in content analysis, it means anything written, visual, or spoken in a communication medium.

tables). In addition, you can reveal difficult-to-see aspects of the text's content. For example, you might watch television commercials and feel that nonwhites rarely appear in commercials for expensive consumer goods (e.g., luxury cars, furs, jewelry, perfume, etc.). By using content analysis, you can document—in objective, quantitative terms—whether your vague feelings from nonsystematic observation are true.

You use coding to create repeatable, precise data about the text of a communication medium. With coding, you turn aspects of text content into quantitative variables. After you have gathered the quantitative data, you use statistics to examine variables in the same way that an experimenter or survey researcher would.

Content analysis is useful for three research issues:

- *Large volumes of text.* With careful sampling and measurement, you can analyze what appears in all television programs of a certain type on five major channels over a five-year period.
- *Topics studied "at a distance".* You can study the writings of someone who has died, or you can study broadcasts in a distant hostile foreign country.
- *Content difficult to see with casual observation.* You can note themes or bias about which a text's creator and people who read it are not aware (e.g., preschool picture book authors who portray children in traditionally stereotyped gender roles).

How to Measure and Code in Content Analysis

In content analysis, you convert a large mass of text information (words or images) into precise, quantitative data. To do this, you carefully design and document procedures in a manner that makes replication possible. It should be possible for someone else to repeat what you have done. To operationalize variables in content analysis, you create a **coding system**. By using a coding system, you observe in a systematic, careful way by consistently following written rules. The rules explain how to categorize and classify observations. As with other kinds of measurement, you want mutually exclusive and exhaustive categories. The written rules make replication possible and improve reliability.

You must tailor the coding system to the specific type of text or communication medium you are examining, such as television dramas, novels, photos in magazine advertisements, and so forth. You must also tailor it to your unit of analysis (you will learn about units of analysis in Chapter 10). The unit of analysis varies widely in content analysis. It can be a television commercial, a phrase, a book's plot, a newspaper article, a film character, and so forth. For this reason, decide on the unit of analysis before you develop measures or record any of the data. If your unit is a full-length film, a television commercial, or a newspaper editorial, you adjust the coding to that type of unit (see Example Study Box 2: Film and Gender Roles).

What Do You Measure? You begin with a preliminary coding system that has rules you can use to conduct a pilot study on a small amount of data. You use pilot study results to refine the coding rules for the full study. As you develop rules, you can measure five characteristics of variables in the text content you will code:

- *Direction.* Note the positive/support or negative/oppose direction of messages in the text relative to an issue, trait, or question. For example, you devise a list of ways an elderly television character can act. Some are positive (e.g., friendly, wise, considerate) and some are negative (e.g., nasty, dull, selfish).
- *Frequency.* Count whether something occurs in the text and how often. For example, how many elderly people appear on a television program within a week? What percentage of all characters are they, or in what percentage of programs do they appear? How frequently do they have speaking parts?
- *Intensity.* Measure the strength of a variable. For example, the characteristic of forgetfulness can be minor (e.g., not remembering to take your keys when leaving home) or major (e.g., not remembering your name, not recognizing your children).

coding system in content analysis, a set of instructions or rules stating how text was systematically measured and converted into variables.

Example Study Box 2 Film and Gender Roles

Lauzen and Dozier (2005) studied gender stereotypes in the most popular U.S. films in 2002. They developed a coding system based on prior studies of prime-time television shows and film. They began with a list of the 100 most popular U.S. films of 2002 and employed three graduate students to work as coders. Their unit of analysis was the film. During an initial training period, Lauzen and Dozier created a coding system and variable definitions. Next, they had the coders practice by coding several films independently of one another. They compared results and discussed the practice coding. Two coders independently coded 10 percent of all the films. This allowed the researchers to calculate intercoder reliability measures (discussed later in this chapter). The intercoder measure for the gender of the major character in the film was 0.99, for occupation of the characters it was 0.91, and for the age of characters it was 0.88. This told the researchers that different coders were coding in a highly consistent way.

- *Space.* Measure the size, volume, and amount of time or physical space. One way to measure space in written text is to count words, sentences, paragraphs, or physical space on a page (e.g., square inches). For video or audio text, you can measure the duration of time. For example, a TV character may be present for a few seconds or continuously in every scene of a two-hour program.
- *Prominence.* Prominence is related to space—is it located in a time or physical location to get a lot of attention? A television show aired in "prime time" versus 3 A.M. has greater prominence. An article on the front page of a newspaper has greater prominence than one buried inside.

4

Coding, Validity, and Reliability. There are two major types of coding in content analysis, manifest and latent.

Manifest Coding. With **manifest coding**, you count the number of times a phrase or word appears in written text, or whether a specific action (e.g., a kiss, a slap) or object (e.g., a gun, a dog) is in a photograph or video scene. The coding system is a list of terms or actions for you to locate in text. For written text, you may be able to use a computer program to search for words or phrases. To do this, you must first develop a comprehensive list of relevant words or phrases, and then put the text into a form that computers can read. Manifest coding is highly reliable because a word, object, or action is either present or not. A weakness of manifest coding is that it cannot take into account the specific meaning, context, and connotations of the words, phrases, objects, or actions. A word, object, or action has multiple meanings, and this weakens the measurement validity of manifest coding.

For example, I read a book with a *red* cover that is a real *red* herring. Unfortunately, its publisher drowned in *red* ink because the editor could not deal with the *red* tape that occurs when a book is *red* hot. The book has a story about a *red* fire truck that stops at *red* lights only after the leaves turn *red*. There is also a group of *Reds* who carry *red* flags to the little *red* schoolhouse. They are opposed by *red*-blooded *red*necks who eat *red* meat and honor the *red,* white, and blue. The main character is a *red*-nosed matador who fights *red* foxes, not bulls, with his *red* cape. *Red*-lipped little *Red* Riding Hood is also in the book. She develops *red* eyes and becomes *red*-faced after eating many *red* peppers in the *red* light district. Her angry mother, a *red*head, gives her a *red* backside.

Latent Coding. In **latent coding**, you read an entire paragraph or book or view an entire film and then decide whether it contains certain themes (e.g., danger, erotic)

manifest coding content analysis coding in which you record information about the visible, surface content in a text.

latent coding coding in content analysis in which you look for the underlying, implicit meaning in the content of a text.

or a mood (e.g., threatening, romantic). Instead of lists of words or actions, a latent coding system has general rules that guide how you interpret text and determine whether themes or moods are present. Compared to manifest coding, latent coding tends to be less reliable because it relies on a coder's in-depth knowledge of language, subtle clues, and social meaning. Training, practice, and clear written rules can improve reliability, especially if several people do the coding. However, even with training and practice, it is difficult to identify themes, moods, and so forth consistently. On the other hand, latent coding can have greater measurement validity. This is because we communicate meaning in many indirect and implicit ways that depend on the context, not just on specific words or actions. Latent coding captures the direct and indirect meanings that may be embedded in a specific text context.

It is very time consuming, but the ideal is to use both manifest and latent coding. If they agree, you can have confidence in the results. If they disagree, you may want to reexamine the operational and theoretical definitions.

Intercoder Reliability. In most situations, you will code text from a very large number of units. You may code the content in dozens of books, hundreds of hours of television programming, or thousands of newspaper articles. In addition to coding personally, you may have assistants to help. You must instruct the assistants on the coding system and train them. The coder-assistants need to understand the variables, carefully follow the coding system, and ask you about ambiguities. As the coding progresses, you must document every decision about how to treat a new coding situation so you will be consistent and have a written record.

If you use assistants as coders, *always* check for consistency across them. To do this, ask several coders to code the same text independent of one another. If you have three assistants coding television commercials, have the three coders independently code the same 15 commercials. Check for consistency across the coders and determine whether they coded the 15 commercials the same. With **intercoder reliability**, you measure the degree of consistency with a statistical coefficient. *Always* report the coefficient along with the results.

There are several intercoder reliability measures. All range from 0 to 1. Perfect agreement among coders is 1.0. Most researchers treat a coefficient of 0.80 or higher as very good and 0.70 as acceptable. When the coding process stretches over a considerable time span (e.g., over three months), you should check coding reliability over time by having each coder independently code samples of text that were previously coded. For example, the assistants code six hours of television episodes in April and recode the same six hours in August without looking at their original decisions. A deviation in coding between the two times means retraining coders and recoding text.

Content Analysis with Visual Material. Using content analysis to study visual "text," such as photographs, paintings, statues, buildings, clothing, and videos and film, is more difficult than doing so for written text. Visual material communicates messages or emotional content indirectly through symbols and metaphors. Moreover, visual images often contain mixed messages and operate at multiple levels of meaning. Learning to "read" visual media takes substantial effort and skill. You need to be aware of multiple symbolic meanings and references.

To conduct a content analysis of visual text, you "read" the meaning(s) within visual text (i.e., you interpret signs or symbols and the meanings they convey). Reading visual text is not mechanical (i.e., image *X* always means *G*) but depends on cultural context. We attach cultural meanings to symbolic images (see Learning from History: Visual Text Is Cultural Bound).

Most people in one culture share a common meaning for its major cultural symbols. However, visual text is often multilayered with several meanings. Different people can read the same symbol differently. For example, one person "reads" graffiti as vandalism that defaces a building, another reads it as a work of art, and a third

intercoder reliability a measure of measurement consistency in content analysis when you have multiple coders.

Learning from History Visual Text Is Cultural Bound

Ingo Jezierski/Photodisc/ Getty Images Royalty Free

Many people associate the swastika with the Nazi government in Germany or extreme racist groups. This is because they first saw the image in history books, films, and news reports. However, the origin of the image goes back over 2000 years. The swastika is on religious buildings across Asia as a good luck symbol, and it is used in decorative art and clothing. People were using the symbol for over a thousand years before the Nazi movement adopted it. Many people use the image without any awareness of the Nazis. This shows how a symbol's meaning depends on when and where it appears. (See Quinn 1994.)

A second example is the smile. We treat a smile as a reflex indicating a positive feeling, and it is nearly a cultural universal. However, it is not always a friendly sign. Its meaning varies by how and when it appears. In some cultures, a smile can signal deceit, insincerity, or frivolity. Smiling depends on the social situation as well as the culture. Smiling at a funeral is appropriate in some cultures but highly disrespectful in others. A smile's meaning can also change over time. Perhaps you noticed that in very old photographs, the people never smiled. This was not because they were always unhappy but because smiling as a social convention when being photographed only developed later (in the 1920s in the United States). (Also see Rashotte 2002)

Bettmann/Corbis

reads it as a mark of a street gang's territory. To conduct a content analysis of images, you need to be aware of possible divergent readings of images or symbols.

Symbol use can be a source of conflict. Sociopolitical groups invent or construct new symbols and attach meanings to them. For example, the Nazis originally used a pink triangle in concentration camps to mark homosexuals who were condemned

Example Study Box 3 Magazine Covers and Cultural Messages

Chavez (2001) conducted a content analysis of the covers of major magazines that dealt with the issue of immigration into the United States. Looking at the covers of 10 magazines from the mid-1970s to the mid-1990s, he classified them into sending one of the following messages: affirmative, alarmist, or neutral and balanced. He also examined the mix of people (i.e., race, gender, age, and dress) in the photographs and whether major symbols, such as the Statute of Liberty or the U.S. flag, appeared. Chavez argued that magazine covers are a cultural site. They are a place where media create and communicate cultural meanings to the public. Visual magazine covers carry multiple levels of meaning. When people see a cover and apply their cultural knowledge, they construct specific meanings. Collectively, the covers convey a worldview and express messages about a nation and its people. For example, we usually see the icon of the Statute of Liberty as strong and full of compassion. Its usual message is, Welcome immigrants. However, when a magazine cover altered this icon to give it Asian facial features, its message shifted to become, Asian immigrants are distorting the U.S. national culture and altering the nation's racial make-up. When a magazine showed this icon holding a large stop sign, its message became, Go away immigrants—we do not want you. The symbolic messages sent by visual images can have a powerful emotional effect on people that is sometimes stronger than written text.

to extermination along with Jews, and other "undesirables." The pink triangle later came to mean gay pride. Competing sociopolitical groups often wrestle to control the meaning of symbols. Thus, some people want to assign a Christian religious meaning to the Christmas tree; others say it represents a celebration of tradition and family values without religious content; others see its origins as an anti-Christian pagan symbol; and still others see it as a profit-oriented commercial symbol. Because a symbol has complex, multilayered meanings, you must make qualitative judgments about how to code images.

How to Conduct Content Analysis Research

STEP 1. Formulate a research question. Start with a topic and research question. When your research question involves variables that are messages or symbols, content analysis may be appropriate. Conceptualize each variable. Let us say you want to study newspaper coverage of a political campaign. Your must refine the idea of "coverage"—do you mean the amount of coverage, prominence of the coverage, or direction of coverage? You must decide how to examine newspaper coverage. You could survey people about what they think of newspaper coverage or examine the newspapers directly using content analysis. Your research question will guide you to the variables to measure. You might have a research question such as, Does the newspaper give more coverage to one presidential candidate over the other as the date of the election gets closer? This suggests the variables of amount of coverage for each candidate and dates of coverage relative to the election.

STEP 2. Identify the text to analyze. Find the communication medium that best matches your research question. Your research question and decision about type of text are usually a single process—candidate coverage and the newspaper as a type of text (versus television, radio, or other media). You still must identify the specific text (such as which newspapers) and its scope (which dates).

STEP 3. Decide on units of analysis. This is a major early decision in content analysis. There are many possible units in content analysis—the page, the episode, the character, and so forth. The unit of analysis determines the amount of text to which you assign a code. For example, for a political campaign, you may code what each newspaper article reports (excluding editorials, letters to the editor, and advertising). In this case, the article is your unit of analysis. You still need to determine how to identify "campaign-related" articles from others (such as by scanning the headlines).

STEP 4. Draw a sample. Random sampling works well for most content analysis studies because you often have a huge collection of units to which you want to generalize (such as all newspaper articles) but only have time to code a small proportion of the units. The steps are as follows:

- Define the population (e.g., all articles, all sentences).
- Select the sampling element (your unit of analysis).
- Create a sampling frame.
- Use a random selection process.

STEP 5. Create a coding system. Once you decide on variables to measure, operationalize them by creating a coding system. To create a coding system, carefully conceptualize each variable and decide whether you will use a manifest or latent coding method or both. For each variable, you decide what it is you wish to measure (a variable's direction, frequency, intensity, space or prominence, or all of them).

STEP 6. Construct and refine coding categories. The coding category is a critical aspect of the coding system. It determines the number and types of distinctions you make within a variable and how you distinguish among them. Let us say you are measuring the variable "violence." You must decide, Do you want high, medium, and low levels of intensity, or are there more levels? How do you distinguish a low

Making It Practical **Sampling in Content Analysis**

Suppose your research question is, How do U.S. weekly newsmagazines portray women and minorities? Your unit of analysis is the article. Your population is all articles published in *Time, Newsweek,* and *U.S. News and World Report* between 1997 and 2007. You will need to define precisely the unit of analysis, the article. Do film reviews count as articles? Does a letter to the editor count? Does an article have a minimum size (two sentences)? Will you count a multipart article as one or two articles?

Next, you examine issues of the three magazines. You need to find out how many articles are in the average issue of the magazine. You might look at two issues of each magazine in the first (1997), middle (2002) and last year (2007). This gives you (3 magazines × 2 issues × 3 time periods = 18) 18 issues to look at and count articles. If each issue contains 45 articles and the magazines publish an issue each week or 52 weeks per year within 10 years, your population of articles has (3 magazines × 45 articles × 52 issues × 10 years = 70,200) 70,200 articles. Your sampling frame is a list of all the articles.

Next, decide on the sample size and design. After looking at your budget and time, you may decide to sample 1404 articles. Your sampling ratio is 2 percent (70,200 × 0.02 = 1404). You must choose a sampling design. Avoid systematic sampling because magazine issues are published cyclically according to the calendar (e.g., an interval of every 52nd issue results in the same week each year). Because issues from each magazine are important, you probably want to use stratified sampling. You stratify by magazine, sampling 1404/3 = 468 articles from each magazine. If you want to ensure that articles represent each of the 10 years, you can also stratify by year. With rounding, this results in (468/10 = 46.8) 47 articles per magazine per year. To simplify matters, you may use cluster sampling, in which the issue of a magazine in a year is the cluster. Since each magazine has 52 issues in a year, you may wish to randomly sample 8 issues of each magazine for each year. You then only have to count all articles in those 8 issues for a year and then draw a random sample of 47. For example, in 2002 you use a random sampling computer program to get 8 numbers from 1 to 52. These are your sample of 8 issues of *Time* magazine from the 52 that were published. Next, you count the total number of articles in all 8 issues and number them. If there are 380 total articles, you create a list of articles from 1 to 380. Now use a random number table or random sampling computer program to select your sample of 47 articles from those 380. You are now ready to apply your coding system to these 47 articles.

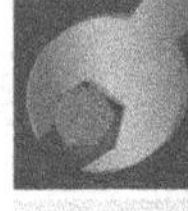

Making It Practical **Coding Systems and Categories**

Suppose your research question is, Has the appearance of people of different races-ethnicities or genders shown in significant leadership roles in U.S. newsmagazines changed over a 10-year period? You must define "significant leadership role" in operational terms. This means creating written rules for classifying people named in an article. For example, if an article discusses the achievements of someone who is now dead, does the dead person have a significant role? What is a significant role—a local Girl Scout leader or a corporate president? You need to record information on the race-ethnicity and gender of people in significant leadership roles. What do you do if the race and sex are not evident in the text or accompanying photographs? How do you decide on the person's race and sex? Are you interested in both positive and negative leadership roles? You can measure this using either latent or manifest coding. With manifest coding, you must create a list of adjectives and phrases. If a sampled article referred to someone using one of the adjectives, then the direction is decided. For example, the terms *brilliant* and *top performer* are positive, whereas *average* and *uninspired* are negative. For latent coding, you must create rules to guide coding judgments. For example, you classify stories about a diplomat resolving a difficult world crisis, a business executive unable to make a firm profitable, or a lawyer winning a case into positive or negative terms.

When planning a research project, you should calculate the time required to complete the research. For example, during a pilot test, you may learn that it takes an average of 15 minutes to read and code one article. This does not include sampling or locating magazine articles. If you have approximately 1400 articles, it means 350 hours of coding—not counting time to verify the accuracy of coding. Because 350 hours is about nine weeks of nonstop work at 40 hours a week, you may consider hiring assistants as coders or making other adjustments.

from a medium level? Do you want to consider different types of violence (e.g., physical, emotional, sexual) and look at the intensity of each?

STEP 7. Code the data onto recording sheets. Once you decide the variables, type of coding, and coding categories, you should construct a sheet (paper- or computer-based) on which to record information. Typically, you will have one recording sheet (piece of paper or word processing page) for each unit or case. If you planned to code 1000 television commercials and the commercial was your unit of analysis, you would have 1000 sheets, one for each. Put general information about the study (title, who does the coding) on each sheet. Also have space for basic information about the unit (the date and time) and space for each variable and its categories. You then code the text by filling in the information on each unit. Place them into spaces on the recording sheet.

STEP 8. Data analysis. Content data analysis is like other quantitative data analysis. You must transfer the data from the recording sheets into a machine readable form that computer programs use. Typically, this is a grid or spreadsheet. Each row

Making It Practical Recording Data in Content Analysis

EXAMPLE OF BLANK RECORDING SHEET

Professor Neuman, Sociology-Anthropology Department Coder:____

Minority/Majority Group Representation in Newsmagazines Project

ARTICLE #____ MAGAZINE:____ DATE:____ SIZE:____ col. in.

Total number of people named____ Number of photos____

No. people with significant roles:____ Article topic:____

Person____:	Race:____	Gender:____	Leader?:____	Field?____	Rating:____
Person____:	Race:____	Gender:____	Leader?:____	Field?____	Rating:____
Person____:	Race:____	Gender:____	Leader?:____	Field?____	Rating:____
Person____:	Race:____	Gender:____	Leader?:____	Field?____	Rating:____
Person____:	Race:____	Gender:____	Leader?:____	Field?____	Rating:____
Person____:	Race:____	Gender:____	Leader?:____	Field?____	Rating:____
Person____:	Race:____	Gender:____	Leader?:____	Field?____	Rating:____
Person____:	Race:____	Gender:____	Leader?:____	Field?____	Rating:____

EXAMPLE OF COMPLETED RECORDING SHEET FOR ONE ARTICLE

Professor Neuman, Sociology Department Coder: Susan J.

Minority/Majority Group Representation in Newsmagazines Project

ARTICLE # 0454 MAGAZINE: Time DATE: March 1–7, 1998 SIZE: 14 col. in.

Total number of people named 5 Number of photos 0

No. people with significant roles: 4 Article topic: Foreign Affairs

Person 1:	Race: White	Gender: M	Leader?: Y	Field? Banking	Rating: 5
Person 2:	Race: White	Gender: M	Leader?: N	Field? Government	Rating: NA
Person 3:	Race: Black	Gender: F	Leader?: Y	Field? Civil Rights	Rating: 2
Person 4:	Race: White	Gender: F	Leader?: Y	Field? Government	Rating: 0
Person ____:	Race: ____	Gender: ____	Leader?: ____	Field? ____	Rating: ___
Person ____:	Race: ____	Gender: ____	Leader?: ____	Field? ____	Rating: ___
Person ____:	Race: ____	Gender: ____	Leader?: ____	Field? ____	Rating: ___
Person ____:	Race: ____	Gender: ____	Leader?: ____	Field? ____	Rating: ___

is a unit or case, and the columns represent variables. You can then use standard analysis techniques for quantitative data.

Limitations of Content Analysis

Generalizations in content analysis are limited to the cultural communication itself. Unfortunately, by itself content analysis cannot do any of the following:

- Determine the truthfulness of an assertion
- Evaluate the aesthetic qualities of literature or visual text
- Interpret the content's significance
- Reveal the intentions of the organizations or people who created the text
- Determine the influence of a message on its receivers

Content analysis can only describe what is in the text and reveal patterns in it. With content analysis, you can say that a certain type of message appears regularly on television, but you cannot say how that message influences the thinking of viewers who receive it. You can build on the content analysis using other research to understand fully the process of how messages influence people's beliefs and behaviors. If you wish to talk about the appearance of a message and its influence, combine content analysis with other types of studies, such as experiments. You can then see both how widespread a message appears and how it affects message receivers. For example, your content analysis shows that children's books contain sex stereotypes. Alone, that does not mean that such stereotypes influence children's beliefs or behaviors. You next conduct a separate research study on how what children read influences their beliefs and behaviors. Putting the two types of research together can give you a complete picture.

MINING EXISTING STATISTICAL SOURCES TO ANSWER NEW QUESTIONS

Thus far, we have discussed research techniques, such as the survey, experiment, or content analysis, in which you create a design and collect data. You are lucky to have mountains of information about the social world already collected and available. Some of it is in statistical documents (books, reports, etc.). Other information is in computerized records. In either case, you can search through collections of information with variables and a research question in mind and then statistically analyze the information to address the research question.

Existing statistics research involves analyzing previously collected public data to answer new research questions. It differs from most other research techniques in that you must learn what data are available before you develop a research question and hypothesis. Recall that in other quantitative research, the process was to (1) begin with ideas or concepts, (2) conceptualize them into variables with definitions, (3) operationalize variables into specific measures, (4) gather data, and (5) analyze the data. For the other research techniques, you start with a research question or hypothesis. Now you must start by learning what is available. The process goes as follows:

1. Search and scan existing statistical information or data.
2. Conceptualize the data you found into variables.
3. Identify variables that have the same unit of analysis and verify the accuracy of the data.
4. Organize hypotheses with independent and dependent variables from the variables you found.
5. Test the hypotheses using statistical data analysis.

An experiment is best for topics in which you can control a situation and manipulate an independent variable. Survey research is best for topics in which you can ask questions and learn about reported attitudes or behavior. Content analysis is best for topics in which you look at the content in a communication medium. The best topics for existing statistics research are ones on which large bureaucratic organizations routinely collect and report quantitative information; many measures in such reports are **social indicators.**

During the 1960s, many social scientists were dissatisfied with the information available to decision makers. Information was limited to a few economic measures. The dissatisfied scientists spawned the "social indicators movement" and developed many new measures, or indicators, of social conditions or well-being. Their goal was to combine data on social conditions with economic indicators (e.g., gross national product, income) to create a more complete picture of social-economic life that could better inform policy-making officials. Social indicators measure negative aspects of social life (the death rate of infants during the first year of life, crime rate, divorce rate, alcoholism) or positive aspects (job satisfaction, volunteering activity, park land, homeownership, housing with indoor plumbing) (see Table 4.1). Organizations also regularly report measures of the physical environment (air pollution) and psychological conditions (reports of stress, mental health visits).

Hundreds of public or private organizations have ongoing data collection and reporting activities for internal policy decisions or as a public service. They rarely collect data to address one specific research question. Existing statistics research is appropriate when you have an issue or question about the various social, economic, and political conditions on which organizations gather and report information. Often organizations collect the data over time or across wide geographic areas. The information is often free or nearly free. For example, free, public existing statistics allow you to determine whether unemployment and crime rates are associated in 150 cities across a 20-year period.

Some of the initial data collection may have been reactive. For example, a measure of the unemployment rate comes from a survey that asks people whether they are looking for work. Other data collection is without reactive effects, such as recording how many people voted in an election or the number of students who received high school diplomas. Organizations collect the data as part of their routine bureaucratic planning and monitoring activities, not for research. Your use of the data to answer research questions is nonreactive. People on whom the information is gathered are unaware of its research use.

You will face three challenges in doing existing statistics research: searching and locating data sources, verifying data quality, and being creative in thinking about how to turn the data into variables that can answer research questions.

social indicator any measure of social conditions or well-being that can be used in policy decisions.

4

Table 4.1 Examples of Publicly Available Social Indicators

Turnout to vote in elections
Number of hours that people volunteer per year
Percent of the population that is literate
Percent of the population that lacks health care coverage
Number of child abuse cases
Average length of time people commute to work
Number and size of parks and recreation areas
Number of crimes reported to police

Example Study Box 4 Pollution, Race, and Housing Choice in Detroit

Downey (2005) conducted an existing statistics study on the topic of black-white racial inequality and living near a toxic pollution site in Detroit. He wanted to test the hypothesis that blacks more than whites lived near toxic waste sites. He used public census data that have years of information on population and housing (including home ownership and race of owner) and on manufacturing facilities (location of factories, where most employees lived). Downey identified the location of polluting factories using the Environmental Protection Agency's (EPA's) inventory of toxic chemicals. His unit of analysis was the census tract (a geographic unit created by the U.S. Census Bureau). So he had information about all his variables from each census tract and combined it with other public information. Downey tested three models of environmental inequality:

1. *Racist site location policy.* Companies and officials placed the toxic sites near existing black residential areas.
2. *Economic inequality.* Low-income people who are disproportionately black moved into areas near toxic sites because that is where the low-cost housing was located.
3. *Residential segregation.* Whites moved into desirable areas and tried to keep out nonwhites. The nonwhites were forced to live in remaining open areas that are near toxic sites.

Downey's data showed greatest support for the residential segregation model. However, his findings differed from his original hypothesis. He discovered that although whites tried to maintain all-white neighborhoods, they also wanted to live close to where they worked. Many whites worked at factories that produced toxic pollution and stored it on site. Paradoxically, this meant whites more than blacks lived close to the toxic pollution sites. The whites had kept blacks from moving into their neighborhoods; neighborhoods that were close to polluting factories.

Locating Data

Governments, international agencies, private companies, and nonprofit organizations gather an enormous volume and variety of quantitative information. The quantity is overwhelming and specifics are difficult to pinpoint. If you plan to conduct an existing statistics research study, discuss your interests with an information professional—in this case, a reference librarian, who can point you in the direction of possible sources. Many existing sources are "free"—that is, publicly available at libraries or over the Internet. Nonetheless, it can take a huge amount of time and effort to search for specific information. There is a paradox: You do not know what information you will find until you look for it, and you do not know what to look for until you begin to search. Professional researchers can spend many hours searching in libraries, searching on the Internet, or contacting specific organizations with requests for information. Once you locate information, you need to record it. Some information is already available in a computer readable format. For example, instead of recording voting data from published books, it is already in a format that computers read (e.g., spreadsheets, statistics programs).

There are so many diverse sources that it is a full-time job for professionals to keep track of it. The single most valuable source of statistical information about the United States is the *Statistical Abstract of the United States* (see Figure 4.1). The U.S. government has published it annually since 1878. It is available in all libraries and on the Internet. The *Statistical Abstract* contains 1400 charts, tables, and statistical

■ Figure 4.1 Example of Page from Statistical Abstract of the United States

Percentage of Adults Engaging in Leisure-Time, Transportation-Related and Household-Related Physical Activity: 2003

[In percent. Covers persons 18 years old and over. Based on responses to questions about physical activity in prior month from the Behavioral Risk Factor Surveillance System. Estimates are age-adjusted to the year 2000 standard population. Based on a survey sample of approximately 257,000 persons in 50 states and the District of Columbia in 2003]

Characteristic	Persons who meet recom-mended activity[1]	Persons not meeting recom-mended activity[2]	Persons who are physically inactive[3]
Total	**46.0**	**54.0**	**24.3**
Male	48.2	51.8	22.0
Female	44.0	56.0	26.3
White, non-Hispanic	49.0	51.0	20.9
Black, non-Hispanic	36.3	63.7	32.7
Hispanic	37.5	62.5	36.0
Other	43.5	56.5	25.2
Males:			
18 to 29 years old	57.8	42.2	17.1
30 to 44 years old	48.7	51.3	20.7
45 to 64 years old	43.2	56.8	24.4
65 to 74 years old	45.7	54.3	24.9
75 years old and over	36.7	63.3	31.0
Females:			
18 to 29 years old	50.1	49.9	21.9
30 to 44 years old	47.7	52.3	23.4
45 to 64 years old	42.6	57.4	26.7
65 to 74 years old	37.1	62.9	31.2
75 years old and over	27.6	72.4	42.0
School years completed:			
Less than 12 years	33.8	66.2	45.7
12 years	43.1	56.9	30.5
Some college (13 to 15 years)	47.5	52.5	21.0
College (16 or more years)	51.9	48.1	13.1
Household income:			
Less than $10,000	34.7	65.3	42.2
$10,000 to $19,999	37.0	63.0	38.9
$20,000 to $34,999	43.6	56.4	29.4
$35,000 to $49,999	47.3	52.7	21.9
$50,000 and over	53.6	46.4	13.6

[1]Recommended activity is physical activity at least 5 times/week × 30 minutes/time or vigorous physical activity for 20 minutes at a time at least 3 times/week. [2]Persons whose reported physical activity does not meet recommended level or report no leisure-time, transportation-related, or household-related physical activity. [3]Persons with no reported physical activity.

Source: U.S. National Center for Chronic Disease Prevention and Health Promotion, "Nutrition and Physical Activity"; and unpublished data: <http://www.cdc.gov/needphp/dnpa>.

Households and Persons Having Problems With Access to Food: 2000 to 2003

[**106,043 represents 106,043,000.** Food secure means that a household had access at all times to enough food for an active healthy life for all household members, with no need for recourse to socially unacceptable food sources or extraordinary coping behaviors to meet their basic food needs. Food insecure households had limited or uncertain ability to acquire acceptable foods in socially acceptable ways. Food insecure households with hunger were those with one or more household members who were hungry at least sometime during the period due to inadequate resources for food. The omission of homeless persons may be a cause of underreporting. The severity of food insecurity and hunger in households is measured through a series of questions about experiences and behaviors known to characterize households that are having difficulty meeting basic food needs. These experiences and behaviors generally occur in an ordered sequence as the severity of food insecurity increases. As resources become more constrained, adults in typical households first worry about having enough food, then they stretch household resources and juggle other necessities, then decrease the quality and variety of household members' diets, then decrease the frequency and quantity of adults' food intake, and finally decrease the frequency and quantity of children's food intake. All questions refer to the previous 12 months and include a qualifying phrase reminding respondents to report only those occurrences that resulted from inadequate financial resources. Restrictions to food intake due to dieting or busy schedules are excluded. Data are from the Food Security Supplement to the Current Population Survey (CPS); for details about the CPS, see text, Section 1 and Appendix III]

Household food security level	Number (1,000)				Percent distribution			
	2000	2001	2002	2003	2000	2001	2002	2003
Households, total	**106,043**	**107,824**	**108,601**	**112,214**	**100.0**	**100.0**	**100.0**	**100.0**
Food secure	94,942	96,303	96,543	99,631	89.5	89.3	88.9	88.8
Food insecure	11,101	11,521	12,058	12,583	10.5	10.7	11.1	11.2
Without hunger	7,785	8,010	8,259	8,663	7.3	7.4	7.6	7.7
With hunger	3,315	3,511	3,799	3,920	3.1	3.3	3.5	3.5
With hunger among children[1]	255	211	265	207	0.7	0.6	0.7	0.5
Adult members	**201,922**	**204,340**	**206,493**	**213,441**	**100.0**	**100.0**	**100.0**	**100.0**
In food secure households	181,586	183,398	184,718	190,451	89.9	89.8	89.5	89.2
In food insecure households	20,336	20,942	21,775	22,990	10.1	10.2	10.5	10.8
Without hunger	14,763	14,879	15,486	16,358	7.3	7.3	7.5	7.7
With hunger[2]	5,573	6,063	6,289	6,632	2.8	3.0	3.0	3.1
Child members	**71,763**	**72,321**	**72,542**	**72,969**	**100.0**	**100.0**	**100.0**	**100.0**
In food secure households	58,868	59,620	59,415	59,704	82.0	82.4	81.9	81.8
In food insecure households	12,895	12,701	13,127	13,265	18.0	17.6	18.1	18.2
Without hunger	12,334	12,234	12,560	12,845	17.2	16.9	17.3	17.6
With hunger among children[1]	562	467	567	420	0.8	0.6	0.8	0.6

[1]One or more children in these households was hungry at some time during the year because of the household's food insecurity. Percent distribution of households with hunger among children excludes households with no child from the denominator. [2]One or more adults in these households was hungry at some time during the year because of the household's food insecurity.

Source: U.S. Department of Agriculture, Economic Research Service, *Household Food Security in the United States, 2003, Food Assistance and Nutrition Research Report No. 42*; October 2004; <http://www.org.usda.gov/briefing/foodsecurity/>.

lists. It is a selected compilation of thousands of more detailed reports from hundreds of government and private agencies. At times, you will want to examine the more specific government documents. It is hard to grasp all that the *Statistical Abstract* contains until you skim through it. Most information is by state or county as the unit of analysis, and often it goes back many years.

Most national and state governments publish similar statistical yearbooks. If the country is your unit of analysis, the United Nations and international agencies (the World Bank, Organization for Economic Cooperation and Development) have their own statistical publications with information on countries (e.g., literacy rates, percentage of the labor force in agriculture, birth rates).

Verifying Data Quality

Despite its low cost and ease of access, six issues can limit your research when using existing statistics:

- Missing data
- Reliability
- Validity
- Topic knowledge
- Fallacy of misplaced concreteness
- Ecological fallacy

1. *Missing data.* Missing data can be a major limitation with existing statistics and documents. Sometimes the data were collected but have been lost. More frequently, no one collected the data. Officials in government agencies decide whether to collect official information, and their political beliefs and values can influence what data are gathered. Government agencies can start or stop collecting information for political, budgetary, or other reasons. For example, the U.S. federal government stopped the collection of several types of information that social researchers had found highly valuable. The official reason was cost cutting, but later some officials revealed it had to do with promoting a political agenda. If the government stopped gathering or publishing information that could document certain inequalities or health risks, critics would find it difficult to make claims of discrimination or unsafe conditions. Missing information is especially a problem when you want to cover a long time period.

A related type of missing data is data collected with less refined categories than you want. Perhaps you are interested in racial-ethnic groups. You want to compare some aspect of whites, blacks, Asians, and Latinos in the United States, but the official data only offer you white and nonwhite as variable categories. The data are not available at the level of refinement needed for your research question.

2. *Reliability.* Reliability problems plague many existing statistics sources. Reliability problems develop when official definitions or methods of collecting information vary over time. For example, the official definitions of *work injury, disability, unemployment*, and the like have changed several times. Even if you learn of the changes, consistent measurement may be impossible. For example, during the early 1980s, the U.S. government changed how it calculated the U.S. unemployment rate. Until then, government agencies calculated it as the number of unemployed people divided by the total number of people in the civilian work force. The new method divided the number of unemployed by the civilian work force, plus all people in the military. A similar complication happens when police departments computerize their records. The number of crimes reported increases not because actual crime increases but due to improved recordkeeping.

3. *Validity.* You can encounter three kinds of measurement validity problems in existing statistics research. First, the agency or organization that collects informa-

tion uses a different conceptual definition from yours. For example, you define a *work injury* as including minor cuts, bruises, and sprains that occur while working on a job. The official definition includes major injuries that required a visit to a physician or hospital. Many injuries you define as work injuries would not be in the official statistics. Another example is that you define a person as being *unemployed* if he or she would work if a job for which he or she is trained is available, if the person is forced to work part time but wants to work full-time, or if after a year of trying the person has given up looking for work. The official definition includes only people now actively seeking any full- or part-time work at any job. Excluded are people who stopped looking, who work only 15 hours a week because they cannot find more hours, or who are not looking because there are no jobs for someone with their special training (e.g., a dentist can only find a job driving a taxi). To add complications, different countries or states often use different official definitions. (See Making It Practical: Official Unemployment Rates versus the Nonemployed.)

A second validity problem arises when official statistics are a proxy for a variable of interest. The official statistics do not really measure what you want, but they are all you have so you use them. Let us say you want to know how many people were robbed in a city last year. You use police statistics on robbery arrests as a proxy. However, many robberies go unreported. If half of robberies are not reported to the police, by using official statistics you are not really measuring the number of people robbed. You have only part of what happened, the number of robberies known to police. Such reporting bias can affect hypotheses testing. Let us say young people are less likely to report a robbery to police than old people. Using official data, you find that most robbery victims are older. In fact, this may not be true but it is due to the reporting bias in official statistics.

Making It Practical **Official Unemployment Rates versus the Nonemployed**

In most countries, the official unemployment rate measures the unemployed as a percent of all working people. It excludes two related categories of not-fully-employed people: involuntary part-time workers and discouraged workers. In some countries (e.g., Sweden and the United States), the unemployment rate would double if these people were included. Most official statistics exclude other nonworking people such as transitional self-employed and the underemployed. Different definitions treat the situation of unemployment differently. An economic policy or labor market perspective sees the unemployment rate as measuring people ready to enter the labor market immediately. It sees nonworking people as a supply of labor that is available to employers, or as an input to the economy. A social policy or human resource perspective sees the unemployment rate as measuring people not currently working to their full potential. The rate tells us who cannot fully utilize their talents, skills, or time. Nonworking people viewed individuals who are unable to be productive, contributing members of society. Thus, a nation's official statistics will include a definition that reflects a particular value perspective or theory of what unemployment means for society. Consider the following list of all nonemployed people:

Categories of Nonemployed/Fully Utilized

- *Officially unemployed.* People who meet three conditions: (1) lack a paid job outside the home, (2) are actively engaged in looking for work, and (3) can begin work immediately if it is offered.
- *Involuntary employed.* People with a job, but who work irregularly or many fewer hours than they are able or willing to, or who are working part time but desire and are able to work full time.
- *Discouraged workers.* People able to work and who had actively sought work for some time, but being unable to find work have stopped looking.
- *Other nonworking.* People not working because they are retired, on vacation, temporarily laid off, semidisabled, homemakers, full-time students, or in the process of moving.
- *Transitional workers.* Self-employed people who are not working full time because they are just starting a business or are going through bankruptcy of a failed business.
- *Underemployed people.* Persons with a temporary full-time job for which they are seriously overqualified. They seek a permanent job in which they can fully apply their skills and experience.

Source: Adapted from *The Economist*, July 22, 1995, p. 74.

A third validity problem arises because you must depend on official agencies that collected the information. Information collecting may have systematic errors (e.g., census people who avoid poor neighborhoods and make up information, or people who put a false age on a driver's license). Or people in an agency may make errors in organizing and reporting the information (e.g., a police department that is sloppy about filing crime reports and loses some). Some errors occur in publishing information (e.g., a typographical error in a table).

An example of such errors in official statistics is illustrated by data on the number of people permanently laid off from their jobs. Official U.S. Bureau of Labor Statistics data on permanent job losses come from a survey of 50,000 randomly selected people. The agency counted percent saying they were laid off based on the number of questionnaires sent out and failed to adjust the data for people who did not respond. Here is an example of what happened. The agency sent 50,000 people questionnaires. In 1993, 8000 returned the questionnaire reporting that they had been laid off. This is 16 percent of the total and is reported as the laid-off rate. In 1996, 4500 returned the questionnaire saying that they had been laid off of work. This is 9 percent of the total. The agency reports a 7 percent decline in laid-off people between 1993 and 1996. However, in 1993, 40,000 people returned their questionnaires. This makes the true rate 20 percent (8000/40,000). In 1996, only 22,500 people returned the questionnaire. This is also 20 percent (4500/22,500). Instead of a 7 percent decline in laid-off people between 1993 and 1996, as officially reported, there was no change. Only a university researcher's careful detective work uncovered the error (see Stevenson 1996).

4. *Topic knowledge.* Because existing statistical data are easily accessible, you may be able to get a lot of data on an issue that you know little about. This can lead to erroneous assumptions or false interpretations of results. Before using any data, you should become informed about the topic. For example, perhaps you are interested in the percent of the U.S. population covered by some form of health insurance. The *Statistical Abstract of the United States* (2006, Table 142) shows that this was 15.6 percent in 2003. However, it is easy to make errors in interpreting results because there are many forms of health insurance coverage. Some are government provided, some are purchased privately, and some are employer provided; some only cover the bare basics and only after a person has paid a great amount personally, whereas others cover all health care visits plus medicine at no cost to a person; some are open and available to anyone, whereas others have very restrictive entry requirements. You may have a statistic, but do you know what it really means? This issue is far greater when using international statistics because the definitions and situations in different countries can vary widely.

5. *Fallacy of misplaced concreteness.* The **fallacy of misplaced concreteness** occurs when you quote statistics in excessive detail to give an impression of scientific rigor and precision. For example, an existing statistics report says that Australia has a population of 19,179,083. It is better to say that it is about 19.2 million, because the exact number is not that precise. The counting of people could easily be higher or lower by a few thousand people. If you calculated the percentage of divorced people in a town as 15.655951, only report it to one decimal place, or 15.7 percent.

6. *Ecological fallacy.* The **ecological fallacy** happens when your research question is about a lower-small unit of analysis (such as individual behavior) but you only have data on a higher-larger unit of analysis (an entire state). Published data are often available on a higher or larger unit of analysis. If you are interested in variables on a much lower level than your data, you may be seriously misled. For example, data may be available on the state level (such as unemployment rate by state), but you are interested in individuals (characteristics of individuals who become unemployed). From existing statistics, you find that states with high unemployed rates also have a high percentage of cigarette smokers. It is an ecological

fallacy of misplaced concreteness when statistical information is reported in a way that gives a false impression of its precision.

ecological fallacy mistaken interpretations that occur when you use data for a higher or bigger unit of analysis to examine a relationship among units at a lower or small unit of analysis.

4

Tips for the Wise Consumer Using Data from Existing Statistical Sources

When you use data from existing statistical documents, do the following:

1. Be certain that the definition and measure of a variable truly fit the variable of interest to you.
2. Watch out for missing data or variable categories that combine distinctions of interest to you.
3. Be aware of the units of analysis used in measures and avoid the ecological fallacy.
4. Know about a topic area that applies to the data you are using.
5. Read statistical tables very carefully, including the details in footnotes and other explanations, so you know exactly what the table offers.

fallacy to say that unemployed people are more likely to smoke. Data for the state as a unit of analysis do not show which individuals smoke. Simply because more smokers are in a state that also has a high unemployment rate does not make the unemployed people more likely to smoke than employed people. If you want to know whether unemployed individuals are likely to smoke, you need data for which the individual is the unit of analysis. Official statistics may not have the data to match your research question, so you must change your question or switch to a different research technique, such as the social survey. You can ask individuals, Do you smoke? What is your employment status? Then see whether the two variables are associated among those individuals.

Creative Thinking About Variables of Interest

When you use existing statistical data, someone else already collected data that represent conceptual variables. At times, the data does not match the exact variable of most interest to you. When using existing data sources, you frequently must be creative to identify a surrogate or proxy for your conceptual variable. To do this, you first search through existing statistical sources looking for data measures that most closely match your concept. Perhaps you are interested in measuring "upper class neighborhood" but no existing data source has such a measure. You nonetheless find data on various social characteristics by city block. If you are careful and creative, you can build a close substitute measure of "upper class neighborhood." Let us say you believe that upper class people tend to own their own house that has a high value (over one million dollars), completed a college degree or more schooling, send their children to expensive private schools, and belong to exclusive country clubs. You find data by city block on percent of owner-occupied houses of a high value and percent of residents with a college degree or more schooling. You also obtain address lists of student at expensive private schools and for members of exclusive private clubs, then match the addresses to city block. You find a dozen city blocks in which most houses are owner-occupied and worth over 1 million dollars, almost all residents have at least a college degree, and that contain addresses of at least ten children attending expensive private schools and at least ten members of an exclusive private club. By merging the existing statistics data measures, you can create your own indicator of an "upper class neighborhood."

Standardization of Data

You have heard of crime rates (e.g., 11 murders per 10,000), birth rates (e.g., 5 births per 1000 women), or the unemployment rate (e.g., 4 percent). Many measures are expressed as rates or percentages. Percentage is a kind of rate, a rate per 100. The rates standardize the value of a variable to allow for valid comparisons. A lot of existing statistics information is standardized. At times, you must standardize it before you can use the information. Without standardization, it is difficult or impossible to compare and very easy to misinterpret the information.

Let us say you are interested in citizen participation in elections in various states. The *Statistical Abstract of the United States* shows that 12,421,000 people in California and 741,000 people in Maine voted in the 2004 presidential election. Does the bigger number mean Californians are more politically active than people in Maine? You might realize that California has more people (population was 35.8 million in 2004) than Maine (1.3 million people in 2004), so California should have more voters. To compare the voting rate or percentage of voters in the two states, you must first standardize the data.

Standardization involves selecting a base and dividing a raw measure by it. The base is simply a number or characteristic that influences how you interpret raw measures. Population size is an example. It is relevant to the number of people who vote. If California and Maine had the exact same number of people, you would not need to standardize. Standardization lets you compare on a common base by adjusting or removing the effect of relevant but different characteristics. It makes important differences visible. You can remove the size difference in the two states to make true differences in voting rates visible. The percentage is a common form of standardization; it standardizes on base 100. We can divide the number of voters in each state by the state's population size. If 12.4 million out of 36.8 million voted in California, about 33.7 percent voted. If 741,000 out of 1.3 million people in Maine voted, then 57 percent voted. Of course, California's population size means it had a bigger impact on the national election's outcome, but if your interest is in active participation in elections, then you need to remove the effect of different state population sizes.

4

You might say wait, not everyone can vote! Recent immigrants, noncitizens, and people under the age of 18 cannot vote but are in the population. The entire state population is not the best base to use. A critical question in standardization is deciding what base to use. The choice is not always obvious. It depends on the variable, and you need to think about it. To get an accurate measure of the percent who voted, we need to divide number of voters by the number eligible voters. In 2004, California had 26.3 million people eligible to vote. If 12.4 million showed up to vote, then California's voter turnout rate in the 2004 presidential election was 47 percent. Maine had 1.04 million eligible voters in 2004. Since 741,000 voted, Maine had a much higher voter turnout rate, 71.6 percent.

Different bases can produce different rates, and the base is influenced by how you define a variable. For example, some define the unemployment rate as the number of people in the work force who are out of work. The overall unemployment rate is given by the following fraction:

$$\text{Unemployment rate} = \frac{\text{Number of unemployed people}}{\text{Total number of people working}}$$

You can also divide the total population into subgroups to get rates for subgroups in the population, such as white males, African American females, African American males between the ages of 18 and 28, or people with college degrees. Rates for subgroups are often relevant to a research question. Perhaps you conceptualize unemployment as an experience that affects an entire household. You can change the base to households, not individuals. The formula for an unemployment rate will look like this:

$$\text{Household unemployment rate} = \frac{\text{Number of households with at least one unemployed person}}{\text{Total number of households}}$$

standardization adjusting a measure by dividing it by a common base to make comparisons possible.

How you conceptualize a variable suggests different ways to standardize, but failing to standardize can produce distorted results. A few years ago, a student announced to me that based on the *Statistical Abstract of the United States*, New York had a terrible child abuse record with over 74,000 child victims, whereas her home state of Utah had only about 13,500. She failed to standardize on population size. Once she adjusted for the number of children in each state, New York had 16.3 victims of child abuse per 1000 children whereas Utah had 18.3 per 1000. Thus, the situation looked worse for Utah. Of course, the detection and follow-up of abuse cases may not be the same across the states, but the importance of standardizing data was clear.

Secondary Sources

Secondary data analysis is similar to existing statistics research in that you analyze data that someone else collected. The difference is that organizations often release official statistical information in aggregate form; or for large, macro units of analysis; or they publish it in descriptive tables that do not have all variables on all units. For example, from official statistics you learn the percent of doctors in a state affiliated with hospitals and the percent of hospitals with certain medical technology (e.g., an MRI [magnetic resonance imaging] machine). You cannot find out the number of doctors affiliated with each separate hospital and what equipment each hospital has. If you are interested in whether the number of doctors at a hospital is associated with it having certain medical equipment, you need data in which the unit of analysis is the hospital, but this may not be in any of the official statistics available to the public.

As opposed to primary data research (e.g., experiments, surveys, and content analysis), you do not focus on collecting data in secondary data analysis. Rather, the focus is on statistically analyzing data. Secondary data analysis facilitates replication and permits asking research questions that the original researchers did not consider. In a way, it is similar to entering the research process after the data collection phase has been completed. Collecting data on a large scale (such as nationally) is very expensive and difficult. A major national survey with rigorous technical support can cost tens of thousands of dollars. Fortunately, several organizations gather, preserve, and share survey data or other types of data. They make their data available for others to analyze. The most widely used source of survey data in the United States is the **General Social Survey (GSS)**. The U.S. government pays for the social survey, and the National Opinion Research Center at the University of Chicago has conducted it nearly annually for over 30 years. Data from it are made available to the public for secondary analysis. In recent years, many other industrialized nations have started similar surveys (see Making It Practical: The General Social Survey and Secondary Data Analysis).

General Social Survey a large-scale survey with many questions of a large national sample of adult Americans conducted almost every year. Data from it are made available to researchers at low or no cost.

4

Making It Practical The General Social Survey and Secondary Data Analysis

The General Social Survey (GSS) is the best-known source of survey data for secondary analysis in the United States. It is available in computer-readable formats. Neither the datasets nor codebooks are copyrighted. Users can copy or disseminate them without obtaining permission. Results using the GSS appear in over 2,000 research articles and books. The National Opinion Research Center (NORC) has conducted the GSS almost every year since 1972. Data comes from face-to-face interviews of a random sample of 1,500 to 4,000 adult U.S. residents. The NORC staff carefully selects and trains its interviewers. The interviews are typically 90 minutes long and contain about 500 questions. The response rate has been 71 to 79 percent. Each year a team of researchers selects questions for inclusion. They repeat some questions and topics each year, include others on a four- to six-year cycle, and add other topics in specific years. You can learn more about the GSS by visiting the NORC web site. You can order a copy of the GSS data or analyze it online. Online analysis of the data is available through several sources, such as Survey Data and Analysis (SDA) at the Computer-assisted Survey Methods Program of the University of California–Berkeley. You will want to begin with a list of survey questions or variables that are available at several online sites. To analyze data in detail you will need statistical analysis software and a raw data file. Several sources sell the data file at low cost, and they pre-format it for major statistics software packages.

Limitations of Secondary Data Sources

Using data collected by others is not trouble free. As with existing statistics research, you first must locate a data source and see what variables it contains. The most common limitation is that secondary data lack the variables you want for a research question. For example, in the GSS you are dependent on other researchers including survey questions on topics that you find interesting. Even when the data are available on variables of interest, the researchers who designed a study and collected the data may have conceptualized them differently. Before you proceed with secondary data analysis, you need to consider units in the data (e.g., types of people, organizations), the time and place of data collection, the sampling methods used, and the specific issues or topics covered in the data. For example, you may want to examine race/ethnic tensions between Latinos and Anglos in the Southwestern and Pacific regions of the United States. However, you find secondary data that include only the Pacific Northwest and New England states. You will have to reconsider the research question or use other data if they exist.

Secondary data analysis seems easier because the data are provided and you only need to know how to use and interpret statistical software programs. However, the other limitations common for existing statistics research, such as validity and topic knowledge, also apply in secondary data analysis. As with existing statistics research, you first need to examine the data and then develop hypotheses and a research question. Let us say you obtain a copy of the GSS. You may discover three limitations to its use:

1. Data are on all adults across the United States and not on specific types of individuals and geographic locations that you need for a research question. Perhaps you are interested in how 18- to 22-year-olds in your state feel about an issue, but the GSS does not allow you to examine this topic.
2. GSS survey questions are not on issues in your research question. Perhaps you are interested in a specific issue, such as whether a person engaged in sexual activity with his or her spouse before marriage, but the GSS did not include such questions.
3. GSS questions are worded differently than you wish or have different answer choices. For example, a long-used GSS question about prayer in public schools asks about whether respondents agree with a U.S. Supreme Court decision banning it. You cannot really learn people's opinions about favoring or opposing specific types of prayer or religious activities in a school. If the GSS offers a two-choice answer, support/oppose abortion under certain conditions, but you want a wide range of choices (strongly support to strongly oppose), you will be restricted.

4

Summary Review Strengths and Limitations of Four Kinds of Nonreactive Research

Nonreactive Research	Major Strengths	Major Limitations
Physical Evidence	Indirect and unobtrusive evidence	Must infer to people's intentions
Content Analysis	Reveal hidden content in communication	Patterns in text, not its effects on people
Existing Statistics	Quantitative data of wide scope, low cost	Measurement reliability and validity
Secondary Analysis	Large-scale survey data, low cost	Limited variables are available

CONDUCTING ETHICAL NONREACTIVE RESEARCH

Ethical concerns are not at the forefront of most nonreactive research because the people who you study are not directly involved. In secondary analysis and content analysis, few ethical concerns arise. The primary ethical concern of physical evidence analysis is to protect people's privacy and the confidentiality of data.

The use of official existing statistics raises other issues. They are social and political products. Implicit theories and value assumptions guide which information researchers collect and how they collect it. Measures or statistics that agencies define as being official and collected regularly can be involved in political disputes. If measuring something one way is official and another way is not, measuring in the official way may benefit certain political positions over others. What information is gathered and made public also shapes public policy decisions. For example, political activity pressured government agencies to collect information on certain social conditions (e.g., the number of patients who died while in public mental hospitals). Government officials previously did not think the condition was sufficiently important to warrant public attention, or preferred to keep it quiet and hidden. Likewise, information on the percentage of nonwhite students enrolled in U.S. schools at various ages only became available in 1953. Nonwhite students attended schools before 1953, but court decisions and public interest in racial discrimination caused government agencies to begin to collect the data. Just as organized concern about an issue stimulates the collection of new official statistics, the collection of official statistics on an issue can stimulate public attention. For example, drunk driving became more of a public issue after government agencies began to collect and publish statistics on the number of automobile accidents and on whether alcohol was a factor in the accidents.

Most official statistics are collected for top-down bureaucratic or administrative planning, not for a researcher's purposes or for people who strongly oppose the bureaucratic decision makers. A government agency may gather data on the number of tons of steel produced, miles of highway paved, and average number of people in a household. It decides not to gather information on drinking-water quality, contamination at food processing plants, or stress-related job illness. Some officials see the gross national product (GNP) as a critical measure of societal progress. However, the GNP omits noneconomic aspects of social life (e.g., time spent playing with one's children) and ignores some types of work (e.g., housework). To a large degree, official statistics reflect the outcome of political debates about what we need to know and the values of officials who head government agencies. It is your ethical-moral decision to question or closely examine the values and decisions that guide which official statistics are collected and made public. It is important to recognize that people in positions of power are making decisions about what information to collect and make public. By not collecting and making public certain information, they may be protecting their position or advancing a social-political value position.

WHAT HAVE YOU LEARNED?

In this chapter, you learned about several types of nonreactive research techniques. You can use these techniques to measure or observe aspects of social life without affecting the people who you study. The techniques can produce numerical information that you can analyze to address research questions. You can use the techniques with other types of quantitative or qualitative social research to address a large number of issues.

As with other quantitative data, you need to be concerned with data quality and measurement. It is easy to take available information from a previously conducted survey or government document, but this does not mean that it is the best measure of what really interests you. Another limitation of nonreactive research stems from the availability of existing information. Existing statistics and secondary data analysis are low-cost research techniques. However, you lack control over or detailed knowledge of the data collection process. This can be a potential source of mistakes and errors, and you must be especially vigilant and cautious.

The analysis techniques apply to quantitative data. Thus far, you have seen how to move from a topic, to a research design and measures, to collecting data.

KEY TERMS

4

coding system *83*
content analysis *82*
ecological fallacy *96*
fallacy of misplaced concreteness *96*
General Social Survey (GSS) *99*
intercoder reliability *85*
latent coding *84*
manifest coding *84*
nonreactive research *80*
social indicator *91*
standardization *98*
text *82*
unobtrusive measures *80*

APPLYING WHAT YOU'VE LEARNED

Activity 1

Locate eight trashcans in public places (such as a classroom, student lounge, or waiting room). Obtain permission from a person in charge of the area and take the content of the trashcan and catalog the types of items you find for each of 10 days, five weekdays in a row, for two weeks. This gives you 10 observations from eight locations. Are there patterns in what you find, either by location or day?

Activity 2

Content analyze television commercials (not including ones for upcoming TV shows or public service advertisements) by first developing a recording sheet. The sheet should have the (1) television network (2) day of week, (3) time of day, and (4) estimated price of product: (a) under $10, (b) $10–$100, (c) $101–$500, (d) $501–$10,000, (e) over $10,000. Pick two TV networks, and four days—two weekdays and both weekend days. Divide the time of day into four parts: morning (8 A.M. to noon), afternoon (noon to 5 P.M.), early evening (5 P.M. to 9 P.M.), and late evening (9 P.M. to midnight). Now observe each network each day for each time slot (you may enlist a friend to help). After you gather the data, do you find patterns by the price of products based on time of day or by day of the week? Are the two networks the same or different?

Activity 3

Go online to the *Statistical Abstract of the United States* (http://www.census.gov/compendia/statab/). Once there, click on Print Version to see many sections (chapters) with the topics they cover. Can you locate the following five pieces of information and the table in which it appears in the *Statistical Abstract*?

a. What percentage of U.S. households reported that they owned a dog as a pet?
b. What percentage of rapes/sexual assaults occurred in the victim's home or place of lodging?
c. What percentage of all youth, aged 12 to 17, engaged in "binge drinking"?
d. In terms of per capita (i.e., per person) consumption, which of the following was the highest (in terms of total pounds eaten)—beef, chicken, fish/shellfish, or pork?
e. For the entire U.S. population (all ages, races, genders), what percent say they have serious limitations in activity caused by chronic health conditions because of a serious physical, mental, or emotional problem?

Activity 4

Go online to the NORC Web site (http://www.norc.org/GSS+Website/). Click on Browse GSS variables, then Subject Index (be sure to look past the blank space in the upper half of the screen). Click on the letter D and find the survey question on the Military Draft. Look at the question Return to the Draft. Click on Trends at the bottom to see the years this question was in the GSS and overall support. What exactly did the GSS ask in this question? During what years did this question appear in the GSS? See if you can find out who is more in favor of the military draft, men or women.

REFERENCES

Chavez, Leo. 2001. *Covering Immigration.* Berkeley: University of California Press.

Downey, Liam. 2005. "The Unintended Significance of Race: Environmental Racial Inequality in Detroit." *Social Forces* 83:971–1007.

Foster, Gary, Richard Hummel, and Donald Adamchak. 1998. "Patterns of conception, Natality and Morality from Midwestern Cemeteries." *Sociological Quarterly* 39:473–490.

Lauzen, Martha, and David Dozier. 2005. "Maintaining the Double Standard: Portrayals of Age and Gender in Popular Films." *Sex Roles* 52:437–446.

Quinn, Malcolm. 1994. *The Swastika: Constructing the Symbol*. New York: Routledge.

Rashotte, Lisa Slattery. 2002. "What Does That Smile Mean? The Meaning of Nonverbal Behaviors in Social Interaction" *Social Psychology Quarterly* 65(1): 92–102.

Rathje, William, and Cullen Murphy.1992. *Rubbish: The Archaeology of Garbage*. New York: Vintage.

Stevenson, Richard W. (Oct. 16, 1996). U.S. to revise its estimate of layoffs. *New York Times*.

CHAPTER 5

Looking at the Past and Across Cultures

Taken from: *Understanding Research,* by W. Lawrence Neuman

The Granger Collection, New York

Do people who immigrate form attachment to their new country or stay connected across international borders? McKeown (2001) asked this question and studied Chinese migrant networks in Peru, Chicago, and Hawaii early in the twentieth century. As part of his study, he examined events taking place over 100 years of history and in three nations. He looked at major international events, national laws, and individual family biographies. Although his study was historical and qualitative, he also examined quantitative data. He provided us with graphs, charts, and tables of statistics. The data included geographic maps, photographs, quotes from 100-year-old telegrams, official government documents, original newspaper reports, and personal letters in three languages. By comparing Chinese migrants over a long period in different social-cultural settings, he traced the formation and operation of transnational communities and social identities. He learned that people had formed social networks that linked back to villages in China and crossed several national borders. These networks helped people to sustain a vibrant, interactive social community. Ties in the village of origin, clan and family, business transactions, and a shared language and customs held the social network together. People in the network helped each another with legal and financial issues. They consulted on major social events or concerns. Their children often intermarried. McKeown discovered an ethnic-immigrant network that mixed local customs and language with those of the country of origin to sustain long-term family and other social relationships across international borders for several generations. People in the network mixed languages and customs. They created business and family relationships that operated across countries. McKeown concluded that if we only see people as individuals inside a nation or treat people as a single ethnic group, we fail to see that they may also be part of a large transnational social community that is a hybrid of several cultures.

WHAT IS HISTORICAL-COMPARATIVE RESEARCH?

You will learn about historical-comparative (H-C) research in this chapter. It is the most relevant research method for explaining and understanding macro-level events—a terrorist attack, a nation going to war, sources of racism, large-scale immigration, violence based on religious hate, or urban decay. The major nineteenth-century founders of the social sciences, such as Emile Durkheim, Karl Marx, and Max Weber, used this method. Researchers used it to study issues in many macro-level topic areas—such as social change, political sociology, social movements, and social inequality—and in other areas—such as health care, criminology, gender relations, race relations, and family. H-C has become increasingly popular. Researchers probably conducted more H-C studies in the past 10 years than in the previous 30 years combined.

H-C studies are ideal when you want to address "big questions," but people question their practical value. True, most H-C research studies address basic rather than applied research questions. In addition, H-C studies can take a long time to complete. It typically requires over a year to complete an H-C study. In contrast, field research studies often take about a year, and many experiments, surveys, or existing statistics research studies are finished within a few months. On the other hand, often there is no better way to answer important questions than H-C research.

H-C research provides answers to questions such as, Why are there has two types of physicians with different medical degrees and different approaches medicine in the United States? Most people are familiar with medical doctors (MDs) but few know about osteopathic physicians (DOs). About 55,000 DOs practice medicine in the United States, representing about 6 percent of all physicians. A DO practices medicine based more on a broad mixture of medical and health remedies and is more holistic than the MD who tends to use laboratory-based pharmaceuticals and surgery. This fast-growing type of medical professional is trained in separate medical schools, licensed in all 50 states, and can practice in all medical specialties.

H-C studies also provide innovative ideas in fields such as education, business, law enforcement, and medical care. Long forgotten practices or practices used in other cultures can stimulate exciting new ways to approach current issues and solve problems. In addition, the methodological issues of H-C research have wider implications in comparison to other research techniques, and being aware of them will build your general research skills.

You use a blend of research techniques in H-C research. Some are like traditional history, some are like field research, and others extend quantitative research such as surveys or existing statistics research. In this chapter, we focus on H-C research that places historical time and/or cross-cultural variation at the center. It is best to use H-C research when your research question involves the flow of history and/or two or more sociocultural contexts. H-C researchers look at how a specific mix of diverse factors have come together in time and place to generate a specific outcome (e.g., civil war). They compare entire societies to see what they share and do not share. They also examine the same social process across several cultural or historical settings (see Example Study Box 1: Women's Right to Vote).

Many people enjoy reading H-C studies because they learn about distant places or the past. However, the studies can be difficult to follow if you lack background knowledge about history or other cultures. H-C studies assume that readers have a minimal level historical-geographic literacy and cultural knowledge. Most people acquire a background in high school or general education college classes. H-C studies extend and build on the existing background knowledge. To appreciate H-C studies and conduct H-C research, you need an awareness of geography, history, and cross-cultural differences (see Example Study Box 2: Race Relations in Different Countries and Learning from History: Conditions in Medieval Western Europe).

Example Study Box 1 Women's Right to Vote

Underwood & Underwood/Corbis

Both Switzerland and the United States have strong democratic traditions and highly individualistic cultures. Both have similar federalist forms of national government and local governments that allow direct democracy (also called public referendums or local ballot initiatives) (see Kriesi and Wisler 1999). In 1920, the United States joined other proactive nations in allowing women to vote in nationwide elections. However, Swiss women did not win the right to vote until 1990. Switzerland was among the last nations to extend the right to vote to women. Banaszak (1996) examined the 70-year difference on this basic issue in countries with numerous political and cultural similarities. In her study, she looked at published studies, official records and documents on women's movements, government, and social-political conditions in each society across a century. She discovered that the United States suffrage movement was very different from the one in Switzerland. The Swiss women's movement favored consensus politics, supported local autonomy, and worked closely with the major political parties. A more confrontational grass-roots suffrage movement emerged in the United States. It worked outside the major political parties and purposely disrupted the established system to win voting rights for women. Thus, the two nations' women's movements differed dramatically in orientation even though their political institutions were alike.

Most H-C researchers use a variety of data to examine a central issue and place it in a context with background knowledge. They generally gather qualitative data and focus on issues of culture. Like field researchers, they want to see things through the eyes of the people they are studying. They examine specific individuals or groups and are sensitive to specific historical or cultural contexts. As with field research and unlike quantitative research, most H-C researchers only make limited generalizations.

How Are Field Research and H-C Research Alike?

First, we consider similarities between H-C research and field research. In the next section, we examine the unique features of historical-comparative research. Field and H-C research have five similarities:

- They incorporate an individual researcher's point of view as part of the research process.
- They examine a great diversity of data types (diaries, maps, official statistics, newspapers, novels).
- They focus on processes, time passage, and sequence.
- They use grounded theory.
- They make limited generalizations.

An individual researcher's characteristics, place in history, and geographic-cultural situation may influence the research process. The time, place, and culture

Example Study Box 2 Race Relations in Different Countries

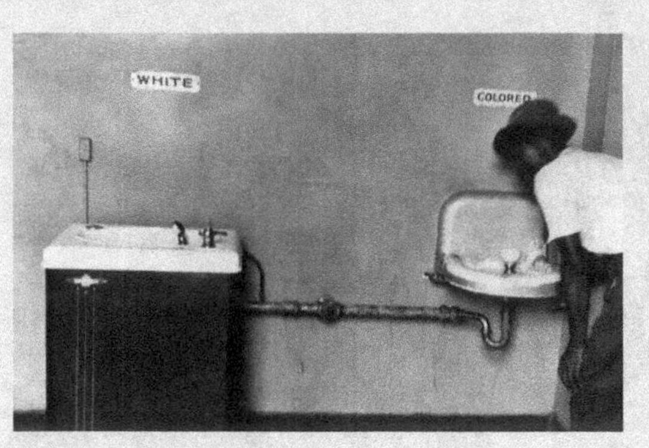

Elliott Erwitt/Magnum Photos Inc.

What are the origins of racism and why did it take very different forms in multiracial countries? Anthony Marx (1998) compared racial relations in Brazil, South Africa and the United States. Each country had black-white racism, but it took different forms based on specific historical conditions and politics in each country. Marx assumed his readers knew basic geography and something about U.S. racial conditions, and he provided background information, such as that Brazil and the United States are geographically large countries with mixed-race populations. Both had large-scale European immigration and slaves taken from Africa from the 1700s to the mid-1800s. By contrast, South Africa had a small European-immigrant population since the 1700s and a large majority native African population. Marx provided many historical and comparative details to build on this foundation of knowledge. To conduct his study, he devoted years to reading hundreds of historical books and articles and examining statistical records and official reports. He traveled to each country and conducted interviews. From the data collected, he shows us how each country developed a different pattern of race relations over time. Brazil developed moderately integrated black-white relations, whereas the Southern U.S. and South Africa both developed highly segregated racial patterns. Marx explains why these differences occurred. In the United States and South Africa, but not in Brazil, social-political elites emphasized racial superiority to unify a white population characterized by internal divisions of social class and other issues (religion, nation of origin). To do this they enforced long-term, legally enforced systems of official racial segregation.

in which you live may affect your data collection and interpretation. Both H-C and field research recognize this feature. In both, you may see specific biographic details of the person who conducted the research included somewhere in the study.

In both types of research, you immerse yourself fully in a huge amount of qualitative data. The goal is to understand in depth the lives, language, and perspective of the people you are studying so you can acquire an empathic understanding of them. You try to capture their subjective feelings and details of their daily lives. Only after an immersion in the data do you narrow the focus to specific areas for analysis. As you acquire an up-close understanding of the people studied, you "translate" from events their worldview for readers of your research report.

In field and H-C research, you devote attention to processes, time passage, and sequence, and you never treat people or social life as being static or unchanging. You treat the passage of time (micro-level clock time as well as long-term historical time) as an essential aspect of the data.

All researchers begin with concepts and ideas, but in H-C and field research you often create new concepts based on the data. The ideas emerge during data collection and analysis in a process of grounded theory (you will read about grounded theory in Chapter 10). As you gain greater knowledge about a particular place and time, it may be difficult to make broad generalizations that apply to all places or times. Typically, field and H-C research offer more limited generalization than quantitative research.

Learning from History Conditions in Medieval Western Europe

You need background information to read H-C studies and put them in context. Perhaps you read about Western Europe in the 1500s. You may already have learned that roughly one-third of the population (75 million people) died in the Black Death and about 90 to 95 percent of the population in that era could not read or write. However, you know that using the number zero was considered the devil's work, using Arabic numbers (the ones we use today) instead of Roman numerals was forbidden, and only a handful of math experts could do simple multiplication or division (what you learned in third or fourth grade). This lack of math skills profoundly affected business, accounting, and engineering. Basic banking—lending or counting money for buying and selling goods—was so primitive that it slowed the growth of trade. Most people considered loaning money for interest or making profits slightly immoral or possibly illegal. This example shows the importance of background knowledge. If you look at some past situation and ask, "Why didn't people do things differently?" you often discover the answer in the many differences from the present. For example, you may it unusual that people looked up to a local 29-year-old scribe as if he was a respected wise man when his scribe skills equaled those of a bright sixth-grader today. This makes sense in a social world where only 5 percent of adults had basic literacy skills (versus 95 percent today) and life expectancy was about 40 years old (versus nearly 80 years old today).

Bettmann/Corbis

5

What Is Unique about H-C Research?

Despite its many similarities to field research, H-C research has important differences. In H-C research, how you conduct research on the historical past and another culture differs from doing field research in the present in your home culture. The H-C researcher learns to do each of the following things:

1. Work with limited evidence.
2. Interpret evidence with minimum distortion.
3. Integrate the micro and macro levels.
4. Use specific as well as transcultural, transhistorical concepts.

1. Build on Limited and Indirect Evidence. In all studies, you construct an understanding of social life based on the empirical evidence you gathered. Historical evidence depends on data that have survived from the past. Even if you have many excellent historical documents (e.g., letters and newspapers), you are limited to what has not been destroyed and what has left a trace or other evidence behind. You cannot directly observe or be involved in the past. In comparative research, only a native member of two cultures can grasp all the similarities and differences. You may learn another language, study a new culture, and spend time in that culture, but unless you grew up in and fully absorbed the other culture, your understanding will always be that of an outsider. To see and feel like a native in both cultures, you must be truly bicultural.

2. Interpret the Meaning of Events in Context. Data in H-C studies are rarely simple and unambiguous. The data usually contain multiple messages from which you extract meaning. Do not expect to get a full understanding based on a quick first glance of the evidence. Immerse yourself in it, absorb its complexity, and place it in context. Only after you reflect on the evidence and consider its many meanings can you interpret what it means.

Perhaps you want to conduct a study on family relations of 120 years ago or in a distant country. To start, you need to learn the social context (e.g., the nature of daily work, forms of communication, transportation technology). You may want to study maps and events of that time and place. You want to be aware of local laws, the nature of health and medical care, types of foods eaten, daily household tasks, and common social practices. You may have data for a simple event, "the visit of a family member." Kinship customs and obligations of the time shape the event. To put the event in context, you need to realize that the roads are made of dirt and mud, traveling is by foot, no one can call ahead of time, and there are few places to stop and rest. Without a full immersion in the evidence, you cannot grasp the meaning of "visit of a family member." As you learn the context, you need to guard against three common types of distortion:

- Supracontext awareness
- Coherence imposition
- Capacity overestimation

Supracontext Awareness. You are aware of events beyond the immediate people or setting that your are studying, such as events that occurred later in time or elsewhere. This knowledge could distort your understanding because you know things that the people you are studying could not know. For example, you study people living in colonial America in 1760. You know that there will soon be a war of independence from Britain and the colonialists will win. However, the people you are studying did not know that. Do not to judge their actions based on what you know happened later. From their perspective, things may have looked different. You must see situations as they saw them. In a comparative study, you may become familiar with another culture but study people who know only their own culture. For example, you notice that there is a food spoilage problem, people spend lots of time storing food, putting it in jars in dark rooms, and people often get sick from spoiled food. You may think, Why don't they store food by wrapping it up as the people of my home culture do? It takes less time than other methods, and the food rarely spoils. It is unfair to evaluate life in one culture based on your awareness of a life in different culture that most people know little or nothing about.

Coherence Imposition. We like consistency and order. If you impose the expectation that people engage in predicable behavior and hold stable beliefs, you may introduce distortion. Prepare to study events or people that are contradictory or have "loose ends" that do not neatly come together. Try not to impose your own sense of order to make people's beliefs or actions coherent, noncontradictory, and consistent more than they actually are. For example, you study people having a birthday party. You expect a clear beginning and ending, with the person having a birthday at the center of attention. You see people wandering in or out, one by one, without signaling that they are leaving, and you cannot even tell whose birthday it is. From an outsider perspective, you may want to organize and impose boundaries around the event, but the people you are studying do not see or experience that way. Instead of interjecting your desire for order, accurately describe how they see/experience the world.

Capacity Overestimation. People learn, make decisions, change direction, and act on (or fail to act on) what they learn. However, people have a limited capacity to learn, make decisions, and modify the course of events. It is easy to overestimate the ability of people to act. Recognize that people may not quickly take actions. For example, you think, Those parents could have met with the teacher about their child's problem. However, from the parents' life situation and point of view, that may not be an easy or realistic option. Do not become frustrated and say, "They could have done X; why did they not act?" Try to grasp their point of view and recognize the constraints they feel.

3. Integrate the Micro and Macro Levels. H-C researchers often examine and integrate data from both the micro (small-scale, face-to-face interaction) and macro (large-scale social structures) levels. For example, you read diaries or letters to get a feel for the everyday lives of individuals who lived in the distant past. You learn about the food they ate, their recreational pursuits, clothing, sicknesses, relations with friends, and so on. You link this micro-level view to macro-level, societal-wide processes (increased immigration, mechanization of production, tightened labor markets, and the like). Perhaps you want to compare schooling in two cultures. You visit and spend time in classrooms, talk to students and teachers, and devote hours to learning the daily routines and micro-culture of schools. In addition, you study the overall structure of education in each culture, such as requirements, graduation rates, numbers and types of schools, the books and tests used in schools, official curriculum guides, teacher training requirements, and so forth. You then integrate the micro-level or face-to-face life in classrooms with the macro-level structure of the national education system in each culture.

4. Use Specific and Transcultural, Transhistorical Concepts. We use many concepts to study and think about the social world. Imagine them on a continuum. At one end are universal concepts. They apply across social settings, historical time, and cultures. They are transcultural or transhistorical. You can use the same idea to exam-

Summary Review A Comparison of Approaches to Research

TOPIC	BOTH FIELD AND H-C RESEARCH	QUANTITATIVE RESEARCH
Researcher's perspective	Include the researcher as an integral part of the research process.	Remove the researcher influence from the research process.
Approach to data	Become immersed in many details to acquire an empathetic understanding.	Precisely operationalize variables.
Theory and data	Use grounded theory, create a dialogue between data and concepts.	Compare deductive abstract theory with empirical data.
Present findings	Translate a meaning system to others.	Test specific hypotheses.
Action/structure	People construct meaning but do so within social structures.	Social forces shape people's behavior whether or not they are aware of them.
Laws/generalization	Make limited generalizations that depend on context.	Discover universal, context-free general laws.

Features of a Distinct H-C Approach to Doing Research

TOPIC	THE HISTORICAL COMPARATIVE RESEARCHER
Evidence	Reconstructs from many fragments and incomplete evidence
Distortion	Guards against using own awareness of factors outside the social or historical context
Human role	Includes the consciousness of people in a context and uses their motives as causal factors
Causes	Sees cause as contingent on conditions, hidden beneath the surface, and due to a specific combination of factors
Micro/macro	Links the micro to macro levels or layers of social reality
Cross-contexts	Moves between concrete specifics in a context and across contexts for more abstract comparisons

ine all times and all cultures. At the opposite end are concepts that apply only to particular social settings, cultures, or historical eras. Of course, many concepts fall between these extremes.

A universal concept, such as fear, exists in all societies in all eras. Specific concepts may be found in one historical era or culture but few if any in others. Perhaps a culture has as an event marking a girl's fourteenth birthday as a major signal of the end of childhood and her being ready for marriage and childbearing. H-C researchers use both types of concepts. Sometimes an event, activity, or social situation is unique in time or place, you grasp this, and you explain and apply it as appropriate. At other times, you can use universal concepts that let you make comparisons across time and culture and build broader explanations. Quantitative studies usually use transcultural, transhistorical concepts; however, they are frequently assumed and rarely examined to see whether they actually apply in different cultures or historical eras.

HOW TO DO A HISTORICAL-COMPARATIVE RESEARCH STUDY

In this section, we discuss how to do H-C research. Like field research, H-C research does not require you to follow a fixed set of steps; nonetheless, it involves several processes that usually occur in order:

- Acquire the necessary background.
- Conceptualize the issue.
- Locate and evaluate the evidence.
- Organize the evidence.
- Synthesize and develop concepts.
- Write the report.

Acquire the Necessary Background

As a preliminary step, learn about the basics of the setting (i.e., historical period and/or cultures). If you are not already familiar with the historical era or culture of your study area, engage in orientation reading (i.e., read several general books on the setting).

Conceptualize the Issue

Early in the process, think through the topic and develop ideas about it with clear definitions. You can begin with a general topic and a few ideas, but after you have background knowledge and start to gather data, start focusing on a specific issue. The focused issue will direct you to relevant evidence but remain flexible. It is impossible to begin research without some assumptions, concepts, and theory. Allow concepts and evidence to interact and stimulate the research direction. As in field research, you can change direction based on what you learn from the data. Start with some preliminary, provisional concepts to "package" evidence and guide you. As you acquire a strong grasp of the details of a specific setting, adjust or refine the concepts. Create new organizing concepts, subdivide the main issue, and develop lists of questions to ask. Often you find that the data do not fit neatly with the original concepts, and you must revise them. For example, you study a restaurant in the distant past or another culture. You begin with a few concepts such as dining pleasure, consumer choice, price competition, and so forth. You quickly discover that the restaurant does not wash dishes in clean water, all of the customers are neighbors who live within a 10-minute walk from the restaurant, there is no written menu, and no one mentions prices. You may rethink what is happening and develop new ideas to make sense of the situation.

Locate and Evaluate the Evidence

You will need to do a lot of bibliographic work, especially for historical research. Historical research requires using indexes, catalogs, and special reference works that list what libraries or other sources contain. Professional researchers may spend months searching for sources in libraries, travel to different specialized research libraries, and read dozens (if not hundreds) of books and articles. For comparative research, this means you must focus on one or more specific nations or areas. Comparative research often requires learning a foreign language and/or travel to another country and then establishing contacts with local people. Once you find evidence, you need to evaluate its accuracy (see the following discussion of primary historical evidence). As you gather evidence, try to keep two questions in mind:

- How relevant is the evidence to emerging research questions and evolving concepts?
- How accurate and strong is the evidence?

Your research focus often shifts. As this happens, evidence that was once relevant becomes less relevant and previously ignored evidence may become highly relevant. Also, you want to constantly evaluate alternative interpretations of the evidence and look for "silences." Silences are situations in which the evidence fails to address an event, topic, or issue. For example, you study a group of leading male merchants in the 1890s. You find a lot of evidence and documents about them and their business dealings. However, there is no evidence about their wives and many servants—who are invisible in the data. To assess the whole situation, you want to notice both what is clearly documented and what has "disappeared."

Organize the Evidence

As you gather and locate sources, you also organize the data. Obviously, it is unwise to take notes madly and let them pile up haphazardly; instead you sort, label, and categorize. Begin with a preliminary analysis by noting themes in the mass of details. As you sort and label, reflect and develop insights that can stimulate new ways to organize data and new questions for your study. Let data and theory interact and influence one another. Evaluate the evidence based on emerging ideas or theory. Your thinking on an issue advances as you reexamine and reorganize evidence. This occurs because you use newly created ideas to look at old data in new ways and the new ideas will guide your search for additional data.

5

Synthesize and Develop Concepts

Once most of the evidence is in, move toward creating an overall picture or general explanation. You want to synthesize and pull the parts together into one story. As you read and reread your notes and you sort and resort them based on various organizing schemes, look for new connections. Try to see the evidence in different ways. By looking for patterns, you can draw out similarities and differences to accompany your analogies. You might organize events into sequences and group them into a step-by-step process. You can synthesize by connecting a body of evidence with an abstract concept or causal mechanism. Many researchers find metaphors useful. For example, you note that relations between a foreman and workers are "like an emotional roller coaster drop" in which things seemed to be getting better and moving higher and higher, and then there is a sudden letdown after expectations have risen very fast. You can use metaphors as organizing and sensitizing devices.

Write the Report

Assembling evidence, arguments, and conclusions into a written report is a crucial step in all research. If anything, this step is more important for H-C than for quantitative research. A carefully crafted, well-written report often "makes or breaks" the success of H-C research. You must distill mountains of evidence into clear exposition, document numerous sources with extensive footnotes, and weave the evidence and arguments together in a manner that communicates a coherent, convincing picture. You gathered mountains of specific details in the study but can only include a few critical examples of the raw evidence. These illustrate and give credence to your larger story. Achieving a good balance between generalization and documented specific details can be difficult, but you want do this as you tell readers a dramatic, compelling story.

RESEARCHING THE PAST

In this section, we look at research into past events or people. Of course, the past begins five minutes ago, but something usually is at least 10 years in the past before we call it history. After about 10 years, direct experience has faded and our perspective shifts. The word *history* is confusing because of its several meanings:

- Actual events that occurred in the past (e.g., it is *history* that the French withdrew troops from Vietnam)
- A documented record of the past (e.g., a *history* of French involvement in Vietnam)
- An academic field in which specialists study the past (e.g., a course in the department of *history*)

Specialists in the field of history, or historians, devote most of their time and efforts to gathering and analyzing historical data. They often use specialized techniques. Nonhistorian social researchers rarely "do history," but they too examine historical data—that is, evidence about actual past events, including documented records. Compared to a professional historian, social researchers often consider a wider scope of historical evidence and have different goals in mind. Let us look at the contrast in goals and activities between the historian and the H-C social researcher. The historian usually

- sees collecting highly accurate historical evidence as a central goal in itself;
- interprets the data's significance in light of other historical events; and
- is not overly concerned about developing a theory to explain social relations or processes.

By contrast, the H-C social researcher

- treats gathering carefully documented, extremely accurate, and highly detailed descriptions of specific past events as important but secondary;
- wants to extend or build a theory or apply social concepts to new situations;
- uses historical evidence as a means to an end (e.g., to explain and understand social relations).

Types of Historical Evidence

Social researchers and historians both draw on four types of historical evidence:

- Primary sources
- Running records
- Recollections
- Secondary sources

The historian's main goal is to locate, collect, validate, and analyze the first one on the list—primary sources (to be discussed shortly). By contrast, a social researcher will look more at secondary sources or running records. Both use recollections. In the study about Chinese immigrants that opened this chapter, McKeown (2001) used all the sources except recollections.

Primary Sources. The letters, diaries, newspapers, magazines, speeches, movies, novels, articles of clothing, photographs, business records, and so forth from people in the past that have survived into the present are called **primary sources**. You can find them in official archives (a place where documents are stored), in private collections, in family closets, or in museums. Today's documents and objects (letters, television programs, menus, commercials, clothing, toys, and automobiles) will become primary sources for future historians. A widely used primary source is a published or unpublished written document. Documents may be in their original form or in preserved form on microfiche or film. They are often the only surviving record we have of the words, thoughts, deeds, and feelings of people in the past. A classic primary source is a bundle of yellowed letters that a traveling businessman wrote to his wife and that the historian discovers in an attic 75 years after both the husband and wife have died.

A limitation of written sources is that elites or people in official organizations write most of the documents. It is easy to overlook the views of the illiterate, the poor, or people outside official institutions. For example, during early nineteenth century, in the United States it was illegal for slaves to read or write. You will find it difficult to locate written sources on how a slave actually experienced slavery. By contrast, most slave owners could read and write. Written documents from the slave era tend to give a slave owner's rather than the slave's point of view.

primary sources sources created in the past and that survived to the present.

Making It Practical Old Newspaper Articles as Sources

A widely used and easily accessible primary source is the newspaper. The "official" national newspaper of the United States is the *New York Times*. Luckily, you can search old copies of it electronically through online services such as Proquest™. For example, you are interested in articles on the topic of immigration between 1900 and 1910. You quickly find 3711 articles, so you narrow the topic. Let us say you want to find out about immigration from one country, Japan. You discover 224 articles discussing the topic in the *New York Times* during those 10 years (see Figure 5.1). As you read, you find one 1902 article about how the Japanese government wanted to protect from discrimination its citizens who came to the United States and distinguish Japanese laborers from Chinese coolies. Japan's government said it would limit who it allowed to immigrate irrespective of U.S. immigration laws. The article says that fewer than 14,000 Japanese live in the United States, excluding Hawaii (at that time a U.S. territory but not a state). To study this topic more fully, you want to read secondary sources and newspapers from the Pacific coast, where the topic was hotly debated. You need background knowledge, such an awareness of hostility toward Asians and rioting against Chinese in Pacific states in the 1880s. This turmoil led to the 1882 Chinese Exclusion Act, which ended most immigration from China. A look at the

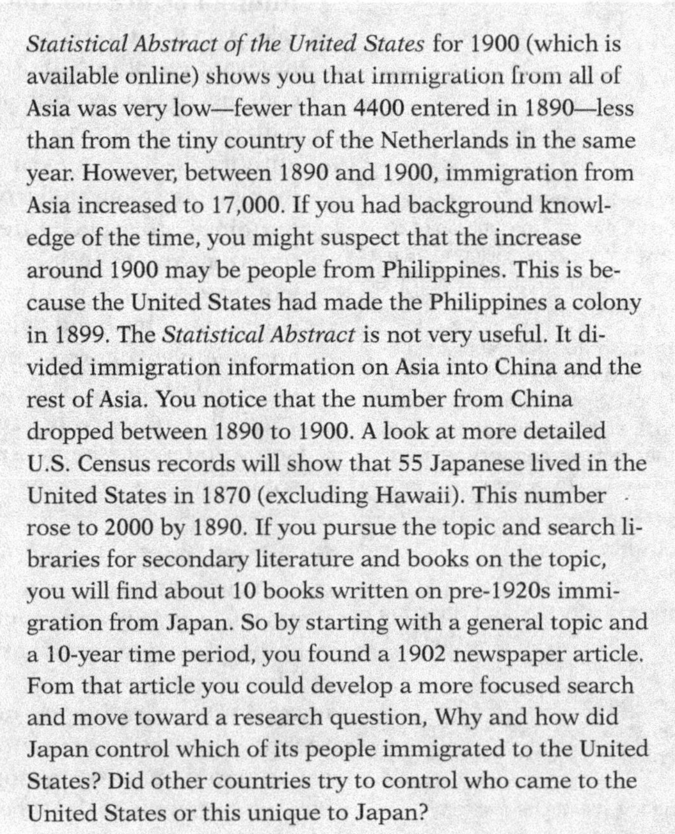

Statistical Abstract of the United States for 1900 (which is available online) shows you that immigration from all of Asia was very low—fewer than 4400 entered in 1890—less than from the tiny country of the Netherlands in the same year. However, between 1890 and 1900, immigration from Asia increased to 17,000. If you had background knowledge of the time, you might suspect that the increase around 1900 may be people from Philippines. This is because the United States had made the Philippines a colony in 1899. The *Statistical Abstract* is not very useful. It divided immigration information on Asia into China and the rest of Asia. You notice that the number from China dropped between 1890 to 1900. A look at more detailed U.S. Census records will show that 55 Japanese lived in the United States in 1870 (excluding Hawaii). This number rose to 2000 by 1890. If you pursue the topic and search libraries for secondary literature and books on the topic, you will find about 10 books written on pre-1920s immigration from Japan. So by starting with a general topic and a 10-year time period, you found a 1902 newspaper article. Fom that article you could develop a more focused search and move toward a research question, Why and how did Japan control which of its people immigrated to the United States? Did other countries try to control who came to the United States or this unique to Japan?

A big concern of primary sources is that only a fraction of what existed in the past has survived into the present. Moreover, what survived is a not a representative sample of what once existed.

As you read primary sources, avoid the distortion of supracontext awareness. You want to "bracket," or hold back, knowledge of subsequent events and modern values. For example, you read a source written in 1840 by a Southern slave owner. Moralizing against the owner based on the evils of slavery or faulting him for not seeing that slavery would soon end is not worthwhile. Instead, withhold judgment and try to see things from the perspective of the person who lived in the past. Researchers who study primary sources try to avoid a specific form of supercontext awareness distortion, **presentism**. Presentism has a parallel distortion in comparative studies, **ethnocentricism**. In both fallacies, you treat your culture and time in history as being "normal" or "the best." You use it as a standard to evaluate other times or places instead of seeing things from another's point of view.

Locating primary documents can be very time-consuming. You must search through specialized indexes and may have to travel to archives or specialized libraries. Once you arrive, you may discover that sources, such as newspapers, diaries, letters, memos, and other records, are stored in a dusty and rarely visited room filled with stacked boxes that contain fading documents. The documents may be incomplete, disorganized, and in various stages of decay. After you locate documents or other primary sources, you must evaluate them with external and internal criticism (see Figure 5.2).

- **External criticism.** You want to be certain that a source is not a fake or a forgery. Relevant questions to ask are, When was the document really created? Where was it really created? Did the person claiming to be the source's author actually produce it? Why was the source created and why did it survive into the present? For example, you find a letter written on a typewriter, but the letter's date is 10 years before the first typewriter was invented. You know that the letter is not authentic.
- **Internal criticism.** After you have determined that a primary source is not a fake, you want to be certain it accurately reflects events, people, and situations. Relevant questions to ask are, Did the source's author directly witness what it contains or is it secondhand information? Is information in the source consistent with other accounts at that time? What conditions (e.g., wartime censorship, an author's desire to appear moral or important) might have influenced what was included in or omitted from a source? You want to place a source in context and examine both explicit (literal, visible) and implicit (subtle connotations, implications) meanings in it. For example, you locate a pile of letters and notes by a women about her dead husband. As you read the material, you notice no references to the husband's alcoholism. The alcoholism is in sources from neighbors and relatives, in arrest records of the husband for public intoxication, and in a large bill of daily charges by the husband at a nearby tavern. You question the credibility of the wife's report on the husband as a complete, accurate picture and wonder whether she was trying to make him appear more respectable in the source documents.

Running Records. Luckily, many organizations maintain files or records for their own purposes that you can use. For example, a country church has records of every marriage, baptism, and funeral from 1880 to the present. By looking at the church's running records in combination with other historical evidence, you can trace the social life of a village for over a century. Two limitations of running records are as follows: (1) Organizations do not always maintain them; and (2) organizations do not record information consistently over time. Changing policy or other events may cause an organization to stop keeping records, or new administrators, clerks, policies, or events may cause changes in the way records are kept and what they record.

presentism the fallacy of looking at past events from the point of view of today and failing to adjust for a very different context at the time.

ethnocenticism as applied in comparative research, the fallacy of looking at the behaviors, customs, and practices of people in other cultures narrowly from your culture's point of view.

external criticism evaluating the authenticity of primary source materials.

internal criticism evaluating the credibility of information in primary source materials.

running records ongoing files or statistical documents that an organization, such as a school, business, hospital, or government agency, maintains over time.

■ **Figure 5.1** *New York Times* Article on Emigration

JAPAN TO STOP EMIGRATION.

Mikado's Government Will Restrict Movement of Coolies to America.

WASHINGTON, April 23.—Information has reached Washington that the Japanese Government itself, without waiting a request from the United States, is about to take steps to restrict the emigration of Japanese coolies to the United States.

It is asserted that the figures relative to this emigration have been magnified, and that, as a matter of fact, there are not more than about 15,000 ot 16,000 Japanese within the limits of the United States, outside of Hawaii. It is said that such emigration as has lately occurred has resulted entirely from the competition of the two great Japanese emigration societies; that the laborers have been practically brought here under the delusion that there were untold opportunities for work at great wages. The Japanese Government is interested in protecting its people from the hardships resulting from impositions and that, it is said, is the reason it intends to establish restrictions on the outward flow.

It is said, however, that the Government would never contemplate with equanimity legislation by the United States directed exclusively against Japanese immigration, for, though perfectly willing to abide by the results of any legislation on the subject of immigration that affects all outside nations alike, discriminations against Japan would certainly have most disastrous effects upon trade. The position of the Japanese Government upon that point is that the Japanese emigrant is not for a moment to be classed with the Chinese coolie.

Source: New York Times (1857–Current file); Apr. 24, 1900; ProQuest Historical Newspapers The New York Times (1851–2003) pg. 10

Before the use of electronic telecommunications, computers, cell phones, and video technology, people usually communicated and kept records in writing. You can examine letters, memos, diaries, ledgers, or newspapers to learn about past communication or ideas. Many of today's communication forms do not leave a permanent physical record (e.g., telephone conversations, e-mails, radio broadcasts) unless they are electronically archived. This could make the work of future historians and H-C researchers more difficult.

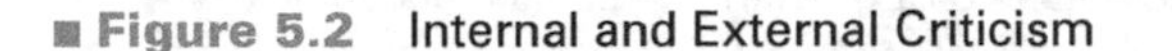

■ **Figure 5.2** Internal and External Criticism

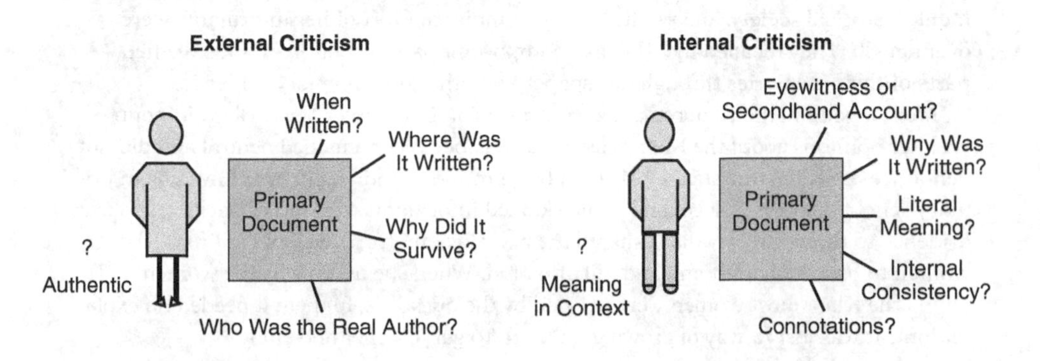

Recollections. People's memories of the past and their experiences originated in the past like primary sources, but they are not a primary source. **Recollections**, such as a written memoir or autobiography, are created afterward from memory. A special type of recollection, the **oral history**, is especially valuable for people who do not keep detailed written diaries and for the illiterate (see Example Study Box 3). Because memory is imperfect, recollections and oral histories can be a distorted picture of the past in ways that primary sources are not. They may not be perfectly accurate, but often they are our only window into the how people living in the past experienced events.

recollections a person's words or writings about past experiences created by the person some time after the experiences took place.

oral history interviews with a person about his or her life and experiences in the past.

Secondary Sources. The strength of primary sources is their authenticity, but they have practical limitations. It can take a huge amount of time to locate, verify, and read primary sources. You may discover thousands of pages of primary source documents to sort and read. In addition, primary sources may cover a short period of

Example Study Box 3 Women of the KKK

Bettmann/Corbis

Blee (1991) was interested in right-wing extremist groups and conducted a historical study on the Ku Klux Klan in the Midwest. Her six years of research illustrates great ingenuity. She focused on the state of Indiana, where 32 percent of the white Protestant population belonged to the Klan at its peak in the 1920s. In addition to reviewing studies on the Klan, she investigated newspapers, pamphlets, and unpublished reports. She conducted library research on primary and secondary materials at over half a dozen college, government, and historical libraries. She provides readers with historical photographs, sketches, and maps to create a feel for the topic and its context.

Bee also conducted oral histories with women about being in the Ku Klux Klan. She noted that, prior to her research, no one had studied the estimated 500,000 women in the largest racist, right-wing movement in the United States. Many people had assumed that women were apolitical and passive. The Klan was a secret society, no membership lists survived, and finding information was difficult. To locate survivors 60 years after the Klan was active, Blee had to be persistent and inventive. She identified Klan women by piecing together a few surviving rosters, locating old newspaper obituaries that identified women as Klan members, and looking for names by scrutinizing historical documents that were public notices or anti-Klan documents. She mailed a notice about her research to every local newspaper, church bulletin, advertising supplement, historical society, and public library in Indiana. Most of her informants were over age 80. They recalled the Klan as an important part of their lives. Blee verified parts of their memories through newspaper and other documentary evidence.

Membership in the Klan remained controversial. In the interviews, Blee did not reveal her opinions about the Klan. She was tested, but Blee remained neutral and did not denounce the Klan. She stated, "My own background in Indiana (where I lived from primary school through college) and white skin led informants to assume—lacking spoken evidence to the contrary—that I shared their worldview" (p. 5). She did not find Klan women to be brutal, ignorant, and full of hatred. When she asked why the women had joined the Klan, most women were puzzled by the question. To them it needed no explanation—it was just "a way of growing up" and "to get together and enjoy."

time or one very specific location. Perhaps they may let you document events in one tiny village for a two-year period, but many research questions are about a longer time and a wider range of locations. H-C researchers rely on secondary sources when they want to address broader questions.

Secondary sources are the dozens of books and articles specialist historians wrote on specific people, places, or events. You can use these sources as information about a broader topic. Historians may have produced over one thousand books and articles on numerous specific, narrow topics about a broad topic that interests you. Secondary sources have a maze of details and interpretations. You must transform the numerous separate studies into an intelligible picture organized around your research question. You need to evaluate the sources and exercise care when using them.

Secondary sources have limitations. Despite producing many studies, historians have not studied every aspect of all topics from the past. There may be holes or gaps in the historical record and few studies on your topic. Other limitations include the issue of inaccurate historical accounts and the historian's interpretation of data. Even if there are many studies on your topic and you locate and read them all, history books contain more than theory-free, objective "facts." Historians frame and organize their primary source data with concepts, ideas, and assumptions. The historian's concepts originate in journalism, the language of past people, ideologies or philosophy, today's language, and theory. Historians do not always define their concepts or apply them consistently. For example, you read a book in which a historian calls 10 families in a nineteenth-century town "upper class." However, the historian never defines "upper class" or ties it to any studies of social class. This makes it difficult for you to know what "upper class" means in the history book.

The historical study does not reveal everything the historian saw in primary sources. The historian might read 10,000 pages of newspapers, letters, and diaries and then reduce those data to summaries and selected quotes in a 180-page history book. You locate the 180-page book and must rely on the historian's judgments about the primary source data. The historian's judgments about what to include contain selection criteria and biases. You rarely know what they were. Perhaps the historian omitted information relevant for your research question.

5

When organizing their data, many historians use a *narrative history* format, which organizes the evidence chronologically around a single coherent "story." They connect each part of the story to other parts by its place in the time order of events. Together, all the parts form a unity or whole. The story often makes interesting reading. However, the historian will emphasize or downplay information based on how it fits into the story. You might read a history book (such as Blee looking for information about information on the Klan in Indiana in the 1920s), but the historian downplayed information relevant to your question (women's activism in the Klan) because it was not central to the historian's story (how financial corruption and infighting weakened the Klan). Also, historians add events in the narrative to enrich the background or to add color. They note what a particular person has done or said but may not analyze unseen influencing factors. Just because a fact is in the history narrative, it may have little theoretical significance. For example, a historian discusses family relations among a group of settlers in seventeenth-century America. The historian focuses on intrafamily gender dynamics but downplays factors such as problems with securing a stable food supply. This does not mean that lack of food was unimportant for your research topic (decisions by settlers to give up and return home). It only means that the historian decided to downplay such factors in his or her narrative. While you read the historian's narrative, you can learn a lot but need to look for details relevant to your own research question even if they are not central to the narrative.

The writing of historians is influenced by the era in which they live and by their outlook or school of historical scholarship. In certain historical periods, various interpretations or themes are popular. You will find similar themes in most historical books written in that period (e.g., an emphasis on immigration, labor-management

secondary sources specific studies conducted by specialist historians who may have spent many years studying a narrow topic. Other researchers use these secondary data as sources.

Making It Practial A Life History Interview

The life history interview is a special kind of recollection in which you interview a middle-aged or elderly person about his or her entire life. You ask many open-ended questions in a sympathetic, nonjudgmental manner to help the person open up and elaborate on specific details of his or her life. You usually begin by asking about events when the person was a child. Be flexible, and do not structure the interview too much. You want to encourage the person to open up and reveal many specific details. You can prepare a long list of possible topics to ask about (family, schooling, work, travel, friendships, and so forth) but also rely on other things you already learned earlier in the interview for new questions. For example, you ask, "Do you remember any details about the year you were six years old? Was that the year your younger brother Jonathan got very sick and almost died?" Anything the person recalls is relevant. You want to capture details, relationships, and events from the point of view of the person you interview. Many people never had an opportunity to sit down and reflect about all the past events in detail. Life history interviews can be therapeutic for some people. Approach the interview with care and consideration. People may block out certain events, and recalling some events may generate great sorrow, anger, or anxiety, even many years later. You can ask about events taking place around the person (major political events, world events, and so forth) to get the person's own perspective on them. Most researchers tape record life history interviews. Depending on the person, you may have six or more hours of interviewing. People tire of a very long interview, so plan to break the interviewing into three or more two-hour interview sessions that are spaced across several days. This not only lets the interviewed person rest but also lets you review the early interviews and return to major turning points or life events to ask for additional details or clarification.

conflicts, or gender issues). Historians tend to follow a school of historical scholarship when they conduct a study, such as diplomatic, demographic, ecological, psychological, Marxist, intellectual, and so forth. Each school has its own priorities about data and key questions. If you use secondary sources, you need to be aware of major themes popular when the historian wrote and the outlook he or she adopted.

RESEARCH THAT COMPARES ACROSS CULTURES

Comparative research is as much an orientation toward research issues as it is a separate research technique. Doing a comparative study is not doing anything dramatically different from other social research; however, many of the issues or problems in social research are greatly magnified in a comparative study. In a sense, a comparative perspective exposes potential weaknesses that can exist in all social research. This awareness of possible concerns can help improve the quality of all social research.

Some comparative research takes place to demonstrate that basic social processes (e.g., psychological orientations, family relations) hold across countries; other research examines differences. The focus is to examine similarities and differences between units of comparison (cultures, nations). In comparative research, you see what is shared across units and what is specific to one unit alone.

The comparative orientation improves measurement and conceptualization. One reason is that when we develop concepts based on comparative research, the concepts are less likely to be restricted to a specific culture. We can develop a concept for a familiar or home culture but be unaware of hidden biases, assumptions, and values until we try to apply it to different cultures. For example, you develop a concept of reverse discrimination based on the U.S. experience. You think it is a general idea, but until you try to apply the concept in many other cultural settings, you do not know whether it is applicable or limited to the U.S. context. By using a concept in a range of cultures, you see whether it applies in diverse settings. Comparative research also reveals important but unrecognized factors. If all the studies of a topic are in one culture, you may not realize that something in the culture but not elsewhere is a cause. For example, gun ownership is 100 times greater in the United States than in other advanced nations. If you only look within the United States, you may not find gun ownership connected with another factor, but if you compare the United States and other nations, the gun ownership rate of the United States may stand out as a key factor.

It is important to look across cultures to see a wider range or variation in a variable. For example, two researchers, Hsi-Ping and Abdul, look at the relationship between the age at which a child is weaned and the onset of emotional problems. Hsi-Ping looks only at U.S. data. They show a range from 5 to 15 months at weaning and indicate that emotional problems increase steadily as age of weaning increases. She concludes that late weaning causes emotional problems. Abdul

Example Study Box 4 Abortion Politics in the United States and Germany

Alex Wong/Getty Images

Ferre, Gamson, Gerhards, and Rucht (2002) conducted a comparative study of abortion politics in the United States and Germany. They specifically looked at public discussions about abortion in the two countries. In both countries, abortion was made legal and became a heated and widely debated moral-political issue. The authors examined four types of data: (1) secondary historical evidence, (2) a content analysis, (3) a survey of leaders in organizations, and (4) open-ended interviews. The secondary evidence came from books about the history, organized movements, court rulings, and public debates about abortion. The authors examined articles in the two major newspapers of both countries for the period 1970–1994, looking for all articles that mentioned the abortion issue in any way. They selected articles meeting certain criteria (such as longer than three paragraphs, not book reviews, no letters to the editor) and found 1243 articles in the United States and 1425 in Germany. They then content analyzed the articles. The authors also sent a questionnaire to 150 abortion-issue organizations. The questionnaire asked about organizational goals, activities, media relations, internal resources, and alliances with other organizations. The authors also interviewed leaders or media directors of 20 U.S. and 23 German abortion-issue organizations and several leading journalists in each country who regularly wrote on the abortion issue. The study produced many findings. One major finding was that people discussed the same issue very differently in the two countries. In Germany, there is less open conflict over the issue, and people discussed abortion in terms of fetal rights and protecting women. In the United States, there was great conflict associated with activism by advocacy organizations outside government or political parties. The issue was framed in terms of individual rights or freedom from government interference, or as a religious-moral issue. Religious and women's organizations related to the issue very differently by country. In the end, the authors identified specific features of the culture, advocacy organizations, mass media, and political institutions in each country that influenced the abortion debate. They found that a country's government structure, media system, legal system, and so forth had a large influence on how people thought about and debated the exact same public issue.

looks at data from 10 cultures. He discovers a range from 5 to 36 months at weaning. He finds that the rate of emotional problems rises with age of weaning until 18 months; it then peaks and falls to a lower level. Abdul has a more complete picture. Emotional problems are likely for weaning between the ages of 6 and 24 months. Weaning either earlier or later reduces the chances of emotional problems. Hsi-Ping reached false conclusions because of the narrow range of weaning age in the United States.

Comparative research is more difficult, costly, and time consuming than research that is not comparative. You may be limited in the types of data that you can collect and have problems with equivalence (see the following discussion). In comparative research, you cannot randomly sample cultures. Sufficient information is not available for all world cultures and is unavailable for a nonrandom subset (poor countries, nondemocratic countries, etc.). In addition, cultures or nations are not equal units. Some have over a billion people and others only 100,000.

Can You Really Compare?

For convenience, most comparative researchers use the nation-state as their unit of analysis. Most people see the globe as divided in terms of nation-state (or country), and this is how official statistics are collected. The nation-state is a socially and politically defined unit. In it, one government has sovereignty (i.e., military control, political authority) over a populated territory. People living in the territory may share a common language, culture, and customs, but the nation-state is not the only possible unit for comparative research.

If you want to compare something clearly within nation-state boundaries, such as legal system, voting and government, or economic relations, then it makes sense to compare nation-states. However, for comparative research, the relevant unit is often the culture. Culture is more difficult to define. It refers to a shared identity, social relations, beliefs, and technology. Cultural differences in language, custom, traditions, and norms often follow nation-state borders, but national borders do not always match cultural boundaries. A single culture may be divided among several governments, or one nation-state may be multicultural with several cultures. If you want to compare cultures, then the nation-state may not be the best unit. For example, the people of one region may have a distinct ethnic background, language, customs, religion, social institutions, and identity, such as Quebec in Canada, Wales in the United Kingdom, and Flanders in Belgium.

Over the centuries, wars and conquests carved new political units onto territory and in the process destroyed, rearranged, or diffused boundaries between cultures. In many world regions, Western empires imposed arbitrary boundaries on distinct cultural groups and made them into colonies. Later the colonies became independent nations. At other times, one nation-state expanded and absorbed the territory of people who had a distinct culture. For example, the U.S. government took over American Indian lands and the islands of Hawaii and Puerto Rico. Likewise, new immigrants or ethnic minorities did not always assimilate into the dominant culture. Such intranational cultures can create tension or regional conflict, since ethnic and cultural identities are the basis for nationalism. In his Presidential speech to the Canadian political science association, McRoberts (2001) argued that Canada is more than multicultural—it is multinational. Multiple nations (British, French, aboriginal) exist within one political structure. This implies that we should treat Canada as three units, not one.

You need to ask, What is the appropriate comparative unit for my research question—the nation, the culture, a region, or a subculture? For example, your research question is, Are income level and divorce related? Your hypothesis is that higher-income people are less likely to divorce. Perhaps income and divorce are related among the people of one culture. However, elsewhere in the same nation-state where

Making It Practical Which Units Should You Use?

How do you decide on the appropriate units of analysis for comparative research? If you want to study two different national cultures, such as the United States and Kenya, is the nation or a smaller unit such as the state, region, or tribe best? The answer hinges on whether a nation-state has a single homogenous culture. You need to be cautious if a country has regional divisions in which people of different regions do not share the same religion, customs, or language. You must to learn about the internal divisions and minority groups within a nation before conducting a study. In some nations, such as Belgium, formal political and geographic divisions separate the country by distinct cultures. In such situations, subnational units may be best. In other countries, such as the United States, the cultural dividing lines are not as sharp and are not in distinct geographic regions.

The appropriate units to study vary by your research question. For example, you are interested in marriage customs and childrearing practices. If there is one homogenous culture, you can study it anywhere in a nation. If the nation has several different cultures and marriage practices might vary by culture, it might be best to limit your study to one or two cultural groups within the nation rather than use the nation as a whole.

a different culture prevails, income and divorce are not related. If you use the nation-state as the unit and mix everyone together, your findings will be unclear and show a weak correlation. If you instead use two separate regions, you will find a strong correlation among the variables in one culture and no correlation in the other. Thus, it is best to ask what is appropriate rather than assume that every nation-state has only one culture. Some cultures do not fit into one geographic region and are scattered. This weakens a distinct culture and makes cultural comparison more complex. The Latino or Chinese-American or African-American are ethno-religious cultures scattered geographically across the U.S. territory. Should we study them as distinct cultures or as ethnic/racial groups?

Learning from History The Galton-Tylor Discovery

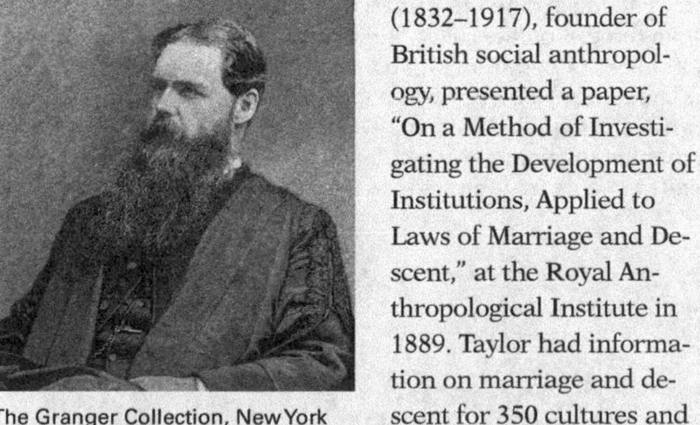

The Granger Collection, New York

Sir Edward B. Tylor (1832–1917), founder of British social anthropology, presented a paper, "On a Method of Investigating the Development of Institutions, Applied to Laws of Marriage and Descent," at the Royal Anthropological Institute in 1889. Taylor had information on marriage and descent for 350 cultures and found correlations between marriage/descent forms and measures of social complexity. He interpreted the results in terms of an evolutionary sequence. Over time, as societies became more complex, they changed from a maternal to a paternal descent line. Francis Galton, a statistical genius also at the Institute, raised objections. He pointed out that the correlation could be a mirage because the cultures may not be totally distinct and separate. Marriage forms could diffuse, cultures could borrow forms, or a marriage form could have a common origin in a different culture that crossed into other cultures. Galton maintained that before we can say that evolving social complexity and marriage forms are correlated, we must first rule out diffusion across different cultures and a common origin. Tylor agreed with Galton, and this sparked an innovation in comparative research called Galton's problem.

Bettmann/Corbis

Galton's Problem

To make a valid comparison, the units must be distinct and non-overlapping. If two units are actually subparts of a single larger unit, relationships you find in both of them may have a common origin. Here is an extreme example to illustrate the idea. Let us say you are interested in the association of two traits: the language people speak and what they use as money. Your research question is, Does the language people use affect what they use as money? Your units are territories in five nations (prefectures in Japan, the states in the United States, Lander in Germany, provinces in Argentina, and governorates [*muhafazat*] in Egypt). You add 47 prefectures, 50 states, 16 Lander, 23 provinces, and 26 governorates for a total of 162 units. You discover a perfect correlation between language and money for your 162 units. Where people speak English, they use the dollar, when they speak Japanese, they use the yen; when they speak Spanish, they use the peso; when they speak German, they use the euro; and when they speak Egyptian, they use the pound as currency. The association between language and currency is not because language and currency are actually related to one another; rather, your units of analysis (i.e., the states, provinces, etc.) are actually subparts of a larger unit (i.e., nations). The larger unit is the common source of both traits. Before you examine the association of two variables/traits, look closely at your units. Galton's problem is important because the boundaries between cultures are unclear or changing (see Figure 5.3). It may be hard to say where one culture ends and another begins. You can think of Galton's problem as a special case of the spurious relationship that you will learn about in Chapter 10.

Gathering Comparative Data

Galton's problem a possible mistake when comparing variables/features of units of analysis, in which an association among variables or features of two units may be due to them both actually being part of one large unit.

5

Comparative researchers use several types of data and combine types together in one study:

- Comparative field research
- Existing qualitative data
- Cross-national survey data
- Existing cross-national quantitative data

Figure 5.3 Galton's Problem.

Galton's problem occurs when a researcher observes the same social relationship (represented by X) in different settings or societies (represented as A, B, and C) and falsely concludes that the social relationship arose independently in these different places. The researcher may believe he or she has discovered a relationship in three separate cases. But the actual reason for the occurrence of the social relation may be a shared or common origin that has diffused from one setting to others. This is a problem because the researcher who finds a relationship (e.g., a marriage pattern) in distinct settings or units of analysis (e.g., societies) may believe it arose independently in different units. This belief suggests that the relationship is a human universal. The researcher may be unaware that in fact it exists because people have shared the relationship across units.

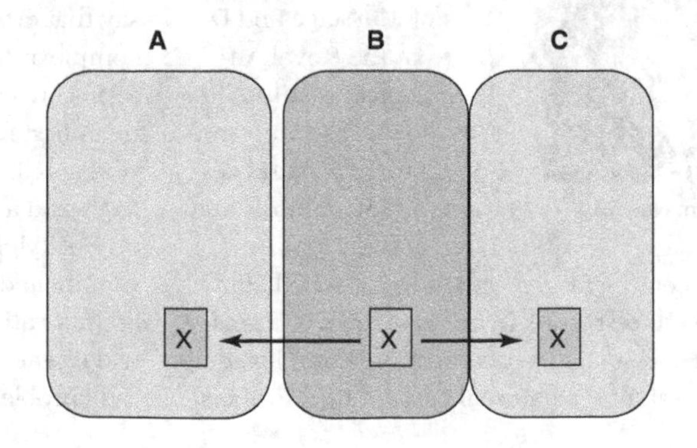

Comparative Field Research. Comparative researchers use field research in cultures other than their own. The training of social-cultural anthropologists prepares them for this type of research. The overlap of research techniques between anthropological and field research suggests modest differences between doing field research in your home culture and in a different culture. Conducting field research in another culture is usually more difficult and places more requirements on a study than doing research in your home culture. You first must immerse yourself in and learn the other culture in depth. This takes time and requires many adjustments, but can it yield new insights and personal as well as professional gains.

Existing Qualitative Data. Comparative researchers use qualitative primary and secondary sources. For example, you want to conduct a comparative study of the Canadian, Chilean, and Chinese school systems. Ideally, you visit each country to learn about each first-hand. Before visiting or if you cannot visit, locate existing qualitative data, such as videos, photos, music, novels, and essays about or by the country's schools, their teachers, and students. Read historical and field-research studies that describe the education systems in the three nations. You can use the descriptive details you learned from these sources as part the evidence for a study.

Cross-National Survey Research. You can conduct a survey in several different countries, but survey research in multiple cultures is more complex and creates additional methodological issues. In principle, the issues also exist in a survey conducted in your home culture, but they differ in magnitude and severity. A survey in a different culture requires knowing the language, norms, practices, and customs. Without such knowledge, you can easily make serious errors in procedure and interpretation. Knowing a language is not enough; cultural expectations and practices are essentials. It is best to work in close cooperation with people who are natives of the other culture.

Substantive (e.g., theory, research question) and practical factors are relevant when choosing cultures for a cross-national survey. You must adjust each step of the survey process (question wording, data collection, sampling, interviewing, etc.) to the culture. People in all cultures do not approach survey research the same. In some cultures, people might see survey interviewing as a strange, frightening experience, somewhat analogous to a police interrogation. You want to check local conditions and learn how people in the culture view surveys.

Cultural context also influences sampling. In addition to concerns about an accurate sampling frame, there are issues such as records privacy, quality of mail or telephone service, and transportation to remote rural areas. You need to be know how often people move, the types of dwellings in which people live, the number of people in a dwelling, the telephone coverage, and typical rates of refusal (i.e., refusal to participate in the survey).

The difficulties of writing a good survey question for your home culture are greatly magnified when you study a different culture. The cultural context affects question wording, questionnaire length, introductions, and the topics you include. You need to learn the local norms and topics that are highly sensitive in a culture. Questions about political beliefs, alcohol use, religion, or sexuality that you might ask in your home culture might be taboo in a different culture. In addition to these cultural issues, translation and language equivalency often pose problems (see the later discussion of lexicon equivalence). It is best to use bilingual people, but it may be impossible to ask the exact same question in a different language/culture.

Cross-cultural interviewing can be difficult. The selection and training of interviewers depends on the education, norms, and etiquette of the culture. An interview situation introduces issues such as norms of privacy, ways to gain trust, beliefs about confidentiality, and differences in dialect. In some cultures, you must spend a day in informal socializing before you achieve the rapport needed for a short interview. In other places, you must get prior approval from an official, headman, or local elder. Elsewhere, a male cannot interview a female without her elder brother, husband, or father being present.

Survey research across nations/cultures can be a challenge, but it can be highly rewarding and produce information not otherwise attainable. More than anything else, you need to be culturally aware at each step. You must evaluate whether you can do the same as in your home or need to make adjustments. This careful, step-by-step evaluation in itself raises your awareness of how to conduct good survey research.

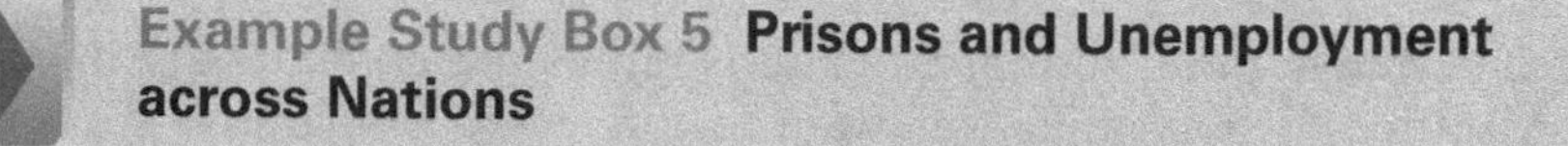

Example Study Box 5 **Prisons and Unemployment across Nations**

Dennis MacDonald/PhotoEdit Inc.

Sutton (2004) conducted a quantitative cross-national study looking at data on 15 nations between 1960 and 1990. For a long time, researchers knew that changes in the crime rate do not predict imprisonment rates. They asked, What does predict them? About 70 years ago, researchers Rusche and Kirchheimer (1939) offered a thesis that unemployment rates cause a rise in imprisonment rates. They argued that prisons are a government social control mechanism. If there are many unemployed young males in a population, they can become unruly and threaten the social order. For this reason, governments adjust policies when many men are unemployed to make it easy to fill prisons with out-of-work males. The government maintains social order by keeping a surplus population of unemployed males in prison. When the economy is booming and jobs go unfilled, national policies shift and the prisons begin to empty out. Sutton tested the Rusche and Kirchheimer thesis by gathering data from government statistical yearbooks, international organizations such as the World Health Organization, and studies on unionization patterns, political party structure, and so forth. He found limited support for the thesis as originally put forth. However, he learned that the association between unemployment and imprisonment was spurious (you will learn about spurious relationships in Chapter 10). Sutton discovered that political-organizational factors in a nation influence both its unemployment and imprisonment rates. In some nations, low-income workers are politically weak compared to the upper middle class and corporation owners. In those nations, both unemployment and imprisonment rates tend to be high. In other nations, low-income workers acquire political power and have strong political influence. In those nations, both the unemployment and imprisonment rates are low. Thus, Sutton found that the political strength of low-income working people is the true causal factor that explains both unemployment and imprisonment rates (see Figure 5.4).

■ Figure 5.4 What Sutton Learned About Unemployment Rates and Prison Populations

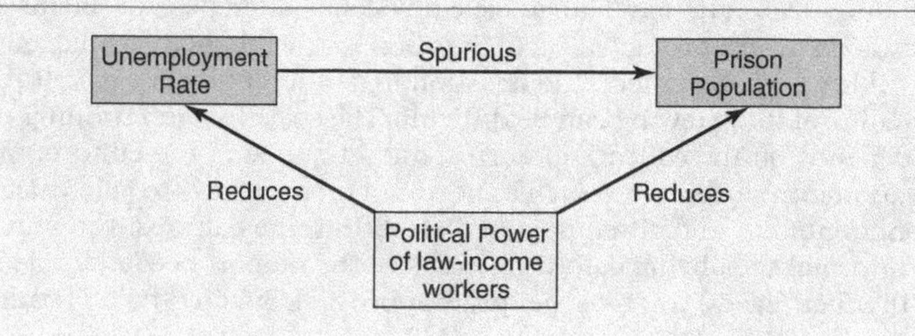

Existing Cross National Quantitative Data. Organizations gather and publish data on numerous features for many nations. A wide variety of data are available in major national data archives in a computer-readable format. This makes it easy to conduct secondary analysis on international existing statistics data. As with existing statistics for a single nation, existing cross-national data have limitations. These limitations are of greater magnitude than is the case for existing statistics on a single nation. The definitions of variables and the reliability of data collection can vary dramatically across nations. Perhaps you want to study statistics on crime in various nations. However, nations vary by what constitutes a crime and by legal system. What is criminal behavior in one nation might be acceptable and legal in another. What one nation treats as a breach of etiquette another nation may see as a serious crime that requires harsh punishment. The standards of legal evidence and law enforcement may also vary widely. Missing information is a common problem in cross-national existing statistics. Intentional misinformation in the official data from some governments is also a problem. Another limitation is the nations for which data is collected. For example, during a 35-year period, new nations come into existence, others change their names or form of governments, and some have different territorial borders.

The Issue of Equivalence

You have probably heard the expression, Compare apples to apples, not apples to oranges. The expression is not about fruit; it is about comparison. You cannot examine the similarities among things that are completely different; what you compare must be equivalent in some way. Equivalence is a critical concern in all types of social research. It is the issue of whether you can compare across divergent social contexts. You cannot easily compare family relations, crime rates, and business patterns for people or societies that are radically different—for example, an advanced urban industrial nation of 300 million with a tiny hunting and gathering tribal society of 1000 people. The technology, material conditions, and social environment differ radically. The units must have some basic similarity in order to make a valid comparison.

The issue of equivalence exists in all social research, but it is especially important for doing H-C research. Without basic equivalence, you cannot apply ideas or measures across different cultures or historical periods. You will misinterpret events in a different era or culture, or there may be no equivalent feature for you to compare. There are several forms of equivalence. They are closely related, but we can subdivide them into four types:

- Lexicon
- Conceptual
- Context
- Measurement

Summary Review Data in H-C Research

Thus far, we have considered four types of historical evidence and four types of comparative data.

4 Types of Historical Evidence	4 Types of Comparative Data
Primary evidence	Comparative field
Recollections	Existing qualitative
Running records	Cross-national survey
Secondary evidence	Existing cross-national quantitative

5

Lexicon Equivalence. **Lexicon equivalence** is easiest to see across two languages. For example, in many languages you use one form of address and pronouns for private settings, intimates (e.g., close friends and family members), and subordinates (e.g., younger persons, lower-status people) and another for address in public settings, with strangers, or for persons of higher social status. Modern English usage lacks this feature, although it once had something similar (the pronouns *thou, thee, thine*, and *thy*). In cultures where age is an important status, many status-based words exist that are absent in English. You cannot say, "my brother" without indicating whether you are talking about an older or younger brother because "my younger brother" or "my older brother" are different words. The meaning of words also varies across historical eras. For example, today the English word *weed* refers to unwanted plants or to marijuana. In Shakespeare's era, *weeds* meant clothing. Linguists study whether what you can express in one language (or the same language long ago) has a precise meaning in another language.

If your study goes into the distant past or involves different languages or dialects, lexicon equivalence can be an issue. Do not assume that a word or expression used in a different cultural or historical context has the same or a simple and comparable meaning. Lexicon equivalence is relevant in four situations of H-C research:

- When you are reading a document from the distant past or written in a different language
- When you are writing a survey questionnaire or talking to people who use or think in a different language
- When you are describing events, activities, or social relations from a different culture or historical era that you have studied to people today, in your home culture
- When you are theorizing and analyzing data or conditions across different cultures or historical eras

5

Conceptual Equivalence. Every day you use many concepts—such as friendship, loyalty, trust, family, parent, employee, and self-esteem—to discuss and examine social life. In a study, you use concepts from the research literature, personal experiences, and background knowledge to analyze and discuss the data or to test and build theory. The concepts you use are from a specific culture and historical era. People discuss concepts in the research literature live in specific cultural and historical settings, but they try to stretch beyond one time and one culture. The issue of conceptual equivalence is whether a concept developed and used in one historical era and culture applies to a very different time or place. The question is whether an idea (e.g., sibling conflict, customer service, blood honor) that may be best for understanding and organizing data in one historical era or culture can be applied in a very different era or culture wherein the idea may be inappropriate and incomprehensible. Conceptual equivalence is part of the broader issue of using universal (transcultural, transhistorical) concepts versus culturally and historically specific ones. Let us say you want to discuss "income." In pre-money bartering societies in which most people grow their own food, make their own furniture and clothing, barter goods, and rarely use money, income means something very different from today's advanced societies. The same concept of "income" may not fit both settings. Likewise, if you study people who believe that spirit forces cause certain diseases or health conditions, you may not have a concept that easily and fully captures the concept of "spirit forces" for comparison with a society that uses concepts such as bacteria, germs, DNA, and so forth. The concept of "attending college" has a different meaning today than in a historical context in which only the richest 1 percent of the population attended college, most colleges had fewer than 300 students, all were private all-male institutions, and the college curriculum consisted of learning classical languages and receiving moral training. The event or idea "attending college" has a different meaning from today.

lexicon equivalence being able to say the same thing with the same meaning across languages or dialects in different cultures or historical eras.

conceptual equivalence being able to apply the same concept across different cultures or historical eras.

At one time we automatically treated the beliefs and ideas of other cultures or eras as inferior or as "superstition" and treated those of own era and culture as "real" or "true." Nowadays, we try to avoid ethnocentrism and presentism. This is an improvement, but it does not provide is a simple, easy solution when doing research.

Cultural anthropologists and historians create new concepts that can capture what they study in a different culture or past era. To compare and discuss similarities and differences, sensitivity to whether a concept fits a setting is essential. You must ask whether a concept you are using really applies to both settings. If it does not, you may have to use different ones for each part of the comparison.

Contextual Equivalence. Our conversations, actions, events, and activities always take place in a social context. The same action (singing, telling a joke) may be acceptable in one social setting but not another. The context helps give meaning to the action. It might be acceptable to sing loudly at a lively party, but it is not acceptable for a physician to sing while carrying out a medical procedure on a patient. How a context shapes an action, event, or activity may vary across cultures and historical times. Perhaps in the historical past or in a different culture, singing during a medical procedure was not only acceptable but expected behavior. You need to evaluate not just what someone does or says, but how it fits into a context, and the influence of a context can vary by historical era or culture. **Contextual equivalence** means you should recognize how a specific context can shape the meaning of an event or activity. The specific context is within a broader culture or historical era. For example, you study a culture in which everyone has to pay a small amount of cash before a government official will do a task (e.g., stamp an official document, approve a driver's license). In your home culture, this may be considered a bribe and clearly inappropriate or illegal. Perhaps in one culture if you want a driver's license application approved, you must slip a five-dollar bill to the clerk with your application. If you do not slip the money, the clerk puts your application in a huge pile that might be processed next year. In the local context, the payment is acceptable as a kind of small service fee. The larger culture shapes the local context. In the larger culture, small amounts are paid regularly to help out the extremely underpaid government officials who work with impossible-to-implement bureaucratic rules. In a different context, paying a fee for a government service (having your passport stamped at the local airport) may be unacceptable. In a local context, government officials want to appear "modern" and impress foreign visitors that one set of rules applies, but when they provide a service to local people, another set of rules applies. To understand what is occurring, you need to be sensitive to the local context and the larger culture. How do you compare this government service event to that occurring in a different culture where handing a cash payment to a government employee would be seen as an unacceptable bribe? In a study, you may only be able to remark on the differences based on the context. The key point is, do not assume that the same activity has the same meaning across different contexts.

Measurement Equivalence. You may identify a concept, event, or activity for your study and adjust for the context and the broader cultural or historical setting. A question remains: Do you measure in the same way if you want to compare it to a different cultural or historical setting? **Measurement equivalence** recognizes that you cannot always use the same measure (such as survey questionnaire or official records such as birth certificates) in different historical or cultural settings. Let us say you are studying two cultures. In one culture, the local police keep a careful record of each household, including each person in a dwelling unit, their kinship or relations to each another, and where each person works or attends school. You want to compare this to another culture, where there is no police record of who lives where, except for the name of the legal owner, and no other information about the people. You cannot use

contextual equivalence seeing the same event or activity in context across different cultures or historical eras.

measurement equivalence using very different ways of measuring across different cultures or historical eras. The measurement method may influence outcomes.

the same measure of household size—looking at official police records in both countries. In one culture, you have to conduct a survey and ask about household size. In the other culture, you use official police records. The issue is whether the two different methods give identical answers if you had used them in the other culture (i.e., use a survey in the culture where police keep records). Perhaps you adjusted the way you measure a concept, event, or activity for a culture or historical setting so that it differs from how you measure it in a different setting. Did the measurement method affect what you learned in each setting, or can you treat the information as the same? There is no simple solution to this issue. You may have to measure differently in various settings and then compare results across settings, and you cannot be certain whether the different measurement methods influenced what you found.

BEING AN ETHICAL H-C RESEARCHER

Ethical concerns in H-C research are similar to those of nonreactive research techniques, especially when using secondary sources or existing cross-national quantitative data. Primary historical sources can introduce special ethical issues. The ethical researcher needs to carefully document where and how primary sources were obtained, make explicit the selection criteria for including some sources and not others, and apply external criticism and internal criticism to the source materials. At times, protecting privacy may interfere with gathering evidence. A person's descendants may want to destroy or hide private papers or evidence of scandalous behavior. We know that political figures (e.g., U.S. presidents) have tried to destroy or hide embarrassing official records.

Comparative researchers want to be sensitive to issues of cross-cultural interaction. Ethical behavior means respecting moral values and beliefs. You should learn what a culture considers to be acceptable or offensive and show respect for the traditions, customs, and meanings of privacy in the host culture. Actions that may be acceptable in your home culture may be unacceptable in a different culture, and vice versa. Be aware of and check your assumptions about what is appropriate behavior. Perhaps in your home culture you can enter a religious building and take photos when there is no service in progress. In another culture, taking a photo of religious buildings, even from the street, may be offensive and unacceptable. If this is the case, is it ethical to take the photo in the other culture? Perhaps you study a culture in which a father invites a male researcher to have sexual relations with his teenage daughter as a friendly gift to a visitor after completing an interview. In your home country, such behavior would be highly unethical and perhaps illegal. Is it unethical in both situations?

If you visit another culture to do research, establish good relations with the host country's government and do not take data out of the country without giving something (e.g., results) in return. At times, the military or political interests of the researcher's home culture or the researcher's personal values may conflict with official policy in the host nation. This introduces complexity. People in the other culture may distrust you and suspect you of being a spy, or your home culture's government may pressure you to gather covert information. In the past, these issues have created serious difficulties for social researchers.

At times, a researcher's presence or findings create diplomatic problems among governments. For example, a researcher examines health care practices in a different culture and then declares that official government policy is ignoring a serious illness and not providing medical care. This may create a major controversy. Likewise, a researcher may be sympathetic to the cause of people who oppose the government. Sometimes even talking to and working with such a group might cause a researcher to be threatened with imprisonment or deported. Anyone who conducts comparative research needs to be aware of such issues and the potential consequences of their actions.

WHAT HAVE YOU LEARNED?

In this chapter, you learned about historical and comparative research. The H-C approach is especially appropriate when you want to ask "big questions" about macro-level change, or when you want to understand social processes operating across historical eras or across cultures. Historical-comparative research involves a different orientation toward research that goes beyond applying specialized techniques. There are several ways to do H-C research, but a distinctly qualitative H-C approach is similar to field research in many respects. H-C has some specialized techniques, such as the external criticism of primary documents. Nevertheless, the most vital feature is how you approach a question, probe data, and move toward explanations.

Historical-comparative research is usually more difficult to conduct than other types of research. The same complexities or difficulties are often present to a lesser degree than in other research. For example, issues of equivalence are present to some degree in all social research. Such issues cannot be treated as secondary concerns in H-C research but are at the forefront of how you do research and seek answers to research questions.

KEY TERMS

conceptual equivalence *128*
contextual equivalence *129*
ethnocentrism *116*
external criticism *116*
Galton's problem *124*
internal criticism *116*
lexicon equivalence *128*
measurement equivalence *129*
oral history *118*
presentism *116*
primary sources *115*
recollections *118*
running records *116*
secondary sources *119*

APPLYING WHAT YOU'VE LEARNED

Activity 1

Locate a family member or neighbor who is elderly, ideally 40–50 years older than you. Ask the person if you can have two 90-minute interviews with him or her. Schedule the open-ended interviews on different days and use a tape recorder. Ask the person to tell you about his or her life, starting when he or she was no more than six years old. Just ask a few guiding questions and let the person talk, following a chronological order if possible. Pay close attention to major life events, such as marriages, deaths, new jobs, and moving to a new town. Ask the person to explain how these events felt at the time. Ask the person to comment on major historical events that occurred during his or her lifetime (e.g., wars, major political events). Allow the person to repeat stories or tell about the same event more than once, and ask for clarification if there is something you do not understand. After you have 2–3 hours of taped interviews, transcribe the interviews onto paper. You now have a record of the person's life, which he or she may read if desired.

Activity 2

Locating newspaper articles that are over 100 years old can be fun and fascinating. You may have to ask your local reference librarian how to get them most quickly from your specific location. Once you access the newspaper articles, identify a topic and narrow it down (as I did with immigration in Making It Practical: Old Newspaper Articles as Sources, p. 303). Read all the articles for a five-year period about that topic. Write an essay on what they learned.

Activity 3

Pick a country with a population of 5 to 50 million and about which you know very little. First, develop some background knowledge by finding out about the country's history, conflicts, internal social divisions, economy, family traditions, culture, form of government, religious beliefs, holidays, and so forth. An online source to check is the *CIA World Factbook*. After you have a basic understanding of the country, pick one feature about it (e.g., marriage practices, school system) and make comparison with your home culture. Develop a list of at least 10 similarities and/or differences. Draw on at least five different sources to develop your comparison list. If you were to visit the country and conduct a study of the feature, what would you want to observe and learn about it?

Activity 4

Two free online sources that have primary historical materials on the United States are: (1) *American Memory* at http://memory.loc.gov/ammem/index.html (Library of Congress), which contains photographs, maps, manuscripts, and sheet music; and (2) *Historical Census Browser* at http://fisher.lib.virginia.edu/collections/stats/histcensus/ (University of Virginia Library), which contains data from the U.S. Census of Population and Housing volumes and provides statistics for each decade from 1790 to 1960. Go to the *American Memory* Web site and then select Culture/folklife, then select Slave Narratives (audio interview 1932–1975) or Slave narratives (federal writer's project 1932–1938). Read what the ex-slaves said in the interviews and identify five people to follow. Go the *Historical Census Browser* Web site. Find the number of slaves in the same state and country at 1850 as each of those five people (first select 1850, then scroll down to slave population). Select the state, and at the bottom of the list of states and territories, select Retrieve County level data. Find out as much as you can about that county in 1850 and write a short essay about the five people's life conditions when they were young children.

5

Activity 5

Go online to locate international existing statistics about many countries. A free online source with lots of information is *Nationmaster* (http://www.nationmaster.com/index.php) and the *World Bank* (http://web.worldbank.org/WBSITE/EXTERNAL/DATASTATISTICS/0,,contentMDK:20535285~menuPK:1192694~pagePK:64133150~piPK:64133175~theSitePK:239419,00.html). Two other online sources are the *Statistical Abstract of the United States* and the *CIA Factbook*. Using these sources, identify a set of 15 countries and 15 variables that are available for all 15 countries (such as infant mortality rate, per capita GDP, and birth rate). Create a 15 × 15 chart. List the countries along the side and put letters A–O in the columns across the top. At the bottom, create a key for the letters with the name of each variable. Using this chart, what patterns do you see?

URLs

World Bank

http://web.worldbank.org/WBSITE/EXTERNAL/DATASTATISTICS/0,,contentMDK:20535285~menuPK:1192694~pagePK:64133150~piPK:64133175~theSitePK:239419,00.html

NATIONMASTER

http://www.nationmaster.com/index.php

CIA Fact Book

https://www.cia.gov/library/publications/the-world-factbook/

Statistical Abstract of the United States

http://www.census.gov/compendia/statab/past_years.html

REFERENCES

Banaszak, Lee Ann. 1998. "Use of the Initiative Process by Women Suffrage Movements." Pp. 99–114 in *Social Movements and American Political Institutions*, (Ed.) A. Costain and A. McFarland. Lanham MD: Rowman and Littlefield.

Blee, Kathleen. 1991. *Women of the Klan*. Berkeley: University of California Press.

Ferree, Myra Marx, William Gamson, Jurgen Gerhards, and Dieter Rucht. 2002. *Shaping Abortion Discourse*. New York: Cambridge University Press.

Kriesi, Hanspeter and Dominique Wisler. 1999. "The Impact of Social Movements on Political Institutions" Pp. 42–65 in *How Social Movements Matter*, (Ed.) M. Giugni, D. McAdam, and C. Tilly. Minneapolis MN: University of Minnesota Press.

Marx, Anthony W. 1998. *Making Race and Nation*. New York: Cambridge University Press.

McKeown, Adam. 2001. *Chinese Migrant Networks and Cultural Change.* Chicago: University of Chicago Press.

McRoberts, Kenneth. 2001. "Canada and the Multinational State." *Canadian Journal of Political Science / Revue Canadienne de Science Politique* 34:683–713.

Rusche, Georg and Otto Kirchheimer. 1939. *Punishment and Social Structure* New York: Russell and Russell.

Sutton, John. 2004. "The Political Economy of Imprisonment in Affluent Western Democracies, 1960–1990." *American Sociological Review* 69:170–189.

CHAPTER 6

Observing People in Natural Settings

Taken from: *Understanding Research,* by W. Lawrence Neuman

Digital Vision/Alamy Royalty Free

Many occupations involve "emotion work." The "work" is labor or effort you expend, usually in return for pay. The "emotion" refers to your feelings, or at least a public display of inner feelings. In emotion work, you are required or expected to show certain feelings as part of a job. Your job is to display certain emotions, and you may have to deny, suppress, or hide your own true feelings. In the travel, hospitality, and entertainment industries; in nursing, social service, and counseling fields; in grief counseling and funeral services; and in many sales jobs a large part of "doing a good job" is to display emotions; emotions help other people to experience certain feelings. Typically, jobs require you to be cheerful, friendly, positive, upbeat, empathetic, or concerned and caring. An employer may have written rules about your emotion work, and supervisors may monitor and enforce proper emotional displays/attitudes. Of course, we may do a kind of emotion work when we negotiate with friends or intimate partners, get along with coworkers, or go take part in daily events. There is a difference when emotion work is not something you decide to do on your own but is required as part of a job. In the *Managed Heart,* Arlie Hochschild (1983) outlined emotional labor and described how she went about studying it among airline attendants. She and others learned that employees put forth serious effort to display a friendly smile and cheerful manner. They did this even when they felt tired or depressed or were thinking about a serious personal, family, or work problem. Emotion work drains people physically and emotionally. Acting pleasant, warm, and comforting toward demanding clients or customers can extract a high personal toll, especially when the customers or clients are hostile, rude, or obnoxious. Some businesses, such as Disneyland, carefully plan, manage, and coordinate staff members' emotion work as a central part of creating a total customer experience (Van Maanan 1991). To study emotion work, researchers gathered first-hand qualitative information by directly participating and observing in natural work settings (i.e., they performed field work). They got a job that required them to do emotion work themselves. They spent many hours in daily contact, both closely observing and talking with people whose jobs involved a lot of emotion work. The field research method is especially well suited for studying emotion work.

WHAT IS FIELD RESEARCH?

Unlike the quantitative research discussed in previous chapters, field research produces qualitative data and involves a different approach to doing research. Field researchers directly observe and participate in a natural social setting. Actually, there are several kinds of field research, including ethnography, participant-observation research, informal "depth" interviews, and focus groups.

If you have heard about field research, it may sound like you simply hang out with a group of people who are unlike you. Maybe it sounds easy. In field research, there are no statistics or abstract deductive hypotheses. You observe a setting and may chat informally with the people you are studying. Unlike quantitative research, you personally engage in direct, face-to-face social interaction with "real people" in a natural setting. Professional researchers may devote months or years to studying people in a setting. They learn about the daily activities, life histories, hobbies and interests, habits, hopes, fears, and dreams of the people they study. Meeting new people and discovering new social worlds can be fun. It can also be tedious, time consuming, emotionally draining, and sometimes physically dangerous.

Field research is ideal for examining the micro-level social world and everyday interactions of ordinary people "up close." It is best suited for studying issues (e.g., classroom behavior, street gangs) that are difficult to study using other methods (e.g., surveys, experiments). In field research, you can get a close-up look and develop insights that may be impossible with other methods. Many areas use field research, such as anthropology, education, health care, marketing, hospitality-tourism, human service delivery, recreation, and criminal justice. Field researchers have explored a wide range of social settings, subcultures, and aspects of social life (see Figure 6.1). Students in my classes conducted successful short-term, small-scale field research studies in a barbershop, beauty parlor, daycare center, bakery, bingo parlor, bowling alley, church, coffee shop, laundromat, police dispatch office, fast food restaurant, elementary school classroom, nursing home, tattoo parlor, gay bar, bridal shop, hospital waiting room, and athletic weight room, among other places.

6

Ethnography

A major type of field research, ethnography, comes from cultural anthropology. *Ethno* means "people" or "folk," and *graphy* means "to describe something." The purpose of **ethnography** is to provide a detailed description and up-close understanding of a way of life from the standpoint of its natives/members/insiders. Ethnography builds on the idea that humans live in cultures, from micro-cultures (a single family or small friendship group) to macro-cultures (entire societies or world regions). We continuously learn, use, and modify cultural knowledge. Cultural knowledge has two parts: explicit and tacit. Explicit knowledge is what we easily see and directly know. We often talk about it. Tacit knowledge is what remains unseen or unstated. We rarely acknowledge it and are often only indirectly aware of it. Cultural knowledge includes assumptions, symbols, songs, sayings, facts, ways of behaving, and objects (e.g., telephones, newspapers, etc.). People learn it by reading, watching television, listening to parents, observing others, and the like. *Tacit knowledge* includes the unspoken cultural norms. It requires making inferences (i.e., going beyond what someone explicitly does or says to what he or she means or implies). Most etiquette and polite behavior rely on tacit knowledge.

ethnography a detailed description of insider meanings and cultural knowledge of living cultures in natural settings.

Ethnography is a study of how people activate and display culture—what they think, ponder, value, or believe to be true. They do this by what they say and do in

Figure 6.1 Examples of Field Research Sites/Topics

Small-Scale Settings

Passengers in an airplane
Battered women's shelters
Camera clubs
Laundromats
Social movement organizations
Social welfare offices
Television stations
Homeless shelters
Waiting rooms

Occupations

Airline attendants
Artists
Cocktail waitresses
Dog catchers
Door-to-door salespersons
Factory workers
Gamblers
Medical students
Female strippers
Police officers
Restaurant chefs
Social workers
Taxi drivers

Social Deviance and Criminal Activity

Body/genital piercing and branding
Cults
Drug dealers and addicts
Hippies
Nude beaches
Occult groups
Prostitutes
Street gangs, motorcycle gangs
Street people, homeless shelters

Community Settings

Retirement communities
Small towns
Urban ethnic communities
Working-class neighborhoods

Children's Activities

Children's playgrounds
Little League baseball
Youth in schools
Junior high girl groups

Medical Settings and Medical Events

Death
Emergency rooms
Intensive care units
Pregnancy and abortion
Support groups for Alzheimer's caregivers

Leisure Industry

Bowling alleys
Hotel lobbies
Restaurants and bars
Resorts

specific natural settings. To figure out or infer the meaning of people's actions, you need to become very familiar with the cultural and social context. You shift from what you actually hear or observe to what an action means in a situation. For example, an adult brother and sister are sitting next to one another at a family Thanksgiving meal. During the entire event, they never exchange a single word. You might infer cool social relations between them.

Often people only become aware of tacit knowledge, such as the proper distance to stand from others, when it is not followed. A violation of social custom or practice can cause unease or discomfort, but people may find it difficult to pinpoint the source of unease. A good ethnographer will describe explicit and tacit cultural knowledge by offering highly detailed descriptions. He or she also analyzes social situations by taking them apart and reassembling them. Recognizing explicit and tacit levels

Making It Practical **Seeing Culture in the American Thanksgiving**

Ethnographers study social gatherings and socio-cultural events, like the U.S. Thanksgiving holiday. Thanksgiving is part of *explicit knowledge*. It is on a Thursday in late November. Most businesses and all schools close on the day. It has some visible symbols and traditions. People say it is a celebration of abundance and dates back to the early settlers. The central focus of this holiday is people joining with family members or close friends to share a large feast that usually includes eating roast turkey. Related activities include parades with floats in some large cities, football games on television, the arrival of Santa Claus for children, and the beginning of Christmas holiday shopping. At the Thanksgiving meal, tacit knowledge says to use forks and knives when eating turkey meat, wait until finishing other parts of the meal before starting dessert, eat with others and not off alone in a corner, and engage in conversation with others who are at the meal. Eating large quantities or overeating is expected behavior. The timing of the main feast varies by family tradition, but it is rarely very early in the morning, as a breakfast, or extremely late at night. Most people eat Thanksgiving dinner between noon and 7 P.M. It is not the same as ordinary dinner. In addition to the turkey, other foods rarely seen on other occasions may be served. Pumpkin pie is the most common dessert. The common color scheme is orange and brown. A few seasonal decorations (e.g., autumn leaves, pilgrims) may be seen but they are usually minor. Gift exchanges are rare. In some parts of the United States, people hunt deer or other wild animals on or around Thanksgiving Day.

Blend Images/Alamy Royalty Free

of knowledge, describing in detail, and analyzing events of a social setting are key ethnographic techniques. Often an ethnographer pays great attention to specific details and considers events in silence or by engaging in ordinary social interaction.

An ethnographer notes how people construct social meanings as ongoing processes in specific daily settings. He or she looks for unwritten scripts or routines. Since social activities and events unfold in real time, they are not always pre-

Example Study Box 1 **Ethnographic Inference in a Hotel**

Thinkstock/Corbis Royalty Free

Rachel Sherman (2006) did field research on luxury hotels (room rates in the range of $500 and up per night). She studied emotion work, workplace relations, and service provided by hotel employees to the wealthy hotel guests. Two luxury hotels in New York were her field sites. She interviewed, observed, and got a job working at the hotels. In the study, she noticed many hundreds of tacit and subtle exchanges among hotel guests and workers. For example, she noticed a service code for employees to provide "unlimited labor" to hotel guests. The employee was supposed to perform the labor in a way that made it appear to be a voluntary favor that he or she wanted to do. A tacit rule was that workers should display emotions of being sincere and truly caring about a guest's needs or desires. She gave an example (2006, p. 42) of when she worked as a housekeeper. Hotel guests asked her to wrap up a large bouquet of flowers for them to take home. She quickly smiled and responded to the request, "I'll deal with it." The guest repeated the phrase "deal with it." She instantly realized that she made a mistake. She should have expressed her joy at the task. The words *deal with it* implied that it might be undesired work. A proper response would have been to smile and say, "I'd be happy to wrap the flowers for you right away, sir."

dictable. Not everyone in a setting sees everything identically. The ethnographer will try to grasp multiple perspectives of people in a social setting. The ethnographer constantly switches perspectives and looks at activities from several points of view simultaneously. This is not easy to do at first, but with practice, it is a skill than can be learned and improved upon.

STUDYING PEOPLE IN THE FIELD

Field research is as much an orientation toward doing research as a set of techniques to apply. Field researchers use a wide variety of techniques in the field to gain information. A principle guiding field research is **naturalism**. Unlike quantitative research in safe settings such as an office, laboratory, or classroom, field research requires you to personally go into the "real world" and become directly involved. You become a part of the social world you study. If you are a beginning field researcher, you will want to start with a relatively small group (20 or fewer people) who regularly interact with each other in a stable setting (e.g., a street corner, church, barroom, beauty parlor, baseball field, etc.). Most field research is by one person alone, although sometimes small teams of two or three have been effective.

Direct, personal involvement in the field can have an emotional impact. Field research can be fun and exciting, but it may disrupt your personal life, unsettle your physical security, or strain your sense of well-being. More than other kinds of social research, field research can reshape your friendships, family life, self-identity, and personal outlook. Direct, personal involvement carries both risks and rewards.

Flexibility is another principle of field research. Field research is less structured than quantitative research. Field researchers recognize and seize opportunities, "play it by ear," and rapidly adjust to fluid, changing situations. Instead of starting with a hypothesis and then following a sequence of steps, you choose techniques based on their value for acquiring information in a specific setting and change direction to follow interesting new leads as they appear.

Flexibility has a down side. Without fixed steps, it is easy to become sidetracked and drift directionless and without focus. Beginning field researchers feel they have little control over events, need focus, and feel that data collection is unmanageable and the task is overwhelming. You may feel that you are collecting too little, too much, or the wrong data. Feelings of emotional turmoil, isolation, and confusion are common. This makes it essential for you to be organized and prepared. After you learn about a setting, you can slowly develop a specific focus for the inquiry. As you develop a focus, your focus will guide you to the qualitative data you need.

In this section, we will examine eight stages of doing a field research study:

1. Preparing for a field study
2. Starting the research project
3. Being in the field
4. Developing strategies for success in the field
5. Observing and taking field notes
6. Conducting field interviews
7. Leaving the field
8. Writing the field research report

1. Preparing for a Field Study

We can divide the early preparation for doing a field study into the following three parts:

- Increasing self-awareness
- Conducting background investigation
- Practice observing and writing

naturalism the principle that we learn best by observing ordinary events in a natural setting, not in a contrived, invented, or researcher-created setting.

Brand X/SuperStock Royalty Free

Example Study Box 2 College Students Selling Door-to-Door

Schweingruber and Berns (2005) studied emotion work among college students who got jobs as door-to-door salespeople over the course of a year. They were directly and personally involved. Both worked for the company in several roles as salespeople. They observed recruitment interviews and went through the training programs themselves. During the summer, they accompanied college-student salespeople across five states on their long, 15-hour days, and during the time-off periods. In addition to working and living with the salespeople to understand their perspective, the researchers also analyzed company documents, engaged in field interviews, and conducted focus groups to "discover social meanings inductively" (Schweingruber and Berns 2005: 687).

Self-Awareness. Human and personal factors have a role in all social research projects, but they are crucial in field research. Direct, personal involvement with other people means your emotional make-up, personal biography, and cultural experiences are highly relevant. There is no room for self-deception. Your personal characteristics (including your physical appearance, gender, age, racial-ethnic background) are often relevant in the research process. You need to be candid and have a solid understanding of who you are. You are directly in the middle of the real, ongoing events, not safely hidden away in a laboratory, office, or computer room.

A good field researcher has a well-developed sense of self but is not self-absorbed. You must have an ability to notice details around you and have empathy for other people. You must also be aware of your own personal concerns, commitments, and inner conflicts. Expect anxiety, self-doubt, frustration, and uncertainty in the field, especially in the beginning. You may feel doubly marginal: an outsider in the field setting, and increasingly distant from friends, family, and other researchers.

6

Background Investigation. As with all research, reading the scholarly literature helps you learn useful concepts, potential pitfalls, data collection techniques, and strategies. Field researchers also use films, novels, or journalistic accounts about the type of field site or topic. They read autobiographies or diaries of people similar to those in the field site to gain familiarity and prepare themselves emotionally. More than a standard literature review, field researchers conduct a wide-ranging background investigation.

Practice Observing and Writing. Field research depends on skills of careful observing and listening, short-term memory, and writing. A good field researcher is observant and notices many details. He or she can also "pull back" to see the whole and grasp what occurs "between the lines." Much of what a field researcher does is to notice ordinary details of situations and to write them down. Attention to subtle details and short-term memory can improve with practice. Before you enter a field site, practice and refine your observation skills. Many people find that keeping a daily diary is good practice for writing field notes. Beyond personal strength and strong social skills, a field researcher needs to be a compulsive, organized note taker.

2. Starting the Research Project

We can divide the process of starting the research project into the following four parts:

- Getting organized
- Selecting a field site
- Gaining access
- Entering the field

Getting Organized. You need to adjust your mind-set and attitude as part of field research preparation. To begin, you want to defocus (i.e., be very open minded and clear your mind of preconceptions). Do not begin with set ideas, stereotypes, or notions about the topic, members, or field site. Be open to what you actually learn in the field, and do not impose preconceptions. You need to maintain a balance between being attentive and informed yet open to new experiences or ideas. You begin the field research process with a general topic, not with a narrow question or specific hypotheses. Avoid locking yourself into a narrow focus quickly, but do not become entirely directionless. Finding the research questions that fit a field situation takes time in the field. You develop the questions only after you know more about a site or situation. Patience is another valuable field research skill.

Selecting a Field Site. Field projects often begin with a chance occurrence or personal interest. Many studies began with a researcher's experiences, such as working at a job, having a hobby, or being a patient or an activist. The term *field setting* or **field site** can be misleading. It is more than a single, fixed physical location. It is a socially defined territory with fluid and shifting boundaries because social groups can interact across several physical sites. For example, a college football team may interact on the playing field, in the locker room, in a dormitory, at a training camp, or at a local hangout. The field site to study a football team includes all five physical locations. You need to recognize the interdependence that may exist among the physical site, the topic, the interacting members, and you, the researcher.

Selecting a field site is a major decision. Researchers often try several sites before settling on one and take notes on the site selection processes. Four factors affect your choice of a field research site: containment, richness of data, unfamiliarity, and suitability.

- **Containment.** It is easier to study field sites in which small groups engage in sustained social interaction within a bounded space. Field research in large, open public spaces where many strangers pass through with little social interaction (such as a shopping mall, large discount store, large outdoor park or parking lot) is much more difficult.
- **Richness.** More interesting data come from sites that have overlapping webs of social relations among people with a constant flow of activities and diverse events.
- **Unfamiliarity.** Despite some initial unease, you can more quickly see cultural events and relations in a setting that is new to you (see "Acquiring an Attitude of Strangeness" later in this chapter).
- **Suitability.** Consider practical issues, such as your personal characteristics and feelings. Also important are your time and skills, your physical safety, ethical protections, conflicts on the site, and your ability to gain access.

6

Gaining Access. Personal characteristics, such as age, gender, and race, can facilitate or limit access. You may find that you are unwelcome or not allowed on a site, or that you face legal and political barriers to entry. We can array field sites on a continuum. At one end are open access public areas (e.g., public restaurants, check-in airport waiting areas). At the other end are closed, private, or semiprivate settings (e.g., exclusive clubs, activities in a person's home). Laws and regulations in institutions (e.g., public schools, hospitals, prisons) can restrict access. In addition, institutional review boards (see Chapter 2) may limit field research on ethical grounds.

Almost all field sites have a **gatekeeper**. The gatekeeper can be the thug on the corner, an administrator of a hospital, a manager of a restaurant, or the owner of a beauty parlor. Informal public areas (e.g., sidewalks, airport waiting areas) often have gatekeepers. Formal organizations have authorities from whom you must obtain explicit permission. Whether or not it is required, it is good practice to identify and ask permission of gatekeepers.

field site any location or set of locations in which field research takes place. It usually has ongoing social interaction and a shared culture.

gatekeeper someone with the formal or informal authority to control access to a field site.

Example Study Box 3 Negotiating with Gatekeepers

In her study of luxury hotels, Rachel Sherman (2006) described gaining access to two five-star hotels. At one hotel, she received permission from the general manager and human resources manager. When she was assigned to be an intern at that hotel, she had to work with other gatekeepers who were managers or supervisors in various areas (such as guest services, "doorman" and parking, front desk). She found that gaining access from a gatekeeper at one level or area did not automatically transfer to other levels or areas. In addition to formal gatekeepers, she had to negotiate with informal gatekeeper-workers as she worked with the hotel employees. At another hotel, the human resource manager was the primary gatekeeper and there was less negotiation with each area. The internal arrangements and authority within each hotel altered access issues.

Expect to negotiate with gatekeepers and bargain for access. In addition to being flexible, a field researcher sets nonnegotiable limits to protect research integrity. For example, a gatekeeper who demands you only say positive things or insists on reading and censoring field notes makes research at a site impossible. If there are many restrictions initially, often you can reopen negotiations later. Gatekeepers may forget their initial demands as trust develops. Dealing with gatekeepers is a recurrent issue as you enter new levels or areas of the social setting.

Entering the Field. When entering a field site, adopt a flexible plan of action. Each site is different, and the way you enter a site depends on your prior experience, contacts, commonsense judgment, and social skills. Three issues to consider are presentation of self, amount of disclosure, and social role.

Presentation of Self. When you begin any new social relationship, including entering a field site as a researcher, you display the type of person you are or would like to be. Consciously or not, you do this through physical appearance, through what you say, by tone and mannerisms, and in how you act. The message may be, "I'm a serious, hard-working student," "I'm a warm and caring person," "I'm a cool jock," or "I'm a rebel and party animal." You can show more than one self, and the self you present can differ by the occasion.

You should be aware of self-presentation processes in the field. Your demeanor—your manner of speaking, the way you walk or sit, your facial expressions and eye contact, your hairstyle and your clothing—"speaks" for you. Be aware of what they are saying to members in the field. For example, how should you dress in the field? The best guide is to respect both yourself and the people you are studying. A professor who studies street people does not have to dress or act like one; to dress and act informally is sufficient. Likewise, if you study corporate or school officials, formal dress and a professional demeanor are expected. You need to be conscious of how self-presentation affects field relations. You want to fit in, but it is difficult to present a very deceptive front or to present a self that deviates sharply from your ordinary self. Your discomfort and awkwardness will show through and can impede developing smooth relations in the field.

Disclosure. A field researcher decides how much to disclose about self and the research to gatekeepers and members in the field. Revealing details of your personal life, such as hobbies, interests, and background, can build trust and help to create intimate relationships with people in the field. It also can result in a loss of privacy. We can think of disclosure on a continuum. At one end is covert research, in which no one in the field is aware that research is taking place. At the opposite end is fully open research, in which everyone becomes familiar with the researcher and is aware of the research project. The degree and timing of disclosure depend on your judgment and the particulars of a setting. Disclosure may unfold over time, as you feel more secure.

Social Roles. You play many social roles in daily life—daughter/son, student, customer, sports fan, friend, and so forth. You can switch roles, play multiple roles, or play a role in a particular way. You choose some roles, and others are prestructured for you. Few of us have a choice but to play the role of son or daughter, although you have some control over *how* you play the role. Some social roles are formal (e.g., bank teller, police chief), others are informal (e.g., flirt, elder states person, buddy).

Field researchers assume and play social roles in the field. At times, they adopt an existing role, such as the role of housekeeper that Rachel Sherman adopted in her study of hotels. Some existing roles provide greater access to all areas of the site. They let you observe and interact with all members and give you freedom to move around the site. Other roles are more restrictive. For example, the role of bartender when studying a tavern permits access to all areas, but it may limit freedom because it requires providing service, protecting the business, and collecting money. At other times, researchers create a new role or modify an existing one. For example, Fine (1987) created a role of the "adult friend" and performed it with little adult authority when studying preadolescent boys. He was able to observe parts of the boys' culture and behavior that were otherwise inaccessible to adults. It may take time to adopt some roles, and you may adopt several different field roles over time.

Your skills, time, and personal features—such as age, race, gender, and attractiveness—influence the roles open to you. You can only control some of these. Such factors can influence gaining access or can restrict available roles. Since many roles are sex typed, your gender is an important consideration. Female researchers have encountered difficulties in a dangerous setting where males are in control (e.g., police work, firefighting). They may be shunned or pushed into limiting gender stereotypes (e.g., "sweet kid," "mascot," "loud mouth," "hard bitch"). For example, Gurney (1985) reported that being a female in a male-dominated setting required extra negotiations and "hassles." Nevertheless, her gender also provided insights and created situations that would have been absent with a male researcher. Race and age can have a similar impact on role selection.

6

3. Being in the Field

Once you have selected a site, gained access, and assumed a social role, you need to settle in. We can divide ongoing observation and research in the field site into five parts:

- Learning the ropes
- Normalizing
- Building rapport
- Negotiating continuously
- Deciding on a degree of involvement

Learning the Ropes. New researchers often face embarrassment, experience discomfort, and become overwhelmed by the details in the field. Maintaining a "marginal" status is stressful. It is difficult to be an outsider who is not fully involved, especially when studying settings full of intense feelings (e.g., political campaigns, religious conversions). Do not be surprised if you feel awkward until you "learn the ropes" (i.e., acquire an understanding of micro-level norms, rules, and customs of a local field site). As you learn the ropes and fit in, you learn how to cope with stress and how to **normalize** the social research.

normalize how a field researcher helps field site members redefine social research from unknown and potentially threatening to something normal, comfortable, and familiar.

Normalizing Social Research. A field researcher not only observes and investigates members in the field, but he or she is also being observed and investigated. Frequently, members are initially uncomfortable with the presence of a researcher. Many may be unfamiliar with field research and confuse sociologists, psychologists, counselors, and social workers. They may see you as an outside critic or spy, or as a savior or all-knowing expert. You need to normalize. To help members adjust to the research process, you may present your own biography, explain field research a little at a time, appear nonthreatening, and accept or ignore minor rule violations in the setting. For example, the clerks at a work setting you are observing sometimes leave 20 minutes early when they should not. You do not report them to a supervisor. Soon, they begin to accept you as less threatening and like one of them.

Building Rapport and Trust. As you overcome your initial bewilderment to an unusual way of talking or system of meaning, you can slowly build relations of trust and establish rapport. This takes time and repeated positive social interactions. To do this you need to "get along with" members in the field. This may require listening sympathetically to complaints, sharing experiences, swapping stories, and laughing or crying with field site members.

Many factors influence building trust and rapport—how you present yourself; your role in the field; and the events that facilitate, limit, or destroy trust. Gaining rapport and trust is a developmental process that builds up through many social nuances (e.g., sharing of personal experiences, story telling, gestures, hints, facial expressions). Trust and rapport are easier to lose once established than to gain in the first place. Maintaining good rapport requires repeated social engagements with almost daily reinforcement. For example, if you establish rapport with a group of people and then disappear for three months, do not expect the same level of rapport instantly when you return. Creating trust often requires taking risks or passing mini social "tests." It also requires continuous reaffirmation, and you re-create it anew as you enter new topics, issues, physical locations, or social groups. Perry (2001) explains how she presented herself and gained rapport in her study of two high schools.

> Although I looked somewhat younger than my age (thirty-eight when the research began), I made concerted efforts to minimize the effects of age difference on how students related to me. I did not associate with other adults on campus. I dressed casually in attire that I was comfortable in, which happened to be similar to the attire students were comfortable in: blue jeans, sandals or athletic shoes, T-shirt or sweatshirt, no jewelry except four tiny hoop earrings—one in one ear, three in the other. I had students call me by my first name, and I did not talk down to them, judge them, or otherwise present myself as an authority figure. To the contrary, I saw the students as the authorities, and they seemed to appreciate that regard. Those efforts, on top of having developed some popular-cultural frames of reference with the students, contributed to my developing some very close relationships with several of the students and fairly wide access to different peer groups and cliques on campus. (Perry 2001:63)

Rapport and trust may be very difficult to achieve in some field sites. Some sites may be filled with fear, tension, and conflict. The local members may be unpleasant, untrustworthy, or untruthful. They may do things that disturb or disgust you. Experienced researchers are prepared for a range of events and relationships. However, it is sometimes impossible to penetrate a setting or get really close to members. Settings in which cooperation, sympathy, and collaboration are impossible may require different techniques.

Building rapport and trust is a step toward obtaining an understanding of the social life of a field site. Rapport helps you to understand the members. The understanding is a precondition for gaining greater access to a deeper level—a member's inner worldview and perspective. The step after seeing an event from a member's point of view is getting inside and grasping how the member thinks, feels, and reacts. You move beyond understanding toward empathy (i.e., seeing, feeling, and experiencing events in the field site as a member does). Empathy is not the same as sympathy, agreement, or approval. It means to see, feel, and think as another person does. Rapport helps to create understanding and ultimately empathy. At the same time, empathy facilitates greater rapport.

Negotiating Continuously. Most field sites have multiple levels or areas. Entry can be an issue for each. Entry is more analogous to peeling the layers of an onion than to opening a door. Moreover, bargains or promises made at entry may not be permanent. You should have fallback plans and expect renegotiation. Perhaps you got permission from the principal and parents to observe young children. After you arrive at the school, you find that two teachers control the children's time closely. They block your access and give you no chance to observe the children playing or interacting spontaneously. Your fallback plan may be to shift to study and spend more time with the two teachers. You try to see the world from their viewpoint. Once you better understand them and win their trust, you might be able to renegotiate with them to observe the children more.

Frequently, the specific focus of a field research study only emerges late in the research process, and it can change. This means you must negotiate for access to new areas as your research focus develops. Also, as you encounter new people in the field site, you may have to negotiate over social relations again with each new person until a stable relationship develops or has to be renewed. Expect to negotiate and explain what you are doing repeatedly. Although you may feel it, try not to express your irritation or impatience with the repetition.

Deciding on a Degree of Involvement. In addition to a social role in the field, you adopt a researcher role. This kind of role is on a continuum by the degree of direct involvement with members in the field and their activities. At one extreme is a detached and remote outsider. You only observe events from the distance and do not directly interact with people. At the opposite extreme is an intimately involved and engaged participant. You fully engage and begin to become just like another member in the field site (see Figure 6.2).

The outsider is faster, easier, and necessary at the start of observation. At the outsider end of the continuum, you need less time for acceptance, and overinvolvement is less likely. At times, people find it easier open up to someone seen as a detached outsider visitor. This role also protects your self-identity. However, you may feel marginal and unable to grasp an insider's experience. You are also more likely to misinterpret events. To understand local social meaning fully, you must participate in the setting with other people.

Roles at the insider end of the continuum facilitate empathy, sharing of a member's experience, and fully experiencing the intimate social world of field site members. However, with little social distance and too much sympathy for members, overinvolvement is possible. Intimate contact can make serious data gathering difficult, and you may lose the distance needed for research analysis. Feelings of loneliness and isolation in the field may combine with a desire for rapport and empathy to create overinvolvement or **going native**. This can destroy a research study because

going native when a field researcher drops a professional researcher role and loses all detachment to become fully involved as a full field site member.

Figure 6.2 Researcher Role by Degree of Involvement in the Field Site

Total Observer ⟷ Complete Participant

being like the others in the field takes priority over doing careful research, observation, or analysis. Maintaining a high degree of involvement without being overly involved is difficult.

4. Strategies for Success in the Field

All field researchers have strategies that they tailor to the specifics of a field site and their own background. In this section, we look at six of the strategies that many field researchers have used:

- Building relationships
- Performing small favors
- Appearing interested and exercising selective inattention
- Being an earnest novice
- Avoiding conflict
- Adopting an attitude of strangeness

Building Relationships. Over time, you develop social relationships with people in the field site (see Learning from History: Taxis, Customers, and Tips). This requires putting in time, remembering personal details about members, and making "small talk" (such as saying good morning, commenting on the weather). Members who are cool at first may warm up later. Alternatively, they may put on a front of initial friendliness, with fears and suspicions surfacing later. You are in a delicate position because early in a study, when you know little about a field site, you may resist forming a close relationship with particular people because you are unfamiliar with the social scene. If you quickly develop one or two close friends, they can become allies and valuable sources of information. They can explain events to you, introduce you to others, defend your presence, and help you to gain access. However, depending on who the first friends are, they can also block you from having access to some parts of the field site or inhibit creating social relations with others in the setting.

You need to notice quickly the social cliques, friendship ties, disputes or tensions, and power relations in a social setting. For example, after two days in a field site you recognize that Samantha and Judy seem to avoid one another and do not get along. George and Roberto appear to be close friends. Minsook looks quiet, shy, and uncertain of herself and has few friends. April appears to be outgoing and confident and seems to be in charge.

As you acquire awareness of the social "lay of the land," you also need to monitor how your own actions or appearance affect others. For example, a physically attractive researcher who interacts with members of the opposite sex often encounters crushes, flirting, and jealousy. You need to be aware of these field relations and manage them. You must maintain some level professional detachment and discipline but not hurt feelings, harm rapport, or close off access. At times, you need to be able to break off relations or withdraw from them. You may discover that to forge social ties with some people, you must break off close social ties with others. As with the end of any friendly relationship, social withdrawal can cause emotional discomfort or pain for both you and the other person. As a field researcher, you must constantly balance social sensitivity with your research goals.

Performing Small Favors. You have probably noticed that social life is full of exchange relationships. You do something for someone else and he or she usually returns the favor. Exchange relationships also develop in a field site. People exchange small favors, including deference and respect. A research strategy for gaining acceptance in the field is to help in small ways but not expect anything in return. As you repeatedly help and perform "small acts of kindness," people in the field incur an informal social obligation. They may feel they should reciprocate by offering you help in the field.

Learning from History Taxis, Customers, and Tips

In a famous article, Fred Davis (1959) analyzed what he learned from field research when he worked as a taxi driver for six months in 1948 in Chicago. He focused on the social relationship between the driver and passenger or fare. He observed that drivers have limited control over the job. They have little choice of passengers and only a few regular clients-customers. Mobile and without a fixed business location, the low-status cabdriver devoted long hours to short-term encounters with many diverse individuals. The encounters were highly variable and contained risk (such as fare jumpers, women in labor, robbers). Customers often ignored the driver or acted as if he or she was not there. Davis noticed that taxis drivers, like others in similar low-status service jobs, "sized-up" and quickly classified their customers. Customer categories were a large part of the taxi driver's daily social world. Using a customer category system added a small degree of control and predictability in a highly uncertain job. It also helped when evaluating risk. Drivers also used it to gain some control and estimate the likelihood of tips. The driver had little discretion over how to perform a service. Beyond careful driving, opening doors, or speedy delivery, using a customer classification let the driver to assert some control and engage in strategic emotion work—smile, make small talk, display kindness—to improve tips.

Appearing Interested and Exercising Selective Inattention. At times, you may feel bored or distracted in the field site. Looking bored is a nearly certain way to break off or weaken a developing social relationship. You should learn to "act" and maintain an **appearance of interest**. Appearing interested in the people and events of a field site with your words and actions (e.g., facial expression, going for coffee, going to a party, listening to jokes), even if you are not truly interested, is an important strategy.

Putting on a temporary front of involvement to be sociable is a common small deception of daily life. It is a part of being polite. Of course, selective inattention (i.e., not staring or appearing not to notice) is also part of acting polite. If someone makes a social mistake (e.g., accidentally uses an incorrect word, passes gas), the polite thing to do is to ignore it. Selective inattention in fieldwork gives an alert researcher an opportunity to learn by casually eavesdropping on conversations or observing events not meant to be public.

Being an Earnest Novice. When you are new to a setting and first forming relationships, you may be curious and ask many questions. One field strategy is to extend this mode of operating for some time. Being the "expert" or "know-it-all" is *not* how you learn about a field site or win friends. As the outsider, your primary mission in the field is to observe, listen, and learn about other people. It is not to brag, talk a lot, promote your opinions, or correct others' mistakes. If anything, you should act slightly less informed and knowledgeable than you really are. This is a good way to learn from people in the field. Being humble and adopting a learner role pays research dividends. You learn more by listening and asking questions. Treating local members as experts encourages them to share confidences with you. You do not want to appear unnecessarily stupid or naive, but you want to ask for explanations rather than assume that you already know what is happening or why things are done in certain ways. By adopting a novice role as someone who wants to learn, you both learn more and help members to feel respected and valuable.

Avoiding Conflicts. Fights, conflict, and disagreements can erupt in the field. You may study people with opposing positions. In such situations, you may feel pressure to take sides. People may test you to see if you can be trusted or are on the enemy's side. In such occasions, it is usually best to stay on the neutral sidelines and try to walk a tightrope between opposing sides. Once you align closely with one side, you will be cut off from access to the other side. In addition, you will only see the situation from one point of view and may get a distorted picture of events.

appearance of interest a micro strategy to build or maintain relationships in a field setting in which a researcher acts interested even when he or she is actually bored and uninterested.

Adopting an Attitude of Strangeness. Life is filled with thousands of details. If you paid attention to everything all the time, you would suffer from severe information overload. We manage life by ignoring much of what is around us and by engaging in habitual thinking. We overlook what is very familiar and assume that other people experience reality the same as we do. We treat our way of living as being natural or normal. We rarely recognize what we take for granted. For example, someone hands you a wrapped gift. You probably say "thank you," open the gift, and then praise it. Yet gift-giving customs vary by culture. In some cultures, people barely acknowledge the gift and quickly put it aside unwrapped. In others, people expect the gift receiver to complain that the gift is inadequate. Habitual thinking and not noticing what is familiar makes doing field research in a familiar setting very difficult. Field researchers adopt an **attitude of strangeness**. With the stranger's perspective, the unspoken, tacit culture of a setting becomes more visible. When you first go to a new, unfamiliar place as a stranger, you are extra sensitive to the physical and social surroundings. You do not know what will happen. By adopting an attitude of strangeness, you retain such an extra-sensitive perspective and use it to look at field events in a new way.

If you visit a very different culture, you will encounter different assumptions about what is important and how to do things. This confrontation of cultures, or culture shock, makes it easier for you to see cultural elements and facilitates self-discovery. By acquiring the attitude of strangeness, you notice more details. You find that reflection and introspection are easier and more intense. As a field researcher, you want to adopt both a stranger's and an insider's point of view. Your understanding will expand if you learn to see the ordinary both from an outsider-stranger's perspective and as an insider-member does. Switching back and forth is key to good field research.

5. Observing and Collecting Data

In this section, we look at ways to get good qualitative field data. Field data are what a researcher experiences, remembers, records in field notes, and makes available for systematic analysis.

6

The Researcher Is a Data Collection Instrument. The good field researcher is a resourceful, talented individual with ingenuity and an ability to think quickly on his or her feet while in the field. In quantitative research, you may use various instruments (e.g., questionnaire, response reaction measures in a computer) to acquire data. In field research, you are the instrument for acquiring field data. This has two implications. First, you must be alert and sensitive to what happens in the field and disciplined about recording data. Second, your social relationships and personal feelings and personal, subjective experiences are field data. They are valuable in themselves and for interpreting events in the field. Instead of trying to be objective and eliminate personal reactions as in quantitative studies, you reflect on your reactions and feelings and then record them as an important data source. For example, a field researcher visits a pornography shop to study what happens inside. He notices an increase in personal unease and anxiety (rapid heartbeat, sweaty palms). He reflects on sources of the unease—is it a fear of discovery, is it excitement from transgressing a moral line, is it uncertainty over someone approaching him in the store to solicit for sex? The researcher's inner anxiety and feelings that have accompanied his observing of customers and clerks at the shop are legitimate field data. He should notice and record them, as Karp (1973) did in his study of porn shops.

What to Observe. In the field site, you must pay very close attention, watch all that is happening, and listen carefully (see Example Study Box 3: Negotiating with Gatekeepers). You use all your senses. Notice what you see, hear, smell, taste, and touch to absorb all sources of information.

attitude of strangeness a perspective in which the field researcher questions and notices ordinary details by looking at the ordinary through the eyes of a stranger.

Example Study Box 4 Noticing Details

In one of the luxury hotels she studied, Rachel Sherman (2006) noticed that management sent contradictory messages to workers: (1) You are part of a family or community and have free choice; (2) you are under surveillance and required to perform your job. How did she arrive at this conclusion? She noticed many details in the employee handbook, at training sessions, in worker-manager interactions, and many little things in general. For example, she saw a sign posted for an upcoming employee meeting. It said, "come enjoy the refreshments," and under this message it said "attendance is mandatory" (2006, p. 75). Through her careful attention to details that she recorded and on which she later reflected, she could build a picture of the corporate culture sustained in each luxury hotel.

The Physical Setting. In the beginning, you want to scrutinize the physical setting and capture its atmosphere. What is the color of the floor, walls, ceiling? How large is the room? Where are the windows and doors? How is the furniture arranged and what is its condition (e.g., new or old and worn, dirty or clean)? What type of lighting is there? Are there signs, paintings, or plants? What are all the sounds or smells?

Why bother with such details? Stores and restaurants often plan lighting, colors, and piped-in music to create a certain atmosphere. Used-car salespeople spray a new-car scent into cars. Shopping malls and stores intentionally send out the odor of freshly made cookies because it attracts customers. To sell a house, people often add a fresh coat of paint. These subtle, unconscious signals influence human behavior. As a field researcher, you want to notice, capture, and record anything in the surroundings that could influence social relations and create "atmosphere."

You may find that field observing is detailed, tedious work, but motivation is based on a deep curiosity about the details. A good field researcher is intrigued with details. The mass of ordinary details can reveal "what's going on here." The mass of ongoing mundane, trivial, and daily minutiae can communicate very important aspects of social life. This is what people often overlook but what field researchers notice and from which they learn.

6

People and Their Behavior. In addition to physical surroundings, you observe people in the field. Notice each person's observable physical characteristics: age, sex, race, and stature. Why? People socially interact differently depending on whether someone is 18, 40, or 80 years old; male or female; white or nonwhite; short, thin, and frail or tall, heavyset, and muscular. For example, an attitude of strangeness can heighten your sensitivity to a group's racial composition. A white researcher in a multiracial society who does not notice that everyone in a group in a field setting is also white is racially insensitive and missing a feature of the setting that could be important for understanding it. The 20-year-old researcher observing a crowded restaurant who notices nothing unusual until an elderly couple walks in is suddenly aware that all people in the restaurant are under 30 years old. The youthfulness of the staff and customers is actually a major feature of the restaurant setting. In her study of luxury hotels, Sherman (2006) noticed a "stark" racial/ethnic division of labor in one hotel—"front office workers, many of whom were European, were white; the only nonwhite worker at the desk was Inga, a young Swede of Asian descent. Three of the four doormen were white. . . . A striking and important feature of the front office workers . . . was their youth. Annie, Jackie, Betsy and, Ginger, white front desk/concierge workers, were all under twenty-three" (pp. 86–97).

You record all the details because something of significance *might* be revealed. You may not become aware of a detail's relevance until later. You want to err by including everything rather than missing potentially significant details. Highly specific, descriptive details capture the setting and events. For example, "a tall, white, muscular 19-year-old male in jeans sprinted into the brightly lit room just as the short, slight black woman in her sixties and a tailored blue dress eased into a battered plastic chair" says more than "one person entered, another sat down."

Physical appearance—such as makeup, neatness, clothing, or hairstyle—sends messages that can influence social interactions. Some people devote a lot of time and money to selecting clothes, styling and combing their hair, putting on makeup, shaving, ironing clothes, and using deodorant or perfumes. This is part of their self-presentation. People who do not groom, shave, or wear deodorant are also presenting themselves and sending messages. No one dresses or looks "normal." Such a statement suggests that you are not seeing the social world through the eyes of a stranger or are insensitive to social signals.

Beyond appearance, people's actions can be significant. Notice where people sit or stand, the pace at which they walk, and their nonverbal communication. People express social information, feelings, and attitudes through nonverbal communication, including gestures, facial expressions, and how they stand or sit (standing stiffly, sitting in a slouched position, etc.). People express relationships by where they position themselves in a group and through eye contact. You want to read social communication by quickly noticing who is standing close together, having a relaxed posture, and making eye contact and who is not.

You also need to notice the context in which events occur: Who was present? Who just arrived or left the scene? Was the room hot and stuffy? Was it late or early in the day? Such details help you assign meaning and learn why events occur. If you fail to notice such details, they are lost. Also lost is a full understanding of the event. In their study of timeshare sales presentations, Katovich and Diamond (1986) documented how sales staff carefully deployed situational details, such as timing, phrasing, and the staging of events, to influence sales.

Lastly, you need to notice exactly what people say, their specific words and phrases. Also note how it is said—the loudness, tone of voice, accent, and so forth. Intense listening is tiring and difficult in a noisy room with many conservations or distracting sounds. If you are not part of a private conversation, listening to what people say is eavesdropping and considered very impolite. Yet a stranger who overhears a loud conversation is not being rude. Eavesdropping is intentionally listening to something meant to be private, but overhearing is unintentionally hearing when speakers show little concern for privacy. Field researchers engage in both, but they exercise care and discretion.

As you hear phrases, accents, and grammar, listen to what is said, how it is said, and what it implies. For example, people often use ambiguous phrases such as "you know" or "of course" or "et cetera." A field researcher tries to discover meaning behind such phrases. If someone fails to complete a sentence but ends with "you know," what does she mean? You hear a 14-year-old boy say, "We all went to the mall and hung out until 2, you know." The phase "you know" may be a sloppy speaking habit. It could mean he expects you to be aware of what 14-year-old boys do with their friends hanging out at a shopping mall for two hours in the middle of the day. Or the phrase could be deflecting attention since he engaged in forbidden behaviors and does not want to tell you.

When "Nothing" Happens. Inexperienced field researchers complain that they observed in a field site but "nothing happened." They get frustrated with the amount of "wasted" time waiting for something to occur. They have not yet learned the importance of serendipity in field research. You do not know the relevance of what you observe until later. Keen observations are useful at all times, even when it appears that "nothing happens." Although "nothing happened" from your perspective, what about from that of members in the field? As a field researcher, you need to operate on other people's schedules and observe events as they occur within their flow of time. You may be impatient to get in, get the research over, and get on with your "real life." For people in the field site, this *is* their real life. You may need to subordinate your personal wants to the flow and demands of the field site.

Field researchers appreciate "wait time." Waiting is a necessary part of fieldwork that can be valuable. Wait time can indicate inactivity and a slow pace, a delay because of scheduling problems, a stalemate in a conflict, or power relations in which unimportant people are expected to wait. Wait time reveals the pace and rhythm of a setting. Also, wait time is not always wasted time. You can use wait time for reflecting, for observing details, for developing social relations, for building rapport, and for becoming a familiar sight to people in the field setting. Wait time also displays that you are committed and serious; perseverance is a significant trait. Like the appearance of interest, it signals to people in the field that you are earnest and committed. It shows them that you believe what occurs in the field site is valuable and important.

Sampling. Field research sampling differs from that of survey research. Field researchers do not use random sampling. They sample by taking selective observations from all possible times, locations, people, situations, types of events, or contexts of interest. You might sample time by observing a setting at different times of the day. For example, in studying a bowling alley you observe at three times of the day, on weekdays and weekends, to get a sense of what remains the same and what changes. It is often best to overlap sampling times (e.g., 9:00 to 11:00 A.M., 10:30 A.M. to noon, 11:30 A.M. to 1:00 P.M.). You may want to sample locations because sitting or standing in different locations provides a better sense of the whole site. Let us say you are studying the emotion work of a waitress. You want to observe interactions in the front area (with customers), in a back area (with cooks, etc.), and in a back break room with coworkers. You would sample all shifts and meal times, both the slow and very busy times. Observations from multiple locations and times will give you a much richer picture of the entire social setting.

You can sample people by focusing attention on different kinds of people (old-timers and newcomers, old and young, males and females, leaders and followers). As you identify all the types of people, or people with various outlooks in a field site, you want to interact with and learn about all of them.

You can also sample three types of field site events: routine, special, and unanticipated.

- **Routine.** Events that occur over and over again the same way (e.g., opening up a store for business every day). Do not be mistaken and think they are unimportant simply because they are routine.
- **Special.** Events announced and planned in advance (e.g., annual office party). These events focus member attention and can reveal aspects of social life not otherwise visible.
- **Unanticipated.** Events that just happen while you are present (e.g., how unsupervised workers act when the manager gets sick and cannot oversee them for a day). In this case, you may see something unusual, unplanned, or rare. Such events might reveal new aspects of a setting, such as how much the workers really respect the manager and follow her rules even when she is not around to observe them.

Becoming a Skillful Note-Taker. Field research data are your memories of observations and experiences and your field notes. Field notes are the permanent record of observations and experiences. Producing good field notes is essential for a high-quality ethnography or field research study. Do not plan to take notes while in the field site. After spending some time in the field, plan to sit down in a quiet place and write from memory. Especially in the beginning, you leave the field to write notes after only one or two hours of observation. Expect to spend nearly as much time writing as you did observing in the field site. If you observed for two hours, you may be writing for two hours.

Types of Notes. Any notes taken directly in the field site differ from full field notes. A common mistake of new field researchers is to try to take the full field notes while still in the field site (see Making it Practical: Recommendations for Taking Field Notes). Only take **jotted notes** in the field site, not full field notes. If you take jotted notes, write them on a small scrap of paper inconspicuously or in private (such as in a bathroom). You use them to get down one or two critical key words or phrases that can stimulate your memory later.

Immediately after you leave the field site, sit down in a quiet place to write notes. Writing field notes requires self-discipline and can be boring, tedious work. You need to make writing notes a compulsion. Your notes should contain extensive descriptive detail drawn from short-term memory. New field researchers find they can recall more details with some effort. Generally, the quality and quantity of notes improve over time. Be sure to keep field notes neat and organized. You will return to them over and again. Always put the date and time of the observation at the top of the first page for a session in the field. Once written, the notes are private and valuable; treat them with care and protect their confidentiality. Sometimes hostile parties, blackmailers, or legal officials will want to read them. Some professional field researchers write their field notes in code. Your mood, state of mind, attention level, and conditions in the field can affect note-taking.

Supplements. Beyond detailed descriptions, your full field notes can contain maps, diagrams, photographs, interviews, tape recordings, videotapes, memos, objects from the field, and jotted notes taken in the field. For a field project of a few weeks, you might fill several notebooks or the equivalent in computer memory. Some professional researchers have produced 40 single-spaced pages of notes from three hours of observation. With practice, even a new field researcher can soon produce four or five pages of notes for each hour in the field.

jotted notes optional, very short notes of a few words written inconspicuously in the field site that are used only to trigger memory later.

6

Making It Practical **Recommendations for Taking Field Notes**

1. Record notes immediately after being in the field. Avoid talking with others until you record observations.
2. Begin the record of each field visit with a new page. Enter the date and start and ending times.
3. Use only the optional jotted notes as a temporary memory aid, with one or two key words or terms.
4. Use wide margins so you can add to your notes at any time. Go back and add things you remember later.
5. Plan to type notes and keep the note levels (to be discussed later) separate so you can easily return to them.
6. Record events in the order in which they occurred. Note their length (e.g., a 15-minute wait, a one-hour ride).
7. Be as specific, concrete, complete, and comprehensible as possible. You can always throw away extra details.
8. Try to recall exact phrases. Use double quotes for exact phases and single quotes for paraphrasing.
9. Record small talk or routines that do not appear to be significant at the time; they may become important later.
10. "Let your feelings flow," and write quickly without worrying about spelling or "wild ideas."
11. Never substitute tape or video recordings completely for written field notes.
12. Include diagrams or maps of the setting. Outline your own movements along with those of other people during observation.
13. Include your own words and behavior in the notes. Also, record your emotional feelings and private thoughts.
14. Avoid evaluative generalizing or summarizing words. For example, rather than writing "The sink looked disgusting," it would be much better to write, "The sink was rust-stained and looked as if it had not been cleaned in a long time. Pieces of food and dirty dishes looked as if they had been piled in it for several days."
15. Reread your notes periodically and record any ideas generated by the rereading.
16. Always make backup copies of your notes and store the copies in different places in case of fire or other disaster.

How to Take Notes. There is more than one way to take field notes. The recommendations here (also see Making It Practical on page 152 and below) are only suggestions. With experience, you may develop your own system. Full field notes have several levels. Keep all the notes for an observation period together, but distinguish the levels of notes by starting each level on a new page or use a new color or font for each level. You will not produce the same amount of notes for each level. If you observe for six hours, you might have a tiny scrap paper of jotted notes, 40 pages of direct observation, 5 pages of researcher inference, and 2 pages in total for the methodological, theoretical, and personal level notes.

Maps and Diagrams. Many field researchers make maps and draw diagrams or pictures. Maps and diagrams help the researcher organize ideas and events in the field, and it helps when conveying life in a field site to other people. For example, you observe a lunch counter with 15 stools. You may draw and number 15 circles to simplify recording (e.g., "Yosuke came in and sat on stool 12; Phoebe was already on stool 10"). Field researchers create three types of maps: spatial, social, and temporal (see Figure 6.3).

- A spatial map orients the data in space or physical location.
- A social map shows connections among people and follows the flow of interactions indicating power, influence, friendship, division of labor, and so on.
- A temporal map shows time starts, endings, and durations for people, goods, services, and communications.

Making It Practical Five Levels of Field Notes

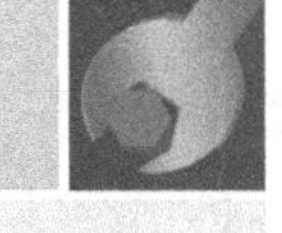

6

Jotted notes. Short, temporary memory triggers such as words, phrases, or drawings taken inconspicuously, often scribbled on any convenient item (e.g., napkin, matchbook). You will incorporate them into direct observation notes. They are never substitutes for full notes.

Direct observation notes. These are the core of your field data and are written immediately after leaving the field site. Order them chronologically, with the date, time, and place on each entry. They are a detailed description of everything you heard and saw in very concrete, specific terms. To the extent possible, they are an exact recording of the particular words, phrases, or actions, never summaries or generalizations.

Researcher inference notes. You need to look and listen without inferring or imposing an interpretation. Observations without inferences go into direct observation notes. *You record inferences in a separate section that is keyed to direct observations.* Keep inferred meanings separate from direct observation because the meaning of actions is not always self-evident. For example, a couple registers at a motel as Mr. and Mrs. Smith. You record what actually happened in the direct observation level but put your inference that they are not married in the inference level. A great deal of social behavior is ambiguous and has multiple possible meanings. Your own feelings, interpretations, and reactions are part of data in the field and should be in the notes, but separated.

Analytic notes. Keep methodological ideas in analytic notes to record plans, tactics, ethical and procedural decisions, and self-critiques. You may have educated hunches or emerging theoretical ideas during data collection, and you should put them in the notes. Analytic notes are a running account of your attempts to give meaning to field events. You can "think out loud" in your analytic notes by suggesting links between ideas, proposing conjectures, and developing new concepts. Your analytical notes can include ethical concerns that you encounter and strategies you invent.

Personal notes. Personal notes serve three functions: They are an outlet for you and a way to cope with stress; they are a source of data about personal reactions; and they are a way to evaluate direct observation or inference notes later when you reread notes. For example, if you were in a good mood during observations, your mood might color what you observed or how you felt about events.

Recordings to Supplement Memory. The novice field researcher could mistakenly think audio or video recorders make field note-taking unnecessary. Professional researchers sometimes use them as supplements in field research but not as substitutes. Recorders provide a close approximation to what occurred and are a permanent record that can help you to recall events. However, machines are never a total substitute for written field notes or your presence in the field. Recording devices have many limitations, including the following:

- You cannot introduce them into all field sites for practical reasons (large area with noise) or legal reasons.
- People in the field will see them as a threat; recording devices frequently create a disruption and raise awareness of surveillance. You can only use them after you have developed rapport and trust.
- Recorders frequently miss action or are out of range, they break down or fail, or they may require your attention and reduce direct personal involvement with what is happening in the field site.
- Recorders rarely save time. You can expect to spend two to three times longer reviewing and transcribing recorded material than the time of the recoding. You may have three hours of recording, but it could take you an additional eight hours to review and transcribe what you recorded.

6. Interviewing in Field Research

Field researchers use unstructured, nondirective, in-depth interviews. These differ from formal survey research interviews in many ways (see Making It Practical: Survey Interviews versus Field Research Interviews). In a field research interview, you ask questions, listen, express interest, and record. The field interview is a joint production between you and a field site member or informant (see the discussion of informants). People you interview are active participants in the discussion process, and their insights, feelings, and cooperation reveal their perspectives and subjective meanings.

You interview in the field or a convenient location and are informal and nondirective. It is acceptable for you to share your background to build trust and encourage the informant to open up. Do not force answers or use leading questions. You want to encourage and guide in a process of mutual discovery.

In field interviews, field members express themselves in their habitual way of speaking, thinking, and organizing reality. You want to retain their expressions, jokes, and narrative stories in a natural form without repackaging them into a standardized format. You want to stay close to the field member's experience. This means you ask questions in terms of concrete examples or situations—for example, "Could you tell me things that led up to your quitting in June?" instead of "Why did you quit your job?"

Field interviews can occur in a series over time. You first build rapport and avoid probing inner feelings until intimacy is established. After several meetings, you may be able to probe more deeply into sensitive issues and seek clarification of less sensitive issues. In later interviews, you can return to topics and check past answers by restating them in a nonjudgmental tone and asking for verification—for example, "The last time we talked, you said that you started taking things from the store after they reduced your pay. Is that right?" The field research interview is a "speech event," closer to a friendly conversation than the stimulus/response model used in a survey research interview. It differs from a friendly conversation in that it has an explicit purpose—to learn about the informant and setting. You may include explanations or requests that diverge from friendly conversations. You may say, "I'd like to ask you about," or "Could you look at this and see if I've written it down right?" The field interview is less balanced than a conversation. You ask more of the questions and may express more ignorance and interest than an ordinary conversation. Repetition is common. You may ask a field site member to elaborate on unclear abbreviations. You do not have to ask every person you interviewed the same questions, but tailor questions to specific individuals and situations.

Types of Questions in Field Interviews. Field researchers ask three types of field interview questions: descriptive, structural, and contrast questions. You can ask all concurrently, but each type is more frequent at a different stage in the research process. When you first enter the field site, you will primarily ask descriptive questions. You can gradually add structural questions until, in the middle stage after analysis has begun, most of the questions are structural. Contrast questions begin in the middle of a study and increase until, by the end, you ask more of them than any other type.

Descriptive Questions. You ask descriptive questions to learn about the setting and members. Descriptive questions can be about time and space—for example, "Where is the bathroom?" "When does the delivery truck arrive?" "What happened Monday night?" They can be about people and activities: "Who is sitting by the window?" "What is your uncle like?" They can be about events or activities: "What happens during the initiation ceremony?" They can be about objects: "When do you use a saber saw?" Questions asking for examples or experiences are descriptive questions: "Could you give me an example of a great date?" "What happens in a perfect game?" You can ask about hypothetical situations: To the new teacher—"If a student opened her book during the exam, how would you deal with it?"

Structural Questions. You use a structural question after spending time in the field and after you started a preliminary analysis of your data. You ask structural questions after you have organized specific field events, situations, and conversations into preliminary conceptual categories and started to figure out how things are organized. You ask them for clarification and confirmation. For example, you observe a highway truck-stop restaurant. Over time, you see that the employees informally classify customers patronizing the truck stop. Based on a preliminary analysis, you think there are five types of customers. Using structural questions, you seek verification of the five types and their features. You might ask whether a category includes features beyond those you already identified—for example, "Are there any types of customers other than regulars, greasers, pit stoppers, road rangers, and long haulers?" You ask for confirmation: "Is a greaser a type of customer you serve early in the morning?" "Would you consider Johnny Jensen to be a long hauler?"

Contrast Questions. After you have verified major categories, processes, or aspects of life in the field with structural questions, you can begin asking contrast questions. Contrast questions focus on the similarities or differences among the categories, processes, or aspects. You ask questions to verify similarities and differences that you believe to exist among categories. You may ask, "You seem to have a number of different kinds of customers come in here. Two types just stop to use the restroom without buying anything—entire families and a lone male driver. Do you call both of them pit stoppers?"

Informants. The term **informant** has a specific meaning in field research. It is someone with whom you develop a relationship and who informs you about life in the field. The ideal informant is a person currently in the field site, completely familiar with its culture, and in position to have witnessed and participated in its significant events. The informant should not be too busy to spend some time talking with you. The ideal informant is nonanalytic. He or she uses ordinary native folk theory or pragmatic commonsense thinking. People who are highly educated and try to analyze the field site by imposing ideas or categories taken from the media or academic work are not good informants. In a long field study, you might interview various types of informants, such as rookies and old-timers, people who recently changed status (e.g., through promotion), and those who are static. You seek out in-

informant a member in a field site with whom a researcher develops a relationship and who tells the researcher many details about life in the field site.

6

Making It Practical Survey Interviews versus Field Research Interviews

TYPICAL SURVEY INTERVIEW

1. It has a clear beginning and end.
2. You ask the same standard questions of all respondents in the same sequence.
3. You appear neutral at all times.
4. You as the interviewer ask all questions, and the respondent only answers.
5. The interview is with one respondent alone.
6. You maintain a professional tone and businesslike focus; you suppress or ignore diversions.
7. Closed-ended questions are common, and probes are rare.
8. You as the interviewer alone control the pace and direction of the interview.
9. You ignore the social context in which the interview occurs.
10. You mold the communication pattern into a standard framework.

TYPICAL FIELD INTERVIEW

1. The beginning and end are not clear. The interview can stop and be resumed later.
2. You tailor the questions you ask and the order in which you ask them to specific people and situations.
3. You show interest in specific answers/responses and encourage elaboration.
4. The typical field interview is somewhat like a friendly conversational exchange, but with more interviewer questions.
5. Field interviews can occur in a group setting or with others in the area.
6. The interview can be interspersed with jokes, asides, stories, diversions, and anecdotes, and you record them.
7. Open-ended questions are common, and probes are frequent.
8. You and the field site member jointly control the pace and direction of the interview.
9. You note the social context of the interview and treat it as important for interpreting the meaning of responses.
10. You adjust to the member's norms and language usage.

formants who are frustrated or needy as well as those who are happy and secure, people at the center of the action and those on the fringes, and the leaders as well as followers. You can expect mixed messages when you interview a range of informants, but this is not a problem. It reflects the multiple points of view that can coexist in a field site.

Most people only reveal highly intimate, confidential information in private settings. Likewise, the field interview varies by its context. You generally want to conduct field interviews in the field member's home environment to increase the comfort level. Context and past interactions between you and an informant can shape what is said and how, so you want to note those things as well as what the informant actually says. You also want to note nonverbal communication in the interview that can add meaning, such as a shrug or a gesture (see Making It Practical: Survey Interviews versus Field Research Interviews).

7. Leaving the Field

A professional field researcher may be in a field site from a few weeks to a dozen years. At some point, work in the field ends. It may end naturally—when learning new things diminishes and theory building reaches a closure. Alternatively, it could go on without end, and you must decide to cut off relations and exit. At times, external factors force an ending (e.g., a job ends, gatekeepers order you to leave, a project deadline arrives).

You should plan for and anticipate the disengaging and exiting process. Depending on the intensity of involvement and the length of time in the field, exiting can be disruptive or emotionally painful. You may feel guilty and depressed immediately before and after leaving. You may find it difficult to let go because of personal and emotional ties. Professionals with a long, intense involvement in a field site sometimes need a month or more of adjustment time after exiting before they feel at home with their original cultural surroundings.

The exit process depends on specifics of the field setting and relationships developed. You have to decide length and form of disengagement. You can leave quickly (simply not return one day) or slowly reduce your involvement over several weeks. You also need to decide how to tell members and how much advance warning to give. If you spend a lot of time in a field site and have intense involvement with members, you should give some warning of the exit. Try to fulfill any bargains or commitments you built up in the field so you can leave with a clean slate. Often a small ritual, such as a going-away party or thanking and shaking hands with everyone, helps to signal the social break.

Anticipate the effect exiting may have on members. Some members may feel hurt or rejected because a close social relationship is ending. They may try to pull you back into the field. Over time, as warm social relations develop and many experiences are shared, members may have forgotten that you were an outsider there for research purposes. Bringing the research aspect of your relationship to the forefront may cause members to grow cold and distant or to become angry and resentful. Some researchers continue to maintain social relations with people they got to know in a field site after the study ends. For example, in her study of luxury hotels, Rachel Sherman (2006) reported that a few years after she left the field site, she continued to get together socially several times a year with workers who she got to know during the research.

8. Writing the Field Research Report

This section provides a brief overview of the field research report. More details on writing research reports are presented in Chapter 11. Field researchers start to think about what will appear in a report while they are still gathering data. More than in other types of social research, the researcher may use first person in the study report and recount his or her personal observations and experiences. More than in other reports, a field research report depends on the researcher's writing skill to fully convey a feeling of the field site, to describe individual people in the field, and to recount events in great depth. Unlike quantitative research reports, field research reports do not follow a fixed pattern. Many field research reports are book-length or are long, descriptive articles. Tables with numbers, graphs, or charts are very rare. In the report, the researcher provides supporting data in the form of photos

6

Tips for the Wise Consumer

You look for different things in a report on a field research study or ethnography than in a quantitative research study. Here are some things to look for:

- Exactly who conducted the study? Was it one person or several? What are the background or other characteristics of the person who conducted the study?
- What is the field site? Exactly when and where was the study conducted?
- Who constitute the members in the field site?
- How did the researcher gain access to the field site? Was it easy or difficult to gain access?
- How long did the researcher spend in the field conducting observations?
- Did the researcher supplement field observations with other types of evidence or documentation?
- What social role and what researcher role did the researcher use?
- Did the researcher conduct interviews for this study?
- How did the author use data to back up statements about themes, concepts, or processes in the field site?

Summary Review The Process of Doing Field Research

1. Preparing for a field research study
   - Self-awareness
   - Background investigation
   - Practice observing and writing
2. Starting the research project
   - Getting organized
   - Selecting a site
   - Gaining access
   - Entering the field
     - Presentation of self
     - Amount of disclosure
     - Selecting a social role
3. Being in the field
   - Learning the ropes
   - Building rapport
   - Negotiating continuously
   - Deciding on a degree of involvement
4. Developing strategies for success in the field
   - Building relationships
   - Performing small favors
   - Being inept but accepted
   - Avoiding conflict
   - Adopting an attitude of strangeness
5. Observing and taking field notes
   - The researcher as instrument
   - What to observe
     - Physical setting
     - People
     - Routines, events, and activities
     - Learning to listen
   - What if nothing happens?
   - Sampling
   - Becoming a skillful notetaker
     - Types of notes
     - Supplements
6. Conducting field interviews
7. Leaving the field
8. Writing the field research report

and quotes or short selections of concrete situations taken from the observations in field notes. The researchers use the quotes both to document and illustrate the concepts or themes that are part of the analysis.

ETHICS AND THE FIELD RESEARCHER

Several ethical issues are introduced by your direct, personal involvement in the social lives of others when doing field research. Often you are alone in the field and must make a quick ethical decision about situations that appear unexpectedly in the field. Privacy is the most common ethical issue. As you gain intimate knowledge in a field site and people give you information in confidence, you incur an ethical obligation to uphold the confidentiality of data. You must keep it confidential from other people in the field as well as from the public. You may want to disguise real names in field notes and in a report for the public.

New field researchers often ask about deception. When do you not fully and honestly disclose your role as a researcher and true purpose for being at a site? Professional researchers debate over covert versus overt field research. Everyone agrees that covert research is not preferred. Some say it is never acceptable. Others see covert research as acceptable and necessary for entering into and gaining knowledge about certain areas of social life, such as a secret society or ring of illegal drug dealers. In general, you should be honest and openly disclose why you are in a site whenever possible. This is especially true if you are a beginning researcher. Covert research raises ethical and sometimes legal issues. It is more difficult to maintain a false front and to be in a constant anxiety over being caught.

Professional researchers who conduct field research on people who engage in illegal behavior face additional ethical issues as well as personal risk. They may know of and are sometimes indirectly involved in illegal activity. Such knowledge is of interest both to law enforcement officials and to other criminals. The researcher faces an extra challenge in building trust and rapport but not becoming so involved as to violate personal moral standards or endanger other people. In such situations, professional researchers often make an explicit arrangement with the members—such as, I will leave when certain serious illegal behavior occurs. Field research with criminals is for experienced researchers who have extra training and a knowledge of the risks involved.

FOCUS GROUPS

What do you think about a male elementary school teacher? Most elementary school teachers are women. A traditional female gender role includes close physical contact with young children and nurturing emotional relationships that are necessary for successful elementary school teaching. By contrast, the traditional male gender role is to be emotionally remote, engage in coarse or rough behavior, and avoid intimate physical contact, such as hugging and touching. A male elementary school teacher may have his masculinity questioned. People may see him as being weak and not ambitious. They may suspect he is a homosexual or a dangerous pedophile. Beyond the gender role issue, males may avoid the job because of its low pay and low status. It is socially defined as "women's work" not appropriate for a "real man."

Christina Kennedy/Photo Edit Inc.

Many observers note that highly gender stratified elementary schools perpetuate and reinforce traditional gender roles. Young boys and girls learn a traditional adult male model, one that they also see daily in the mass media and among many adults. They learn that a male is supposed to be emotionally cool and aggressive. They are indirectly "taught" that adult men are not emotionally expressive and caring. Having male elementary teachers promotes social equality and gives young children a positive male role model. Young children learn gender roles in which it is acceptable for an adult male to express emotional intimacy and be nurturing. Having male elementary school teachers also enables males who enjoy working with active young children and who do not repress the caring, emotionally warm side of their self to have a rewarding professional career.

The **focus group** is a special qualitative research technique that differs from traditional ethnography. It does not require an extended period of detailed observation in a field site. It is similar in that you acquire qualitative data from a small number of selected people participating in a naturalistic open group conversation.

Focus group research has rapidly grown over the last 20 years. In it, you informally interview people in a group-discussion setting. It can take place in a natural field setting (e.g., restaurant, break room of work site) or a special setting (e.g., classroom, conference room). To create the group you gather together 4 to 12 people in a room with a trained moderator to discuss a few issues. The group members should be homogeneous but not include close friends or relatives. Most focus group sessions are 45 to 90 minutes long. The moderator must be nondirective and facilitate free, open discussion among all group members. The moderator offers open-ended questions and does not let one person dominate the discussion. In a typical study, you might create four to six separate focus groups. All would discuss the same questions or focus on the same topic.

focus group a qualitative research technique that involves informal group interviews about a topic.

To understand why men become elementary level teachers and how they feel about the reactions of others, Cushman (2005) conducted a focus group study with male elementary teachers.

Cushman (2005) contacted 17 practicing elementary teachers to participate in 90-minute focus group discussions. Three or four teachers were together in each group with a moderator. The semistructured discussion centered on several questions, such as the following:

- What aspects of elementary school teaching initially attracted you to this career?
- What sort of reaction did you get when you told family and friends?
- Did you go straight from school or try other career options first?
- Was the salary or status of an elementary teacher a concern to you?
- Do you face any challenges being part of a school staff in which males are a minority?
- To what extent does having physical contact with young children concern you?

Cushman found that all the teachers overwhelmingly chose the career because of the intrinsic joy they got from working with children. They found the play aspect of teaching young children to be most rewarding. Many also liked the strong service aspect of teaching. They tended to value intrinsic over extrinsic rewards (e.g., job satisfaction versus salary). Reactions by others to their decision varied but were often negative. Fathers were the most negative about the career choice. Positive reactions were most common when the men had teachers in their fami-

Summary Review **Advantages and Limitations of Focus Groups**

ADVANTAGES

- They are fast, easy to do, and inexpensive.
- They occur in a more natural setting that helps to increase external validity.
- They provide exploratory researchers with new insights and give survey researchers ideas for questions and answer categories.
- They give quantitative researchers a window into how people naturally discuss topics and aid in the interpretation of quantitative results.
- They allow research participants to query one another and explain their answers to each other.
- They encourage open expression among members of marginalized social groups who may not otherwise speak.
- They help people to feel empowered by a group setting, especially in action-oriented research projects.

LIMITATIONS

- You cannot generalize the discussion outcomes to a large, diverse population.
- They create a "polarization effect" such that attitudes become more extreme after group discussion.
- They are limited to discussing one or a few topics in a session.
- A moderator may unknowingly limit full, open, and free expression by all group members.
- Focus group participants tend to produce fewer ideas than in individual interviews.
- A large quantity of open-discussion results can be difficult to analyze.
- Reports on focus groups rarely report all the details of study design/procedure.
- Researchers find it difficult to reconcile differences that arise between responses given by an individual-only interview and those from a focus group.

Making It Practical Using Focus Groups to Learn Why Students Picked a Private High School

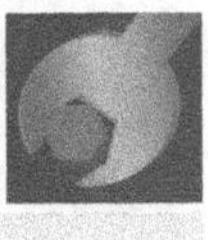

Several years ago, I used focus groups as part of an applied study on why parents and students chose a private high school. I formed six focus groups. Each group had 8 to 10 student volunteers from the high school. A trained college-student moderator asked questions, elicited comments from group members, and made sure that no one person dominated the discussions. The six groups contained male and female members from either one grade level or two adjacent grades (e.g., freshmen and sophomores). For 45 minutes, students discussed their reasons for attending the high school. They were asked about the importance of specific factors in the decision. These included parent pressure, participating in school sports, academic reputation, cost of the school, being with their friends, siblings or parents who went to the same school, school size, and the school's religious orientation. We tape-recorded the discussions and then analyzed the tapes to understand what the students saw as most important to their decisions. In addition, the data helped us to interpret survey data on the same topic. We used the results to design three survey questionnaires. One questionnaire was for all high school students, another for a sample of parents, and a third for students at junior high schools that often sent students to the high school. Results were part of a written report and presented at an open meeting of the parents and the school's administration.

lies. Many men came to elementary teaching after having tried other career options and only after developing a strong sense of self and their major life priorities. All were aware that homophobic communities made false accusations against male teachers. They knew that false accusations could have tragic consequences for a teacher.

Researchers have examined many topics using the focus group technique. Topics include issue attitudes (e.g., race relations, workplace equality), personal behaviors and relations (e.g., how to live with a child who has disabilities), a new product (e.g., breakfast cereal), or a political candidate. The focus group procedure has its own strengths and weaknesses (see Summary Review: Advantages and Limitations of Focus Groups).

WHAT HAVE YOU LEARNED?

In this chapter, you learned about the field research process, including its logic, choosing a site and gaining access, developing relations in the field, observing and collecting data, and conducting a field interview. You saw how field research differs from quantitative research; field researchers begin data analysis and theorizing as they collect data. In field research, you as the researcher are directly involved with the people you study. You become immersed in the social life of a natural setting to learn about it. More than quantitative research, doing field research can have a large impact on your emotions, personal life, and sense of self. Field research is a way to study parts of the social world that you otherwise could not study.

To do good field research requires a combination of skills. You need a strong sense of self, an excellent ability to listen and absorb details, tremendous patience, sensitivity and empathy for other people, superb social skills, a talent to think very quickly on your feet, the ability to see subtle interconnections among people/events, and an ability to express yourself in writing. Field research is especially valuable for studying micro-level social life and face-to-face interactions among small groups of people who interact with one another. It is less effective when the concern is macro-level processes and social structures, such as events that occurred in the distant past or that stretch across decades. Historical-comparative research, discussed in the previous chapter, is better suited to investigating these types of concerns.

KEY TERMS

analytic notes *153*
appearance of interest *147*
attitude of strangeness *148*
ethnography *136*
field site *141*
focus group *159*
gatekeeper *141*
going native *145*
informant *155*
jotted notes *152*
naturalism *139*
normalize social research *143*

APPLYING WHAT YOU'VE LEARNED

Activity 1

A good way to learn about ethnography and field research is to read studies that use them. Locate three field research studies on different settings or topics. Many studies are book-length, but two journal sources are the *Journal of Contemporary Ethnography* and *Qualitative Sociology*. You can also try a keyword search of scholarly articles using the terms *ethnography*, *participant observation*, or *field research*. Look for the features outlined in Tips for the Wise Consumer box of this chapter.

6

Activity 2

Doing detailed field research observation takes practice. Find a public social location that meets the criteria of a good field site and assume a total observer role for 30 minutes. Return to the same location 24 to 48 hours later for a second 30-minute observation period. During your first visit, notice everything about the physical setting using all your senses. After you leave the site, try to write down everything you can recall. During your second visit, (1) notice what you missed about the physical setting the first time that helps produce its atmosphere; and (2) notice the people—their number, age, gender, ethnicity—and entry/exit location. After you leave the site, try to write down everything you can recall. Two days later, reread your notes for both observations and add any other details you recall.

Activity 3

You can learn to see social settings in a new light by drawing three types of field site maps: temporal, social, and spatial. Find a social location that meets the criteria of a good field site and assume a total observer role for 20 minutes. Return to the same site five times. Pick different days of the week and times of the day. After leaving the site, try to create each type of map. The spatial is usually the easiest, the temporal and social more difficult. Can you begin to see how the three types of maps capture and together begin to present a picture of life in the field site?

Activity 4

Conduct an informal, open-ended interview for about 15 minutes with someone who works full time as a waiter or waitress at a sit-down restaurant about "emotion work." Do not use that term. Instead ask about specifics—do they have to "act nice," "say pleasant things," "smile when dealing with people who are difficult or rude," and so forth? Try to get a sense of how they deal with unpleasant customers, the pressure on them from management, or tips to be nice and friendly. Have them recount specific instances or tell stories. Ask whether there is a gap between how they really feel and how they must act on the job. Do they hide their true emotions and feelings as part of the job? Have they ever let their true feelings show when they should not have?

REFERENCES

Cushman, Penni. 2005. "It's Just Not a Real Bloke's Job: Male Teachers in Primary Schools." *Asia-Pacific Journal of Teacher Education* 33:321–338.

Davis, Fred. 1959. "The Cabdriver and His Fare: Facets of a Fleeting Relationship." *The American Journal of Sociology* 65:158–165.

Fine, Gary Alan. 1987. *With the Boys: Little League Baseball and Preadolescent Culture*. Chicago: University of Chicago Press.

Gurney, Joan Neff. 1985. "Not one of the guys: The female researcher in a male-dominated setting." *Qualitative Sociology* 8(1): 42–62.

Hochschild, Arlie. 1983. *The Managed Heart: Commercialization of Human Feeling*. Berkeley: University of California Press.

Katovich, Michael A., and Ron L. Diamond 1986. "Selling Time: Situated Transactions in a Noninstitutional Environment." *Sociological Quarterly* 27(2): 253–271.

Perry, Pamela. 2001. "White Means Never Having to Say You're Ethnic: White Youth and the Construction of "Cultureless" Identities." *Journal of Contemporary Ethnography* 30(1): 56–91.

Schweingruber, David, and Nancy Berns. 2005. "Shaping the Selves of Young Salespeople through Emotion Management." *Journal of Contemporary Ethnography* 34:679–706.

Sherman, Rachel. 2006. *Classic Acts: Service and Inequality in Luxury Hotels*. Berkeley: University of California Press.

Van Maanen, John. 1991. "The Smile Factory: Work at Disneyland." in P. Frost, L. Moore, M. Luis, C. Lundberg, and J. Martin (eds.), *Reframing Organizational Culture* (pp. 58–76). Thousand Oaks, CA: Sage.

CHAPTER 7

Qualitative Interviewing

Taken from: *Basics of Social Research: Qualitative and Quantitative Approaches*, Canadian Edition, by W. Lawrence Neuman and Karen Robson

INTRODUCTION

This chapter shifts from the quantitative style of the past several chapters to the qualitative research style. The qualitative and the quantitative styles can differ a great deal.

Survey researchers also interview study members, but qualitative interviews differ from survey research interviews. This section introduces the qualitative interview.

Research Questions Appropriate for Qualitative Interviewing

Social science researchers also use less structured, nondirective, in-depth interviews, which differ from formal survey research interviews in many ways (see Table 7.1). The **qualitative interview** involves asking questions, listening, expressing interest, and recording what was said. It is a joint production of a researcher and an interviewee. Interviewees are active participants whose insights, feelings, and cooperation are essential parts of a discussion process that reveal subjective meanings.

Qualitative interviewing is often used in field research. It should be noted, however, that qualitative interviewing is a method that is separate from field research and that field researchers use qualitative interviewing often in addition to other data-collection techniques.

Qualitative interviews go by many names: unstructured, semi-structured, in-depth, ethnographic, open-ended, informal, and long. Generally, they involve one or more people being present and are informal and nondirective (i.e., the respondent may take the interview in various directions).

A qualitative interview involves a mutual sharing of experiences. A researcher might share his or her background to build trust and encourage the informant to open up, but does not force answers or use leading questions. She or he encourages and guides a process of mutual discovery.

Table 7.1 Survey Interviews versus Qualitative Interviews

Typical Survey Interview	Typical Qualitative Interview
1. It has a clear beginning and end.	1. The beginning and end are not clear. The interview can be picked up later.
2. The same standard questions are asked of all respondents in the same sequence.	2. The questions and the order in which they are asked are tailored to specific people and situations.
3. The interviewer appears neutral at all times.	3. The interviewer shows interest in responses, encourages elaboration.
4. The interviewer asks questions, and the respondent answers.	4. It is like a friendly conversational exchange, but with more interviewer questions.
5. It is almost always with one respondent alone.	5. It can occur in a group setting or with others in an area, but varies.
6. It has a professional tone and businesslike focus; diversions are ignored.	6. It is interspersed with jokes, asides, stories, diversions, and anecdotes, which are recorded.
7. Closed-ended questions are common, with rare probes.	7. Open-ended questions are common, and probes are frequent.
8. The interviewer alone controls the pace and direction of interview.	8. The interviewer and member jointly control the pace and direction of the interview.
9. The social context in which the interview occurs is ignored and assumed to make little difference.	9. The social context of the interview is noted and seen as important for interpreting the meaning of responses.
10. The interviewer attempts to mold the framework communication pattern into a standard.	10. The interviewer adjusts to the member's norms and language usage.

Source: Adapted from Briggs (1986), Denzin (1989), Douglas (1985), Mishler (1986), Spradley (1979a).

In qualitative interviews, study participants express themselves in the forms in which they normally speak, think, and organize reality. A researcher retains members' jokes and narrative stories in their natural form and does not repackage them into a standardized format. The focus is on the members' perspectives and experiences. In order to stay close to a member's experience, the researcher asks questions in terms of concrete examples or situations—for example, "Could you tell me things that led up to your quitting in June?" instead of "Why did you quit your job?"

Qualitative interviews can occur in a series over time. A researcher begins by building rapport and steering conversation away from evaluative or highly sensitive topics. He or she avoids probing inner feelings until intimacy is established, and even then, the researcher expects apprehension. After several meetings, he or she may be able to probe more deeply into sensitive issues and seek clarification of less sensitive issues. In later interviews, he or she may return to topics and check past answers by restating them in a nonjudgmental tone and asking for verification—for example, "The last time we talked, you said that you started taking things from the store after they reduced your pay. Is that right?"

Similarities and Differences between Qualitative Interviews and Friendly Conversations

The qualitative interview is closer to a friendly conversation than the stimulus/response model found in a survey research interview. You are familiar with a friendly conversation. It has its own informal rules and the following elements: (1) a greeting ("Hi, it's good to see you again"); (2) the absence of an explicit goal or purpose (we don't say, "Let's now discuss what we did last weekend"); (3) avoidance of repetition (we don't say, "Could you clarify what you said about . . . "); (4) question asking ("Did you see the race yesterday?"); (5) expressions of interest ("Really? I wish I could have been there!"); (6) expressions of ignorance ("No, I missed it. What happened?"); (7) turn taking, so the encounter is balanced (one person does not always ask questions and the other only answer); (8) abbreviations ("I prefer CFL, but I'll watch NFL if it's on TV," not "I prefer Canadian Football League, but I will watch the American National Football League games if they are on television"); (9) a pause or brief silence when neither person talks is acceptable; (10) a closing (we don't say, "Let's end this conversation"; instead, we give a verbal indicator before physically leaving: "I've got to get back to work now—see you tomorrow").

The qualitative interview differs from a friendly conversation. They are similar in that both involve asking questions. Qualitative interviews, however, have an explicit purpose—to learn about the informant and setting. A researcher includes explanations or requests that diverge from friendly conversations. For example, he or she may say, "I'd like to ask you about . . ." or "Could you look at this and see if I've written it down right?" The qualitative interview is less balanced. A higher proportion of questions come from the researcher, who expresses more ignorance and interest. Also, it includes repetition, and a researcher asks the member to elaborate on unclear abbreviations. Table 7.2 summarizes some important differences between qualitative interviews and friendly conversations.

Albanese (2006) used in-depth interviews in her study of women in Quebec whose children were in provincial child care (discussed in Chapter 3). Interviews lasted about an hour. Albanese was interested in how the provincial daycare system impacted on domestic and community life. She asked the women about the school readiness of their children before and after being placed in the daycare program. She also asked the women how they chose the child-care facility and what impact the use of these programs had had on their relations at home. Open-ended interviewing allowed her to see how the women thought the daycare program had impacted on their own lives, the lives of their families, and the general quality of life in the wider community.

Table 7.2 Friendly Conversations versus Qualitative Interviews

Friendly Conversation	Qualitative Interview
A casual or friendly greeting often initiates a conversation.	Often it begins by obtaining consent from the interviewee
There is no explicit goal or purpose.	There is an explicit purpose—to answer the research question
There is avoidance of repetition.	Repetition is included to ensure that researcher's interpretation is correct.
Expressions of interest and ignorance can be balanced	Researcher expresses more interest and ignorance.
There is turn taking, so the encounter is balanced	Much less balanced—the majority of questions are asked by the interviewer.
Often includes abbreviations and jargon that are familiar to both people	Researcher asks about abbreviations and jargon so that there is no misunderstanding between the interviewer and interviewee.
A pause or brief silence when neither person talks is acceptable.	Pauses can be used by the interviewer to get the interviewer to elaborate on a previous point.
End of conversation is verbal indicator followed by physical departure.	A formal closing that acknowledges the interview is over.

THE PROCEDURE OF QUALITATIVE INTERVIEWING

As with any research method, the researcher should have a clearly defined research question before interviewing participants for his or her study. Unlike quantitative research methods, researchers using qualitative interviewing rarely have hypotheses that they are testing. Rather, they have an inductive approach to theorizing and will build a theory from the evidence that emerges from the interviews they conduct.

Sampling in Qualitative Interviews

Social scientists typically select interview participants through nonprobability sampling, which was discussed in Chapter 3. With this particular data-collection technique, snowball and purposive sampling are often used for recruiting potential interviewees. This is because the topics that researchers are interested in studying through the use of qualitative interviewing do not easily lend themselves to probability sampling. If you recall from Chapter 3, probability sampling requires the use of a sampling frame—the list of all elements in a population. In the examples that follow, there was no official list of all of the members of the target populations. It should be said, however, that not all research that uses qualitative interviewing as a form of data collection uses nonprobability sampling—but the vast majority does.

In Lewis' (2006) study of exotic dancers in southern Ontario, interviewees were selected through purposive sampling so that as much diversity as possible could be incorporated into the sample. The researcher conducted interviews with 30 female dancers, ranging in age from 18 to 38. All but two interviewees were Caucasian but they varied according to educational and marital status. One-quarter, for example, were attending some form of schooling. Half of the dancers had partners, while one-third of the dancers had children.

Baron (2001) in his study of street youth in Edmonton, used a snowball sampling technique to recruit participants for interviews. Baron approached some street youth and explained the study to them and invited them to participate. Additional participants were recruited through these initial contacts. Baron would visit the same location where he met the original participants daily in order to initiate contact with more street youth or would be introduced to them through one of the original participants. Albanese (2006) also used snowball sampling in her study of mothers using daycare facilities in Quebec. She knew some mothers using daycare facilities in Quebec and then she asked them for the names of other mothers in similar situations. She also made contact with local child-care providers through the names given by the women that she interviewed.

As addressed in Chapter 3, hidden populations refer to people who belong to subcultures whose members are difficult to locate and therefore difficult to study. Many researchers who are interested in studying hidden populations rely on qualitative interviewing as a data-collection technique. Clearly, no sampling frame exists for members of hidden populations, such as gangs, members of clandestine religious orders, or illegal drug users, for example. Researchers interested in studying hidden populations often rely on nonprobability sampling techniques, particularly snowball sampling. After making contact with some members of the hidden population, the researchers can then ask members of the hidden population if they would refer them to other potential study participants.

How Many People to Interview?

Research that uses qualitative interviewing as its method of data collection is typically inductive in nature—that is, theory is derived from the data. As discussed in Chapter 3, the process of theoretical sampling goes hand in hand with the grounded theory approach. Theoretical sampling, to recap, means that a researcher does not know in advance how many individuals he or she needs to interview. The researcher continues to interview subjects until the same general themes continue to emerge from the data and no new findings are being revealed. This is known as theoretical saturation.

In reality, however, the number of people interviewed in a study employing qualitative interviewing as the data-collection method is usually dictated by the time and resources available to the researcher. Locating suitable interviewees who are willing to participate can be a time-consuming process, especially if you are studying a hidden population or do not know any contacts that can put you in touch with potential subjects. As discussed below, transcribing interview data is also very time demanding, and if a researcher decides to employ a transcriptionist, this can be very costly. A one-hour interview, in the authors' personal experience, takes about six hours to transcribe, but this can vary according to your typing speed, the type of equipment you are working with, and the quality of the interview recording.

Incentives

Often, because interviews can be time consuming for the interviewee, the researcher offers the potential interviewee an **incentive** for his or her participation. This can be a cash payment, vouchers, being entered into a draw, or simply being offered a copy of the final research report when it is finished. It is important to use an incentive that is appropriate to your target sample. For example, in Baron's (2001) study of street youth, he used an incentive for participation, which was ten dollars worth of vouchers to a popular fast-food restaurant. It is unlikely that a copy of his final paper would have been much of an incentive for this group of participants.

As well, instead of one-on-one incentives to individual participants, researchers who are doing research in a community or organization may make a gift offering to the entire community or organization at the end of their research project.

Interview Sites

Researchers using qualitative interviews as a form of data collection recognize that the type of conversation that occurs in a private office may not occur in a crowded lunchroom. Often, interviews take place in the member's home environment so that he or she is comfortable. This is not always best. If a member is preoccupied or there is no privacy, a researcher will move to another setting (e.g., restaurant or university office). For example, Baron (2001) interviewed street youth in the sheltered and more comfortable conditions of one of the many malls in downtown Edmonton.

The interview's meaning is shaped by its gestalt, the whole interaction of a researcher and a member in a specific context. For example, a researcher notes nonverbal forms of communication that add meaning, such as a shrug, a gesture, and so on. The gestalt of an interview is more than just the words that are exchanged between the interviewer and interviewee. The act of the interview is a social process unto itself that is characterized by several factors, including body language, the relationship between the interviewer and interviewee, and the context in which the interview takes place.

Recording and Transcribing

The researcher usually audio-records the interview and jots down notes while the interview takes place. There are many new digital recording devices that have better sound quality, are more dependable, and are more portable than what researchers have had to use in the recent past. Transcribing qualitative interviews is a time-consuming process but should be done as soon as possible after the interview has taken place so that the researcher has a better chance of deciphering audio material that may be difficult to understand. When the interview is "fresh" in the researcher's mind, it is more likely that he or she will have a clearer recollection of the interview and be able to fill in gaps where sound quality might be compromised.

Sometimes researchers do not transcribe their interviews in full and undertake what is called **selective transcription**. Selective transcription is usually done when the researcher feels it is unnecessary to fully transcribe the interviews in order to answer his or her research question. Rather that transcribing the entire interview, he or she will opt to only transcribe the parts that are most relevant to the research question that is being asked. In order for qualitative data to be as trustworthy as possible (according to the criteria suggested by Lincoln and Guba) and to ensure dependability of our findings, we should make our data available for other researchers to examine. Fully transcribed interviews are the best way to ensure that our findings are dependable and trustworthy.

Informants

An **informant** or key actor in qualitative research is a member with whom a researcher develops a relationship and who tells about, or informs on, the aspects of the research setting.[1] Who makes a good informant? The ideal informant has four characteristics.

1. The informant is very familiar with the culture and is in a position to witness significant events. He or she lives and breathes the culture and engages in routines in the setting without thinking about them.
2. The individual is currently involved in the culture that the researcher is trying to understand. Ex-members may provide useful insights, but the longer they have been away from direct involvement, the more likely it is that they have reconstructed their recollections.
3. The person can spend time with the researcher. Interviewing may take many hours, and some members are simply not available for extensive interviewing.

4. Nonanalytic individuals make better informants. A nonanalytic informant is familiar with and uses native folk theory or pragmatic common sense. This is in contrast to the analytic member, who preanalyzes the setting, using categories from the media or education.

A researcher may interview several types of informants. Contrasting types of informants who provide useful perspectives include rookies and old-timers; people in the centre of events and those on the fringes of activity; people who recently changed status (e.g., through promotion) and those who are static; frustrated or needy people and happy or secure people; and the leader in charge and the subordinate who follows. The researcher expects mixed messages when he or she interviews a range of informants.

In Lewis' (2006) study of exotic dancers, three of her key informants worked with her research team as research assistants. Each of her key informants had experience in various positions in strip clubs and was able to give the researchers important information about how these types of organization operated.

ASKING QUESTIONS IN QUALITATIVE INTERVIEWS

In Chapter 9, we will discuss how structured interviewers required trained interviewers to ask the same questions to interviewees, that the questions were asked in the same order, and that the questions were asked in the same way. In qualitative interviewing, the interview takes on much different characteristics.

Kvale Question Types

Kvale (1996) has created a typology of nine different question types that can occur during a qualitative interview. According to Kvale, there are introducing questions, follow-up questions, probing questions, specifying questions, direct questions, indirect questions, structuring questions, interpreting questions, and silence. Box 1 provides examples of these question types from an actual interview.

Introducing questions are general opening questions where the interviewee is prompted to give his or her account of a situation or experience. For example, the interviewee might be asked, "Could you tell me about the first time you remember experiencing racism?" or "Do you remember a time when you experienced being treated differently because of your ethnicity?" It is anticipated that such questions will result in rich, detailed descriptions from the interviewee and will be at the core of answering the research question.

Follow-up questions are those that are asked by the interviewer to get additional description about topics just discussed by the interviewee. The goal of follow-up questions is to get additional details of events or experiences. Follow-up questions can simply be the interviewer repeating words that seem important in the interviewee's account. For example, if an interviewee says, "I felt that I was receiving a very negative reaction from the teacher," the interviewer could follow that up by repeating "Negative reaction?"—at which point the interviewee would more than likely elaborate on what he or she meant by this.

Probing questions are very much like probes used by structured interviewers. Sometimes, an interviewer will respond to a question with a yes or no answer, for example. Or the interviewee may give a very brief description of an event or experience. An interviewer can probe such answers by asking if the interviewee could give more details about the event or if he or she has any other examples that he or she could share. Probing questions are different from follow-up questions. With follow-up questions, the interviewer asks the interviewee to expand on a particular point; with probing questions, the interviewer asks for general expansion without indi-

Box 1 Kvale Question Types in an Actual Interview Transcript

Introducing question

- "I was just wondering how you think of bullying. When you think of it, what kinds of things come to your mind?

Follow-up questions

- "Ok, during what years in school did you feel this happened to you?"
- "And did they all last for the duration of the school year?"
- "So, when you would tell your teachers, you felt it worsened the situation?"

Probing questions

- "You didn't develop any interests . . . ?"
- "So it was all basically just physical abuse and . . ."
- "You didn't develop any interests . . . computer games or something?"

Specifying questions

- "And did they all last for the duration of the school year?"
- "What kinds of things would they do to you?"
- "What made you decide to start fighting back?"

Direct questions

- "Do you think having been bullied as a child has affected how you are today?"
- "So, when you think about those things, how do you say they affected your experience going to school?"
- "Do you think that having been abused by your peers has any effect on your ability to feel empathy?"

Indirect questions

- "Why do you think they picked you to harass?"

Structuring questions

- "OK. Do you think that . . . I know we've already talked about this, but do you think that bullying has had any effect on your personal relationships in your adult life?"
- "So, when you think about those things, how do you say they affected your experience going to school?"

Interpreting questions

- "From what you were saying, you weren't really safe at school?"
- "So you kind of take those things and make it into a game, then?"
- "So your closest friends basically weren't in school with you?"
- "So you think you'd outsmart them?"

Silence

- "Wow." (pause)
- "Interesting." (pause)

cating which part of the answer he or she is interested in getting more information about. A general probing question would be, "Could you tell me more about that?" or "Do you have any other examples?"

Specifying questions are those that the researcher asks to get more detailed descriptions about specific aspects of the interviewee's descriptions. In response to a statement, the interviewer may ask, "How did you react then?" Additionally, a simple probe of "uh-huh" can be used to encourage the interviewee to continue speaking.

Direct questions are usually introduced by the interviewer toward the end of the interview in order to address specific topics that may not have been covered yet—for example, "Have you ever left a job due to perceived racist treatment?"

Indirect questions are those that the interviews asks in order to get a sense of how the interviewee believes other people think, behave, or feel. The researcher must be careful in his or her interpretation of such answers because it must be clear whether the opinion expressed through indirect questioning is actually that of the interviewee or what she or he thinks that other people think. An example of an indirect question is, "How do you think other employees regard racist behaviours in the workplace?"

Structuring questions are used by the interviewer to keep the interview on track if it has gone off topic, or if he or she believes the answer to a question has been fully exhausted. Structuring questions are also used to keep the interview moving along. An example of a structuring question is, "I would now like to discuss another issue . . . "

How we interpret our interview data is at the heart of how we answer our research question. We listen to the interviewee, and his or her answers to our questions are filtered through our own minds. **Interpreting questions** help us to ensure that we are interpreting what the interviewee is saying as correctly as possible. We can ask the interviewee if our own interpretations are accurate by asking questions that begin, "From what I understand, you mean that . . ." or "From what you've told me, your experience can be summed up like . . ."

You may also ask your interviewee to make connections between different pieces of information that he or she has disclosed to you in the interview: e.g., "Do you see a connection between how you were bullied at school and the racism you experienced in the workplace?"

While "silence" is not technically a question, using **silence** can encourage interviewees to continue talking. You've probably noticed that among people that you do not know very well, there is a tendency for pauses in conversation to feel rather awkward. Typically, people try to fill in these gaps in the conversation. If researchers use the technique of allowing for pauses, it is likely that interviewees will continue talking and will elaborate on their answers.

Interview Guide

Keeping the research question in mind, the researcher should develop an **interview guide**. An interview guide is a list of questions that the researcher wants to ensure is covered during the course of the interview. It does not have to be followed chronologically but serves as a guide for the interviewer during the course of the interview. He or she can refer to the guide to introduce a structuring question, for example. When the interview is nearing its end, the researcher can also refer to the guide to make sure all the topics are covered. In Box 2, the interview used for the bullying study undertaken by one of the authors (Robson) is presented.

ADVANTAGES AND LIMITATIONS OF QUALITATIVE INTERVIEWS

Just like any data-collection technique, there are advantages and limitations of qualitative interviews. The discussion below, while not an exhaustive list of the pluses and minuses of this approach, summarizes some of the more vocal arguments for and against this particular data-collection technique.

From the Perspective of the Interviewee

One of the major advantages of qualitative interviews is that they allow the researcher to see the world from the perspective of his or her interviewees. The differences between the types of data a person collects in survey research methods and qualitative interviewing are very pronounced. While survey respondents are often required to answer from a fixed set of possible answers, the types of responses possible in qualitative interviewing are much more varied and allow the "voice" of the interviewee to be heard. Qualitative interviewees are free to respond in whatever way they wish, using whatever words they feel best express their accounts of experiences, feelings, or opinions. Reading research reports that use qualitative interviewing as a data-collection method is very engaging, and creates a sense of intimacy between the researcher, interviewees, and reader that cannot be captured in research reports full of statistics and graphs.

Box 2 Interview Guide for Research on the Long-Term Effects of Childhood Bullying

1. As you know, when I was looking for participants to volunteer for this project, I indicated that I was interested in talking to adults who had experienced bullying as children. You identified yourself to me as someone who had experienced this. In this interview, I am going to ask you some questions about your experiences as a child.
   To begin, could you just start by telling me what "bullying" means to you, as someone who experienced it?
2. During what years in school did you feel that your peers abused you?
3. How long did this last?
4. Why do you think you were picked on?
5. Who were the people that bullied you? Was there some kind of bullying group? A leader of it? What was your relationship to it?
6. Many people find talking about these events very difficult, but if you could, do you think you could tell me some of things that occurred to you in general?
7. Where did this bullying occur?
8. How did these events affect your overall school experience?
9. Did you ever do something to prevent these things from happening? Did you ever skip classes, stay home from school, or hide?
10. Did you ever do other things to help you forget about these experiences? What were they? Did it help?
11. Did you ever participate in bullying anyone? If so, what did you do? Why?
12. Did you ever have a "safe" environment of peers you could turn to? (i.e., if bullying occurred at school, did you have neighbourhood friends, for example?)
13. Did your parents or teachers ever try to intervene? If so, how? Did it help the situation?
14. Do you feel that parents or teachers improved or worsened the situation?
15. When did you begin to feel like you were no longer a victim of bullying?
16. What did you do during the time between being a victim and a nonvictim? How did you make the transition?
17. Was there a specific moment when you finally felt free of the bullies?
18. Did you receive any help from others in freeing yourself of them?
19. Now that you are an adult, do you think about your experiences as a victim of bullying?
20. Do you think that being bullied as a child has shaped who you are today? How?
21. Have you been able to recover feelings of self-worth? If not, do you think you ever will?
22. What kinds of effects has it had on your personal relationships?
23. Do you think that being bullied has influenced your ability to feel empathy toward others? Has it improved your ability to understand how others feel? If so, why do you think this is so?
24. Are there things that you do or have done in order to cope with the memories that resulted from being bullied as a child? What kinds of things? Have they helped?
25. Have you been able to forgive your bullies?
26. What would you do if your children were bullied?
27. What would you do if your child was a bully?
28. Is there anything you would like to add?

Data Rich with Description

The types of data collected in qualitative interviews are often rich with descriptive detail. Indeed, the more descriptive detail that is available in the data, the better. This is what qualitative interviewers are seeking when conducting an interview of this sort—that the interviewee will give plenty of description and explanation around the events, experiences, opinions, or feelings that he or she is describing. As a result, qualitative interview transcripts can be very long and the amount of data that needs to be analyzed even in a small study of ten people can be rather overwhelming.

The techniques involved in the analysis of qualitative interview data are very different from those used in structured survey interviews (where answers are converted to numbers and then analyzed statistically) and can be very time consuming.

Development of New Theories

Because researchers using qualitative interviewing usually have an inductive approach to theory (theory emerges from data), it is through qualitative interviewing (and other qualitative approaches) that new theories are developed using the grounded theory approach. Researchers look for themes to emerge from their interview data to create theories of social behaviour. While quantitative research is primarily concerned with testing and refining existing theories, data from qualitative interviews can contribute to the development of new theories where none had previously existed. This is particularly true in the case of studying hidden or marginalized groups on which there has been very little previous research (see Chapter 3).

Development of New Avenues of Research

As mentioned above, qualitative interviewing is a particularly valuable research method for studying understudied or previously unstudied populations. In addition to learning about groups about which very little information exists, qualitative interviewing data can create theories that can feed into the future research of other social scientists, including those who use quantitative techniques. Theories that are developed through the grounded theory approach can be used to later develop structured interview questions (i.e., surveys) where greater numbers of individuals from these populations can be studied, which can lead to a greater understanding of these individuals and more generalizable research findings.

Problems with Validity and Reliability

One of the biggest criticisms launched against qualitative interviewing as a method of data collection is that it encounters unique problems in relation to data validity and reliability. Sample sizes are usually small in comparison to those used in quantitative work, and therefore members of the research community question whether the results of such studies are actually applicable to a wider population beyond those in the interview sample.

The archiving of qualitative interview data so that it is available for scrutiny and further analysis by other members of the research community has been very rare. This is steadily changing, with more and more researchers depositing their data with established data banks (discussed below).

Lincoln and Guba (1985) have suggested that qualitative data be evaluated according to their trustworthiness. To increase the trustworthiness of qualitative interview data, researchers can ensure that their data is made available to other interested researchers who may want to reanalyze it. Researchers using qualitative interviews can also maximize the transferability (or generalizability) of their findings to populations beyond their immediate sample by selecting participants who are not entirely homogeneous. For example, in Lewis' study of exotic dancers, interviewees were chosen who were from a variety of ages and dance clubs. The interviewees also represented a variety of marital and motherhood statuses.

FOCUS GROUPS

The **focus group** is a special qualitative research technique in which people are informally "interviewed" in a group-discussion setting.[2] Sometimes, focus groups are called *group interviews*. Focus group research has grown over the past 20 years. It is also a particularly popular way for market researchers to test their products, although social scientists use the technique extensively. Many students in our methods courses have told us that they have been part of focus group research, often for market research purposes. Focus group topics might include public attitudes (e.g., race relations, workplace equality), personal behaviours (e.g., avoiding sexually transmitted infections), a new product (e.g., breakfast cereal), a political candidate, and so on.

The Focus Group Procedure

In very general terms, a researcher gathers together 6 to 12 people in a room with a moderator to discuss a few issues. The **moderator** is the person who leads the focus group and asks questions to prompt group discussion. Most focus groups last about 90 minutes. Often, focus groups are held in rooms equipped with audio and video recording facilities so that the sessions can be accurately transcribed afterward.

The Role of the Moderator

The moderator is trained to be nondirective and to facilitate free, open discussion by all group members. Moderators are also called *facilitators*. The moderator does not typically interfere in the discussion but starts the group off with the general topic. As in regular qualitative interviewing, the moderator follows an **interview guide** to make sure that all the topics related to answering the research question are answered. (See Box 3 for an example of an interview guide used in focus group research.)

The moderator's job is also to ensure that the conversation stays on track and does not veer too far off the topic determined by the research question. Moderating a focus group is a special skill that should not be underestimated. Effective moderators have extensive experience and are able to gently control several people at one time. The moderator is always aware in advance of the problems that might occur in the focus group and is trained to intervene in specific circumstances. For example, the moderator ensures that a single person does not dominate the discussion, and conversely can "probe" quieter individuals for their opinions. The moderator will also know how to effectively diffuse arguments between people. Because there are several people to manage concurrently, there are more possibilities for problems that the moderator will have to handle compared to one-on-one interviews.

Composition of Focus Groups

Who is in a focus group is largely determined by the research question at hand. In general, group members should be homogeneous but not include close friends or relatives. If researchers have reason to believe that opinions will vary by some kind of demographic factor, for example sex or ethnicity, then additional groups should be included where these characteristics are represented.

In a study of adolescents' perceptions of abuse in heterosexual dating relationships, Sears and associates (2006) recruited adolescents from four francophone and three anglophone schools in New Brunswick. The students were in Grades 9 and 11 and were predominantly white. The researchers used a total of 26 focus groups and divided them by sex so that 13 comprised only males and 13 comprised only females. In half of the groups, the focus of the discussion was on psychological abuse, while for the other half of the groups, the focus was on physical abuse. It is reasonable to think that perceptions of inappropriate behaviour in dating relationships would vary according to sex, so this division of participants by sex could identify whether this was the case. Focus groups also included only individuals who were in the same grade. Again, perceptions in appropriate dating behaviour among adolescents likely varies by age, so by keeping the participants in different groups according to grade, the researchers would be able to investigate if any differences in opinions emerged that could be attributed to maturity.

Box 3 The Interview Guide for a Focus Group

Just as in qualitative interviewing with a single participant, focus group interviews use interview guides to direct the discussion within a focus group. The interview guide serves not only to ensure that the questions necessary to answer the research question are asked, it also serves to give some structure to the focus group event and helps the moderator to steer the conversation back on track if it veers off topic.

In the example of adolescents' perception of inappropriate dating behaviour, the following interview guide was used to investigate the adolescents' perceptions of psychological abuse in heterosexual dating relationships:

Interview Guide

Psychological Abuse

1. Question
   We are meeting to talk about your views, opinions, and feelings about dating violence. To begin, when I talk about dating violence, what kinds of things do you think about?
2. Transition Question
   There is much talk these days about the kinds of violence that occur in relationships, including teenage dating relationships. Are there things that go on between dating teenagers that you would call violence?
3. Key Questions
   a. One type of problem that is talked about quite a bit is emotional abuse. This term is often associated with particular behaviours between partners, including insults, controlling, pressuring, and yelling at one's partner. Let's discuss these one at a time: (a) insulting one's partner, (b) controlling one's partner, (c) pressuring one's partner, (d) yelling at one's partner.
   b. How would you explain the finding that boys and girls are about equal in their use of emotional abuse in dating relationships?
   c. When emotional abuse does happen, is it important enough to do something about it? Why?
4. Ending Question
   Given everything we have discussed during the past hour or so, what stands out as most important to you? Is there any point you would have liked to comment on further?
5. Summary
   A summary of the group's main points is provided. Is my summary of our discussion accurate or are there important points that I have not mentioned?
6. Final Question
   Is there anything we have missed? Are there other questions that need to be discussed in reference to emotional abuse?

(From Sears et. al, 2006: 1204.)

The Number of Groups in a Focus Group Study

There is no set number of groups that a researcher interviews to answer his or her research question. The number of groups has a lot to do with the number of demographic factors that he or she wants to "control" or account for. In the example above, the researchers used a total of 26 groups, but this is atypical. In a typical study, a researcher uses four to six separate groups. The researchers studying adolescent attitudes to appropriate dating behaviour, however, had a number of characteristics by which they wanted to make their groups as homogeneous as possible: age, sex, and language. As well, they also had two research questions that they were investigating (psychological abuse and physical abuse), which essentially doubled the number of groups they required.

As with qualitative interviewing, time and money often dictate the number of interviews that a researcher can undertake. The grounded theory approach discussed in Chapter 3, however, should ideally be the yardstick by which researchers decide on their number of focus groups. Recall that theoretical sampling requires that the researcher continues to collect and analyze data until he or she reaches **theoretical saturation**—that is, the same themes and concepts keep emerging from the data. In other words, if similar themes appear after four groups, then data collection is complete. However, for some research questions, the number of groups may be much higher. It cannot be known in advance and the researcher must continue running focus group sessions until saturation is achieved. The analysis of both qualitative interview data and focus group data often follows the principles of grounded theory, where theory is developed from analysis of the data.

Researchers often combine focus groups with quantitative research, and the procedure has its own specific strengths and weaknesses (see Box 4).

Several years ago, one of the authors (Neuman) conducted an applied study on why parents and students chose a private high school. In addition to collecting quantitative survey data, he formed six focus groups, each with eight to ten students from the high school. A trained university student moderator asked questions, elicited comments from group members, and prevented one person from dominating discussions. The six groups were mixed sex and contained members of either one grade level or two adjacent grades (e.g., grade 10 and grade 11). Students discussed their reasons for attending the high school and whether specific factors were important. The author tape-recorded the discussions, which lasted about

Box 4 Advantages and Limitations of Focus Groups

Advantages

- The natural setting allows people to express opinions/ideas freely.
- Open expression among members of marginalized social groups is encouraged.
- People tend to feel empowered, especially in action-oriented research projects.
- Survey researchers are provided with a window into how people talk about survey topics.
- The interpretation of quantitative survey results is facilitated.
- Participants may query one another and explain their answers to each other.

Limitations

- A "polarization effect" exists (attitudes become more extreme after group discussion).
- Only one or a few topics can be discussed in a focus group session.
- A moderator may unknowingly limit open, free expression of group members.
- Focus groups produce the possibility of groupthink.
- It is not clear who the members of the focus group are representing—themselves, social groups, or their membership to the focus group.
- Focus group participants produce fewer ideas than in individual interviews.
- Focus group studies rarely report all the details of study design/procedure.
- Researchers cannot reconcile the differences that arise between individual-only and focus group-context responses.

45 minutes, then analyzed the tapes to understand what the students saw as important to their decisions. In addition, the data helped when interpreting the survey data.

Focus Groups as Social Groups

Unlike individual qualitative interviews, focus groups have the additional characteristic of being a group, and as social scientists, we know that groups have their own social dynamics. The study of the impact of the focus group itself on opinions expressed within them has become a topic of study in its own right. There are a number of concerns about focus groups that relate to their characteristic of using the group interview.

The first is whether or not the opinion expressed during the focus group is actually representative of any definable population. Hydén and Bülow (2006:306) ask

> Do the participants represent various groups outside the focus group, like professional or social groups; or do they just represent themselves as individuals; or do they act as members of the focus group? Further, do they talk and act as the same type of representatives throughout the entire focus group session, or is it possible that they shift positions?

Researching these questions themselves, the researchers concluded that focus group participants speak from many "voices," depending on how other members of the focus group are contributing and how they are being instructed by the moderator.

A related topic of concern about focus groups is tied to the notion of **groupthink**. The term *groupthink* was coined by prominent American sociologist William H. Whyte, who first used the term in *Fortune* magazine (March 1952, p. 114). The term generally refers to a person's natural desire to avoid conflict and lean toward group consensus, even when the opinion of the group does not reflect his or her own personal opinions. Obviously, this can be a major problem for the validity of focus group data. But how do we tackle the problem of groupthink if it is caused by human nature? MacDougall and Baum (1997) have recommended that researchers using focus groups employ the selective use of a devil's advocate to prevent groupthink from occurring. The term **devil's advocate** generally refers to a person whose role it is to argue against a dominant idea. MacDougall and Baum suggest that the role of the devil's advocate in a focus group would be someone who could introduce new questions and new ways of thinking into the group so as to prevent the tendency toward group conformity. The devil's advocate is not played by the moderator but rather by a pretrained member of the focus group who is identified at the outset as having this particular role.

QUALITATIVE DATA RESOURCES

Data archives and data centres that store quantitative data are available for researchers to analyze. There are also similar resources for researchers interested in analyzing previously collected qualitative data. In the United Kingdom, there is a data archive that was especially created for qualitative data—the Qualitative Data Service, or Qualidata. Qualidata is part of the larger UK Data Archive (located at the University of Essex), which is home to many quantitative data sources as well. Adding qualitative data has been a major project for Qualidata for the past several years, and they continue to encourage qualitative researchers to archive their research materials there. Qualidata has a searchable online catalogue, which can be found through the Qualidata's main webpage at www.qualidata.essex.ac.uk.

In recent years the efforts to archive qualitative data have really begun to materialize into publicly accessible archives. The amount of work that has to go into converting qualitative material into archivable materials is appreciable: audio materials must be digitized, notes scanned in, and interviews fully transcribed. The Qualidata is, by far, the most established of all of these efforts. Other notable qualitative data archives include the following:

The International Consortium for Political and Social Research (ICPSR) at the University of Michigan, a resource for quantitative data, also has a limited number of qualitative data sources. There is a searchable catalogue that can be accessed at www.icpsr.umich.edu/ICPSR.

The Center for Oral History and Cultural Heritage at the University of Mississippi has over 1000 transcripts of interviews with individuals about the history of Mississippi. Oral histories are very much like qualitative interviews, although their focus is on accounts of history—either cultural history or personal history. Many of the transcripts from this project can be viewed online at www.usm.edu/msoralhistory.

The University of Mississippi also stores oral history transcripts related to a project called The Civil Rights Documentation Project, which can be found at www.usm.edu/crdp.

Another project that publishes its transcript data online is the results of the First Black Women at Virginia Tech History Project. As the name suggests, the project chronicles the experiences of the first African American women to study, work, or teach at Virginia Tech, which highlight the role of race and gender in the mid- 1960s. Selected transcripts are available at http://spec.lib.vt.edu/blackwom.

The Online Archive of California (http://findaid.oac.cdlib.org/texts) also has a searchable catalogue with links to transcribed oral histories. Major topics at this archive include oral histories of Japanese Americans interned during the Second World War and Black History in California.

Texas Tech University also has an online archive of oral histories associated with the Oral History Project of The Vietnam War. The interviews are fully transcribed and available online at www.vietnam.ttu.edu/oralhistory/interviews/index.htm and often have associated streaming-audio files to accompany them.

As part of the Oral History Archives of World War II, the Korean War, the Vietnam War, and the Cold War, Rutgers University has a large collection of interviews available online at http://oralhistory.rutgers.edu.

As this list of resources suggests, there is no one body that organizes the archiving of qualitative data in Canada. As technological innovations increase the ease at which these data can be digitized, however, the numbers of secondary sources available online are increasing. It is just a matter of time before major North American data archives initiate a major effort in archiving these materials.

QUALITATIVE RESEARCH RESOURCES

The Qualitative Research and Resource Centre at York University (affiliated with the Department of Sociology) was created to promote the practice of qualitative research methods. The Centre has a range of research facilities available, including focus group facilities (including audio and videotaping), transcription equipment, qualitative data analysis software, expert consultation, and an extensive collection of reference materials. More information about the Centre can be found at www.arts.yorku.ca/soci/qrrc/index.html.

The International Institute for Qualitative Methodology is an interdisciplinary institute affiliated with the Faculty of Nursing at the University of Alberta. It has onsite facilities for individuals to use and also hosts a number of workshops and seminars over the course of the year. The Institute also has an extensive onsite library. See www.uofaweb.ualberta.ca/iiqm.

CONCLUSION

In this chapter, you learned about qualitative interviewing and the qualitative interviewing process (finding interviewees, preparing an interview guide, asking questions). You also learned about the group interview, or focus group. You learned about how the composition of groups is decided, how the number of groups is determined, and the moderator's role within the group. Both qualitative interviewers and focus group researchers begin data analysis and theorizing during the data-collection phase.

The analysis of qualitative interview data and focus group data is very time consuming and requires that the researcher go through the transcriptions of the session to look for emerging theories.

Good qualitative interviewing and focus group moderation require a distinct set of skills. The best qualitative interviewers are able to make interviewees feel at ease and able to talk freely about the topic at hand, even if it is a sensitive area. Qualitative interviewers must have the ability to listen and establish a good rapport with their interviewees, and they also much display the correct amounts of sensitivity and empathy for the people that have agreed to be in their study.

Field research often uses qualitative interviewing to supplement observational data. Qualitative interviewing and field research are distinct approaches in their own right, but often field researchers use qualitative interviews "in the field" with individual members of the group they are studying in order to enhance their interpretation of characteristics of the group.

KEY TERMS

devil's advocate *178*
direct questions *171*
focus group *174*
follow-up questions *170*
groupthink *178*
incentive *168*
indirect questions *171*
informant *169*
interpreting questions *172*
interview guide *172*
introducing questions *170*
moderator *175*
probing questions *170*
qualitative interview *165*
selective transcription *169*
silence *172*
specifying questions *171*
structuring questions *171*
theoretical saturation *177*

ENDNOTES

1. Field research informants are discussed in Dean and associates (1969), Kemp and Ellen (1984), Schatzman and Strauss (1973), Spradley (1979a:46–54), and Whyte (1982).
2. For a discussion of focus groups, see Bischoping and Dykema (1999), Churchill (1983:179–184), Krueger (1988), Labaw (1980:54–58), and Morgan (1996).

CHAPTER 8

Case Studies

Taken from: *Qualitative Research Methods for the Social Sciences*, Seventh Edition, by Bruce L. Berg

THE NATURE OF CASE STUDIES

Case study method is sometimes criticized as being somewhat of a *weak sister* among social science methods, in spite of the fact that it is quite extensively used across a number of different disciplines (Swanson & Holton, 2005). Nonetheless, as a methodology, it has sometimes been considered less rigorous and less systematic than other forms of research. The case study method is defined and understood in various ways. Some sources define the case study method as an attempt to systematically investigate an event or a set of related events with the specific aim of describing and explaining this phenomenon (see, e.g., Bromley, 1990). Bogdan and Biklen (2003, p. 54) define case study as "a detailed examination of one setting, or a single subject, a single depository of documents, or one particular event" (see also Gomm, Hammersley, & Foster, 2000; Yin, 2003a). Hagan (2006, p. 240) simply defines the case study method as "in-depth, qualitative studies of one or a few illustrative cases." Previous editions of my own book (see Berg, 2004, 2007) define case study as a method involving systematically gathering enough information about a particular person, social setting, event, or group to permit the researcher to effectively understand how the subject operates or functions. Interestingly, Creswell (2007) points out that Stake (2005a) actually suggests that case study research is not really a methodology at all; rather, Stake (2005a) claims that it involves a choice in what is to be studied. Taken together, these various definitions and explanations suggest that case study is an approach capable of examining simple or complex phenomenon, with units of analysis varying from single individuals to large corporations and businesses; it entails using a variety of lines of action in its data-gathering segments and can meaningfully make use of and contribute to the application of theory (Creswell, 2007; Yin, 2003a).

Given the scope of the method, case studies can be rather pointed in their focus or approach a broad view of life and society. For example, an investigator may confine his or her examination to a single aspect of an individual's life such as studying a medical student's actions and behaviors in a medical school. Or the investigator might attempt to assess the social life of an individual and his or her entire background, experiences, roles, and motivations that affect his or her behavior in society. Extremely rich, detailed, and in-depth information characterize the type of information gathered in a case study. In contrast, the often extensive large-scale survey research data may seem somewhat superficial in nature (Champion, 2006).

Many qualitative investigators use the case study approach as a guide to their research. By concentrating on a single phenomenon, individual, community, or institution, the researcher aims to uncover the manifest interaction of significant factors characteristic of this phenomenon, individual, community, or institution. But, in addition, the researcher is able to capture various nuances, patterns, and more latent elements that other research approaches might overlook. The case study method tends to focus on holistic description and explanation; and, as a general statement, any phenomenon can be studied by case study methods (Gall, Borg, & Gall, 1995, 1998). Others suggest a type of *embedded case study* approach (Hancock & Algozzine, 2006; Scholz & Tietje, 2002). Embedded case studies involve looking at one case study but including several levels or units of analysis. In other words, this case study approach includes examination of a subunit, or several subunits, of the overall focus of the research. For instance, let's say a given case study seeks to explore a single organization such as a community hospital; the analysis might additionally include focus and outcomes about clinical services, staff in specialty nursing units (such as ICU, CCU, etc.), or other staff employed by the hospital. In a study examining post-prison community reintegration, several programs involved in the overall effort of some agency might be evaluated, and this too would represent a kind of embedded case study (Yin, 2003a).

The case study method is not a new style of data gathering and analytic technique. The fields of medicine and psychology, for example, by their very nature, require physicians and psychologists to examine patients case by case. Case studies are commonly used in business, information systems, and law curricula to help students bridge the gap between foundational studies and practice. The use of diaries and biographies, a popular method among some feminist and other social scientists, approaches the case study method, as does ethnobiography (Hesse-Biber & Yaiser, 2004; Reinharz, 1992). In education, case studies abound and include studies of unique people and programs, as well as special programming (Herreid, 2006; McLeod, 1994; Stake, 1995). In fact, case studies by certain social scientists represent classical research efforts in sociology and criminology. Consider, for example, Edward Sutherland's (1937) *The Professional Thief*; Clifford R. Shaw's (1930) *The Jack Roller*; Robert Bogdan's (1974) lengthy life history/autobiography, *Being Different: The Autobiography of Jane Fry*; and Rettig, Torres, and Garrett's (1977) *Manny: A Criminal Addict's Story.*

THEORY AND CASE STUDIES

Yin (2003a) indicates that there has been a revived interest in the role of theory and case studies. Interestingly, a cursory review of the literature suggests that a vigorous renewal of this interest appears to occur in the areas of business, marketing, and information systems, as well as in the social sciences (see, e.g., Alexander & Bennett, 2005; Fernandez, 2005; Woodside & Wilson, 2004). Typically, although not exclusively, case study methods are found in the literature associated with theory building rather than theory testing Woodside & Wilson, 2004), but some sources suggest the utility of case study strategies in theory testing or in combining both theory development and testing (Alexander & Bennett, 2005; Woodside & Wilson, 2004).

How does the case study method inform theory? Case studies can provide a kind of deep understanding of phenomenon, events, people, or organizations, similar to Geertz's (1973) notion of "thick description." In essence, case studies open the door to the processes created and used by individuals involved in the phenomenon, event, group, or organization under study (Weick, 1995). Sensemaking is the manner by which people, groups, and organizations make sense of stimuli with which they are confronted how they frame what they see and hear, how they perceive and interpret this information, and how they interpret their own actions and go about solving problems and interacting with others.

Yin (2003a, pp. 4–5) tends to endorse a theory-before-research model and indicates that theory development prior to the collection of case study data can be important for the following reasons:

- It can assist selecting the cases to be studied and whether to use a single-case or multiple-case design.
- It helps the researcher specify what is being explored when undertaking exploratory case studies.
- It aids in defining a complete and appropriate description when undertaking descriptive case studies.
- It can stimulate rival theories when undertaking explanatory cases studies.
- It can support generalizations the researcher may seek to make to other cases.

Others, however, argue that case studies can be used to generate theory (grounded theory) and follow a pattern similar to theory after research. Fernandez (2005, p. 47) cites Eisenhardt (1989, pp. 546–547), for instance, arguing that using case data to build grounded theory has three major strengths:

1. Theory building from case studies is likely to produce theory; this is so because "creative insight often arises from juxtaposition of contradictory or paradoxi-

cal evidence" (p. 546). The process of reconciling these accounts using the constant comparative method forces the analyst to a new gestalt, unfreezing thinking and producing "theory with less research bias then theory built from incremental studies or armchair, axiomatic deduction" (p. 546).
2. The emergent theory "is likely to be testable with constructs that can be readily measured and hypotheses that can be proven false" (p. 547). Because of the close connection between theory and data, it is likely that the theory can be further tested and expanded by subsequent studies.
3. "resultant theory is likely to be empirically valid" (p. 547). This is so because a level of validation is performed implicitly by constant comparison, questioning the data from the start of the process. "This closeness can lead to an intimate sense of things . . . that often produces theory which closely mirrors reality" (p. 547).

In other words, theory can be uncovered and informed as a consequence of the data collection and interpretations of this data made throughout the development of the case study—hence, a grounded theory case study. What might this process look like? The researcher would start with some sort of research idea, then develop a plan—including whether to use a single- or multiple-case approach—identify the location of the study (in what group or organization), determine how access is to be obtained, and consider what data-collection strategies to use. Once access is obtained, data must be collected; as the data is collected, the researcher constantly considers what is being unearthed, making comparisons between information (data) collected and assessments with other researchers (to assure unbiased interpretations and analysis) and the literature. The investigator then must reflect on the information collected and the problem(s) initially addressed to deliberate over what the findings mean and what their implications may be. Finally, the researcher can offer some theoretical implications for whatever problems or issues were being explored, described, or explained in the study. Figure 8.1 offers a visualization of this model of developing grounded theory through the case study method.

THE INDIVIDUAL CASE STUDY

As in any other research situation, one must determine how broad an area of social life will be covered. In most research, this decision is largely dictated by the research question and the nature of the research problem under investigation. When examining an individual case study, a similar type of assessment must be undertaken. In some instances, a single lengthy interview may yield sufficient information to produce answers to the research question(s). In other circumstances, several interviews may be necessary, and these may require supplementation by field notes during direct observation, copies of journal or diary entries from the subject, or other forms of documentation.

Several reasons may make it necessary for a broader, more sweeping investigation. First, the research may itself focus on a broad area such as the subject's relationships in a particular group, necessitating that the group also be examined. It would be unwise, for example, to examine various aspects of changes in the quality of life of hemodialysis patients without also examining how family members perceive changes occurring in the family group itself.

A second reason for broadening a case study is the realization that all the aspects of an individual's social life are interconnected and often one of them cannot be adequately understood without consideration of the others.

■ **Figure 8.1** Developing Grounded Theory through the Case Study Method

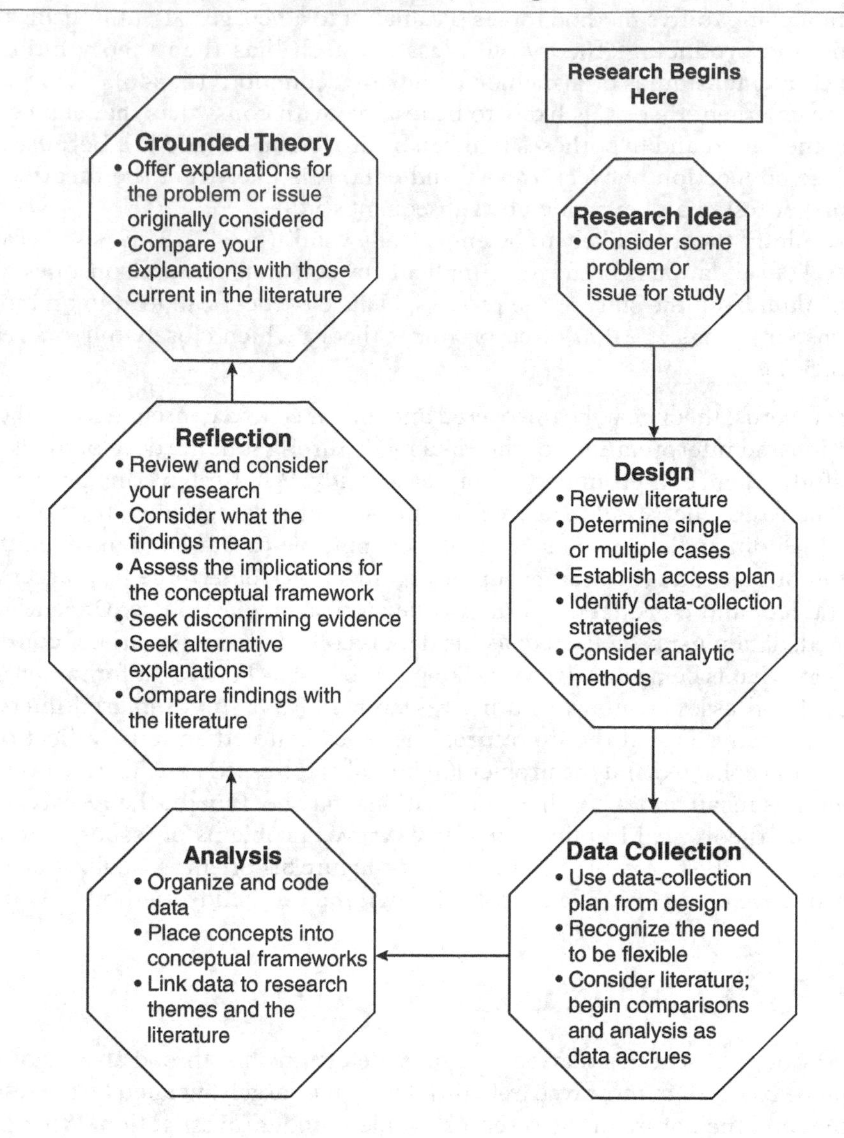

The Use of Interview Data

The particular focus of a study might be a woman's adjustment to becoming "the boss" in some predominantly male corporate organization. In order to fully understand this adjustment, it would be helpful to learn how she adjusts to changes in other situations, perhaps adjustments in her home or among friends or in social organizations. These may be accomplished using various standard techniques of interviewing to collect data.

Of these areas of additional study, perhaps the most generally rewarding to the subject is found to be her home and family background. The physical aspects of the home—its size, its neatness or disorder, its furnishings, indications of intellectual, athletic, or aesthetic interests such as books, pictures, records, sporting equipment, and the like—can all be of value in this case study. Even evidence of social support from family members should be observed and included in the research. Obviously, to understand the subject's adjustments to the work role, the researcher must observe the subject in the work site and speak with various coworkers. It should be likewise obvious that to understand the subject's role in her family, several visits to the home will be necessary. Also it may be fruitful to speak with (interview) various family members (husband, children, or other relatives in the home) who can provide various pieces of background information and insights.

Unless an individual is exceptionally isolated, he or she is likely to have some role in the neighborhood community. Some people enjoy an elevated position of respect and position in their business, social, or political life. Others may hold no particularly high level of respect but function as participants in various activities. Still others may actually be social outcasts. This type of information could be very useful for understanding how a woman business executive adjusts to her new position in the company. Visits to neighbors, various social organizations to which the subject may be a member, conversations with local tradespersons, and the subject's clergy person all may supply useful information.

Yin (1998) identifies five researcher skills associated with conducting good case studies. To a large extent, these are similar and an extension to three skills offered by Merriam (2001). The first is an *inquiring mind* and the willingness to ask questions before, during, and after data are collected, as well as to constantly challenge oneself about why something appears to have happened or be happening. The second is the ability of the investigator to *listen*, to include *observation* and *sensing* in general, and to assimilate large amounts of new information without bias. Third is *adaptability* and *flexibility* to handle unanticipated events and to change data-collection strategies if they do not seem to be functioning effectively and to use alternative sources of data that may be more fruitful. Fourth is a thorough *understanding of the issues* being studied in order not merely to record data but to interpret and react to these data once collected. The researcher must be able to determine, for example, if different sources of data are adequate or if additional sources are required. The fifth quality is *unbiased interpretation of the data*. Yin suggests that a good test for bias is the degree to which the researcher is open to contradictory findings. He recommends reporting preliminary findings to colleagues, who may offer alternative explanations that would require further investigation. This notion is similar to a researcher taking an intellectual risk by providing sufficient information for others to replicate the research and potentially to find contradictory results.

Throughout the preceding paragraphs, the chief suggestions for information (data) gathering have been the use of interviews and observation. As implied earlier, however, it is often also useful to supplement this information with various documentary sources. You should, therefore, be familiar with the possible use of records concerning the life course of the subject. These may include birth, marriage, divorce, property ownership, and educational records of the subject. They may additionally include an assortment of other more or less official documents such as police actions, court records, evaluations of work records, and so forth. All of these official documents are potentially valuable sources of information in a case study.

The Use of Personal Documents

Personal documents involve any written record created by the subject that concerned his or her experiences. The common types of documents classified under this label include autobiographies, diaries and journals, letters, and memos written by a subject in a research investigation. In addition, and given the extent to which people use photographic and video equipment today, these items may also serve as categories of personal documents.

Autobiographical documents include a considerable variety of written material. They may be published or unpublished documents, cover an entire life span, or focus on only a specific period in a subject's life or even a single event. Even a written confession to a crime may be seen by some researchers as a type of autobiographical document.

Diaries and journals also may arise in a number of varieties. A diary may be kept with no purpose in mind beyond the writer's personal desire to maintain a record of daily events. It may be maintained in order to provide some therapeutic release or as a kind of log and chronological listing of daily events during new experiences, such as an internship. Or a diary or journal may be created at the specific request of a researcher as a contribution to some study. In the latter case, one may consider the material in a solicited document.

Letters provide an intriguing view into the life of the author. Typically, letters are not created by the writer with the intention of having them used by a researcher. As a result, they frequently reflect the inner worlds of the writer. They may record the writer's views, values, attitudes, and beliefs about a wide variety of subjects. Or they may describe the writer's deepest thoughts about some specific event or situation about which they report. Historians have long seen the value of letters to document events during the past. Letters written by military figures and politicians, for example, may allow researchers to better understand how and why certain battles have been fought. Letters written by criminals such as serial killers and bombers provide insight into how the culprit thinks and potential explanations for their actions. Letters are simply replete with potentially useful information.

For example, Elizabeth Roberson (1998) explored the letters of Eli Landers, a young Confederate soldier (see also Wasta & Lott, 2002). Landers wrote letters from the battlefield to his mother and sister that express his emotional views of the war, his personal losses, as well as specific details about the Civil War.

The use of memoranda has become commonplace in virtually all work settings. Memos may contain strictly work-related information or casual insider jokes and communications. They may reflect the tone and atmosphere of a work setting as well as the potential level of anxiety, stress, and morale of the writer. Moreover, they may even show the research aspects of the workplace culture or work folkways. Also, they may contain information relevant to understanding the general organizational communications network used in the setting, the leadership hierarchy, various roles present in the setting, and other structural elements. Thus, a memorandum can provide an interesting self-disclosing aspect of its creator, or various aspects of a group or organization, when used as data in a case study.

Photographic and video equipment has become so inexpensive that many people now regularly record their lives and the lives of their family members in this manner. It becomes important, therefore, for researchers to consider how these items may illustrate various aspects of the subject's life and relationships. This may involve stepping back and examining the entire photograph in terms of what it shows in general; it may include an examination of the expressions of people shown in the picture; it could involve consideration of where the picture or video was taken or recorded such as on a vacation, in the home, or at a party; or it may involve determination of the reason the photograph or video was created—as a simple family record to commemorate some situation, to have as a keepsake, to document some event or situation, and so forth.

The literal value of personal documents as research data is frequently underestimated in contemporary research texts and courses. Although such documents are certainly extremely subjective in their nature, these data should not be viewed as a negative or, in this case, even as some sort of limitation or shortcoming. It is the very fact that these documents do reflect the subjective views and perceptions of their creators that makes them useful as data in a case study. It is precisely through this subjectivity that these documents provide information and insight about the subject that might not be captured through some other more pedestrian data-collection technique.

INTRINSIC, INSTRUMENTAL, AND COLLECTIVE CASE STUDIES

Stake (1994, 1995) suggests that researchers have different purposes for studying cases. He suggests that case studies can be classified into three different types: *intrinsic, instrumental*, and *collective*.

Intrinsic case studies are undertaken when a researcher wants to better understand a particular case. It is not undertaken primarily because it represents other cases or because it illustrates some particular trait, characteristic, or problem. Rather, it is because of its uniqueness or ordinariness that a case becomes interesting (Creswell, 1998, 2007; Stake, 1994, 2000). The role of the researcher is not to understand or test abstract theory or to develop new or grounded theoretical explanations; instead, the intention is to better understand intrinsic aspects of the particular child, patient, criminal, group, organization, or whatever the case may be (Munhall, 2007).

Instrumental case studies provide insights into an issue or refine a theoretical explanation, making it more generalizable (Creswell, 2002; Stake, 1994). In an instrumental case study, the researcher focuses on a single issue or concern and identifies a single case to illustrate this item of focus or concern (Creswell, 2007). In these situations, the case actually becomes of secondary importance, playing a supportive role (Denzin & Lincoln, 2005). It serves only a supportive role, a background against which the actual research interests will play out. Instrumental case studies are often investigated in depth, and all aspects and activities are detailed but not simply to elaborate the case per se. Instead, the intention is to help the researcher better understand some external theoretical question, issue, or problem. Instrumental case studies may or may not be viewed as typical of other cases. However, the choice of a particular case for study is made because the investigator believes that his or her understanding about some other research interest will be advanced.

Stake (1994, 2000) also points out that because researchers often have multiple interests, there is no solid line drawn between intrinsic and instrumental studies. In fact, a kind of "zone of combined purpose separates them" (Stake, 1994, p. 237).

Collective case studies (Stake, 1994, 2000, 2005b) are also known as multiple-case studies, cross-case studies, comparative case studies, and contrasting case studies (Gerring, 2006; Merriam, 2001). Thus, collective case studies involve extensive study of several instrumental cases, intended to allow better understanding, insight, or perhaps improved ability to theorize about a broader context. Yin (2003a) argues that multiple cases may be selected in order to try replicating insights found in individual cases or to represent contrasting situations. Regardless of one's purpose, Yin (2003a, p. 46) indicates that multiple-case studies are frequently "considered more compelling, and the overall study is therefore regarded as more robust."

CASE STUDY DESIGN TYPES

According to Yin (1994, 2003a) and Winston (1997), there are several appropriate designs for case studies: exploratory, explanatory, and descriptive. These three approaches consist of either single- or multiple-case studies in which the cases studied are actual replications, not sampled cases. Each approach is discussed next.

Exploratory Case Studies

When conducting exploratory case studies, fieldwork and data collection may be undertaken before defining a research question. This type of study may be seen as a prelude to a large social scientific study—which may or may not in itself involve case studies. From my perspective, the study must have some type of organizational framework that has been designed prior to beginning the research. Others, however, such as Yin (2003b, p. 6), suggest that these exploratory cases studies may follow "intuitive paths often perceived by others as sloppy." But, as Yin (2003b) also points out, the goal in these studies may be justified when they seek to discover theory through directly observing some social phenomenon in its natural and raw form. The sort of exploratory study may be useful as a pilot study, for example, when planning a larger, more comprehensive investigation (Swanson & Holton, 2005).

Explanatory Case Studies

Explanatory case studies are useful when conducting causal studies. Particularly in complex studies of organizations or communities, one might desire to employ multivariate cases to examine a plurality of influences. This might be accomplished using a pattern-matching technique suggested by Yin and Moore (1988). *Pattern-matching* is a situation in which several pieces of information from the same case may be related to some theoretical proposition.

Descriptive Case Studies

Descriptive case explorations require that the investigator present a descriptive theory, which establishes the overall framework for the investigator to follow throughout the study. What is implied by this approach is the formation and identification of a viable theoretical orientation before enunciating research questions (Hancock & Algozzine, 2006; Munhall, 2007). The investigator must also determine before beginning the research what exactly the unit of analysis in the study will be.

In creating formal designs for case-study investigations, Yin (1994, p. 20) recommends five component elements:

- Study questions
- Study propositions (if any are being used) or theoretical framework
- Identification of the unit(s) of analysis
- The logical linking of the data to the propositions (or theory)
- The criteria for interpreting the findings

A study's *questions* are generally directed toward *how* and *why* considerations, and their articulation and definition are the first task of the researcher. Sometimes, the study's *propositions* derive from these how and why questions and assist in developing a theoretical focus. Not all studies will have propositions. An exploratory study, rather than having propositions, may have a stated purpose or criteria that will provide guidance and a kind of operating framework for the case study to follow. The *unit of analysis* defines what the case study is focusing on (what the case is), such as an individual, a group, an organization, a city, and so forth. *Linkages between the data and the propositions* (or theory) *and the criteria for interpreting the findings*, according to Yin (1994), typically are the least developed aspects of case studies.

Jason Jensen and Robert Rodgers (2001, pp. 237–239) offer a typology of types of case studies:

1. **Snapshot case studies.** Detailed, objective studies of one research entity at one point in time. Hypothesis testing by comparing patterns across subentities (e.g., comparing departments within the case study agency).
2. **Longitudinal case studies.** Quantitative and/or qualitative studies of one research entity at multiple time points.
3. **Pre–post case studies.** Studies of one research entity at two time points separated by a critical event. A critical event is one that on the basis of a theory under study would be expected to impact case observations significantly.

4. **Patchwork case studies.** A set of multiple case studies of the same research entity, using snapshot, longitudinal, and/or pre–post designs. This multi-design approach is intended to provide a more holistic view of the dynamics of the research subject.
5. **Comparative case studies.** A set of multiple case studies of multiple research entities for the purpose of cross-unit comparison. Both qualitative and quantitative comparisons are generally made.

Unfortunately, researchers do not always have good theories to work with, in a given situation, particularly when exploring cutting-edge issues. In these situations, a logic model, or what Patton (2001) calls a "theory of action," may be developed. This *theory of action* will define how the researcher expects an intervention, event, or process to take a case from one situation to the next. In effect, this theory of action will define the issues to be examined during the analysis, thereby providing linkages among the research question(s), propositions, and analytic criteria.

THE SCIENTIFIC BENEFIT OF CASE STUDIES

The scientific benefit of the case study method lies in its ability to open the way for discoveries (Shaughnessy, Zechmeister, & Zechmeister, 2008). It can easily serve as the breeding ground for insights and even hypotheses that may be pursued in subsequent studies. However, whenever one considers the scientific value of case studies, two points should be addressed. First, does this procedure involve too many subjective decisions made by the investigator to offer genuinely objective results? Second, does this method offer information that can be seen as useful beyond the individual case? In other words, can findings be generalized? Let us consider each of these questions separately.

Objectivity and the Case Method

Objectivity is a somewhat elusive term. For some researchers, it involves the creation of analytic strategies in an almost sterile environment. Often, qualitative research of any type is viewed as suspect when questions of objectivity are asked. However, objectivity is actually closely linked with reproducibility (replication). The question is not simply whether or not an individual researcher has made some subjective decision regarding how the researcher should progress or how the study is designed. These types of considerations are regularly undertaken by all who undertake social scientific research—whether quantitatively or qualitatively oriented.

When a quantitative methodologist identifies which level of statistical acceptability he or she will use for some statistical measure, it is often a subjective decision. For example, let's say the researcher sets the level at .05. Does that alter the findings when it is statistically significant at the .05 level but not at the .001 level? Thus, objectivity apparently lies someplace other than in the kinds of decisions made by a researcher regarding various aspects of the research strategy.

For many researchers, objectivity rests on the ability of an investigator to articulate what the procedures are so that others can repeat the research if they so choose. It also has the effect of placing the researcher's professional ego on the line. It is akin to saying, "Here is how I did my research, and here are my results. If any reader has questions or challenges, go out and repeat the study to see what you find." From this perspective, case studies, like any other research procedure, require that the investigator clearly articulate what areas have been investigated and through what means. If someone has doubts about the findings, he or she is free to replicate the research with a similar case subject.

If the investigator's findings and analysis were correct, subsequent research will corroborate this. If the research produced from a case study is faulty, in error, or inaccurate, this too will be shown by subsequent research. As in any scientific research, findings from a single study are seldom accepted immediately without question and additional research investigations. In this light, case methods are as objective as any other data-collection and analysis strategies used by social scientists.

Generalizability

The second concern addresses the question of generalizability. For many, the question is not even necessary to ask. This is because there is clearly a scientific value to gain from investigating some single category of individual, group, or event simply to gain an understanding of that individual, group, or event. For those with a more positivist orientation who have concern about generalizing to similar types of individuals, groups, or events, case methods are still useful and, to some extent, generalizable.

When case studies are properly undertaken, they should not only fit the specific individual, group, or event studied but also generally provide understanding about similar individuals, groups, and events. This is not to say that an explanation for why one gang member is involved in drug dealing immediately informs us about why *all* drug-dealing gang members are also involved in this activity. It does, however, suggest an explanation for why some other gang members are likely to be involved in these behaviors. The logic behind this has to do with the fact that few human behaviors are unique, idiosyncratic, and spontaneous. In fact, if this were the case, the attempt to undertake any type of survey research on an aggregate group would be useless. In short, if we accept the notion that human behavior is predictable—a necessary assumption for all behavior science research—then it is a simple jump to accept that case studies have scientific value. "It is the task of the researcher to determine what it is he or she is studying; that is, of what is this a case?" (Bogdan & Biklen, 1992, p. 66).

CASE STUDIES OF ORGANIZATIONS

Case studies of organizations may be defined as the systematic gathering of enough information about a particular organization to allow the investigator insight into the life of that organization. This type of study might be fairly general in its scope, offering approximately equal weight to every aspect of the organization. For instance, you might conduct an organizational case study on a police department. During this investigation, you may examine subunits such as the juvenile division, traffic division, criminal investigations, homicide, and so forth. The results will be a thorough understanding about how the agency operates and how each subunit fits together and serves the overall objectives of the organization. For instance, Barbara French and Jerry Stewart (2001) examined how contemporary law enforcement agencies engage in new organizational practices that focus on empowering line officers, encouraging teamwork, and creating an atmosphere conducive for participative management.

On the other hand, you may specialize, during an organizational case study, by placing particular emphasis on a specific area or situation occurring in the organization. For example, Susan Slick (2002) explored how a learning community operated among a cohort of graduate students in education attending a special pilot master's degree program at the University of Wisconsin-Stevens Point campus. This learning community fostered group goals and values for working and learning collaboratively.

There are a number of reasons that a particular organization may be selected for a case study. For example, a researcher may undertake a case study of an organization to illustrate the way certain administrative systems operate in certain types of organizations. Or the researcher may be interested in accessing how decisions are made in certain types of organizations or even how communications networks operate. In fact, the case method is an extremely useful technique for researching relationships, behaviors, attitudes, motivations, and stressors in organizational settings.

CASE STUDIES OF COMMUNITIES

A *community* can be defined as some geographically delineated unit within a larger society. Such a community is small enough to permit considerable cultural (or subcultural) homogeneity, diffuse interactions and relationships between members, and to produce a social identification by its members. The literal application of the term *community* is somewhat fluid. However, it does not actually include an entire nation, a state, or even a large city. It would, however, include a particular neighborhood within a city such as a Chinatown, a Little Italy, or the Jewish section, or even an enclave of Amish farmers all residing within a 4- or 5-mile radius.

A case study of a community may, however, address a larger entity by placing its focus on a smaller unit of analysis, perhaps a group or social institution such as the Catholic church. Linkogle (1998), for example, undertook a study of the role of popular religion in social transformation in Nicaragua from 1979 to 1998. He examined some general issues around popular religion in Latin America and its relationship to the practice and pronouncements of the Catholic church. Linkogle's primary focus was how popular religious practices may impact and shape gender and political and religious identities.

Case studies of communities can be defined as the systematic gathering of enough information about a particular community to provide the investigator with understanding and awareness of what things go on in that community; why and how these things occur; who among the community members take part in these activities and behaviors, and what social forces may bind together members of this community. As with other variations of case studies, community case studies may be very general in their focus, offering approximately equal weight in all of the various aspects of community life. Or community case studies may specifically focus on some particular aspect of the community or even some phenomenon that occurs within that community. For example, you may consider a community in general, such as examining an Amish farming community. In such an investigation, you may be interested in the various daily routines of members as well as their social interactions. You might consider any political ideologies that predominate among members of the community and how these affect behaviors among both insiders and outsiders, and so forth. On the other hand, you may be interested in a particular phenomenon occurring within the Amish community. For instance, you may be interested in how social control mechanisms operate in the community. Will the community handle an errant youth who may have shoplifted some petty item such as a magazine, or will the outside, non-Amish community's laws apply? Of course, if you investigate the latter phenomenon, to remain a community case study, this exploration would have to be undertaken against the backdrop of the life of the community. Although there are other styles of research that might explore a particular question in isolation from the background of the community, these would not be accurately called case studies.

Robert and Helen Lynd's study of Middletown, first published in 1929, stands as a classic example of how community case studies operate. This research was among the earliest systematic studies of an American community where the purpose was primarily to develop a scientific understanding of community life.

Data Collection for Community Case Studies

The various data-collection strategies used in community case studies are, for the most part, those already discussed in this chapter. However, in addition, community case studies frequently make use of maps. These may include existing maps used for various human ecological purposes, as well as maps created by the researcher in order to indicate physical and social proximity of items and events occurring in the community.

Human ecological concerns have long been important foci in community case studies. Human ecology is concerned with the interrelationships among people in their spatial setting and physical environment. An ecological focus might consider how various physical environmental elements shape the lives of people in a community or the life of the community itself. Do rivers block a community's expansion? Are railroad tracks or major highways located close enough to encourage industry in a community? Has a coal mine played out and closed down, sending hundreds of community members to unemployment, and so forth? Maps are frequently the basic tool necessary for a consideration of such ecological concerns in a community case study.

Community Groups and Interests

In a manner similar to how one might break down a community into its constituent physical parts, its human members too can be divided into groups. These groups may be classified in a number of different ways. For example, there may be different ethnic groups all residing in the same community. Although some ethnic groups are sufficiently large enough and homogeneously located to constitute a community in themselves, this is not always the case. In many communities several distinct ethnic groups reside in both physical and social proximity but manage to retain their own individual ethnic identity. In some cases, the ethnic groups may retain certain of their distinctive ethnic features but merge or assimilate into their surrounding social life. In such a case, one would need to consider this ethnic group both as a thing apart from the community, as well as an element of the larger community.

The study of any group in a community begins much as you would begin any research study, namely, in the library. The logical place to begin considering community groups is in published sources. In addition, community case studies may include an examination of census data, local histories, newspaper accounts of group activities and events, any official records of various organizations related to the group or community, and so on. As with other variations of case studies, interviews may provide useful information or even historical explanations for various groups or the presence of certain conditions in the community. Researchers even use fairly traditional strategies of observation to learn about groups in a community. Observations may include consideration of the types of homes and housing in the community, places used for leisure or amusement, schools and religious institutions in the community, and so forth.

Interest groups are another way you might divide up the inhabitants of a community. In this case, you may include street gangs, various social clubs or organizations in the community (Boy and Girl Scouts, YMCAs, Little Leagues, Bowling Leagues, and so forth), lodges and fraternal organizations, political clubs, business associations, and the like. Membership in many of these interest groups is rather ephemeral and transient. Even the more stable of interest groups are likely to lack the continuity of ethnic or religious groups. Direct observation of these interest groups, along with interviews with members, is probably the best general method for studying these kinds of groups.

Social classes may also be viewed as a type of grouping that allows the researcher to divide up a community. Although you might argue about what division labels to actually use as categories of class, some categorical labeling schema can be conceived. In keeping with the community case study mode, you could consider how members of each social class operate in the community and how these categories fit together to form the entire community.

In essence, there are numerous ways of grouping together people of a community for the purpose of systematically exploring life in that community. Community case studies are large-scale undertakings. They may be time-consuming and expensive if they are to be comprehensive. The community is a sufficiently large segment of society that it permits a wide and diverse array of social phenomena to occur and to be observed. Although not as popular in recent years as they were during the 1930s and 1960s, especially in areas of urban sociology and urban ecology, community case studies continue to offer an important and valuable means to understanding communities and community members.

TRYING IT OUT

Suggestion 1

Using available archival information located in your school's library and various administrative offices, conduct an organizational case study of your college or university. This will involve using at least some historical tracings.

Suggestion 2

Select an adult relative and conduct a modified case study. For this project, examine only the roles and behaviors of the individual during some aspect of his or her life. This may be during school activities, work life, home life, and so forth. Limit the time on this project to one week of data collection. Remember, this is simply practice, not actual research.

REFERENCES

Alexander, G. L., & Bennett, A. (2005). *Case Studies and Theory Development in the Social Sciences*. Cambridge, MA: MIT Press.

Berg, B. (2004). *Qualitative Research Methods for the Social Sciences* (5th ed.). Boston: Allyn and Bacon.

Berg, B. (2007). *Qualitative Research Methods for the Social Sciences* (6th ed.). Boston: Allyn and Bacon.

Bogdan, R. (1974). *Being Different: The Autobiography of Jane Fry*. New York: John Wiley and Sons.

Bogdan, R. C., & Biklen, S. K. (1992). *Qualitative Research for Education*. Boston: Allyn and Bacon.

Bogdan, R. C., & Biklen, S. K. (2003). *Qualitative Research for Education* (4th ed.). Boston: Allyn and Bacon.

Bromley, D. B. (1990). Academic contributions to psychological counseling: A philosophy of science for the study of individual cases. *Counseling Psychology Quarterly 3*(3), 299–307.

Champion D. J. (2006). *Research Methods for Criminal Justice and Criminology* (3rd ed.). Upper Saddle River, NJ: Pearson/Prentice Hall.

Creswell, J. W. (1998). *Qualitative Inquiry and Research Design: Choosing Among Five Traditions*. Thousand Oaks, CA: Sage.

Creswell, J. W. (2002). *Educational Research: Planning, Conducting, and Evaluating Quantitative and Qualitative Research*. Upper Saddle River, NJ: Merrill Prentice Hall.

Creswell, J. W. (2007). *Qualitative Inquiry and Research Design: Choosing Among Five Traditions* (2nd ed.). Thousand Oaks, CA: Sage.

Denzin, N. K., & Lincoln, Y. S. (2005). *The Sage Handbook of Qualitative Research* (3rd ed.). Thousand Oaks, CA: Sage.

Eisenhardt, K. (1989). Building theories from case study research. *Academy of Management Review 14*(4), 532–550.

Fernandez, W. (2005). The grounded theory method and case study data in IS research: Issues and design. In D. N. Hart & S. D. Gregor (Eds.), *Information Systems Foundations: Constructing and Criticising*. Canberra, Australia: Australian National University E-Press, pp. 43–60.

French, B., & Stewart, J. (2001). Organizational development in a law enforcement environment. *The FBI Law Enforcement Bulletin 70*(9), 14.

Gall, M. G., Borg, W. R., & Gall, J. P. (1995). *Educational Research and Introduction*. New York: Longman Publishing Group.

Gall, M. G., Borg, W. R., & Gall, J. P. (1998). *Applying Educational Research*. New York: Longman Publishing Group.

Geertz, C. (1973). *The Interpretation of Culture*. New York: Basic Books.

Gerring, J. (2006). *Case Study Research: Principles and Practices*. New York: Cambridge University Press.

Gomm, R., Hammersley, M., & Foster, P. (Eds.). (2000). *Case Study Method*. Thousand Oaks, CA: Sage.

Hagan, F. E. (2006). *Research Methods in Criminal Justice and Criminology* (7th ed.). Boston: Allyn and Bacon.

Hancock, D. R., & Algozzine, R. (2006). *Doing Case Study Research: A Practical Guide for Beginning Researchers*. New York: Teachers College Press.

Herreid, C. F. (2006). *Start With a Story: The Case Method of Teaching College Science*. Arlington, VA: National Science Teachers Association.

Hesse-Biber, S. N., & Yaiser, M. L. (2004). *Feminist Perspectives on Social Research*. New York: Oxford University Press.

Jensen, J. L., & Rodgers, R. (2001). Cumulating the intellectual gold of case study research. *Public Administration Review 61*(2), 236–246.

Linkogle, S. (1998). The revolution and the Virgin Mary: Popular religion and social change in Nicaragua. *Sociological Research Online 3*(2). Available online at www.socresonline.org.uk/socresonline/3/2/8.html.

Lynd, R. S., & Lynd, H. M. (1929). *Middletown*. New York: Harcourt, Brace.

McLeod, B. (1994). *Language and Learning: Educating Linguistically Diverse Students*. Albany, NY: SUNY Press.

Merriam, S. B. (2001). *Qualitative Research and Case Study Applications in Education*. San Francisco: Jossey-Bass.

Munhall, P. L. (2007). *Nursing Research: A Qualitative Perspective* (4th ed.). Boston, MA: Jones & Bartlett Publications.

Patton, M. Q. (2001). *Utilization-Focused Evaluation: The New Century Text* (4th ed.). Thousand Oaks, CA: Sage.

Reinharz, S. (1992). *Feminist Methods in Social Research*. New York: Oxford University Press.

Rettig, R. P., Torres, M. J., & Garrett, G. R. (1977). *Manny: A Criminal Addict's Story*. Boston: Houghton Mifflin.

Roberson, E. W. (1998). *Weep Not for Me Dear Mother: The Letters of Eli Landers*. New York: Pelican.

Scholz, R. W., & Tietje, O. (2002). *Embedded Case Study Methods: Integrating Quantitative and Qualitative Knowledge*. Thousand Oaks, CA: Sage.

Shaughnessy, J. J., Zechmeister, E. B., & Zechmeister, J. S. (2008). *Research Methods in Psychology* (8th ed.). New York: McGraw-Hill.

Shaw, C. R. (1930). *The Jack Roller*. Chicago: University of Chicago Press.

Slick, S. (2002). Teachers are enthusiastic participants in a learning community. *The Clearing House 75*(4), 198–202.

Stake, R. E. (1994). Case studies. In N. K. Denzin & Y. S. Lincoln (Eds.), *Handbook of Qualitative Research*. Thousand Oaks, CA: Sage.

Stake, R. E. (1995). *The Art of Case Study Research*. Thousand Oaks, CA: Sage.

Stake, R. E. (2000). Case studies. In N. K. Denzin & Y. S. Lincoln (Eds.), *Handbook of Qualitative Research* (2nd ed., pp. 435–454). Thousand Oaks, CA: Sage.

Stake, R. E. (2005a). Qualitative case studies. In N. K. Denzin & Y. S. Lincoln (Eds.), *Handbook of Qualitative Research* (2nd ed., pp. 443–466). Thousand Oaks, CA: Sage.

Stake, R. E. (2005b). *Multiple Case Study Analysis*. New York: Gilford Publications Incorporated.

Sutherland, E. H. (1937). *The Professional Thief*. Chicago: University of Chicago Press.

Swanson, R. A., & Holton III, E. F. (2005). *Research in Organizations: Foundations and Methods of Inquiry*. San Francisco, CA: Berrett-Koehler Publishers, Inc.

Wasta, S., & Lott, C. (2002). Eli Landers: Letters of a Confederate soldier. *Social Education 66*(2), 122–130.

Weick, K. E. (1995). *Sensemaking in Organizations*. Thousand Oaks, CA: Sage.

Winston, T. (July 1997). An introduction to case study. *The Qualitative Report 3*(2). Available online at www.nova.edu/ssss/QR/QR3-2/tellis1.html.

Woodside, A. G., & Wilson, E. J. (2004). Case study research methods for theory building. *Journal of Business & Industrial Marketing 18*(6/7), 493-508.

Yin, R. K. (1994). *Case Study Research: Design and Methods* (2nd ed.). Beverly Hills, CA: Sage.

Yin, R. K. (1998). The abridged version of case study research: Design and method. In L. Bickman & D. J. Rog (Eds.), *Handbook of Applied Social Research Methods*. Thousand Oaks, CA: Sage.

Yin, R. K. (2003a). *Case Study Research* (3rd ed.). Thousand Oaks, CA: Sage.

Yin, R. K. (2003b). *Applications of Case Study Research* (2nd ed.). Thousand Oaks, CA: Sage.

Yin, R., & Moore, G. (1988). The use of advanced technologies in special education. *Journal of Learning Disabilities 20*(1), 60.

CHAPTER 9

Survey Research

Taken from: *Basics of Social Research: Qualitative and Quantitative Approaches,* Canadian Edition, by W. Lawrence Neuman and Karen Robson

INTRODUCTION

Someone hands you a sheet of paper full of questions. The first reads: "I would like to learn your opinion of the Neuman and Robson research methods textbook. Would you say it is (a) well organized, (b) adequately organized, or (c) poorly organized?" You probably would not be shocked by this. It is a kind of survey, and most of us are accustomed to surveys by the time we reach adulthood.

The survey is the most widely used data-gathering technique in sociology, and it is used in many other fields, as well. In fact, surveys are almost too popular. People sometimes say, "Do a survey" to get information about the social world, when they should be asking, "What is the most appropriate research design?" Despite the popularity of surveys, it is easy to conduct a survey that yields misleading or worthless results. Good surveys require thought and effort.

All surveys are based on the professional social research survey. In this chapter, you will learn the main ingredients of good survey research, as well as the limitations of the survey method.

Research Questions Appropriate for a Survey

Survey research developed within the positivist approach to social science. The survey asks many people (called *respondents*) about their beliefs, opinions, characteristics, and past or present behaviour.

Surveys are appropriate for research questions about self-reported beliefs or behaviours. They are strongest when the answers people give to questions measure variables. Researchers usually ask about many things at one time in surveys, measure many variables (often with multiple indicators), and test several hypotheses in a single survey.

Although the categories overlap, the following can be asked in a survey:

1. **Behaviour.** How frequently do you brush your teeth? Did you vote in the last city election? When did you last visit a close relative?
2. **Attitudes/beliefs/opinions.** What kind of job do you think the mayor is doing? Do you think other people say many negative things about you when you are not there? What is the biggest problem facing the nation these days?
3. **Characteristics.** Are you married, cohabiting, single, divorced, separated, or widowed? Do you belong to a union? What is your age?
4. **Expectations.** Do you plan to buy a new car in the next 12 months? How much schooling do you think your child will get? Do you think the population in this town will grow, shrink, or stay the same?
5. **Self-classification.** Do you consider yourself to be liberal, moderate, or conservative? Into which social class would you put your family? Would you say you are religious or not religious?
6. **Knowledge.** Who was elected mayor in the last election? About what percentage of the people in this city are non-white? Is it legal to own a personal copy of Karl Marx's *Communist Manifesto* in this country?

Researchers warn against using surveys to ask "why?" questions (e.g., Why do you think crime occurs?). "Why?" questions are appropriate, however, if a researcher wants to discover a respondent's subjective understanding or informal theory (i.e., the respondent's own view of "why" he or she acts a certain way). Because few respondents are fully aware of the causal factors that shape their beliefs or behaviour, such questions are not a substitute for the researcher developing a consistent causal theory of his or her own that builds on the existing scientific literature.

An important limitation of survey research is that it provides data only of what a person or organization says, and this may differ from what he or she actually does. This is illustrated by Rubenson and associates (2006). The researchers found that 83 percent of persons responding to the Canadian Election survey had said that they had voted in the 2000 federal election. The actual official voter turnout, however, was substantially lower—approximately 61 percent. In other words, 83 percent of people said they voted—but only about 61 percent *actually did.*

THE LOGIC OF SURVEY RESEARCH

What Is a Survey?

Survey researchers sample many respondents who answer the same questions. They measure many variables, test multiple hypotheses, and infer temporal order from questions about past behaviour, experiences, or characteristics. For example, years of schooling or a respondent's race are prior to current attitudes. An association among variables is measured with statistical techniques. Survey researchers think of alternative explanations when planning a survey, measure variables that represent alternative explanations (i.e., control variables), then statistically examine their effects to rule out alternative explanations.

Survey research is often called *correlational.* Survey researchers use questions as control variables to approximate the rigorous test for causality that experimenters achieve with their physical control over temporal order and alternative explanations. In other words, control variables are other characteristics that the researcher accounts for so as to minimize the possibility of spuriousness.

Steps in Conducting a Survey

The survey researcher follows a deductive approach. He or she begins with a theoretical or applied research problem and ends with empirical measurement and data analysis. Once a researcher decides that the survey is an appropriate method, basic steps in a research project can be divided into the substeps outlined in Figure 9.1.

In the first phase, the researcher develops an instrument—a survey questionnaire or interview schedule—that he or she uses to measure variables. Respondents read the questions themselves and mark answers on a *questionnaire.* An **interview schedule** is a set of questions read to the respondent by an interviewer, who also records responses. To simplify the discussion, we will use only the term *questionnaire.*

A survey researcher conceptualizes and operationalizes variables as questions. He or she writes and rewrites questions for clarity and completeness, and organizes questions on the questionnaire based on the research question, the respondents, and the type of survey. (The types of surveys are discussed later.)

When preparing a questionnaire, the researcher thinks ahead to how he or she will record and organize data for analysis. He or she pilot-tests the questionnaire with a small set of respondents similar to those in the final survey. If interviewers are used, the researcher trains them with the questionnaire. He or she asks respondents in the pilot test whether the questions were clear and explores their interpretations to see if his or her intended meaning was clear. The researcher also draws the sample during this phase.

After the planning phase, the researcher is ready to collect data. This phase is usually shorter than the planning phase. He or she locates sampled respondents in person, by telephone, or by mail. Respondents are given information and instructions on completing the questionnaire or interview. The questions follow, and there is a simple stimulus/response or question/answer pattern. The researcher accurately records answers or responses immediately after they are given. After all respondents complete the questionnaire and are thanked, he or she organizes the data and prepares them for statistical analysis.

Survey research can be complex and expensive, and it can involve coordinating many people and steps. The administration of survey research requires organization

■ **Figure 9.1** Steps in the Process of Survey Research

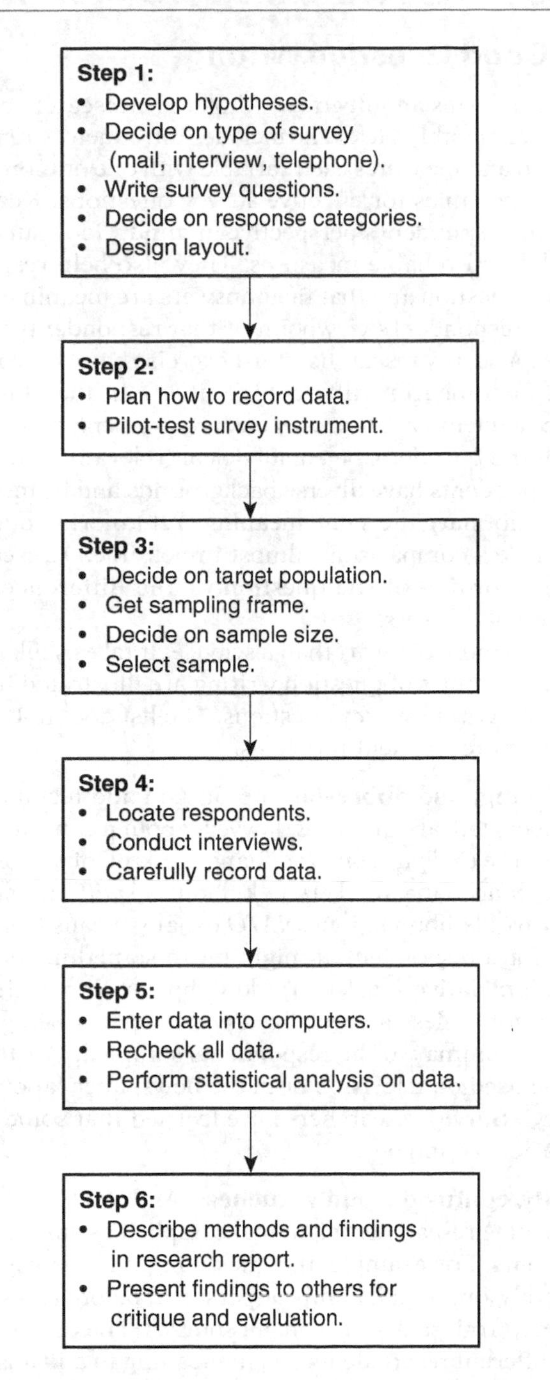

and accurate record keeping. The researcher keeps track of each respondent, questionnaire, and interviewer; for example, he or she gives each sampled respondent an identification number which also appears on the questionnaire. He or she then checks completed questionnaires against a list of sampled respondents. Next, the researcher reviews responses on individual questionnaires, stores original questionnaires, and transfers information from questionnaires to a format for statistical analysis. Meticulous bookkeeping and labelling are essential. Otherwise, the researcher may find that valuable data and effort are lost through sloppiness.

CONSTRUCTING THE QUESTIONNAIRE

Principles of Good Question Writing

A good questionnaire forms an integrated whole. The researcher weaves questions together so they flow smoothly. He or she includes introductory remarks and instructions for clarification and measures each variable with one or more survey questions.

There are three principles for effective survey questions: Keep it clear, keep it simple, and keep the respondent's perspective in mind. Good survey questions give the researcher valid and reliable measures. They also help respondents feel that they understand the question and that their answers are meaningful. Questions that do not mesh with a respondent's viewpoint or that respondents find confusing are not good measures. A survey researcher must exercise extra care if the respondents are heterogeneous or come from different life situations than his or her own.

Researchers face a dilemma. They want each respondent to hear exactly the same questions, but will the questions be equally clear, relevant, and meaningful to all respondents? If respondents have diverse backgrounds and frames of reference, the same wording may not have the same meaning. Yet tailoring question wording to each respondent makes comparisons almost impossible. A researcher would not know whether the wording of the question or the differences in respondents accounted for different answers.

Question writing is more of an art than a science. It takes skill, practice, patience, and creativity. The principles of question writing are illustrated in the following 12 things to avoid when writing survey questions. The list does not include every possible error, only the more frequent problems.

1. **Avoid jargon, slang, and abbreviations.** Jargon and technical terms come in many forms: Plumbers talk about *snakes,* lawyers about a contract of *uberrima fides,* psychologists about the *Oedipus complex.* Slang is a kind of jargon within a subculture—for example, marijuana smokers talk about a *spliff* and snowboarders talk about a *fakie.* Also avoid abbreviations. *NATO* usually means North Atlantic Treaty Organization, but for a respondent, it might mean something else (National Auto Tourist Organization, Native Alaskan Trade Orbit, or North African Tea Office). Avoid slang and jargon unless a specialized population is being surveyed. Target the vocabulary and grammar to the respondents sampled. For the general public, this is the language used on television or in the newspaper (about an eighth-grade reading vocabulary). Survey researchers have learned that some respondents may not understand basic terminology.

2. **Avoid ambiguity, confusion, and vagueness.** Ambiguity and vagueness plague most question writers. A researcher might make implicit assumptions without thinking of the respondents. For example, the question, "What is your income?" could mean weekly, monthly, or annual; family or personal; before taxes or after taxes; for this year or last year; from salary or from all sources. The confusion causes inconsistencies in how different respondents assign meaning to and answer the question. The researcher who wants before-tax annual family income for last year must explicitly ask for it.[1]

Another source of ambiguity is the use of indefinite words or response categories. For example, an answer to the question, "Do you jog regularly? Yes _____ No _____," hinges on the meaning of the word *regularly.* Some respondents may define *regularly* as every day, others as once a week. To reduce respondent confusion and get more information, be specific—ask whether a person jogs "about once a day," "a few times a week," "once a week," and so on. (See Box 1 on improving questions.)

3. **Avoid emotional language.** Words have implicit connotative as well as explicit denotative meanings. Words with strong emotional connotations can colour how respondents hear and answer survey questions.

Box 1 Improving Unclear Questions

Here are three survey questions written by experienced professional researchers. They revised the original wording after a pilot test revealed that 15 percent of respondents asked for clarification or gave inadequate answers (e.g., don't know). As you can see, question wording is an art that may improve with practice, patience, and pilot testing.

Original Question	**Problem**	**Revised Question**
Do you exercise or play sports regularly?	What counts as exercise?	Do you do any sports, physical activities, or exercise, including walking, on a regular basis?
What is the average number of days each week you have butter?	Does margarine count as butter?	The next question is just about butter—not including margarine. How many days a week do you have butter?
[Following question on eggs] What is the number of servings in a typical day?	How many eggs is a serving? What is a typical day?	On days when you eat eggs, how many eggs do you usually have?

	Responses to Question		**Percentage Asking for Clarification**	
	Original	*Revision*	*Original*	*Revision*
Exercise question (% saying "yes")	48%	60%	5%	0%
Butter question (% saying "none")	33%	55%	18%	13%
Egg question (% saying "one")	80%	33%	33%	0%

Source: Adapted from Fowler (1992).

Use neutral language. Avoid words with emotional "baggage," because respondents may react to the emotionally laden words rather than to the issue. For example, the question, "What do you think about a policy to pay murderous terrorists who threaten to steal the freedoms of peace-loving people?" is full of emotional words (*murderous, freedoms, steal,* and *peace*).

4. **Avoid prestige bias.** Titles or positions in society (e.g., prime minister, expert) carry prestige or status. Issues linked to people with high social status can colour how respondents hear and answer survey questions, resulting in **prestige bias**. Avoid associating a statement with a prestigious person or group. Respondents may answer on the basis of their feelings toward the person or group rather than addressing the issue. For example, saying, "Most doctors say that cigarette smoke causes lung disease for those near a smoker. Do you agree?" affects people who want to agree with doctors. Likewise, a question such as, "Do you support the prime minister's policy regarding Kosovo?" will be answered by respondents who have never heard of Kosovo on the basis of their view of the prime minister.

5. **Avoid double-barrelled questions.** Make each question about one and only one topic. A **double-barrelled question** consists of two or more questions joined together. It makes a respondent's answer ambiguous. For example, if asked, "Does this company have pension and health insurance benefits?" a respondent at a company with health insurance benefits only might answer either yes or no. The response has an ambiguous meaning, and the researcher cannot be certain of the respondent's intention. A researcher who wants to ask about the joint occurrence of two

things—for example, a company with both health insurance and pension benefits—should ask two separate questions.

6. **Do not confuse beliefs with reality.** Do not confuse what a respondent believes with what you, the researcher, measure. A respondent may think that a relationship exists between two variables but this is not an empirical measurement of variables in a relationship. For example, a researcher wants to find out if students rate teachers higher who tell many jokes in class. The two variables are "teacher tells jokes" and "rating the teacher." The wrong way to approach the issue is to ask students, "Do you rate a teacher higher if the teacher tells many jokes?" This measures whether or not students *believe* that they rate teachers based on joke telling; it does not measure the empirical relationship. The *correct* way is to ask two separate empirically based questions: "How do you rate this teacher?" and "How many jokes does the teacher tell in class?" Then the researcher can examine answers to the two questions to determine if there is an association between them. People's beliefs about a relationship among variables are distinct from an actual empirical relationship.

7. **Avoid leading questions.** Make respondents feel that all responses are legitimate. Do not let them become aware of an answer that the researcher wants. A **leading (or loaded) question** is one that leads the respondent to choose one response over another by its wording. There are many kinds of leading questions. For example, the question, "You don't smoke, do you?" leads respondents to state that they do not smoke.

Loaded questions can be stated to get either positive or negative answers. For example, "Should the mayor spend even more tax money trying to keep the streets in top shape?" leads respondents to disagree, whereas "Should the mayor fix the potholed and dangerous streets in our city?" is loaded for agreement.

8. **Avoid asking questions that are beyond respondents' capabilities.** Asking something that few respondents know frustrates respondents and produces poor-quality responses. Respondents cannot always recall past details and may not know specific factual information. For example, asking an adult, "How did you feel about your brother when you were six years old?" is probably worthless. Asking respondents to make a choice about something they know nothing about (e.g., a technical issue in foreign affairs or an internal policy of an organization) may result in an answer, but one that is unreliable and meaningless. When many respondents are unlikely to know about an issue, use a full-filter question form (to be discussed).

Phrase questions in the terms in which respondents think. For example, few respondents will be able to answer, "How many litres of gasoline did you buy last year for your car?" Yet respondents may be able to answer a question about gasoline purchases for a typical week, which the researcher can multiply by 52 to estimate annual purchases.[2]

9. **Avoid false premises.** Do not begin a question with a premise with which respondents may not agree, then ask about choices regarding it. Respondents who disagree with the premise will be frustrated and not know how to answer. For example, the question, "The post office is open too many hours. Do you want it to open four hours later or close four hours earlier each day?" leaves those who either oppose the premise or oppose both alternatives without a meaningful choice.

A better question explicitly asks the respondent to assume a premise is true, then asks for a preference. For example, "Assuming the post office has to cut back its operating hours, which would you find more convenient, opening four hours later or closing four hours earlier each day?" Answers to a hypothetical situation are not very reliable, but being explicit will reduce frustration.

10. **Avoid asking about intentions in the distant future.** Avoid asking people about what they might do under hypothetical circumstances far in the future. Responses are poor predictors of behaviour removed far from their current situa-

tion or far in the future. Questions such as, "Suppose a new grocery store opened down the road in three years. Would you shop at it?" are usually a waste of time. It is better to ask about current or recent attitudes and behaviour. In general, respondents answer specific, concrete questions that relate to their experiences more reliably than they do those about abstractions that are beyond their immediate experiences.

11. **Avoid double negatives.** Double negatives in ordinary language are grammatically incorrect and confusing. For example, "I ain't got no job" logically means that the respondent does have a job, but the second negative is used in this way for emphasis. Such blatant errors are rare, but more subtle forms of the double negative are also confusing. They arise when respondents are asked to agree or disagree with a statement. For example, respondents who *dis*agree with the statement, "Students should not be required to take a comprehensive exam to graduate" are logically stating a double negative because they *disagree* with *not* doing something.

12. **Avoid overlapping or unbalanced response categories.** Make response categories or choices mutually exclusive, exhaustive, and balanced. *Mutually exclusive* means that response categories do not overlap. Overlapping categories that are numerical ranges (e.g., 5–10, 10–20, 20–30) can be easily corrected (e.g., 5–9, 10–19, 20–29). The ambiguous verbal choice is another type of overlapping response category—for example, "Are you satisfied with your job or are there things you don't like about it?" *Exhaustive* means that every respondent has a choice—a place to go. For example, asking respondents, "Are you working or unemployed?" leaves out respondents who are not working but do not consider themselves unemployed (e.g., full-time homemakers, people on vacation, students, people with disabilities, retired people, etc.). A researcher first thinks about what he or she wants to measure and then considers the circumstances of respondents. For example, when asking about a respondent's employment, does the researcher want information on the primary job or on all jobs? On full-time work only or both full- and part-time work? On jobs for pay only or on unpaid or volunteer jobs as well?

Keep response categories *balanced.* A case of unbalanced choices is the question, "What kind of job is the mayor doing: outstanding, excellent, very good, or satisfactory?" Another type of unbalanced question omits information—for example, "Which of the five candidates running for mayor do you favour: Eugene Oswego or one of the others?" Researchers can balance responses by offering polar opposites. It is easy to see that the terms *honesty* and *dishonesty* have different meanings and connotations. Asking respondents to rate whether a mayor is highly, somewhat, or not very *honest* is not the same as asking them to rate the mayor's level of *dishonesty.* Unless there is a specific purpose for doing otherwise, it is better to offer respondents equal polar opposites at each end of a continuum.[3] For example, "Do you think the mayor is very honest, somewhat honest, neither honest nor dishonest, somewhat dishonest, or very dishonest?" (See Table 9.1.)

Aiding Respondent Recall

Recalling events accurately takes more time and effort than the five seconds that respondents have to answer survey questions. Also, one's ability to recall accurately declines over time. Studies in hospitalization and crime victimization show that although most respondents can recall significant events that occurred in the past several weeks, half are inaccurate a year later.

Survey researchers recognize that memory is less trustworthy than was once assumed. It is affected by many factors—the topic, events occurring simultaneously and subsequently, the significance of an event for a person, situational conditions (question wording and interview style), and the respondent's need to have internal consistency.

■ **Table 9.1** Summary of Survey Question Writing Pitfalls

Things to Avoid	Not Good	A Possible Improvement
1. Jargon, slang, abbreviations	Did you drown in brew until you were totally wasted last night?	Last night, approximately how much beer did you drink?
2. Vagueness	Do you eat out often?	In a typical week, about how many meals do you eat at a restaurant, cafeteria, or other eating establishment?
3. Emotional language 4. Prestige bias	"The respected Gomery Commission documents that millions of our tax dollars were being completely wasted through poor procurement practices, bad management, sloppy bookkeeping, defective contract management, personnel abuses, favouritism, and other wasteful practices. Is cutting pork barrel spending and eliminating government misspending of public funds a top priority for you?"	How important is it to you that the House of Commons adopt measures to reduce government waste? Very Important Somewhat Important Neither Important or Unimportant Somewhat Unimportant Not Important At All
5. Double-barrelled questions	Do you support or oppose raising social welfare benefits and increased spending for the military?	Do you support or oppose raising social welfare benefits? Do you support or oppose increasing spending on the military?
6. Beliefs as real	Do you think highly educated people smoke less?	What is your education level? Do you smoke cigarettes?
7. Leading questions	Did you do your patriotic duty and vote in the last election for mayor?	Did you vote in last month's mayoral election?
8. Issues beyond respondent capabilities	Two years ago, how many hours did you watch TV every month?	In the past two weeks, approximately how many hours do you think you watched TV on a typical day?
9. False premises	When did you stop beating your girlfriend/boyfriend?	Have you ever slapped, punched, or hit your girlfriend/boyfriend?
10. Distant future intentions	After you graduate from college, get a job, and are settled, will you invest a lot of money in the stock market?	Do you have definite plans to put some money into the stock market within the coming two months?
11. Double negatives	Do you disagree with those who do not want to build a new city swimming pool?	There is a proposal to build a new city swimming pool. Do you agree or disagree with the proposal?
12. Unbalanced responses	Did you find the service at our hotel to be Outstanding, Excellent, Superior, or Good?	Please rate the service at our hotel: Outstanding, Very Good, Adequate, or Poor.

The complexity of respondent recall does not mean that survey researchers cannot ask about past events; rather, they need to customize questions and interpret results cautiously. Researchers should provide respondents with special instructions and extra thinking time. They should also provide aids to respondent recall, such as a fixed time frame or location references. Rather than ask, "How often did you attend a sporting event last winter?" they should say, "I want to know how many sporting events you attended last winter. Let's go month by month. Think back to December. Did you attend any sporting events for which you paid admission in December? Now, think back to January. Did you attend any sporting events in January?"

Types of Questions and Response Categories

Threatening Questions. Survey researchers sometimes ask about sensitive issues or issues that respondents may believe threaten their presentation of self, such as questions about sexual behaviour, drug or alcohol use, mental health problems, or deviant behaviour. Respondents may be reluctant to answer the questions or to answer completely and truthfully. Survey researchers who wish to ask such questions must do so with great care and must be extra cautious about the results[4] (see Table 9.2).

Table 9.2 Threatening Questions and Sensitive Issues

Topic	Percentage Very Uneasy
Masturbation	56
Sexual intercourse	42
Use of marijuana or hashish	42
Use of stimulants and depressants	31
Getting drunk	29
Petting and kissing	20
Income	12
Gambling with friends	10
Drinking beer, wine, or liquor	10
Happiness and well-being	4
Education	3
Occupation	3
Social activities	2
General leisure	2
Sports activity	1

Given that this list was published in 1980, would you expect some of these to have changed? Do you think that some of these items may have moved up or down on this list? Not all things that were considered "taboo" topics in 1980 are still as stigmatized.

Source: Adapted from Bradburn and Sudman (1980:68).

Threatening questions are part of a larger issue of self-presentation and ego protection. Respondents often try to present a positive image of themselves to others. They may be ashamed, embarrassed, or afraid to give truthful answers, or find it emotionally painful to confront their own actions honestly, let alone admit them to other people. They may underreport or self-censor reports of behaviour or attitudes they wish to hide or believe to be in violation of social norms. Alternatively, they may overreport positive behaviours or generally accepted beliefs (social desirability bias is discussed later).

People are likely to underreport having an illness or disability (e.g., cancer, mental illness, venereal disease), engaging in illegal or deviant behaviour (e.g., evading taxes, taking drugs, consuming alcohol, engaging in uncommon sexual practices), or revealing their financial status (e.g., income, savings, debts) (see Table 9.3).

Table 9.3 Over- and Underreporting Behaviour on Surveys

Percentage Distorted or Erroneous Answers			
	Face-to-Face	*Phone*	*Self-Administered*
Low Threat/Normative			
Registered to vote	+15	+17	+12
Have own library card	+19	+21	+18
High Threat			
Bankruptcy	–32	–29	–32
Drunk driving	–47	–46	–54

Source: Adapted from Bradburn and Sudman (1980:8).

Survey researchers have created several techniques to increase truthful answers to threatening questions. Some techniques involve the context and wording of the question itself. Researchers should ask threatening questions only after a warm-up when an interviewer has developed rapport and trust with the respondents, and they should tell respondents that they want honest answers. They can phrase the question in an "enhanced way" to provide a context that makes it easier for respondents to give honest answers. For example, the following enhanced question was asked of heterosexual males: "In past surveys, many men have reported that at some point in their lives they have had some type of sexual experience with another male. This could have happened before adolescence, during adolescence, or as an adult. Have you ever had sex with a male at some point in your life?" In contrast, a standard form of the question would have asked, "Have you ever had sex with another male?"

Also, by embedding a threatening response within more serious activities, it may be made to seem less deviant. For example, respondents might hesitate to admit shoplifting if it is asked first, but after being asked about armed robbery or burglary, they may admit to shoplifting because it appears less serious.

Socially Desirable Questions. **Social desirability bias** occurs when respondents distort answers to make their reports conform to social norms. People tend to overreport being cultured (i.e., reading, attending high-culture events), giving money to charity, having a good marriage, loving their children, and so forth. For example, one study found that one-third of people who reported in a survey that they gave money to a local charity really did not. Because a norm says that one should vote in elections, many report voting when they did not. In Canada, those under the greatest pressure to vote (i.e., highly educated, politically partisan, highly religious people who had been contacted by an organization that urged them to vote) are the people most likely to overreport voting.

Questionnaire writers try to reduce social desirability bias by phrasing questions in ways that make norm violation appear less objectionable and that presents a wider range of behaviour as acceptable. They can also offer multiple response categories that give respondents "face-saving" alternatives.

Knowledge Questions. Studies suggest that a large majority of the public cannot correctly answer elementary geography questions or identify important political documents (e.g., the *Canadian Charter of Rights and Freedoms*). Researchers sometimes want to find out whether respondents know about an issue or topics, but knowledge questions can be threatening because respondents do not want to appear ignorant. Surveys may measure opinions better if they first ask about factual information, because many people have inaccurate factual knowledge.

Some simple knowledge questions, such as the number of people living in a household, are not always answered accurately in surveys. In some households, a marginal person—the boyfriend who left for a week, the adult daughter who left after an argument about her pregnancy, or the uncle who walked out after a dispute over money—may be reported as not living in a household, but he or she may not have another permanent residence and consider himself or herself to live there.[5]

A researcher pilot-tests questions so that questions are at an appropriate level of difficulty. Little is gained if 99 percent of respondents cannot answer the question. Knowledge questions can be worded so that respondents feel comfortable saying they do not know the answer—for example, "How much, if anything, have you heard about. . . ."

Skip or Contingency Questions. Researchers avoid asking questions that are irrelevant for a respondent. Yet some questions apply only to specific respondents. A **contingency question** is a two- (or more) part question. The answer to the first part of the question determines which of two different questions a respondent next receives. Contingency questions select respondents for whom a second question is relevant. Sometimes they are called *screen* or *skip questions*. On the basis of the answer to the first question, the respondent or an interviewer is instructed to go to another or to skip certain questions.

The following example is a contingency question, taken from the 2004 Canada Campus Survey,[6] discussed in chapter 3. In this questionnaire, there is a large section that deals with the drinking behaviour of students. A contingency question is used at the beginning of the section on drinking to immediately redirect students who never drink, as the questions that follow on drinking behaviours would not be relevant to them.

1. During the past 12 months, how often, on average, did you consume alcoholic drinks?
   Every day ☐
   4-6 times a week ☐
   2-3 times a week ☐
   Once a week ☐
   1-3 times a month ☐
   Less than once a month ☐
   Never ☐ → SKIP TO QUESTION 17
2. During the past 12 months, on the days when you drank, how many drinks did you usually have? (PLEASE WRITE NUMBER OF DRINKS)
   Number of drinks ☐☐

Open versus Closed Questions

There has long been a debate about open versus closed questions in survey research. An **open-ended** (unstructured, free response) **question** asks a question (e.g., "What is your favorite television program?") to which respondents can give any answer. A **closed-ended** (structured, fixed response) **question** both asks a question and gives the respondent fixed responses from which to choose (e.g., "Is the prime minister doing a very good, good, fair, or poor job, in your opinion?").

Each form has advantages and disadvantages (see Box 2). The crucial issue is not which form is best. Rather, it is under what conditions a form is most appropriate. A researcher's choice to use an open- or closed-ended question depends on the purpose and the practical limitations of a research project. The demands of using open-ended questions, with interviewers writing verbatim answers followed by time-consuming coding, may make them impractical for a specific project.

Large-scale surveys have closed-ended questions because they are quicker and easier for both respondents and researchers. Yet something important may be lost when an individual's beliefs and feelings are forced into a few fixed categories that a researcher created. To learn how a respondent thinks, to discover what is really important to him or her, or to get an answer to a question with many possible answers (e.g., age), open questions may be best. In addition, sensitive topics (e.g., sexual behaviour, liquor consumption) may be more accurately measured with closed questions.

The disadvantages of a question form can be reduced by mixing open-ended and closed-ended questions in a questionnaire. Mixing them also offers a change of pace and helps interviewers establish rapport. Periodic probes (i.e., follow-up questions by interviewers) with closed-ended questions can reveal a respondent's reasoning.

Having interviewers periodically use probes to ask about a respondent's thinking is a way to check whether respondents understand the questions as the researcher intended. However, probes are not substitutes for writing clear questions or creating a framework of understanding for the respondent. Unless carefully stated, probes

Box 2 Closed versus Open Questions

Advantages of Closed

- It is easier and quicker for respondents to answer.
- The answers of different respondents are easier to compare.
- Answers are easier to code and statistically analyze.
- The response choices can clarify question meaning for respondents.
- Respondents are more likely to answer about sensitive topics.
- There are fewer irrelevant or confused answers to questions.
- Less articulate or less literate respondents are not at a disadvantage.
- Replication is easier.

Disadvantages of Closed

- They can suggest ideas that the respondent would not otherwise have.
- Respondents with no opinion or no knowledge can answer anyway.
- Respondents can be frustrated because their desired answer is not a choice.
- It is confusing if many (e.g., 20) response choices are offered.
- Misinterpretation of a question can go unnoticed.
- Distinctions between respondent answers may be blurred.
- Clerical mistakes or marking the wrong response is possible.
- They force respondents to give simplistic responses to complex issues.
- They force people to make choices they would not make in the real world.

Advantages of Open

- They permit an unlimited number of possible answers.
- Respondents can answer in detail and can qualify and clarify responses.
- Unanticipated findings can be discovered.
- They permit adequate answers to complex issues.
- They permit creativity, self-expression, and richness of detail.
- They reveal a respondent's logic, thinking process, and frame of reference.

Disadvantages of Open

- Different respondents give different degrees of detail in answers.
- Responses may be irrelevant or buried in useless detail.
- Comparisons and statistical analysis become very difficult.
- Coding responses is difficult.
- Articulate and highly literate respondents have an advantage.
- Questions may be too general for respondents who lose direction.
- Responses are written verbatim, which is difficult for interviewers.
- A greater amount of respondent time, thought, and effort is necessary.
- Respondents can be intimidated by questions.
- Answers take up a lot of space in the questionnaire.

might shape the respondent's answers or force answers when a respondent does not have an opinion or information. Yet flexible or conversational interviewing in which interviewers use many probes can improve accuracy on questions about complex issues on which respondents do not clearly understand basic terms or about which they have difficulty expressing their thoughts. For example, to the question, "Did you do any work for money last week?" a respondent might hesitate, then reply, "Yes." An interviewer probes, "Could you tell me exactly what work you did?" The respondent may reply, "On Tuesday and Wednesday, I spent a couple hours helping my buddy John move into his new apartment. For that he gave me $40, but I didn't have any other job or get paid for doing anything else." If the researcher's intention was only to get reports of regular employment, the probe revealed a misunderstanding. Researchers also use **partially open questions** (i.e., a set of fixed choices with a final open choice of "other"), which allows respondents to offer an answer that the researcher did not include.

Open-ended questions are especially valuable in early or exploratory stages of research. For large-scale surveys, researchers use open questions in pilot tests, then develop closed- question responses from the answers given to the open questions.

Researchers writing closed questions have to make many decisions. How many response choices should be given? Should they offer a middle or neutral choice? What should be the order of responses? What should be the types of response choices? How will the direction of a response be measured?

Answers to these questions are not easy. For example, two response choices are too few, but more than five response choices are rarely effective. Researchers want to measure meaningful distinctions and not collapse them. More specific responses yield more information, but too many specifics create confusion. For example, rephrasing the question, "Are you satisfied with your dentist?" (which has a yes/no answer) to "How satisfied are you with your dentist: very satisfied, somewhat satisfied, somewhat dissatisfied, or not satisfied at all?" gives the researcher more information and a respondent more choices.

Nonattitudes and the Middle Positions. Survey researchers debate whether to include choices for neutral, middle, and nonattitudes (e.g., "not sure," "don't know," or "no opinion").[7] Two types of errors can be made: accepting a middle choice or "no attitude" response when respondents hold a nonneutral opinion, or forcing respondents to choose a position on an issue when they have no opinion about it.

Many fear that respondents will choose nonattitude choices to evade making a choice. Yet it is usually best to offer a nonattitude choice, because people will express opinions on fictitious issues, objects, and events. By offering a nonattitude (middle or no opinion) choice, researchers identify those holding middle positions or those without opinions.

The issue of nonattitudes can be approached by distinguishing among three kinds of attitude questions: standard-format, quasi-filter, and full-filter questions (see Box 3). The **standard-format question** does not offer a "don't know" choice; a respondent must volunteer it. A **quasi-filter question** offers respondents a "don't know" alternative. A **full-filter question** is a special type of contingency question. It first asks if respondents have an opinion, then asks for the opinion of those who state that they do have an opinion.

Many respondents will answer a question if a "no opinion" choice is missing, but they will choose "don't know" when it is offered, or say that they do not have an opinion if asked. Such respondents are called **floaters** because they "float" from giving a response to not knowing. Their responses are affected by minor wording changes, so researchers screen them out using quasi-filter or full-filter questions. Filtered questions do not eliminate all answers to nonexistent issues, but they reduce the problem.

9

Agree/Disagree, Rankings or Ratings? Survey researchers who measure values and attitudes have debated two issues about the responses offered.[8] Should questionnaire items make a statement and ask respondents whether they agree or disagree with it, or should it offer respondents specific alternatives? Should the questionnaire include a set of items and ask respondents to rate them (e.g., approve, disapprove), or should it give them a list of items and force them to rank-order items (e.g., from most favoured to least favoured)?

It is best to offer respondents explicit alternatives. For example, instead of asking, "Do you agree or disagree with the statement, 'Men are better suited to. . . .'" instead ask, "Do you think men are better suited, women are better suited, or both

Box 3 Standard-Format, Quasi-Filter, and Full-Filter Questions

Standard Format

Here is a question about another country. Do you agree or disagree with this statement? "The Russian leaders are basically trying to get along with America."

Quasi-Filter

Here is a statement about another country: "The Russian leaders are basically trying to get along with America." Do you agree, disagree, or have no opinion on that?

Full Filter

Here is a statement about another country. Not everyone has an opinion on this. If you do not have an opinion, just say so. Here's the statement: "The Russian leaders are basically trying to get along with America." Do you have an opinion on that? If yes, do you agree or disagree?

Example of Results from Different Question Forms

	Standard Form (%)	*Quasi-Filter (%)*	*Full Filter (%)*
Agree	48.2	27.7	22.9
Disagree	38.2	29.5	20.9
No opinion	13.6*	42.8	56.3

*Volunteered

Source: Adapted from Schuman and Presser (1981:116–125). Standard format is from Fall 1978; quasi- and full-filter are from February 1977.

are equally suited?" Less-educated respondents are more likely to agree with a statement, whereas forced-choice alternatives encourage thought and avoid the **response set** bias—a tendency of some respondents to agree and not really decide.

Researchers create bias if question wording gives respondents a reason for choosing one alternative. For example, respondents were asked whether they supported or opposed a law on energy conservation. The results changed when respondents heard, "Do you support the law or do you oppose it because the law would be difficult to enforce?" instead of simply, "Do you support or oppose the law?"

It is better to ask respondents to choose among alternatives by ranking instead of rating items along an imaginary continuum. Respondents can rate several items equally high, but will place them in a hierarchy if asked to rank them.[9]

Wording Issues

Survey researchers face two wording issues. The first, discussed earlier, is to use simple vocabulary and grammar to minimize confusion. The second issue involves effects of specific words or phrases. This is trickier because it is not possible to know in advance whether a word or phrase affects responses.

The difference between *forbid* and *not allow* illustrates the problem of wording differences. Both terms have the same meaning, but many more people are willing to "not allow" something than to "forbid" it. In general, less-educated respondents are most influenced by minor wording differences.

Certain words seem to trigger an emotional reaction, and researchers are just beginning to learn of them. For example, Smith (1987) found large differences (e.g., twice as much support) in U.S. survey responses depending on whether a question asked about spending "to help the poor" or "for welfare." He suggested that the word *welfare* has such strong negative connotations for Americans (lazy people, wasteful and expensive programs) that it is best to avoid it. Research in Canada by Hunter and Miazdyck (2003) has shown that Canadians are somewhat less receptive to the word "welfare" compared to "help for the poor" as well, but not to the extent as their American counterparts.

Many respondents are confused by words or their connotations. For example, respondents were asked whether they thought television news was impartial. Researchers later learned that large numbers of respondents had ignored the word *impartial*—a term the middle-class, educated researchers assumed everyone would know. Less than half the respondents had interpreted the word as intended with its proper meaning. Over one-fourth ignored it or had no idea of its meaning. Others gave it unusual meanings, and one-tenth thought it was directly opposite to its true meaning. Researchers need to be cautious, because some **wording effects** (e.g., the difference between *forbid* and *not allow*) remain the same for decades, while other effects may appear.[10]

Questionnaire Design Issues

Length of Survey or Questionnaire. How long should a questionnaire be or an interview last? Researchers prefer long questionnaires or interviews because they are more cost effective. The cost for extra questions—once a respondent has been sampled, has been contacted, and has completed other questions—is small. There is no absolute proper length. The length depends on the survey format (to be discussed) and on the respondent's characteristics. A five-minute telephone interview is rarely a problem and may be extended to twenty minutes. A few researchers stretched this to beyond thirty minutes. Mail questionnaires are more variable. A short (three- or four-page) questionnaire is appropriate for the general population. Some researchers have had success with questionnaires as long as ten pages (about 100 items) with the general public, but responses drop significantly for longer questionnaires. For highly educated respondents and a salient topic, using questionnaires of fifteen pages may be possible. Face-to-face interviews lasting an hour are not uncommon. In special situations, face-to-face interviews as long as three to five hours have been conducted.

Question Order or Sequence. A survey researcher faces three issues of question sequence: organization of the overall questionnaire, question order effects, and context effects.

Organization of Questionnaire. In general, you should sequence questions to minimize the discomfort and confusion of respondents. A questionnaire has opening, middle, and ending questions. After an introduction explaining the survey, it is best to make opening questions pleasant, interesting, and easy to answer to help a respondent feel comfortable about the questionnaire. Avoid asking many boring background questions or threatening questions first. Organize questions into common topics. Mixing questions on different topics causes confusion. Orient respondents by placing questions on the same topic together and introduce the section with a short introductory statement (e.g., "Now I would like to ask you questions about housing"). Make question topics flow smoothly and logically, and organize them to assist respondents' memory or comfort levels. Do not end with highly threatening questions, and always end with a "thank-you."

Order Effects. Researchers are concerned that the order in which they present questions may influence respondent answers. Such "**order effects**" appear to be strongest for people who lack strong views, for less-educated respondents, and for older respondents or those with memory loss.[11] For example, support for an unmarried woman having an abortion rises if the question is preceded by a question about abortion being acceptable when a fetus has serious defects, but not when the question is by itself or before a question about fetus defects. An example of order effects is presented in Box 4.

Respondents may not perceive each issue of a survey as isolated and separate. They respond to survey questions based on the set of issues and their order of presentation in a questionnaire. Previous questions can influence later ones in two ways: through their content (i.e., the issue) and through the respondent's response. For example, a student respondent is asked, "Do you support or favour an educational contribution for students?" Answers vary depending on the topic of the preceding question. If it comes after, "How much tuition does the average Canadian student pay?" respondents interpret "contribution" to mean support for what students will pay. If it comes after "How much does the Swedish government pay to students?" respondents interpret it to mean a contribution that the government will pay. Responses can be also influenced by previous answers, because a respondent having already answered one part will assume no overlap. For example, a respondent is asked, "How is your wife?" The next question is, "How is your family?" Most respondents will assume that the second question means family members other than the wife because they already gave an answer about the wife.[12]

Context Effects. Researchers found powerful context effects in surveys. As a practical matter, two things can be done regarding context effects. Use a **funnel sequence** of questions—that is, ask more general questions before specific ones (e.g., ask about health in general before asking about specific diseases). Or, divide

Box 4 Question Order Effects

In order to study how question order affected questionnaire responses, Bassili and Krosnick (2000) administered a telephone survey to a random sample of 621 University of Toronto students. The questionnaire asked the respondents about their opinions on a wide range of topics. The researchers were interested to see how the students would respond to the following questions on abortion, depending on which on which one was presented first:

Question 1

"Would you tell me whether or not you think it should be possible for a pregnant woman to obtain a legal abortion if she is married and does not want any more children?"

Question 2

"Please tell me whether or not you think it should be possible for a pregnant woman to obtain a legal abortion if there is a strong chance of serious defect in the baby."

When Question 1 was asked first, 69% of the respondents answered in favour of the woman's right to obtain an abortion. However, when Question 1 was preceded by Question 2, 64% reported being in favour of the woman's right to choose an abortion. Upon further examination of the data, the researchers found that people who tended to have more "extreme" attitudes on other questionnaire items were more likely to be affected by question order.

The context created by answering the first question affects the answer to the second question.

Source: Adapted from Bassili and Krosnick (2000).

the number of respondents in half and give half of the questions in one order and the other half in the alternative order, then examine the results to see whether question order mattered. If question order effects are found, which order tells you what the respondents really think? The answer is that you cannot know for sure.

For example, a few years ago, students in one of the author's (Neuman) classes conducted a telephone survey on two topics: concern about crime and attitudes toward a new anti-drunk-driving law. A random half of the respondents heard questions about the drunk-driving law first; the other half heard about crime first. Neuman examined the results to see whether there was any **context effect**—a difference by topic order. He found that respondents who were asked about the drunk-driving law first expressed less fear about crime than did those who were asked about crime first. Likewise, they were more supportive of the drunk-driving law than were those who first heard about crime. The first topic created a context within which respondents answered questions on the second topic. After they were asked about crime in general and thought about violent crime, drunk driving may have appeared to be a less important issue. By contrast, after they were asked about drunk driving and thought about drunk driving as a crime, they may have expressed less concern about crime in general.

Respondents answer all questions based on a context of preceding questions and the interview setting. A researcher needs to remember that the more ambiguous a question's meaning, the stronger the context effects, because respondents will draw on the context to interpret and understand the question. Previous questions on the same topic and heard just before a question can have a large context effect. For example, Sudman and associates (1996:90–91) contrasted three ways of asking how much a respondent followed politics. When they asked the question alone, about 21 percent of respondents said they followed politics "now and then" or "hardly at all." When they asked the question after asking what the respondent's elected representative recently did, the percentage who said they did not follow nearly doubled, going to 39 percent. The knowledge question about the representative made many respondents feel that they did not really know much. When a question about the amount of "public relations work" the elected representative provided to the area came between the two questions, 29 percent of respondents said they did not follow politics. This question gave respondents an excuse for not knowing the first question—they could blame their representative for their ignorance. The context of a question can make a difference and researchers need to be aware of it at all times.

Format and Layout. There are two format or layout issues: the overall physical layout of the questionnaire and the format of questions and responses.

Questionnaire Layout. Layout is important, whether a questionnaire is for an interviewer or for the respondent. Questionnaires should be clear, neat, and easy to follow. Give each question a number and put identifying information (e.g., name of organization) on questionnaires. Never cram questions together or create a confusing appearance. A few cents saved in postage or printing will ultimately cost more in terms of lower validity due to a lower response rate or of confusion of interviewers and respondents. Make a **cover sheet** or face sheet for each interview, for administrative use. Put the time and date of interview, the interviewer, the respondent identification number, and the interviewer's comments and observations on it. A professional appearance with high-quality graphics, space between questions, and good layout improves accuracy and completeness and helps the questionnaire flow.

Give interviewers or respondents instructions on the questionnaire. Print instructions in a different style from the questions (e.g., in a different colour or font, or in all capitals) to distinguish them. This is so an interviewer can easily distinguish between questions for respondents and instructions intended for the interviewer alone.

Layout is crucial for mail questionnaires because there is no friendly interviewer to interact with the respondent. Instead, the questionnaire's appearance persuades the respondent. In mail surveys, include a polite, professional cover letter on letterhead stationery, identifying the researcher and offering a telephone number for questions. Details matter. Respondents will be turned off if they receive a bulky brown envelope with bulk postage addressed to Occupant or if the questionnaire does not fit into the return envelope. Always end with "Thank you for your participation." Interviewers and questionnaires should leave respondents with a positive feeling about the survey and a sense that their participation is appreciated.

Question design matters. One study of university students asked how many hours they studied per day. Some students saw five answer choices ranging from 0.5 hour to more than 2.5 hours; others saw five answer choices ranging from less than 2.5 hours to more than 4.5 hours. Of students who saw the first set, 77 percent said they studied under 2.5 hours versus 31 percent of those receiving the second set. When the mail questionnaire and telephone interview were compared, 58 percent of students hearing the first set said under 2.5 hours, but there was no change among those hearing the second set. More than differences in response categories were involved, because when students were asked about hours of television watching per day with similar response categories and then with the alternative response categories, no differences between the two were found. What can we learn from this? Respondents without clear answers tend to rely on questionnaire response categories for guidance and more anonymous answering formats tend to yield more honest responses (see Dillman 2000:32–39 for more details).

Question Format Survey. researchers decide on a format for questions and responses. Should respondents circle responses, check boxes, fill in dots, or put a 3 in a blank? The principle is to make responses unambiguous. Boxes or brackets to be checked and numbers to be circled are usually clearest. Also, listing responses down a page rather than across makes them easier to see (see Box 5). As mentioned before, use arrows and instructions for contingency questions. Visual aids are also helpful. For example, hand out thermometer-like drawings to respondents when asking about how warm or cool they feel toward someone. A **matrix question** (or grid question) is a compact way to present a series of questions using the same response categories. It saves space and makes it easier for the respondent or interviewer to note answers for the same response categories.

Nonresponse. The failure to get a valid response from every sampled respondent weakens a survey. Have you ever refused to answer a survey? In addition to research surveys, people are asked to respond to many requests from charities, marketing firms, candidate polls, and so forth. Charities and marketing firms get low response rates, whereas government organizations get much higher cooperation rates. Nonresponse can be a major problem for survey research because if a high proportion of the sampled respondents do not respond, researchers may not be able to generalize results, especially if those who do not respond differ from those who respond.

Public cooperation in survey research has declined over the past 20 to 30 years across many countries.[13] There is both a growing group of "hard core" refusing people and a general decline in participation because many people feel there are too many surveys. Other reasons for refusal include a fear of crime and strangers, a more hectic lifestyle, a loss of privacy, and a rising distrust of authority or government. The misuse of the survey to sell products or persuade people, poorly designed questionnaires, and inadequate explanations of surveys to respondents also increase refusals for legitimate surveys.

Survey researchers can improve eligibility rates by careful respondent screening, better sample-frame definition, and multilingual interviewers. They can decrease

Box 5 Question Format Examples

Example of Horizontal versus Vertical Response Choices

Do you think it is too easy or too difficult to get a divorce, or is it about right?
• Too Easy • Too Difficult • About Right

Do you think it is too easy or too difficult to get a divorce, or is it about right?
- Too Easy
- Too Difficult
- About Right

Example of a Matrix Question Format

	Strongly Agree	*Agree*	*Disagree*	*Strongly Disagree*	*Don't Know*
The teacher talks too fast.	■	■	■	■	■
I learned a lot in this class.	■	■	■	■	■
The tests are very easy.	■	■	■	■	■
The teacher tells many jokes.	■	■	■	■	■
The teacher is organized.	■	■	■	■	■

Examples of Some Response Category Choices

Excellent, Good, Fair, Poor
Approve/Disapprove
Favour/Oppose
Strongly Agree, Agree, Somewhat Agree, Somewhat Disagree, Disagree, Strongly Disagree
Too Much, Too Little, About Right
Better, Worse, About the Same
Regularly, Often, Seldom, Never
Always, Most of Time, Some of Time, Rarely, Never
More Likely, Less Likely, No Difference
Very Interested, Interested, Not Interested

refusals by sending letters in advance of an interview, offering to reschedule interviews, using small incentives (i.e., small gifts), adjusting interviewer behaviour and statements (i.e., making eye contact, expressing sincerity, explaining the sampling or survey, emphasizing importance of the interview, clarifying promises of confidentiality, etc.). Survey researchers can also use alternative interviewers (i.e., different demographic characteristics, age, race, gender, or ethnicity), use alternative interview methods (i.e., phone versus face-to-face), or accept alternative respondents in a household.

A critical area of nonresponse or refusal to participate occurs with the initial contact between an interviewer and a respondent. A face-to-face or telephone interview must overcome resistance and reassure respondents.

Research on the use of incentives found that prepaid incentives appear to increase respondent cooperation in all types of surveys. They do not appear to have negative effects on survey composition or future participation.

There is a huge literature on ways to increase response rates for mail questionnaires (see Box 6).[14] Heberlein and Baumgartner (1978, 1981) reported 71 factors affecting mail questionnaire response rates.

Box 6 Ten Ways to Increase Mail Questionnaire Response

1. Address the questionnaire to specific person, not "Occupant," and send it first class.
2. Include a carefully written, dated cover letter on letterhead stationery. In it, request respondent cooperation, guarantee confidentiality, explain the purpose of the survey, and give the researcher's name and phone number.
3. *Always* include a postage-paid, addressed return envelope.
4. The questionnaire should have a neat, attractive layout and reasonable page length.
5. The questionnaire should be professionally printed and easy to read, with clear instructions.
6. Send two follow-up reminder letters to those not responding. The first should arrive about one week after sending the questionnaire, the second a week later. Gently ask for cooperation again and offer to send another questionnaire.
7. Do not send questionnaires during major holiday periods.
8. Do not put questions on the back page. Instead, leave a blank space and ask the respondent for general comments.
9. Sponsors that are local and are seen as legitimate (e.g., government agencies, universities, large firms) get a better response.
10. Include a small monetary inducement if possible.

TYPES OF SURVEYS: ADVANTAGES AND DISADVANTAGES

Mail and Self-Administered Questionnaires

Advantages. Researchers can give questionnaires directly to respondents or mail them to respondents who read instructions and questions, then record their answers. This type of survey is by far the cheapest, and it can be conducted by a single researcher. A researcher can send questionnaires to a wide geographical area. The respondent can complete the questionnaire when it is convenient and can check personal records if necessary. Mail questionnaires offer anonymity and avoid interviewer bias. They can be effective, and response rates may be high for an educated target population that has a strong interest in the topic or the survey organization.

Disadvantages. Since people do not always complete and return questionnaires, the biggest problem with mail questionnaires is a low response rate. Most questionnaires are returned within two weeks, but others trickle in up to two months later. Researchers can raise response rates by sending nonrespondents reminder letters, but this adds to the time and cost of data collection.

A researcher cannot control the conditions under which a mail questionnaire is completed. A questionnaire completed during a drinking party by a dozen laughing people may be returned along with one filled out by an earnest respondent. Also, no one is present to clarify questions or to probe for more information when respondents give incomplete answers. Someone other than the sampled respondent (e.g., spouse, new resident) may open the mail and complete the questionnaire without the researcher's knowledge. Different respondents can complete the questionnaire weeks apart or answer questions in a different order than that intended by researchers. Incomplete questionnaires can also be a serious problem.

Researchers cannot visually observe the respondent's reactions to questions, physical characteristics, or the setting. For example, an impoverished 70-year-old white woman living alone on a farm could falsely state that she is a prosperous 40-year-old Asian male doctor living in a town with three children. Such extreme lies are rare, but serious errors can go undetected.

The mail questionnaire format limits the kinds of questions that a researcher can use. Questions requiring visual aids (e.g., look at this picture and tell me what you see), open-ended questions, many contingency questions, and complex questions do poorly in mail questionnaires. Likewise, mail questionnaires are ill suited for the illiterate or near-illiterate in English. Questionnaires mailed to illiterate respondents are not likely to be returned; if they are completed and returned, the questions were probably misunderstood, so the answers are meaningless (see Table 9.4).

Web Surveys

Access to the internet and email has become widespread since the late 1990s across most advanced nations. For example, 18 percent of the Canadian population had email in 1994; only 11 years later about 68 percent of the population used the internet for personal or nonbusiness reasons.

Advantages. Web-based surveys over the internet or by email are very fast and inexpensive. They allow flexible design and can use visual images, or even audio or

Table 9.4 Types of Surveys and Their Features

	Type of Survey			
Features	*Mail Questionnaire*	*Web Survey*	*Telephone Interview*	*Face-to-Face Interview*
Administrative Issues				
Cost	Cheap	Cheapest	Moderate	Expensive
Speed	Slowest	Fastest	Fast	Slow to moderate
Length (number of questions)	Moderate	Moderate	Short	Longest
Response rate	Lowest	Moderate	Moderate	Highest
Research Control				
Probes possible	No	No	Yes	Yes
Specific respondent	No	No	Yes	Yes
Question sequence	No	Yes	Yes	Yes
Only one respondent	No	No	Yes	Yes
Visual observation	No	No	No	Yes
Success with Different Questions				
Visual aids	Limited	Yes	None	Yes
Open-ended questions	Limited	Limited	Limited	Yes
Contingency questions	Limited	Yes	Yes	Yes
Complex questions	Limited	Yes	Limited	Yes
Sensitive questions	Some	Yes	Limited	Limited
Sources of Bias				
Social desirability	Some	Some	Some	Most
Interviewer bias	None	None	Some	Most
Respondent's reading skill	Yes	Yes	No	No

video in some internet versions. Despite great flexibility, the basic principles for question writing and for paper questionnaire design generally apply.

Disadvantages. Web surveys have three areas of concern: coverage, privacy and verification, and design issues. The first concern involves sampling and unequal internet access or use. Despite high coverage rates, older, less-educated, lower-income, and more rural people are less likely to have good internet access. In addition, many people have multiple email addresses, which limits using them for sampling purposes. Self-selection is a potential problem with web surveys. For example, a marketing department could get very distorted results of the population of new car buyers. Perhaps half of the new car buyers for a model are over age 55, but 75 percent of respondents to a web survey are under age 32 and only 8 percent are over age 55. Not only would the results be distorted by age but the relatively small percentage of over-55 respondents may not be representative of all over-55 potential new car buyers (e.g., they may be higher income or more educated).

A second concern is protecting respondent privacy and confidentiality. Researchers should encrypt collected data, only use secure websites and erase nonessential respondent identification or linking information on a daily or weekly basis. They should develop a system of respondent verification to ensure that only the sampled respondent participates and does so only once. This may involve a system such as giving each respondent a unique PIN number to access the questionnaire.

A third concern involves the complexity of questionnaire design. Researchers need to check and verify the compatibility of various web software and hardware combinations for respondents using different computers. Researchers are still learning what is most effective for web surveys. It is best to provide screen-by-screen questions and make an entire question visible on the screen at one time in a consistent format with drop-down boxes for answer choices. It is best to include a progress indicator (as motivation), such as a clock or waving hand. Visual appearance of a screen, such as the range of colours and fonts, should be kept simple for easy readability and consistency. Be sure to provide very clear instructions for all computer actions (e.g., use of drop-down screens) where they are needed and include "click here" instructions. Also, make it easy for respondents to move back and forth across questions. Researchers using web surveys need to avoid technical glitches at the implementation stage by repeated pretesting, having a dedicated server, and obtaining sufficient broadband to handle high demand.

Telephone Interviews

Advantages. The telephone interview is a popular survey method because about 95 percent of the population can be reached by telephone. An interviewer calls a respondent (usually at home), asks questions, and records answers. Researchers sample respondents from lists, telephone directories, or random digit dialing, and can quickly reach many people across long distances. A staff of interviewers can interview 1500 respondents across a nation within a few days and, with several call-backs, response rates can reach 90 percent. Although this method is more expensive than a mail questionnaire, the telephone interview is a flexible method with most of the strengths of face-to-face interviews but for about half the cost. Interviewers control the sequence of questions and can use some probes. A specific respondent is chosen and is likely to answer all the questions alone. The researcher knows when the questions were answered and can use contingency questions effectively, especially with computer-assisted telephone interviewing (CATI) (to be discussed).

Disadvantages. Higher cost and limited interview length are among the disadvantages of telephone interviews. In addition, respondents without telephones are impossible to reach, and the call may come at an inconvenient time. The use of an interviewer reduces anonymity and introduces potential interviewer bias. Open-ended questions are difficult to use, and questions requiring visual aids are impossible. Interviewers can only note serious disruptions (e.g., background noise) and respondent tone of voice (e.g., anger or flippancy) or hesitancy.

Face-to-Face Interviews

Advantages. Face-to-face interviews have the highest response rates and permit the longest questionnaires. Interviewers also can observe the surroundings and can use nonverbal communication and visual aids. Well-trained interviewers can ask all types of questions, can ask complex questions, and can use extensive probes.

Disadvantages. High cost is the biggest disadvantage of face-to-face interviews. The training, travel, supervision, and personnel costs for interviews can be high. Interviewer bias is also greatest in face-to-face interviews. The appearance, tone of voice, question wording, and so forth of the interviewer may affect the respondent. In addition, interviewer supervision is less than for telephone interviews, which supervisors monitor by listening in.[15]

INTERVIEWING

The Role of the Interviewer

Interviews to gather information occur in many settings. Survey research interviewing is a specialized kind of interviewing. As with most interviewing, its goal is to obtain accurate information from another person.[16]

The survey interview is a social relationship. Like other social relationships, it involves social roles, norms, and expectations. The interview is a short-term, secondary social interaction between two strangers with the explicit purpose of one person's obtaining specific information from the other. The social roles are those of the interviewer and the interviewee or respondent. Information is obtained in a structured conversation in which the interviewer asks prearranged questions and records answers, and the respondent answers. It differs in several ways from ordinary conversation (see Table 9.5).

An important problem for interviewers is that many respondents are unfamiliar with the survey respondents' role. As a result, they substitute another role that may affect their responses. Some believe the interview is an intimate conversation or therapy session, some see it as a bureaucratic exercise in completing forms, some view it as a citizen referendum on policy choices, some view it as a testing situation, and some consider it as a form of deceit in which interviewers are trying to trick or entrap respondents. Even in a well-designed, professional survey, follow-up research found that only about half the respondents understand questions exactly as intended by researchers. Respondents reinterpreted questions to make them applicable to their idiosyncratic, personal situations or to make them easy to answer.[17]

The role of interviewers is difficult. They obtain cooperation and build rapport, yet remain neutral and objective. They encroach on the respondents' time and privacy for information that may not directly benefit the respondents. They try to reduce embarrassment, fear, and suspicion so that respondents feel comfortable revealing information. They may explain the nature of survey research or give hints about social roles in an interview. Good interviewers monitor the pace and direction of the social interaction as well as the content of answers and the behaviour of respondents.

Survey interviewers are nonjudgmental and do not reveal their opinions, verbally or nonverbally (e.g., by a look of shock). If a respondent asks for an interviewer's opinion, he or she politely redirects the respondent and indicates that such questions are inappropriate. For example, if a respondent asks, "What do you think?"

Table 9.5 Differences between Ordinary Conversation and a Structured Survey Interview

Ordinary Conversation	The Survey Interview
1. Questions and answers from each participant are relatively equally balanced.	1. The interviewer asks and the respondent answers most of the time.
2. There is an open exchange of feelings and opinions.	2. Only the respondent reveals feelings and opinions.
3. Judgments are stated and attempts made to persuade the other of a particular point of view.	3. The interviewer is nonjudgmental and does not try to change the respondent's opinions or beliefs.
4. A person can reveal deep inner feelings to gain sympathy or as a therapeutic release.	4. The interviewer tries to obtain direct answers to specific questions.
5. Ritual responses are common (e.g., "Uh-huh," shaking head, "How are you?" "Fine").	5. The interviewer avoids making ritual responses that influence a respondent and also seeks genuine answers, not ritual responses.
6. The participants exchange information and correct the factual errors that they are aware of.	6. The respondent provides almost all information. The interviewer does not correct a respondent's factual errors.
7. Topics rise and fall and either person can introduce new topics. The focus can shift directions or digress to less relevant issues.	7. The interviewer controls the topic, direction, and pace. He or she keeps the respondent "on task," and irrelevant diversions are contained.
8. The emotional tone can shift from humour, to joy, to affection, to sadness, to anger, and so on.	8. The interviewer attempts to maintain a consistently warm but serious and objective tone throughout.
9. People can evade or ignore questions and give flippant or noncommittal answers.	9. The respondent should not evade questions and should give truthful, thoughtful answers.

Source: Adapted from Gorden (1980:19–25) and Sudman and Bradburn (1983:5–10).

the interviewer may answer, "Here, we are interested in what *you* think; what I think doesn't matter." Likewise, if the respondent gives a shocking answer (e.g., "I was arrested three times for beating my infant daughter and burning her with cigarettes"), the interviewer does not show shock, surprise, or disdain but treats the answer in a matter-of-fact manner. He or she helps respondents feel that they can give any truthful answer.

You might ask, "If the survey interviewer must be neutral and objective, why not use a robot or machine?" Machine interviewing has not been successful because it lacks the human warmth, sense of trust, and rapport that an interviewer creates. An interviewer helps define the situation and ensures that respondents have the information sought, understand what is expected, give relevant answers, are motivated to cooperate, and give serious answers.

Interviewers do more than interview respondents. Face-to-face interviewers spend only about 35 percent of their time interviewing. About 40 percent is spent in locating the correct respondent, 15 percent in travelling, and 10 percent in studying survey materials and dealing with administrative and recording details.[18]

Stages of an Interview

The interview proceeds through stages, beginning with an introduction and entry. The interviewer gets in the door, shows authorization, and reassures and secures cooperation from the respondent. He or she is prepared for reactions such as, "How did you pick me?" "What good will this do?" "I don't know about this," "What's this about, anyway?" The interviewer can explain why the specific respondent is interviewed and not a substitute.

The main part of the interview consists of asking questions and recording answers. The interviewer uses the exact wording on the questionnaire—no added or omitted words and no rephrasing. He or she asks all applicable questions in order, without returning to or skipping questions unless the directions specify this. He or she goes at a comfortable pace and gives nondirective feedback to maintain interest.

In addition to asking questions, the interviewer accurately records answers. This is easy for closed-ended questions, where interviewers just mark the correct box. For open-ended questions, the interviewer's job is more difficult. He or she must listen carefully, must have legible writing, and must record what is said verbatim without correcting grammar or slang. More important, the interviewer never summarizes or paraphrases. This causes a loss of information or distorts answers. For example, the respondent says, "I'm really concerned about my daughter's heart problem. She's only ten years old and already she has trouble climbing stairs. I don't know what she'll do when she gets older. Heart surgery is too risky for her and it costs so much. She'll have to learn to live with it." If the interviewer writes "concerned about daughter's health," much is lost.

The interviewer knows how and when to use probes. A **probe** is a neutral request to clarify an ambiguous answer, to complete an incomplete answer, or to obtain a relevant response. Interviewers recognize an irrelevant or inaccurate answer and use probes as needed.[19] There are many types of probes. A three- to five-second pause is often effective. Nonverbal communication (e.g., tilt of head, raised eyebrows, or eye contact) also works well. The interviewer can repeat the question or repeat the reply and then pause. She or he can ask a neutral question, such as, "Any other reasons?" "Can you tell me more about that?" "How do you mean?" "Could you explain more for me?" (see Box 7).

The last stage is the exit, when the interviewer thanks the respondent and leaves. He or she then goes to a quiet, private place to edit the questionnaire and record other details, such as the date, time, and place of the interview; a thumbnail sketch of the respondent and interview situation; the respondent's attitude (e.g., serious, angry, laughing); and any unusual circumstances (e.g., "Telephone rang at question 27 and respondent talked for four minutes before the interview started again"). He or she notes anything disruptive that happened during the interview (e.g.,

Box 7 Example of Probes and Recording Full Responses to Closed Questions

Interviewer Question: What is your occupation?
Respondent Answer: I work at General Motors.
Probe: What is your job at General Motors? What type of work do you do there?

Interviewer Question: How long have you been unemployed?
Respondent Answer: A long time.
Probe: Could you tell me more specifically when your current period of unemployment began?

Interviewer Question: Considering the country as a whole, do you think we will have good times during the next year, or bad times, or what?
Respondent Answer: Maybe good, maybe bad, it depends, who knows?
Probe: What do you expect to happen?

Record Response to a Closed Question

Interviewer Question: On a scale of 1 to 7, how do you feel about capital punishment or the death penalty, where 1 is strongly in favour of the death penalty, and 7 is strongly opposed to it?

(Favour) 1 ___ 2 ___ 3 ___ 4 ___ 5 ___ 6 ___ 7 ___ (Oppose)

Respondent Answer: About a 4. I think that all murderers, rapists, and violent criminals should get death, but I don't favour it for minor crimes like stealing a car.

"Teenage son entered room, sat at opposite end, turned on television with the volume loud, and watched a music video"). The interviewer also records personal feelings and anything that was suspected (e.g., "Respondent became nervous and fidgeted when questioned about his marriage").

Training Interviewers

A large-scale survey requires hiring multiple interviewers. Few people appreciate the difficulty of the interviewer's job. A professional-quality interview requires the careful selection of interviewers and extensive training. As with any employment situation, adequate pay and good supervision are important for consistent high-quality performance. Unfortunately, professional interviewing has not always paid well or provided regular employment. In the past, interviewers were largely drawn from a pool of middle-aged women willing to accept irregular part-time work.

Good interviewers are pleasant, honest, accurate, mature, responsible, moderately intelligent, stable, and motivated. They have a nonthreatening appearance, have experience with many different types of people, and possess poise and tact. Researchers may consider interviewers' physical appearance, age, race, sex, languages spoken, and even the sound of their voice.

Professional interviewers receive a training course. It includes lectures and reading, observation of expert interviewers, mock interviews in the office and in the field that are recorded and critiqued, many practice interviews, and role playing. The interviewers learn about survey research and the role of the interviewer. They become familiar with the questionnaire and the purpose of questions, although not with the answers expected.

Although interviewers largely work alone, researchers use an interviewer supervisor in large-scale surveys with several interviewers. Supervisors are familiar with the area, assist with problems, oversee the interviewers, and ensure that work is completed on time. For telephone interviewing, this includes helping with calls, checking when interviewers arrive and leave, and monitoring interview calls. In face-to-face interviews, supervisors check to find out whether the interview actually took place. This means calling back or sending a confirmation postcard to a sample of respondents. They can also check the response rate and incomplete questionnaires to see whether interviewers are obtaining cooperation, and they may re-interview a small subsample, analyze answers, or observe interviews to see whether interviewers are accurately asking questions and recording answers.

Interviewer Bias

Reducing interview bias goes beyond reading each question exactly as worded. Ideally, the actions of a particular interviewer will not affect how a respondent answers, and responses will not vary from what they would be if asked by any other interviewer.

Survey researchers know that interviewer expectations can create significant bias. Interviewers who expect difficult interviews have them, and those who expect certain answers are more likely to get them (see Box 8). Proper interviewer behaviour and exact question reading may be difficult, but the issue is larger.

The social setting in which the interview occurs, including the presence of other people, can affect answers. For example, students answer differently depending on whether they are asked questions at home or at school. In general, survey researchers do not want others present because they may affect respondent answers. It may not always make a difference, however, especially if the others are small children.[20]

An interviewer's visible characteristics, including race and gender, often affect interviews and respondent answers, especially for questions about issues related to race or gender. For example, Black and Asian respondents may express different policy positions on race- or ethnic-related issues depending on the apparent race or ethnicity of the interviewer. This occurs even with telephone interviews when a

Box 8 Interviewer Characteristics Can Affect Responses

Example of Interviewer Expectation Effects

Asked by Female Interviewer Whose Own	*Female Respondent Reports That Husband Buys Most Furniture*
Husband buys most furniture	89%
Husband does not buy most furniture	15%

Example of Race or Ethnic Appearance Effects

	Percentage Answering Yes to:	
Interviewer	*"Do you think there are too many Jews in government jobs?"*	*"Do you think that Jews have too much power?"*
Looked Jewish with Jewish-sounding name	11.7	5.8
Looked Jewish only	15.4	15.6
Non-Jewish appearance	21.2	24.3
Non-Jewish appearance and non-Jewish-sounding name	19.5	21.4

Note: Racial stereotypes held by respondents can affect how they respond in interviews.
Source: Adapted from Hyman (1975:115, 163).

respondent has clues about the interviewer's race or ethnicity. In general, interviewers of the same ethnic-racial group get more accurate answers.[21] Gender also affects interviews both in terms of obvious issues, such as sexual behaviour, as well as support for gender-related collective action or gender equality.[22] Survey researchers need to note the race and gender of both interviewers and respondents.

Computer-Assisted Telephone Interviewing

Advances in computer technology and lower computer prices have enabled professional survey research organizations to install **computer-assisted telephone interviewing (CATI)** systems.[23] With CATI, the interviewer sits in front of a computer and makes calls. Wearing a headset and microphone, the interviewer reads the questions from a computer screen for the specific respondent who is called, then enters the answer via the keyboard. Once he or she enters an answer, the computer shows the next question on the screen.

Computer-assisted telephone interviewing speeds interviewing and reduces interviewer errors. It also eliminates the separate step of entering information into a computer and speeds data processing. Of course, CATI requires an investment in computer equipment and some knowledge of computers. The CATI system is valuable for contingency questions because the computer can show the questions appropriate for a specific respondent; interviewers do not have to turn pages looking for the next question. In addition, the computer can check an answer immediately after the interviewer enters it. For example, if an interviewer enters an answer that is impossible or clearly an error (e.g., an H instead of an M for "Male"), the computer will request another answer. Innovations with computers and web surveys also help to gather data on sensitive issues (see Box 9).

Several companies have developed software programs for personal computers that help researchers develop questionnaires and analyze survey data. They provide guides for writing questions, recording responses, analyzing data, and producing reports. The programs may speed the more mechanical aspects of survey research—such as typing questionnaires, organizing layout, and recording

Box 9 Computer-Aided Surveys and Sensitive Topics

The questioning format influences how respondents answer questions about sensitive topics. Formats that permit the respondent greater anonymity, such as a self-administered questionnaire or the web survey, are more likely to elicit honest responses than one that requires interaction with another person, such as in a face-to-face interview or telephone interview. One of a series of computer-based technological innovations is called *computer-assisted self-administered interviews (CASAI)*. It appears to improve respondent comfort and honesty in answering questions on sensitive topics. In CASAI, respondents are "interviewed" with questions that are asked on a computer screen or heard over earphones. The respondents answer by moving a computer mouse or entering information using a computer keyboard. Even when a researcher is present in the same room, the respondent is semi-insulated from human contact and appears to feel comfortable answering questions about sensitive issues.

responses—but they cannot substitute for a good understanding of the survey method or an appreciation of its limitations. The researcher must still clearly conceptualize variables, prepare well-worded questions, design the sequence and forms of questions and responses, and pilot-test questionnaires. Communicating unambiguously with respondents and eliciting credible responses remain the most important parts of survey research.

THE ETHICAL SURVEY

Like all social research, people can conduct surveys in ethical or unethical ways. A major ethical issue in survey research is the invasion of privacy. Survey researchers can intrude into a respondent's privacy by asking about intimate actions and personal beliefs. People have a right to privacy. Respondents decide when and to whom to reveal personal information. They are likely to provide such information when it is requested in a comfortable context with mutual trust, when they believe serious answers are needed for legitimate research purposes, and when they believe answers will remain confidential. Researchers should treat all respondents with dignity and reduce anxiety or discomfort. They are also responsible for protecting the confidentiality of data.

A second issue involves voluntary participation by respondents. Respondents agree to answer questions and can refuse to participate at any time. They give "informed consent" to participate in research. Researchers depend on respondents' voluntary cooperation, so researchers need to ask well-developed questions in a sensitive way, treat respondents with respect, and be very sensitive to confidentiality.

A third ethical issue is the exploitation of surveys and pseudosurveys. Because of its popularity, some people use surveys to mislead others. A **pseudosurvey** is when someone who has little or no real interest in learning information from a respondent uses the survey format to try to persuade someone to do something. Charlatans use the guise of conducting a survey to invade privacy, gain entry into homes, or "suggle" (sell in the guise of a survey). During elections, you may hear about "suppression polls" or "push polls." These are pseudosurveys that are used to spread negative information about political candidates. Under the guise of conducting a poll, a person is called and asked about his or her political views, such as who he or she will vote for. If the person favours a candidate other than the one the caller is campaigning for, the interviewer would then ask whether the respondent would still support that candidate if he or she knew that the candidate had an unfavourable characteristic (e.g., had been arrested for drunk driving, used illegal drugs, raised the wages of convicted criminals in prison). The goal of such push polls is not to measure candidate support; rather, it is to identify a candidate's supporters, then attempt to suppress voting.

Another ethical issue is when people misuse survey results or use poorly designed or purposely rigged surveys. Why does this occur? People may demand answers from surveys that surveys cannot provide and may not understand a survey's limitations. Those who design and prepare surveys may lack sufficient training to conduct a legitimate survey. Unfortunately, policy decisions are sometimes made based on careless or poorly designed surveys. They often result in waste or human hardship. This is why legitimate researchers conducting methodologically rigorous survey research are important.

The media report more surveys than other types of social research, yet sloppy reporting of survey results permits abuse.[24] Few people reading survey results may appreciate it, but researchers should include details about the survey (see Box 10) to reduce the misuse of survey research and increase questions about surveys that lack such information. Survey researchers urge the media to include such information, but it is rarely included. Most of the reporting on surveys in the mass media fails to reveal the researcher who conducted the survey, and only a handful provide details on how the survey was conducted.[25] Currently, there are no quality-control standards to regulate the opinion polls or surveys reported in the Canadian media. The Canadian Broadcasting Corporation claims to have standards, but does not specify exactly what they are.[26] Researchers have made unsuccessful attempts since World War II to require adequate samples, interviewer training and supervision, satisfactory questionnaire design, public availability of results, and controls on the integrity of survey organizations.[27] As a result, the mass media report both biased and misleading survey results and rigorous, professional survey results without making any distinction. It is not surprising that public confusion and a distrust of all surveys occur.

Box 10 Ten Items to Include When Reporting Survey Research

1. The sampling frame used (e.g., telephone directories)
2. The dates on which the survey was conducted
3. The population that the sample represents (e.g., Canadian adults, Australian college students, housewives in Singapore)
4. The size of the sample for which information was collected
5. The sampling method (e.g., random)
6. The exact wording of the questions asked
7. The method of the survey (e.g., face to face, telephone)
8. The organizations that sponsored the survey (paid for it and conducted it)
9. The response rate or percentage of those contacted who actually completed the questionnaire
10. Any missing information or "don't know" responses when results on specific questions are reported

CONCLUSION

In this chapter, you learned about survey research. You also learned some principles of writing good survey questions. There are many things to avoid and to include when writing questions. You learned about the advantages and disadvantages of three types of survey research: mail, telephone interviews, and face-to-face interviews. You saw that interviewing, especially face-to-face interviewing, can be difficult.

Although this chapter focused on survey research, researchers use questionnaires to measure variables in other types of quantitative research (e.g., experiments). The survey, often called the sample survey because random sampling is usually used with it, is a distinct technique. It is a process of asking many people the same questions and examining their answers.

Survey researchers try to minimize errors, but survey data often contain them. Errors in surveys can compound each other. For example, errors can arise in sampling frames, from nonresponse, from question wording or order, and from interviewer bias. Do not let the existence of errors discourage you from using the survey, however. Instead, learn to be very careful when designing survey research and cautious about generalizing from the results of surveys.

KEY TERMS

closed-ended question *209*
computer-assisted telephone interviewing (CATI) *225*
context effect *215*
contingency question *208*
cover sheet *215*
double-barreled question *203*
floaters *211*
full-filter question *211*
funnel sequence *214*
interview schedule *200*
leading question *204*
matrix question *216*
open-ended question *209*
order effects *213*
partially open question *211*
prestige bias *203*
probe *223*
pseudosurvey *226*
quasi-filter question *211*
response set *212*
social desirability bias *208*
standard-format question *211*
threatening questions *207*
wording effects *213*

9

ENDNOTES

1. Sudman and Bradburn (1983:39) suggested that even simple questions (e.g., "What brand of soft drink do you usually buy?") can cause problems. Respondents who are highly loyal to one brand of traditional carbonated sodas can answer the question easily. Other respondents must implicitly address the following questions to answer the question as it was asked: (a) What time period is involved—the past month, the past year, the past ten years? (b) What conditions count—at home, at restaurants, at sporting events? (c) Does this refer to buying for oneself alone or for other family members? (d) What is a "soft drink"? Do lemonade, iced tea, mineral water, or fruit juices count? (e) Does "usually" mean a brand purchased as 51 percent or more of all soft drink purchases, or the brand purchased more frequently than any other? Respondents rarely stop and ask for clarification; they make assumptions about what the researcher means.
2. See Dykema and Schaeffer (2000) and Sudman and colleagues (1996:197–226).
3. See Ostrom and Gannon (1996).
4. See Bradburn (1983), Bradburn and Sudman (1980), and Sudman and Bradburn (1983) on threatening or sensitive questions. Backstrom and Hursh-Cesar (1981:219) and Warwick and Lininger (1975:150–151) provide useful suggestions as well.
5. For more on how the question "Who knows who lives here?" can be complicated, see Martin (1999) and Tourangeau et al. (1997).
6. The questionnaire from the Canadian Campus Survey can be downloaded from the CAMH website at www.camh.net/research/areas_of_research/Population_li fe_ course_studies/population_life_course.html.
7. For a discussion of the "don't know," "no opinion," and middle positions in response categories, see Backstrom and Hursh-Cesar (1981:148–149), Bishop (1987), Bradburn and Sudman (1988:154), Brody (1986), Converse and Presser (1986:35–37), Duncan and Stenbeck (1988), and Sudman and Bradburn (1983:140–141).
8. The disagree/agree versus specific alternatives debate can be found in Bradburn and Sudman (1983:149–151), Converse and Presser (1986:38–39), and Schuman and Presser (1981:179–223).
9. The ranking versus ratings issue is discussed in Alwin and Krosnick (1985) and Krosnick and Alwin (1988). Also see Backstrom and Hursh-Cesar (1981:132–134) and Sudman and Bradburn (1983:156–165) for formats of asking rating and ranking questions.
10. See Foddy (1993) and Presser (1990).
11. Studies by Krosnick (1992) and Narayan and Krosnick (1996) show that education reduces response-order (primacy or recency) effects, but Knäuper (1999) found that age is strongly associated with response-order effects.
12. This example comes from Strack (1992).
13. For a discussion, see Couper, Singer et al. (1998), de Heer (1999), Keeter et al. (2000), Sudman and Bradburn (1983:11), and "Surveys Proliferate, but Answers Dwindle," *New York Times*, October 5, 1990, p. 1. Smith (1995) and Sudman (1976:114–116) also discuss refusal rates.
14. Bailey (1987:153–168), Church (1993), Dillman (1978, 1983), Fox and colleagues (1988), Goyder (1982), Heberlein and Baumgartner (1978, 1981), Hubbard and Little (1988), Jones (1979), and Willimack and colleagues (1995) discuss increasing return rates in surveys.
15. For a comparison among types of surveys, see Backstrom and Hursh-Cesar (1981:16–23), Bradburn and Sudman (1988:94–110), Dillman (1978:39–78), Fowler (1984:61–73), and Frey (1983:27–55).
16. For more on survey research interviewing, see Brenner and colleagues (1985), Cannell and Kahn (1968), Converse and Schuman (1974), Dijkstra and van der Zouwen (1982), Foddy (1993), Gorden (1980), Hyman (1975), and Moser and Kalton (1972:270–302).
17. See Turner and Martin (1984:262–269, 282).
18. From Moser and Kalton (1972:273).
19. The use of probes is discussed in Backstrom and Hursh-Cesar (1981:266–273), Gorden (1980:368–390), and Hyman (1975:236–241).
20. See Bradburn and Sudman (1980), Pollner and Adams (1997), and Zane and Matsoukas (1979).
21. The race or ethnicity of interviewers is discussed in Anderson and colleagues (1988), Bradburn (1983), Cotter and colleagues (1982), Davis (1997), Finkel and colleagues (1991), Gorden (1980:168–172), Reese and colleagues (1986), Schaffer (1980), Schuman and Converse (1971), and Weeks and Moore (1981).
22. See Catania and associates (1996) and Kane and MacAulay (1993).
23. CATI is discussed in Bailey (1987:201–202), Bradburn and Sudman (1988:100–101), Frey (1983:24–25, 143–149), Groves and Kahn (1979:226), Groves and Mathiowetz (1984), and Karweit and Meyers (1983).
24. On reporting survey results in the media, see Channels (1993) and MacKeun (1984).
25. See Singer (1988).
26. According to www.cbc.radio-canada.ca/accountability/journalistic/surveys.shtml, "To ensure the validity and reliability of their results, surveys of public opinion must be conducted according to tested methods and recognized standards. Any departure from methods or standards and other relevant information on the techniques or funding of such research should be known to the public."
27. From Turner and Martin (1984:62).

PART III

Planning and Writing a Research Report

CHAPTER 10

Planning a Study

Taken from: *Understanding Research*, by W. Lawrence Neuman

Rick Friedman/Corbis

Do you have a tattoo? Have you ever wondered why people get tattoos? Your curiosity about tattoos can be the start of a research study. You might begin by looking at the several books and 25 social research articles on tattooing published in the past five years. This may help you turn the broad topic of tattoos into a research question for a study. You might ask, Why are tattoos popular for people in certain cultures or times? This question directs you to look at the cultural and historical development of tattoos—their use to brand people or in religious rituals. You might learn that the word *tattoo* originated from the Tahitian word *tatau*. Tattoos were used thousands of years ago in what is today Japan, Siberia, India, Peru, and Egypt. Certain peoples, such as the Maori in New Zealand, some Amazon tribes, and certain subcultures, such as Japanese crime gangs or Neo-Nazi skinheads, regularly tattoo. Alternatively, you might ask, How many people in the United States today have tattoos and what types of people get them? To answer these questions you might conduct survey research. One 2003 survey found that 16 percent of the U.S. population has a tattoo. This rises to 28 percent of people under the age of 25. There is no difference in the male–female tattoo rate. Democrats are slightly (18 percent) more likely to get them than Republicans (14 percent) and gay-lesbian-bisexuals (31 percent) more than straights and so forth (Harris Interactive 2003). Maybe you want to ask, How do others think about people who have tattoos? To answer this question, you might conduct an experiment similar to that by Hawkes, Senn, and Thorn (2004). They looked at people's reactions to college females with a tattoo. Participants in the study read about women. The researchers varied details about each woman's characteristics and her tattoo (its size and location). They also measured related factors, such as how people view gender roles. If your question is about tattoos on people in music videos, you could conduct a content analysis study of music videos to see what tattoos are shown and who has them. Maybe you are curious about the business of tattooing. You could examine existing statistics and records to find the number of tattooing businesses, suppliers, and tattoo artists. If you are curious about subjective beliefs of people who get tattoos, you could conduct a qualitative field research study like that by Atkinson (2004). He spent a lot of time with tattooed people and tattoo artists and got to know them very well. Alternatively, you might focus on field research with a specific subgroup, such as gang members or Neo-Nazis, to see whether they see their tattoos differently. Many young people in North America today who get a tattoo say that it signals a rejection of authority, is a statement about control over their body, indicates group membership, or is a form of spiritual-artistic self-expression. Of course, once top celebrities or most of your friends get a tattoo, you may get one to mimic an idol or to conform to peer pressure. This example of tattoos shows how to turn a topic into the start of a research study. In this chapter, we will look at how to take a topic and design a research study to examine that topic in depth.[1]

You are now ready to look at the specifics of study design. Recall the steps of the research process: Begin with a general topic, narrow it into a specific research question, and then decide how to conduct a study that can address the research question. Before gathering data, you might prepare a **research proposal**, which is written a detailed plan for doing a study.

PICKING A STUDY TOPIC

Topics arise from many sources: past studies, television or film, personal reactions or experiences, discussions with friends and family, or ideas from a book, magazine, or newspaper. A topic may be something that arouses your curiosity, something about which you hold deep commitments, or something you believe is wrong and want to change. A topic appropriate for social research is one that you *generalize* about social *patterns* that operate in *aggregates* and are *empirically observable*. Let us look at these four features briefly:

- *Generalize.* The topic is beyond one isolated unique instance; it is likely to reappear and applies to a broad scope of people, places, times, or events.
- *Social pattern.* The topic has regularity or some kind of structure/form that describes interconnections among a set of events, situations, or relationships in a condensed way.
- *Aggregates.* The topic applies to a collection of people or other units (e.g., families, businesses, schools, hospitals, or neighborhoods). The people/units do not have to be connected to one another or even be aware of the others. There could be as few as ten or as many as hundreds of millions.
- *Empirically observable.* The topic appears in the observable world in a way that we can detect and observe it using our senses (sight, sound, touch, smell) directly or indirectly.

These four features rule out some topics. They eliminate particularistic situations (e.g., why your boy/girlfriend dumped you yesterday, why your friend's little sister hates her third grade teacher) and a single case (e.g., your own family). Nonetheless, patterns (boyfriends of this type tend to act in this way, children often dislike third grade teachers for one of four main reasons) help us understand particular situations. Also ruled out are things impossible to observe, even indirectly (e.g., unicorns, alien space creatures, or ghosts with supernatural powers). We cannot study imaginary objects, but we can study people's beliefs about them (e.g., what types of people tend to believe in ghosts and why).

research proposal a detailed plan for conducting a study on a specific research question, that includes a literature review and specific techniques to be used.

CONDUCTING A REVIEW OF PAST STUDIES

An early step when doing study is to read past studies, or to conduct a **literature review**. The "literature" refers to past research reports on a topic. Reading the literature serves several functions.

- It helps you to narrow down a broad topic by showing you how others conducted their studies. You can use other studies as a model of how narrowly focused your research question should be.
- It provides you with examples of research designs, measures, and techniques that you might use.
- It informs you about what is known about a topic. Past studies teach you the key ideas, factors, terms, and issues surrounding a topic. You may wish to replicate, test, or extend what others already found.
- It presents you with examples of what final research reports look like, their parts, form, and writing style.
- It can help you to improve writing skills and learn subtle elements of conducting a good research study.
- It is often fun and may stimulate your creativity and curiosity.

Before you go off to search for the published reports of studies, it is essential to be organized. To prepare a well-written, complete literature review, you have to schedule your time and develop a search plan. The ideal literature review is a carefully crafted summary of the recent studies on a topic. It discusses both study findings and how researchers reached the findings. In the review, you must carefully document all sources.

Doing a literature review is rooted in an assumption that knowledge accumulates. We build on what others have done. Recall that research is the collective effort of many people who share their results with one another. We pursue knowledge as a community. This is why researchers constantly compare, replicate, or criticize other studies. Certain studies may be especially important and a few individual researchers may become famous, but each research project is just one small part of the larger, collective process of expanding what we know. The study you do today builds on those of the past, and studies you or others conduct in the future will build on the studies being conducted today. As Sir Isaac Newton put it, "If I have seen further it is by standing on the shoulders of giants."[2] Every research achievement builds on those who came before.

Where Do You Find the Research Literature?

You can find research reports in several locations. This section briefly discusses each type and provides you with a simple road map for how to access them.

Periodicals. You can learn about social research in newspapers, in popular magazines, on television or radio broadcasts, and in Internet news summaries. They can be the start of a topic or research question, but they are not sufficient for preparing a literature review. They are not the full, complete reports of a study that you need for a literature review. Media reports are selected and highly condensed summaries journalists prepare for a general audience. They lack many essential details required to evaluate a study. Textbooks and encyclopedias contain condensed summaries of studies to introduce readers to a topic. They are also inadequate for a literature review because essential details are absent. To conduct a literature review, you must locate the complete report of a study. The full reports first appear in specialized periodicals.

A periodical (or "serial," in librarian terminology) is any publication (print or electronic) that appears regularly over time (such as daily, weekly, monthly, quarterly, or annually). There are thousands of periodicals and they come in a vast array

literature review a summary of previously conducted studies on the same topic or research question.

Making It Practical A Literature Review Search Plan

Evaluate resources: How much time can you devote to the search? Do you have access to a college or university library? Do you know what computerized literature search tools are available at the library and how to use them? Do you want to locate a minimum number of studies? Can you easily distinguish an empirical research study from other articles? After answering these questions, you may wish to start preparing a time schedule with benchmarks or self-created deadlines for each step. The more practice you have in published studies, the faster it will go. A first-time search by a novice can take three or more times longer than one by an experienced person.

Select and narrow the topic: You search a specific question, not a general topic. The faster you can focus on a specific research question, the quicker you can proceed. Some people devote days or weeks to focusing on a research question; this is not always necessary. The question you begin with is preliminary because you can adjust and refine it as you learn more from reading past studies.

Learn to use literature search tools: Use computerized search tools (discussed later in this chapter) to search the literature. The tools require that you convert your research question's central ideas and terms into keywords. It takes time and practice to become skilled at using specific tools. Librarians can help or may offer workshops that teach about the tools. If you have never used a tool, expect to spend an hour or more to learning to use it.

Plan to locate and scan read articles: The search tools yield a list of articles with your keywords, but they cannot determine the true relevance of the articles for your research question. You must decide their relevance by scanning the articles' titles, abstracts (to be discussed later), or first few paragraphs. Based on a quick scan-read, you decide what is relevant. If the search tool locates 35 articles, it may take two hours to scan-read all of them and decide their relevance. You may end with 10 relevant, useful studies to read in depth.

Allow time to extract the major findings: Reading a scholarly research study is a skill that improves with practice. Most have a sophisticated vocabulary and technical information. It takes time to know what to look for. As you read, ask three questions: What was this study really about? How did researchers conduct the study (i.e., gather data), and What is the study's main finding or outcome? You want to extract the essential elements from a research report and write them as notes. Plan how to take notes and record all key source details (discussed later in this chapter). You might spend one hour reading and taking notes on each relevant article.

Final stage—synthesize: Once you have enough articles (because there are no more, you are learning nothing new with additional ones, or you ran out of time), you must pull together and integrate what they said. You might use a few quotes, but you mostly want to paraphrase (put in your own words). Integrating different studies and synthesizing what they really say in combination is a difficult thinking and writing task. Plan to reread what each study said more than once and return to the full article for clarification and verification.

Figure 10.1 Advancing Knowledge

of types. It is easy to be confused about the types of periodicals. With skill, you can learn to distinguish among the following five types:

- Peer-reviewed scholarly journals in which researchers present reports of studies
- Popularized social science magazines for an educated general audience
- Practitioner advice/opinion/news-technical publications, newsletters, and magazines
- Opinion magazines in which scholars and experts debate and express their views
- "Mass market" or "trade" newspapers and magazines that are written for the general public

You want to locate scholarly journals because that is where full reports of empirical research appear. Articles in the other types of periodicals may discuss study findings, but they lack essential details about the study. Popularized social science magazines offer the interested, educated public a simplified version of study findings without all the details. Most professions have news/communication newsletters for working professionals in which you may find discussions of a research study or its implications, but they lack full study details. Experts and scholars write articles for serious opinion/public issue magazines about topics on which they may also conduct empirical research (e.g., welfare reform, prison expansion, voter turnout, new marketing techniques). These publications differ in purpose, look, and scope from scholarly journals. They are an arena for debates about issues, not where researchers present a full report of their studies. Mass market publications provide the general public with news, opinion, and entertainment. You can find them at large newsstands, public libraries, or bookstores. They are source for many current events, but they do not contain reports of research studies.

You can find full reports of research studies in the following six outlets:

- *Scholarly journals.* The main place to look; they are stored for long periods in many locations and have a well-developed system to help you locate relevant articles;
- *Books.* In-depth and valuable for some topics, but difficult to find and time-consuming to read;
- *Government documents.* Only some are relevant and access may be limited, difficult to find;
- *Ph.D. dissertations.* Can be very valuable for an extensive review but difficult to find and access;

PhotoAlto/James Hardy/Getty Images Royalty Free

Summary Review **Different Types of Periodicals**

Periodical Type	Example	Authors	Purpose	Strength	Weakness
Peer-reviewed scholarly journal	*Social Science Quarterly, American Educational Research Journal, Journal of Applied Psychology, Social Forces*	Professors and professional researchers	Report on empirical research studies to professionals and build scientific knowledge	Highest quality, most accurate and most objective with complete details	Technical, difficult to read, requires background knowledge or training, not always about current issues
Semischolarly professional publication	*American Prospect, Society, Psychology Today, American Demographics*	Professors, professional policy makers, politicians	Disseminate and discuss new findings and their implications for professionals and the educated public	Generally accurate, somewhat easy to read	Lacks full detail and explanation, often includes opinion mixed in with discussion
Practitioner magazine or newsletter	*Coach & Athletic Director, Military Police, Retail Merchandiser, Mental Health Weekly*	Working professionals and some professors or "experts"	Provide a communication forum for working professionals	Current news and debates on relevant issues	Narrow focus and rarely builds general knowledge
Opinion magazine	*Nation, Human Events, Public Interest, Commentary*	Professors, professional policy makers, politicians	Present value-based ideas and opinions for professionals and educated public	Carefully written and reasoned	One-sided view and highly value based
Mass market magazines for the public	*Time, Esquire, Ebony, Redbook, Forbes, Fortune*	Professional journalists and other writers	Entertain, present, and discuss current events for lay public	Easy to read, easy to locate	Often inaccurate and incomplete

- *Policy reports.* Often relevant but are difficult to locate and only available for short periods of time; and
- *Presented papers.* Very difficult to locate, many are later published in scholarly journals.

A Special Type of Periodical: Scholarly Journals. The primary place where researchers disseminate information about studies is in scholarly journals (e.g., *Advances in Nursing Science, American Educational Research Journal, American Political Science Review, Journal of Marketing, American Journal of Sociology, Criminology, Nursing Research,* and *Social Science Quarterly*). Scholarly journals are essential to a literature review because they have the complete reports of research. You rarely find them outside of college and university libraries (or an online service connected with a college library). Many have *journal* or *review* in their title but not all do. They have the following features:

1. Most if not all of the articles are reports about original research studies.
2. Articles are peer-reviewed (see discussion in next section).
3. The articles have a reference or bibliography section that lists sources in detail.
4. Articles are part of an indexing location system accessible with **article search tools** (discussed later).

Peer review is a type of quality assurance system for the publication of research. After a researcher completes a study and writes a report about it, he or she presents it in several forums. The most frequently used and respected forum is a scholarly journal. It demands the highest level of rigor and is widely read by knowledgeable professional researchers. A critical feature of scholarly journal is that articles are **peer reviewed**. This means a study report went through the following peer review process:

1. A researcher prepares the detailed report of a study in a specific format and sends it (in pre-publication form it is called a manuscript) to the editor of a scholarly journal for consideration for possible publication.
2. The editor (a respected, experienced researcher with a deep knowledge of the field) looks at the manuscript and makes certain it meets minimal standards and is relevant for the specific journal.
3. The editor selects several (two to six) respected peer researchers to be volunteer reviewers. Each reviewer independently reads and evaluates the manuscript. He or she looks for a study's contribution to advancing knowledge, its originality, the quality of research design and execution, and the technical correctness of the research procedures. The editor also evaluates the report's completeness, organization, use of sources, and writing quality.
4. Each peer reviewer returns to the editor a written evaluation with criticisms, comments, and suggestions.
5. The editor examines all the evaluations from the reviewers and then decides to accept the manuscript as is and publish it; to ask the researcher to revise and resubmit the report for a second round of evaluation; or to reject the manuscript.

Most scholarly journals use a "blind review" version of the peer review process. In it, a researcher does not know the identity of the peer reviewers who evaluate the manuscript, and reviewers do not know who conducted the study. A blind review ensures that reviewers judge the manuscript solely on its own merits. Personal relationships with the author and his or her reputation do not influence decision making.

Many scholarly journals accept one-half to one-fourth of what they receive for consideration. Some highly prestigious and widely read journals publish 10 percent of the submitted manuscripts. That is, they turn down 90 percent of what researchers have sent to them. When you read articles in the high-prestige journals, you are seeing the top 10 percent of current research.

article search tool an online service or publication that provides an index, abstract list, or database with which you can quickly search for articles in numerous scholarly journals by title, topic, author, or subject area.

peer reviewed a scholarly publication that has been independently evaluated for its quality and merits by several knowledgeable professional researchers and found acceptable.

Scholarly journals feature more than reports of research. They also contain letters to the editor, theoretical essays, book reviews, legal case analysis, and comments on other published studies. Some specialized journals have only have book reviews; others only have literature review essays *(e.g., Annual Review of Psychology, Annual Review of Nursing Research, Annual Review of Law and Social Science, Annual Review of Public Health)* in which a researcher gives a "current state of the field" essay.

Except for peer review, there is no simple "seal of approval" to distinguish scholarly journals from other periodicals. Once you find a peer-reviewed scholarly journal, you need to distinguish an empirical research study from other types of articles. This takes judgment skills or the advice of experienced researchers or professional librarians. The best way to learn to distinguish among types of publications and articles is to read many articles in scholarly journals.

The Internet has a full copy of some, but not all, scholarly journal articles. Most journals charge a fee to access articles over the Internet; your college library may allow you free access (because the library paid the fee). Internet services sometimes provide a full, exact copy of the article, but some may only provide a short summary. Many services feature articles for a limited number of years and only from certain scholarly journals. Someday the Internet may replace print versions. For now, 99.5 percent of full scholarly journal articles are available in print, and about one-half of those from the past decade are available on the Internet in full form.

Photo Courtesy of Annie Pickert, Permission granted by Wiley-Blackwell for reproduction of *Social Science Quarterly*, March 2008, Volume 89, Number 1

You need to use an online library service to find articles. Once you locate a scholarly journal (see Making It Practical: Locating Scholarly Journals), you need to check that it is an article with study results and not another type (e.g., opinion essay, book

abstract short summary, usually on the first page of a scholarly journal article.

Making It Practical Locating Scholarly Journals

Your college library has a section for scholarly journals and magazines, or, in some cases, it mixes them with books. Look at a map of library facilities or ask a librarian to find this section. Many libraries place the most recent issues, which look like thin paperbacks or thick magazines, in a "current periodicals" section. The library stores them temporarily until it receives all the issues of a volume. After the library has an entire volume, staff members bind all issues together and place the volume in the library's collection. They place scholarly journals from different fields together with other periodicals or serials. Libraries post a list of the periodicals to which they subscribe.

Scholarly journals are published as rarely as once a year or as frequently as weekly. Most appear four to six times a year. For example, *Sociological Quarterly* appears four times a year, where as the *Annual Review of Nursing Research* appears once a year. Librarians and scholars created a system for tracking articles in scholarly journals. Every scholarly journal has a year, volume number, and issue number. When a journal begins, it is with volume 1, issue 1, and the numbers increase thereafter. The volume is a year of articles, and an issue is a part of the volume with several articles. Each issue has a table of contents with the title, author(s), and pages of articles. Most journals number pages by volume, not by issue or article. Page 1 is the first issue of a volume. Not all journals begin their publishing cycle in January. Issue 1 might begin in July or September. Page numbering continues throughout the entire volume and articles on consecutive pages. One issue may have from 1 to 50 articles, but most have 8 to 18 articles. Articles are 5 to 50 pages long. Because one volume is one year, a journal issue with volume 52 usually means that it has been operating for 52 years.

To locate an article, we use journal name, volume, year, issue, author, article title, and page numbers. These details are the **"citation"** of a source in the reference section of an article or literature review. Most journal articles have an **abstract**. A good abstract tells you the topic, research question, method, and findings. There are hundreds of scholarly journals in most fields. Each journal charges an annual subscription fee ($100 to $3000). For this reason, only the largest research libraries subscribe to most of them. If an article is not available on the Internet or at your local library, you can often obtain a copy from a distant library through an interlibrary loan service, a system by which libraries lend materials to other libraries.

review). It is easier to identify quantitative studies because most have a methods or data section and charts, statistical formulas, and tables of numbers. Qualitative research articles are easy to confuse with theoretical essays, literature review articles, idea-discussion essays, policy recommendations, book reviews, and legal case analyses.

Books. Books communicate information, provoke thought, and entertain. There are many types of books: picture books, textbooks, short story books, novels, popular fiction or nonfiction, religious books, children's books, and others. Some books report on original research or are collections of research articles. Libraries shelve and assign call numbers to them as with other types of books. You can find information on them (e.g., title, author, and publisher) in the library's catalog system. Only college or university libraries have books that report on research. It is difficult to distinguish them from other books. Some publishers, such as university presses, specialize in publishing them. Qualitative types of research are more likely to appear in a book format, as are the results of long, complex studies that may also be published in scholarly journal articles. Because they are not in the article search tool system, finding studies in books is difficult. Three types of books can contain research reports:

- *Monographs.* Contain the details of a long complex study or a set of interconnected studies.
- *Readers.* Contain articles on a topic, original or gathered from journals. Often the editor of the book has modified the research (i.e., shortened and simplified it) to make it easier for nonexperts to read.
- *Edited collection.* A collection of new research reports, articles reprinted from scholarly journals, or a mixture of both on a common topic.

Dissertations. All graduate students who receive the Ph.D. degree are required to do original research. They write the study as a dissertation thesis. Dissertations are in the library of the university that granted the Ph.D. About one-third of dissertation results are published later as books or articles. Because dissertations report on original research, they can be valuable sources of information. Specialized indexes list dissertations. *Dissertation Abstracts International* (online and print version) lists dissertations with their authors, titles, and universities (see Figure 10.2). To get a copy of the dissertation, you must borrow it via interlibrary loan from the degree-granting university, if that university permits this, or purchase a photocopy of it.

Government Documents. The U.S. federal government, the governments of other nations, state- or provincial-level governments, the United Nations, and international agencies such as the World Bank, all sponsor research studies and publish research reports. Many college and university libraries have some of these documents in their holdings, often in a special government documents section. Most libraries hold only the most frequently requested documents and reports. You can use specialized lists of publications and indexes to search for them, but usually you will need the help of a librarian. Some are also available online.

Policy Reports. Research institutes and policy centers (e.g. Brookings Institute, Rand Corporation) publish papers and reports (see Example Study Box 1: Sexual Harassment). An organization might list its reports on its Internet site and make copies available on the Internet. To find all of them, you need to contact the organization and request a list of reports. Sometimes organizations charge a fee for their reports.

Presented Papers. Each year, the professional associations in various fields (e.g., criminal justice, education, marketing, nursing, political science, psychology, recreation, sociology) hold annual meetings. At them hundreds of researchers gather to deliver, listen to, or discuss oral reports of recent research, with many

■ **Figure 10.2** Example Dissertation Abstract

Title: Learning English in a midwestern urban high school: A case study of an ELL Vietnamese student
Author(s): Fan, Yanan
Degree: Ph.D.
Year: 2006
Pages: 00179
Institution: Michigan State University; 0128
Advisor: Adviser Anne Haas Dyson
Source: DAI, 67, no. 10A (2006): p. 3686
Standard No: **ISBN:** 978-0-542-90694-7
Abstract: The goal of this ethnographic case study is to examine what it means to learn English within the sociocultural contexts of a mid-sized Midwestern urban high school, focusing on a Vietnamese teenager. The data set consists of fieldnotes from key educational sites; interviews of students, teachers, and a first language aide; and collected artifacts (e.g., photocopies of student's written work, class handouts and syllabi, audiotaped interactions of the student in classrooms, visual images of sites, and site documents). Based on an inductive analysis of the data set, I asserted that the student's learning experiences are embedded in and influenced by the sociopolitical assumptions of a larger educational system that defines second-language learning. The student was lost in the institution's inconsistent vision of literacy while negotiating expectations and opportunities for participation in varied classrooms with little support and resources. In the meantime, the student's language proficiency, immigrant history, ethnicity, race, gender, and the model minority rhetoric all figure into her identity formation in the peer self-segregation of her school. This study extends the understanding of the complexities of second language learning, of the challenges adolescent immigrant students face in secondary schools, and of the cultural construction of the model minority rhetoric. It also contributes to the methodological discussion on conducting ethnographical studies by offering a reflection of the researcher's own negotiation of her relationship with the participants, considering issues of membership, reciprocity, and power.

Source: Copy of an abstract from *Dissertation Abstracts*, International.

Example Study Box 1 **Sexual Harassment**

In December 2005 the AAUW (American Association of University Women) Educational Foundation released a 72-page report, "Drawing the Line: Sexual Harassment on Campus." It is an advocacy policy report that describes an applied research study on sexual harassment. Instead of an abstract, as in a scholarly journal, it contains a three-page executive summary, and research methods are described in an appendix. Data for the study came from a stratified random sample and an online survey. A professional survey organization sent people in its national database password-protected e-mail invitations to participate in a survey. Organization employees randomly selected a sample of students enrolled in public and private postsecondary schools that offered two- and four-year degrees. In total, they interviewed 2036 U.S. residents ages 18 to 24 enrolled in college in 2005. The average interview lasted 17 minutes.

The executive summary shows you that this was a descriptive study. Its research questions were as follows: How common is sexual harassment, who is being harassed, who is doing the harassing, how are students being affected by harassment, and what do students think should be done about it? Key findings are that one-third of students experience sexual harassment in their first year of college. Most harassment is verbal, but about one in three of the harassed students also experienced physical harassment. Men and women are both likely to be harassed but in different ways. Harassed students feel upset, embarrassed, angry, less confident, afraid, worried, and confused. They are likely to be disappointed in their college experience. Lesbian, gay, bisexual, or transgender (LGBT) students are more likely than heterosexual students to experience sexual harassment. Males harass more than females, with nearly one-half of male college students saying that they sexually harassed someone. The harassing men thought it was funny or thought the victim wanted attention. They did not consider it serious or think about the consequences. Less than 10 percent of harassed students file a report with university officials. The study report contains charts and statistics. It also contains quotes from individual students about their ideas on and experiences with sexual harassment. A hard copy of the report is for sale from the AAUW for $12, 1111 Sixteenth Street NW, Washington, DC, 20036, helpline@aauw.org, or you can download a free copy if you complete an information form at. http://www.aauw.org/research/dtl.cfm.

also in written form. People who attend can pick up a copy. If you do not attend, you can obtain a meeting program with a list of each paper with its title, author, and author's place of employment. You can write directly to the author to request a copy.

How to Conduct a Literature Review: A Six-Step Process

In this section, we examine six steps (see Figure 10.3) in locating research reports and preparing a literature review.

STEP 1. Refine the topic. Your search begins with a research question, not a topic. It is impossible to examine a broad topic with any depth or seriousness. A topic such as "divorce" or "crime" or "patient care" is too broad. Narrow the topic to something such as, "the stability of families with stepchildren" or "economic inequality and crime rates across 50 nations" or "long-term care of elderly patients with a heart condition." You further narrow this into a research question by adding conditions and limiting the range of cases/situations to which it applies (see discussion later in this chapter). Searching the literature itself also helps you focus a research question.

STEP 2. Design your search. (1) Decide on the review's extensiveness by fixing parameters for your search: how much time can you devote to it, how many years back will you look, what is the minimum number of reports you will examine, how many libraries you can visit, if you will look at both articles and books or only articles, and so forth. Expect to make multiple visits to a library (online or physically). If you have 15 hours to do a literature review, do not expect to locate and include

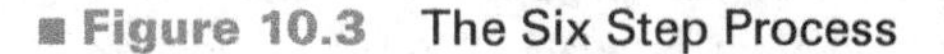

■ Figure 10.3 The Six Step Process

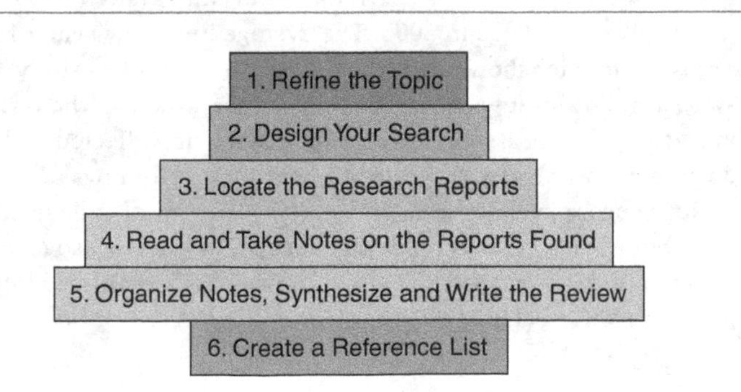

more than 10 to 12 research reports. (2) Decide which article search tools to use (discussed later in this chapter). (3) Decide how you will record the bibliographic information for each source and how to take notes (e.g., in a notebook, on 3 × 5 cards, in a computer document).

STEP 3. Locate the research reports. Searching varies by type of research report (article, book, or dissertation). Scholarly journal articles are usually the most valuable and least time-consuming to find. Locating a full copy of the reports can take time. After you find a full copy, you must read and take notes on it.

Articles in Scholarly Journals. Most studies are reported in scholarly journals. However, there are hundreds of journals, most go back several decades, and each may have over a hundred articles each year. Luckily, article search tools (sometimes called indexes or research literature services) make the task easier (See Making It Practical: Using Article Search Tools).

Many article search tools only provide author, titles—and abstract, not the full text of an article. Once you get search results, you can scan the titles and abstracts for relevant articles. Articles usually contain reference sections with leads to additional sources. For example, the article discussed in Figure 10.4 on a content analysis study of the media contained 53 references. The article on sexual harassment of college women listed 93 items, including journal articles, books, and other research reports. Reading the reference section can point you to relevant sources that you might not find using an article search tool.

Making It Practical Using Article Search Tools

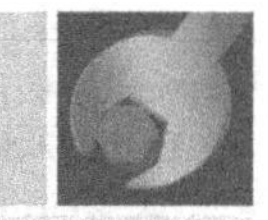

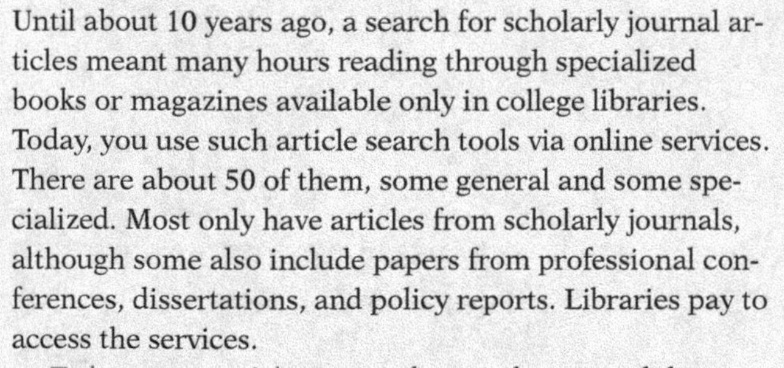

Until about 10 years ago, a search for scholarly journal articles meant many hours reading through specialized books or magazines available only in college libraries. Today, you use such article search tools via online services. There are about 50 of them, some general and some specialized. Most only have articles from scholarly journals, although some also include papers from professional conferences, dissertations, and policy reports. Libraries pay to access the services.

To locate an article you use keywords or search by author name. Many article search tools are titled *abstracts* or *indexes* (e.g., *Psychological Abstracts, Social Sciences Index,* and *Gerontological Abstracts*). For education-related topics, the Educational Resources Information Center (ERIC) system is valuable; for medicine, MEDLINE is widely used. The name *abstract* is from an article's "abstract" or a short summary, usually placed at the beginning of an article. It does not contain all the findings or details of a study, but you can use abstracts to screen articles for relevance. Some are highly organized and contain specific details whereas others are less structured (see Figure 10.4).

You can search by author, subject, or keyword. Search tool subjects are limited to a few popular ones. Unless you know that a specific researcher did a study or you are at a late stage in searching, you probably will not use the author name for a search. For most searches, you will use keywords. You must develop key terms for your research question. The question *Are illegal drugs more common in urban than rural high schools?* might include keywords such as *drug abuse, substance abuse, drug laws, illegal drugs*. You can combine these with keywords as *high schools, high school students, rural schools, urban schools,* and *secondary schools*.

You should consider several synonyms for keywords. For example, a search with the keyword *homicide* may not find articles that use the word *murder*, so you want to try both. Most search tools look for a keyword in a title or the abstract. Often you can use multiple keywords using the connectors *or* or *and*. If you choose very board keywords or many connected by *or* you will get a huge number of irrelevant articles. Narrow keywords or several keywords connected with *and* may yield zero articles. To learn what works best, try experimenting with alternatives. The best search tools are only available to students or employees through a college library.

Figure 10.4 Examples of Two Abstracts from Scholarly Articles

Example abstract of journal article: Highly Structured

Article title: Measuring Media Bias: A Content Analysis of Time and Newsweek Coverage of Domestic Social Issues, 1975–2000
Authors: Tawnya J. Adkins Covert and Philo C. Wasburn
Publication Information: *Social Science Quarterly* Vol. 88 (3), pp. 690–706 [September 2007].

Abstract

Objective. This study is an effort to produce a more systematic, empirically-based, historical-comparative understanding of media bias than generally is found in previous works. **Methods.** The research employs a quantitative measure of ideological bias in a formal content analysis of the United States' two largest circulation news magazines, Time and Newsweek. Findings are compared with the results of an identical examination of two of the nation's leading partisan journals, the conservative National Review and the liberal Progressive. **Results.** Bias scores reveal stark differences between the mainstream and the partisan news magazines' coverage of four issue areas: crime, the environment, gender, and poverty. **Conclusion.** Data provide little support for those claiming significant media bias in either ideological direction.

Example abstract of journal article: Less Structured

Article title: The Moderating Roles of Race and Gender-Role Attitudes in the Relationship Between Sexual Harassment And Psychological Well-Being
Authors: Juliette C. Rederstorff, Nicole T. Buchanan, and Isis H. Settles
Publication Information: *Psychology of Women Quarterly* Vol. 31 (1), pp 50–61 [March 2007]

Abstract

Although previous research has linked sexual harassment to negative psychological outcomes, few studies have focused on moderators of these relationships. The present study surveyed Black (n = 88) and White (n = 170) female undergraduates who endorsed experiences of sexual harassment to examine whether traditional gender attitudes differentially moderated the relationship between sexual harassment and three outcomes: posttraumatic stress symptoms, general clinical symptoms, and satisfaction with life. We replicated past findings that sexual harassment is related to negative outcomes. Further, the results supported our hypothesis that less traditional gender attitudes (i.e., more feminist attitudes) would buffer the negative effects of sexual harassment for White women, whereas the same attitudes would exacerbate its negative effects for Black women. We discuss reasons for these differences, including Black women's double consciousness and differences in the meaning of feminist and traditional gender attitudes for Black and White women.

Example Study Box 2 Sexual Harassment, Literature Search

Here is a search I conducted using article search tools. My general topic was "sexual harassment." I narrowed the topic to "sexual harassment of female college students." I looked for peer-reviewed articles published from 2001 to 2006. I started with the article search tool called "EBSCO-Host Academic Elite." This tool examines 1500 peer-reviewed journals for all academic fields back to the late 1990s for most journals. Other article search tools contain information from different journals or cover different time spans. My first keywords were *sexual harassment* and *university*. The search located 199 articles. I found that many were not about college students. The search tool had picked up the word *university* from where the author worked. A search with *sexual harassment* and *student* yielded 80 articles. Some were about high school students and some were about males being harassed by females, but many were relevant. I narrowed my search further to *sexual harassment* and *college female* and got 28 articles. Not all were on my topic of interest. I noticed that "gender-related harassment" and "unwanted sexual encounters" appeared in some articles. This gave me the idea to use them as alternative keywords for sexual harassment. I next used three other article search tools with the same restrictions and used the same keywords as before. I found that the four article search tools located many of the same articles, but at times one search tool found articles not located by a different article search tool. This suggests that is usually best to use more than one search tool.

Number of Articles Found Using Different Article Search Tools
(peer reviewed articles, 2001–2006)

	Article Search Tool			
Keywords Used	**EBSCO-Host**	**Wilson-Web**	**Pro-quest**	**CSA-Illumina**
Sexual harassment & *university*	199	24	35	321
Sexual harassment & *student*	80	27	39	115
Sexual harassment & *college* & *female*	28	6	11	79

Specific article databases within each Article Search Tool: EBSCO-Host: Academic Elite; Wilson Web: Social Sciences, Education; Pro-quest: Criminal Justice, Gender Watch; CSA-Illumina: Social Services Abstracts & Sociological Abstracts.

Books. It is very difficult to find studies in books. The subject lists in library catalog systems are broad and not very useful. Moreover, they list only books in a particular library system. Professional librarians can help you locate books from other libraries. There is no sure-fire way to locate relevant books. Use multiple search methods, including a look at journals that contain book reviews and the bibliographies of articles.

Other Outlets. (Government documents, Ph.D. dissertations, Policy Reports, and Presented Papers) Locating studies in other outlets is far more difficult and time-consuming. A specific study might be highly relevant to your question, but few beginning researchers have the time or skills to search other outlets systematically.

STEP 4. Read and take notes on the reports found. It is easy to feel overwhelmed as you gather studies. To help, develop a system for taking notes. The old-fashioned approach is to write notes onto index cards. You then shift and sort the note cards, placing them in piles, then look for connections among them. This method still works. Today, most people use word-processing software and gather photocopies or printed versions of many articles.

10

Create Source and Content Files. Several strategies are used in literature searches and article reading. My strategy is to create two kinds of files: a *source file* and a *content file*. I recommend that you adopt a similar strategy.

In the source file, I record *all* the bibliographic information for each source, even if I may not use some of the articles. This includes journal name, full article title, date, volume and issue number, starting and ending page numbers, and the full names of all authors. It is easier to erase an unused source than to try to locate bibliographic information later when needed. The source file allows me to create a list of complete references very quickly.

I put substantive details in the content file. This file contains major findings, details of methodology (such as if it was a survey or experiment, the number of

■ **Figure 10.5** Web Page from EBSCO-Host Academic Elite Advanced Search

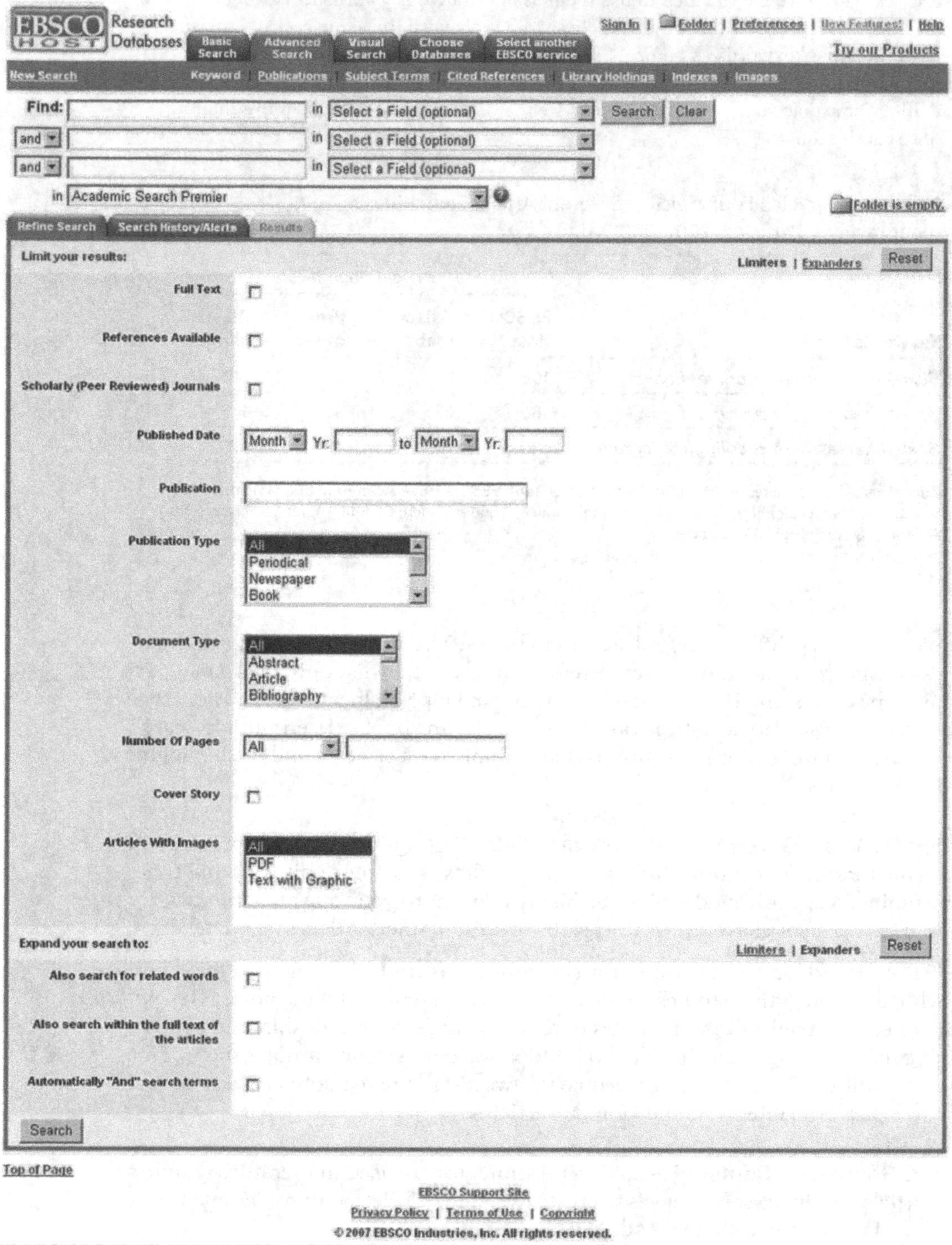

EBSCO HOST Research Databases

Basic Search | Advanced Search | Visual Search | Choose Databases | Select another EBSCO service

Sign In | Folder | Preferences | New Features! | Help

Try our Products

New Search | Keyword | Publications | Subject Terms | Cited References | Library Holdings | Indexes | Images

Find: in Select a Field (optional) Search Clear

and in Select a Field (optional)

and in Select a Field (optional)

in Academic Search Premier

Folder is empty.

Refine Search | Search History/Alerts | Results

Limit your results: Limiters | Expanders Reset

Full Text

References Available

Scholarly (Peer Reviewed) Journals

Published Date Month Yr: to Month Yr:

Publication

Publication Type: All, Periodical, Newspaper, Book

Document Type: All, Abstract, Article, Bibliography

Number Of Pages: All

Cover Story

Articles With Images: All, PDF, Text with Graphic

Expand your search to: Limiters | Expanders Reset

Also search for related words

Also search within the full text of the articles

Automatically "And" search terms

Search

Top of Page

EBSCO Support Site

Privacy Policy | Terms of Use | Copyright

Making It Practical How to Read a Scholarly Journal Article

1. Read with a clear purpose in mind. Are you reading to gain background knowledge on a broad topic or to find information for a very specific research question?
2. First read the title and abstract for an article's relevance and general content. Next, quickly scan subheadings and the introduction and conclusion sections.
3. Form a mental image of the article's topic, major findings, method, and general conclusion.
4. Consider your own opinion about or bias toward the topic, the method, the publication source. How might your own opinion color how you read and evaluate the study?
5. Marshal external knowledge. What do you know about the topic and the research methods used?
6. As you read the entire article, evaluate. What errors might be present? Does the discussion of findings follow the data? Is the article's conclusion consistent with its approach?
7. Summarize. Prepare your own abstract. Include the topic, the methods used, and the main findings. Next, take notes, including quotation from the article and page numbers for quotes or ideas.
8. Review the reference section or bibliography for additional sources.

participants), definitions of major concepts, how concepts were measured, and interesting quotes. When quoting, I *always* record the specific page number(s) on which the quote appears. On each content note, I put the author's last name and the publication year, which allows me to link multiple cards or computer notes in the content file to a specific source in the source file.

What to Record in Notes. It is best to be consistent when writing notes—use all computer files or all note cards of the same size. As you decide what to record about an article, book, or other source, it is better to err by writing a little too much rather than not enough. Your notes should answer the following questions:

- What is study's basic topic and question? Does it state expectations of what the data will show based on a theory? Often a study will look at multiple questions, but only one is of interest to you.
- How did the authors define and measure their major ideas?
- What is the study's basic design? What procedures and techniques did the author use (e.g., was it an experiment, a survey, a field research study, and so forth)?
- What is the data, group, or sample? What units were examined (individuals, families, companies, towns, or nations). How many were examined (5 or 5000)? How were units chosen?
- What findings are relevant to your research question? Studies often have multiple findings, and the findings most relevant for your research could be buried deep inside an article.

Critically reading research reports is a skill that takes time and practice to develop. Despite a peer review procedure, errors and sloppy logic can slip into research reports. Sometimes titles, abstracts, and the introduction are misleading; they may not fully explain the study's method and results. A good article is logically tight, and all its parts fit together. Weak articles make huge leaps in logic or omit transitional steps.

As you read for details and take notes, you develop a mental image of how researchers conducted a study. This is why reading many studies will expand your research design skills. If you read a study in which the authors were disorganized or did not clearly provide all the details, you will see quickly the importance of good organization and clearly specifying all details. As mentioned earlier, look at the reference section to find new sources.

You may encounter unfamiliar terms, new theoretical ideas, advanced technical vocabulary, or sophisticated statistical charts, graphs, and results beyond your back-

Figure 10.6 Example of Notes on an Article

ENTRY IN SOURCE FILE

Bearman, Peter, and Hannah Bückner. 2001. "Promising the Future: Virginity Pledges and First Intercourse." *American Journal of Sociology* Volume 106, pages 859–912, January, issue number 4.

CONTENT FILE

Bearman and Bückner 2001

Background: Since 1993, the Southern Baptist Church sponsored a movement among teens. Teens make a public pledge to remain virgins until marriage. Over 2.5 million teens have made the pledge. This study looks at whether the pledge influenced the timing of first sexual intercourse and whether pledging teens differ from those who did not pledge. Critics say the pledge supporters often reject sex education, hold an unrealistic and overly romanticized view of marriage, and push teens to follow to traditional gender roles.

Questions/expectations: Adolescents try to engage in behaviors that adults enjoy but that are forbidden to them. When social controls are high, adolescent opportunities to engage in forbidden behavior is limited. Expectation 1: Teens from nontraditional families will have fewer social controls, more freedom and less supervision. They are more likely to engage in forbidden behavior (sexual intercourse) than those from traditional families and close to their parents. Teens from traditional families experience greater social control and delay sexual activity. Expectation 2: Teens closely tied to an "identity movement" outside the family will modify their behaviors based on the norms taught by the movement. As a result, family influence on them will not be as strong.

Definitions and measures: Identity movement is a social movement that emphasizes a self-identity separate from the larger society and being the member of a select group. Movements recruit members who modify their identity. The abstinence pledge movement recruits through the Internet, church groups, and Christian music and rallies. A person sustains his or her movement-pledge identity by repeated interactions with other pledging members. Pledge—A public shift in identity. The study measured it by asking unmarried teens if they have "ever taken a public or written pledge to remain a virgin until marriage." Family type—The study measured three types: living with both biological parents; living with only a mother or father; and living with two adults one or both of whom are step- or foster parents Religiosity—Measured with three behavioral items: frequency of praying, church attendance, and self-report of the importance of religion in the person's life.

Research Design: U.S. teens who were in randomly sampled public or private schools in 1994–1995 completed a questionnaire on a single day within one 45-60-minute class period. About 80 percent of students in a school completed it. Researchers also interviewed a subset of the students at home for 90 minutes. All students were asked about their parent's educational and occupational background, household structure, risk behaviors, visions of the future, self-esteem, health status, contacts with friends, and the sports and extracurricular activities in which they participated. The in-home interview measured sensitive health risk behaviors, such as drug and alcohol use, sexual behavior, criminal activities and family dynamics.

Data or Subjects: 90,000 students in grades 7–12 in 141 schools. Schools varied from under 100 to more than 3,000 students. 20,000 of the 90,000 students completed a second questionnaire.

Findings: Teens who pledged substantially delayed the timing of first sexual intercourse. However, pledging teens were largely in social contexts where abstinence was already a social norm. Pledging teens were more religious, less developed physically, and from traditional family backgrounds. Once social context is considered, the pledging itself had little effect on the delay of sexual activity compared to teens who did not pledge. In short, teens from traditional social backgrounds, strong religious beliefs and close family ties were less likely to engage in early sexual activity whether or not they pledged. Teens from non-traditional backgrounds, weak religious beliefs and few family ties are more likely to engage in early sexual activity whether or not they pledged. Another finding was that pledging teens who engaged in sexual intercourse were less likely to use contraceptives than non-pledgers.

ground. This is because professional researchers are the primary audience for research reports. The technical terms and results communicate important information to this audience. Do not be overly concerned if you cannot follow everything. As a novice researcher and consumer of studies, you should not expect to have the sophisticated knowledge of an expert researcher. A lack of knowledge might prevent you from fully evaluating all aspects of a study, but you can still learn from and build on the studies. Even if parts are over your head now, you can improve and expand your understanding over time. Be prepared to read an article more than once.

Photocopying all the relevant articles can save time in recording notes, and you will have the entire report and can write on the photocopy. Although photocopying sounds like the easy route, it has several downsides:

- The time and cost of photocopying can add up (30 articles of 20 pages = 600 pages, at 7 cents = $42, at 10 minutes to copy each article = 300 minutes).
- Be aware of copyright laws. U.S. copyright laws permit photocopying for personal research use.
- Be certain to include all citation details (title, page numbers, volume, etc.) of each article.
- Organizing many articles can be cumbersome. Plus, you may use several parts of a single article for different ideas or purposes.
- You may have to reread articles more than once unless you highlight carefully or take good notes.

STEP 5. Organize notes, synthesize, and write the review. Synthesizing and discussing findings with clear writing is the most difficult step in preparing a literature review. After gathering information, you need to organize specific findings to create a mental map of how they fit together. Your organizing method depends on the purpose of the review. Usually, it is best to organize findings around your research question or around a few core shared findings. Most professionals try several organizing schemes before they settle on a final one. Organizing is a skill that improves with practice. Some people place notes into several piles, each representing a common theme. Others draw charts or diagrams to show the connections among different findings. Others create lists of how the many study findings agree and disagree. Organizing notes is a process. Often you will find that some references and notes are no longer relevant, and you will discard them. You may discover gaps or new areas that you did not consider previously. This may require return visits to the library to refine your search.

A common error when writing a first literature review is to list summaries of articles, one study after another. This indicates an incomplete process that stopped before synthesis. To synthesize means to combine parts or elements into an integrated whole. You want to blend the findings, methods, or statements from separate studies and end up with a coherent whole in which the studies fit together as one integrated picture. Like fitting together the pieces of a jigsaw puzzle, all the parts fit to present an overall picture. However, with jigsaw puzzles someone started with the picture and then cut it up. In a literature review, there is no preexisting picture. You create one out of the many studies. It is more like weaving cloth from many separate threads. The threads start separate and different but end up as one piece of cloth or clothing tightly held together.

You use all the skills of good writing to produce a literature review. Your goal is to produce a compact document that clearly summarizes what many studies say about a research question. A literature review is a neutral summary-description. It does not include your personal opinion or conjecture. The rules of good writing (e.g., clear organizational structure, an introduction and conclusion, transitions between sections, etc.) apply.

A good literature review communicates its purpose to the reader by its organization. If you write a review by listing a series of summaries, you to communicate a sense of purpose; your review reads as notes strung together. You want to organize

Making It Practical What a Good Literature Review Looks Like

EXAMPLE OF WEAK REVIEW

Sexual harassment has many consequences. Adams, Kottke, and Padgitt (1983) found that some women students said they avoided taking a class or working with certain professors because of the risk of harassment. They also found that men and women students reacted differently. Their research was a survey of 1000 men and women graduate and undergraduate students. Benson and Thomson's study in *Social Problems* (1982) lists many problems created by sexual harassment. In their excellent book *The Lecherous Professor*, Dziech and Weiner (1990) give a long list of difficulties that victims have suffered.

Researchers study the topic in different ways. Hunter and McClelland (1991) conducted a study of undergraduates at a small liberal arts college. They had a sample of 300 students, and students were given multiple vignettes that varied by the reaction of the victim and the situation. Jaschik and Fretz (1991) showed 90 women students at a mideastern university a videotape with a classic example of sexual harassment by a teaching assistant. Before it was labeled as *sexual harassment*, few women called it that. When asked whether it was sexual harassment, 98 percent agreed. Weber-Burdin and Rossi (1982) replicated a previous study on sexual harassment, but they used students at the University of Massachusetts. They had 59 students rate 40 hypothetical situations. Reilley, Carpenter, Dull, and Bartlett (1982) conducted a study of 250 female and 150 male undergraduates at the University of California at Santa Barbara. They also had a sample of 52 faculty. Both samples completed a questionnaire in which respondents were presented vignettes of sexual-harassing situations that they were to rate. Popovich et al. (1986) created a nine-item scale of sexual harassment. They studied 209 undergraduates at a medium-sized university in groups of 15 to 25. They found disagreement and confusion among students.

EXAMPLE OF BETTER REVIEW

The victims of sexual harassment suffer a range of consequences, from lowered self-esteem and loss of self-confidence to withdrawal from social interaction, changed career goals, and depression (Adams, Kottke, and Padgitt, 1983; Benson and Thomson, 1982; Dziech and Weiner, 1990). For example, Adams, Kottke, and Padgitt (1983) noted that 13 percent of women students said they avoided taking a class or working with certain professors because of the risk of harassment.

Research into campus sexual harassment has taken several approaches. In addition to survey research, many have experimented with vignettes or presented hypothetical scenarios (Hunter and McClelland, 1991; Jaschik and Fretz, 1991; Popovich et al., 1987; Reilley, Carpenter, Dull, and Barlett, 1982; Rossi and Anderson, 1982; Valentine-French and Radtke, 1989; Weber-Burdin and Rossi, 1982). Victim verbal responses and situational factors appear to affect whether observers label a behavior as harassment. There is confusion over the application of a sexual harassment label for inappropriate behavior. For example, Jaschik and Fretz (1991) found that only 3 percent of the women students shown a videotape with a classic example of sexual harassment by a teaching assistant initially labeled it as *sexual harassment*. Instead, they called it "sexist," "rude," "unprofessional," or "demeaning." When asked whether it was sexual harassment, 98 percent agreed. Roscoe et al. (1987) reported similar labeling difficulties.

common findings or arguments together, address the most important ideas first, logically link findings, and note discrepancies or weaknesses in the research (see Making It Practical: What a Good Literature Review Looks Like for an example).

STEP 6. Create the Reference List. The last step is to create a reference list, works cited list, or bibliography. Works cited and reference list are the same thing—an alphabetical list of sources cited or to which you referred. They differ from a bibliography, which is an alphabetical list of all the materials you consulted, whether or not you cited them. For a literature review, use a reference list of sources you discussed in the review.

How you indicate sources in the text of your review and in the reference list is very important. There are several format styles, each with separate rules. Different fields (e.g., psychology, history) use specific formats. In the text of a review itself, an in-text citation format in most common. It has the author or authors' last name and year of publication for a general statement, with page numbers for specific details or quotes. To discuss an article on abstinence pledges, I might say, *Bearman and*

Brückner (2001) studied the identity movement in which teens pledge to stay virgins until marriage. Alternatively, I could state, *In a study of the identity movement, teens pledged to stay virgins until marriage (Bearman and Brückner 2001).* A quote from a specific page might look like this: *The movement has been successful in organizing mass rallies in which speakers extol the benefits of abstinence to stadiums full of eager adolescents. Its growth rate has been phenomenal, and with it, the movement has spawned a whole new subculture in which it is "cool" to say no to sex (Bearman and Brückner 2001: 860).*

The order and format of source **citation** information can vary greatly. You need to learn which format style an instructor or publication requires. The citation format style precisely specifies how to organize details of source information in a reference list. Two reference books on the topic in social science are the *Chicago Manual of Style,* which contains nearly 80 pages on bibliographies and reference formats, and the *American Psychological Association Publication Manual,* which devotes about 60 pages to the topic.

The entry for a book is shorter and simpler than for an article. It has the following: author's name, book title, year of publication, place of publication, publisher's name. Article entries are more complex than book entries. They require the names of all authors, article title, journal name, and volume and page numbers. Some formats require the authors' complete first names whereas others use initials only. Some require the issue or month of publication; others do not (see Figure 10.7 for four styles, MLA [Modern Language Association], ASA [American Sociological Association], APA [American Psychological Association] and Chicago [*Chicago Manual of Style*]).

citation documenting a source of information in a standardized format.

Figure 10.7 Different Reference Citations for a Book and a Journal Article

Style	Book with One Author in Reference List
MLA	Pillow, Wanda S. Unfit Subjects: Educational Policy and the Teen Mother. New York: Routledge, 2004.
ASA	Pillow, Wanda S. 2004. *Unfit Subjects: Educational Policy and the Teen Mother.* New York: Routledge.
APA	Pillow, W.S. (2004). *Unfit subjects: Educational policy and the teen mother.* New York: Routledge.
Chicago	'Same as MLA for the arts, literature or history. Same as ASA for science fields.
Style	**Journal Article with Two Authors in Reference List (Journal Pagination by Volume)**
MLA	Bearman, Peter and Hannah Bückner. "Promising the future: Virginity pledges and first intercourse." American Journal of Sociology 106 (2001) 859–912.
ASA	Bearman, Peter and Hannah Bückner. 2001. "Promising the Future: Virginity Pledges and First Intercourse." *American Journal of Sociology* 106:859–912.
APA	Bearman, P., and Bückner, H. (2001). Promising the future: Virginity pledges and first intercourse. *American Journal of Sociology* 106, 859–912.
Chicago	Same as APA for science fields. Same as MLA for arts, literature and history.
Others	Bearman, Peter and Hannah Bückner, 2001. "Promising the future: Virginity pledges and first Intercourse." *Am. J. of Sociol.* 106:859–912. Bearman, P. and Bückner, H. (2001). "Promising the Future: Virginity Pledges and First Intercourse." *American Journal of Sociology* 106 (January): 859–912. Bearman, Peter and Hannah Bückner. 2001. "Promising the future: Virginity pledges and first Intercourse." *American Journal of Sociology* 106 (4):859–912. Bearman, P. and H. Bückner. (2001). "Promising the future: Virginity pledges and first intercourse." American Journal of Sociology *106, 859–912.* Peter Bearman and Hannah Bückner, "Promising the Future: Virginity Pledges and First Intercourse," American Journal of Sociology 106, no. 4 (2001): 859–912.

Format styles for sources in a reference list.

10

Tips for the Wise Consumer Using the Internet for Social Research

The Internet has revolutionized research. Only fifteen years ago, few people used it. Today, researchers and others use it Internet regularly to review the literature, to communicate with others, and to search for information. The Internet has been a mixed blessing. It has not proved to be the panacea that some people first thought it might be. It is an important way to find information, but it remains one tool among others. It is a supplement rather than a replacement for traditional library research. On the positive side, it is easy, fast, and cheap. On the negative side, there is no quality control over what gets on the Internet. Unlike standard academic publications, there is no peer review process, or any review at all. Anyone can put almost anything on a Web site. It may be poor quality, undocumented, highly biased, totally made up, or fraudulent.

Many excellent sources and important resource materials for social research are not available on the Internet. Most information is available only through library subscription services. Contrary to popular belief, the Internet has not made all information free and accessible to everyone. Internet sources can be "unstable" and difficult to document. After you conduct a search on the Internet and locate Web sites, note the specific URL (uniform record locater) or "address" (usually it starts http://) where it resides and the date you saw it. This address refers to an electronic file sitting in a computer somewhere. If the computer file moves, it may not be at the same address two days later. Unlike a journal article stored on a shelf in hundreds of libraries for many decades and available for anyone to read, Web sites can quickly vanish. This means it may not be possible to check Web references easily, verify a quote, or go back to original materials. It is easy to copy, modify, or distort and then reproduce copies of a Web source, so you may find several variations on the same material. A few rules can help you locate the best sites on the Internet—ones that have useful and truthful information. Sources that originate at universities, research institutes, or government agencies usually are more trustworthy. Many Web sites fail to provide complete information to make citation easy. Better sources will provide complete information about the author, date, location, and so on.

FOCUSING ON A RESEARCH QUESTION

By now you know that before you conduct a literature review or develop a proposal for a study, you need to focus on a research question that is much narrower than a topic. The way you do this varies depending on whether your study follows one of two general approaches to research, an inductive or deductive approach. A study that is **inductive** starts with by evidence and then slowly builds toward generalizations, patterns, or summary ideas. A **deductive** study starts with a summary idea or an "educated guess" of what you think might occur and then moves toward specific, observable evidence to test or verify the ideas.

Many studies are not strictly inductive or deductive, but most emphasize one approach over the other. There is no rigid rule; however, the type of data and purpose of a study is a guide. Most often, an inductive approach goes with qualitative data and the deductive approach with quantitative data. Most exploratory studies use the inductive approach, explanatory studies use the deductive approach, and descriptive studies use both.

10

If you follow a deductive approach with quantitative data, you will need to devote significant time early in a research study to specifying the research question precisely and planning most study details. Once you design the study, the other steps (i.e., collecting and analyzing data) can proceed in a fairly straightforward way. By contrast, if you follow an inductive approach with qualitative data, you can devote less time to developing a research question and planning study details in advance. However, you must spend far more time and effort during the subsequent stages of a study (i.e., collecting and analyzing data).

It takes time to develop the judgment skills to decide whether a deductive-quantitative or an inductive-qualitative study works best for a research question. Three things can help you pick most effective type:

- Reading many past studies
- Appreciating the specific features of qualitative and quantitative data

inductive research in which you start many specific observations and move toward general ideas or theory to capture what they show.

deductive research in which you start with a general idea or theory and test it by looking at specific observations.

■ **Figure 10.8** Inductive or Deductive Approach

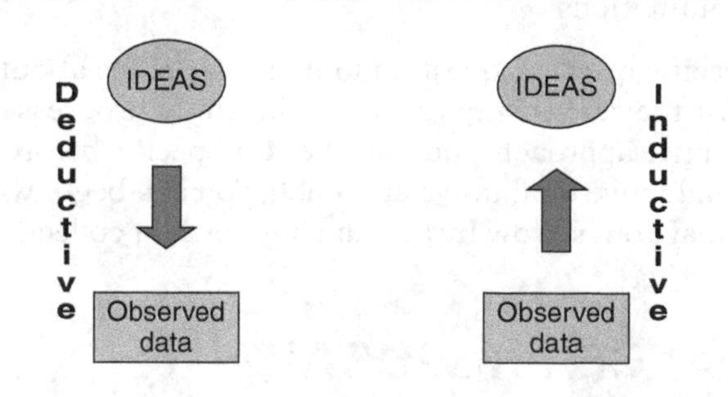

Making It Practical Narrowing a Topic into a Research Question

You want the research question to be empirically testable and specific. Here are four ways to do this:

Examine the research literature. From a literature review, you may decide to replicate a past study exactly or with slight variations. You can also explore unexpected findings discovered in past research. In many reports, authors offer suggestions for future research that you can follow. You can also extend an existing explanation to a new topic or setting. For example, a study of workplace relations in a hospital found that nurses and other staff cooperate and are more productive under certain arrangements. You might conduct a study to see whether the same arrangements have the same outcome in a nonmedical setting (e.g., a large legal office). You can examine the intervening process. For example, a study found that increased police foot patrols produced more calls to police when trouble occurred. You might examine exactly how this occurred—did the foot patrols increase familiarity, feelings of trust, and belief in the honesty in police?

Talk over ideas with others. Ask people who are knowledgeable about the topic for questions. It is often useful to seek out those who hold opinions that differ from yours on the topic and discuss possible research questions with them. A research question might help resolve different positions on an issue.

Specify the context. Apply a finding or topic a specific time, society, geographic unit, or category of people. Let us say you want to study divorce. Your research question might examine divorce in a particular era (divorce in the 1950s versus the early 2000s), location (Southwest versus New England states), or category of people (among people of different religions versus a shared religion).

Specify the purpose of your study. Do you want the study to be an exploratory, descriptive, explanatory, or evaluation study? Tailor your research question to one or another purpose.

COMPARING GOOD AND NOT-SO-GOOD RESEARCH QUESTIONS

Not-So-Good Research Questions

Not empirically testable, nonscientific questions. Should abortion be legal? Is it right to have capital punishment?

General topics, not research questions. Treatment of alcohol and drug abuse. Sexuality and aging.

Set of variables, not questions. Capital punishment and racial discrimination. Urban decay and gangs

Too vague, ambiguous. Do police affect delinquency? What can be done to prevent child abuse? How does poverty affect children?

Good Research Questions for Parallel Structure

Exploratory questions. Has the actual incidence of child abuse changed in California in the past 10 years? Is a new type of abuse occurring?

Descriptive questions. Is child abuse, violent or sexual, more common in families that have experienced a divorce than in intact, never-divorced families? Are children raised in impoverished households more likely to have medical, learning, and social-emotional adjustment difficulties than children raised in nonimpoverished households?

Explanatory Questions. Does the emotional instability created by experiencing a divorce increase the chances that divorced parents will physically abuse their children? Is a lack of sufficient funds for preventive treatment a major cause of more serious medical problems among children raised in families in impoverished?

Evaluative Questions. Has the new patient tracking system produced higher satisfaction ratings? Does the automatic arrest of abusive males in domestic violence calls to police reduce later violent domestic abuse incidents? Will third-grade children's readings scores show larger improvements under the new program than the existing reading program? Does calling customers to remind them of their appointment a day in advance reduce the percent of customer no-shows at the service center?

- Understanding how to use various research techniques and recognizing their strengths and limitations

You need a specific research question to make decisions about study design, although you adjust the research question as the study progresses. If you adopt a deductive-quantitative approach, you must be very specific before you can proceed. If you adopt the inductive-qualitative approach, you can begin with a general a research question that you narrow further during the data collection process.

THE RESEARCH PROPOSAL

As stated at the start of this chapter, the research proposal is a written document in which you review the literature and provide a detailed plan for research study. Your proposal will vary depending on whether the approach and research evidence is primarily deductive-quantitative or inductive-qualitative. A mixed approach with both types of data is also possible and has many advantages.

A Proposal for Quantitative or Qualitative Research

In all empirical research studies, you systematically collect and analyze data. If your data are qualitative in the form of words, sentences, photos, symbols, and so forth, you must use different strategies and data collection techniques than if the data are numbers. Techniques appropriate for qualitative data may be wholly inappropriate for quantitative data, and vice versa. One data form is not always superior; rather, each has strengths. Your goal is to fit the form of data to a specific research question and situation in a way that utilizes its strengths. The form of data affects how to conduct a study and influences your research proposal as follows:

1. When and how you do focus the research question?
2. To what universe can you generalize from a study's findings?
3. Will you follow a linear or nonlinear path when doing research?
4. Do you examine variables and hypotheses or cases and contexts?
5. How will you analyze patterns in the data that you gather?
6. What type of explanation will you use to give meaning to the patterns in the data?
7. What are your units of analysis in your study?
8. What is the level of analysis of your study?

1. When Do You Focus the Research Question? If you plan to conduct research gathering quantitative data, you need to develop a specific focus early in the process, before gathering any data. The research question directs you to the particular data you will need to gather. Past studies, theories, or a few discussions might help you focus. For example, your question tells you to collect data about the attendance of students in specific grades, and to measure their learning (using test scores, course grades, teacher notes) in specific subject areas. If you intend to gather qualitative data, you proceed slowly and focus on a research question after you gather data. You will need a topic, such as how do high school students actually learn course material, but do not have to focus on a specific question at first. You may spend many hours gathering data by talking with, observing, and interacting with students, teachers, and parents. After examining the data, you develop a specific question to direct later stages of data collection. The research question emerges slowly, in an ongoing, interactive process of data gathering.

universe a broad category of cases or units to which the study findings apply.

2. To What Universe Can You Generalize from a Study's Findings? As you move to focus on a research question, you will also specify the **universe** to which you can generalize an answer to the question. Only rarely do you want to restrict findings to the specific units or cases you happened to study. Instead, you want to extend them to a broader category of people, organizations, and other units. For example, your research question is, Does a new attendance policy help high school students learn more? You plan to study three high schools in one U.S. city in 2008. The universe, in this case, is all high school students. You want to generalize what you learn beyond the specific students in three high schools of one U.S. city in 2008 to all high school students, or at least all U.S. high school students in the early twenty-first century.

3. Which Type of Research Path Do You Follow? A path is a metaphor for the sequence of activities you do. It is a way of thinking and a way of looking at issues. In general, with quantitative data you will follow a **linear path**. You follow a relatively fixed sequence of steps in one direction. It is like a staircase, a straight pathway that moves upward without deviation and takes you to a single location. When gathering qualitative data, the pathway is less a straight line or fixed sequence; the set of steps is somewhat flexible, multidirectional, and nonlinear. A **nonlinear path** makes successive passes through steps and moves sideways before going forward. You advance slowly but not directly. It is more of a spiral. At each cycle or repetition, you collect data and gain new insights, then move ahead.

If you are accustomed to the direct, linear approach with fixed steps, the nonlinear path may look inefficient and sloppy. A nonlinear approach does not have to be disorganized and is never an excuse for doing poor-quality research. It has its own discipline and rigor. It can be highly effective when adjusting to a fast-changing, fluid situation. It can create a feeling for the whole, allow grasping subtle shades of meaning, pull together divergent information, and permit switching perspectives. If you are used to a nondirect approach, the linear approach may appear to be rigid and artificial. It may look so set, fixed, and standardized as to miss what is most interesting and important in dynamic human relations. The linear path can offer a highly efficient, disciplined, and simple-to-follow sequence that makes it easy to spot a mistake and to repeat a past study.

linear path a relatively fixed sequence of steps in one forward direction, with little repeating, moving directly to a conclusion.

nonlinear path advancing without fixed order that often requires successive passes through previous steps and moves toward a conclusion indirectly.

Making It Practical **Practical Limitations on Study Design**

Designing a perfect research project is an interesting academic exercise, but if you actually carry out a study, practical limitations have an impact on its design. You need to ask the following questions:

- How much time you can devote to the study?
- What is the cost of conducting the study and do you have the required funds?
- Can you gain access to needed resources, people, and locations?
- Do you have required approval of authorities or officials?
- Have you addressed all ethical concerns?
- Do you have the needed skills, expertise, and knowledge?

If you can devote 10 hours a week for five weeks to a study but answering a research question requires a five-year study, narrow the research question. It is difficult to estimate accurately how much time you will need to conduct a study. The research question, research technique you use, and the amount and types of data you collect will all have an impact. Consulting with experienced researchers is the best way to get a good estimate.

Access to resources is a common limitation on a study. Beyond money and time, required resources include the expertise of others, special equipment, and information. For example, you have a research question about burglary rates and family income in the 20 largest nations. This is almost impossible to answer because information on burglary and income is not available for most countries. Some questions require the approval of authorities (e.g., to see medical records) or involve violating basic ethical principles (discussed in chapter 2). Your expertise or lack of it can be a limitation. Answering some research questions may require knowledge of research techniques, a statistical ability, or foreign language skills that you do not yet have.

4. What Do You Examine? The **variable** is a central idea in quantitative research. Simply defined, a variable is a concept that varies. Research with quantitative data uses a language of variables and emphasizes relationships among variables. Once you begin to look for them, you will see variables everywhere. For example, gender is a variable; it can take on two values: male or female. Marital status is a variable; it has the values of never married single, married, divorced, or widowed. Type of crime is a variable; it can take on values of robbery, burglary, theft, murder, and so forth. Family income is a variable; it can take on values from zero to billions of dollars. A person's attitude toward abortion is a variable; it ranges from strongly supporting the right to a legal abortion to strongly opposing abortion.

It is easy to confuse a variable with the categories or values of variables. Confusion arises because a category in one variable can itself become a separate variable with a slight change in definition. "Male" is not a variable; it describes a category of the variable gender. A related idea, "degree of masculinity," is a variable. It describes the intensity or strength of attachment to attitudes, beliefs, and behaviors associated with being masculine within the broader idea of gender. "Married" is a category of the variable "marital status." Related ideas such as "number of years married" or "depth of commitment to a marriage" are variables. If you wish to gather quantitative data, you must convert most of your ideas into the language of variables.

Types of Variables. We can classify variables into three basic types, depending on their location in a cause-effect statement. The cause variable is the **independent variable**. The result or effect variable is the **dependent variable**. The independent variable is "independent of" prior causes that act on it. The dependent variable "depends on" the cause.

It is not always easy to determine whether a variable is independent or dependent. Two questions help identify the independent variable:

- Does it come earlier in time? Independent variables always come before any other type.
- Does it have an impact on another variable? Independent variables have an impact on other variables.

You can reword most research questions in terms of the dependent variables because dependent variable is what you will explain. If your research question is about reasons for an increase in the crime rate in Dallas, Texas, then your dependent variable is the Dallas crime rate.

A simple cause-effect relationship requires only an independent and a dependent variable. A third type of variable, the **intervening variable**, appears in complex relations. It shows the link or mechanism between the independent and dependent variable. To advance knowledge, we both document simple cause-and-effect relationships and try to specify the mechanisms within a causal relation. In a sense, the intervening variable acts as a dependent variable with respect to the independent variable and as an independent variable toward the dependent variable.

Here is a three-variable example. The famous French sociologist Emile Durkheim developed a theory about a causal relationship between marital status and suicide rates. He found that married people are less likely to commit suicide than single people and believed it was because married people were more socially integrated (i.e., had feelings of belonging to a group or family). We can restate his theory as the following: Being married (independent variable) increases social integration (intervening variable), which in turn reduces the suicide rate (dependent variable).

Specifying the chain of variables clarifies the linkages in a causal explanation. Complex theories have multiple independent, intervening, and dependent variables. They link together a string of intervening variables. You notice that people from disruptive family settings have lower incomes as adults. Why? Family disruption causes lower self-esteem among children, which causes greater psychological depres-

variable a feature of a case or unit that represents multiple types, values, or levels.

independent variable the variable of factors, forces, or conditions acting on another variable to produce an effect or change in it.

dependent variable the variable influenced by and changes as an outcome of another variable.

intervening variable a variable that comes between the independent and dependent variable in a causal relationship.

■ Figure 10.9 Chain of Variables

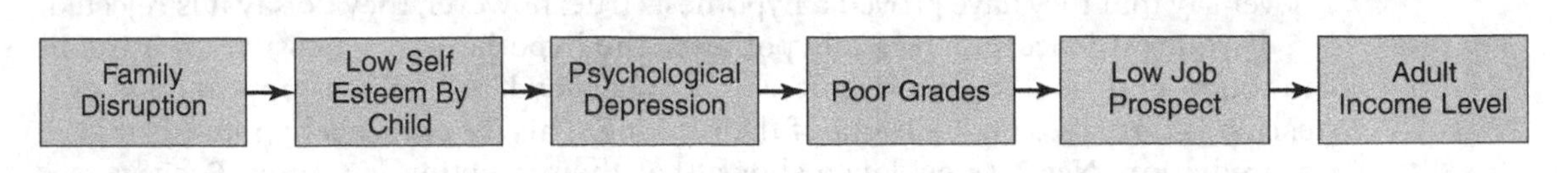

sion, which causes poor grades in school, which causes reduced prospects for getting a good job, which causes a lower adult income (see Figure 10.9).

Family disruption is the independent variable. Adult income level is the dependent variable. All the rest are intervening variables. Two explanations of the same dependent variable may use different independent variables, or agree about the independent and dependent variables but differ on the intervening variable. Both may say that family disruption causes lower adult income. One holds that disruption encourages children to join deviant peer groups that are not socialized to norms of work and thrift. Another emphasizes the impact of the disruption on childhood depression and poor academic performance.

In a single study, you usually test only a part of a complex causal explanation. Even though you might test one small part, you want to link it to a larger explanation. In a study, you connect independent and dependent variables with the hypothesis. A **hypothesis** is a tentative statement of a relationship between two variables. It is a guess about how the world works and can be restated as a prediction about what you expect to find. A causal hypothesis has the following five characteristics:

- It has at least two variables.
- It specifies how the variables are connected, which is the cause, and which is the effect.
- It includes a time order assumption (what comes first).
- You can restate it as a prediction or expected finding.
- You can show that it is supported or false with empirical data.

Example: The more a couple attends religious services together, the lower the chances that they will divorce.

- Two variables: (1) attendance at religious services, (2) probability of divorce.
- Connection: Lower attendance causes higher chance of divorce, and vice versa.
- Time order: attendance is earlier and divorce comes later.
- Prediction: Couples who attend religious services together very often will have fewer divorces than couples who never or rarely attend religious services together.
- Testable with empirical data: We can look at 1000 couples and ask how often they attend religious services together, then see how many of them are still married to one another 10 years later.

Knowledge cannot advance far with one test of a single hypothesis. In fact, you may get a distorted picture of the research process if you focus too much on a single study that tests one hypothesis. Knowledge develops over time as many researchers test many hypotheses. It grows out of the shifting and winnowing of many findings about hypotheses. If data fail to support some hypotheses, researchers gradually drop them from consideration. If data support a hypothesis, they keep it in contention. Researchers constantly create new hypotheses that challenge existing ones that have received support. Over time, if a hypothesis continues to receive empirical support in test after test and it stands up as better than alternative hypotheses, we can begin to accept it as likely to be true. To gain acceptance, the hypothesis needs multiple tests with consistent and repeated empirical support.

The Null Hypothesis. Our confidence in the truthfulness of a hypothesis grows as it defeats its competitors in repeated tests. A curious aspect of hypothesis testing is that we treat evidence in support of a hypothesis differently than evidence that

hypothesis a statement about the relationship of two (or more) variables yet to be tested with empirical data.

negates it. We give the negative evidence greater importance. Technically, researchers never say that they have proved a hypothesis true; however, they do say it is rejected.

If your evidence supports a hypothesis, the hypothesis is a possibility; it is still in the running and the case is not closed. When evidence fails to support a hypothesis, it is tarnished and falls out of the running. This is because a hypothesis makes a prediction. Negative evidence shows that the prediction is wrong. Positive evidence is less critical, because alternative hypotheses may make the same prediction. Confirming evidence may reinforce your belief in a hypothesis, but it does not automatically beat out the alternative hypotheses making the same prediction. Whereas negative evidence seriously weakens a hypothesis, piling up more and more evidence in favor of a hypothesis is not as significant.

Researchers test hypotheses in two ways: a straightforward way and by using the **null hypothesis**. Most of us talk about a hypothesis as a way to predict a relationship between two variables. The null hypothesis does the opposite; it predicts no relationship. Many quantitative researchers, especially experimenters, use a null hypothesis. They look for evidence that will let them accept or reject the null hypothesis. For example, Sarah believes that students who live on campus in dormitories get better grades than students who live off campus and commute. Her null hypothesis is that residence and grades are unrelated. She matches the null hypothesis with a corresponding alternative hypothesis. It is that a relationship exists; more specifically that a student's on-campus residence has a positive effect on grades.

null hypothesis a hypothesis that there is no relationship between two variables, that they do not influence one another.

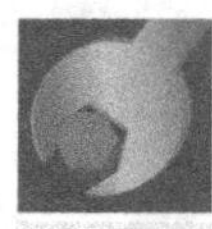

Making It Practical From the Research Question to Hypotheses

Going from a well-formulated research question to a hypothesis is a short step. A good research question has hints about the hypothesis. The hypothesis is a tentative answer to the research question. Consider the research question, "Is age at marriage associated with chances of divorce?" It has two variables: "age at marriage" and "chances of divorce." Age at marriage is the independent variable because marriage must logically come before divorce. Beyond stating that two variables are connected, you need to decide the direction of the relationship. You have two choices: (1) The lower the age at time of marriage, the greater the chances that of divorce; (2) the higher the age at time of marriage, the greater the chances of divorce. A hypothesis makes a prediction, with choice (1) it says that people who marry younger are more likely to divorce. This may help you to better focus the research question, "Are couples who marry younger more likely to divorce?"

You can create several hypotheses from one research question. The question was, "Is age at marriage associated with chances of divorce?" Here is another hypothesis from it: "The smaller the difference between the ages of the marriage partners at the time of marriage, the lower the chances of divorce." Here age at marriage is specified differently. You can also specify conditions under which a relationship works. For example, "The lower the age at time of marriage, the greater the chances that the marriage will end in divorce, unless it is a marriage between two members of a tight-knit traditional religious community in which early marriage is the norm."

Besides answering a research question, a hypothesis can be an untested proposition from a theory. You can express a hypothesis at two levels: (1) an abstract, conceptual level of general theory; and (2) a concrete, measurable level that you actually test in a study. The theory explains why the prediction in your hypothesis is true. We can continue with the same example but now put it in the form of a theoretical statement.

> Adults stabilize their self-identity and develop mature coping abilities as they move from their late teens to their late twenties. A stable self-identity and mature coping abilities help people to sustain a long-term committed intimate relationship, such as marriage. If two adults enter into a marriage relationship before they have a stable a self-identity and mature coping abilities, the marriage is unlikely to last many years.

Now let us look at the same hypothesis but phrased as empirically testable statement with specific measures:

> The rate of divorce within the first 10 years of a marriage is much higher when both partners are 21 years old or younger at the time of a marriage than when both marriage partners are 28 years old or older.

You may feel that the null hypothesis is a backward way of hypothesis testing. It rests on the assumption that hypothesis testing should make finding a relationship between variables very demanding. With the null hypothesis approach, you directly test the null hypothesis. If evidence supports the null hypothesis (technically—you accept it as true), you are forced to conclude that the alternative hypothesis is false. On the other hand, if the evidence rejects the null hypothesis, then the alternative hypothesis remains as a possibility. You keep it in contention. As you repeatedly test and reject the null hypothesis, the alterative hypothesis looks stronger over time. Researchers use the null hypothesis because they are extremely cautious. They hesitate to say that a relationship exists until they have mountains of evidence. This is similar to the Anglo-American legal idea of innocent until proved guilty. Assume that the null hypothesis is correct until reasonable doubt suggests otherwise.

Quantitative data studies emphasize variables. By contrast, studies with qualitative data examine cases and contexts. A researcher who uses qualitative data may not think in terms of variables or testing hypotheses. He or she sees many areas of social life, human relations, and social activities as being intrinsically qualitative. Rather than try to convert fluid qualitative social life into variables or precise numbers, he or she retains the loose images or ideas that people use in natural social contexts.

Qualitative researchers usually examine a limited number of cases in depth. The cases are usually the same as a unit of analysis (discussed later). Instead of precise numerical measures of a very large number of cases, as in quantitative data analysis, in a qualitative study you examine in detail many aspects of a few cases. The rich detail and astute insight into the cases replace precise measures across numerous cases. Because you closely examine the same case or a few over time, you can see an issue evolve, a conflict emerge, or a social relationship develop. This places you in a good position to detect and observe processes. In historical research, the passage of time may involve years or decades. In field research, it may be days, weeks, or months. In both, you observe what unfolds and can quickly notice when something unusual or important occurs.

The social context is very important for studies with qualitative data. This is because an event, social action, or statement's meaning depends, in an important way, on the context in which it appears. When you remove an event, social action, or conversation from its social context, or ignore the context, you can seriously distort its meaning. Without the context, its real importance or significance is often lost. This requires you to pay close attention to what surrounds an action, event, or statement. It also implies that the same actions, events, or statements can have different meanings in different situations, cultures, or historical eras.

Let us say you studied voting. Instead of simply counting votes across time or cultures, you might ask, What does voting mean in the context? The same action (e.g., voting for a presidential candidate) may differ depending on the context, such as intense argument and competition among several parties, no difference among candidates, or a situation of total one-party dominance. Until you place the parts of social life into a larger whole, you may not grasp the part's meaning. It is hard to understand a baseball glove without knowing about the game of baseball. If you look at it as a glove, like a mitten for cold weather, a pair of driving gloves, or gloves to use for working in the garden, the baseball glove has little meaning. The glove's meaning comes from its use and placement within the flow of a baseball game. The whole of the game—innings, bats, curve balls, hits—gives meaning to each of the parts. Each part without the whole has little meaning.

5. How Do You Look for Patterns in the Data? Researches look for patterns in both the quantitative and qualitative data but do so differently. With quantitative data you rearrange, examine, and discuss numbers by using charts, tables, and statistics to see patterns. They reveal patterns in the numerical data. You connect the patterns with your research question. In a way, the hypothesis is both an answer to the research question and a prediction about what will appear in your charts, tables, and statistics.

With qualitative data, you look for patterns by rearranging, examining, and discussing textual or visual data. You do this in a way that conveys an authentic voice, or that remains true to the original understandings of the people and situations that you studied. Instead of relying on charts, statistics, and displays of numbers, you identify patterns (i.e., sequences, cycles, contrasts) in the data, (i.e., observed events, conversations, or situations) as they appear in a specific context. You might discuss the patterns in terms of themes or as narratives. A narrative is a story that has a beginning and ending and major actors or forces that pull the reader from start to finish. Qualitative data are often more complex and filled with specific meaning than numbers. Essentially, you must translate, or make understandable, the data for people who lack a direct experience with the specific research setting. For example, you describe a 30-second social interaction in which no one spoke.

> A middle-aged man in a business suit rushes into a coffee shop, opens his wallet, and puts a five-dollar bill on the counter. Without a word, the clerk at the shop quickly pours a cup of coffee into a take-away container and adds cream for the man. The man picks up the container, turns, and quickly walks out the door.

You create a translation based on observations, conservations, and the context. The man is a regular patron of the coffee shop near a train station. He has been coming each morning for five years. Today he is in a rush to catch a commuter train to his office downtown. He will drink the coffee while on the train. The clerk knows the man and knows what he wants. The man orders the same thing every day. In return, the clerk rushes to take care of the man each time. When the man is very rushed, he just puts down a five-dollar bill. The coffee only costs \$1.50; the money covers the cost of the coffee, \$1.50 for the newspaper that the man took from outside the front of the coffee shop before entering, and a \$2.00 tip. On the days that he has time, the man sits and chats with the clerk about baseball and current events.

Summary Review **Quantitative versus Qualitative Research**

Overall Type of Study	Quantitative Research	Qualitative Research
Approach	Approach is usually deductive.	Approach is usually inductive.
Research Question	Developed and refined before gathering data	Developed and refined while gathering data
Path	Path is linear.	Path is non-linear.
Main goal	Test a hypothesis that you started with.	Discover/capture the meaning of a social setting.
Concepts and Ideas	Are expressed in the form of distinct variables	Are expressed in the form of themes and motifs
Measurement	Plan precise measurements before data collection	Create measures ad hoc as gathering data
Data	In the form of numbers	In the form of words and images
Theory	Theory is largely causal.	Can be causal or other.
Data Analysis	Data analysis includes statistics, tables, or charts with relationships among numbers.	Often includes narrative story with a detailed description of a social setting.

6. What Type of Explanation Will You Use? We use the word *explanation* in two ways. One is an everyday type, in which *explanation* means making something clear or comprehensible to another person with examples or everyday reasons. The other is a research study type that means answering the why question and making something comprehensible by placing it within a relevant structure of theory, ideas, or set of circumstances.

When doing explanatory research, you create a research explanation. There are several research explanations, but the most common one is a **causal explanation** In it you explain by finding one or more causes for an effect or outcome. The cause in the explanation corresponds to your independent variable and the effect to your dependent variable. A causal explanation is usually inside a larger theory or idea framework and has the following three elements:

- *Time order:* The cause must come earlier in time than the effect or the result it produces.
- *Association:* The cause and effect are associated or they go together and vary with one another. Some people call it correlation, although technically correlation is a specific measure of association.
- *Alternative causes ruled out:* There is no better or stronger cause than the one you identified.

To be a cause (an independent variable), something must happen first. Usually you can observe or logically determine time order. Two factors that occur together are associated: that is, when one factor is present or at a high level, the other one is also present or at a high level. Several statistics measure an association. The most well known is the correlation. The last item in the list is the most difficult one to document or observe. If you claim that one factor causes another, there should not be any stronger, truer, or better cause present that you are not including. This is an important element because there can be multiple causal factors, some obvious and some hidden. If you say that a factor causes another but an unacknowledged and stronger cause is present, it is misleading. You try to rule out other possible causes (see the discussion of spuriousness later in this chapter).

In a causal explanation, you make a generalization and specific instance of it, as follows:

A causes B generally.
This situation is A, therefore, we expect to find B.
Example: People who spent many years in prison have difficultly finding stable, well-paid work after their release. Joe Brown was imprisoned for many years; he is having difficulty finding stable, well-paid work after his release.

You fit a specific observable instance within the more general rule or pattern. You can covert a causal explanation into independent and dependent variables.

Independent variable: Whether a person was previously imprisoned for many years
Dependent variable: Amount of difficulty in finding stable, well-paid work

Sometimes researchers who use qualitative data use causal explanation. At other times they do not but instead develop ideas or theories during the data collection process. They build up from specific data to general ideas. Instead of a causal connection between two variables, their explanation is in the form of motifs, themes, or distinctions. Many explanations with qualitative data take the form of **grounded theory**. In a grounded theory explanation you build the explanation by making comparisons. For example, you observe an event (e.g., a police officer confronting a speeding motorist). You look for similarities and differences. You ask, Does the police officer always radio in the car's license number before proceeding? After radioing the car's location, does the officer ask the motorist to get out of the car sometimes but at other times casually walk up to the car and talk to the seated driver? When data collection and theorizing are interspersed, theoretical questions arise that

causal explanation a type of research explanation in which you identify one or more causes for an outcome, and place cause and effect in a larger framework.

grounded theory ideas and themes that are built up from data observation.

■ Figure 10.10 Quick Checklist of Study Design Issues in a Research Proposal

When do you focus the research question?	Very early or it emerges later
What is the universe of your study?	The broad set of units to which you can generalize
What is your research path?	Linear or nonlinear
What do you examine?	Variables and hypotheses or cases and contexts
How do you interpret patterns in the data?	Statistics and charts or themes and narratives
What type of explanation do you use?	Causal explanation or grounded theory
What are your units of analysis?	The cases or units you measure
What is your level of analysis?	Micro to macro

suggest future observations. You collect new data so they can answer theoretical questions that came from thinking about previous data.

7. What Are the Units of Analysis in Your Study? Every study contains units of analysis. They are critical for clearly thinking through and planning a research study. Few researchers explicitly identify units of analysis as such. Your research question shapes the unit of analysis, which in turn influences study design, so being aware of them will help you to design a better study and to avoid errors. The **unit of analysis** is the unit on which you measure variables and gather data. Common units are the individual, the group (e.g., family, friendship group), the organization (e.g., corporation, university), the social category (e.g., social class, gender, race), the social institution (e.g., religion, education, the family), and the society (e.g., a nation, a tribe). Say you want to conduct a descriptive study to find out whether colleges in the North spend more on their football programs than do colleges in the South. Your variables are college location and amount of spending for football, and the unit of analysis in this situation is the college. It flows from the research question.

In social research the individual is the most commonly used unit of analysis, but it is by no means the only one. Different questions imply one or another unit of analysis, and different research techniques work best for specific units. For example, the individual is the unit of analysis in the survey of students about sexual harassment (see Example Study Box 1: Sexual Harassment). On the other hand, you might conduct a study to compare the level of sexual harassment at 20 different colleges. Perhaps you think harassment is greater at colleges with more alcohol-related problems. You could measure the number of alcohol-related behavior problems/arrests at the colleges and measure degree of harassment by the number of harassment reports filed and amount of hours counselors devote to sexual harassment at the colleges. Your unit of analysis would be the organization, or specifically the college. This is because you are comparing characteristics of the colleges. Units of analysis influence how to gather data and the level of analysis (see below).

8. What Is the Level of Analysis of Your Study? The social world operates on a continuum from small scale or micro level (e.g., a few friends, a small group) to large scale or macro level (e.g., entire civilizations or a major structure of a society). The **level of analysis** is the level of reality you examine. It is a mix of the number of people, the expanse of geographic space, the scope of the activity, and the length of time. A micro-level study might involve 30 minutes of interaction among five people in a small room. A macro-level study could involve a billion people on three continents across a century. The level of analysis delimits the kinds of assumptions, concepts, and theories you will use. It also influences the appropriate units of analysis. Let us look at examples at each end of the continuum.

unit of analysis the case or unit on which you measure variables or other characteristics.

level of analysis the level of reality to which explanations refer, micro to macro.

Micro Level: Suppose you want to study the topic of dating among college students. A micro-level analysis uses ideas such as interpersonal contact, mutual friendships, and common interests among individual students. Suppose you believe that students tend to date someone with whom they have had personal contact in a class, share friends in common, and share common interests. You might gather data from 100 students on their friends, contacts, and relationships. The individual student is your unit of analysis.

Macro Level: Suppose you want to learn how social-economic inequality affects violent behavior in a society. You may be interested in the degree of inequality (e.g., the distribution of wealth, property, income, and other resources) throughout a society. Likewise, you may look at patterns of societal violence (e.g., aggression against other societies, level of violent crime, violent feuds between families, organized crime with gangs, bandits, and warlords, religious-racial-based conflicts). You develop a macro-level explanation because of the topic and the level of social reality. You gather data on the level of inequality in each of 50 countries for 20 years, as well as data on how many acts of violence occurred in each country. The country is your unit of analysis.

Warning: Avoid Spuriousness. As you design a study with a causal explanation, you need to be aware of an issue that may totally upset your explanation. As you learned previously, you need three things for a causal explanation: time order, association, and ruling out of alternative causal factors. You can observe or test the first two, but the third element can be tricky. It involves making certain that there are no alternative causes. The alternative cause may not be obvious. If an unseen alternative cause strongly affects your dependent variable, then claims you make about the cause (independent variable) could be false. Having time order and a strong association between two variables does not mean you can relax. It could be an illusion, just like the mirage that resembles a pool of water on a road during a hot day.

Spuriousness is an illusionary relationship due to an unacknowledged other variable that is a cause of both the independent and the dependent variable. You could have a strong correlation between the two variables, but the two variables may be not really be cause and effect. You must also check for spuriousness to claim causality.

Spuriousness may seem complicated, but it uses common-sense logic. You already know that there is an association between the use of air conditioners and ice cream cone consumption. If you measured the number of air conditioners in use and the number of ice cream cones sold each day, you would find a strong correlation. More cones are sold on the same days when more air conditioners being used. However, you know that eating ice cream cones does not cause people to turn on air conditioners, or turning on an air conditions does not produce a craving for ice cream. Instead, a third factor causes both variables: hot days.

spuriousness when two variables appear to be causally connected but in reality, they are not because an unseen third factor is the true cause.

Learning from History **Night-Lights and Spuriousness**

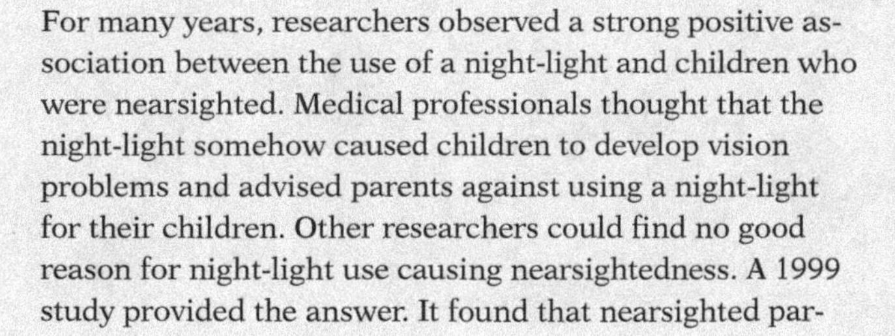

For many years, researchers observed a strong positive association between the use of a night-light and children who were nearsighted. Medical professionals thought that the night-light somehow caused children to develop vision problems and advised parents against using a night-light for their children. Other researchers could find no good reason for night-light use causing nearsightedness. A 1999 study provided the answer. It found that nearsighted parents are more likely to use night-lights. Parents also genetically pass on their vision deficiency to their children. The study found no link between night-light use and nearsightedness once the effect of parental vision was considered. Thus, the initial causal link was misleading or spurious once the previously unrecognized impact of parental vision impairment and night-time behavior was considered (see *New York Times,* May 22, 2001).

You may ask, How can you tell whether a relationship is spurious? How do you discover the mysterious third factor? As you prepare a research proposal, how can you build in a safeguard against spuriousness? You can deal with spuriousness in different ways using different research techniques. The internal design of an experiment helps to control for spuriousness. In survey data and existing statistical sources, you must decide on control variables that measure possible alternative causes. You then use statistical techniques (discussed later in this book) to test whether an association is spurious. In all situations, including qualitative data analysis, you need a theory, or at least a good guess, about what alternative causes might influence what you see as the cause and effect, and then take them into consideration. One way to grasp the idea of spuriousness is with an example (see Learning from History: Night-Lights and Spuriousness).

Let us look a spurious relationship. Does taking illegal drugs cause more suicide, school dropouts, and violent acts? Many people point to positive correlations between taking drugs and being suicidal, dropping out of school, and engaging in violence. They argue that ending drug use will end such problems. A second position argues that many people turn to drugs to cope with their emotional problems or high levels of disorder in their communities (e.g., high unemployment, unstable families, high crime, few community services, and lack of civility). At the same time, people with emotional problems or who live in disordered communities are often in such straits that they are more likely to commit suicide, drop out of school, and engage in violence. It may be that reducing emotional problems and community disorder will end both drug use and the other problems. Reducing drug taking alone will have a limited effect because it does not address the root causes (i.e., emotional problems and community disorder). If the second position is correct, the apparent relationship between illegal drugs and the problems stated is spurious and misleading. This is because emotional problems and community disorder are the true and initially unacknowledged alternative causes (see Figure 10.11).

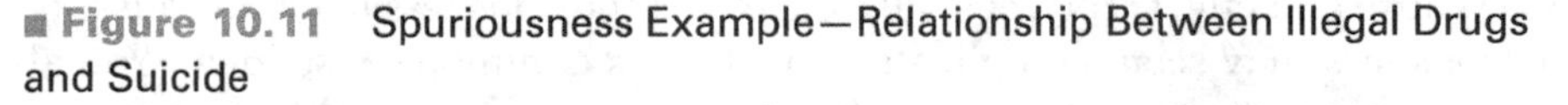

Figure 10.11 Spuriousness Example—Relationship Between Illegal Drugs and Suicide

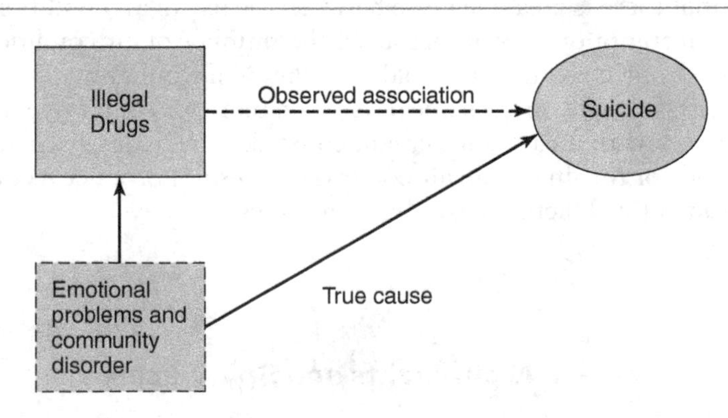

WHAT HAVE YOU LEARNED?

In this chapter, you encountered the groundwork to begin a study. You saw how to conduct a literature search, narrow a topic into a focused research question, and identify units and levels of analysis. The decision to use qualitative or quantitative data suggests a different sequence of decision making as you get started. Choosing a qualitative or quantitative approach (or a mix of both) depends on your topic, your purpose and intended use of study results, as well as your own assumptions.

If you decide that quantitative data are best, you take a linear path and emphasize objectivity and use explicit, standardized procedures and a causal explanation. You use the language of variables and hypotheses testing. The process is a set of discrete steps that precede data collection: Narrow the topic to a more focused question, transform concepts into variables, and develop hypotheses to test. In actual practice, you move back and forth, but the general process flows in a single, linear direction. Your explanations usually take a cause-effect form.

If you decide that qualitative data are best, you follow a nonlinear path that emphasizes becoming intimate with the details of a natural setting or a particular context. You use fewer standardized procedures or explicit steps, and you must devise on-the-spot techniques. You use a language of cases and contexts that directs you to examine particular cases or processes in detail. You do not separate planning and design decisions into a distinct pre–data collection stage, but you continue to develop the study design throughout early data collection. You slowly evolve toward a specific focus based on what you learn from the data. As you reflect on the data, you can develop a grounded theory explanation.

The qualitative and quantitative distinction is overdrawn and is not a rigid dichotomy. You can mix the two types. Before you mix the data types, you need to understand each and appreciate each on its own terms. You should recognize that quantitative and qualitative data each have strengths and limitations. Your ultimate goal is to better understand and explain events in the social world, and the best way to do so is to appreciate the value of each style of data collections has to offer.

KEY TERMS

article search tool *238*
abstract *239*
causal explanation *261*
citation *251*
deductive *252*
dependent variable *256*
grounded theory *261*
hypothesis *257*
independent variable *256*
inductive *252*
intervening variable *256*
level of analysis *262*
linear path *255*
literature review *235*
nonlinear path *255*
null hypothesis *258*
peer reviewed *238*
research proposal *234*
spuriousness *263*
unit of analysis *262*
universe *254*
variable *256*

APPLY WHAT YOU'VE LEARNED

Activity 1

Go to your college library (physically or via its Web site) and locate article search tools. You may have to ask your librarian about which specific services at available at the library; some common ones are JSTOR, EBSCO, WilsonWeb, and Proquest. Pick one of the article search tools and conduct a search using the term *tattoo*. Restrict your search to peer-reviewed scholarly publications. Then answer the following:

- How many total studies have been conducted on the topic of tattoos during the past 10 years? ____

- How many total studies have been conducted on the topic of tattoos during the past 5 years? _____
- Based on the article title or abstract, what percent of studies in the past 5 years appear to be about medical issues (e.g., infection, etc.)? _____

Activity 2

Repeat Activity 1 but with a different article search tool. What differences did you discover? What accounts for the differences?

Activity 3

Take the five most recent scholarly journal articles you found in Activity 1 or 2. Prepare a reference/bibliography using the ASA (American Sociological Association) format. Be sure to put the articles in alphabetical order by the last name of the first author. Note that in a scholarly journal article that has more than one author, the first listed author usually did more work on the study than the others, so you want to retain name order.

If you Google "American Sociological Association style" you will find many college library sites that have additional help on how to organize the references. You can also find information on the ASA format at the following Web site: http://www.asanet.org/page.ww?name=Quick+Style+Guide§ion=Sociology+Depts

Activity 4

Design the first part a study using quantitative data on a topic of interest to you. Complete each of the following parts of the design:

Topic: ______________________________
Research question: ______________________________
Hypothesis: ______________________________
Your independent variable of the hypothesis above: ______________________________
Your dependent variable of the hypothesis: __________
The unit of analysis for your study: ______________

Activity 5

Identify the unit of analysis, Universe, and dependent variable in each of the three articles from the scholarly journal *Social Science Quarterly* listed below.

1. "The Effects of Visual Images in Political Ads: Experimental Testing of Distortions and Visual Literacy" (*Social Science Quarterly,* 2000, 81:913–27) by Gary Noggle and Lynda Kaid.
2. "The Politics of Bilingual Education Expenditures in Urban Districts" (*Social Science Quarterly,* 2000, 81:1064–72) by David Leal and Fred Hess.
3. "Symbolic Racism in the 1995 Louisiana Gubernatorial Election" (*Social Science Quarterly,* 2000, 81:1027–35) by Jon Knuckey and Byron Orey.

REFERENCES

Atkinson. Michael. 2003. *Tattooed: The Sociogenesis of a Body Art*. Toronto: University of Toronto Press.

Atkinson, Michael. 2004. "Tattooing and Civilizing Processes: Body Modification as Self-control." *Canadian Review of Sociology & Anthropology* 41(2):125–146.

Caplan, Jane (editor). 2000. *Written on the Body*. Princeton NJ: Princeton University Press.

DeMello, Margo. 2000. *Bodies of Inscription*. Durham NC: Duke University Press.

Fisher, Jill A. 2002. Tattooing the Body, Marking Culture. *Body & Society* 8 (4):91–107.

Harris Interactive. 2003 "A Third of Americans With Tattoos Say They Make Them Feel More Sexy" http://www.harrisinteractive.com/harris_poll/index.asp?PID=407 (downloaded 3/25/08).

Hawkes, Daina, Charlene Seen and Chantal Thorn 2004. Factors That Influence Attitudes Toward Women With Tattoos. *Sex Roles* 50 (9/10):593–604.

Horne, Jenn, David Knox, Jane Zusman, and Marty Zusman, 2007. "Tattoos And Piercings: Attitudes, Behaviors, and Interpretations of College Students." *College Student Journal* 41 (4):1011–1020.

Kang, Miliann, and Katherine Jones. 2007. "Why do people get tattoos." *Contexts* 6(1):42–47.

ENDNOTES

1. For more on the topic of tattoos see Atkinson (2003, 2004), Caplan (2000), DeMello (2000), Fischer (2002), Horne, Knox, Zusman, and Zusman (2007) and Kang and Jones (2007).
2. Sir Isaac Newton in letter to Robert Horne, Feb. 5, 1676. http://en.wikiquote.org/wiki/Isaac_Newton

CHAPTER 11

Writing a Research Report

Taken from: *Understanding Research*, by W. Lawrence Neuman

Stephan Hoeck/Stock 4B/Getty Images

A crucial phase in the research process takes place *after* you have gathered and analyzed the data. You must communicate what you learned to others. Whether your study was in chemistry, criminology, education, engineering, marketing, nursing, psychology, public policy, or another field, you need to communicate how you conducted it and its findings. Your communication can be oral but should also be in a written form. As with all written communication, you want to maximize readability. Readability indicates how accessible the writing is, and how effectively it will reach a given reading audience. An audience's ability to read and understand your writing will depend on their knowledge and reading skills. These vary widely. Medical doctors differ from teens. Whatever your audience, try to make your writing both highly accurate and easy to understand. Do this by using precise wording, a clear organizational structure, and a logical flow of ideas.

In previous chapters, you learned how to design studies, gather data, and analyze the data. Yet research is not complete until you share results with other people. Communicating how you conducted a study and its results with others is a critical stage of the research process. It is usually in the form of a written report. In this chapter, you will learn how to write a report on research.

Example Study Box 1 Who Writes How

Hartley, Pennebaker, and Fox (2003) examined the readability of research reports. They noted that past studies suggested that men and women wrote differently, and that individuals writing alone differ from people who write together. To see whether this happened in research reports, they looked at reports in the *Journal of Educational Psychology* for 1997–2001. They found 21 articles that individual men wrote, 21 by individual women, and 19 written by pairs of men and 19 by pairs of women. They examined each article's abstract, and most of its Introduction and Discussion sections. They measured readability with two computer-based writing style programs. They did not find gender differences or group versus individual author differences. However, they did find differences among article sections that replicated findings from past studies. The Introduction sections were harder to read than Discussion sections. In addition, Introduction sections had more specific quotations from other authors than the Discussion sections.

WHY WRITE A REPORT?

After you complete a study or a significant phase of a large project, you need to communicate to others what you learned through a research report. You can learn a lot about writing a research report by reading many reports or taking a course in scientific and technical writing. A **research report** is organized in a particular way. It requires writing that differs from other types, such as news stories, personal autobiography, and creative fiction. The report communicates the methods and findings in a straightforward and serious manner. More than a quick summary, it is a full, complete, and detailed record of the entire research process.

Do not wait until you finish all research activities to begin thinking about the report. Instead, begin to think ahead while early in the research process. The report is one reason to keep careful records while you are conducting research. In addition to the findings, the report includes the reasons for initiating a study, a description of the research procedures, a presentation of evidence, and a discussion of how the evidence relates to the research question. It has a reference section of the literature that you cited in the report. The references provide background on the research question and show how your study fits within past research.

The purpose of a report is to tell others what you did, how you did it, and what you discovered. People write research reports for many reasons: to fulfill a course, academic degree, or job assignment; to meet an obligation to an organization that paid for the research; to persuade a professional group about specific aspects of a problem; or to tell the general public about findings. Telling the public what you learned is a second stage of disseminating findings. The first stage is to communicate with people who are knowledgeable about the study topic and the research process. They can seriously evaluate the research in the report; they are also in the best position to understand what you did in the study and why.

Assume that people who will read the report are scientifically literate. Hurd (1998) suggested that a scientifically literate person can

- distinguish experts from uninformed people, theory from dogma, data from myth, empirical evidence from propaganda, facts from fiction, and knowledge from opinion;
- understand that the research process is cumulative, tentative, and skeptical; as well as understand the limitations of scientific inquiry and causal explanations;

research report a written document that summarizes the way a study was conducted and its major findings, and is a complete report on the research process.

the need to gather sufficient evidence to support or reject claims; and the influence of society on research; and
- analyze and process data, and be aware that problems often have more than one accepted answer and that many issues are multidisciplinary with political, judicial, ethical, and moral dimensions.

THE WRITING PROCESS

There are many good books on how to write a research report. My favorite is by Howard S. Becker and is titled *Writing for Social Scientists: How to Start and Finish Your Thesis, Book, or Article* (University of Chicago Press, 2007). It has many tips and tricks, as well as a general philosophy of writing, social relationships, and doing research. Many other books focus more on step-by-step mechanics. In this section we discuss the general consensus on writing research reports.

Know Your Audience

Professional writers tell us, Always know for whom you are writing. This is because communication is most effective when you tailor it to a specific audience. You should write a research report differently depending on whether the primary audience is an instructor, students, professional social scientists, practitioners, or the lay

Making It Practical **Tailoring a Report to the Audience**

- *Writing for instructors.* An instructor assigns a research report for different reasons and may place requirements on how you are to prepare it. In general, instructors want to see good writing and an organization that reflects clear, logical thinking. They want to see a report that demonstrates a solid grasp of substantive and methodological concepts. They want to see you only using technical terms explicitly *when appropriate,* and not used excessively or incorrectly. Often instructors are concerned more with how the report demonstrates your thought process, specific details about research steps, and use of the correct format than with your findings.
- *Writing for other students.* You want to define all technical terms and clearly label each part of a report. Your discussion section should proceed in a very logical, step-by-step manner. You should offer many specific examples. You will want to use less formal language to explain how and why you conducted the various steps of the research project. One strategy is to begin with the research question, then structure the rest of the report as an answer to that question.
- *Writing for expert professionals and scholars.* You do not need to define technical terms or explain why you used research standard procedures (e.g., random sampling). Professionals are interested in how the research links to theory or past findings in the literature. They want to see a compact but detailed description of the research process. They will pay close attention to how you measured variables and gathered data. They like a condensed, tightly written, but extensive section on data analysis, with a precise and meticulous discussion of the results.
- *Writing for practitioners, managers, and policy makers.* Provide a short summary of how you conducted the study, and present the main results in a few simple charts and graphs that are easy to read and understand. Practitioners like to see an outline of alternative paths of action implied by results with the practical outcomes of pursuing each path. Practitioners focus on the main findings, but you may have to caution practitioners not to overgeneralize from the results of one study. For practitioner reports, you want to place the details of research design and the long version of the results in an appendix.
- *Writing for the public.* You need to use simple language, provide concrete examples, and focus on the practical implications of findings for specific issues or problems. You do not have to include many details of research design or of results. You need to be very careful not to make unsupported claims when writing for the public, because people can easily misinterpret findings. Informing the public is an important service. It helps nonspecialists make better judgments about public issues.

public. In all cases, the writing should be clear, accurate, and organized. This usually takes hard work and practice.

Pick a Style and Tone

Write reports of research studies in a narrow range of styles with a distinct tone. They have one primary purpose—to communicate clearly the research method and findings.

Style refers to the type of words, length and form of sentences, and pattern of paragraphs. In the report, avoid a poetic or flowery style with many extra colorful adjectives and illusions. Also avoid a highly formal, dense, and turgid style that is common in government and bureaucratic documents. Such documents use passive voice and are full of long, complex sentences and unnecessary technical jargon (see Making It Practical: Suggestions for Rewriting later in this chapter). Research reports have a formal and succinct style (they say a lot in few words).

Tone is the attitude or relation toward the subject matter that you express as a writer. For example, an informal, conversational way of writing (e.g., colloquial words, idioms, clichés, and incomplete sentences) with a personal tone (e.g., these are my personal feelings) is appropriate if you are writing a letter or e-mail to a close friend. You may use comedy or a whimsical tone to express humor. This is inappropriate for research reports. The tone in a research report expresses some distance from the subject matter. It is professional, semidetached, and serious. Field researchers sometimes use an informal style and a more personal tone, but this is the exception. Also, avoid moralizing and "preaching" a specific point of view. Your goal is to inform, not to advocate a position or to entertain. You persuade through systematic empirical evidence and using accepted research techniques.

Your research report should be accurate and clear. You must check and recheck details (e.g., page references in citations) and fully disclose how you conducted the research project. If readers detect carelessness in your report, they may question the research itself. The details of a research study can be complex. This complexity makes confusion possible. It also makes clear thinking and plain writing essential. To achieve these goals, think and rethink your research question and study design. You should explicitly define major terms, write in short declarative sentences, and limit the conclusions to what you can support with empirical evidence.

Organize Your Thoughts

Writing is serious, time-consuming work. It does not happen magically or simply flow automatically when you put pen to paper (or fingers to keyboard). Think of writing as a process. It has a sequence of steps and activities that result in a final product. Writing a research report is not radically different from other types of writing. The steps may differ and the level of complexity may be greater, but what a good writer does to write a long letter, a poem, a set of instructions, or a short story also applies to writing a research report.

Go Back to the Library

Few researchers totally finish the literature review before they complete the study. You should be familiar with the literature before you start, but expect to return to the literature after completing data collection and analysis. The following are three reasons for doing this:

- Time has passed between the beginning and the end of a research project, and new studies may have been published.
- After completing a research project, you will know better what is or is not central to the study and may have new questions in mind as you reread studies in the literature.

Making It Practical Getting Started in Writing

1. *Have something about which to write.* The "something" in the research report includes the topic, research question, design and measures, data collection techniques, results, and implications.

2. *Get organized.* When you have many parts to write about, organization is essential. The most basic tool for organizing writing is the outline. Outlines help you ensure that all ideas are included and that the relationship among them is clear. Outlines have topics (words or phrases) or sentences. Most of us are familiar with the basic form of an outline (see Tips for the Wise Researcher: Outlining and Figure 11.1).

3. *Avoid procrastination and writer's block* Some people become afflicted with a strange ailment when they sit down to compose writing—the mind goes blank, the fingers freeze, and panic sets in. **Writer's block** also occurs when procrastination becomes writing constipation! After many delays, you cannot get the writing process moving. You stall without ideas or motivation. Many people delay writing until the last possible moment and then, under great pressure or panic, force themselves to write. This is not a successful strategy for professional writing. The pressure of a deadline might be motivation, but frantic, rapid writing is only useful as a prewriting activity (discussed later), not as a final draft. Writers from beginners through experts occasionally experience writer's block. If you experience it, calm down and work on overcoming it. There are many tricks to overcome it (e.g., taking a walk, getting a back rub, organizing files, sharpening pencils). A common technique is to identify small parts of a larger task that you can easily accomplish and do them first. Set a reasonable schedule for such parts. After you finish a part, give yourself a small reward (e.g., have a special dessert). The best way to avoid writer's block is by writing, at least a little, all the time. Set aside a small amount of time to write every day. If you are always writing something, even if you later throw it away, you are less likely to be blocked.

Somos Images/Corbis Royalty Free

4. *Engage in prewriting activities.* Writing is an ongoing process, not a one-time event. Sometimes it helps to build up momentum. Writing starts with prewriting activities—creating self-imposed deadlines and a schedule, arranging your notes, preparing lists of ideas, drafting rough outlines, making certain that bibliographic references are complete, and reviewing the data analysis. Of course, there is a danger that you will get distracted and sidetracked by such activities. Self-discipline is central to the writing process.

- As you write the report, you may find that your notes are not complete enough or a detail is missing in the citation of a reference source. The visit to the library after data collection is less extensive and more selective or focused than that conducted at the beginning of research, but it may be necessary to fill in missing details.

When writing a research report, you will probably discard some of the notes and sources that you gathered. This does not mean that your initial library work and literature review were a waste of time and effort. Researchers expect that some of the notes (e.g., 25–30 percent) taken before completing the study will become irrelevant as the study gains greater focus. Do not include notes or references in a report that are no longer relevant. They will distract from the flow of ideas and reduce the report's clarity.

You return to the library to verify and to complete references. Going back to the library also helps you avoid plagiarism (discussed in Chapter 2), a very serious form of cheating. Take careful notes and identify the exact source of phrases or ideas to avoid unintentional plagiarism. Cite the sources of what you directly quote and of ideas that you paraphrase. For direct quotes, always include the specific location of the quote with page numbers in the citation. Using another person's words and failing to give credit is always clearly wrong. **Paraphrasing** is not using another's exact words; rather, you restate someone else's ideas in your own words. Researchers regularly paraphrase and cite the source. To paraphrase, you need a solid

writer's block a temporary inability to write that some people experience when they have a writing task to complete.

paraphrasing restating another person's ideas in your own words, condensing at the same time.

Tips for the Wise Researcher Outlining

Outlines can help you as a writer. However, they can also become a barrier if you use them improperly. An outline is a tool that helps you organize ideas. With it you do three things:

1. Put ideas in a sequence (e.g., what will be said first, second, and third);
2. Group related ideas together (e.g., these are similar to each other, but differ from those); and
3. Separate the more general, or higher-level, ideas from more specific ideas, and the specific ideas from very specific details.

Some students feel they must have a complete outline before they can start to write, and that once they prepare an outline, they cannot deviate from it. Few professional writers begin with a complete, detailed outline and stick to it rigidly. Your initial outline can be sketchy, because until you write everything down, it is impossible to put all ideas in a sequence, group them together, and separate the general from the specific. For most writers, new ideas develop or become clearer in the process of writing itself.

Your beginning outline may differ from the final outline by more than its degree of completeness. The process of writing not only reveals and clarifies ideas, it also stimulates new ideas, new connections among ideas, a new sequence of parts, or new relations between the general and the specific. In addition, the writing process may stimulate you to reanalyze or reexamine the literature or findings. This does not mean beginning all over again. Rather, it means you need to maintain an open mind to new insights and be candid about reporting how you conducted the research.

■ **Figure 11.1** Outline Form

I. First major topic	High level of importance
A. Subtopic of topic I	Second level of importance
1. Subtopic of A	Third level of importance
a. Subtopic of 1	Fourth level of importance
b. Subtopic of 1	"
(1) Subtopic of b	Fifth level of importance
(2) Subtopic of b	"
(a) Subtopic of (2)	Sixth level of importance
(b) Subtopic of (2)	"
i. Subtopic of (b)	Seventh level of importance
ii. Subtopic of (b)	"
2. Subtopic of A	Third level of importance
B. Subtopic of topic I	Second level of importance
II. Second major topic	High level of importance

understanding of what you paraphrase. It is more than replacing another's words with synonyms; you condense statements to the core ideas and give credit to the source.

Engage in Prewriting Activities

Many people find that getting started is difficult. Beginning writers often jump to the second step and go from there. This often results in poor-quality writing. **Prewriting** means that you begin with a file folder full of notes, outlines, and lists. You spend thinking time to consider the form of the report and audience. Thinking time often occurs in spurts over time before the bulk of composing begins.

11

Many writers begin to compose by **freewriting**. Freewriting creates a link between a rapid flow of ideas in the mind and writing. As you freewrite, do not stop to reread what you wrote, do not ponder the best word, do not worry about correct grammar, spelling, or punctuation—just get your ideas on paper (or on screen) as quickly as possible to get and keep the creative juices or ideas flowing. You can later clean up what you wrote.

prewriting activities that prepare you for a serious writing process.

freewriting a way to begin serious writing in which you write down everything you think of as quickly as it enters your mind, not worrying about correct grammar or spelling.

Writing and thinking are intertwined. It is impossible to know where one ends and the other begins. If you plan to sit and stare at the wall, the computer output, the sky, or whatever until your thoughts are totally developed and clear before you begin to write, you probably will not get anything written. Writing itself ignites the thinking process, which, in turn, feeds further writing.

Rewrite Your Report

Perhaps one in a million writers is a creative genius who can produce a first draft that communicates with astounding accuracy and clarity. For everyone else, writing means that rewriting—and rewriting again—is necessary. For example, Ernest Hemingway is reported to have rewritten the end of *A Farewell to Arms* 39 times. Professional researchers may rewrite a report a dozen times. If rewriting sounds daunting to you, do not become discouraged. If anything, rewriting reduces the pressure; it means you can start writing and just produce a rough draft that you will polish later. Plan to rewrite a draft at least three or four times. A draft is a complete report, from beginning to end, not a few rough notes or an outline.

Making it Practical **Suggestions for Rewriting**

1. *Mechanics.* Check grammar, spelling, punctuation, verb agreement, verb tense, and verb/subject separation with each rewrite. Remember that each time you add new text, new errors can creep in. Many mistakes are distracting, and they weaken the confidence readers place in the ideas you express.

2. *Usage.* Reexamine terms, especially key terms. When you rewrite, check to see whether you are using a word that best expresses your intended meaning. Do not use technical terms or long words unnecessarily. Use the plain word that best expresses a clear meaning. Get a thesaurus and use it. A thesaurus is an essential reference tool, like a dictionary. It has words of similar meaning and can help you locate the exact word for a meaning you want to express. Precise thinking and expression requires precise language. Do not say *average* if you intend to use *mean*. Do not say *mankind* or *policeman* when you intend *people* or *police officer* (i.e., strive for gender neutrality in your writing). See Pitt (1994) or url: http://www.jeanweber.com/newsite/?page_id=55 for advice on gender neutral writing. Do not use *principal* for *principle*, *there* for *their*, or *than* for *then*. Also avoid unnecessary qualifying language, such as *seems to* or *appears to*.

3. *Voice.* Some writers make the mistake of using the passive voice in a research report instead of the active voice. It may appear to be authoritative, but the passive voice obscures the actor or subject of action. Compare the voice in these two examples: PASSIVE: "The relationship between grade in school and more definite career plans was confirmed by the data." ACTIVE: "The data confirm the relationship between grade in school and more definite career plans." PASSIVE: "Respondent attitude toward abortion was recorded by an interviewer." ACTIVE: "An interviewer recorded respondent attitude toward abortion."

4. *Coherence.* Make the sequence of ideas logically tight. Include transitions between ideas. Try reading the entire report one paragraph at a time. Does each paragraph contain a unified idea? Does it have a topic sentence? Did you include transitions between the topics and paragraphs within the report?

5. *Repetition.* Remove repeated ideas, wordiness, and unnecessary phrases. It is best to state ideas once, forcefully, rather than repeatedly in an unclear way. When revising, eliminate deadwood (words that add nothing) and circumlocution (the use of several words when one precise word will do). Directness is preferable to wordiness. Here is an example: WORDY: "To summarize the above, it is our conclusion in light of the data that x has a positive effect of considerable magnitude on the occurrence of y, notwithstanding the fact that y occurs only on rare occasions." LESS WORDY: "In sum, the effect of x on y is large and positive but occurs infrequently."

6. *Structure.* Make the organization of your research report transparent. Move sections around as necessary to fit the organization. It is wise to use headings and subheadings. A reader should be able to follow a report's logical structure with great ease.

7. *Abstraction.* A good research report mixes abstract ideas with concrete examples. A long string of abstractions without specifics is difficult to read. Likewise, a mass of specific concrete details without a periodic generalization to summarize the main point can also lose readers.

8. *Metaphors.* Many writers use metaphors to express ideas. They use phrases such as "the cutting edge," "the bottom line," and "penetrating to the heart" to express their ideas. Metaphors can be an effective method of communication if you use them sparingly and with care. A few well-chosen, consistently used, fresh metaphors can communicate ideas quickly and effectively; however, excessively using metaphors, especially overused metaphors (e.g., the bottom line), is a sloppy, unimaginative method of expression.

Rewriting helps you to express yourself with a greater clarity, smoothness, precision, and economy of words. When rewriting, focus on clear communication; do not use unnecessary pompous or complicated language. When rewriting, you slowly read what you have already written. Some people read what they wrote out loud to see whether it sounds right. It is always wise to share your writing with others. Professional writers have others read and criticize their writing. New writers quickly learn that friendly, constructive criticism is very valuable. Sharing your writing with others may be difficult at first. It means exposing your written thoughts and encouraging criticism. Yet the purpose of the criticism is to clarify the writing. A good critic is doing you a favor.

Rewriting involves two processes: revising and editing. **Revising** is inserting new ideas, adding supporting evidence, deleting or changing ideas, moving sentences around to clarify meaning, and strengthening transitions and links between ideas. **Editing** is cleaning and tightening up the mechanical aspects of writing, such as spelling, grammar, usage, verb tense, sentence length, and paragraph organization. As you rewrite, go over a draft and revise it brutally to improve it. You will find this is easier to do if you allow some time to pass between writing a draft and rewriting. Phrases that seemed satisfactory in a draft may look fuzzy or poorly connected a week later.

Even if you have not acquired typing or keyboarding skills, it is a good idea to type and print out at least one draft before the final draft. It is easier to see errors and organization problems in a clean, typed draft. Freely cut and paste, cross out words, and move phrases on the printed copy. Serious professionals find that the time they invest in building keyboard skills and learning to use a word processor pays huge dividends later. Word processors make editing much easier. They also check spelling, offer synonyms, and check grammar. Do not rely on the computer program to do all the work; the computer can miss errors (e.g., if you have used *their* when you should have used *there*), but it makes writing easier.

revising part of the rewriting process in which you move ideas around or add and subtract ideas or evidence.

editing part of the rewriting process in which you focus on improving the mechanical aspects of writing, such as spelling or sentence structure.

One last suggestion: Write the introduction and title after you finish a draft of the report. This ensures that they will accurately reflect what you have said. Make titles short and descriptive. They should communicate the topic and the major variables. They can describe the type of research (e.g., "An experiment on") but should not have unnecessary words or phrases (e.g., "An investigation into the").

Summary Review **Steps in the Writing Process**

The way to learn to write is by writing. Writing takes time and effort and improves with practice. There is no single correct way to write, but some ways are better than others are. The writing process has three steps:

1. *Prewriting.* Prepare to write by arranging notes on the literature, making lists of ideas, outlining, completing bibliographic citations, and organizing comments on data analysis.
2. *Composing.* Get your ideas onto paper as a first draft by freewriting, drawing up the bibliography and footnotes, preparing data for presentation, and writing a draft introduction and conclusion.
3. *Rewriting.* Evaluate and polish the report by improving coherence, proofreading for mechanical errors, checking citations, and reviewing voice and usage.

SHOW CAUSE-EFFECT RELATIONS

In many research studies, you want to demonstrate cause-effect relations. You want to see whether one or more factors, conditions, or variables cause another factor or variable. You saw this earlier in Chapter 10, with an independent (cause) and dependent variable (effect) in a simple hypothesis. Although most common in quantitative data research, causal relations can appear in all types of studies. If you wish to show a cause-effect relationship in a study, you need to think about how you will write about and explain it to readers.

Experimental researchers can demonstrate cause-effect relations most clearly. Experiments best meet the three conditions required to show causality: temporal order, association, and control over alternative causes. Hard-core experimenters tend to think that only an experiment can show cause-effect relations, and they question it in other types of research. You show cause-effect in an experiment by introducing the independent variable at a specific time, looking for an association in data on dependent variable measures, and creating an experimental design to control for factors that could influence the outcome (internal validity). Of course, the experimental approach has limitations, including a lack of random samples, difficulties with generalizing (external validity), the need to examine a single variable at a time, and an emphasis on micro-level relationships. If you conduct an experiment, you can talk about causal relations in a report by showing a strong association between the independent and dependent variable in results and a high degree of internal validity in the experimental design.

Researchers who use survey or existing statistical methods also want to show cause-effect relations. Of the three conditions for causality, they can best demonstrate an association among variables. However, as you already learned, an association or correlation alone is not enough for causality. Demonstrating time order in survey or existing statistics data requires extra effort. For example, a respondent may answer all survey questions at one point in time. If some questions ask about past events (e.g., what did you do in high school, or how much education did you parents receive?) whereas others are about present events or attitudes, you can establish time order by carefully looking at the time of a variable in a survey question or variable. This is how a survey or existing statistics researcher argues for temporal order. Survey and existing statistics researchers also control for alternative explanations. They cannot exercise physical control through experimental design as experimenters do. Instead, they measure any variables that might indicate an alternative explanation. These are control variables. Advanced statistical methods allow researchers to add control variables along with the main causal variables and check whether the main variables are still association, net of the control variables. If you conduct survey or existing statistics research, you can talk about causal relations by showing a strong association among variables, by noting the temporal ordering of variables, and by ruling out alternative explanations by using control variables. By using control variables and logically arguing that alternatives are unlikely, you can say that an association among variables supports a causal relationship and is not spurious.

Many field researchers and historical-comparative researchers also want to show cause-effect relations. They observe events over time, so meeting the temporal order condition is usually easy. Showing an association is more difficult. To do this, they carefully note the co-occurrence of events in the qualitative data. For example, a researcher studying a small work setting notices that employees become upset and make a lot of complaints about work conditions and superiors for a week or two several times during a year of field observation. The researcher notes when this occurred and what occurred before, during, and after the employee dissatisfaction peaks. Each peak of complaints occurred shortly after employees returned from a holiday or vacation. During weeks before a holiday or vacation, employees appeared happy and satisfied, but during the week or two following they complained. Listening to the informal talk among employees, the researcher learned that employees often spent vacation or holiday time with adult friends, family members, and neighbors who worked in other jobs. In postholiday informal conversations, the employees talked about how their friends, family members, or neighbors had nice, rewarding jobs. The researcher observed an association between (1) expressions of dissatisfaction and (2) the opportunity the employees had to compare their work situations to the jobs held by other people.

Eliminating alternative explanations is the most difficult condition to satisfy. Researchers do this by becoming intimately familiar with a setting and providing in-depth details and specifics about a particular context. They think about alternatives while conducting the research and try to look for evidence of possible alternative explanations. For example, is it having time away from work on a vacation or holiday and not comparing jobs with friends, family, and neighbors that increased dissatisfaction? If you conduct a field or H-C study, you can talk finding a causal relationship in a report if you show a sequence of events and can document events that occurred earlier or at the same time. To eliminate alternative explanations, be familiar with the literature on the topic and note whether anyone suggested or found evidence for alternative explanations. You can also suggest potential alternatives along with any evidence you found for them with your judgment of whether they might be present.

THE QUANTITATIVE RESEARCH REPORT

The principles of good writing apply to all types of reports, but the parts of a report differ depending on whether your study used quantitative or qualitative data. It is always wise to read many reports on the same kind of research for models and ideas. We begin by looking at the quantitative research report. The sections of the report roughly follow the sequence of steps of a research project.

Abstract or Executive Summary

Quantitative research reports begin with a short summary or abstract (you read about the abstract of a study in Chapter 10). The size of an abstract varies; it can be as few as 50 words (this paragraph has 82 words) or as long as a full page. Most scholarly journal articles have abstracts on the first page of the article. The abstract has information on the topic, the research problem, the basic findings, and any unusual research design or data collection features.

Applied research reports for practitioners substitute a long summary, the **executive summary**, for an abstract. The executive summary has more detail than an article abstract and is longer (often three to five pages). It has most major findings, the implications of findings, and major recommendations. The executive summary has more in it because many practitioners and policy makers only read the executive summary and then just skim parts of the full report.

Abstracts and executive summaries tell a reader what is in a report. They help the reader looking for specific information to screen many reports and decide whether to read the entire report. An abstract also gives serious readers who intend to read the full report a quick overview of it. This makes reading the report easier and faster. Although the abstract or executive summary are the first thing someone reads, you should write them last. Write them after you have finished the rest of report so you know what the report contains.

executive summary a summary of a research report that is longer than an abstract and used in applied research studies for practitioners.

Presentation of the Problem

The first section of a report is very important because in it you introduce readers to the main topic, research question, and overall tone of the report. Your goal is to present the research question, define major concepts, and begin to guide a reader through your report. The introductory section has several possible headings, such as "Introduction," "Problem Definition," "Literature Review," "Hypotheses," or "Background Assumptions." Although the headings vary, the contents include a statement of the research problem/question and a rationale for its importance. Here, you explain the significance of and provide background on the research question. Explain the significance of your study by showing how different solutions to the problem lead to different applications or theoretical conclusions. This section is where you place the literature review and link the specific question of your study to past studies. You also define key concepts and present the main hypotheses in general, conceptual terms.

Description of the Method

The next section of the report describes how you designed the study and collected the data. It goes by several names (e.g., "Methods," "Research Design," or "Data") and may be subdivided into other parts (e.g., "Measures," "Sampling," or "Manipulations"). It is the most important section for the professional when he or she is evaluating the quality of research methodology. This section answers several questions for the reader:

1. What type of study (e.g., experiment, survey) did you conduct?
2. Exactly how did you collect the data (e.g., study design, type of survey, time and location of data collection, experimental design used)?
3. How did you measure/introduce each variable? Are the measures reliable and valid?
4. Did you sample? How many participants are in the study? Exactly how did you select them? What are their characteristics (age, gender, race-ethnicity, and so forth)?
5. Did any ethical issues or specific design concerns arise, and, if so, how did you deal with them?

Results and Tables

After you described how you sampled, collected data, and measured variables, you present the data. In this section you present—not discuss, analyze, or interpret—the data. Researchers often combine the "Results" section with the next section, called "Discussion" or "Findings," but many keep the sections separate. You have a few choices in how to present the data. When you analyzed the data, you looked at dozens of univariate, bivariate, and multivariate tables and statistics to get a feel for the data. Do not put every statistic and table you looked at in a final report. Rather, select the minimum number of charts or tables that fully informs a reader. Charts or tables should summarize the data and show any tests of hypotheses (e.g., frequency distributions, tables with means and standard deviations, correlations, and other statistics). Your goal is to give readers a complete picture of the data without overwhelming them—not to provide data in excessive detail or present irrelevant data. Readers can make their own interpretations by examining the data. Detailed summary statistics and very technical explanations belong in appendixes.

Discussion

In the discussion section, give the reader a concise, unambiguous interpretation of the data's meaning. The discussion is not a selective emphasis or partisan interpretation. You candidly discuss what is in the results section. You separate the discussion section from the data results section to allow a reader to examine the

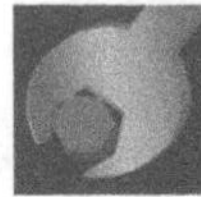

Making It Practical Writing the Discussion Section of a Report on Quantitative Research

Many beginning researchers find it difficult to organize a discussion section. Reading many research reports can help you see how to do it. One approach is to organize the discussion according to hypotheses. You can discuss how the data relate to each hypothesis. In addition to reporting how data relate to your hypotheses, you should discuss unanticipated findings that look interesting. Also, give possible alternative explanations of results. Your may also note the weaknesses or limitations of your study. Many beginning researchers find it unusual to point out limitations. Remember that a major principle of the research process is to be fully open and candid, not to hide or defend a particular outcome. Readers will have more confidence in your report if you openly disclose its limitations.

data and arrive at his or her own interpretations. Organize your discussion to make it easy for a reader to follow. One way to do this is to repeat hypotheses and describe how the findings specifically support, modify, or reject each hypothesis. After reading the discussion section, a reader should leave with a clear picture of the findings.

Conclusions

In the conclusion or summary section, you restate the research question and summarize major findings. This is a place to highlight limitations of the study and possible implications for the future. The only sections after the conclusion are notes, references, and appendixes (if any). You should only include sources you referred to in the references section. If you have an appendix, place additional detailed information on methods of data collection (e.g., questionnaire wording) or specialized results in it. Use footnotes or endnotes sparingly to expand or elaborate on information in the text. Put secondary information (information that clarifies your in-text statements) in notes to avoid distracting readers from the flow of your text.

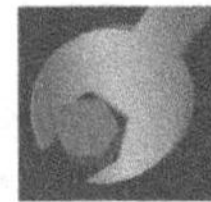

Making It Practical Looking at the Parts of a Published Quantitative Data Study

Regarding the quantitative data study by Weitzer and Tuch (2005), from the abstract, a reader learns the following five things:

1. The topic of this study is racial bias by police, specifically racial profiling in the United States.
2. The study is important because the extent of police racial bias and public perceptions of it are not well known.
3. Data for this study are a national survey on citizens' views of and experiences with police bias.
4. Findings of the study are that three factors shape a person's views on the issue: race, prior experiences with police discrimination, and exposure to news media.
5. The study finds support for a group-position theory of race relations.

The authors divided the introduction section into a short introductory paragraph that outlines the topic and research question, a section with the literature review, and the hypotheses they test. The researchers present three hypotheses; each has two parts. The authors also outline alternative explanations or theories that they will consider. The next section, Methods and Data, is divided into several parts: Sampling, Panel Representation (repeated measures of the same people over time), Independent, Dependent, and Control Variables. In the methods section, the authors also present readers with basic descriptive statistics for each variable in a table. The Results section combines results and discussion. There are many tables with numbers in this section. The authors organized the discussion of results by each hypothesis. The Conclusion section is three pages long. In it, the authors discuss the significance of their study, repeat their major findings, and point to directions for future research. After the conclusion are endnotes and references.

THE QUALITATIVE RESEARCH REPORT

Compared to a quantitative data research report, most people find writing a report on qualitative research to be more difficult. It has fewer rules and is less structured. Nevertheless, all reports have the same the purpose: to communicate how you conducted a study, what data you collected, and what you learned from a through examination of the data.

In a quantitative research report, you present hypotheses and evidence in a logically tight and condensed style. By contrast, a report on a qualitative study can be longer and less compact. In fact, book-length reports on qualitative research are common. Reports on qualitative research are longer for several reasons:

- It is difficult to condense data that are in the form of words, pictures, or sentences.
- Providing evidence often means offering readers specific quotes and extended examples.
- You want to create a subjective sense of empathy and understanding of real people, events, and settings. It takes more words to give highly detailed descriptions of specific settings and situations.
- In qualitative data studies, you use less standardized techniques for gathering data, creating analytic categories, and organizing evidence. You may create new the techniques for a particular setting. This means you must explain in depth exactly what you did in the study and why rather than simply referring to a well-known standard technique.
- Many qualitative data studies construct new concepts or theories. It takes more words to develop new concepts and explain the relationships among them than to use existing concepts. Because theory flows from the evidence, you need to show readers how the concept is linked to the evidence.
- Many writers use a variety of writing styles in a qualitative data report. This freedom to depart from a precise, standard style tends to increase overall length. You may employ literary devices to tell a story or recount a colorful tale.

Report on Field Research

Reports on field research rarely follow a fixed format with standard sections. You can use a less objective and formal tone when writing about field research. You can write a report on field research in first person (i.e., using the pronoun *I*) because you, as an individual person, were directly involved in the setting and interacted face-to-face with the people studied. Your decisions or indecisions, feelings, reactions, and personal experiences are legitimate parts of the field research process.

In the report, you do not separate theoretical ideas from data into distinct sections. Instead, you intertwine generalizations with the empirical evidence. This takes the form of detailed description with frequent quotes. You must balance the presentation of data and analysis. Too much data without analysis and too much analysis with supporting data are both problems to avoid.

Data reduction is a major issue in field research. Field research data are in the form of a huge volume of field notes, but you can only share a very small percent of observations or recorded conversations with the readers.

Field researchers organize reports in several ways. Two major ways are by chronological natural history and by themes. When you use natural history organization, you present the sequence of ideas and data in the same time order as you discovered or came across them. When you use a thematic organization, you present a theme and then provide data that illustrate or support it. You can choose between using abstract analytic themes from the scholarly literature or your own thinking, and using themes that are used by the people you studied. Both have advantages. The former makes it easier to connect your study with other studies or more abstract theory. The latter gives readers a vivid description of the setting and lets you display

Learning from History *Boys In White*

The book *Boys In White* (Becker et al. 1961) describes the pioneering study by Howard Becker and his colleagues into how medical students become doctors. It is a classic ethnographic study that details the lives of young men at the University of Kansas—their schedules, efforts to find out what professors wanted from them, "latent culture," and assimilation of medical values. It also describes how they learned to negotiate a hospital or clinic in all its complexity as well as develop a perspective on their futures. The clarity and thoughtfulness of the method used and its write-up are equally important as the findings. The authors started with about 5000 pages of single-spaced field notes. Of these, they put less than 5 percent in the book-length report as quotations. The remaining 95 percent were not wasted. The field notes are a rich, deep reservoir of empirical evidence from which the authors created the report. As you prepare a report, carefully select quotes and indirectly convey the rest of the data to readers.

the language, concepts, categories, and beliefs of the people you studied. You can use a mix of both types of themes.

In a field research report, you discuss the methods used in the report, but its location and form vary. One technique is to interweave a description of the setting, the means of gaining access, the role of the researcher, and the subject/researcher relationship into the discussion of evidence and analysis. A chronological or theme-based organization allows you to put the data collection method near the beginning or the end. In book-length reports, most authors put a discussion of methodological issues in a separate appendix at the end.

Field research reports can contain transcriptions of tape recordings, maps, photographs, and charts illustrating analytic categories. They supplement the discussion and are placed near the discussion they complement. Qualitative field research can use creative formats that differ from the usual written text with examples from field notes. The photographs give a visual inventory of the settings described in the text and present the meanings of settings in terms of those being studied. For example, field research articles have appeared in the form of all photographs, a script for a play, or a documentary film.

Direct, personal involvement in the intimate details of a social setting heightens ethical concerns. Researchers write in a manner that protects the privacy of people they study. They usually change the names of members and exact locations in field reports. Personal involvement in field research leads researchers to include a short autobiography. For example, in the appendix to *Street Corner Society*, the author, William Foote Whyte (1955), gave a detailed account of the occupations of his father and grandfather, his hobbies and interests, the jobs he held, how he ended up going to graduate school, and how his research was affected by his getting married.

Making it Practical **Organization of a Report on Field Research**

1. Introduction
    a. Most general aspects of situation
    b. Main contours of the general situation
    c. How you collected materials
    d. Details about the setting
    e. How the report is organized
2. The situation
    a. Analytic categories
    b. Contrast between situation and other situations
    c. Development of situation over time
3. Strategies
4. Summary and implications

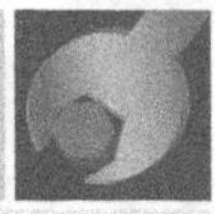

Making It Practical Looking at the Parts of a Published Qualitative Data Study

From the abstract in the qualitative data study by Perry (2001), a reader learns the following five things:

1. The topic is the processes by which people construct white racial identities.
2. The study examined white youth in two high schools: one predominantly white, the other multiracial.
3. The researcher used ethnographic techniques and in-depth interviews.
4. A main idea is that racial superiority is based on whites having no culture, because their culture is the norm.
5. The study has implications for "critical white studies," sociology of education, and racial identity formation.

The report begins with an open-end question that Perry asked a participant and a quote of the participant's response. The introduction section has a description of the field sites (two high schools) and major organizing concepts (white culture, naturalization, a claim to be cultureless, and rationalization). The next section is the literature review. After reviewing the literature and elaborating on the study topic, Perry provides the reader with a method and reflections section. In it she describes her own study of existing statistics and other sources to acquire a background on setting and topic, describes the two field sites in greater depth, and explains in detail how she did the study, such as spending two and one-half years observing and interviewing, as well as her specific activities in the field sites. She tells her age and how she dressed and techniques she used to gain rapport with field participants. She also describes types of participants she interviewed, where she conducted the interviews, and for what length of time (about two hours). Her results are not in a section by that name, but she presents results for each of the two field sites, one after the other, mixed with conceptual categories. The results include description and analysis intermixed with frequent quotes from field notes or interviews. The conclusion section summarizes major findings and concepts and outlines implications of the study. It is followed by endnotes and references.

Report on Historical-Comparative Research

There is no single best way to write a report on historical-comparative research. Most frequently, researchers "tell a story" and describe details in general analytic categories. They go beyond description to include some limited generalizations. Thus, a major feature is to connect abstract concepts with specific empirical details.

Researchers rarely describe their methods in any detail in a report on historical-comparative research. The methods may have involved visiting many specialized libraries or obtaining documents, but beyond listing sources, other details are not necessary. You will rarely see an explicit section of a report or an appendix describing the methods used. Occasionally, a book-length report contains a bibliographic essay that discusses major sources used. More often, you see numerous detailed footnotes or endnotes. For example, a 20-page report on quantitative or field research typically has 5 to 15 notes or sources. A report on historical research of equal length may have over 60 notes or sources.

Historical-comparative reports often have photographs, maps, diagrams, charts, or tables of statistics. You see them throughout the report sections that discuss evidence that relates to them. The charts, tables, and so forth are less the "make or break" evidence of a quantitative research report. Instead, they are part of a slow build-up of a large quantity of diverse evidence. You put them in the report to give readers a more complete picture and better feel for the places and people in the study. You use them in conjunction other evidence, as part of creating a broad web of meaning with many descriptive details. Skill at organizing the large amounts of qualitative evidence is itself a way to convey interpretations and generalizations to a reader.

You can organize a report of historical-comparative research in two major ways: by topic and chronologically. Most writers mix the two types. For example, you can organize information chronologically within topics, or organize by topic within chronological periods. If the report is truly comparative, you have additional options, such as making comparisons within topics. Some historical-comparative researchers mimic the quantitative research report and use quantitative research techniques. Their reports follow the model of a quantitative research report.

Many researchers use a narrative style of report writing, in which they "tell a story." If you use a narrative style, you organize the data chronologically and try to "tell a story" around specific individuals and events.

THE RESEARCH PROPOSAL

In Chapter 10 you learned about research proposals. You write a proposal for a supervised project submitted to instructors as part of an educational degree (e.g., a honor's or master's thesis or a Ph.D. dissertation) or for a funding source. The proposal's purpose is to convince reviewers that you, the researcher, are capable of successfully conducting the proposed research. Reviewers will have confidence that you can successfully complete the study if your proposal is well written and organized and if you demonstrate careful planning. A proposal is similar to a research report, but you write it before the research begins. A proposal describes the research problem and its importance and gives a detailed account of the methods that you will use and why they are appropriate. See Chapter 16 for example proposals.

Proposals for Research Grants

The purpose of a research grant is to provide the resources needed to help complete a worthy project. Researchers whose primary goal is to use funding for personal benefit or prestige, to escape from other activities, or to build an "empire" are less successful. The strategies of writing proposals and "winning" grants are separate skills in themselves.

There are many sources of funding for research proposals. Colleges, private foundations, and government agencies have programs that award grant funds to researchers (see Figure 11.2). You may use the money for purchasing equipment, for paying salaries, for research supplies, for travel to collect data, or for help with the publication of results. The degree of competition for a grant varies a great deal depending on the source. Some sources fund more than three out of four proposals they receive; others fund fewer than one in twenty.

Tips for the Wise Researcher Quantitative and Qualitative Research Proposals

A proposal for quantitative research has most of the parts of a research report: a title, an abstract, a problem statement, a literature review, a methods or design section, and references. It lacks results, discussion, and conclusion sections. It is a plan for data collection and analysis (e.g., types of statistics) and frequently includes a schedule of the steps to be undertaken and an estimate of the time required for each step.

A proposal for qualitative research is more difficult to write. This is because the research process itself is less structured and preplanned. You prepare a problem statement, literature review, and references. You can demonstrate an ability to complete a proposed qualitative project in two ways:

1. Your proposal is well written, with an extensive discussion of the literature, significance of the problem, and sources. This shows reviewers your familiarity with qualitative research and the appropriateness of the method for studying the problem.
2. Your proposal describes a qualitative pilot study. This demonstrates motivation, familiarity with research techniques, and ability to complete a report about unstructured research.

■ **Figure 11.2** Examples of Announcements to Fund Research.

Spencer Foundation
Eligibility: Principal Investigators applying for a Research Grant must be affiliated with a school district, a college or university, a research facility, or a cultural institution. The Foundation accepts proposals from institutions and/or researchers from the U.S. and internationally. Researchers must also have an earned doctorate in an academic discipline or professional field or appropriate experience in an education-related profession. Budget Restrictions: Indirect costs may not be charged to proposed budgets with less than $50,000 in direct costs. Proposals exceeding $500,000 in direct costs require particularly close scrutiny and are generally developed in close consultation with Spencer staff prior to submitting a proposal.

Determine whether your project fits within one or more of the Foundation's current areas of interest:

- The Relation between Education and Social Opportunity;
- Organizational Learning in Schools, School Systems, and Higher Education Institutions;
- Teaching, Learning, and Instructional Resources; and
- Purposes and Values of Education.

In addition to proposals in these defined areas, the Foundation will continue to accept proposals that do not fit one of these areas.

Deadlines: There are no deadlines for preliminary proposals. They are welcome at any time.

If invited, full proposals in the Major Research Grants Program are considered four times per year.

Blue Cross Foundation Announces Letter of Inquiry Deadlines for Minnesota Projects
Grants up to $150,000 will be provided to Minnesota nonprofits and government organizations for programs focusing on the health/well-being of immigrants or children. . . .

Deadline: Various

Komen for the Cure Seeks Applications for Washington, D.C. Area Community Grants
Grants of up to $700,000 will be awarded to nonprofits, government agencies, and educational institutions working to reduce breast cancer disparities in Washington, D.C., and seven surrounding counties. . . .

Deadline: August 20, 2007

You need to investigate funding sources so you can direct your proposal to the funding source with which it has the greatest chance of success. Ask questions:

- What types of projects get funded—applied versus basic research, specific topics or research techniques?
- What are the deadlines and proposal format requirements (page length, font size)?
- What kind of proposal is necessary (e.g., short letter, detailed plan)?
- How large have most previous grants been?
- What parts of doing the research (e.g., equipment, personnel, travel) are or are not funded?

There are many sources of information on funding sources. Librarians or officials responsible for research grants at a college are good resource people.

Many funding agencies periodically issue **requests for proposals (RFPs).** These ask for proposals to conduct research on a specific issue (see Figure 11.3). In evaluating proposals, funding agencies look for a record of past success. The researcher in charge of a study is the **principal investigator (PI)** or project director. Proposals usually include a curriculum vitae or academic resumé, letters of support from other researchers, and a record of accomplishments. The reviewers of proposals feel safer investing funds in a project headed by someone who already has research experience than in a novice. You can build a record with small research projects or by assisting an experienced researcher before you seek funding as a principal investigator.

requests for proposals (RFPs) an announcement by a founding source that it seeks research proposals to fund.

principal investigator (PI) the main researcher who conducts a study that is funded by a grant.

Figure 11.3 Example RFP

ANNOUNCEMENT OF AVAILABILITY OF FUNDS, TRAINING, AND TECHNICAL ASSISTANCE IN JUVENILE JUSTICE AND DELINQUENCY PREVENTION

KEEP THIS ANNOUNCEMENT TO REFER TO WHILE COMPLETING THE APPLICATION FORM.

A. **ISSUING OFFICE.** This announcement of availability of federal funds, training, and technical assistance is issued for the State of Colorado by the Colorado Department of Public Safety, Division of Criminal Justice (DCJ), in conjunction with the Juvenile Justice and Delinquency Prevention (JJDP) Act of 1974 (42 U.S.C. 5601), as amended. DCJ is the sole point of contact concerning this Announcement. All communications must be done through the Division of Criminal Justice.

B. **APPLICATION PROCESS AND INQUIRIES.** An application and application instructions may be obtained by mailing or faxing the attached "Intent to Apply" form to the address/fax number listed on that form, or e-mailing the same information to the e-mail address on the form.

C. **ELIGIBLE APPLICANTS. General:** Eligible applicants are public and private state-level agencies or local agencies, including local law enforcement, courts, probation offices, district attorneys' offices, schools, school districts, BOCES, and community-based not-for-profit organizations. Applicants may propose to subcontract any or all of the required activities but are not required to do so. Subcontractors can be other public state or local agencies or private not-for-profit organizations as identified under Section 501(c)(3) of the federal tax code. The applicant agency must certify that all participating agencies/organizations have collaborated in the design of the project and agree that the identified lead agency is appropriate.

Specific: For **Program 1, Juvenile-Focused Community Policing Programs,** eligible applicants are local law enforcement agencies or local public/private community-based agencies collaborating with law enforcement. Applications must include Memoranda of Understanding signed by all project participants, which delineate the role(s) of the community partners in the support and implementation of the project. The applicant agency must certify that all participating agencies/organizations have collaborated in the design of the project and agree that the identified lead agency is appropriate. Applicants that are not law enforcement agencies must provide written endorsement of the proposal from the primary law enforcement agency for the area and demonstrate the project's relationship to community policing programs/philosophy. Likewise, applications submitted by law enforcement agencies must provide written endorsement from the community organization(s) that is/are collaborating in the problem-solving effort.

For **training and technical assistance for comprehensive delinquency prevention planning,** requests must come from units of local government, including departments such as law enforcement and social services, and from advisory groups associated with the local government.

D. **BACKGROUND AND AVAILABLE FUNDS.** These federal funds are available under Title II Formula and Challenge Grant Programs of the Juvenile Justice and Delinquency Prevention (JJDP) Act. The Colorado Juvenile Justice and Delinquency Prevention (JJDP) Council oversees these grant programs and has prioritized and budgeted funds for the following four areas:

1. the expansion of both the restorative justice philosophy in programs that focus on juvenile accountability and juvenile-focused community policing programs ($150,000)
2. the implementation of interventions to address the over representation of minority youth in the juvenile justice system ($200,000)
3. the provision of quality female-specific services in the juvenile justice system ($150,000)
4. an in-depth look, through a pilot site, at the quality of and access to counsel for juveniles ($70,000)

The purposes and principles identified for each area are described below under Item E. Awards will be made, on a competitive basis, for twelve-month periods (unless otherwise stated), beginning October 1, 2001. Individual award amounts (minimum of $5,000) will be determined by the number and quality of eligible applicants, and funds available. These funds cannot be used to supplant (replace) existing dollars from other sources; however, they may enhance or expand an existing program.

The Colorado Juvenile Justice and Delinquency Prevention Council will judge the merits of the proposals received in accordance with the evaluation factors listed in this announcement. Failure of the applicant to provide any information requested in this announcement and the application form may result in disqualification of the application. The responsibility is that of the applicant. The plan of the Council will be to fund those applicants whose proposals are most responsive to the specifications in this announcement, within the available funds.

Source: Logo Courtesy of the Colorado Department of Public Safety

11

■ **Figure 11.3** *Continued*

E. **PURPOSES, PRINCIPLES, AND GUIDELINES FOR FUNDED PROGRAMS.** It is the intent of the Council and DCJ to allow applicants to design their projects to meet local needs. However, there are several primary principles which must be included in the application problem statement, project description, goals and objectives, and evaluation plan. These are listed by program area below.

1. **Juvenile-Focused Community Policing and Restorative Justice.** ($150,000)

Juvenile-Focused Community Policing These funds are intended for projects that use community policing principles to foster positive relationships with the community, involve the community in the quest for better delinquency control and prevention, and pool resources with those of the community to address the most urgent needs of community members regarding youth crime.

OJJDP has defined community policing as "a policing philosophy that promotes and supports organizational strategies to address the cause and reduce the fear of crime and social disorder through problem-solving tactics and community-police partnerships." It should empower law enforcement and the community to implement specific problem-solving strategies that address the underlying causes of the youth-focused problematic issues.

Example of the Community Policing Problem-Solving Approach:

Problem Statement/Identification: Repeat calls for service for juvenile loitering activity in the community. Large number of kids, ages 12–14 years, are without recreational activity. Youths in the neighborhood need recreational activities. Current facilities close early and are outside the area.

Action Plan: To provide recreational activities at the local baseball field and elementary schools to develop art programs and team sports of baseball, basketball and volleyball.

Risk/Protective Factor Addressed: Provide access to resources, provide supportive networks and social bonds to community.

Anticipated Results: Reduced youth-related police calls for service, increased involvement of residents in youth activities and increased neighborhood participation in the neighborhood association.

Evaluation: Are calls for juvenile loitering reduced in the area during programmed activities? Are the youth involved in the program seeking alternative activities once the program is compete?

Under the community policing model, the citizen is asked to assume a greater responsibility and contribute individually and collectively to public safety. By relying on expertise and resources which already exist in communities, police can perform their duties more effectively and will give the members of the larger community a key role in problem solving.

Project dollars must be for the specific purpose of development, enhancement, implementation, or evaluation of *youth-focused*, neighborhood-based community policing programs. The geographic boundaries of the neighborhood or community must be clearly defined. The problem identification process must be documented: How did the community verify *what* is occurring; *who* is it affecting; *when* is it occurring; *where* is it occurring; and *how* is it impacting the community? Memoranda of Understanding, delineating the roles and responsibilities of the law enforcement and community partners, must be included.

*Please do not staple your proposal pages.

Reviewers who evaluate a proposal first ask whether the proposal project is appropriate to the funding source's goals. For example, programs that fund basic research have the advancement of knowledge as a goal. Programs to fund applied research often have improvements in the delivery of services as a goal. Instructions specify page length, number of copies, deadlines, and the like. Follow all instructions exactly.

Your proposal should be neat and professional looking. The instructions for proposals may ask for a detailed plan for the use of time, services, and personnel. State them clearly and be realistic. Excessively high or low estimates, unnecessary add-ons, and omitted essentials will result in a less favorable evaluation. Creating a budget for a proposed research project can be complicated and requires technical assistance. There are official pay rates, fringe benefit rates, and so on. It is best to

Simon Battensby/Photographer's Choice/Getty Images

consult a grants officer at a college or an experienced proposal writer. In addition, endorsements or clearances of regulations are often necessary (e.g., IRB approval). The proposal should also include specific plans for disseminating results (e.g., publications, presentations before professional groups) and a plan to evaluate whether the project met its objectives.

The proposal is a type of contract between the researcher and the funding source. Funding agencies often require a final report. It includes details on how funds were spent, the findings, and an evaluation of whether the project met its objectives. A failure to spend funds properly, complete the project as described in the proposal, or file a final report has serious consequences. The funding agency may sue for a recovery of funds or a researcher might be banned from receiving future funding. A serious misuse of funds may result fines, jail terms, or the penalties for the institution (school, hospital, research institute) where the research was to occur.

The process of reviewing proposals after they are submitted takes from a few weeks to almost a year. In most cases, reviewers rank a large group of proposals, and only highly ranked proposals receive funding. Most government agencies or research centers use a peer review process. Private foundations may have a mix of nonresearcher lay people and professional researchers review proposals. Instructions on preparing a proposal indicate whether you are to write for professional specialists or for an educated general audience. As with writing a research report, it is always a good idea to have others read it and give you comments and to revise as necessary before you submit your proposal.

If your proposal is funded, celebrate, but only for a short time. If your proposal is rejected, do not despair. Given the competition, funding sources reject a majority of proposals the first or second time they are submitted. Many funding sources provide you with written reviewer evaluations of the proposal. You should always request evaluations if they are available. Sometimes a courteous talk on the telephone with a person at the funding source will reveal the reasons for rejection. You should strengthen and resubmit a proposal based on the reviewer comments. Most funding sources accept repeated resubmissions of revised proposals. Propos-

Making It Practical A Successful Research Grant Proposal

Before you submit a grant proposal, be certain that the funding agency is looking for proposals on your topic or research question. If you are uncertain, check with the funding agency officials first. If you submit a proposal to an appropriate funding source, reviewers are more likely to rate it higher when the following are present:

1. For basic research: Your proposal addresses an important research question, clearly builds on past studies, and represents a substantial advance in knowledge. For applied research: Your proposal carefully documents a major social problem, shows an awareness of all alternatives, and offers solutions.
2. You have followed all instructions in detail.
3. You submitted the proposal well within the deadline. Funding agencies automatically reject late proposals.
4. The proposal is written clearly and has easy-to-follow objectives. Many proposals provide charts or diagrams that make it easy for a reader to following all details.
5. You completely described your research procedures and used high standards of research methodology. The research techniques you describe are the most appropriate ones for your specific research question.
6. You included specific plans for how you will disseminate the results and evaluate all project objectives.
7. You provided a study design that shows serious planning and realistic budgets and schedules.
8. You have the experience or background required to complete the study successfully and/or include other researchers with technical background and experience as consultants.
9. You include letters of support from knowledgeable people or involved organizations.

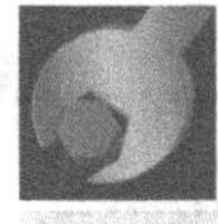

Making It Practical Select Undergraduate Research Sources

Council on Undergraduate Research
Council on Undergraduate Research
734 15th St. N.W. Suite 550 Washington, DC 2005
PHONE: (202) 783-4810 WEB SITE: http://www.cur.org/
National Conference on Undergraduate Research
http://www.ncur.org/
National Science Foundation: Research Experiences for Undergraduates
http://128.150.4.107/pubs/2005/nsf05592/nsf05592.htm
Undergraduate Research Community for the Human Sciences
http://www.kon.org/urc/undergrad_research.html

Stewart Cohen/Blend Images/Corbis Royalty Free

als that have been revised based on past reviews tend to be stronger in subsequent competitions.

UNDERGRADUATE RESEARCH

Many people engage in social research—high school students, undergraduates, graduate students working on master's or doctoral degrees, and professionals in many fields. Learning to do research has long been an essential part of earning advanced degrees. Learning research skills often begins while a student is an undergraduate. The Council on Undergraduate Research (CUR), founded in 1978, promotes research by all undergraduates. The CUR has grown to include 900 colleges and universities. The CUR hosts an undergraduate research conference, produces a scholarly journal, and provides special Institutes on undergraduate research for students and faculty. In addition to CUR, other national organizations and many colleges and universities actively promote undergraduate research as a highly engaging and effective form of learning and professional growth. They offer small grant programs or summer research opportunities to assist students in conducting research.

WHAT HAVE YOU LEARNED?

In this chapter you learned about the research report and the process of writing such a report. You saw how features of a research study, such as qualitative versus quantitative data, affect the organization and content of a report. You also learned about the process of preparing a research proposal and seeking funding for research, as well as the fast growing area of programs and support for undergraduate research.

Clearly communicating results is a vital part of the research process, as are the ethics and politics of social research. I urge you, as a consumer of social research or a new social researcher, to be self-aware. Be aware of the place of research in society and of the societal context in which social research can thrive. Social researchers bring a unique perspective to the larger society.

KEY TERMS

editing *276*
executive summary *278*
freewriting *274*
paraphrasing *273*
prewriting *274*
principal investigator (PI) *285*
request for proposals (RFPs) *285*
research report *270*
revising *276*
writer's block *273*

APPLYING WHAT YOU'VE LEARNED

Activity 1

Practice preparing an outline for a research report. To do this, first identify five scholarly journal articles that report on the same type of research on one topic. Develop of an outline of each research report. Notice what is similar and what is different about each. After outlining each and conducting a comparison, develop an outline of your own in two stages. First, develop general categories with major headings and no more than one secondary level in the outline. You should have four or five major headings and two or three subcategories under each. Second, refine your outline by developing two levels of greater detail, so that you have major headings, first-level headings, second-level headings, and one more level of subheadings. There should be two or more items at each level.

Activity 2

Locate five RFPs for a topic of interest. You can find a few with a general search on the Internet, but many are only available in specialized publications or databases. A good one to check is the U.S. government's *Federal Register*. It is available in most college libraries and online, and it has an overwhelming amount of information. It is often easier to locate specific private foundations or government agencies at the national, state, or city level. For example, specific agencies such as Big Brothers or Big Sisters to might ask for RFPs for applied research, or a state Department of Education might seek RFPs to evaluate its bilingual education programs. The RPF may be active or have already had a deadline that passed. Once you found five RFPs, answer the following six questions about each:

1. What is the name of the funding source?
2. From whom are applications sought, or who is eligible to apply for funding?
3. What topics or research questions does the funding source want to be examined?
4. How much money is provided either in total or as the maximum for a proposal?
5. What is the submission deadline for a proposal, and are there specifications for how the proposal should be delivered?
6. Are there specifications for the format of the proposal (e.g., page length, specific sections)?

Activity 3

Go onto the Internet and conduct a search using Google. Enter the term *Undergraduate Research*. Create three lists. In list 1, include colleges and universities that have a program for undergraduate research. In list 2, place government or private agencies that provide financial support for undergraduate research. In list 3, put all scholarships, summer institutes, and research grant support for undergraduates. Note whether the funding is for a specific academic field (e.g., chemistry) or is open to all fields.

REFERENCES

Becker, Howard S. et al. 1961. *Boys in White: Student Culture in Medical School.* Chicago: University of Chicago Press.

Hartley, James, James Pennebaker, and Claire Fox. 2003. "Using New Technology to Assess the Academic Writing Styles of Male and Female Pairs and Individuals." *Journal of Technical Writing and Communication* 33(3):243–261.

Hurd, P. D. 1998. "Scientific Literacy: New Minds for a Changing World." *Science Education* 82:407–416.

Perry, Pamela. 2001. "White Means Never Having to Say You're Ethnic: White Youth and the Construction of 'Cultureless' Identities." *Journal of Contemporary Ethnography* 30(1):56–91.

Pitt, M. J. 1994. "A Practical Guide to Gender Neutral Language" *Management Decision* 32(6):41–44.

Weitzer, Ronald and Steven Tuch. 2005. "Racially Biased Policing Determinants of Citizen Perceptions." *Social Forces* 83(3):1009–1030.

Whyte, William Foote. 1955. *Street Corner Society: The Social Structure of an Italian Slum.* Chicago: University of Chicago Press.

CHAPTER 12

Sample Research Proposals

Taken from: *Understanding Research,* by W. Lawrence Neuman

EXAMPLE RESEARCH PROPOSAL, QUALITATIVE EXPLORATORY STUDY OF ANIME FANS IN THE UNITED STATES

INTRODUCTION AND RESEARCH TOPIC

Anime, or Japanese-origin animation, has become widely popular among some teens and young adults. Enthusiasts watch many hours of the films, collect the films, read magazines about characters and films, attend fan conventions, create Internet sites with fan information, and dress up as their favorite characters. While the public might be familiar with a few box-office hits, such as *Spirited Away* or children's cartoons, there is an entire world of fans in their teens through twenties who avidly follow anime.

A few studies have been conducted on the cinematic form and industry of Japanese animation and its spill-over to Japanese popular culture products, but almost nothing is written about the anime fan subculture in America. It appears to have arisen in 1990s and greatly expanded during the early 2000s. Casual observation suggests it is about equally among popular both genders and all ethnic-racial groups. It primarily attracts young people from the pre-adolescence and early teens (11–15) through early adulthood (25–28). Apparently, children discover the Japanese-style cartoons, and some become attracted to more sophisticated animation forms as well as video game spin offs.

The scant journalistic commentary on anime fans implies that many are "social misfits" or "geeks." They do not cause trouble or break laws, but they do not fit in with mainstream peers. Many U.S. fans have self-adopted the Japanese term *otaku* (which translates as an obsessed misfit/geek and has negative connotations) as a badge of honor. Some apparently excel at academics, but few appear seriously involved in sports or other social activities common for their age group. There is speculation is that these young people are bright and pulled into a fantasy world that offers rapid action escape, adventure, morality tales, and intrigue. Somewhat socially separated from peers, they apparently seek out others with the same interest. While most appear socially adjusted and operate in daily life without serious difficulties, a few withdraw and devote more time in the fantasy world of animation than in reality. Reactions by parents and other adults who work with young people (teachers, librarians) are not known.

There are many forms of anime. Most genres have an adventure-fantasy theme, but some offer elaborate alternative worlds, and others are very violent or graphically pornographic. With little formal adult or institutional support, the fans seek one another out to form clubs at schools, libraries, or community centers at which they watch and discuss their favorite characters and tales. They organize conventions at the state, regional, or national level. The role of the anime production and distribution industry in these is unknown. At the conventions, they discuss and analyze the animation stories and also engage in dress-up or "cosplay" (a Japanese term for costume play). It appears that many young people dress as their favorite characters then admire one another's costumes and interact in ways that mimic the character. There are many products (posters, clothing, trinkets) sold to fans but little is known about the people who produce and sell these products.

RESEARCH OBJECTIVE AND PROCEDURE

1. Research Objective

This is an exploratory, qualitative study, in which we seek to describe the anime fan culture. Our goal is to gather preliminary information that can be used for a future study.

2. Research Participants

The principal investigator and/or trained assistant will locate anime fans at clubs, anime conventions, and through referrals. The exact number is not clear since this is an exploratory and uncharted area. Additional fans will be located using purposive and snowball (referral) sampling. We hope to locate a least 30 fans for interviews. The age, race, gender make-up is unknown but will probably involve an equal mix of gender, all racial-ethnic groups, and persons aged 13 to 30 years. Persons under the age of 13 will be excluded.

3. Research Procedure

The principal investigator and/or trained adult college student assistants will personally observe fans in public places using participant observation techniques, conduct informal small talk-conversations, and make arrangements to interview participants at a later time. We may take a few brief notes (such as a person's name and address or phone number) in the field setting, but take extensive notes of the club activities and convention events after the observation.

While at meetings and conventions, we will gather names for future interviews or conduct interviews after club meetings or during conventions. The interviews will be open-ended and tape-recorded. See Appendix for questions/topics in the interviews. Prior to interviewing or tape-recording, we will explain the purpose of the study to participants and tell them that their involvement is voluntary. We will collect the names of participants but hold them in confidence. Personal identifiers (age, gender, etc.) will be released to the public in a way that protects the identity of participants. Because some anime fans may be under the age of 18, we will obtain parental permission prior to interviews.

We expect interviews to vary in length (ten minutes to an hour) and may take place on more than one occasion in a semi-private location (e.g., room alcove, table or booth in a restaurant). Interview questions will not be fixed prior to interviewing but will follow a general list of topics (see below). We may ask different participants different questions based on their early responses. We will listen to tape recordings and take notes, but not transcribe the interviews. We may take photos, with permission, of conventions and participants, and will collect artifacts (e.g., announcements, brochures on conventions, etc.). We will document the types of products (shirts, posters, etc.) sold to fans at the conventions to identify patterns and trends.

4. Anticipated Results

As an exploratory study into a relatively unknown area, we can only speculate about possible results. We will describe anime fan activities (clubs, conventions, etc.) and characteristics of the fans we interview. We will identity repeated themes and patterns within the clubs/conventions and examine themes in anime fan conversations, and about fan social activities. We will use the results to develop a more systematic study into the anime subculture.

5. Schedule and Budget

Schedule

Months 1–2	Locate fan clubs and conventions and scan Internet sites.
Months 3–4	Visit clubs and conventions, interview fans.
Months 5–6	Assemble and organize collected materials and field notes to analyze them.

Budget

Supplies
- notebooks
- tape recorder and supplies (batteries)

Travel
- To clubs and conventions

APPENDIX

Questions in the interviews will include the following topics:

- What is your age? If in college, what is your major and GPA?
- Do you have a part-time job, what is it?
- What are your career goals and aspirations for the future?
- What is your favorite anime film/character? Has this changed over time?
- At what age did you first develop an interest in anime? Explain, please.
- What got you interested in anime?
- Have your interests/favorites changed over time?
- About how many hours per week do you watch anime?
- How many anime films do you personally own?
- How often do you get together with friends to discuss anime?
- Of all those who you consider close friends, how many follow anime?
- Do you engage in cosplay or other anime social activities?
- What other hobbies or interests do you have besides anime?
- If you have social activities, what proportion are centered on anime?
- About how much money do you spend on anime per month?
- Do you have any other Japan-related interests other than anime?
- Do you have friends who were once interested in anime but dropped out?
- What do you and your anime friends talk about?
- What interests you in anime, how does it make you feel?
- Do you ever get very angry or upset watching anime?
- What types of anime do you like? Dislike?
- What types do you feel excited by or bored by?
- What do you think about people who do not like anime?
- Do you watch/play video games related to anime?
- In general, what type of student are you?
- In what ways, if any, does anime relate to your school work?
- Do you have any other hobbies or interests based on your anime interest?
- Do you think you will always love anime? Why or why not?
- Do you encourage people younger than yourself to learn about anime?

- How would you describe your relations with your parents?
- Does anime relate to your sexuality and interest in sex in any way?

QUESTION TOPICS FOR ADULT PARTICIPANTS (18 AND OLDER) ONLY

- Do you currently consume alcohol or recreational drugs while viewing anime?
- Did you consume alcohol or recreational drugs while viewing anime when you were younger, under 18?
- Of your sexual partners, do many share your interest in anime?
- Do you get sexually aroused when you watch anime?

EXAMPLE RESEARCH PROPOSAL A QUANTITATIVE STUDY OF ANIME ENTHUSIASTS IN THE UNITED STATES

INTRODUCTION AND THEORY

We all "consume" many popular cultural products, such as media forms (e.g., video or music), food dishes, electronic devices, and so forth. Most achieve a mass distribution, but some are specialized. Specialized products can attract a small number of people who become enthusiasts. At times, the enthusiasts develop social relations with one another, exchange information, and discuss product details. More than being casual consumers, their interest includes studying, collecting, and becoming experts on the products. By communicating and interacting, they might develop a distinct subculture around the products. A cultural product subculture is likely to develop when the cultural product is unusual or obscure, requires special knowledge, or has devotees in a geographic region or specific age group.

Early in subculture formation, the devotees may meet to exchange information, create publications, or form clubs. Fans set themselves apart from "outsiders" unfamiliar or not yet entranced by the product. Their skill and expertise with the product helps them develop self-esteem and gain respect from their like-minded peers. Even more than other cultural products, media forms change "fashion" very quickly. Young people tend to be more interested in new media that appeared in the late 20th and early 21st centuries. With fewer family or job responsibilities and a disposable income, young people are the primary consumers of popular media and may develop a "fan" following around specific products, artists, musicians, or a genre. With globalization, some cultural productions, and particularly new media, are shared across international borders and marketed to people in many countries. The cultural products are part of a developing international youth culture.

RESEARCH QUESTION

This study examines the U.S. fans of the cultural media product Japanese animation, or anime. Artists, writers, and producers in Japan create anime. It has a "different" foreign or exotic look compared to most American-created animated media. Compared to traditional U.S. animation, Japanese anime is more diverse, has more complicated plots and developed characters, and appeals to a wider age range. Anime takes some themes from Japan and builds on Japanese settings or situations that are not widely known in the United States. This study looks at several questions about anime:

1. Does anime with its "foreignness" attract people who feel somewhat outside the U.S. cultural mainstream?
2. Are males and females attracted to different aspects or themes in anime that relate to emerging gender issues?
3. Over time do anime fans develop an interest in the country or culture of its origin, Japan?

Each research question has broader implications. With globalization, more products from other countries for people are available. It could be that some people that are not part of a somewhat homogenized mainstream culture find foreign products more attractive and a way to express their feelings of difference or individuality. One aspect of a foreign cultural product is that they might offer an alternative set of social relations or cultural viewpoint, even it if is not realistic or easy to act upon. When a cultural product of foreign origin includes some elements of the foreign culture or country, avid consumers of the product may develop an interest in the foreign country or culture as an ancillary effect of their devotion and interest in the cultural product.

LITERATURE REVIEW

Several studies of anime productions have documented the themes and situations borrowed from Japanese culture in the stories, characters, and situations (see references). Anime films fall into a set of categories (fantasy, adventure, and so forth) and is somewhat differentiated by age and gender. Both male and female characters are often shown with superpowers, and changing or ambiguous gender of characters is present in several anime series (reference). Other studies of the anime industry emphasize its rapid growth and connection to other media, Japanese-style comics and video games (reference). A few theorists emphasized anime as part of an transnational youth culture (reference).

Only two studies (see reference) have looked at anime fans. One unpublished study found that college student anime fans were first attracted to anime but knew very little about Japan or had little interest in Japan. Another study that was a doctoral dissertation found that while many anime fans fit a "geek" or "nerd" stereotype, this was not universal. All did share a strong interest in media (watching film) and related media product (video games), and most began at a young age.

HYPOTHESES

HY 1: Persons with fewer "mainstream" hobbies or interests, and with fewer "mainstream" close friends are likely to be stronger anime fans.

HY 2: Female anime fans identify more with androgynous/ambiguous gendered characters than male fans.

HY 3: Intense and committed anime fans are the most likely to want to learn about Japanese culture, learn the Japanese language, and/or wish to visit the country of Japan.

METHOD

1. Sample

The *population* is self-identified anime fans between the ages of 13 and 26. A fan is defined as someone who attends club meetings or a convention that is focused on anime, or who describes his or her main hobby as watching anime films, dressing and acting as anime characters, and/or talking with others anime enthusiasts about anime films.

We will draw a stratified random sample of 200 fans from university, school, and community anime clubs in the area and conventions. First, we will identify ten anime clubs or conventions and attend multiple meetings to obtain lists of members or attendees. Next, we will create a *sampling frame* that has the names, ages, addresses, phone numbers, and e-mails of the members, attendees, and self-described fans at the clubs or conventions. Next, we will divide the sampling frame into two age groups: (1) fans aged 13–18, and (2) those aged 19–26. Finally, we will draw a random sample of 100 names from each age group.

We will contact each sampled person to set up an interview. For persons under 18 years of age, we will use a two-stage process. First, we will contact the sampled person and request the name, address, and phone number of a parent or legal guardian. Before scheduling an interview, we will mail the parent or legal guardian an informed consent form that explains the study and asks permission to interview the legal minor along with a stamped return envelope. We will telephone parents who fail to respond in seven days to make an oral request and offer a second informed consent form.

If we cannot contact or obtain permission to interview a sampled name after six tries using phone, regular mail, and e-mail, we will randomly draw a replacement name from the same age-stratified sampling frame until we have 200 people who agree to be interviewed.

2. Data Collection Procedure

We will conduct face-to-face or telephone interviews with each respondent. We estimate that about one-half will be face-to-face and one-half by telephone, depending on logistics and scheduling. We will ask permission to tape record all telephone interviews. After obtaining permission to record, we will read an informed consent statement prior to interviewing. For face-to-face interviews, we will ask each respondent to sign an informed consent form. Informed consent will be obtained for persons under 18 in addition to a parent or guardian consent form.

We will conduct the face-to-face interviews in any public place (school grounds, shopping mall, or restaurant) but without another person participating and no one listening in. After completing a questionnaire, we will offer to send a copy of the report to a respondent and provide contact information should he or she have further questions. We will number and store the questionnaires and begin to enter data from each questionnaire into a statistical computer program after the first twenty are completed.

We anticipate spending 10 minutes per interview locating and arranging for the interview, and the interview itself to take about 15 minutes to complete. We estimate about 20 minutes to travel to and meet with people for each face-to-face interview and 20 minutes to transcribe each of the telephone interviews. To complete the 200 interviews it will take about 33 hours for locating and scheduling, 50 hours for actual interviewing, and 67 hours for traveling and transcribing.

3. Variable Measurement

We will create three general measures by combining multiple survey questions to measure: (1) being a "nerd" or "geek" or being outside the mainstream of U.S. culture, (2) being a committed anime fan based on years of watching anime, spending time with anime and other fans, and expressing a strong interest in anime, and (3) having an interest in learning about Japan and Japanese culture. We anticipate the questionnaire will have about 40 items. Examples of some preliminary questions to be in the final questionnaire are listed below.

Variable Name	Questionnaire Item
1. Gender	Are you, _____ Male _____ Female _____ GBLT
2. Age	How old are you now? _____
3. School	Do you now attend school? If No Next, If Yes, what school/grade _____
4. Start	At what age did you first start watching anime regularly? _____
5. Games	Do you play video games? If No skip to #8, If Yes, how often? _____ daily _____ 2–3 times a week _____ weekly _____ less often
6. Games 1	What are your favorite two games (1)_____________________________
7. Games 2	(2)____________________
8. Own	How many anime DVDs do you personally own? _____
9. Often	How often do you watch anime? _____ every day _____ 3–5 times a week _____ about once a week _____ several times a month _____ less than once a month
10. Where	Where do you usually watch anime films? _______________
11. Friends	Of your five best friends, how many are anime fans? _____
12. Alone	Think back to the last 10 times you watched an anime film. How many of those 10 times were you watching it alone? _____
13. Favorite1	Name your four favorite anime films of all time, (1) __________
14. Favorite2	(2) __________
15. Favorite3	(3) __________
16. Favorite4	(4) __________
17. Character1	Name your two favorite anime characters of all time, (1) __________
18. Character2	(2) __________
19. Products	Do you own any anime-related products, such as posters, clothing, stuffed animals, etc.? If No skip to #21,
20. Type	If Yes, what products do you own, type and number? ____________________________
21. Cosplay	Do you ever dress up in a costume as an anime character? _____ Yes _____ No
22. Japan1	Have you ever read a book about Japanese history or society?
23. Japan2	Have you ever traveled to Japan? If Yes #25, If No,
24. Japan3	How interested are you in traveling to Japan? _____ Extremely _____ Very _____ Somewhat _____ A little _____ Not at All
25. Club	Do you belong to an Anime Club, No _____ Yes _____
26. Conven1	Have you ever attended an anime convention? If No skip to #28, If Yes,
27. Conven2	How many conventions have you attended in the past three years? _____
28. FriendG	Of your five closest friends, how many are your same gender? _____
29. Internet	How often do you go to anime related sites on the Internet? _____ Never _____ once a month _____ several x a month _____ Weekly _____ Daily or more
30. Magazine	Do you subscribe to an anime magazine? _____ Yes _____ No

Time Schedule

Month 1	Obtain IRB approval, continue literature review, prepare draft of complete questionnaire, develop list of anime clubs and conventions
Months 2–3	Visit anime clubs and conventions to collect names and create sampling frame, pilot test questionnaire
Month 4	Draw a random sample of names and contact under 18 sample for parental permissions, revise questionnaire, begin to schedule interviews
Months 5–7	Contact and arrange for all interviews, begin interviewing
Month 8	Complete last interviews, and start to code data into computer program
Month 9	Finish coding, and analyze data using statistics program
Month 10	Write up results as a report and present findings

Budget Extimate

Supply and Service Expenses
- Printing and postage
- Tape recorder and supplies
- Telephone

Travel Expenses
- To go to anime clubs and conventions
- To go to interviews
- To go to professional meeting to present final report

Labor Expenses
- General clerical help
- Interviewing help
- Tape transcription help
- Data entry help
- Statistical analysis

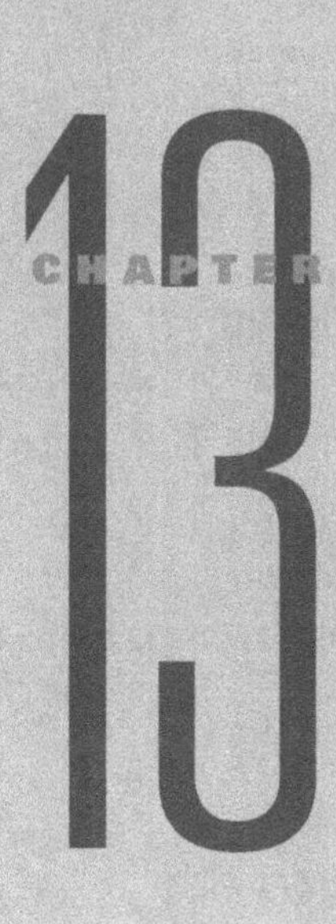

CHAPTER 13

Drafting the Paper in an Academic Style

Taken from: *The Essential Guide to Writing Research Papers,* Canadian Edition, by James D. Lester, James D. Lester, Jr., and Patricia I. Mochnacz.

As you draft your paper, you should adopt an academic style that reflects your discipline. Present a fair, balanced treatment of the subject. Mentioning opposing viewpoints early in a paper gives you something to work against and may strengthen your conclusion. Your early draft is a time for discovery. Later, during the revision period, you can strengthen skimpy paragraphs, refine your prose, and rearrange material to maintain the momentum of your argument.

WRITING IN A STYLE APPROPRIATE FOR YOUR FIELD OF STUDY

Each discipline has its own special language, style of expression, and manuscript format. You will, in time, learn fully the style for the field in which you major. Meanwhile, a few characteristics to guide your writing for papers in the humanities, social sciences, and sciences are identified in the following examples.

Academic Style in the Humanities

Writing in the humanities will require you to adopt a certain style, as shown in the following example written in CMS (Chicago).

> Organ and tissue donation is the gift of life. Each year many people confront health problems due to diseases or congenital birth defects. Tom Taddonia explains that tissues such as skin, veins, and valves can be used to correct congenital defects, blindness, visual impairment, trauma, burns, dental defects, arthritis, cancer, vascular and heart disease.[8] Steve Barnill says, "More than 400 people each month receive the gift of sight through yet another type of tissue donation—corneal transplants. In many cases, donors unsuitable for organ donation are eligible for tissue donation."[9] Barnill notes that tissues are now used in orthopedic surgery, cardiovascular surgery, plastic surgery, dentistry, and podiatry.[10] Even so, not enough people are willing to donate organs and tissues.

Writing in the humanities often displays these characteristics:

- Preoccupation with the quality of life, of art, of ideas (as shown in the first sentence of the example and as echoed in the final sentence).
- Personal involvement in ethical standards.
- Use of the present tense to indicate that this problem is an enduring one for humans of past ages as well as the present and the future.
- Use of CMS note style or MLA style for documenting the sources.
- Discussion of theory as supported by the literature.

Academic Style in the Social Sciences

A social science student might write the same passage in APA style:

> Organ and tissue donation has been identified as a social as well as a medical problem in North America. On one side, people have confronted serious problems in securing organs and tissue to correct health problems; on the other, people have demonstrated a reluctance to donate their

13

> organs. This need has been identified by Barnill (1999), Ruskin (2000), Taddonia (2001), and others. This hypothesis remains: People are reluctant to sign their donor cards. Consequently, this study will survey a random set of 1000 persons who have driver's licences to investigate the reasons for signing or not signing for donation. Further investigation can then be conducted to determine ways of increasing participation by potential donors.

Writing in the social sciences typically displays these characteristics:

- An objective approach to the topic.
- Fewer quotations from the sources, anticipating that readers will examine the literature for themselves.
- Use of past tense or the past participle in references to the source material.
- Use of APA style for documenting the sources.
- Discussion of theory as supported by the literature.
- Awareness that this research will prompt further study.

Academic Style in the Physical and Medical Sciences

A science student might write on this same topic in this way:

> Taddonia (1) has shown that human tissue can be used to correct many defects. Barnill (2) showed that more than 400 people receive corneal transplants each month. Yet the health profession needs more donors. It has been shown (3–6) that advanced care directives by patients with terminal illnesses would improve the donation of organs and tissue and relieve relatives of making any decision. Patients have been encouraged to complete organ donation cards (7) as well as to sign living wills (5, 8), special powers of attorney (5), and DNR (Do Not Resuscitate) Orders (5, 8). It is encouraged that advanced care directives become standard for the terminally ill.

Scientific or medical writing typically displays some of these characteristics:

- An objective approach to the topic without signs of personal commitment.
- A search for a professional position (i.e., on organ donation).
- A preference for the passive voice and the past tense.
- Use of the CBE number system or, in some cases, the name and year system.
- A reluctance to quote from the sources.
- A willingness to let a number represent the literature that will be cited with full documentation in the references section.

FOCUSING YOUR ARGUMENT

Your writing style in the research paper needs to be factual, but it should also reflect your thinking on the topic. Drafting the paper will happen more quickly if you focus on the central issues. Each paragraph will develop your primary claim.

Persuading, Inquiring, and Informing

Establishing a purpose for writing is one way to focus your argument. Do you wish to persuade or inquire and inform? *Persuasion* means that you wish to convince the reader that your position is valid and, perhaps, to ask the reader to take action. For example:

> Research has shown that homeowners and wild animals cannot live together in harmony. *Thus, we need to establish green zones in every city of this country to control the sprawl in urban areas and to protect a segment of the natural habitat for the animals.*

Inquiry is an exploratory approach to a problem in which you examine the issues and *inform* the reader of the results of the inquiry without the insistence of persuasion. You may need to examine, test, or observe in order to discuss the implications of the research. For example:

> Many suburban home dwellers complain that deer, raccoons, and other wild animals ravage their gardens, flowerbeds, and garbage cans; however, the animals were there first. This study will examine the problem in one subdivision of 142 homes. How have animals been affected by the intrusion of human beings? How have homeowners been harassed by the animals? *The research will examine each side of the conflict by interviews with homeowners and observation of the animals.*

Note: In the above examples the thesis statement has been italicized.

Maintaining a Focus with Ethical and Logical Appeals

As an objective writer, you will need to examine the problem, make your claim, and provide supporting evidence. Moderation of your tone, even during argument, suggests control of the situation, both emotionally and intellectually. Your tone alerts the audience to your point of view in two ways:

1. **Ethical appeal**. If you project the image of one who knows and cares about the topic, the reader will recognize and respect your deep interest in the subject and the way you have carefully crafted your argument. The reader will also appreciate your attention to research conventions.
2. **Logical appeal**. For readers to believe in your position, you must provide sufficient evidence in the form of statistical data, paraphrases, and direct quotations from authorities on the subject.

The issue of organ donation, for example, elicits different reactions. Some people argue from the logical position that organs are available and should be used for those in need. Others argue from the ethical position that organs might be harvested prematurely or that organ donation violates religious principles. Some people are objective in their views; others are subjective. As a writer, you must balance your ethical and logical appeals to your readers.

Refining the Thesis Statement

A thesis is a statement or theory supported by arguments. Make sure your thesis statement satisfies all the following requirements:

1. Sets the argument to give focus to the entire paper.
2. Gives order to details of the essay by providing unity and a sense of direction.
3. Specifies to the reader the point of the research.

For example, Jennifer Kroetsch crafted this thesis:

> Consumers must consider the use of herbal remedies cautiously because of the possibility of dangerous side effects and the limited research on these products.

This statement focuses the argument on the side effects of, and lack of research into, herbal remedies.

Using Questions to Focus the Thesis

If you have trouble focusing a thesis statement, ask yourself a few questions. In the previous example, Jennifer might have asked: What are the advantages of herbal remedies? How do they work? What are the serious side effects? What research on herbal remedies is available?

The next thesis developed from the question: "Do I have a new approach to guilt's impact on teen suicide?"

> **Thesis** Recent research demonstrates that self-guilt often prompts a teenager to commit suicide.

The next thesis developed from the question: "What effect does poverty have on the crime statistics of juveniles?"

> **Thesis** Personal economics is a force to be reckoned with; hence, poverty, not greed, forces many youngsters into a life of crime.

While questions may help develop the thesis, the thesis sentence makes a declarative statement that focuses the argument toward an investigative issue that will be resolved in the paper's discussion and conclusion.

Note: Even a "final" thesis may need adjustment as you develop the paper.

Using Key Words to Focus the Thesis

Use the important words from your notes and rough outline to refine your thesis statement. For example, during your reading of several novels by Margaret Laurence, you might have jotted down certain repetitions of image, theme, or character. The key words might be "liberation," "acceptance of self," "personal fulfillment," or other issues that Laurence explored time and again. These specific ideas might point you toward a general thesis:

> In her Manawaka novels, Margaret Laurence depicts women who break free from the roles imposed on them by their prairie small-town backgrounds.

Final Thesis Checklist

The thesis will fall short of expectations if it fails to answer "yes" to each of these questions:

1. Does it express your position in a full, declarative sentence that is not a question, not a statement of purpose, and not merely a topic?
2. Does it limit the subject to a narrow focus that grows out of research?
3. Does it establish an investigative, inventive edge to the interpretation or to the theoretical presentation?

DESIGNING AN ACADEMIC TITLE

A clearly expressed title, developed early in the composing process, like a good thesis statement, will control your writing and keep you on course. Although writing a final title may not be feasible until the paper is written, the preliminary title can provide specific words of identification to help you stay focused. For example, one writer began with the title "Diabetes." Then the writer made it more specific: "Diabetes Management." As research developed and she recognized the role of medicine, diet, and exercise, she refined the title even more: "Diabetes Management: A Delicate Balance of Medicine, Diet, and Exercise." Thereby, she and her readers had a clear idea that the paper was about three methods of managing the disease.

Long titles are standard in scholarly writing. Your task is to give the reader a clear concept about the contents of the research paper, so use one of these strategies for writing your title:

1. Name a general subject, followed by a colon and a phrase that renames the subject ("Computer Control: Software Safeguards and Computer Theft").
2. Narrow a general subject with a prepositional phrase ("Religion in Public Schools").
3. Name a general subject and cite a specific work that will clarify the topic ("The Immigrant Experience in Brian Moore's *The Luck of Ginger Coffey*").
4. Name a general subject, followed by a colon, and followed by a phrase that describes the type of study ("Black Dialect in the Short Stories of Arna Bontemps: A Language Study").
5. Name a general subject, followed by a colon, and followed by a question ("Nuclear Energy: Do the Risks Outweigh the Benefits?").
6. Establish a specific comparison ("Women's Rights in Henrik Ibsen's *A Doll's House* and Alice Munro's *Lives of Girls and Women*").

Be sure to avoid fancy literary titles that may fail to label issues under discussion.

Poor "Let There Be Hope"

Better "Let There Be Hope: A View of Child Abuse"

Best "Child Abuse: A View of the Victims"

DRAFTING THE PAPER

As you begin drafting your research paper, follow a few general guidelines:

1. Work systematically through a preliminary plan or outline to keep order as your notes expand your research.
2. Leave wide margins, use triple spacing, and put blank spaces between paragraphs. Open areas in your writing will leave room for later revisions.
3. Use your notes, photocopies, downloaded material, and research journal to transfer materials directly into the text, either by hand or on your computer.
4. Provide quotations and paraphrases of key sentences, but avoid the temptation of borrowing too much.
5. Do not quote an entire paragraph unless it is crucial to your discussion and you cannot easily reduce it to a précis.
6. Let the writing find its own way, guided, but not controlled, by your outline or paradigm.
7. Use different models and methods of development for different papers.
8. Do not expect a polished product at first. Initial drafts are exploratory and usually require additional reading, researching, and note taking.

These additional tips for drafting your paper may help:

Be practical. Begin by writing portions of the paper when you are ready, not only when you have a complete outline.

Be uninhibited. Initial drafts must be attempts to get words on the page rather than to create a polished document. Write without fear or delay.

Be judicious. Treat the sources with respect by citing names, enclosing quotations, and providing page numbers to the sources.

Drafting with a Computer

If you have developed your outline and notes on a computer, you can draft the paper from your outline and notes. You can do this in several ways:

1. Expand your outline to become the first draft of your research paper. Do this by importing your notes to a specific location of the outline and entering information underneath any of the outline headings as you develop ideas.
2. If you have placed all your notes within one file, begin writing your paper in a new file. As the writing progresses, find the note you wish to transfer, then CUT and COPY it. Go back to your text file and PASTE the note into your text.
3. In the file where you have placed all your notes, begin drafting the paper at the top of this file, which will push the notes below as you write. When you need a note, use FIND or SEARCH with the code word or title, then CUT and PASTE the note into your text.

Writing in the Proper Tense

Verb tense often distinguishes a paper in the humanities from one in the natural and social sciences. MLA style and CMS footnote style both require the present tense to cite an author's work (e.g., "Kozyrskyj *explains*" or "the work of Johnson and Stewart *shows*"). In contrast, APA style and CBE style both require the past tense or present perfect tense to cite an author's work (e.g., "Kozyrskyj *discovered*" or "the work of Johnson and Stewart *has demonstrated*"). When writing a paper in the humanities, use the historical present tense, as shown here in MLA style:

> Spear argues that Gentileschi's painting is clearly "a cathartic expression of the artist's private, and perhaps repressed, rage" (569).

Use the past tense in a humanities paper only for reporting historical events. In the next example, past tense is appropriate for all sentences *except* the last:

> In 1876, Alexander Graham Bell invented the telephone. Signals, sounds, and music had been sent by wire before, but Bell's instrument was the first to transmit speech. Bell's story, a lesson in courage and determination, is one worthy of study.

See Chapter 14, "Using APA Style" for additional discussion about using the correct tense in scientific style.

Using the Language of the Discipline

Every discipline and every topic has its own vocabulary. Therefore, while reading and taking notes, jot down words and phrases relevant to the study. Get comfortable with the vocabulary of your topic so you can use it effectively. Nothing will betray a writer's ignorance of the subject more quickly than awkward and distorted technical terminology. For example, a child abuse topic requires the language of sociology, psychology, and medicine, thereby demanding an acquaintance with terms like:

aggressive behaviour	formative years	social worker
battered child	hostility	stress
behavioural patterns	maltreatment	trauma

Writing in the Third Person

Write your paper with an impersonal narration that avoids the use of the first person such as "I believe" or "It is my opinion." Rather than say, "I think objectivity on television is nothing more than an ideal," say, "Objectivity on television is nothing more than an ideal." Readers will understand that the statement is your thought.

Also avoid "we," "our," "you," and "your." Rather than say, "We must learn to be discriminating in our choice of television shows," use the third person and say, "Viewers must be discriminating in their choice of television shows."

Writing in the Passive Voice

Instructors often caution students against using the passive voice, which is often less forceful than using an active verb. However, research writers sometimes need to use the passive voice, as shown here:

> Forty-three students of a Grade 3 class at Barksdale School were observed for two weeks.

This usage of the passive voice is fairly standard in the social sciences and the natural or applied sciences. The passive voice is preferred because it keeps the focus on the subject of the research, not the writer.

Writing with Unity and Coherence

Unity gives writing a single vision; coherence connects the parts. Your paper has *unity* if it explores one topic in depth, with each paragraph carefully expanding upon a single aspect of the narrowed subject. A good organizational plan will help you achieve unity. Your paper has *coherence* if the parts are connected logically by

- repetition of key words and sentence structures
- the judicious use of pronouns and synonyms
- the effective placement of transitional words and phrases (e.g., *also, furthermore, therefore, in addition,* and *thus*)

The next passage moves with unity and coherence:

> Talk shows are spectacles of dramatic entertainment; therefore, members of the studio audience are acting out parts in the drama, like a Greek chorus, just as the host, the guest, and the television viewers are actors as well. Furthermore, some sort of interaction with the "characters" in this made-for-television "drama" happens all the time. While attending this "play," viewers analyze the presentation, determining for themselves what the drama means to them.

Note the use of the third person in the last sentence of the above passage.

Using Source Material to Enhance Your Writing

Readers want to discover *your* thoughts and ideas. For this reason, a paragraph should seldom contain source material only; it needs at the very least a topic sentence to establish a point for the research evidence. Every paragraph should explain, analyze, and support a thesis, not merely string together research information. Write with caution when working from photocopied pages of articles or books. You will be tempted to borrow too much. Quote or paraphrase key phrases and sentences; do not quote an entire paragraph unless it is crucial to your discussion and you cannot easily reduce it to a précis. The following passage, written in APA style, cites effectively two different sources.

> Tabloid television is not so much news as entertainment. Pungente and O'Malley (1999) note: "The [long-running] *Today* show [. . .] gives viewers both information and entertainment, though sometimes the entertainment seems to take over, resulting in 'infotainment'" (p. 155). Another source notes that since "the networks live by the dictum 'keep it short and to the point,'" there is a concerted effort to make the news "lively" (Kuklinski and Sigelman, 2000, p. 821). Sadly, in some newscasts, viewer reaction seems to dictate the presentation of the facts.

This passage illustrates four points. A writer must

- weave the sources effectively into a whole
- cite each source separately, one at a time
- provide different in-text citations
- use the sources as a natural extension of the discussion

Placing Graphics Effectively

Use graphics to support your text. Place graphics as close as possible to the parts of the text to which they relate. It is acceptable to use full-colour art if your printer will print in colours; however, use black for the captions and date. Place a full-page graphic design on a separate sheet after making a textual reference to it (e.g., "see Table 7"). Place graphic designs in an appendix when you have several complex items that might distract the reader from your textual message.

Avoiding Sexist and Biased Language

The best writers exercise caution against words that may stereotype any person, regardless of gender, race, nationality, creed, age, or disability. The following are some guidelines to help you avoid discriminatory language.

Age. Review the accuracy of your statement. It is appropriate to use *boy* and *girl* for children of high school age and under. *Young man* and *young woman* or *male adolescent* and *female adolescent* can be appropriate, but *teenager* carries a certain bias. Avoid *elderly* as a noun; use *older persons.*

Gender. *Gender* is a matter of our culture that identifies men and women within their social groups. *Sex* tends to be a biological factor. (See below for a discussion of sexual orientation.)

- Use plural subjects so that non-specific, plural pronouns are grammatically correct. For example, you may specify that Judy Jones maintains *her* lab equipment in sterile condition or indicate that technicians, in general, maintain *their* own equipment.
- Reword the sentence so that a pronoun is unnecessary, as in *The doctor prepared the necessary surgical equipment without interference.*
- Use pronouns that denote gender only when necessary when gender has been previously established, as in *Mary, as a new laboratory technician, must learn to maintain her equipment in sterile condition.*
- The use of *woman* and *female* as adjectives varies. Use *woman* or *women* in most instances (e.g., *a woman's intuition*) and use *female* for species and statistics, (e.g., *four female subjects*). Avoid the use of *lady,* as in *lady pilot.*
- In MLA and CMS styles the first mention of a person requires the full name (e.g., Charles Dickens or Carol Shields) and thereafter requires only the use of the surname (e.g., Dickens or Shields). In general, avoid formal titles (e.g., Dr., Gen., Mrs., Ms., Lt., Professor). Avoid their equivalents in other languages (e.g., Mme, Dame, Monsieur).
- Avoid unequal phrasing such as *man and wife* or *7 men and 16 females.* Keep the terms parallel by saying *husband and wife* or *man and woman* and *7 male rats and 16 female rats.*

Sexual Orientation. The term *sexual orientation* is preferred to the term *sexual preference.* It is preferable to use *lesbians* and *gay men* rather than *homosexuals.* The terms *heterosexual, homosexual,* and *bisexual* can be used to describe both the identity and the behaviour of subjects.

Ethnic and Racial Identity. The preferred term in Canada is *Aboriginal*, rather than *Native*, because Aboriginal is a broader term that includes Status, Non-status, Inuit, and Métis persons. In historical contexts the terms *Native* and *Indian* are acceptable. The term *First Nations* should be used judiciously because it includes Status and Non-status Aboriginal persons but excludes Métis and Inuit persons. In the United

States, *Native American* is a broad term that includes Samoans, Hawaiians, and American Indians.

Some persons prefer the term *Black*, others prefer *African American*, and still others prefer *a person of colour*. The terms *Negro* and *Afro-American* are now dated and not appropriate. Use *Black* and *White*, not the lowercase *black* and *white*. In like manner, some individuals may prefer *Hispanic, Latino, Mexican,* or *Chicano*. Use the term *Asian, Asian Canadian* or *Asian American* rather than *Oriental*. A good general rule is to use a person's nationality when it is known (*Mexican, Korean,* or *Nigerian*).

Disability. In general, place people first, not their disability. Rather than *a learning disabled person*, say *a person with a learning disability*. Instead of saying *a challenged person* or *a special child*, say *a person with a spinal cord injury* or *a child with Down syndrome*. Avoid making reference to a disability unless it is relevant to the discussion.

CREATING AN INTRODUCTION, BODY, AND CONCLUSION

Writing the Introduction

Use the first few paragraphs of your paper to establish the nature of your study. It should be long enough to establish the required elements described in the checklist below.

Checklist for the Introduction

Subject	Does your introduction identify your specific topic, and then define, limit, and narrow it to one issue?
Background	Does your introduction provide relevant historical data or discuss a few key sources that touch on your specific issue?
Problem	Does your introduction identify a problem and explain the complications that your research paper will explore or resolve?
Thesis statement	Does your introduction have a thesis statement that establishes the direction of the study and points your readers toward your eventual conclusions? Is your thesis statement placed at or near the end of the introduction?

How you work these essential elements into the framework of your opening will depend upon your style of writing. They need not appear in this order. Nor should you cram all these items into a short, opening paragraph. Feel free to write a longer introduction by using more than one of these techniques:

- Open with a quotation.
- Use an anecdote as a hook.
- Relate your topic to the well known.
- Provide background information.

- Review the literature briefly.
- Provide a brief summary.
- Define key terms.
- Supply data, statistics, and special evidence.
- Take exception to critical views.
- State the thesis (usually at the end of your one- or two-paragraph introduction).

The following sample of an introduction in MLA style gives background information, establishes a persuasive position, takes exception, gives key terms, and states the thesis in the last sentence.

> Michel Tremblay's Les Belles-Soeurs premiered in Montreal in 1968. It is a funny, thought-provoking, controversial drama about 14 working-class women in east-end Montreal in the late 1960s who gather one evening to help their relative and neighbour, Germaine Lauzon, stick one million Gold Star stamps into booklets so she can redeem them for "valuable prizes." During this stamp-sticking party, the women vent their frustrations—about being poor, about being oppressed by men and the Church, about being women, and about being Québécoise. Tremblay's play has been acclaimed as "a classic" which "shocked and revolutionized Quebec Theatre" (Cottrell). Indeed, Tomson Highway has indicated that his award-winning portrayal of Aboriginal women in The Rez Sisters owes much to Tremblay's work. In spite of critical acclaim, however, the coarse language (*joual*) and daring themes in Les Belles-Soeurs stirred up much controversy in the late 1960s, and the successful revivals of the 1990s still shocked some audiences. Mixed reaction to Les Belles-Soeurs may well be because at the heart of this drama lies a disquieting theme: "the emotional turbulence of a people struggling to win a protected place in which they can develop in their own unique way" (Clarkson).

Avoiding Certain Mistakes in the Opening

Avoid a purpose statement, such as "The purpose of this study is . . ." unless your paper reports speculative research associated with the sciences.

Avoid repetition of the title, which should appear on the title page or first page of the text anyway.

Avoid a quotation that has no context; that is, you have not blended the quotation into the discussion clearly and effectively.

Avoid complex or difficult questions that may puzzle the reader; however, general rhetorical questions are acceptable.

Avoid simple dictionary definitions, such as "*The Canadian Oxford Dictionary* defines *monogamy* as the practice or state of being married to one person at a time."

Writing the Body

When writing the body of the paper, you should trace, classify, compare, and analyze the various issues. Keep in mind three elements, as shown in the checklist below.

Checklist for the Body of the Paper

Analysis	Classify the major issues of the study and provide a careful analysis of each in defence of your thesis.
Presentation	Provide well-reasoned statements at the beginning of your paragraphs and supply evidence of support with proper documentation.
Paragraphs	Vary development to compare, show process, narrate the subject's history, show causes, and so forth.

Use these techniques to build substantive paragraphs for your paper:

- Relate a time sequence.
- Compare or contrast issues, critics, and literary characters.
- Develop cause and effect.
- Issue a call to action.
- Define key terminology.
- Show a process.
- Ask questions and provide answers.
- Cite evidence from source materials.

The following paragraph in MLA style demonstrates the use of several techniques—establishing an overview of the problem, citing a source, comparing issues, showing cause and effect, noting key terms, and describing process.

> To burn or not to burn the forests in the national parks is the question. The pyrophobic public voices its protests while environmentalists praise the rejuvenating effects of a good forest fire. It is difficult to convince people that not all fire is bad. The public has visions of Smokey the Bear campaigns and mental images of Bambi and Thumper fleeing the roaring flames. Perhaps the public could learn to see beauty in fresh green shoots, like Bambi and Faline as they returned to raise their young. Chris Bolgiano explains that federal policy evolved slowly "from the basic impulse to douse all fires immediately to a sophisticated decision matrix based on the functions of any given unit of land" (23). Bolgiano declares that "timber production, grazing, recreation, and wilderness preservation elicit different fire-management approaches" (23).

Writing the Conclusion

The conclusion is not a summary; it is a discussion of beliefs based on your reasoning and on the evidence that has been presented. Use the following checklist.

Checklist for the Conclusion

Thesis	Reaffirm the thesis statement and the central mission of your study. If appropriate, state your support for or criticism of an original hypothesis.
Judgments	Discuss and interpret the findings. Give answers. Now is the time to draw inferences, emphasize a theory, and find relevance in the details of the results.
Directives	Based on the theoretical implications of the study, offer suggestions for action and new research.

Use these techniques to write the conclusion:

- Restate the thesis and reach beyond it.
- Close with an effective quotation.
- Return the focus of a literary study to the author.
- Compare the past to the present.
- Offer a directive or a solution.
- Give a call to action.

Notice in the following example in MLA style how the writer begins the conclusion by restating the thesis and then uses other techniques to bring the essay's ideas to a conclusion:

> Real or unreal, objectivity is something seldom, if ever, found on television. Ultimately, the media analyst must question why by 1998 both The Jerry Springer Show and The Oprah Winfrey Show were both averaging nearly seven million viewers a day (Pungente and O'Malley 158), and why the first morning talk show, Today, has lasted close to half a century. According to one critic, talk shows provide "instant, vivid, and easy to consume information about a wide and growing range of public affairs" (Kuklinski and Sigelman 810). As well, tabloid television gives people a way to feel good about themselves. Philip Marchand notes in The Toronto Star on January 4, 1997, that "(viewers) can watch these people and still feel . . . a valuable and attractive member of the human race." While watching the chronicles of the rich and famous or the struggles of people with bizarre problems, television viewers are helping to define their own subjective reality within the boundaries of the objective world and the symbolic reality of television.

Avoiding Certain Mistakes in the Conclusion

Avoid including afterthoughts or additional ideas; the conclusion is the place to end the paper, not begin new thoughts. If new ideas occur as you write your conclusion, don't ignore them. Explore them fully in the context of your thesis, and consider adding them to the body of your paper or slightly modifying your thesis. Scientific studies often discuss options and possible alterations that might affect test results.

Avoid the use of "thus," "in conclusion," or "finally" at the beginning of the last paragraph. Readers will be able to see that you are concluding the paper.

Avoid ending the paper without a sense of closure.

Avoid asking questions that raise new issues; however, writing rhetorical questions that restate the issues is acceptable.

REVISING THE ROUGH DRAFT

Revision can turn a passable paper into an excellent one and change an excellent paper into a brilliant research project. First, you should revise your paper on a global scale, moving blocks of material around to the best advantage and into the proper format. Second, revise your introduction, body and conclusion in more detail. Finally, edit the draft and proofread the final manuscript.

Global Revision Checklist

1. Skim through the paper to check its unity. Does the paper maintain a central proposition from paragraph to paragraph?
2. Transplant paragraphs, moving them to more relevant and effective positions.
3. Delete sentences that do not further your cause.
4. Revise your outline to match these changes if you must submit the outline with the paper.

Revising the Introduction, Body, and Conclusion

Examine your **introduction** for the presence of several items:

1. Your thesis statement
2. A clear direction or plan of development
3. A sense of involvement that invites the reader into your investigation of a problem

Use the following as a guide for revising each paragraph in the **body** of your paper:

1. Cut out wordiness and irrelevant thoughts. Delete sentences that contribute nothing to the paper.
2. Combine any short paragraphs with others, or build a short paragraph into one of substance.
3. Revise long, difficult paragraphs by dividing them or by using transitions effectively. (See "Writing with Unity and Coherence".)
4. Omit paragraphs that seem short, shallow, or weak, or add more commentary and evidence to them, especially quotations from the primary source or critical citations from secondary sources.

13

5. Add your own input to paragraphs that rely too heavily on source materials.
6. Examine your paragraphs for transitions that move the reader effectively from one paragraph to the next.

Finally, examine the ending for a **conclusion** that (1) you have drawn from the evidence, (2) you have developed logically from the introduction and the body, and (3) has been determined by your position on the issues. (See also "Writing the Conclusion of the Paper".)

EDITING AND PREPARING THE FINAL MANUSCRIPT

The cut-and-paste revision period is complemented by a session devoted to editing your sentences and your word choices. Use the following techniques to improve your final draft.

1. Cut phrases and sentences that do not advance your main ideas or that merely repeat what your sources have already stated.
2. Determine that coordinated, balanced ideas are appropriately expressed and that minor ideas are properly subordinated.
3. Change most of your "to be" verbs (e.g., *is, are, was*) to stronger active verbs.
4. Maintain the present tense in most verbs in MLA and CMS style manuscripts and the past tense in APA and CBE style manuscripts.
5. Convert passive structures to active if appropriate.
6. Confirm that you have introduced paraphrases and quotations so they flow smoothly into your text.
7. Language should be elevated slightly in its formality, so avoid clusters of monosyllabic words that fail to advance ideas. Examine your wording for its effectiveness within the context of your subject.

PROOFREADING THE FINAL MANUSCRIPT

After you have edited the text to your satisfaction, print a copy of the manuscript. Check for double spacing, one-inch margins, running heads with page numbers, and so forth. Even if you used available software to check your spelling, grammar, and style, you must nevertheless proofread this final version.

Proofreading Checklist

1. Check for errors in sentence structure, spelling, and punctuation.
2. Check for hyphenation and word division. Remember that no words should be hyphenated at the ends of lines. If you are using a computer, turn off the automatic hyphenation.
3. Read each quotation for accuracy of your own wording and of the words within your quoted materials. Look, too, for your correct use of quotation marks.
4. Double check in-text citations to be certain that each one is correct and that each source is listed on your "Works Cited" (MLA and CMS) or "References" (APA and CBE) page at the end of the paper.
5. Double check the format: the title page, margins, spacing, and many other elements.

PART IV

Style Guides of the Social Sciences

Using APA Style

Taken from: *The Essential Guide to Writing Research Papers,* Canadian Edition, by James D. Lester, James D. Lester, Jr., and Patricia I. Mochnacz.

You may be required to write a research paper in APA style, which is governed by the *Publication Manual of the American Psychological Association.* This style has gained wide acceptance in academic circles. APA style is used in psychology and the other social sciences, and versions similar to it are used in business and the biological and earth sciences.

The American Psychological Association has established websites that, among other things, explain its method for citing electronic sources. This chapter conforms to the stipulations of the fifth edition of the APA style manual with adjustments based on APA's current websites. Consult www.apastyle.org/elecref.html and www.apastyle.org/ faqs.html.

ESTABLISHING A CRITICAL APPROACH

In scientific writing, the thesis usually takes a different form. It appears as a *hypothesis* or *statement of principle.* The hypothesis is a theory that needs testing and analysis, which you will do as part of your research. It is an idea expressed as a truth for the purpose of argument and investigation. It makes a prediction based upon the theory. Here is an example:

> It was predicted that patients who suffer a compulsive bulimic disorder would have a more disrupted family life.

In a similar fashion, the statement of principle makes a declaration in defence of an underlying but unstated theory, as shown here:

> The most effective recall cue is the one that is encoded within the event that is to be remembered.

Your work would attempt to prove this principle. Be careful to avoid false assumptions in your hypothesis or statement of principle.

WRITING IN THE PROPER TENSE FOR AN APA STYLE PAPER

Verb tense is an indicator that distinguishes papers in the humanities from those in the natural and social sciences. MLA style uses the present tense when you refer to a cited work ("Kozyrskyj *stipulates*" or "the work of Johnson and Stewart *shows*"). In contrast, APA style uses the past tense or present perfect tense ("Kozyrskyj *stipulated*" or "the work of Johnson and Stewart *has demonstrated*"). The APA style does require present tense when you discuss the results (e.g., *"the results confirm"* or *"the study indicates"*) and when you mention established knowledge (e.g., *"the therapy offers some hope"* or *"salt contributes to hypertension"*). This example shows correct usage for APA style:

> Howes et al. (1996) **found** that few clinical psychology supervisors in Canada received sufficient formal training; Johnson and Stewart (2000) **have reported** similar findings.

However, as shown in the next example, use the present tense (*do not have*) for established knowledge. The past tense (*conducted*) is correct for a reference to completed research.

> Psychologists in Canada **do not have** prescription privileges; Walters (2001) **conducted** a meta-analysis of opinion survey data on this issue.

BLENDING SOURCES INTO YOUR WRITING

The APA style uses these conventions for in-text citations.

- Cite last names only.
- Cite the year, within parentheses, immediately after the name of the author.
- Cite page numbers always with a direct quotation, seldom with a paraphrase.
- Use "p." or "pp." before page numbers.

Citing Last Name Only and the Year of Publication

An in-text citation in APA style requires the last name of the author and the year of publication.

> Montague (2000) has advanced the idea of combining the social sciences and mathematics to chart human behaviour.

If you do not use the author's name in your text, place the name(s) within the parenthetical citation followed by a comma and the year.

> One study has advanced the idea of combining the social sciences and mathematics to chart human behaviour (Montague, 2000).

Providing a Page Number

If you quote the exact words of a source, provide a page number and *do use* "p." or "pp." Place the page number in one of two places: after the year or at the end of the quotation.

> Montague (2000) has advanced the idea of "soft mathematics," which is the practice of "applying mathematics to study people's behaviour" (p. B4).

Citing a Block of Material

Present a quotation of 40 words or more as a separate block, indented five to seven spaces, or one-half inch from the left margin. (*Note:* MLA style uses 10 spaces or one inch.) Because the quotation is set off from the text in a distinctive block, do not enclose it with quotation marks. Do not single space. Do not indent the first line an extra five spaces; however, do indent the first line of any additional paragraphs that appear in the block an extra five spaces, that is, 10 spaces from the left margin. Set parenthetical citations outside the last period.

Johnson and Stewart (2000) reported that:

> Canadian programs and internship sites have failed to adequately prepare students to undertake a central professional demand (clinical supervisory responsibilities).
>
> However, although relatively few respondents received training in supervision, those who did have such training appear to have benefited from it. (pp. 314–315)

Citing a Work with More Than One Author

When one work has two or more authors, use *and* in the text, but use & in the citation.

> Battiste and Barman (1995) stressed the importance of spirituality in Aboriginal education.

but

> It has been emphasized (Battiste & Barman, 1995) that spirituality is central to the education of Aboriginal children.

For three to five authors, name them all in the first entry (e.g., Torgerson, Andrews, Smith, Lawrence, & Dunlap, 2001), but thereafter use "et al." (e.g., Torgerson et al., 2001). For six or more authors, employ "et al." in the first and in all subsequent instances (e.g., Fredericks et al., 2001).

Citing More Than One Work by an Author

Use lowercase letters (a, b, c) to identify two or more works published in the same year by the same author, for example, (Thompson, 2001a) and (Thompson, 2001b). Then use "2001a" and "2001b" in your list of references. (See "Author, Two or More Works by the Same Author, page 280–281, for an example). If necessary, specify additional information:

> Horton (2000; cf. Thomas, 1999a, p. 89, and 1999b, p. 426) suggested an intercorrelation of these testing devices. But after multiple-group analysis, Welston (1998, esp. p. 211) reached an opposite conclusion.

Citing Two or More Works by Different Authors

List two or more works by different authors in alphabetical order by the surname of the first author cited:

> Several studies (Baer and Lambert, 1995; Lennard 1987; Nakhaie & Brym 1999) have investigated the political attitudes of professors in Canadian universities.

Citing Indirect Sources

Use a double reference to cite somebody who has been quoted in a book or an article. That is, use the original author(s) in the text and cite your source for the information in the parenthetical citation.

> In other research, Massie and Rosenthal (1997) studied home movies of children diagnosed with autism, but determining criteria was difficult due to the differences in quality and dating of the available videotapes (cited in Osterling & Dawson, 1998, p. 248).

Citing from a Textbook or Anthology

If you make an in-text citation to an article or chapter of a textbook, casebook, or anthology, use the in-text citation to refer only to the person(s) you cite; the References page will clarify the nature of this citation to Tanner.

> One writer described the Innu of Labrador as a "threatened people" (Tanner, 2000, p. 75).

Abbreviating Corporate Authors in the Text

Corporate authors may be abbreviated after a first, full reference:

> One group has actively lobbied the Canadian government to label alcoholic beverages as hazardous if consumed during pregnancy (Canadian Medical Association [CMA], 2000).

Thereafter, refer to the corporate author by initials: (CMA, 2000).

Citing a Work with an Anonymous Author

When a work has no author listed, cite the title as part of the in-text citation or use the first few words of the material.

> The cost per individual student has continued to rise rapidly ("Money Concerns," 1998, p. 2).

However, when a work's author is identified as "Anonymous," use this form:

> It has been shown that student expenses can be expected to rise for the next several years (Anonymous, 2002).

Citing Personal Communications

The *Publication Manual of the American Psychological Association* stipulates that personal communications, (e-mail, telephone conversations, interviews, memos, and conversations) which others cannot retrieve, should be cited in the text only and not mentioned at all in the references list (bibliography). In the in-text citation, give the initials as well as the last name of the source, provide the date, and briefly describe the nature of the communication.

> B. A. Frost (personal communication, August 24, 2001) described the potential adverse effects of herbal products.

Citing Electronic Sources

In most cases, omit page numbers for articles you find on the Internet. Monitors differ, as do printers, so do not count pages on the screen and do not use the page numbers of your printouts. Electronic text is searchable, so readers can find your quotation quickly with the Find feature of a browser after locating the Internet address in your References list. However, if an article on the Internet has numbered paragraphs, by all means supply that information in your citation. (Jones, 2001, ¶5) or (Jones, 2001, para.5).

> The most common type of diabetes is non-insulin-dependent-diabetes mellitus (NIDDM), which "affects 90% of those with diabetes and usually appears after age 40" (Larson, 1996, para. 3).

Abstract

> "Psychologically oriented techniques used to elicit confessions may undermine their validity" (Kassim, 1997, abstract).

Aggregated Database on a Server or CD-ROM. *The Canadian Encyclopedia Plus* (2001) has described social sciences as a category of disciplines which include anthropology, economics, political science, psychology, and sociology, and sometimes criminology, education, geography, law, psychiatry, philosophy, [and] religion.

E-mail. Treat e-mail as a personal communication, cited only in the text and not in the bibliography. However, electronic chat groups have gained legitimacy in recent years, so in the text give the exact date and e-mail address *only* if the citation has scholarly relevance and *only* if the author has made public the e-mail address with the expressed wish for correspondence.

> One technical writing instructor (March 8, 1997) has bemoaned the inability of hardware developers to maintain pace with the ingenuity of software developers. In his e-mail message, he indicated that educational institutions cannot keep pace with the hardware developers. Thus, "students nationwide suffer with antiquated equipment, even though it's only a few years old" (ClemmerJ@APSU01.APSU.EDU).

If the e-mail is part of a network or online journal, it *may* be listed in the bibliography. In such cases, use the form shown under "Listserv."

Government Document

> The website *Herbal and Homeopathic Products* (1998) has provided the report of the Canadian Pharmacists Association's Advisory Panel on Herbal Remedies, in which 10 recommendations are made to the House of Commons Standing Committee on Health.

Listserv (E-mail Discussion Group)

> Chang (February 14, 2002) has recommended the book *Canadian Guidelines for Sexual Health Education* as a helpful resource for teachers.

Online Magazine

Canadian Geographic (2001) contended that Toronto is "arguably the most multicultural city in the world."

Website

Carpentier (2000), who teaches a graduate course on government information at McGill University, stressed that "a knowledge of the organization and functions of governments is required for an understanding of government publications and information."

WRITING THE LIST OF REFERENCES IN APA STYLE

Use the title "References" for your bibliography page. Alphabetize the entries and double space throughout. Every reference used in your text should appear in your alphabetical list of references at the end of the paper. An exception to this rule exists for untraceable sources like e-mail, personal letters, and phone conversations. Identify these sources in your text, as explained in "E-mail" above.

Use the hanging indentation shown below when preparing your reference list. Type the first line of each flush left, and indent succeeding lines five spaces or one half inch. Italicize names of books, periodicals, and volume numbers, as shown in the next example:

Whittaker, J.C. (2000). Alonia and Dhoukanes: The ethnoarcheology of threshing in Cyprus. *Near Eastern Archaeologist*, 63. Retrieved June 26, 2001, from www.asor.org/nea/632.pdf

Bibliography Form—Books

Enter information for books in the following order. Items 1, 3, and 8 are required; add other items according to the rules that follow:

1. **Author**
2. Chapter or part of the book
3. **Title of the book**
4. Editor, translator, or compiler
5. Edition
6. Volume number of the book
7. Name of the series
8. **Place, publisher, and date**
9. Page numbers
10. Total number of volumes

The following list explains and gives examples of the correct form for books and parts of books.

Author

Thadani, M. B. (1999). *Herbal remedies: Weeding fact from fiction*. Winnipeg: Cantext.

List the author (surname first with initials for given names), year of publication within parentheses, title of the book italicized with *only* the first word of the title and any subtitle capitalized (but do capitalize proper nouns), place of publication, and publisher. In the publisher's name, omit the words *Publishing, Company,* or *Inc.,* but otherwise give a full name: Victoria University Press, Pearson Education Canada, HarperCollins. Indent the second line five spaces, or use the tab key for whatever indentation your computer font provides.

Authors, Two to Six. Give surnames and initials for up to six authors:

Castellano, M. B., Davis, L., & Lahache, L. (Eds.). (2000). *Aboriginal education: Fulfilling the promise.* Vancouver: UBC Press.

For seven or more, give surnames and initials for the first six authors; thereafter, use "et al.," which means "and others" (not italicized and with a period after "al").

Author, Two or More Works by the Same Author. List chronologically, not alphabetically, two or more works by the same author; for example, Fitzgerald's 1997 publication would precede his 1998 publication.

Fitzgerald, R. F. (1997). *Water samples* . . . .
Fitzgerald, R. F. (1998). *Controlling* . . . .

References to the same author in the same year are alphabetized and marked with lower case letters—a, b, c—immediately after the date:

Cobb, R. A. (1990a). *Circulating systems* . . . .
Cobb, R. A. (1990b). *Delay valves* . . . .

Author, Anonymous. If no author is listed, begin with the title of the article.

Canadian expatriates in show business. (2000). *The Canadian Encyclopedia.* New York: Harper.

Author, Corporation or Institution. List author, year, title of the work (italicized), place, and publisher. Use the word *Author* when the publisher and the author are the same.

Canadian Psychological Association. (2001). *Practice guidelines for providers of psychological services* (3rd ed.). Ottawa: Author.

Component Part of Anthology, Textbook, or Collection. List author(s), date, chapter or section title, editor (with name in normal order) preceded by "In" and followed by "(Ed.)" or "(Eds.)," the name of the book (italicized), page numbers to the specific section of the book cited (placed within parentheses), place of publication, and publisher.

Tanner, A. (2000). The Innu of Labrador, Canada. In M. M. Freeman (Ed.), *Endangered peoples of the Arctic: Struggles to survive and thrive* (pp. 75–92). Westport, CT: Greenwood Press.

Cross-References to Works in an Anthology, Textbook or Collection. Make a primary reference to the anthology, textbook, or collection:

Vesterman, W. (Ed.). (1991). *Readings for the 21st Century.* Boston: Allyn & Bacon.

Thereafter, make cross references to the primary source, in this case to Vesterman, as in the following examples:

Bailey, J. (1988). Jobs for women in the nineties. In Vesterman, pp. 55–63.

Fallows, D. (1982). Why mothers should stay home. In Vesterman, pp. 69–77.

Steinem, G. (1972). Sisterhood. In Vesterman, pp. 48–53.

Vesterman, W. (Ed.). (1991). *Readings for the 21st Century.* Boston: Allyn & Bacon.

Note: These entries should be mingled with all others on the reference page in alphabetical order so cross references may appear before or after the primary source. The year cited should be the date when the cited work was published, not when the Vesterman book was published; such information is usually found in a headnote, footnote, or list of credits at the front or back of the anthology.

Edition. Cite all editions except the first.

Campbell, N. A., & Reece, J. B. (2001). *Biology* (6th ed.). New York: Pearson Education.

Editor or Compiler. Place "(Ed.)" or "(Eds.)" after the name of the editor(s) and before the date:

Ghosh, R., & Ray, D. (Eds.). (1995). *Social change and education in Canada* (3rd ed.). Toronto: Harcourt Brace.

Encyclopedias, Dictionaries, and Other Alphabetized Reference Books

Corelli, R. (1999). How are Canadians different from Americans? *The Canadian Encyclopedia.* Toronto: McLelland & Stewart.

Kiosk: Word history. (1992). In *The American heritage dictionary of the American language* (3rd ed., p. 993). Boston: Houghton Mifflin.

Note: Give the volume number for multi-volume works (Vol. 4, pp. 19–20).

Bibliography Form—Periodicals

For journal or magazine articles, use the following order. Items 1, 2, 3, 7, and 8 are required.

1. **Author**
2. **Title of the article**
3. **Name of the periodical**
4. Series number (if it is relevant)
5. Volume number (for journals)

6. Issue number (if needed)
7. **Date of publication**
8. **Page numbers**

Abstract of a Published Article

Misumi, J., & Fujita, M. (1982). Effects of PM organizational development in supermarket organization. *Japanese Journal of Experimental Social Psychology, 21*, 93–111. Abstract obtained from *Psychological Abstracts*, 1982, 68, Abstract No. 11474.

Abstract of an Unpublished Work

Brownridge, D. A. (2000). The etiology of male partner violence against women in common-law and marital unions: An analysis of a national survey in Canada. Abstract of unpublished doctoral dissertation, University of Manitoba. (UMI-ProQuest Digital Dissertations, Abstract No. AAT NQ51631).

Abstract Retrieved from *InfoTrac, Silverplatter, ProQuest,* or Other Servers

Rapin, I. (1997). Autism [rev. of article]. *The New England Journal of Medicine, 337*, 97–104. Abstract retrieved August 4, 1997, from *Expanded Academic Index*, Abstract No. A19615909.

Note: Do not quote from the abstract unless the server stipulates that the author wrote the abstract.

Article in a Journal

Zboril-Benson, L. R. (2002). Why nurses are calling in sick: The impact of health-care restructuring. *Journal of Nursing Research 33*(4), 89–108.

Include the issue number if each issue is paged anew.

Article in a Journal, Two to Six Authors

Johnson, E. A., & Stewart, D. W. (2000). Clinical supervision in Canadian academic and service settings: The importance of education, training, and workplace support for supervisor development. *Canadian Psychology, 41*, 124–130.

Follow the same guidelines outlined above for books, giving surnames and initials for up to six authors, and using "et al.," for seven or more authors.

Article in a Magazine

Deacon, J. (2001, March 26). Rink rage. *Maclean's, 114*, 13.

Article in a Newspaper

Devlin, K. (1997, August 8). "Soft" mathematics can help us understand the human mind. *Chronicle of Higher Education*, pp. B4–B5.

Review

Daneman, M. (2001). [Review of the book *Converging methods for understanding reading and dyslexia*]. *Canadian Psychology, 42*, 143–145.

Jones, S. L. (1991). The power of motivation [Review of the motion picture *Body Heat*]. *Contemporary Film Review, 31*, 18.

Report

The Bureau of Tobacco Control. (1999). *Report on Tobacco Control*. Ottawa: Health Canada.

Bibliography Form—Non-Print Material

Corborn, W. H. (1990, November 3). On facing the fears caused by nightmares [Interview]. Lexington, KY.

Tabata, S. (Producer). (1998). *Transitions to postsecondary learning: Video and instructional material for students with learning disabilities and/or attention deficit disorder* [Videotape]. Vancouver: Eaton Coull Learning Group.

Bibliography Form—Electronic Sources

When citing Internet sources, include page numbers only if you have that data from a printed version of the journal or magazine. If the periodical has no volume number, use "p." or "pp." before the numbers; if the journal has a volume number, omit "p." or "pp." End the entry with the word "Retrieved" followed by the date of access and the URL. (URLs can be quite long, but you must provide the full data for other researchers to find the source.)

Abstract

Bowman, M. L. (2000). The diversity of diversity: Canadian-American differences and their implications for clinical training and APA accreditation. [Abstract]. *Canadian Psychology, 41.4*. Retrieved March 30, 2002, from www.cpa.ca/cp/tc-cpnov00.html

Article from an Online Journal

Dow, J. (2000). External and internal approaches to emotion: Commentary on Nesse on mood. *Psycoloquy*. Retrieved September 23, 2000, from www.cogsci.soton.ac.uk/cgi/psyc/newpsy?3.01

Article from a Printed Journal, Reproduced Online

Bowler, D. M., & Thommen, E. (2000). Attribution of mechanical and social causality to animated displays by children with autism. [Electronic version]. *Autism, 4,* 147–172.

Note: Add the URL and date of access if page numbers are not indicated.

Article from a Printed Magazine, Reproduced Online

Vincent, M. (2001, January/February). Canadians at home, work and play in 1900, 1950 and 2001. *Canadian Geographic*. Retrieved June 26, 2001, from http://www.cangeo.ca/

Article from an Online Magazine, No Author Listed

Health-care inflation: It's baaack! (1997, March 17). *Business Week,* 56–62. Retrieved March 18, 1997, from http://www.businessweek.com/1997/11/b351852.html

Article from an Online Newspaper

Kennedy, M. (2001, April 9). Ottawa to set up national organ donor program. *National Post Online*. Retrieved April 27, 2001, from http://www.nationalpost.com/

Bulletins and Government Documents

Canadian Pharmacists Association. (1998). *Herbal and homeopathic products: Ensuring safe choices for Canadians: Report of the advisory panel on herbal remedies*. Retrieved June 28, 2001, from http://www.cdnpharm.ca/cphanew/nv/herbrief.htm

Canada. Parliament. House of Commons. (1999, October 14). *Youth Criminal Justice Act*, Bill C-3, First Reading (36th Parliament, 2nd Session). Retrieved September 19, 2001, from www.parl.gc.ca/36/2/parlbus/chambus/house/bills/government/C-3/C-3_1/C-3TOCE.html

Listserv (E-mail Discussion Group)

Fitzpatrick, B. T. (2000, November 5). Narrative bibliography. Message posted to e-mail: bryanfitzpatrick@mail.csu.edu

News Groups

Haas, H. (2000, August 5). Link checker that works with cold fusion. Fogo archives. Message posted to impressive.net/archives/fogo/200000805113615.AI4381@w3.org

Review, Online

Ebert, R. (2001, January 5). *Traffic* [Review of the motion picture *Traffic*]. Retrieved April 5, 2001, from www.suntimes.com/ebert/ebert_reviews/2001/01/010501.html

Bibliography Form—CD-ROM and Aggregated Databases

Material from a CD-ROM requires that you identify the database server or the name of the diskette, as shown in the following examples.

Abstract

Figueredo, A. J., & McCloskey, L. A. (1993). Sex, money, and paternity: The evolutionary psychology of domestic violence. *Ethnology and Sociobiology, 14,* 353–79. Abstract retrieved June 12, 2001, from Silverplatter database.

Encyclopedia Article

Social sciences in Canada (2001). *The Canadian Encyclopedia* 2001. Toronto, ON: McClelland & Stewart. Retrieved Mar 25, 2002, from CD-ROM.

Full-Text Article

Borman, W. C., Hanson, M. A., Oppler, S. H., Pulakos, E. D., & White, L. A. (1993). Role of early supervisory experience in supervisor performance. *Journal of Applied Psychology, 78,* 443–449. Retrieved May 23, 2001, from PsycARTICLES database.

FORMATTING THE PAPER IN APA STYLE

Place your materials in this order:

1. Title page
2. Abstract
3. Text of the paper
4. References
5. Appendix (optional)

Title Page

In addition to the title of your paper, your name, and your academic affiliation, the title page should establish the running head that will appear on every page, preceding the page number. The APA style requires a shortened form of the paper's title as the running head.

Abstract

You should provide an abstract with every paper written in APA style. An abstract is a quick but thorough summary of the contents of your paper. For theoretical papers, the abstract should include the following:

- The topic in one sentence, if possible.
- The purpose, thesis, and scope of the paper.
- A brief reference to the sources used (e.g., published articles, books, personal observation).
- The conclusions and the implications of the study.

For a report of an empirical study, the abstract should include the four items listed above for theoretical papers with the addition of three more:

- Description of the subjects (e.g., species, number, age, type).
- Description of the methodology, including procedures and apparatus.
- The findings produced by the study.

Text of the Paper

Double-space throughout your entire paper. In general you should use subtitles as side heads and centred heads in your paper.

Follow your instructor's guidelines for formatting your paper (e.g., margins, indentations, use of fonts). Otherwise, prepare your paper as shown in the student example on the following pages.

References

Present the entries with a hanging indentation.

Appendix

The appendix is the appropriate place for material that is not germane to your text but nevertheless is pertinent to the study: graphs, charts, study plans, observation and test results.

SAMPLE PAPER IN APA STYLE

The following paper demonstrates the format and style of a paper written in APA style, with a title page, a running head, an abstract, in-text citations to name the author and year of each source, and a list of references.

Aboriginal 1

The running head will appear at the top of each page.

Aboriginal Education in Canada:
A Work in Progress

by
C. Turenne

129.181 School and Society
Dr. C. Crippen
21 February 2001

Place the abstract separately on page 2.

Do not use a paragraph indentation for the abstract.

The abstract should not exceed 120 words.

Aboriginal 2

Abstract

To develop an education system which reflects their cultural and spiritual values, yet remains compatible with provincial systems and post-secondary institutions, Aboriginal people must not only set educational goals but also redefine their relationship to the federal government. In 1972, the residential school system (described as both "cultural genocide" and "internal colonialism") was replaced by band- and community-controlled education, but this "control" was affected by lack of funding, poorly constructed schools, and a shortage of trained Aboriginal teachers. Aboriginals must now take their educational destinies into their own hands, determining their educational direction and promoting decolonization. The way they handle this empowerment and the non-Aboriginal societal response will significantly affect the evolution of this educational work in progress.

Aboriginal 3

As the Aboriginal people of Canada can confirm, colonization is an infantilizing process, taking a vigorous culture and forcing it into a childlike dependency on another (Perley, 1993). In 1972, however, with *Indian Control of Indian Education (ICIE)*, a policy paper from the National Indian Brotherhood, Aboriginal people emerged from that "childhood" into a kind of "adolescence" by declaring their right to determine their identities, their futures, and their relationship to the rest of Canada. This metaphorical adolescence, as with any adolescence, is a difficult period of choices and tensions for Aboriginals, as they not only set educational goals, but also redefine their relationship to the authority figure (in this case, the federal government).

Cite the year immediately after the name of the source.

Through experiential learning, Aboriginal children had always been taught the particular skills needed in the environment that would support them (Kirkness, 1992). However, the arrival of the European settlers and the establishment of the residential school system disrupted and contradicted this process entirely. Mercredi (1999) noted that "residential schools are the most common experience for contemporary aboriginal adults." Because of the expressed design of eradicating the language and customs of the First Nations of Canada, the character of Aboriginal education thereafter has been described as "cultural genocide" (Chrisjohn & Young, 1997; Pauls, 1996), and as "internal colonialism" (Perley, 1993, p. 129).

Do not cite a page number for Internet sites.

Use & in citations, but not in the text.

In an attempt to end this situation, in 1969 the federal government proposed that Aboriginal children should no longer be treated as wards of the state but instead as citizens of the provinces in which they lived. Aboriginals' rejection of this proposal (because it was not the government's place to direct that change, whether or not it would be beneficial) was formalized in the policy paper, *Indian Control of Indian Education* (National Indian Brotherhood, 1972). Hereafter, control of Aboriginal education began to devolve to local bands and communities.

Aboriginal 4

[A portion of this paper has been omitted]

Aboriginals, in short, have to take their destinies into their own hands. What they will do with their empowerment, though, is where the challenge lies. Essentially the goals of education are to prepare children to acquire life skills and promote a sense of cultural identity (Charleston, 1988). Many, including Archibald (1995), argued that curricula should reflect the learners' heritage and be created with local Aboriginal people. However, all parties acknowledge the importance of an education system that is compatible with both provincial or territorial systems, and with post-secondary institutions (Charleston, 1988). How educators balance compatibility and uniqueness seems a daunting task.

[A portion of this paper has been omitted]

Several questions remain: How do educators design a Native education that does not just assimilate or undermine Aboriginal values and customs? How will Native cultures adapt and create curricula that embrace the reality of diverse populations, without unwittingly abandoning their children outside the reach of such curricula? Unfortunately, the literature provides few answers, although LaFrance (2000), Watt-Cloutier (2000), and Williams (2000) have described several innovative projects in Akwesasne (ON), Nunavik (QC), and Vancouver (BC), respectively. These programs affirmed that Aboriginal education is growing, strengthening, and maturing. Education is the most significant function a society can perform, and all societies have developed it according to their needs and interests. Castellano, Davis, and Lahache (2000) stressed:

> The old story is one of destruction and pain, while the emerging one is that of the ongoing vitality of Aboriginal people, from whose experience we can learn. Aboriginal people believe that education is an integral way of helping the new story unfold. (p. ix)

Use the past tense or present perfect tense when citing sources.

Indent long quotations of 40 words or more five additional spaces, and omit the quotation marks.

Aboriginal 5

Naturally, given the human condition of imperfection, mistakes will be made. However, it is the unnatural relationship of colonialism that makes non-Natives think that they have the right or responsibility to "prevent" mistakes and that Aboriginals have to "accept" this wisdom. Throughout this work in progress, as the planning of Aboriginal education develops and matures, the societal response of non-Aboriginal people must also develop and mature.

Aboriginal 6

References

Book

Primary reference to an anthology

Cross reference to the primary source (Castellano, Davis, & Lahache)

Internet source

Alladin, M. I. (Ed.). (1996). *Racism in Canadian Schools*. Toronto: Harcourt Brace.

Archibald, J. (1995). To keep the fire going: The challenge for First Nations education in the year 2000. In Ghosh & Ray, pp. 342–357.

Castellano, M. B., Davis, L., & Lahache, L. (Eds.). (2000). *Aboriginal education: Fulfilling the promise*. Vancouver: UBC Press.

Charleston, M. (Ed.) (1988). Quality of First Nations education. In National Indian Brotherhood, Assembly of First Nations, *Tradition and education: Towards a vision of our future* (pp. 71–83). Summerstown, ON: Author.

Chrisjohn, R., & Young, S. (1997). *The circle game: Shadows and substances in the Indian residential school experience in Canada*. Penticton: Theytus. Also available in *For seven generations: An information legacy of the Royal Commission on Aboriginal Peoples*. [CD-ROM]. Ottawa: Libraxus.

Ghosh, R., & Ray, D. (Eds.). (1995). *Social change and education in Canada*. Toronto: Harcourt Brace.

Kirkness, V. J. (1992). *First Nations and schools: Triumphs and struggles*. Toronto: Canadian Education Association.

Lafrance, B. T. (1993). Culturally negotiated education in First Nations communities: Empowering ourselves for future generations. In Castellano, Davis, & Lahache, pp. 101–113.

Mercredi, O. (1999, March). Aboriginal education: Ovide Mercredi reflects. *Professionally Speaking*. Retrieved January 15, 2001, from www.oct.on.ca/english/ps/march_1999/ovide.htm

National Indian Brotherhood. (1972). *Indian control of Indian education*. Policy paper presented to the Minister of Indian Affairs and Northern Development. Ottawa: Author.

Pauls, S. (1996). Racism and Native schooling: A historical perspective. In Alladin, pp. 22–41.

Aboriginal 7

Perley, D. G. (1993). Aboriginal education in Canada as internal colonialism. *Canadian Journal of Native Education* 20, 128–138.

Watt-Cloutier, S. (1993). Honouring our past, creating our future: Education in northern and remote communities. In Castellano, Davis, and Lahache, pp. 114–128.

Williams, L. (1994). Urban Aboriginal education: The Vancouver experience. In Castellano, Davis, & Lahache, pp. 129–146.

Journal article

CHAPTER 15

Using the CMS (Chicago) Note Style

Taken from: *The Essential Guide to Writing Research Papers*, Canadian Edition, by James D. Lester, James D. Lester, Jr., and Patricia I. Mochnacz.

15

The fine arts and some fields in the humanities, but not literature, employ traditional footnotes or endnotes, which should conform to standards set by *The Chicago Manual of Style,* 14th edition, 1993.

BLENDING SOURCES INTO YOUR WRITING

With this system, you must employ superscript numerals within the text (like this[15]) and place documentary notes either as footnotes on corresponding pages or as endnotes that appear together at the end of the paper.

Although a "Bibliography" page (the equivalent of the "Works Cited" or "Sources Cited" page in MLA and the "References" page in APA and CBE) is not always required in CMA, some instructors may ask for one at the end of the paper. This page may be entitled "Selected Bibliography," "Works Cited," or "Sources Cited." Consult your instructor about the preferred title. Running heads and an abstract are optional in this style.

The following discussion assumes that notes will appear as footnotes. However, some instructors accept endnotes; that is, all notes appear together at the end of the paper, not at the bottom of individual pages.

If available, use the footnote or endnote feature of your software. It will not only insert the raised superscript numeral but also keep your footnotes arranged properly at the bottom of each page. In most instances, the software will first insert the superscript numeral and then skip to the bottom of the page so you can write the footnote. It will not, of course, write the note automatically; you must type in the essential data in the correct style.

It is customary to write in the present tense when using the Chicago footnote style.

15

Writing with Superscript Numerals in the Text

Use Arabic numerals typed slightly above the line (like this[12]). Place this superscript numeral at the end of quotations or paraphrases, with the numeral following without a space after the final word or mark of punctuation, as in this sample:

> Under Louis XIV the church in Canada became subordinate to the needs and dictates of the state. The crown determined the number of clergy, defined their roles in the colony, and provided up to 40 percent of the church's revenue.[18] The church's main role was to ensure the subordination of colonists to spiritual and secular authority.[19] The church "attempted to cultivate an ethic of obligation and obedience, of simplicity and austerity."[20]

The superscript numerals go outside the marks of punctuation. Avoid placing one superscript numeral at the end of a long paragraph because readers will not know if it refers to only the final sentence or to the entire paragraph. If you introduce borrowed materials with an authority's name and then place a superscript numeral at the end, you direct the reader to the full extent of the borrowed material.

> Kirkness notes that before the Europeans arrived, education in Aboriginal society was already evolved: every adult had the responsibility to ensure that every child learned "how to live a good life."[1] Kirkness adds, "Not only was education geared to teaching the values of the society, but also its economics."[2]

An advantage of the Chicago footnote style is that, unlike MLA or APA, you can include content or explanatory notes.

FORMATTING THE NOTES IN CMS STYLE

Place your footnotes at the bottom of pages to correspond with superscript numerals (see immediately above). Whether you directly quote, paraphrase, or use the ideas of your source, you must credit each source in a footnote with a page number. Note that "p" and "pp" are not used in footnotes or endnotes. Some papers will require footnotes on almost every page. Follow these conventions:

1. **Spacing and indention.** Single space individual footnotes, but double space between footnotes. Indent the first line five spaces, as you would a normal paragraph.
2. **Numbering.** Number the notes consecutively throughout the entire paper. The raised superscript numeral is preferred if your computer software provides it.
3. **Placement.** Collect at the bottom of each page all footnotes to citations made on that page.
4. **Distinguish footnotes from text.** Separate footnotes from the text by triple spacing.

Writing Notes for Books

Begin with the footnote number, followed by a period and a space, if the number is typed on the line. If you use a superscript numeral, it is *not* followed by a period or a space. Both methods are demonstrated in the following examples citing books. For the rest of the examples, superscript numerals are used. Follow the number with the name of the author in regular order, that is, first name followed by last name, followed by a comma; the title (italicized or underlined); the publication information (place, publisher, and year within parentheses); and a page reference.

Book, One to Three Authors

[1]Orest Martynowych, *Ukrainians in Canada: The Formative Period, 1891–1924* (Edmonton: Canadian Institute of Ukrainian Studies Press, 1991), 25.

2. Marilyn J. Boxer and Jean H. Quataert, eds., *Connecting Spheres: European Women in a Globalizing World, 1500 to the Present*, 2nd ed. (New York: Oxford University Press, 2000), chap. 2, esp. 33.

Book, More Than Three Authors

[3]Alison Prentice et al., *Canadian Women: A History*. 2nd ed. (Toronto: Harcourt Brace Canada, 1996), 531.

Book, Part of an Anthology or Collection

[4]Barry Came, "The Red River Flood, Spring, 1997," in *In the Face of Disaster: True Stories of Canadian Heroism from the Archives of* Maclean's. ed. Michael Benedict (Toronto: Viking, 2000), 71.

[5]George Hersey, "Female and Male Art: *Postille* to Garrard's *Artemisia Gentileschi*," in *Parthenope's Splendour: Art of the Golden Age in Naples*, ed. Jeanne Porter and Susan Munshower (University Park, PA: Pennsylvania State University Press, 1993), 325.

Writing Notes for Periodicals

Article from a Journal

[6]Herb Enns, "Achieving the Modern: Abstract Painting and Design in the 1950's," *Canadian Architect* 38 (1993): 26.

Article from a Magazine

[7]Ken MacQueen, "Wild Woman of the West: Who Were You, Emily Carr?" *Maclean's*, 11 June 2001, 62.

Article from a Newspaper

[8]Peter Crossley, "Leathers on Art Buying," *Winnipeg Free Press*, 4 November 1967, A11.

Review Article

[9]Griselda Pollock, review *of Artemisia Gentileschi: The Image of the Female Hero in Italian Baroque Art*, by Mary Garrard, *Art Bulletin*, 15 March 1994, 505.

Writing Notes for Electronic Sources

The Chicago Manual of Style (CMS) uses brackets to describe the type of electronic source, shows when it was first cited, published, or accessed, and gives an electronic address. The CMS does not supply a great deal of information on citing electronic sources, but the University of Chicago Press suggests consulting *Online! A Reference Guide to Using Internet Sources* by Harnack and Kleppinger (available in print and online at www.bedfordstmartins.com/online/cite7.html) which contains a chapter entitled "Using Chicago Style to Cite and Document Sources."

Article from an Online Journal

[10]Gao Yi, "French Revolutionary Studies in Today's China," *Canadian Journal of History* 32 (1997), <www.usask.ca/history/cjh/> (19 June 2001).

Article from an Online Magazine

[11]Robert Smith, "Escape from Culloden," *British Heritage*, February/March 2001, <www.thehistorynet.com/BritishHeritage/articles/2001/02012_cover.htm> (20 April 2001).

Book Online

[12] D. H. Lawrence, *Lady Chatterly's Lover*, 1928, <http://bibliomania.com/fiction/dhl/chat.html> (16 May 2001).

CD-ROM Source

[13]Aurelio J. Figueredo and Laura Ann McCloskey, "Sex, Money, and Paternity: the Evolutionary Psychology of Domestic Violence," *Ethnology and Sociobiology* 14 (1993): 355, PsycLIT [CD-ROM]; available from Silverplatter.

Electronic Bulletin Board

[14]Rosemary Camilleri, "Narrative Bibliography," <listserv@H-RHETOR @msu.edu> (March 1997).

E-mail. Because e-mail is not retrievable, do not document with a note or bibliography entry. Instead, mention the name of the source within your text by saying something like this:

Walter Wallace argues that teen violence stems mainly from the breakup of the traditional family (e-mail to the author).

Government Document Online

[15]Canada. House of Commons. Standing Committee on Canadian Heritage. *The Challenge of Change: A Consideration of the Canadian Book Industry.* The Report of the Standing Committee on Canadian Heritage, Ottawa: Public Works and Government Services Canada, 21 June 2000, <www.cmhc-schl.gc.ca/en/index.cfm?pMenu=72> (11 July 2001).

Scholarly Project Online

[16]*British Poetry Archive*, ed. Jerome Mcgann and David Seaman, 1999, <http://etext.lib.virginia.edu/britpo.html> (7 March 2002).

Writing Notes for Other Sources

Biblical Reference

[17]Rom. 6:2.

[17]1 Cor. 13.1–3.

Encyclopedia

[18]*The World Book Encyclopedia*, 2000 ed., s.v. "Raphael."

Note: sub verbo ("s.v.") means "under the word(s)."

Government Documents

[19]Canada. Commission of Inquiry into the Deployment of Canadian Forces to Somalia. *Dishonoured Legacy: The Lessons of the Somalia Affair: Report of the Commission of Inquiry into the Deployment of Canadian Forces to Somalia: Executive Summary,* by Gilles Letourneau. Ottawa: Minister of Public Works and Government Services Canada: Canada Communications Group, 1997.

[20]United Kingdom, *Coroner's Act*, 1954, 2 & 3 Eliz. 2, ch. 31.

Non-print Source: Lecture, Sermon, Speech, Oral Report

[21]JoAnne G. Bernstein, "The Renaissance Nude: Studio Practice and the Modern Gaze," Lecture (University of California, San Diego, 27 April 1994).

Television

[22]Holly Doan, *Frida, Georgia and Emily Carr* (Winnipeg: WTN, 10 June 2001).

Film

[23]*Surviving Picasso*, 35mm, 123 min., Warner Brothers, 1996.

Musical Work

[24]Wolfgang A. Mozart, *Symphony no. 41 in C major, K. 551 "Jupiter,"* The London Classical Players, Roger Norrington, EMI 7 54090 2.

CITING SUBSEQUENT FOOTNOTES AFTER THE FIRST

After a first full reference, subsequent footnotes should be shortened to author's name and page number, for example, "Bumsted, 92." When an author has two works mentioned, employ a shortened version of the title, for example, "Friesen, *River,* 25." In general, avoid Latinate abbreviations such as *loc. cit.* or *op. cit.;* however, whenever a note refers to the source in the immediately preceding note, you may use "Ibid." to refer to the same page number of the preceding entry or use "Ibid." with a new page number as shown below (note especially the differences between notes 2, 7, and 8).

WRITING A NOTES SECTION FOR ENDNOTES

If you are using endnotes rather than footnotes, put all your notes together in a Notes section at the end of your paper. Most computer software programs offer features that help you with this task. The disadvantage of this method is that the reader has to flip back and forth to follow your citations. Follow these conventions:

1. **Form.** Use the form explained earlier.
2. **Title.** Begin the notes on a new page at the end of the text. Entitle the page "Notes" centred and placed two inches from the top of the page.
3. **Indention.** Indent the first line of each note five spaces, type the note number in regular Arabic numerals, or use superscript numerals placed slightly above the line. Begin the note and use the left margin for succeeding lines.
4. **Spacing.** Triple space between the heading and the first note. Single space the notes and double space between the notes, as shown in this example of notes from a paper on the women's movement in Canada in the last half of the 20th century.

Notes

[1]Alvin Finkel, Margaret Conrad, and Veronica Strong-Boag, *History of the Canadian Peoples 1867 to the Present* (Toronto: Copp Clark Pitman, 1993), 543.

[2]Ibid., 545.

[3]Barry Came and Bruce Wallace, "The Lepine Massacre, December 6, 1989" in Michael Benedict, ed., *In the Face of Disaster: True Stories of Canadian Heroism from the Archives of Maclean's* (Toronto: Viking, 2000), 160.

[4]Nancy Sheehan, "Sexism in Education" in *Social Change and Education in Canada*, 3rd. ed. Ratna Ghosh and Douglas Ray (Toronto: Harcourt Brace Canada, 1995), 328.

[5]Came and Wallace, 163.

[6]Carol Gilligan, *In a Different Voice* (Boston: Harvard University Press, 1982), 25.

[7]Finkel, Conrad, and Strong-Boag, 545.

[8]Ibid.

[9]Sheehan, 333.

[10]Finkel, Conrad, and Strong-Boag, 555.

WRITING CONTENT OR EXPLANATORY NOTES

Use a content endnote to explain research problems, to resolve or report conflicts in the testimony of the critics, to provide interesting tidbits, and to credit people and sources not mentioned in the text. Content or explanatory footnotes should be intermingled with your documented footnotes. Here is an example:

40. There are three copies of the papal brief situated on Via S. Nicola da Tolentino. The document is printed in Thomas D. Culley, *Jesuits and Music* (Rome and St. Louis, 1979), 1: 358–59.

For additional discussion and examples, see footnote number 2 in the sample paper at the end of this chapter.

WRITING A BIBLIOGRAPHY PAGE FOR A PAPER THAT USES FOOTNOTES OR ENDNOTES

In addition to footnotes or endnotes, you may need to supply a separate bibliography page that lists sources used in developing the paper. Check with your instructor before preparing one because it may not be required. Use a heading that represents its contents, such as "Selected Bibliography," "Sources Consulted," or "Works Cited."

Separate the title from the first entry with a triple space. Use a hanging indent; type the first line of each entry flush left; indent the second line and other succeeding lines five spaces. Alphabetize the list by last names of authors. Single space the lines of each item, but double space between the items. List alphabetically by title two or more works by one author. The basic forms are as follows:

Book

Finkel, Alvin, Margaret Conrad, and Veronica Strong-Boag, *History of the Canadian Peoples 1867 to the Present*. Toronto: Copp Clark Pitman, 1993.

Schirokauer, Conrad. *A Brief History of Japanese Civilization*. New York: Harcourt, 1993.

Journal Article

Silvers, Annette. "Has Her(oine's) Time Now Come?" *Journal of Aesthetics and Art Criticism* 48 (1990): 365–79.

Newspaper

Fine, Sean. "Aboriginal Languages Face Extinction." *The Globe and Mail*, 20 June 2001.

See also the bibliography page that accompanies the sample paper.

SAMPLE PAPER USING THE CMS (CHICAGO) FOOTNOTE SYSTEM

The following paper demonstrates the correct form for a research paper using the CMS (Chicago) note system. The writer's instructor may have requested that her paper be submitted in MLA style.

Breaking the Mould:
Artemisia Gentileschi's Contribution to Art

by
Katrina A. T. Senyk

54.124 Art History
Dr. M. Steggles
March 10, 2002

Most instructors require a title page. The running head (optional in Chicago style) starts on page 2 and will appear at the top of each page.

15

Katrina identifies the issue and cites sources in her opening to confirm the serious nature of the discussion.

Katrina uses raised superscript numerals.

Katrina expresses her thesis in a sentence at the end of the introduction.

Katrina adds an explanatory note to the Garrard reference (one of the advantages of the footnote system).

Senyk 2

Many people believe that artists view the human condition from the unique perspective of their individuality and unconsciously illustrate their perspective via their art, in much the same way that "personality theories are strongly influenced by personal and subjective factors . . . (and) reflect the biographies of their authors."[1] If this is so, then artists' perceptions of the world are translated into their works of art. Moreover, Mary Garrard states that, historically, the "assignment of sex roles has created fundamental differences between the sexes in their perception, experience, and expectations of the world . . . that cannot help but be carried over into the creative process."[2]

Artemisia Gentileschi (1593–c.1652) portrayed her subjects from her unusual perspective as a female artist in the 17th century. Viewers frequently question why Gentileschi painted such powerful female protagonists; by examining Gentileschi's perception of her world, the viewer can better understand what her art represented to her as a woman in a male-dominated profession. Gentileschi's work explores women's demands to be justly represented.

In the 17th century options for women were limited to marrying and raising children, or devotion to the Catholic Church as a nun. Alternatives were not viewed as appropriate. However, Artemisia Gentileschi was more fortunate than her peers; having been born to a painter, she was raised in "an environment where she could acquire the basic skills necessary for a professional artist."[3] Although it was "difficult for women to become artists during this time . . . [Gentileschi] was able to gain access to a world that would normally have been forbidden."[4]

[1]B. R. Hergenhahn and Matthew H. Olson, *An Introduction to Theories of Personality*, 5th ed. (Toronto: Prentice Hall Canada, 1999), 569.

[2]Mary Garrard, *Artemisia Gentileschi: The Image of the Female Hero in Italian Baroque Art* (Princeton: Princeton UP, 1989), 202. For a detailed discussion of the heroic image see Garrard's whole work.

Senyk 3

Her father, Orazio, one of the first followers of Caravaggio, trained Gentileschi from an early age, but he recognized his limits as a teacher when her talent surpassed his. Orazio hired Agostino Tassi to tutor her in perspective, but the perspective Tassi imparted to Gentileschi had nothing to do with any artistic technique. During one of his "lessons," Tassi raped her, and continued sexual relations with promises of marriage. However, when it became apparent that Tassi had no intention of marrying Gentileschi, Orazio sued Tassi for ruining her honour.[5]

During the early 17th century, as Spear notes:

> legal and social dimensions of violent rape centred on questions of family and marriageability, in which women resembled (male) property for exchange . . . usually poor girls sought not the rapist's imprisonment, but either his hand in marriage or payment of a dowry . . . . Marriage, it must be emphasized, rather than rape, was the core substance of the litigation.[6]

Long quotations are indented four spaces.

Gentileschi, as an unmarried woman, was classified as "damaged property." She was subjected to torture, a humiliating public trial, and a medical examination to prove that she was a virgin before the rape.[7] The sexual assaults, compounded by the ordeal of the trial, no doubt caused a "crystallizing moment of recognition of sexuality and gender power" in Gentileschi.[8]

3 Wendy Slatkin, *Women Artists in History: From Antiquity to the Present* (Toronto: Prentice-Hall Canada, 1990), 49.

4 Rebecca Corbell and Samantha Guy, "Artemisia Gentileschi and the Age of Baroque," 1995, <http://rubens.anu.edu.au/student.projects/artemisia/Artemisia.html> (25 February 2001).

5 Slatkin, 49.

6 Richard Spear, "Artemisia Gentileschi: Ten Years of Fact and Fiction," *Art Bulletin* 82 (September 2000): 570.

Note that the reference to Corbell and Guy does not have a page number because it is an Internet source.

15

15

Senyk 4

The emotional chaos resulting from the assaults and the trial is most likely expressed in Gentileschi's work, *Judith Decapitating Holofernes*, painted shortly after the trial was dismissed.[9] Gentileschi's interpretation of this biblical story is particularly gruesome; she uses vivid colours, indicating strong, vehement emotion and enhancing the sense of violence and movement.[10] This painting is clearly a "cathartic expression of the artist's private, and perhaps repressed, rage."[11] Rebecca Corbell and Samantha Guy suggest that "the violence her Judith wreaks on Holofernes is strongly suggestive of the turmoil she must have been experiencing."[12]

Caravaggio also depicts this scene in his *Judith and Holofernes*. Both artists depict the moment when Judith severs Holofernes' head, but Caravaggio positions the figures across the picture surface, weakening the overall effect; the characters seem less active in decapitating Holofernes and more like passive witnesses. Gentileschi, instead, chooses to intersect the arms of all three figures in the centre of the picture plane, "fixing the viewer's attention inescapably on the grisly act much more convincing[ly] than Caravaggio."[13] Caravaggio depicts Judith as a weak, ineffective female, drawing back distastefully, almost cringing at the sight of blood, whereas Gentileschi's Judith looks "as if she is [angrily] struggling to pull the sword through Holofernes' [neck]."[14] Perhaps Gentileschi is expressing the anger she feels about her helplessness and vulnerability as a woman.

Footnotes are separated from the text by triple spacing. Items in footnotes are separated by commas for author, work, and publication data.

[7]Corbell and Guy.

[8]Griselda Pollock, review of *Artemisia Gentileschi: The Image of the Female Hero in Italian Baroque Art*, by Mary Garrard, *Art Bulletin* 72 (September 1990): 503.

[9]Corbell and Guy.

[10]Ibid.

[11]Spear, 569.

[12]Corbell and Guy.

Senyk 5

With a new perspective on the world after the experiences of the sexual assaults and the charade of a trial, Artemisia Gentileschi went on to develop her unique style combining dynamic, gruesome naturalism with innovative interpretations of typical Renaissance and Baroque themes. "She adapted some of Caravaggio's devices to forge an original style of strength and beauty. She expressed her identity as a woman and as an artist."[15] As a woman, Gentileschi identified with the plight of the heroine, whereas her male colleagues identified with the villain's anticipated pleasure.

Artemisia Gentileschi's great contribution to art is found in the "categorically different treatment of major themes around the well-established topos of the heroic woman." [16] Because most artists and patrons have historically been men, naturally most paintings would represent the perspective of the male; and as Garrard notes, ". . . [men have been] drawn by instinct to identify more with the villain than with the heroine."[17]

Katrina now advances her conclusion.

[13]Slatkin, 51.
[14]Corbell and Guy.
[15]Slatkin, 54.
[16]Pollock, 50.
[17]Garrard, 194.

15

Senyk 6

As a result of her experiences, Gentileschi began to reinterpret traditional themes from the viewpoint of the dynamic, assertive female protagonist. In her television documentary, "Artemisia," Adrienne Clarkson asserts that this artist "(broke) the constraints of her female condition to become arguably the most remarkable woman painter of the post-modern period."[18] Through her body of work, Gentileschi explores in depth women's demands to be justly represented.

[18]Adrienne Clarkson, "Artemisia," *Adrienne Clarkson Presents* (Toronto: CBC-TV, 25 January 1993).

Senyk 7

Works Cited

Clarkson, Adrienne. "Artemisia." *Adrienne Clarkson Presents.* Toronto: CBC-TV, 25 January 1993.

Corbell, Rebecca, and Samantha Guy. "Artemisia Gentileschi and the Age of Baroque." <http://rubens.anu.edu.au/student.projects/artemisia/Artemisia.html> (25 February 2001).

Garrard, Mary. Artemisia Gentileschi: The Image of the Female Hero in Italian Baroque Art. Princeton: Princeton UP, 1989.

Hergenhahn, B. R., and Matthew H. Olson. *An Introduction to Theories of Personality.* 5th ed. Toronto: Prentice Hall Canada, 1999.

Pollock, Griselda. Review Artemisia Gentileschi: The Image of the Female Hero in Italian Baroque Art, by Mary Garrard. *Art Bulletin* 72 (September 1990): 499–505.

Slatkin, Wendy. *Women Artists in History: From Antiquity to the Present.* Toronto: Prentice-Hall Canada, 1990. 49–54.

Spear, Richard. "Artemisia Gentileschi: Ten Years of Fact and Fiction." *Art Bulletin* 82 (September 2000): 568–579.

The references (Works Cited) go on a separate page.

Katrina's bibliography demonstrates the citation form for books, journal articles, an Internet source, and a television program.

CHAPTER 16

Discipline Perspectives

Taken from: *A Brief Introduction to Anthropology and Anthropological Research,* by Edwin W. Holland

A BRIEF INTRODUCTION TO ANTHROPOLOGY AND ANTHROPLOGICAL RESEARCH

What is Anthropology?

Anthropology is, literally, the study of humankind. Anthropologists study all aspects of human life—the biological, the social, and the humanistic—at all times and in all places. They are interested in the evolution of the human species and its closest relatives, the monkeys and apes, as well as in the physical and genetic diversity of living human beings. They study ancient, historic, and modern peoples and how their lives have changed over time. And they also address the arts, religions, and philosophies of all these peoples. The aim of Anthropology in taking such a broad approach to the study of humankind is two-fold. The first is descriptive: to know what are the things that characterize human life. The second is analytic: to understand and explain why these things are the way they are.

The earliest use of the term Anthropology was in the 1840s in France, where it was applied specifically to the study of human skeletal measurements. Modern Anthropology developed at the end of the Nineteenth Century in the United States. One of its defining features was its reliance on *field research* to obtain information on the actual nature and lives of people. Before this development, Anthropologists and other social scientists depended on the reports of travellers, missionaries, and government officials for information about the peoples of the world. Their reports were frequently superficial and not always accurate. Often their accounts reflected their own biases and beliefs rather than an attempt to objectively describe the people and objects they encountered. In an effort to remedy this and provide accurate and detailed information on all aspects of people and their lives, Anthropologists began to travel themselves to observe and record information as accurately and objectively as possible. To do this they spent months, and even years, living with the people they studied or carefully excavating the remnants of peoples long gone. Until the 1950s, Anthropology was the only social science that used field research as the major method of gathering information for its studies.

In their efforts to analyze and interpret this information, to understand why things were the way they were, Anthropologists developed two crucial and distinctive approaches to the study of human life: the *Concept of Culture* and the *Holistic Perspective.*

Culture, in its Anthropological sense, was first defined by Edward Burnett Tylor in the later part of the Nineteenth Century. To him it was the essential characteristic of the human species and was the Acomplex whole including . . . all habits and capabilities acquired by man as a member of society. In the 1870s this was a decidedly radical view of human life. Most scholars at the time viewed differences in customs, manners, morals, religion, and even language as biological differences among the people of the world; Tylor proposed that these differences were learned. Further, he defined these as part of a Acomplex whole, that is, these elements of peoples' lives were not isolated and independent bits and pieces, but were interrelated in a coherent fashion.

Tylor's view of culture as the defining characteristic of mankind is still central to modern Anthropology, but has been developed and expanded. By the end of the Nineteenth Century, Franz Boas had developed the idea of *Cultural Relativism,* the view that since cultures are internally consistent, they can only be fully understood on their own terms, and that evaluating them in comparison to one's own culture, *Ethnocentrism*—a common practice in the Nineteenth and early Twentieth Centuries, only leads to misunderstanding. Additionally, the idea that the apparently different parts of human life are actually interrelated has led modern Anthropology to take a Holistic Perspective on human life. In short, this perspective is the view that human life is systemic, that all its aspects—the biological, the social, the economic, the linguistic, and so on—are interconnected, and that to fully understand any aspect of human life one must understand its relationship to other aspects.

Since Anthropology is interested in all aspects of life, it draws on many other disciplines for information, research methods, and theories. The fields of Biology, Medicine, and Genetics have contributed greatly to our study of human evolution and human physical diversity. Mathematics has given us methods of quantitative analysis. From History we have learned to make effective use of documentary evidence. Philosophy and the Humanities have helped us address questions of values and aesthetics as well as the nature of knowledge itself. Geography has offered information on the earth and the distribution of peoples over it that add to our understanding of the relationship of people to their environment. And from each of the other Social Sciences, such as Economics, Political Science, Psychology, and Sociology, we have also drawn valuable methods, data, and theories to help in our understanding of human life and lives. Anthropology has, of course also developed its own methods of research, collected its own data, and developed its own theories to explain mankind, and all these other disciplines have also borrowed from Anthropology in order to further study and understand the aspects of human life which concern them.

The Sub-fields of Anthropology and their Research Methods

While the aim of Anthropology as a discipline is to study all aspects of human life and the relationships among them, it is impossible for any one Anthropologist to study everything about people. As a result, Anthropologists generally specialize in different *sub-fields* of the discipline. There are four of these sub-fields: Physical Anthropology, Archaeology, Anthropological Linguistics, and Cultural Anthropology. Even within these there are further specializations. Because of the holistic perspective of Anthropology, however, there is much overlap among them, and most Anthropologists do look at the relationships between the area of human life in which they specialize and the other sub-fields.

Physical Anthropology is concerned primarily with the biological aspects of human life, though human behavior, particularly for early man, is also considered important in this sub-field. There are three main focuses of interest in Physical Anthropology. *Human Palaeontology* studies the evolution of the human species and its close relative, the monkeys and apes. *Human Heterography* looks at how and why living humans vary physically and genetically. *Primatology* studies the living monkeys and apes to understand their behavior and adaptation to their environments.

Physical Anthropologists all collect the data for their studies through field research. In Palaeontology this involves locating sites with relevant fossils, carefully excavating the sites, and collecting not just the fossils but all materials from the site that may provide evidence of the environment in which the fossilized organisms originally lived and of how they died. Human Heterographers collect data on physical and genetic characteristics of samples of people from all over the world to see how these vary and to identify the environmental and social factors that may help explain why these characteristics are distributed in the way they are. Primatologists spend years, and sometimes their whole life as does Jane Goodall with the chimpanzees of Ngombe, carefully observing monkeys and apes in order to identify patterns of behavior.

Archaelogy is the study of culture and history through the physical remains left by human activity. Originally it dealt only with prehistoric and ancient societies, but, starting in the 1970s, it expanded to include historic societies. Data is collected mostly through systematic and detailed excavation of sites where there is evidence of past human activity. From this data, Archaeologists attempt to reconstruct the lives of the peoples who left the evidence and to trace and explain changes in the lives of these peoples over time. *Prehistoric Archaeology* provides the only history of societies which left no written records. *Historical Archaeology* focuses on the material aspects of cultures and societies which do have written records and thus adds depth to our knowledge and understanding of how these people lived. More recently some Archaeologists have directed their techniques and theories towards contemporary societies and study everything material from architecture to garbage to see how these are related to the lives people lead.

Anthropological Linguistics is interested in all aspects of language as a distinctively human system of communication. It studies the origins of language and the diversification of languages over time, the structure of languages, and how language is used in society and culture. Linguists collect their data by interviewing speakers of a language, by observing and recording speech interactions among people, and, for ancient languages, systematically analyzing the written texts that are available. *Structural Linguistics* analyzes collections of utterances to identify the significant sounds, elements of meaning, and rules of grammar in specific languages. In Structural Linguistics, it is the speakers of the language who are considered the experts who know how to speak the language properly. The Linguist can only analyze the language as it is actually used, and cannot decide on how it should be used. *Historical Linguistics* compares languages to trace relations among them and to reconstruct what the parent language of related languages may have been like. *Sociolinguistics* studies the way language is used in different social contexts.

Cultural Anthropology is the study of peoples living today or in the recent past and is concerned with all aspects of their lives, including how they adapt to their environment, make their livings and exchange goods and services, organize their families and their societies, as well as with their politics, art, music, customs, values, religious and philosophical beliefs, and history. In short, Cultural Anthropology is interested in peoples' cultures: how they see the world (*world view*) and how they live in that world (*ethos*).

The primary method of collecting data in Cultural Anthropology is through *participant observation.* Cultural Anthropologists generally spend at least one year in the field living with people of another culture, participating as much as possible in their lives and observing their activities in order to describe their lives. *Interviewing* is also an important part of this process as the Anthropologist will often ask detailed questions in order to understand what the people are doing and why they are doing it. Anthropologists commonly return to the community they have studied to learn more about them. As with Linguistics, it is the people themselves who Anthropologists consider the experts. The Anthropologist's job is to learn the culture from them. This process of describing cultures as objectively as possible is called *Ethnography,* and its results are the data Cultural Anthropologists attempt to analyze.

The analysis and interpretation of ethnographic data takes two forms. The first concerns specific cultures and is directed at understanding how the different aspects of a particular culture fit together. This is often a significant part of the *ethnographic monograph,* that is, the book the Anthropologist writes to present a description and explanation of a culture. The second, *cross-cultural research,* has as its aim the analysis of similarities and differences among cultures in order to better understand culture in general and how and why it varies throughout the world and over time. It utilizes the *comparative method,* comparing different cultures selected on the basis of specific characteristics to see what may account for both the similarities and the differences among them.

There are numerous specializations within each of the sub-fields, and many of them are based in the relations between the sub-fields. *Forensic Anthropology,* for example, draws on the methods and findings of both Physical Anthropology and Archaeology to collect and interpret data about crimes, and *Palaeopathology* makes use of forensic methods and findings to address issues in archaeology. Within Cultural Anthropology, *Ethnohistory* integrates written records, oral traditions, and archaeological data to develop comprehensive and accurate histories of peoples.

Opportunities for Anthropological Research by College Students

There are numerous possibilities for college students to undertake their own original studies in any of the sub-fields of Anthropology for their courses in Research Methods and Integrating in the Social Sciences. It is essential, of course, to read other researcher's studies of the topic in which you are interested in order to develop your own thesis and to see the methods that the other researchers used to develop your own approach. The opportunities for research are only limited by the feasibility of collecting data and the need for specialized knowledge and abilities in order to successfully conduct the studies. These limitations mostly affect Physical Anthropology, Archaeology, and Linguistics, but there are still many areas in these sub-fields which students may pursue for their own research.

Physical Anthropology, in general, requires a degree of specialized biological knowledge that most social science students do not possess. If you have taken Introduction to Anthropology and Human Evolution, however, there are a number of areas which you may be able to pursue. While it is impossible for you to collect your own original material, there is a wealth of available data on human fossils that you can utilize to test your own thesis on some aspect of human evolution. There is also much data available on human genetic and physical variation and interested students can make effective use of this for their own studies.

In the area of human variation there are some possibilities for students to collect and analyze their own data. Early in the 20th Century, for example, Boas studied stature of immigrants and found that the children born and raised in New York were significantly taller than their parents who had been born and raised in Europe. If you have access to an immigrant population here, you could duplicate Boas' study to see if the same effect holds a century later. In a study such as this you would have to make sure that the families you studied all came from the same area in the Old World (since stature does vary throughout the world anyway), that you only measured their full-grown children, and that you recorded your measurements accurately and systematically. The analytic techniques you learn in Quantitative Methods will provide you with the tools for testing for a significant difference between generations using means, standard deviations, and a t-test.

If you are interested in Primatology, you could consider undertaking your own field observations of Primate behaviour at the Granby Zoo or Parc Safari Africain. Here you could do a study comparing captive primate behaviour to that of the same species in the wild as reported by other field researchers. In observational studies it is important both to record all behaviour in specific detail and to observe for a long enough time to observe regularities in behaviour.

Archaeology also requires specialized knowledge and skills for the collection of much of its data, and since this usually entails a detailed excavation of an archaeological site, it is generally not feasible for a college student to undertake original field research. Once again, however, there are opportunities for students to undertake some forms of original research.

As with Physical Anthropology, there are numerous sources of available data for archaeological research. When a site is excavated, the archaeologists make a record of everything found in the site. These records are often published as *site reports,* and the information in them can be used as a primary source of data for your own study. You might analyze information from a single site report to reconstruct some aspect of the lives of the people who left the site that was not addressed by the original researchers, or you might utilize a number of site reports to undertake a comparative study.

There are also possibilities for field research without excavation through collecting and analyzing historic materials that are still visible or even still in use. Cemeteries contain artifacts—the gravestones—that span many years and thus offer many accessible opportunities for research in material history. James Deetz, for example, studied changes in gravestone inscriptions and styles in early 19th Century cemeteries in New England and found that these were related to changes in religious attitudes. If you are studying a small cemetery, you would make a census of all the grave markers; for a large cemetery, you would select a representative sample of stones for your study. In either case it is important to record all the details of each stone, and you should construct a data sheet to ensure that you collect all the information you need and that you collect comparable information for all the markers. The kind of information you need about the stones includes the date erected, the material it is made of, the size and shape, the finish of the surfaces, carvings or other decorations, and the inscriptions on it. Here is an example of a data sheet for a cemetery study:

Cemetery:	Marker Number:	Year erected:
Shape:	Dimensions:	
Material:	Colour:	
Description:	Sketch:	
Inscription:		

Data sheets like this can be full-sheet or 5×8 index-card size. A photograph of the marker should be attached to the sheet (on the reverse for card-sized); even better, print a digital photo directly onto your data sheet.

Some areas of *Anthropological Linguistics*, such as structural or historical linguistics, require specialized knowledge and skills, but sociolinguistics offers many opportunities for original research by students with a more general knowledge of the field. A major area of interest here is in how people use their language differently in different social situations. When college students speak to their professors, for example, they generally not only speak of different things then when they speak to other students, they also tend to speak differently about the things. That is, their speech tends to be more formal in structure—the kinds of sentences they speak—and to make use of different vocabulary—slang words are much more common when they speak to their friends and fellow students.

If you were interested in a topic such as this, you would collect data by observing people's conversations in different social settings. Your observations would have to be detailed and systematic so as to ensure a reasonable degree of objectivity and avoid the tendency to record only what you want to hear for your thesis. In this kind of linguistic research it would be best to tape record the conversations in their entirety if the speakers agree to it. Otherwise you have to try to write down everything said. You should take notes during the conversation anyway, but the taped record will give you an accurate body of data to which you can refer. Since you would be comparing speech in different social situations, it is absolutely important that you make note of all the details of the situation, including who are the people having the conversation, why they are having it, what it is about, and where it is taking place. You can then systematically compare the data from the different situations to see if there are significant differences in how the people used their language.

Cultural Anthropology may offer the greatest number of possibilities for original student research in the discipline. While a full-scale ethnography would not be feasible for student work, there are many smaller-scale projects which students can undertake. Participant observation is the primary method of data collection here, and it can be used to study many different aspects of culture. Your general reading in Anthropology will give you knowledge of these different aspects of culture that anthropologists study and may stimulate your interest in pursuing research into one of them. Alternatively, you may have already informally observed some aspect of culture in which you became interested. If this is where you interest arises, you will need to read some anthropological studies of it in order to develop your own study.

For student research it is generally best to focus on a specific cultural event, such a religious service, a wedding, a political meeting, or even a dinner. That is, you should study something that is discrete, and not part of a continuous stream of action or behaviour. This will allow you to observe something in its entirety and will enable you to collect data on a specific aspect of culture which you wish to understand and explain. If you were interested in kinship relations, for example, you could participate in and observe a family holiday dinner to see how the different relatives interacted. A religious service, as another example, could provide an opportunity for participant observation research into how participants define their identity and acknowledge their shared beliefs and values.

Your aim in undertaking participant observation research is to provide a detailed description of what you have observed; it is, therefore, imperative that you observe in detail. You should record the data during the event, using notebook or tape recorder, providing the people you observe do not object. If you cannot take notes during the event, record your observations immediately afterwards; the longer you wait to record the data, the less you will remember.

The aspects of the event you should observe include (but are not limited to): the location of the event, the day and time it takes place, its duration, the architecture (if it is in a building), the surroundings (if it is outdoors), demographic characteristics of the participating population (number of people, age and sex distributions), clothing worn by the participants, the arrangement of people at the event, noticeable differentiation among the participants (leaders and followers, for example), and, of course, the activities the participants engage in. Discuss the event with some of the participants if at all possible in order to gain some understanding of the event from their perspective.

Your notes on the event should be as detailed and specific as possible. Maps, diagrams, photographs, and printed materials may all contribute to your observations and should be included in your collection of data if possible.

There is no formula for analyzing a cultural event; your approach is mostly interpretive. You should describe the event as fully, clearly, and coherently as possible from the perspective of the aspect of it you are aiming to explain. The paper you write on the topic, therefore, should reflect the structure of the event, your understanding of it, and your own style of writing.

Anthropological Research: A Brief Bibliography of Sources

There are many sources of information on anthropological research in the John Abbott College Library. The following bibliography is not exhaustive, and covers only cultural anthropology and archaeology. Feel free to search the library for more, and remember that the specific studies you read for your research also include information on the methods of research and analysis used in those studies.

Epstein, A.L. (ed.). 1967. *The Craft of Social Anthropology.* London: Tavistock.

Glazer, Myron. 1972. *The Research Adventure: Promise and Problems of Field Work.* NY: Random House.

Hodder, Ian. 1991. *Reading the Past: Current Approaches to Interpretation in Archaeology.* Cambridge: Cambridge Univ. Press.

Jacobson, David. 1991. *Reading Ethnography.* Albany: State University of New York Press.

Joukowsky, Martha. 1986. *A Complete Manual of Field Archaeology: Tools and Techniques of Field Work for Archaeologists.* NY: Prentice-Hall.

Kelley, Jane H. and Marsha P. Hanen. 1988. *Archaeology and the Methodology of Science.* Albuquerque: Univ. of New Mexico Press.

Kottak, Conrad Phillip (ed). 1982. *Researching American Culture: A Guide for Student Anthropologists.* Ann Arbor: Univ. of Michigan Press.

Krohn, Kaarle. 1971. *Folklore Methodlogy Formulated by Julius Krohn and Expanded by Nordic Researchers.* Austin: University of Texas Press.

Langness, L.L. 1981. *Lives: An Anthropological Approach to Biography. Novato: Chandler & Sharp.*

Rosaldo, Renato. 1989. *Culture & Truth: the Remaking of Social analysis.* Boston: Beacon Press.

Shaffir, William B., Robert A. Stebbins, and Allan Turowetz (eds). 1980. *Fieldwork Experience: Qualitative Approaches to Social Research.* NY: St. Martin's Press.

Spradley, James P. 1979. *The Ethnographic Interview.* NY: Holt, Rinehart and Winston.

Spradley, James P. 1980. *Participant Observation.* New York: Holt, Rinehart and Winston.

WRITING AN HISTORICAL RESEARCH PAPER

Taken from: *Writing an Historical Research Paper,* by Bill Russell

Writing an historical research paper involves explaining and presenting a solution to an historical problem or question. This solution is derived by incorporating your thoughts on the subject-matter with those presented in published print. Having done the research and reading and note-taking for your paper, the next step is to write the first draft. The explanation of the historical problem is presented in the form of a coherent argument based on a clear arrangement of the subject-matter, and composed of facts that are drawn from various sources and synthesised into a paper. In short, the argument consists of a series of premises that follow into a conclusion—the point of the argument. The validity of the conclusion of an argument hinges on how logically and effectively the premises of the argument serve to support the conclusion. The general plan or organisation of the paper is presented in the outline—a skeleton of the argument which will provide you with organisation and focus. The outline is complemented by facts that constitute historical evidence and then by *your* own interpretations of the facts. The purpose of the argument is to explain and convey your conclusion, or thesis-statement—a proposed solution to a historical problem that is derived from and proven with facts and interpretations.

Define the scope and purpose of the paper in the introduction by presenting the background information and stating what aspect of the problem will be examined. Present a brief description of the historical problem that you will attempt to solve and the solution that you will attempt to prove (the thesis-statement). Define a specific thesis that is as narrow and clear as possible. The body of the paper follows the introduction, consisting of the presentation of the evidence, interpretations, and the general structure of the argument. Successive paragraphs follow the pattern of the argument as it is defined in the outline and lead into the conclusion. A summary of the discussion and a proposed solution to the problem are presented in the conclusion. Remember that your conclusions must be supported by the evidence that has been-presented in your work. Reconsider the plan of the outline if it does not serve to produce a logical and coherent development of your argument.

The organisation of the facts that follow the outline are integrated with your interpretation deduced from the facts. Both the evidence and the interpretations are needed to present and argue the case that you'll be stating in your conclusion. Determine what the various components of the historical problem are, then bring them into focus by showing how they relate to it. These components generally take the form of causes for events. Use your imagination to determine how and why the causes of an event were brought about (the how and why of what happened), as if you were designing exam questions on the subject. For example, why did Soviet authorities impose a blockade on the western occupation sectors of Berlin in 1948, and how was this decision brought about? The causes for this drastic action should be examined in the light of the breakdown of joint allied cooperation in postwar Germany. Historical writing that does not include interpretation can be described as a form of superficial journalism, or old news. The narrative entails merely a reconstruction of the past events as they happened, i.e. one thing after another, while interpretation discusses how and why events turned out the way that they did. Remember that your work must have as much interpretation as possible added to the story-telling. Defend these interpretations by basing them on the evidence that you present. When trying to draw conclusions from the narrative, talk about your work to someone can discuss and criticise what you've written, such as your teacher or a fellow student. This kind of "shop-talk" can spark new ideas for your work while you're still in the process of philosophising over what you've got written out up to that point.

The outline, facts, and the interpretations are to be organised into a logical, clear, and cogent argument that should prove and maintain your thesis-statement. Try to determine how the evidence can be pieced together to substantiate an answer, or solution, to the historical problem. The initial draft will put your argument and conclusions to the test, i.e. determine the effectiveness of the structure of the argument and how effectively it establishes the credibility of the thesis-statement. The arrangement of the subject-matter and the focus in developing the argument in deriving your conclusions are perfected in the writing stage. The writing stage will give you direction and shape to the argument. If you find that your thesis cannot be maintained or proven effectively, "go back to the drawing board" and redefine the development of the argument.

A good argument is based on facts. You need not limit yourself to a predetermined number of sources. Preliminary research and reading and note-taking will enable you to produce a first draft to work from, i.e. edit and work on the paper's shortcomings. Successive drafts and subsequent revisions will enable you to bring more clarity and direction to the development, as well as make corrections and improvements on the writing style. If you lack sufficient evidence to support your thesis, resume the research and reading in order to find the evidence to maintain it more thoroughly. By doing so, a more credible argument will be presented, and thus a more valid solution to the historical problem.

The last stage in writing every successive draft is editing. Since nobody is born a good writer, there are always corrections to be made. Judge each draft by determining how effectively the facts and interpretations have been fused together, and how effectively the thesis-statement is presented and communicated. Present the flow of the discussion clearly, as if you were explaining it verbally. Pay close attention to the sentence and paragraph structure. The desired result is a continuous flowing prose holding the complete narrative together, with the end of each paragraph leading into the subject of the next. Your overall thesis should be evident throughout the paper, following a common thread from the statements presented in the introductory paragraph(s), linked to the thoughts and evidence presented throughout the body, until finally leading into the concluding paragraph(s).

Keep these essential tools at arm's length when you're writing each draft: a dictionary, preferably an Oxford to avoid American spellings; a thesaurus to provide synonyms and thereby help avoid the overuse of particular words; and a style manual, such as the MLA handbook to make sure that the presentation of the paper is correct and to avoid stylistic errors such as not italicising or underlining foreign or technical words (your word-processor should provide these tools). If you've got a problem with writing, go to the learning centre and ask them to for help. What they can do is recommend an English course that can help you overcome your writing problems. Or else, pick up a style manual, such as *The Elements of Style* by Strunk and White, or any high school grammar book that will help you polish your writing skills on your own. Here are some pointers on editing papers: solemnly abide by the long-accepted usages of grammar and syntax; make sure every sentence expresses a single thought; every paragraph should be at least three sentences long; watch for subject-verb-object agreement; avoid using the passive voice; make sure you've said what you meant to say by presenting your thoughts directly and plainly in your own words; avoid slang, jargon terms and highfalutin' language. Good writing clearly expresses itself. The writer's thoughts should be clearly presented and explained, and therefore making it unnecessary for the reader to think about what is stated. Be sure to proofread your final draft before you hand it in. Read it backwards in order to detect any typographical errors without getting caught up in the content, or ask someone to read it over for you.

Glossary of Terms

Abstract A brief summary of a journal article summarizing the thesis, method and findings.

Accretion in Nonreactive Measurement Accumulation of physical evidence suggests behaviour.

Active Membership Used in field research. The researcher assumes a membership role and goes through a similar induction into membership and participates like a member.

Analytic Notes Notes that are taken in the field about how to proceed with research in the future.

Annotation Summary of the contents of a book or article.

Bibliography Alphabetical listing of sources on a selected topic.

Census A sample that includes each unit or score in the population or includes information on characteristics of the entire population.

Central Limit Theorem Used in conjunction with sampling distribution theory, central limit theorem states that as the size of the sample gets infinitely large, the shape of the sampling distribution of the sample mean ($\bar{x}$) approaches a normal distribution with mean equal to m and standard deviation equal to $\sigma/\Sigma\bar{n}$.

Circular Argument (Begging the Question) Refers to instances where something is assumed as a premise and then stated as a conclusion.

Cluster Sampling A procedure in which individuals or other elements in the population are not sampled independently but rather in clusters or groups. Within each cluster, all or almost all of the elements or people serve in the sample.

Coding Sheet (Recording Sheet) Instrument used as described in the coding system to gather information using the content analysis research methodology.

Coding System A set of instructions or rules on how to systematically observe and record content from text.

Complete Membership Used in field research. Occurs when the researcher "goes native." Here, the researcher must leave the field to return to being a researcher.

Conceptual Equivalence The ability to use the same concept across divergent cultures or historical eras.

Confidence Interval A statement of two values (or a range of scores) within which you believe the true population parameter value is found. The values or range of scores are generally selected according to a procedure that provides a certain probability that such intervals will include the value of the population parameter. The most common confidence intervals are for the population mean (m) and population proportion (P). The most generic confidence interval is the estimate ± margin of error.

Content Analysis A technique used for gathering information based on the content of the text being viewed. Note that the text in this context can be most any form of communication medium, including written spoken or visual. In content analysis, a researcher uses objective and systematic counting and recording procedures to produce a quantitative description of the symbolic content in a text.

Contextual Equivalence The correct application of terms or concepts in different social or historical contexts.

Control Group The group of subjects in an experiment who do not receive the treatment being tested in experimental design.

Control Variable A variable that is related to the dependent variable, the influence of which needs to be removed.

Convenience Sampling or Haphazard Sampling Refers to a sampling procedure in which the researcher selects a sample primarily because it is accessible and reasonably representative of the population of interest.

Correlation A statistical relation between two variables.

Correlational Research describes the relationship that certain events might have to one another.

Count Behaviour in Nonreactive Measurement Information gained from counting a particular phenomenon in social research.

Cross Tabulations Present the distribution (frequencies and percents) of one variable (usually the dependent variable) across the categories of one or more additional variables (usually the independent variable).

Dependent Variable A variable that is measured to see whether the treatment or manipulation of the independent variable had an effect.

Descriptive Research describes the characteristics of an existing phenomenon.

Deviant Case Sampling When the researcher selects cases that differ from the predominant pattern or that differ from the predominant characteristics of other cases.

Direct Observation Notes Notes a researcher writes immediately after leaving the field, which he or she can add to later.

Double-Blind Experiment An experiment designed to control researcher expectancy. In this context, neither the participants nor the experimenters know who belongs to the experimental group and who belongs to the control group.

Ecological Validity The degree to which the social world described by the researcher matches the world of its members.

Element Particular unit of analysis or case in a sample or population

Erosion in Nonreactive Measurement Wear suggests greater usage

Ethnography Describing a culture and understanding another way of lie from a native point of view.

Evading the Issue Occurs when a writer wittingly or unwittingly gloss over a flaw or gap in their argument by shifting focus away, but not completely, from the relevant point.

Experiment Deliberate imposition of some treatment on individuals in order to observe their responses.

Experimental Group The group of subjects that receives the treatment under consideration.

Exploratory Discourse Asks a question, diagnoses a problem, or provides a "tentative definition" of some term or concept.

External Appearance in Nonreactive Measurement Appearance indicates social factors.

Extraneous Variable A variable that is related to the dependent variable or independent variable that is not part of the experiment.

Faulty Generalization Refers to the instances where the conclusions are not adequately supported by the evidence.

Faulty Premise Occurs when the facts the researcher purports to explain are untrue.

Field Research A qualitative style in which a researcher directly observes and participates in small scale social settings.

Focus Group A qualitative research technique in which people are informally interviewed in a group discussion setting.

Free Writing An exercise that requires non-stop writing for a page or so to develop valuable phrases, comparisons, personal anecdotes, and specific thoughts that help focus issues of concern.

Gatekeeper Someone with formal or informal authority to control access to a site.

Historical Research A research agenda that examines how events in the past affect current or future events.

Hypothesis reflects the general problem statement or question that was the motivation for the underlying research study. An educated guess.

Independent Variable A variable that is manipulated to examine its impact on a dependent variable.

Informative Discourse Answers a question by reporting on events, facts, and ideas.

Intercoder Reliability Required when a researcher using a content analysis approach has several coders. A statistical coefficient that tells the degree of consistency across many coders.

Interval/Ratio Level of Measurement Tells us about the ordering of categories and indicates the distance between them. Generally based on an underlying scale of equal intervals.

Interview Schedule A set of questions read to the respondent by an interviewer, who also records the responses.

Jotted Notes Short notes written in the field. They are usually incorporated into direct observation notes but never substituted for them.

Latent Coding Used in content analysis. Coding the implicit or underlying meaning in the content of a text.

Lexicon Equivalence The correct translation of words and phrases, or finding a word that means the same thing as another word.

Manifest Coding Used in content analysis. Coding the visible or surface content in a text.

Measurement Equivalence Measuring the same concept in different settings.

Member Validation Occurs when a researcher takes field results back to members, who judge their adequacy.

Moderator Variable A variable that is related to the dependent variable or independent variable and has an impact on the dependent variable.

Natural History A detailed description of how the project was conducted.

Naturalism Involves observing ordinary events in natural setting, not in contrived, invented, or research-created settings.

Nominal Level of Measurement Involves placing cases into categories and counting their frequency of occurrence. Usually, the nominal level requires the categories to be mutually exclusive and collectively exhaustive.

Nonexperimental Research does not set out, nor can it test any causal relationships between variables. Types of nonexperimental research include descriptive, historical, correlational, and qualitative research.

Nonreactive Research or Measurement Begins when a researcher notices something that indicates a variable of interest. The people being studied are unaware of this fact.

Null Hypothesis Estimates the likelihood that the sample data collected from a population would have been found if the null hypothesis were true. Generally, what is believed to be true about the population in regard to a population parameter value.

Ordinal Level of Measurement Yields information about the ordering of categories but does not indicate the magnitude of differences.

Parameter (Population) A numeric value summarizing a characteristic of a population.

Participant-Observation Research See field research.

Peripheral Membership Used in field research. Involves maintaining a distance between self and those being studied.

Personal Notes Notes taken be the researcher that records the personal feelings and emotional reactions that the researcher sees, hears, and feels in the field. A personal journal kept by the researcher.

Population All possible cases of interest sometimes referred to the universe.

Posttest The measurement of the dependent variable after the introduction of a treatment in an experiment.

Pretest The measurement of the dependent variable prior to the introduction of a treatment in an experiment.

Primary Source People or documentation that presents original research. More specifically, these are the original words of a writer, such as a novel, speech, eyewitness account, letter, autobiography, interview, or the original written report of original research.

Primary Source of Historical Data Letters, diaries, newspapers, novels, articles of clothing, photographs, and so forth of those who lived in the past and have survived to the present.

Purposive Sampling Uses the judgement of an expert in selecting cases or it selects cases with a specific purpose in mind.

Qualitative Research is used to examine human behaviour in the social, cultural, and political contexts in which they occur.

Quasi-Experimental Research is an experimental situation where participants are preassigned to groups based on some pre-determined characteristic or quality. Also called post hoc or after the fact research.

Quota Sampling Involves stratifying on a large number of demographic variables to end up with target numbers of respondents from very specified subgroups.

Random Digit Dialing A special sampling technique used in research projects in which the general public is interviewed by telephone.

Reactive in experiments and survey research occurs when the people being studied are aware of that fact.

Recollections The words or writings of individuals about their past lives or experiences.

Research is an activity based on the research of others.

Researcher Inference Notes Notes taken by the researcher that infers a particular situation in the field that is not directly observable.

Research Hypothesis The hypothesis postulated by the researcher states what he or she expects to find; it usually states the direction of the expected results.

Research Problem Involves any question or issue around which there is uncertainty or doubt, which will be addressed or resolved by the research.

Rhetorical Strategy The different organizational patterns that recur in expository writing.

Running Records Files or existing statistical documents maintained by organizations.

Running Records in Nonreactive Measurement Using regularly produced public records to reveal behaviour or information.

Sampling Distribution A frequency distribution of a statistic calculated from many different samples, all of the same size and all randomly drawn from the same population.

Scientific Discourse Attempts to answer a research question either by arguing from accepted premises or by generalizing from particular examples.

Scientific Method (1) A process that results in a reasonable and sound answer to important questions that will further our understanding of human behaviour. (2) The set of steps that social scientist follow to ensure a common basis for conducting research.

Secondary Analysis Using existing statistical data and processes in the research process.

Secondary Sources Writings of specialist Historians who have spent years studying primary sources. More specifically, these are writings about the primary sources and about the authors who produce them.

Sequential Sampling Occurs when the researcher tries to find as many relevant cases as possible, until time, financial resources, or his or her energy is exhausted.

Snowball Sampling A multistage sampling technique, which begins with one or a few cases and spreads out on the basis of links to the initial cases.

Spurious Relationship Occurs when a correlation between two factors may be a by product of a third factor.

Statistic (Sample) A numeric value summarizing a characteristic of a sample.

Statistical Significance Occurs when the observed outcome or effect could not have occurred by chance. More specifically, a statistical significance level is a value that relates to the probability of getting scores from a sample drawn from a population with a parameter equal to that of the null hypothesis (H_o).

Stratified Random Sampling Similar to stratified sampling in which the individuals are chosen from within each stratum.

Stratified Sampling A selection procedure that can be used when the population of interest is divided up into mutually exclusive subgroups called strata.

Structured Observation Used in measurement of variables in content analysis. The systematic, careful observation based on the written rules.

Subjects The cases or people used in research projects and on whom variables are measured.

Survey Method Research methodology where the primary instrument of data collection is the survey.

Systematic Sampling A procedure in which every nth person in the sampling frame whose responses are available is sampled.

Theoretical Sampling What the researcher is sampling is carefully selected as the researcher develops the grounded theory.

Theory helps us to organize new information into a coherent body, a set of related ideas that explain events that have occurred and predict events that may happen.

Thesis Statement See research hypothesis.

Treatment The stimulus applied to the members of the experimental group in an experiment.

True Experimental Research involves the determination of causal relationships between variables (explanatory and response variables). Participants are assigned to groups based on the treatment variable (or treatment condition).

Type I Error Occurs in hypothesis testing when the researcher rejects the null hypothesis (H_o) when the null hypothesis is true.

Type II Error Occurs in hypothesis testing when the researcher retains (or accepts) the null hypothesis (H_o) when the null hypothesis is false.

Unobtrusive Observation Data collection method whereby the collector of the data is not directly involved in the interaction of what is being observed.

Variable represents a class of outcomes that can take on more than one value.

Index